Profiles in Leadership

Profiles in Leadership

Alan Axelrod

Prentice
Hall Press

A member of PenguinPutnam Inc.
375 Hudson Street
New York, N.Y. 10014
www.penguinputnam.com

CIP data is available from the Library of Congress.

Printed in the United States of America

10 9 8 7 6 5 4 3 2 1

ISBN 0-7352-0256-7

To Anita—

Whom I would follow anywhere

Introduction

Putting Your Finger on the Pulse of Power

As an A-to-Z guide to history's most powerful and effective people, *Profiles in Leadership* is a new kind of encyclopedia, but one built on a very old idea. The ultimate achievers of the world have always sought out the stories of power. George Washington steeped himself in Caesar's *Gallic Wars,* George S. Patton read everything he could on Napoleon, and Winston Churchill reveled in the study of Elizabeth I. There was a time when aspiring young businesspeople voraciously devoured biographies of American heroes, in search of inspiration, in search of models, in search, finally, of the secrets of power and success. If that desire to learn strikes us these days as quaint or naive—suited to a time when American life had more of a Horatio Alger feel to it—maybe it's because most of us are just too busy *doing* to devote much time to *learning.* In the 60 or 70 hours of today's workweek, who has time to mine a mountain of biographies in search of a nugget or two?

Profiles in Leadership offers the nuggets without the mountain. Its 158 penetrating entries distill the lives and leadership secrets of the men and women who have moved, motivated, and molded the world in a positive, powerful way from ancient times to modern times.

LIFE PROGRAMS FOR SUCCESS

The idea of collecting between the covers of a book the lives of influence, power, and success is not new. The biographical dictionary has been a solid publishing category at least since Plutarch wrote his *Lives of the Noble Grecians and Romans* in the second century A.D. But, as an encyclopedia of powerful people, *Profiles in Leadership* offers something entirely new: *subjects specifically selected, targeted, and treated as lessons in leadership.*

The lives and careers offered here are presented not as mere accretions of biographical fact, just "for the record," but are analyzed as life programs for success.

CATEGORIES OF ACHIEVEMENT

The analysis begins with the 14 categories of leadership achievement:

Character model	Problem solver
Conqueror	Profit maker
Improviser	Rescuer
Innovator	Strategist
Leverager	Systems creator
Mentor	Tactician
Motivator	Visionary

Each of the leaders profiled in the entries is classified in terms of usually three or more of these categories. This system of classification not only reduces each life and career to its essential leadership elements, it also makes *Profiles in Leadership* a dynamic reference tool. A special index lists the leaders by category, so that a reader interested in finding examples of the tactician type can quickly jump to just those entries. Similarly, a reader who needs to find motivators can instantly locate those, and so on, as required.

ACHIEVEMENT ANALYZED

The biographical entries are sufficiently detailed to provide a vivid portrait of each subject's achievement. Each entry is broken down in this way:

- Name of subject, with birth and death dates

- Leadership category or categories: one or more of the 14 leadership types that apply to the subject

- *Leadership achievements:* A bullet list of the subject's accomplishments and principal claims to fame

- *Life:* A concise but eminently readable narrative of the subject's life, with emphasis on career

- *Leadership lessons:* A bullet-list presentation highlighting the leadership lessons offered by the subject of the entry

Many entries also include key leadership quotations from the subject in a section called "In His Own Words" or "In Her Own Words."

T H E   S C O P E   O F   T H I S   B O O K

Leaders are people, and people come in all shapes, sizes, and colors, from all nations, and from all times; they are equipped with divergent attitudes, approaches, talents, abilities, and liabilities. But it is also a fact that, whatever they are and however they do it, leaders are leaders. In business, in industry, in government, in the military, in democracy, in dictatorship, yesterday and today, leaders are leaders. Accordingly, *Profiles in Leadership* takes the broadest possible view. Included here are generals, conquerors, revolutionaries, political leaders, presidents, dictators, humanitarians, and reformers from biblical times, to ancient times, to classical times, to medieval times, to Renaissance times, to the 17th, 18th, 19th, 20th, and 21st centuries. The common denominators among this diverse group are only two: significance of achievement and excellence of execution.

H O W   T O   U S E   T H I S   B O O K

Encyclopedias are designed to provide specific, on-demand information, and this one, alphabetically arranged, is no different. But one of the great pleasures of an encyclopedia is simply dipping into it at random. A good way to get acquainted with *Profiles in Leadership* is to skim the names and the leadership classifications, pausing at whatever strikes you. What you will ultimately discover is that leadership style and leadership achievement are dazzling in their variety, but the key principles of leadership are surprisingly few. Read any 10 entries in this book, from B.C. times to the century just passed, and you will find persistent themes among the variations. The most valuable lessons of leadership are the lessons we discover for ourselves.

Contents

Contents

Contents xxiii

Abbas the Great

Born: 1571   Died: 1629

Conqueror   Motivator   Strategist   Tactician

LEADERSHIP ACHIEVEMENTS

✦

Reversed the decline of the Persian Empire

✦

Inspired loyalty and patriotism

✦

Modernized and redesigned his armies

✦

Maintained an unflagging level of energy that drove a will to conquer

✦

Used a dynamic strategy, making and ending alliances as necessary to achieve his goals

LIFE

Abbas was a shah who greatly strengthened the Persian empire by combining a tireless drive to conquer with the wisdom to create a highly disciplined and professional military force. A fierce enemy, he was also a cunning ally.

Abbas became shah of Persia when his father, Mohammed Khudabanda, abdicated in 1587. Before this, since 1581, he had served as governor of the province of Khorasan, where he gained experience as an administrator and leader. Abbas's first act as shah was not to make war, but peace. Understanding the need to form strategic alliances, he approached his father's traditional enemies, the Ottoman Turks, and ceded to them some western provinces of Persia to cement an alliance that would enable him to focus his forces on fighting the Uzbeks, who posed a continual threat of invasion. Beginning in 1590, Abbas waged an unremitting military campaign against them, which lasted through 1598. He defeated an Uzbek force in the Battle of Herat in 1597, but lost the decisive Battle of Balkh the next year. Nevertheless, his performance in the long war put him in a position to negotiate a very favorable peace. He had also used the war to build Persian patriotism.

Having neutralized the Uzbek menace, Abbas turned against the Ottoman Turks, storming Tabriz in 1602 and settling in for a siege that lasted until October 21, 1603, when this key trading city at last surrendered to him. While the Turks prepared a counteroffensive from 1604 to 1605, Abbas devoted his energies to modernizing his army. This stood him in good stead when the Ottoman army under Sultan Ahmed attacked at the Battle of Sis in 1606. Abbas's forces won a decisive victory.

From 1613 to 1615, Abbas invaded Georgia, which, in defeat, was obliged to acknowledge his sovereignty. This conquest touched off a new war with the Turks, who repeatedly attacked Tabriz during 1616–18. Abbas not only held the Turks off, he won the Battle of Sultania in 1618 and, later that same year, concluded yet another peace agreement with Turkey. Abbas was able to overturn the provision of the treaty of 1612 that had required Persia to pay tribute to the Ottomans.

Abbas made a fresh alliance in 1622, this time with a culturally foreign nation, Britain, whose ships he enlisted to fight the Portuguese and expel them from Hormuz. Also in 1622, Abbas invaded the Mongol Empire, capturing Kamdahar in 1623. This once again provoked war with Turkey and forced Abbas to lead an army to the relief of Baghdad during 1624–25. The shah did not stay on the defensive for long, but aggressively attacked the Turkish besiegers, so demoralizing the enemy that the Turks were forced to withdraw because of a mutiny. Although border clashes continued intermittently during the balance of Abbas's reign, he had generally succeeded in expanding the Persian empire and securing its sovereignty.

LEADERSHIP LESSONS

✦

Look for opportunities to turn defensive situations into positive occasions of aggressive action.

✦

Provide adequate, cutting-edge resources for your "troops."

✦

Negotiate as generously as possible; be prepared to make strategic concessions. Do not put opponents in a nothing-more-to-lose position.

✦

Do not become statically wedded to outmoded alliances.

Abd-el-Kader

Born: 1808   Died: 1883

Character model   Leverager   Motivator   Rescuer   Strategist

LEADERSHIP ACHIEVEMENTS

✦

Won personal control of much of Algeria

✦

Won a measure of independence from French colonial domination

✦

Served as an inspirational model of anticolonial perseverance

LIFE

Abd-el-Kader (sometimes spelled Abd-al-Kadir) was the third son of Mahi-el-Din, leader of the Hashim tribe and the fundamentalist Sufi Qadariyya religious sect. Abd-el-Kader became emir of Mascara following his father's death in 1832 and renewed the jihad (holy war) his father had fought against the French colonizers of Algeria. Abd-el-Kader was intelligent and charismatic. He built up his power with consummate skill and great sophistication. At one point, he even concluded an alliance with the hated French in order to drive out Turkish forces in July 1834. This daring political maneuver allowed him to achieve, by the end of the year, supremacy as the principal native leader in the region.

Once the Turks had been ejected from Algeria, Abd-el-Kader wasted no time in once again turning against the French. He won a decisive victory at the Battle of La Macta on June 28, 1835—although this did not stop the sack of el-Kader's native Mascara by forces under French general Bertrand Clausel in December. Another blow came at the Battle of Sikkah (July 6, 1836), where el-Kader was defeated by General Thomas R. Bugeaud. Following this loss, el-Kader negotiated the Peace of the Tama, a treaty whereby the French sanctioned el-Kader's authority over the various tribes of the region. The Treaty of the Tama is a stunning example of el-Kader's pragmatic brilliance. Even as he suffered defeat and with the tribes on the verge of deserting the anticolonial cause, Abd-el-Kader negotiated a

surrender that actually strengthened his position among the native population. In short, he successfully leveraged his own defeat.

As a government leader, el-Kader organized an efficient theocracy over
the two-thirds of Algeria still in native hands. Through his government el-
Kader did not merely maintain tribal loyalty to him, but actually strengthened it. To the consternation of the French, the tribes now rallied into
renewed resistance. When the French stormed Constantine on October 13,
1837, capping a program of colonial expansion, el-Kader confidently declared
a new jihad in November 1839. He organized a well-disciplined army of
40,000 men, only to meet with disaster in 1842 when he lost Tlemcen. In the
long aftermath of this defeat, his great force was dispersed by a mere 2,000
troops under the Duke of Aumale at the Battle of Smala (May 10, 1843).

Yet, even now, Abd-el-Kader did not give up. His reputation was so
powerful that, after retreating into Morocco, he was able to reorganize a
new army of 45,000 men. French general Bugeaud defeated even this
mighty army, however, and Abd-el-Kader was formally declared an outlaw
by the Moroccan government. It hardly mattered to him and he seized
upon an ongoing rebellion in the Dahra area, north of the Chelif River, to
cover his surreptitious return to Algeria. Rallying yet more forces, el-Kader
won a series of victories, after which massed French forces again drove him
back into Morocco, from which he united the Rif tribes in resistance. In
response, the Moroccan government declared war on el-Kader. Defeated,
he was transported to France, where he was imprisoned from 1848 to
October 16, 1852, when Napoleon III personally ordered his release. After
briefly living in Turkey and Damascus, Abd-el-Kader settled in France
from 1863 to 1865 and then returned quietly to Damascus, where he lived
in retirement until his death.

LEADERSHIP LESSONS
✦
Enmities and alliances change with time and circumstance. Be prepared to
make pragmatic alliances with rivals.
✦
Seize all opportunity. Even in defeat, you may be able to negotiate from a
position of some strength. Leverage *whatever* resources you have.
✦
Never give up. You are not defeated until you declare yourself beaten.

Abrams,
Creighton Williams, Jr.

Born: 1914   Died: 1974

Innovator   Motivator   Problem solver   Rescuer   Strategist   Tactician

LEADERSHIP ACHIEVEMENTS

✦

Led the relief of the 101st Airborne Division in the Battle of the Bulge

✦

Radically revised U.S. strategy and tactics in Vietnam,
better adapting them to the conditions of the war

✦

Scored a spectacular tactical success in leading the defense
against the 1968 Tet Offensive

LIFE

U.S. general Creighton Abrams served in World War II and the Korean War, but he is best remembered for his service during the difficult and painful late phase of America's involvement in the Vietnam War. A native of Springfield, Massachusetts, Abrams enrolled at West Point, from which he graduated in 1936, 18th in a class of 276. Commissioned a second lieutenant of cavalry, he was promoted to captain in 1940 and transferred to armor. In Europe, during World War II, he proved a brilliant commander of the 37th Tank Battalion. In the make-or-break Battle of the Bulge, he led the 4th Armored Division into Bastogne on December 6, 1944, spearheading the relief of the beleaguered 101st Airborne Division, sole bulwark against the massive German offensive. No less a leader than General George S. Patton remarked: "I'm supposed to be the best tank commander in the Army, but I have one peer—Abe Abrams."

After the war, in 1945, Abrams was promoted to temporary colonel and subsequently received an appointment to the Armor School at Fort Knox, Kentucky, as its director. After serving in this post from 1946 to 1948, he was graduated from the Command and General Staff School in 1949. His next combat service came in the Korean War, when he served successively as chief of staff for the I, X, and IX Corps from June 1950 through July 1953. Following the 1953 cease-fire, Abrams was appointed to the General Staff and attended the Army War College. Promoted to brigadier general in February 1956, Abrams was named deputy assistant chief of staff for reserve components on the Army General Staff. He became a major general in May 1960 and continued to serve in various command and staff posts. From September 1962 through May of the following year, he was given the critically sensitive and difficult mission of leading federal troops dispatched to Mississippi to quell riots associated with the enforcement of civil rights legislation.

Late in the summer of 1963, Abrams was promoted to lieutenant general and given command of V Corps in Germany. A year later, in September 1964, he received his fourth star and was named army vice chief of staff.

The rise of Creighton Abrams had been sure and steady, but he came to public prominence as the Vietnam War escalated and he was named deputy commander of the U.S. Military Assistance Command Vietnam (MACV) in May 1967. His greatest challenge came as director of operations in northern South Vietnam during the Tet Offensive of January 30 through February 29, 1968, when the communist forces suddenly and massively attacked on all fronts, in an effort to destroy South Vietnamese resistance in a single stroke. Although a war-weary United States public tended to see the Tet Offensive as a defeat for South Vietnamese and U.S. forces, it was, in military terms, a failure for the North Vietnamese. Of an estimated 84,000 Communist attackers, it is believed as many as 45,000 were killed. By any tactical standard, the defense against Tet was a triumph, and Abrams was named to succeed General William Westmoreland as commander of U.S. MACV.

The new MACV commander departed abruptly from Westmoreland's overall strategy of search and destroy, adopting instead a plan of patrol and ambush, which was better suited to the guerrilla nature of the conflict and was indeed effective in disrupting the support and supply lines of the North Vietnamese forces. Abrams served as MACV commander during the long phase of "Vietnamization" (the transfer of the burden of the war from U.S. to South Vietnamese forces), and, during the presidential administration of Richard M. Nixon, he directed the ordered reduction of American forces in Vietnam through July 1972, when he was appointed chief of staff of the army.

Abrams served as chief of staff until his death in 1974. In recognition of his service as a great commander of armored forces, the army named its principal tank, the M-1, in his honor.

IN HIS OWN WORDS

"We cannot let tomorrow's promises deter us from meeting today's requirements."
—*Military Review* 4, April 1985

"Bad news is not like fine wine—it does not improve with age."
—*Parameters*, 1987

"By 'people' I do not mean 'personnel.' I do not mean 'end strength.' I mean living, breathing, serving human beings. They have needs and interests and desires. They have spirit and will, and strengths and abilities. They have weaknesses and faults; and they have names. They are the heart of our preparedness."
—*Parameters*, 1987

LEADERSHIP LESSONS

✦

Know your job and focus on your mission. Become task- and goal-oriented.

✦

Examine prevailing methods and be willing to revise or discard them,
if necessary.

✦

Analyze problems with the objective of devising the best means to achieve
the designated ends.

✦

Be aware that tactical success may or may not bring strategic victory.

✦

A leader must sometimes embrace inherently thankless missions.

Adams, John

Born: 1735   Died: 1826

**Character model   Innovator   Mentor   Motivator   Problem solver
Rescuer   Strategist   Systems creator   Tactician   Visionary**

LEADERSHIP ACHIEVEMENTS

✦

Was instrumental in laying the philosophical foundation of the American
Revolution

✦

Was willing to take unpopular positions to promote liberty

✦

Responded to the Stamp Act in a way that molded political opinion and
helped to shape the independence movement

✦

Was a principal architect of American independence

✦

Created the Massachusetts constitution

✦

Guided the course of the Revolution and helped keep it focused on the
highest ideals and ultimate goals

✦

Was a key negotiator of the Treaty of Paris, ending the Revolution and
winning American independence

✦

Was the first U.S. vice president and second president

✦

Navigated the nation between radicalism and tyranny—even at the
expense of his own party

LIFE

Second president of the United States, John Adams was also a principal
architect of the American Revolution. He was a New England organizer of
the independence movement; a Massachusetts delegate to the Continental
Congress; a diplomat, during and after the Revolution, who was instrumental in securing European recognition of American independence;

and the nation's first vice president, under George Washington. In a group of extraordinarily intelligent "founding fathers," Adams was among the most brilliant.

Adams was born in Braintree—present-day Quincy—Massachusetts, to a family long established in New England. In 1751, John Adams entered Harvard intending to prepare for the ministry, but soon became absorbed in almost everything else: philosophy, science, the law, and medicine. Upon graduation in 1755, he was still undecided as to his career and took a teaching post in Worcester, Massachusetts, while he pondered his future.

It soon became apparent to Adams that the life of a village schoolmaster was not for him, but it did give him entry into the intellectual circles of Worcester. Among the worthies Adams encountered was James Putnam, a highly capable attorney, with whom Adams decided to apprentice in the law. In 1758, Adams left provincial Worcester to return to more cosmopolitan Braintree, where the prominence of his family helped him join the Boston bar. His early legal work was routine and centered on the affairs of Braintree, but he began spending increasing amounts of time in Boston, where he became deeply involved in the politics of independence. With his new Boston friends James Otis, Jr., and Samuel Adams (a distant cousin), he attended various trade organization meetings and became a founding member of the Sodalitas, a society of Boston lawyers who blended scholarly conversation with debates on the legality of the Stamp Act of 1765.

Although in 1764 he had married Abigail Smith and was now concerned about raising a family in the security of stable respectability, Adams became increasingly passionate about the tyranny represented by the Stamp Act. As a result of his Sodalitas meetings, he wrote a series of anonymous articles for the *Boston Gazette* (later collected and reprinted as *A Dissertation on Canon and Feudal Law*), in which he did no less than trace the origin and rise of leading ideas of liberty. Whether deliberately or not, Adams had begun to lay the philosophical and legal foundation for revolution. He concluded that the rights of Englishmen were derived neither from king nor Parliament, but from God. This point of view led Adams to draw up for his hometown of Braintree a protest against the Stamp Act that went far beyond its local purpose, becoming a model for many similar protests produced throughout New England. He judged the Stamp Act as not only an unnecessary financial burden, but an unconstitutional one, since, as he wrote, "No free man can be separated from his property but by his own act or fault."

Adams's writing on the Stamp Act catapulted him to a leadership position in the growing colonial independence movement, and, in 1768, he moved to Boston. Yet even as he spoke out in the cause of liberty, he refused to be tied down to any political dogma or factional allegiance. He was an intensely moral man, and in 1770, he and fellow colonial lawyer Josiah Quincy volunteered their legal services to defend the soldiers accused of murder in the Boston Massacre. Many radical Patriots criticized Adams for taking the case—and even more for winning acquittals or reductions of charges and sentences—but Adams understood that his leadership in this case was the strongest possible argument for liberty.

Although Adams served in the Massachusetts legislature—called the General Court—he felt himself becoming too intensely involved in a welter of issues related to independence and liberty, so he decided in 1771 to leave public life, at least for a time, to contemplate what course of action would be best. For 16 months he lived in semiretirement, only to return to Boston and resume his work on behalf of independence. When radical Bostonians staged the Boston Tea Party to protest the odious Tea Act of 1773, which interfered with colonial commerce, Adams applauded, and when the Crown responded to the dumping of the tea in Boston Harbor by enacting harshly punitive legislation against Massachusetts, Adams was fully radicalized and became a delegate to the First Continental Congress in 1774. For the next three years in Philadelphia, where the Congress met, Adams led that body in its most decisive moves toward separation from Britain.

In 1778, Adams was sent to replace Silas Deane, one of the American diplomatic agents in Paris charged with negotiating an all-important commercial and military alliance with France. However, the treaty was concluded before Adams arrived, and he rushed back to Massachusetts to serve as a delegate to the state's constitutional convention. It was Adams who wrote most of the articles of the state constitution, which was adopted in 1780. No sooner did he complete this work than he was

appointed minister plenipotentiary—essentially chief negotiator—in antic-
ipation of an upcoming peace treaty with Britain.

Adams immediately set off for Paris to await the start of negotiations,
but friction with Benjamin Franklin, America's longtime senior minister in
France, prompted Adams to travel to the Netherlands, where he quickly
secured not only Dutch recognition of American independence, but also a
badly needed loan and a treaty of amity and commerce. Returning to Paris
in triumph in October 1782, Adams joined John Jay and Franklin in negotiating peace with the British representatives assembled there.

During 1783–84, Adams also negotiated further loans for the United
States in the Netherlands and commercial treaties in France. Then, in
1785, he was appointed first U.S. minister to Britain. This proved a thankless job, and Adams was unable to win trade concessions from the British.
During this period, however, Adams forged a warm friendship with
Thomas Jefferson, then U.S. minister to France, and he wrote the ambitious three-volume *Defence of the Constitutions of Government of the United States,*
which was published in 1787. This work was highly useful to those who
labored in the Constitutional Convention of 1787. It outlined Adams's balanced approach to government, but it also emphasized what he saw as the
need for a strengthened federal government, even at the expense of some
states' rights.

In 1788, in the first election under the new Constitution, Adams was
chosen vice president of the United States. In his two terms as vice president, he presided over the Senate, often casting the deciding vote in that
evenly divided body, and typically promoting measures to increase the
powers of the federal government and the authority of the presidency.

When Washington declined to stand for a third term as president,
Adams ran, but, by this time, national politics was divided between the
Federalism that Adams espoused—an essentially conservative politics,
which concentrated power in the national government—and the more liberal politics epitomized by Jefferson, which would give more power to the
individual states and to the people themselves. Taking his cue from
Washington, Adams disdained party politics, which prompted him to
relinquish control of the Federalist Party to Alexander Hamilton, who
lacked Adams's moderation and who was indeed aggressively autocratic.

Rather than reducing partisan bitterness, Adams's relinquishment of the Federalist reins to Hamilton exacerbated partisanship. In an extremely close race between Adams and Jefferson, Adams emerged the victor—by just three electoral votes—and, in the system then used, Jefferson, his rival, became vice president.

Inaugurated on March 4, 1797, Adams, perhaps belatedly, delivered a message of political harmony, but he encountered only difficulty and dissension, much of it emanating from his own vice president and from the ambitious Hamilton, who continued to serve as secretary of the treasury.

Adams did not allow partisan politics to distract him from what he saw as imminent threats to the United States. He prepared for war with the nation's erstwhile ally, radical France, and, in the most controversial measure adopted during his administration, he approved four bills to control internal subversion, the Alien and Sedition Acts of 1798. The most infamous of these acts levied severe penalties on anyone who criticized the government. To Adams's credit, he saw to it that the potentially tyrannical law was never applied ruthlessly.

Adams himself was wary of Hamilton's growing power within the cabinet and his willingness to exploit deteriorating relations with France as an excuse to introduce a strong strain of militarism into American government. Recognizing this, the president acted skillfully to reduce immediate tensions and avert war by overseeing the negotiation of a treaty with France in 1800. The cost of Adams's conflict with Hamilton and his hardline Federalists was the splintering of the Federalist party. Adams understood this only too well, but he cherished American liberty over the advancement of any political faction. In the elections of 1800, Adams lost the presidency to Thomas Jefferson, and the Federalists never regained their former power.

After Adams left office in 1801, he returned to an active private life in Quincy. Reconciled with his old friend and political rival Jefferson late in life, he conducted a correspondence with him that is one of the monuments of American political thought. Adams died on July 4, 1826, the 50th anniversary of the Declaration of Independence, and, coincidentally, the very day on which, unknown to Adams, Jefferson also died.

IN HIS OWN WORDS

"A government of laws, and not of men."
  —*Novanglus* No. 7, 1774

"The happiness of society is the end [purpose] of government."
  —*Thoughts on Government,* 1776

"Virtue is not always amiable."
  —*Diary,* February 9, 1779

LEADERSHIP LESSONS

✦

Define a body of ideals and remain true to them.

✦

Do not sacrifice high principles and ultimate goals to the passions of the
moment, no matter how popular.

✦

Effective leaders communicate effectively.

✦

Much of leadership is nothing more or less than navigating between
extreme positions.

✦

Determine your priorities. Leadership decisions often involve hard sacrifices.

✦

Do not try to avoid conflict by relinquishing authority.

Agricola, Gnaeus Julius

Born: 37   Died: 93

Character model   Conqueror   Strategist   Systems creator   Tactician

LEADERSHIP ACHIEVEMENTS

◆

Not only conquered, but held Britain for Rome

◆

Combined bold energy with a careful method in successful campaigns
of conquest

◆

Created a high degree of stability in Roman Britain

LIFE

Agricola conquered and then governed Britain. He was born at Forum Julii
(Fréjus) in Gallia Narbonensisi (Rhone Valley region) to the family of a
senator. The execution of his father at the hands of the Emperor Caligula
did not impede Agricola's political rise. His first appointment was as tribune on the staff of Suetonius Paulinus in Britain from 59 to 61. Next,
Agricola became quaestor in Asia during 64 and the people's tribune two
years later. In 68, he was made praetor, at which time he joined the forces
of Vespasian during the civil war of 68–69.

Agricola was given command of the XX ("Valeria Victrix") Legion
serving in Britain during 70, and, when he returned to Rome in 73, he was
elevated to patrician rank. In 74, Agricola was appointed governor of
Aquitania (southern France), where he served until 77, when he was named
consul and governor of Britain. The Britons were a rebellious people, and
ruling them was a formidable challenge. Agricola immediately launched an
expedition to subdue northern Wales and the Island of Mona (Anglesey).
He also conquered the Ordovices. This accomplished, he sought to protect
his conquests by building a fortress for the II Legion at Deva (modern
Chester) during 78–79. From this base, he pushed his conquests northward, reaching the Tay River by 80. Along the northern reaches of Roman
Britain, Agricola created a series of fortified outposts during 81–83. Once

these were in place, he attacked the Caledonians beyond the River Forth (in modern Scotland) and destroyed their army in 84 in a battle at Mons Graupius.

Following his conquest of the Caledonians, Agricola built a large legionary fortress at Inchtuthil (near modern Dunkeld, Scotland) and then returned to Rome, where he retired from public life. Never covetous of glory or power for its own sake, Agricola declined an appointment as proconsul of Asia.

Agricola was not only a brilliant, bold, but always systematic military tactician, he was a conqueror who understood that taking a territory is only part of the task of conquest. Once a region was acquired, it had to be defended and held. Agricola accomplished this by thoroughness and sound method. Moreover, he romanized Britain by refusing to practice persecution and undue coercion. He leavened conquest with a high degree of toleration, permitting a good deal of self-rule among those conquered. He also fostered urbanization in the south of Britain.

IN HIS OWN WORDS

"For myself I have long been convinced that neither for an army nor for a general is retreat safe. Better, too, is an honorable death than a life of shame, and safety and renown are for us to be found together."
—Address before battle, 83

LEADERSHIP LESSONS

✦

Energy and bold action are important in leadership, but system, efficiency, and method must not be sacrificed to them.

✦

Follow through. Having won an objective, create systems to retain and maintain the benefits of the victory.

✦

An effective leader demands as little abject obedience as possible. Within the limits of your program and objectives, give others as much autonomy as possible.

Agrippa, Marcus Vipsanius

Born: ca. 63 B.C. Died: 12 B.C.

Character model   Conqueror   Motivator   Strategist   Tactician

LEADERSHIP ACHIEVEMENTS
✦
Worked in partnership with Augustus to defeat rebels against Rome
✦
Developed a highly effective personal leadership style
✦
Systematically rose within the power structure of Rome
✦
Commanded and returned absolute loyalty

LIFE

A Roman general, Agrippa was an ally of Octavian (later, Caesar Augustus or, more formally, Gaius Julius Caesar Octavionus Augustus) and was instrumental in the defeat of Mark Antony at Actium in 31 B.C. He was born in or near Rome and, as a child, befriended Octavian. Agrippa was with his friend in the spring of 44, when Octavian returned to Rome after the assassination of Julius Caesar. Agrippa became Octavian's chief ally and strong right hand. He raised an army on his behalf, and it is likely that he fought at the battles of Philippi during October–November 42 and played a key role in Octavian's campaign against Lucius Antonius and Fulvia (Mark Antony's sister) during 41. Agrippa's victory at the Battle of Perusia (41) was of even greater consequence, as Agrippa managed to trap the entire rebel force and bring about their capitulation.

In 40, following the great triumph at Perusia, Agrippa was named *praetor urbanis* (magistrate) of Gaul. Almost immediately, he was elevated to governor, serving until 37, when he was recalled after the defeat of Octavian by Pompey. Agrippa took this defeat in stride, turning immediately to the task of creating a new fleet and harbor at Naples. He personally trained the crews to man the vessels of his fleet, which, in 36, he led against the Pompeian forces at Mylae and Naulochus, winning splendid victories in both battles. After these wins, he assumed command of Octavian's campaign against the Illyrians during 35–34, and then resumed command of the fleet during operations against Mark Antony. Agrippa was in personal command at the decisive Battle of Actium (September 2, 31), the final defeat of Mark Antony.

With the fall of Antony, Octavian became the Emperor Caesar Augustus, and he, in turn, elevated Agrippa to consul during 28 and 27. Agrippa served as the emperor's chief lieutenant and troubleshooter, especially in provincial matters. It was Agrippa to whom Augustus entrusted his signet ring when he fell gravely ill in 23, and Agrippa took as his third wife Julia, the daughter of Augustus.

During 23–21, Agrippa served in the East; from 21 to 19, he served in Gaul and Spain. Augustus gave his friend and ally the special title of *tribunicia potestas* in 18, making him the second most powerful man in the empire. Augustus dispatched Agrippa to the East as chief governor of the region. From 17 until his death in 12 B.C., Agrippa founded Roman cities throughout the East and brought peace between the Roman Empire and the Bosporian kingdom, as well as with Herod the Great. Agrippa died of an illness in 12 B.C. He had consolidated, under Augustus, Roman rule in the East, in Gaul, and in Spain. His personal fortune he largely contributed to Rome in the form of funding for great public works, including the Pantheon and the first public baths.

LEADERSHIP LESSONS

✦

A leader need not be the top boss; effective leaders are sometimes great partners and allies.

✦

Loyalty is an asset of inestimable value and power.

✦

Plan the course of your rise, then do what you must to follow it.

✦

A great leader is ultimately selfless. He gives back to the enterprise in no small measure.

Akbar

Born: 1542   Died: 1605

**Character model   Conqueror   Mentor   Strategist
Systems creator   Tactician   Visionary**

LEADERSHIP ACHIEVEMENTS

✦

Was the greatest of India's Mogul emperors

✦

Amassed an empire that encompassed most of India

✦

Combined ruthlessness with justice to create an enduring empire

✦

Followed up conquest with sound administration that benefitted the people
he governed

✦

Fostered loyalty through a combination of conquest and quid pro quo

LIFE

Akbar was the greatest of the Mogul emperors of India, extending his dynasty's rule over most of the Indian subcontinent. He was descended from no less a figure than Genghis Khan and other Mongol conquerors. Born into the ruling class of the Moguls, northern India's Muslim invaders, he did not inherit a stable kingdom. Indeed, shortly after Akbar was born, his father, Hemayun, was driven from his capital, Delhi, by the Afghan usurper Sher Shah Sur. For the first decade of his life, Akbar grew up with his family as an exile in Afghanistan and Iran. However, after he managed to recruit troops from the shah of Iran, Hemayun triumphantly returned to northern India and overthrew Sher Shah Sur. He appointed Akbar governor of the Punjab, a role explicitly intended to groom him for the throne.

Less than a year after returning to India, Hemayun died, leaving the entire northern Indian empire in the hands of 13-year-old Akbar, who ruled for five years under a regent, Bairam Khan. The young king and his regent rarely saw eye to eye, and no sooner did Akbar reach his majority than he forced Bairam Khan from his court. Now a ruler entirely in his own right,

Akbar, beginning in 1561, embarked on an ambitious program of savage conquest of the Indian subcontinent. His vision was of unifying all India under a single ruler—the only way, he believed, to maintain power in the fractious and volatile region.

Akbar behaved with absolute resolve, treating those he conquered fairly, but giving no quarter to those tribes and people who resisted him. In cases of resistance, his solution was to take no prisoners, but to annihilate his opponents. The only exception were the Rajputs, who, although they did resist, Akbar allowed to submit to his overlordship. They rendered to him a yearly monetary tribute and the service of troops. In return, Akbar granted the Rajputs a limited degree of local autonomy and other privileges. Thus Akbar maintained the loyalty of the Rajputs, whose armies he would use as the principal instruments of his further conquests.

By the turn of the century, Akbar had imposed his rule over the Indian subcontinent north of the Godavari River in central India. He did not content himself with mere conquest, however, but radically and thoroughly reformed the administration of all the territory he acquired. He centralized the government of his expanding empire, thereby minimizing the abuses of local administrators and tax collectors. This not only benefitted his reign, but was a positive improvement for those he ruled.

Established through violent and tyrannical means, the government of Akbar nevertheless became an institution in which free expression was encouraged, and it came to be regarded as a model for future rulers of the region.

LEADERSHIP LESSONS

Assert yourself early and absolutely.
✦
Understand the nature of ruthless action. Do not squander it by employing
it gratuitously.
✦
Know the limits of ruthlessness. It may be an efficient means of acquiring
power, but it is rarely effective in maintaining power.
✦
Wise administration of the quid pro quo can purchase active loyalty.
✦
Give value to those you lead. To endure, leadership must produce benefits
beyond those that accrue to the leader.

Akhenaton
(Amenhotep IV)

Reigned: 1379–62 B.C.

Innovator   Visionary

LEADERSHIP ACHIEVEMENTS

✦

Brought a new system of belief to Egypt

✦

Marshaled the resources of a great kingdom in a massive effort of physical
and spiritual rebuilding

✦

Shifted—for a time—the focus of Egyptian society from the afterlife to the
here and now

✦

Centralized the Egyptian government and economy

LIFE

Akhenaton may well have been the most remarkable of ancient Egyptian
rulers. He created a great religious revolution across Egypt, replacing the
old gods with a new monotheistic deity, Aton, thereby ushering in a brief,
but extraordinary flowering of Egyptian art and culture.

He was born Amenhotep, the son of Amenhotep III, a hunter whose
prowess was the stuff of legend and a military leader who brought to its
apex the Eighteenth Dynasty's territorial growth in Asia and Africa. In
contrast to Amenhotep III, Akhenaton was physically frail. His interests
were less military than spiritual, artistic, and intellectual.

It is not known whether Akhenaton succeeded to the throne after his
father's death or whether he ruled alongside his father for a time. In either
case, shortly after he assumed the throne, Amenhotep IV embraced a new
monotheistic cult dedicated to the nature deity Aton. In the sixth year of
his reign, he changed his name to Akhenaton—He Who Serves the Aton—
and built great new temples dedicated to this deity at Karnak, site of the
temples dedicated to the old gods. He then relocated his capital from
Thebes more than 200 miles north to a place now called Armana, on the
east side of the Nile. There he founded a totally new city, which he called

Akhetaton, erecting magnificent public buildings and additional temples. Unlike previous Egyptian royals, Akhenaton, his wife Nefertiti (she whose beauty is preserved in a graceful and much-reproduced bust of the period), and the couple's six daughters freely mingled with the people of their new city, worshiping Aton in a temple open to the sunlight.

The worship of Aton engendered a fertile production of works of art, which are very different from anything that had come before. The painting and sculpture of Akhenaton's reign is naturalistic and sensual, in contrast to the two-dimensional, highly stylized art from earlier periods.

Akhenaton may have lived and worshiped among his people, but he was hardly a democrat in the modern sense. His massively ambitious program of building and of fostering the arts put great demands on the resources of Egypt. To finance his projects, he redesigned Egyptian society and politics, to a great extent centralizing Egypt's economy, appropriating vast tracts of land, levying heavy taxes, and stripping the old ruling class of much of its power.

On his death, Akhenaton was succeeded briefly by Smenkhkare and then by a son-in-law, Tutankhaton, who soon changed his name to Tutankhamen—popularly known in modern times as King Tut. This name change signified his public repudiation of his father-in-law's all-consuming god, Aton, and his embrace of Amon, the old god Aton had displaced. Akhenaton's short-lived revolution was thus undone, although its heritage of art and architecture lived on.

LEADERSHIP LESSONS

✦

The strength of a vision is proportional to the degree that it is shared.

✦

Ambition is an engine of great potential and power.

✦

Great things can be achieved by intensely focusing energy on well-defined goals—although this can be a risky approach to leadership.

✦

Despite his achievements, Akhenaton was a flawed leader, who allowed his focus on achieving his religious and cultural goals to blind him to his kingdom's other needs.

Alanbrooke, Sir Alan Francis Brooke

Born: 1883 Died: 1963

**Character model   Improviser   Leverager   Problem solver
Rescuer   Strategist   Tactician**

LEADERSHIP ACHIEVEMENTS

◆

Achieved recognition for his mastery of strategy and tactics

◆

Was instrumental in the rescue of British forces at Dunkirk

◆

Was one of the chief strategists behind the D-Day invasion of Europe

◆

Mentored a generation of British military officers

◆

Was a great team player content to work behind the scenes

LIFE

Alanbrooke was one of the great strategists and field commanders of World War II. Born in Ireland, at Bagnéres de Bigorre, he was sent to the Continent for his education. Upon his return to England, he joined the army as a junior artillery officer in 1902 and saw service on the Western Front during World War I, where he led Canadian and Indian troops. His command ability was quickly recognized, including his natural grasp of tactics and strategy. Immediately after the war, he was assigned as an instructor at the Staff College, Camberley, where he served periodically through 1927. In that year, he was reassigned to the Imperial Defense College, where he taught in 1927 and then from 1932 to 1934.

In 1936, Alanbrooke was appointed director of military training at the War Office, serving until the following year. Concurrently with this assignment, he commanded the Antiaircraft Command and the Southern Command, serving in these capacities prior to and through the early months of World War II (1937–40). In 1940, he was given command of II Corps of the British Expeditionary Forces (BEF) and displayed great skill, coolness, and presence of mind during the disastrously premature invasion of the Continent, the desperate withdrawal to Dunkirk, and, most of all, the evacuation back to England during May–June 1940. Alanbrooke's leadership presence and his ability to coordinate great, complex actions under the most pressing of circumstances ensured that the imperiled British forces were saved from annihilation in this battle.

Following Dunkirk, Alanbrooke was named commander in chief of home forces in July 1940, and then succeeded Sir John Dill as chief of the Imperial General Staff in December 1941. In this capacity, Alanbrooke participated in all the major strategic decisions of the war, including plans for Operation Overlord, the D-Day invasion of Normandy. Although Alanbrooke lobbied vigorously to obtain direct overall command of the operation, command was entrusted to Dwight David Eisenhower. Always the consummate professional, Alanbrooke refused to allow any personal disappointment he may have felt to interfere with the successful execution of the invasion. He worked smoothly and wholeheartedly with Eisenhower and other American officers. Indeed, Alanbrooke was a leader without ego. He had an uncanny ability to work productively with American as well as Soviet military and civilian leaders. He earned the respect of President Franklin D. Roosevelt, British prime minister Winston Churchill, and—perhaps most importantly—the friendship and goodwill of Soviet premier Joseph Stalin.

LEADERSHIP LESSONS

✦

A great leader is essentially selfless.

✦

A great leader is a great team player.

✦

Never panic. Identify the problem; then work on the problem you have identified.

✦

Do not let personal goals interfere with the enterprise you lead.

✦

Derive satisfaction from achievement rather than from acclaim for achievement.

Alcibiades

Born: ca. 450 B.C.   Died: 404 B.C.

**Conqueror   Improviser   Leverager   Mentor   Motivator
Strategist   Tactician   Visionary**

LEADERSHIP ACHIEVEMENTS

✦

Was a supreme example of leadership presence and leadership
by example

✦

Was a highly flexible and resilient leader

✦

Accepted any and all obstacles as opportunities to achieve greatness

LIFE

The son of a military commander, Alcibiades was born to the Athenian nobility and enjoyed a privileged upbringing. After his father was killed at Coronea in 447 or 446 B.C., Alcibiades was delivered into the family of his kinsman, the great statesman Pericles. The classical biographer Plutarch observes that Pericles must have served the boy as an extraordinary example of statecraft, yet it is also true that Pericles was far too busy with matters of government to devote much attention to his ward. The result of this brilliant neglect was that Alcibiades grew into a handsome, intelligent, and clever youth who was also supremely self-centered and undisciplined. Alcibiades' early association with Socrates, with whom he served in a military campaign at Potidaea in 432 B.C. and in the Battle of Delium in 424, apparently failed to instill a greater degree of self-control.

During the 420s, Alcibiades built a legendary, but entirely justified, reputation as a daring and brilliant military commander of limitless personal courage. He was a skilled strategist and tactician who also tirelessly motivated his troops through his personal example. To these qualities may be added prodigious skill as a persuasive political speaker coupled with physical beauty and charisma. Alcibiades used his personal qualities to draw to him an intensely loyal following, who fixed their dedication upon him, even at the expense of the state.

Alcibiades was a visionary who conceived, early in his career, a passion for making peace between the ever-warring states of Athens and Sparta. He believed that a strategic alliance between these states of sharply different character—Athens the cradle of philosophy and statecraft, Sparta the nursery of great generals and armies—would create the greatest force the world had ever seen. His plan was to bring into play his own ancient family connections with the Spartans, bypassing the powers that be. The scheme failed, however, because Sparta chose to negotiate through more established political channels. At this, Alcibiades turned against the chief Athenian negotiator Nicias and, in 420, as general of an Athenian army, urged Athens into an alliance with Argos, Elis, and Mantineia *against* Sparta. This bold move ended any chance for peace between the two great powers. Two years later, at the Battle of Mantineia, the Spartans defeated Alcibiades and his three-state alliance. This defeat should have ended his political and military career, but Alcibiades seemed capable of drawing on infinite inner resources. When he was threatened with banishment, he made an immediate about-face to ally himself with the autocratic Nicias in opposition to the demagogue Hyperbolus. Such was his personal magnetism that Nicias embraced alliance with his former enemy.

Having once again secured a position of power in the management of the state, Alcibiades redeemed himself in the eyes of the people by his spectacular performance in the Olympic chariot races of 416 (he took first, second, and fourth places). This restored his popular reputation, putting him in a position to persuade Athens to send a military expedition against Syracuse in 415, with himself as co-commander. The campaign was sabotaged by the discovery that the Hermae—ritual busts of Hermes, messenger of Zeus and patron of travelers—had been deliberately damaged, apparently to bring disaster on the Syracusan campaign. Alcibiades was accused not only of this sacrilege, but also of having profaned the Eleusinian Mysteries.

While Alcibiades was in Syracuse, his enemies continued to conspire against him, maneuvering a conviction *in absentia* for treason. Learning that he had been condemned to death, Alcibiades defected to Sparta. He masterminded the fortification of Decelea, which seriously undermined the Athenian position. In another move against Athens, Alcibiades incited a revolt in Ionia in 412 B.C., but this time it was Sparta that turned on him. Nevertheless, Alcibiades preserved his agility and was able to escape to the Persian city of Sardis. From Sardis, he conspired with a cabal of Athenian oligarchs bent on overthrowing the democracy in Athens. Alcibiades believed that he could charm the Persians into financing the overthrow. He did not succeed, and soon his co-conspirators abandoned him.

In the meantime, the Athenian fleet, which was loyal to the democracy Alcibiades had sought to overthrow, was being menaced by the fleet of Sparta. The Athenian commanders were willing to forgive Alcibiades' transgressions in return for his aid in this crisis. Alcibiades seized the opportunity and, from 411 to 408, performed with great effectiveness against the Spartan forces, leading the Athenian fleet to victory in the Hellespont in 411 and at Cyzicus the following year.

By 407, Alcibiades was ready to return to Athens, where he was greeted tumultuously and given supreme command of the armed forces in the ongoing war against Sparta. But this adulation was not long lived. After his lieutenants suffered a trivial naval defeat late in 407, Alcibiades' many political enemies succeeded in turning the populace against him. He retired to a Thracian stronghold, from which he continued to participate in Athenian politics. In 405, despite Alcibiades' warnings, the Athenians lost their entire fleet to a surprise Spartan attack. Alcibiades was forced to flee Thrace and take refuge with the Persian governor of Phrygia. Spartan intriguers induced the governor to order the assassination of his guest.

LEADERSHIP LESSONS

✦

Cultivate and exploit a personal leadership style.

✦

Value courage.

✦

Be prepared to adapt to changing circumstances, no matter how extreme.
Keep all options open.

✦

Know your craft. Make yourself valuable by performing at a high level
of excellence.

Alexander the Great
(Alexander III)

Born: 356 B.C.   Died: 323 B.C.

Conqueror   Mentor   Strategist   Tactician

LEADERSHIP ACHIEVEMENTS

✦

Conquered virtually the entire known world

✦

As a military commander, was undefeated

✦

Trained the greatest army of his time

✦

Triumphed over Darius III of Persia, perhaps history's single most decisive
military victory

✦

Built a vast empire over an astoundingly short span of years

LIFE

In a remarkably short period of time, this Macedonian king conquered virtually the entire known world and, in the process, laid the foundation of the Hellenic Empire. History remembers him as the prototypical conqueror and builder of empire.

Born at Pella, Macedonia, Alexander was the son of King Philip II. For a tutor to Alexander, his father secured the greatest mind of the age, Aristotle. Thus Alexander ascended the Macedonian throne in 336 B.C. as well-educated a monarch ever to assume power.

Young Alexander had a clear vision of leadership priorities. He began by ensuring the security of his court, liquidating a number of rivals in a quick bid to consolidate his political power. This accomplished, Alexander looked to expand the empire. In the spring of 334, he commenced the military expeditions that would occupy the rest of his brief life.

He saw as Macedonia's great rival the Persian Empire, and he resolved to liberate from Persian suzerainty the Greek city-states of Asia. Crossing the Hellespont with an army of about 40,000 men, he defeated the Persian army, subdued other enemies in western Asia Minor, and then, in July 332, stormed the key trading city of Tyre. He conquered and occupied Palestine and Phoenicia, and then turned toward Egypt, which he subdued through a series of lightning campaigns during 332–31.

Returning to Tyre in 331, Alexander marched his army across the expanse of Mesopotamia and conquered Babylon, which he occupied. The following year, he entered Media to the north and captured its capital. This put him into direct confrontation with the Grand Army of Persian emperor Darius III. Alexander set out to defeat this force, considered the most formidable army in the world, at the Battle of Arbela-Gaugamela in 331. Alexander knew that he was overwhelmingly outnumbered. Against his 40,000 infantrymen and 7,000 cavalrymen, Darius may have fielded as many as 250,000 troops. But Alexander also knew that his troops were far better trained than those of Darius—because he had trained them himself. Alexander used a portion of his force to lure Darius into attacking with everything he had. This, Alexander correctly believed, would result in chaos strategy as the vast numbers of Darius's force became unwieldy, the Persian cavalry in effect blocking the Persian infantry. This relieved pressure on Alexander's center and left, allowing them to take the offensive, which Alexander led personally. His forces attacked with such ferocity that they incited panic throughout the vastly superior Persian lines. The result was a terrible Persian slaughter. Estimates of Persian casualties range from 40,000 to 90,000, while Alexander may have lost no more than 500 men (some estimates are as low as 100).

The defeat at Arbela-Gaugamela sent the Persian Empire into irreversible decline and stands as one of the most decisive battles in history— a strategic as well as tactical masterpiece, and a masterpiece, too, of personal leadership.

Although Darius III escaped after the Battle of Arbela-Gaugamela, he died the following year, and Alexander assumed the title Basileus (great king), adding rule of Persia to that of Macedonia. In midsummer 330, Alexander embarked for central Asia, where he fought for the next three years to subjugate the wild region. To secure the territory he gained, Alexander married Roxane, a woman of the Iranian nobility, and he compelled 91 of his officers to marry Iranian women as well. In addition, he conscripted 30,000 Iranian boys into his army and absorbed the Iranian cavalry into his own. These moves may have been diplomatically astute, but they created dissension within Alexander's court and within the ranks of his army. Not all of his officers relished the forced marriages. As a result, Alexander's court descended into scandal and intrigue. Nevertheless, Alexander continued his program of conquest, founding during this period eight important cities, each named for himself—Alexandria.

The last campaign of Alexander the Great was in India. Crossing the Indus River in 326, he set about acquiring territories that extended as far as the Hyphasis and the lower Indus. The only substantial threat to his juggernaut came from King Porus of Paurava. At the Hydaspes River in 326, Alexander defeated Porus by boldly marching across the great river in the very face of the advancing Paurava army. This maneuver, unheard of, cut off the advance of Porus and brought about his total defeat. Alexander now overran the Punjab, but ultimately had to turn back, not because of any defeat in battle, but because his army simply refused to follow him farther. In 324, his officers, bitter over having to command an army of Iranians indiscriminately mixed with Macedonians and also still resentful of the marriages they had been forced to make, came close to outright mutiny.

That he could no longer fully rely on his army did not stop Alexander from pressing ahead with conquest. During the last year and a half of his life, he increasingly used Iranian troops and, with them, prepared to launch a vast Arabian campaign. While making his preparations, however, Alexander fell ill, probably of pernicious malaria, and died in Babylon on June 10, 323. He was only 33.

Alexander was a peerless military leader. But his military achievements outstripped his talent for administration. Among many of the people he conquered, he did not create loyalty and allegiance.

IN HIS OWN WORDS

"They will be fighting for pay—and not much of it at that; we, on the contrary, shall fight for Greece, and our hearts will be in it."
—Address before the Battle of Issus, 333 B.C.

"I wake earlier than you—and watch, that you may sleep."
—Address to troops, 323 B.C.

"Does any man among you honestly feel that he has suffered more for me than I have suffered for him? Come now—if you are wounded, strip and show me your wounds, and I will show mine. There is no part of my body but my back which has not a scar; not a weapon a man may grasp or fling the mark of which I do not carry upon me. I have sword cuts from close fight, arrows have pierced me, missiles from catapults bruised my flesh; again and again I have been struck by stones or clubs—and all for your sakes: for your glory and your gain."
—Address to troops, 323 B.C.

"Next day, despite a sword wound in his thigh, Alexander went round to see the wounded. . . ."
—Arrian, *The Anabasis of Alexander,* A.D. 150

"The end and perfection of our victories is to avoid the vices and infirmities of those whom we subdue."
—Quoted in Plutarch, *Lives,* A.D. 100

"To the strongest."
—Last words, on being asked to whom he bequeathed his empire

LEADERSHIP LESSONS

✦

Tactical and strategic brilliance will go far, but they do not entirely compensate for political naivete and diplomatic insensitivity.

✦

Victory is a strong ingredient in building loyalty, but it gives no license to neglect the needs of those you lead.

✦

Surprise your opponent with daring actions that creatively break the rules.

✦

Incite panic in your opponent, and then exploit your opponent's panic.

✦

Conquest brings responsibility, which cannot be evaded long by additional conquest.

Alexius I Comnenus

Born: 1048   Died: 1118

Conqueror   Leverager   Rescuer   Strategist   Tactician

LEADERSHIP ACHIEVEMENTS

✦

Maintained his enterprise and leadership even under multiple assaults

✦

Won important military victories

✦

Exploited internal instability to achieve power

✦

Leveraged his resources and his alliances

✦

Budgeted his military assets carefully

LIFE

Alexius I Comnenus was a Byzantine emperor who exemplified fine leadership under the tremendous pressures of a radically changing world. He was born in Constantinople, the third son of John Comnenus and the nephew of Emperor Isaac I Comnenus. Trained as a military commander, Alexius first saw combat against the Seljuk Turks during 1068–69 and 1070–71, and then fought against rebels during the insurrections that menaced the reigns of Michael VII Ducas (1071–78) and Nicephorus III Botaniates (1078–81). In each of the campaigns he fought, Alexius distinguished himself. Fighting in the service of Nicephorus III Botaniates, he scored a decisive victory over the rebel Nicephorus Briennus at the Battle of Calavryta (in Thrace, 1079). Nicephorus III, however, proved himself an inept ruler, a circumstance that gave Alexius an opportunity to seize power for himself. Alexius took on and defeated all comers, and, on April 4, 1081, was crowned the new emperor of Byzantium.

The volatility that had brought Alexius to the Byzantine throne also soon threatened his tenure on it. Immediately after he became emperor, he was faced with threats from the Normans (led by Robert Guiscard) as well as the Seljuk Turks. Alexius decided that he could not successfully prosecute a two-front war, so he made peace with the Seljuks, granting them extensive concessions. It was a high price to pay, but it freed him to concentrate his forces against Guiscard, who controlled southern Italy. Alexius next concluded an alliance with Venice, and sent a combined Byzantine and Venetian fleet to engage the forces of Robert Guiscard off the coast of Durazzo in 1081. While the Normans were defeated at sea, Alexius had to make heavy concessions to Venice in return. Worse, the Byzantines did not fare well in the land campaign. Guiscard's cavalry dealt the Varangian Guard a severe blow in October 1081, and the Normans advanced across Greece. In 1082, an army under Bohemund laid siege to the Byzantine town of Larissa on the Vardar River. Here, however, Alexius was able to halt the Norman advance by defeating Bohemund's forces. Nevertheless, the war dragged on until 1085, when Robert Guiscard died.

Within a year after the conclusion of the war with the Normans, Alexius found himself confronting a rebellion by the Bogomils, who were allied with the Petcheneg nomads. Alexius sought alliance with the Cumans. At first, the emperor's forces fared poorly against the combined armies of the Bogomils and Petchenegs, the most stunning defeat coming in 1086 at the Battle of Durostorum. Yet it took four more years before the Bogomils and Petchenegs seriously threatened Constantinople. Alexius assumed personal command of his forces and succeeded in turning back the rebel assault on his capital at the Battle of Mount Levunion (April 29, 1091). The victory was total; the Petchenegs were annihilated. The victory also stood Alexius in good stead as he faced down the Serbs during 1091–94.

In the midst of triumphs against the Bogomil-Petcheneg rebels, Alexius's Cuman allies suddenly rose against him (1094), led by Constantine Diogenes, who claimed to be the son of Romanus IV. Alexius acted quickly to disperse Constantine's forces, which were pushed back across the Danube. On the eastern front, in the meantime, Alexius depended on diplomatic intrigue rather than military means to keep the Seljuks at bay. Through adroit political maneuvering, he managed to stir trouble among the Seljuk tribes, which disputed among themselves so vehemently that they were unable to organize a credible threat against the empire. Alexius even concluded a treaty with a major Seljuk leader, Kilij Arslan, in 1091.

During 1096–97, it was the arrival of the forces of the First Crusade— ostensibly Christian allies of the Byzantines—that upset the balance Alexius had established in Asia Minor. Even so, Alexius managed to turn the Crusaders' presence to his advantage, judiciously supplying them with aid and supplies, and using them, during May 14 through June 19, 1097, to capture Nicaea. This triumph, however, resulted in a jealous dispute between Alexius and the Crusaders, who left the Byzantines in order to continue their advance into Seljuk territory. For his part, Alexius used the momentum of the Crusade to capture Smyrna (Izmir), Ephesus, and Sardos (east of Smyrna) in addition to lesser cities throughout southwestern Asia Minor.

When the Crusaders took Antioch in 1098, which had formerly belonged to the Byzantine Empire, ties between Alexius and the Crusaders were completely severed, save for an alliance with Raymond of Toulouse. Among the Crusaders was Bohemund, whom Alexius had fought in 1082 and who now demanded that Alexius assist him in conquering Turkish towns. Thoroughly alienated from the Crusader cause, Alexius not only refused to help, but began ejecting Crusaders from various Byzantine territories. Using these rebuffs as a pretext, Bohemund returned to Europe in 1105, raised a new army, and attacked at Durazzo in October 1107. Soundly defeated, he surrendered and yielded himself as vassal to Alexius, who granted him Antioch as a fief the following year.

Thus peace came to Byzantium, but it was not destined to endure. In 1110, the Seljuks invaded Anatolia in an effort to retake what Alexius had seized in 1097. At first, the Byzantine forces were repeatedly defeated; however, after some years of fighting, Alexius once again put himself at the head of his forces and led them to a great victory at the Battle of Philomelion in 1116. The defeated Seljuks sued for peace. Two years after this, Alexius died, leaving the empire far stronger than it was when he had assumed the throne.

LEADERSHIP LESSONS

◆

Watch for leadership vacuums and be prepared to fill them.

◆

Husband your resources. Attempt to manage problems without spreading your assets too thinly.

◆

Be prepared to pay for cooperation, but always proportion means to ends, cost to value received.

◆

Keep alliances flexible. Do not allow yourself to be burdened by a bad alliance.

Alfonso VIII

Born: 1155   Died: 1214

Conqueror   Motivator   Strategist   Tactician

LEADERSHIP ACHIEVEMENTS

✦

Skillfully consolidated his power in Castile and the power of Castile on the
Iberian peninsula

✦

Made strategic alliances

✦

Was capable of turning defeat into victory

✦

Was capable of delivering great inspiration

✦

Refused ever to concede defeat

LIFE

Alfonso, king of Castile and León, was one of the great warrior-rulers of
medieval Spain. His signal achievement was overwhelming victory against
the forces of Islam on the Iberian peninsula. The son of Sancho III,
Alfonso succeeded his father to the Castilian throne when he was only
three years old. During Alfonso's minority, the King of Navarre repeatedly
attempted to dominate Castile. Alfonso's marriage, in 1170, to Eleanor the
Younger of Aquitaine, daughter of England's King Henry II of England,
brought Castile an ally that put an end to interference from Navarre. In
1179, Alfonso concluded the pact of Cazorla, which divided Spain between
himself and Henry II. He further consolidated his power in 1188, by securing the homage of his cousin Alfonso IX of León, with whom he assembled a very large army to fight the Muslim Almohades. At the Battle of
Alarcos in 1195, the two Alfonsos suffered a severe defeat. To make matters worse, when Alfonso VIII and his forces limped back to Castile, they
discovered that the realm had been invaded by Navarre and by León, as
well as by the Almohades, who had now taken the offensive.

Surrender seemed the only viable option, but Alfonso would have none of it. He rallied his forces, which succeeded in pushing all of the invaders out of Castile. Nor was Alfonso content to remain on the defensive. He regrouped and quickly mounted an offensive against the Almohades, allying himself with many elements throughout the Angevin Empire (originally, lands held by Henry II and his sons Richard I and John, including England, Anjou, Normandy, and Aquitaine; by 1204, only England and parts of Aquitaine). By 1212, Alfonso VIII was once again in command of a huge army, which he led into Andalusia. At the momentous Battle of Las Navas de Tolosa on July 16, 1212, Alfonso scored a victory that forever ended Almohad power in Spain. Over the course of the next four decades, the Muslims would be pushed back into the tiny kingdom of Granada, and the Iberian peninsula emerged as a Christian-dominated region.

Alfonso's triumph at Las Navas de Tolosa gained much for his empire, but cost him his health. He returned, weak and ill, to Castile, where he died on October 6, 1214.

LEADERSHIP LESSONS

✦

Make strategic alliances to consolidate power.

✦

Set goals and be tenacious in achieving them.

✦

You are not defeated until you concede defeat.

✦

Rarely content yourself with a defensive position; seize the initiative quickly.

✦

Realize that defeat need not be permanent. Do not be afraid to use defeat as a springboard to victory. Rally your forces.

Allenby, Edmund Henry Hynman, 1st Viscount

Born: 1861   Died: 1936

**Character model   Conqueror   Improviser   Innovator   Leverager
Motivator   Problem solver   Strategist   Tactician**

LEADERSHIP ACHIEVEMENTS

✦

Mastered his craft

✦

Refused to yield to discouragement

✦

Led by example and inspiration

✦

Transformed a losing organization into a victorious one

✦

Leveraged all resources to the maximum

✦

Devised an economical, devastatingly effective approach to victory

✦

Effectively formulated strategy, and then effectively executed it

LIFE

Although he was consigned to one of the conflict's more marginal fronts, the Middle East, Edmund Allenby emerged as perhaps the greatest of Britain's commanders in World War I. Not only did he greatly elevate the morale of the disaffected troops under his command, he planned and executed the Battle of Megiddo, the military masterpiece of World War I and one of the most brilliant victories ever achieved by any commander in any conflict.

Allenby was born in Nottinghamshire and, in 1882, at an early age, joined the Inniskilling Dragoons. He served with the dragoons in the Bechuanaland (Botswana) expedition of 1884–85. In African service he earned the attention and admiration of his superiors. During the Second Anglo-Boer War (the Great Boer War) in South Africa, during 1900–02, he served on the staff of the senior commander, Lord Kitchener, as well as in the field. At the conclusion of the war, in 1902, he returned to England, where he was assigned command of the 5th Lancers from 1902 to 1905.

When World War I began in August 1914, Allenby was put in command of the cavalry division (later the cavalry corps) of the British Expeditionary Forces (BEF), serving in that capacity until November, when he was assigned command of V Corps. In October 1915, he was promoted to command of the British Third Army and performed well. During the Battle of Arras, April 9–15, 1917, he even performed with brilliance—however, he also exhibited an individualistic style of command and an unremitting aggressiveness that did not find favor with the British high command. He was, therefore, transferred from the Western Front, the war's principal theater, and sent, in June 1917, to one of the war's backwaters, the Middle East, where he replaced the inept Sir Archibald Murray as commander of British forces in Egypt.

Allenby understood that his transfer was hardly a reward for services rendered on the Western Front. But if he felt any disappointment or resentment, he never allowed himself to exhibit or express these feelings. Indeed, he set about transforming an undermanned, underequipped, hitherto poorly led, and thoroughly demoralized organization into a proud army. He resolved not merely to hold positions against the German-allied Turks, but to take the offensive.

By the early autumn of 1918, the Turks were under the command of the highly skilled German general Liman von Sanders. Sanders deployed the 36,000 men of the Turkish Fourth, Seventh, and Eighth armies in very formidable defensive works running from the Mediterranean Sea north of Jaffa all the way to the Jordan Valley. Despite a continual drain on his manpower—British high command always needed fresh troops for duty on the Western Front—Allenby managed to build up an army of 57,000 infantrymen and 12,000 cavalry, in addition to 540 big guns. While this was a substantial body of men, Allenby was well aware that even a significantly superior force could be wiped out by defenders who were entrenched behind solid fortifications, as the Turks were. He therefore formulated strategy to concentrate on what he saw as the most vulnerable point in the Turkish lines, the Mediterranean seashore. It was a strategy at once bold and complex, calling for not only decisive action but precise coordination between cavalry and infantry components.

The opening action of Allenby's great offensive was the Battle of Megiddo. It began at 4:30 A.M. on September 19, 1918, with a brief and intense artillery barrage followed by the advance of the entire British line. Thanks to his careful preparation, Allenby achieved total surprise. As he had planned, his XXI Corps ripped a wide gap through the Turkish line along the seacoast. Through this, the British Desert Mounted Corps rode while British fliers bombed rail junctions and all of the Turks' headquarters, thereby knocking out communications. As the British cavalry pushed through the Turkish Eighth Army, the British infantry maneuvered in a great wheeling pattern, sweeping all stunned resistance before it. By September 20, the Turkish Eighth Army had been crushed, and the Seventh, routed, fell back in disarray. Megiddo was certainly the most brilliant British action of World War I—possibly of any modern war. Allenby destroyed three enemy armies and took 76,000 prisoners. The cost to his own forces was almost trivial by comparison: 853 killed, 4,482 wounded, 385 missing.

After the Battle of Megiddo, from September 22 to October 30, Allenby relentlessly pursued the fleeing survivors of the Turkish army. Damascus fell on October 1, 1918, to an assault that combined Allenby's troops with Arab allied forces led by the eccentric T. E. Lawrence (Lawrence of Arabia). Lawrence was under Allenby's command, and it is a further measure of the general's leadership genius that he recognized Lawrence's uncanny talent for working with Arab guerrillas and that he gave Lawrence free rein in leading them.

The day after the fall of Damascus, Beirut came under British control. While elements of Allenby's infantry occupied Damascus and Beirut, his Desert Mounted Corps advanced deeper into enemy territory, capturing the Syrian city of Homs and then Aleppo on the Syrian border with Turkey itself. Having taken the British army to the Turkish doorstep, Allenby compelled the Turks to surrender on October 30, 1918.

IN HIS OWN WORDS

"Once you have taken a decision, never look back on it."
—Quoted in Archibald Wavell, *Allenby, Soldier and Statesman,* 1943

"Think to a finish!"
—1902

"In pursuit you must always stretch possibilities to the limit. Troops having beaten the enemy will want to rest. They must be given as objectives, not those that you think they will reach, but the farthest they could possibly reach."
—Order to XXI Corps, 1917

LEADERSHIP LESSONS

✦

"There are no small roles," the great acting teacher Stanislavski said, "only small actors." Make the most of whatever assignment you are given. Creating even a small masterpiece may have a profound effect.

✦

Devote time and care to planning.

✦

Never neglect morale and inspiration in leadership. They are always important.

✦

Express your pride and pleasure in leading the enterprise. Expressing disappointment or discouragement is rarely productive.

✦

Follow through. Execute plans fully. Exploit all advantages gained.

✦

Emphasize efficiency. Leverage your resources.

✦

In approaching any problem, look for a workable point of entry. Do not merely throw your resources at a problem. A sharp, focused approach is almost always more effective than battering away with a blunt instrument. Allenby's victory at Megiddo began when he devised a way to breach the enemy's line at a single, vulnerable point.

Arnold,
Henry Harley ("Hap")

Born: 1886   Died: 1950

**Innovator   Leverager   Mentor   Motivator   Strategist
Systems creator   Tactician   Visionary**

LEADERSHIP ACHIEVEMENTS

✦

Envisioned and then championed the creation of an air force

✦

Became a consummate advocate for his enterprise

✦

Mastered the art and science of aviation before taking a leadership role in it

✦

Created efficient patterns and systems of operation

✦

Fathered the U.S. Air Force

LIFE

Hap Arnold is an example of the leader as visionary innovator. Steeped in the tradition of the U.S. Army, he was also an aviation pioneer who instantly grasped the scope of the role aviation would play in warfare. He is generally regarded as the father of the U.S. Air Force.

Arnold was born in Gladwyne, Pennsylvania, and received an appointment to West Point, from which he graduated in 1907 with a second lieutenant's commission in the infantry. He saw service in the Philippines during 1907–09, but soon became passionately interested in flying—at the time, hardly a promising career path for an ambitious young officer.

In 1911, just eight years after the Wright brothers' first flight at Kitty Hawk, he transferred to the aeronautical section of the Signal Corps and volunteered for flight training with the brothers in Dayton, Ohio. Arnold then went on to make several pioneering contributions to military aviation. He was the first to demonstrate, in October 1912, how the airplane could be used for reconnaissance and was awarded the first McKay flying trophy for his efforts. He earned the first military aviator's badge and expert aviator's certificate, and he established a world altitude record of 6,540 feet.

Despite Arnold's extraordinary efforts—as well as the work of other early military aviation advocates—the army showed little interest in the airplane as a weapon. In April 1913, Arnold was transferred back to the infantry, but was returned to the air service three years later. Promoted to captain in May 1916, he was put in charge of the army's aviation training schools the following year, when the United States entered World War I. Arnold directed aviation training from May 1917 through 1919, earning a reputation as a great teacher.

Following the armistice in November 1918, sharp reductions in military funding retarded the development of American military aviation. Never discouraged, however, Arnold continued to work with whatever he had toward the goal of developing a viable Army Air Corps. His efforts did not go unrecognized. The army sent him to its prestigious Command and General Staff school, from which he graduated in 1929 with the rank of lieutenant colonel. In 1931, he was given command of the 1st Bomb Wing and the 1st Pursuit Wing at March Field, California, a post he held through February 1935. During July and August 1934, he led a flight of ten B-10 bombers on a round trip from Washington, D.C., to Fairbanks, Alaska, winning a second MacKay trophy for having proven the endurance capabilities of the modern bomber.

After promotion to brigadier general, Arnold took command of 1st Wing, GHQ Air Force in February 1935 and became assistant chief of staff of the Air Corps in December of that year. With the death of General Oscar Westover in September 1938, Arnold was given a temporary promotion to major general and named chief of staff. He used this position to institute a program to improve the combat readiness of the Air Corps, but was, as always, hampered by a lack of funding and a stubborn reluctance among tradition-bound military planners to back a fully effective air force. Yet, as always, the validity of Arnold's efforts did receive recognition: He was named acting deputy chief of staff of the Army for air matters in October 1940, and then chief of the Air Corps, after it was renamed the U.S. Army Air Forces in June 1941. Shortly after the December 7, 1941, bombing of Pearl Harbor and America's entry into World War II, Arnold was promoted to the temporary rank of lieutenant general. In March of the following year, he was named commanding general of Army Air Forces, and in 1943 was promoted to the temporary rank of general.

Arnold now served at the very highest level of policy and strategic planning in the U.S. military. Serving on the Joint Chiefs of Staff, he played a key role in shaping Allied strategy in the European as well as Pacific theaters of World War II. To conduct an effective bombing campaign against Japan, Arnold organized the 20th Air Force in April 1944, which answered directly to his command as a representative of the Joint Chiefs. This was a bold leadership step with profound implications because it took the Army Air Forces closer to becoming an independent service. The Army generally resisted the creation of an independent air force, but Arnold had come to believe that only in an independent service could military air power ever reach its full potential.

In December 1944, along with generals Dwight D. Eisenhower, Douglas MacArthur, and George C. Marshall, Hap Arnold was elevated to the special rank of general of the army—a five-star general. He continued to command the Army Air Forces through the end of the war, retiring in March 1946. Just a year later, on September 18, 1947, thanks in great measure to the foundation Arnold had laid, the Army Air Forces became an independent service, the U.S. Air Force.

LEADERSHIP LESSONS

Have the courage and perseverance to realize your dreams and visions.

Have the patience to endure disappointment without losing sight
of your goals.

Become the champion and advocate of your vision. Carry it through the
system. Do not give up.

Be prepared to demonstrate and justify your project or enterprise.

Learn to change the system by working within the system.

Follow through on your vision by creating and implementing practical
systems motivated by that vision.

Ashoka

Born: 273 B.C.   Died: 232 B.C.

Character model   Conqueror   Mentor   Motivator   Visionary

LEADERSHIP ACHIEVEMENTS

✦

Greatly augmented the vast Mauryan empire in India

✦

Abandoned destructive, violent forms of conquest for the beneficent
doctrine of "conquest by *dharma*"

LIFE

One of ancient India's greatest leaders, Ashoka (or Asoka) was king of
Magadha and third and last major emperor of the great Mauryan dynasty.
He began his career as a ruthless conqueror, but ended by adopting a
pacific policy of "conquest by *dharma*" (the practice of honesty, compassion,
benevolence, nonviolence, selfless asceticism, and general civility toward
all living things).

Ashoka was the grandson of Chandragupta and one of many sons of
Bindusara. The ancient *Ceylonese Chronicles* record that he fought a bloody
war of succession with his brothers, killing 99 of them in order to ascend
the throne. Other sources—most notably inscriptions left by Ashoka himself—make no mention of this. What is beyond doubt, however, is the ruthlessness of Ashoka's early wars, which were fought in the eighth year of his
reign against the peoples of Kalinga on India's east coast. Through these
bloody campaigns Ashoka greatly expanded his realm until it encompassed
all but the southern tip of India. Yet the misery these wars created greatly
grieved Ashoka, who turned to the teachings of Buddha, pledging to live
and to govern by Buddha's teachings and to spread the religion through his
realm.

From this point forward, Ashoka renounced war, advocated religious
tolerance, and instilled lofty ethics in all matters of government and commerce. He ordered the construction of many public works, including rest

houses throughout his realm for the benefit of travelers. In addition to planting many trees, he founded a chain of medical facilities for the treatment of people as well as animals. He is said to have ordered the construction of 84,000 *stupas* (reliquary mounds) throughout India and is generally credited with having established the basic sites of Buddhist pilgrimage and with personally providing a supreme example of Buddhist piety.

Ashoka dedicated himself to the Buddhist concept of *dharma*. This policy was apparently quite effective in maintaining his realm during his lifetime, but it did not survive his death in about 232 B.C. (Some authorities put it at about 238 B.C.) At this point, the Mauryan empire quickly disintegrated.

LEADERSHIP LESSONS

✦

Never discount the possibility of change in your life and career.

✦

Never discount the role of inspiration in leadership.

✦

Do well by doing good. What goes around comes around.

✦

Always look for better leadership methods; use them when you find them.

✦

You may find that leadership directed toward achieving common benefits is superior to leadership based on coercion.

Ashurnasirpal II

Died: 859 B.C.

Conqueror   Innovator   Strategist   Tactician

LEADERSHIP ACHIEVEMENTS
◆

Vastly expanded the reach of the Assyrian empire
◆

Virtually invented the "modern" empire
◆

Created the most formidable military machine of his age

LIFE

The facts surrounding the birth and early life of this important Assyrian king are lost in time. What is known is that Ashurnasirpal II vastly expanded his realm by forging the most powerful military machine the world had yet seen. With this army he brought destruction upon Mesopotamia, Kurdistan, and Syria.

Ashurnasirpal ascended the Assyrian throne after the death of his father, Tukulti-Ninurta, whose reign lasted only from 884 to 883 B.C. No sooner had he assumed power than Ashurnasirpal brought war against the hill tribes north of the Tigris River in what is now Kurdistan. These peoples had long menaced Assyria's borderlands, and Ashurnasirpal began his reign by neutralizing that threat. Next, in 883, he sacked the city of Nishtun and, the following year, put down a revolt begun in the city of Suru and backed by the Syrian kingdom of Bit-Adini. During 881–80, he crushed the Aramaeans and went on to defeat an alliance of tribes situated east of the Tigris.

While he campaigned, Ashurnasirpal continually built up, trained, and equipped his army. In 878, he judged his forces ready for a campaign against Babylon, and, in the same year, captured Suhu, another rebellious city of his own realm. With Babylon largely neutralized and internal threats suppressed, the king pushed into Syria, where he defeated Bit-Adini, and then crossed the Orontes River to extort tribute payment from the cities of Phoenicia during 875–74. Ashurnasirpal's final campaign was a successful expedition against the Kashiari hill tribes, which were in rebellion on the northwest borderlands of Assyria during 866.

The military achievements of Ashurnasirpal would be remarkable in any age. In the ninth century B.C., they were not only remarkable, but revolutionary. The age of Ashurnasirpal was one not of nations, but of isolated city-states and loosely constituted tribes. Within this political and social context, Ashurnasirpal created an empire, a vast, integrated realm governed by a central authority from a central location. To accomplish this, Ashurnasirpal remade his realm into a military society governed by institutionalized terror. A very able military leader who equipped his well-trained army with the world's most advanced iron and bronze weaponry, a commander who made skillful tactical use of archers and a formidable corps of combat charioteers, Ashurnasirpal was merciless with his enemies. He routinely impaled and mutilated military prisoners. As for conquered populations, Ashurnasirpal did not scruple to press them into abject slavery. He was, without a doubt, a tyrant and a dictator, yet he sowed the seeds of the modern concept of empire.

LEADERSHIP LESSONS

✦

Some leaders are, first and foremost, inventors, whose innovations may change the culture of a department or corporation, the direction of an industry, or the politics of the world.

✦

Ashurnasirpal decided what he needed to dominate his world—a great military machine—and he focused all of his resources on developing it.

✦

Understand and accept the values necessary to achieve your goals; in the case of Ashurnasirpal, these values included absolute authority enforced by ruthless terror—which is unacceptable today, of course, but was commonplace among rulers of Ashurnasirpal's age.

✦

Do not fight external wars without having first achieved control of internal dissent.

Askia Muhammad (Mohammad I Askia, Muhammad ibn abi Bakr Ture)

Died: 1538

Conqueror Motivator Systems creator

LEADERSHIP ACHIEVEMENTS

✦

Was a strong personal leader

✦

Achieved greatness as the emperor of the Songhai Empire

✦

Brought the Songhai to its greatest height

✦

Was a skilled and tireless military commander, but also understood when it was time to break off a campaign that ultimately threatened his empire

✦

Structured his empire's government wisely and efficiently

LIFE

Born in obscurity and of unknown ancestry, Askia Muhammad went on to become the greatest emperor of the Songhai Empire of North Africa and the founder of the Askian dynasty. He first appears in history as a military commander under Sonni Ali Ber, ruler of Songhai. On Sonni's death in 1492, Askia Muhammad used his charismatic personality to recruit an army that defeated the numerically superior forces of Sonni Baru, son of Sonni Ali Ber, in the Battle of Anfao on April 12, 1493. This earned Askia the throne.

Immediately upon taking power, Askia Muhammad instituted a series of empire-wide reforms. He purged the realm of paganism and put in its place the orthodox observance of Islam. He rationalized and bureaucratized the government, creating distinct ministries to handle finance, justice, affairs of the interior, and agriculture. He devoted his greatest effort to building a well-organized standing army and a navy consisting of war canoes that patrolled the Niger River.

After making a pilgrimage to Mecca in 1495–97, Askia Muhammad commenced a series of ruthless campaigns to expand the Songhai Empire while simultaneously spreading Islam. He began by conquering the Mossi of Yatenga (Upper Volta) during 1498–1502, then attacked the Tuaregs of the Aïr massif (and the vicinity of Agadez, Niger) during 1505–06. For the next seven years, from 1507 to 1514, Askia advanced toward Senegal and to the borderlands of modern-day Niger and Nigeria to fight the Fulani and the Borgu. These last two campaigns, long and arduous, failed to subjugate the Fulani and Borgu, but Askia was able to defeat the Bornu of northeastern Nigeria.

Following the great campaigns of expansion, one of Askia's subordinates, the Karta of Kabi, rebelled against him. During 1516–17, Askia suppressed the Karta's revolt, but the action made clear to him that it was time to halt the expansion of Songhai. Years of uninterrupted military campaigning had created too much internal dissension. Indeed, the children of Askia Muhammad soon fell to disputing over who should succeed their father. As the disputes became increasingly discordant, Askia became increasingly bitter. His health declined. Ill and nearly blind, he was deposed by his son Musa (who took the name Askia Musa) in 1528 and was sent into internal exile on a small island in the Niger River. When another of Askia Muhammad's sons, Ismaïl, ascended the throne, however, he brought his father out of exile. The grateful old ruler bestowed upon Ismaïl his turban and sword, dying a short time later in the Songhai capital of Gao.

LEADERSHIP LESSONS

✦

A leader's authority comes in large part from his ability to persuade others of that authority.

✦

Personal, direct leadership is important, but a successful organization also requires efficient systems.

✦

Always focus on the homefront; be prepared to alter goals to preserve the enterprise.

Atatürk, Mustafa Kemal

Born: 1881   Died: 1938

Innovator   Mentor   Motivator   Rescuer   Systems creator   Visionary

LEADERSHIP ACHIEVEMENTS

✦

Advanced from obscure poverty to a military leadership position

✦

Won the loyalty of those he led

✦

Wholly identified himself with the enterprise he led

✦

Almost single-handedly created the modern Turkish nation

LIFE

Deservedly called the father of modern Turkey, Atatürk almost single-handedly transformed his nation from a moribund Islamic state to a forward-looking country bridging Europe and Asia.

Born in Salonika, Greece—then a part of Ottoman-controlled Macedonia—Mustafa Kemal (Atatürk's given name) was the son of a lower-middle-class customs clerk and his peasant wife. The death of his father left the family in dire straits, but the boy was selected, on scholarship, to attend a state-run military academy, followed by the Senior Military School and, finally, in 1899, the Ottoman Military Academy in Istanbul. In addition to receiving advanced military training, Kemal was exposed to a liberal education. He was particularly attracted to the works of Rousseau, Voltaire, Hobbes, and the other seminal social thinkers of Europe, especially of the Enlightenment. A brilliant student, Kemal, at the age of 20, was promoted to the General Staff College.

It was here that Kemal met like-minded young officers, determined to rescue their nation from its agonizingly slow but certain death as a corrupt, decaying empire. Kemal and his comrades founded the Vatan, a secret revolutionary society. When the Vatan failed to grow beyond its small initial membership, Kemal joined the Committee on Union and Progress, which was aligned with the Young Turk Movement, the principal movement working toward radical government reform. Although Kemal was not directly associated with the Young Turks and their coup d'etat of 1908, he worked closely with many of their key leaders.

At the outbreak of World War I, Kemal was appalled when the sultan aligned the Ottoman Empire with the Germans, whom he distrusted and despised. Yet he put aside his personal feelings to lead his troops with great skill on every Ottoman front during World War I.

With World War I ended, the victorious Allies all but licked their chops over the Ottoman Empire, eager to carve it up and maintain Turkey as a puppet empire; however, Kemal was determined to create an independent, vigorous Turkish state. When government officials sent him to Anatolia in 1919 to put down unrest there, he instead organized that dissent and used it as the nucleus of a movement to combat the numerous "foreign interests" that had invaded his country.

Kemal established a provisional government in Anatolia and was promptly elected its president. From this position, he organized a unified resistance to foreigners. In response, the Ottoman sultan ordered a *jihad,* or holy war, against the Nationalists, as Kemal's party was called. However, when the sultan signed the Treaty of Sèvres in August 1920, which effectively handed the Ottoman Empire over to the Allies in exchange for their promise to keep him in power, public support went overwhelmingly to Kemal, who was enabled to lead his Nationalist Army successfully against the Ottoman capital, Istanbul. The Allies looked to Greece to send troops to resist the Nationalists, but after 18 bitter months of very bloody combat, the Greeks were finally defeated in August 1922. On November 1, 1922, the Grand National Assembly formally dissolved the sultanate of Mehmed VI, and on October 29, 1923, Mustafa Kemal was elected president of the new Republic of Turkey.

Although he was called president, Kemal ruled as a dictator—outlawing all competing political parties, and engineering repeated reelection until his death—although he is more properly considered a benevolent despot, for Kemal wanted no personal glory. He sought, rather, to resurrect Turkey, and he thoroughly reformed its government and society.

Kemal's most sweeping reforms came in the areas of the economy and the social structure. He opened up the Turkish economy to the industrialized West, he secularized the state, he ended the Islamic suppression of women, and, generally, he forced the Western way of life on his people.

Upon proclaiming the creation of the Turkish Republic, Kemal became the recipient of a new name, Atatürk (father of the Turks).

IN HIS OWN WORDS

"Only the teachers and educators are the saviors of nations. A nation wanting of these cannot yet be called a nation. It may be called an ordinary mass but not a nation."
—1925, quoted in Yilmaz Oz, *Quotations from Mustafa Kemal Atatürk,* 1982

"Full pleasure and happiness in life can be found only in working for the honor and happiness of future generations."
—1937, quoted in Yilmaz Oz, *Quotations from Mustafa Kemal Atatürk,* 1982

LEADERSHIP LESSONS

✦

Do not allow your circumstances to limit your options.

✦

Cultivate vision. Do not shun vision as mere idealism.

✦

Do not hesitate to inspire.

✦

Identify yourself, wholeheartedly and publicly, with the enterprise you lead.

✦

Create a definite program for leadership, with clearly defined goals that are ambitious but attainable.

Attila the Hun

Died: 453

Conqueror   Motivator   Profit maker   Strategist   Tactician

LEADERSHIP ACHIEVEMENTS

✦

Acquired territories so vast that he earned a place as history's most famous conqueror

✦

Perfected an ability to move masses of men quickly and in perfect order, and to attack swiftly, with overwhelming strength

✦

Combined ferocity with a high degree of discipline

✦

Consistently turned conquest to profit

LIFE

Attila was known in his own time as the "Scourge of God" and to history simply as Attila the Hun, a name synonymous with ruthless conquest. By any measure, he was a remarkable leader, who, contrary to popular belief, did not rely on the savagery of the troops he led, but on his brilliant skill in managing masses of men in overwhelming attacks.

Attila and his brother Bleda became joint chieftains of the Huns, a warlike tribe of Germanic nomads, in 433, upon the death of their uncle Ruas. A great leader in his own right, Ruas had brought the Huns to a position of unprecedented power in central Europe. Theodosius II, emperor of mighty Rome, agreed to pay Ruas a tribute and to make him a general in the Roman army, thereby effectively ceding to the Huns sovereignty over the province of Panonia (modern Hungary). On the death of Ruas, Attila and Bleda renewed the treaty with Theodosius, exacting from him an even heavier tribute: 700 pounds of gold per annum.

Despite the high cost, it was a wise investment that bought the Roman Empire half a dozen years of peace, as Attila and Bleda focused on conquering the non-Roman world, including Scythia, Media, and Persia. At last, however, during 441–43, the Vandal king Gaiseric paid Attila to invade Rome's Eastern Empire. Abrogating the treaty with Theodosius, Attila advanced into Illyricum, leading his Huns into Moesia and Thrace and up to the walls of Constantinople itself. The Huns quickly destroyed the imperial army of Aspar, which left Attila free to raid throughout the Balkans. In desperation, Theodosius concluded, in August 443, a new treaty, offering to Attila an even higher tribute payment.

In 445, Attila murdered his brother in order to become sole ruler of the Huns. His realm now reached from southern Germany in the west to the Volga River in the east, and from the Baltic in the north to the Danube, the Black Sea, and the Caucasus in the south.

In 447, Attila invaded the Eastern Empire again. Constantinople was thrown into total panic because its walls, on which the defenders successfully relied during the first invasion, had been badly damaged by a recent earthquake. Despite this, East Roman forces were able to blunt Attila's advance at the Battle of Utus. The reversal was temporary, as Attila mounted a fresh attack that defeated the imperial army; however, Attila's conquests typically relied on speed, the rapid delivery of overwhelming force. Once he had lost momentum against Constantinople, Attila turned his army away from the capital of the Eastern Empire and instead advanced on Greece. In Greece, Attila attacked but failed to take the great fortress city of Thermopylae.

Even though he did not attack Constantinople, Attila had made his point. Theodosius negotiated yet another treaty, agreeing to pay Attila three times the original tribute, in addition to ceding to him a 50-mile-wide strip along the right bank of the Danube, from Singidunum (modern Belgrade) to Novae (Svistov, in modern Bulgaria).

This did not sate Attila's appetite for conquest. In 450, he turned from the Eastern Empire to the Western. He seized on a convenient pretext for an invasion: Gaiseric of the Vandals wanted an ally in the West; one of two heirs to the Frankish throne asked Attila for an alliance; and, finally, Attila sought redress for the rebuff he had suffered from Valentinian III, ruler of the Western Empire, when he had sought the hand in marriage of his sister Honoria. In 451, therefore, Attila crossed the Rhine and attacked Gaul with a force reported to have numbered half a million (but which modern scholars believe was closer to 100,000). The commander attempted to persuade the Visigoth ruler Theodoric to join the battle, but the Roman general

Aetius convinced Theodoric to ally the Visigoths with Rome. Thus Aetius assembled a coalition of imperial forces, Visigoths, and others—principally the Alans, fickle kinsmen of the Huns—to confront Attila's horde.

During May and June of 451, Attila besieged Orléans and brought it to the verge of surrender when Aetius arrived to relieve it. The Roman commander pursued Attila's army as far as the Catalaunian Plains, near Châlons-sur-Marne. Aetius won a decisive victory at the ensuing Battle of Châlons during mid-June 451. It proved to be a contest of momentous consequences. A Hun victory would have meant the end of Roman—and Christian—civilization.

But Attila was not victorious. Indeed, badly defeated, he barely managed to retreat with his surviving forces intact. His defeat did not discourage him from renewing his suit for the hand of Honoria the following year. Again, however, Valentinian refused him. This time, Attila responded by invading Italy, destroying Aquileia, and forcing the withdrawal of the people of Venetia (who, fleeing to islands off the Italian coast, contributed to the founding of Venice). Attila's troops leveled Padua and attacked Minicio. However, Attila's army was being eroded by famine and pestilence, which prompted Attila to withdraw from Italy without further battle. He died the next year.

LEADERSHIP LESSONS

✦

Focus single-mindedly on your goal.

✦

Value swift, decisive action; typically, this requires careful advance
planning and then resolute execution.

✦

Emphasize training. Swift, flawless execution can be achieved consistently
only by a thoroughly competent team.

✦

Understand your purpose; in the case of Attila, conquest meant not merely
the acquisition of land, but the accumulation of profit.

✦

Consider pushing the envelope by demanding somewhat more than you
believe you can get.

Augustus, Gaius Julius Caesar Octavianus

Born: 63 B.C. Died: A.D. 14

**Character model   Conqueror   Innovator   Motivator
Systems creator   Visionary**

LEADERSHIP ACHIEVEMENTS

✦

Rose from relative obscurity to a position of greatest power and prestige in
the world's mightiest empire

✦

Combined courage with a persuasive personal and political appeal

✦

Was a leader as adept on the field of battle as in the chamber
of the Senate

✦

Left Rome with a system of government that survived poor leadership

✦

Gave Rome years of relative peace

✦

Created an enduring and unparalleled cultural legacy for Rome

LIFE

Augustus was the first emperor of Rome. While he scrupled at virtually
nothing to attain absolute power, once he had attained it, Augustus ruled
with moderation and wisdom. He was called Octavian before the Senate
honored him with the title Augustus in 27 B.C. He was born on September
23, 63 B.C., the son of Gaius Octavius, a senator, and Atia, niece of Julius
Caesar. The bright and valiant Octavian quickly became Caesar's favorite
and accompanied him on his Spanish campaign in 44 B.C. In his will,
Caesar posthumously adopted Octavian. Thus, after Caesar's assassination on March 15, 44 B.C., Octavian styled himself Gaius Julius Caesar and
won the support of Caesar's loyal veterans, whom he mustered into an illegal private army to oppose Mark Antony.

In January 43, the Senate, which greatly distrusted Antony, made
young Octavian a senator and thereby legitimated his military command. In

the spring of 43—probably in April—Octavian led his army to victory over Antony at Mutina (modern-day Modena), then marched on Rome, and promoted his own election as consul on August 19. Octavian deftly forged an alliance with the defeated Antony and Marcus Aemilius Lepidus. Thus united, they were able to coerce the Senate into naming them triumvirs—joint rulers—on November 27, 43 B.C., their term of rule to last for five years. Their mandate from the Senate was to reform and reorganize the republic. Acting under cover of this, they began their administration by vigorously purging the government of enemies political and personal. This accomplished, in September 42, Antony and Octavian invaded Greece to crush republican conspirators under the command of Brutus and Cassius. Victories at the two battles of Philippi in Macedonia, on October 26 and November 16, 42 B.C., achieved this objective.

Following the triumph in Greece, Antony remained in the East to rule that portion of the empire, while Octavian returned to Italy, where he put down a rebellion (41 B.C.) in Perusia led by Lucius Antonius, Mark Antony's brother. This nearly provoked a break with Antony, but the two came to an accord by means of the Treaty of Brundisium in 40 and through the marriage of Antony to Octavian's sister in 37. In recognition of their successes, the Senate extended the triumvirate for another five years.

From 40 to 36, Octavian campaigned against Sextus Pompeius. In the meantime, in 38, he married Livia Drusilla, a prominent daughter of the republican aristocracy, thereby signaling a desire to come to an accommodation with the republicans. In 36, he engineered the removal of Lepidus from power and assumed control of the African provinces himself. In 34, he led a military expedition to Dalmatia, Illyria, and Panonia in eastern Europe. When Antony's affair with the Egyptian monarch Cleopatra became known, Octavian seized the opportunity to turn political and popular opinion against his fellow triumvir, accusing him in 33 of despotic designs against the republic. The next year, Italy and all of the western provinces professed their allegiance to Octavian, but most of the Senate sided with Antony. On September 2, 31, Octavian met and defeated Mark Antony at the Battle of Actium, capturing most of Antony's army, and then launching an invasion of Egypt, which he conquered by the summer of 30. A defeated Antony committed suicide, as did his paramour Cleopatra. Octavian, now sole ruler of Rome, returned to the capital in triumph the next year. He proclaimed the restoration of the republic, and, with a grand sense of political theater, declared in 27 B.C. that he was stepping down. The Senate, beseeching Octavian not to abandon the state, named him *Augustus* and *Imperator*—emperor. In 23 he was made tribune for life, in 12 he became *pontifex maximus,* head of Roman state religion, and in 2 B.C. he was endowed with the title *Patris Patriae,* Father of His Country.

Having attained the ultimate position of power through craft, intimidation, and ruthlessness, Augustus refused to become a tyrant. Instead of an absolute tyranny, he created the *principate*—the rule of the princeps ("first citizen"), a system in which the army and the people pledged allegiance to the imperator (emperor) and to a collaborative government of the emperor and the two ruling social classes: the senators and the equestrians. In effect, Augustus ensconced himself less in an absolute monarchy than in a constitutional one. He brought a high degree of peace to Rome and fostered literature, the arts, and learning to create the moral and cultural high point of Rome.

LEADERSHIP LESSONS

✦

Give 100 percent and focus all on achieving goals. Most important projects
require no less.

✦

Cultivate the friendship and collegiality of powerful people.

✦

The most persuasive ideas are those we believe are our own. Maneuver
others into proposing the course of action you wish to pursue.

✦

Foster the conditions of worthwhile creativity in the enterprise you lead.

Bajan

Died: 609

Conqueror Profit maker Rescuer Strategist

LEADERSHIP ACHIEVEMENTS

✦

Despite a number of defeats, expanded the holdings of the Avar people

✦

Halted the disintegration of the Avar position in Europe

✦

Reaped great economic gains from the Byzantine Empire

✦

Essentially created the Avars as a nation

LIFE

The warrior-king Bajan led the Avars, a loose confederation of nomadic tribes related to the Huns, expanding their conquests and uniting them as a nation. Nothing is known about the birth and early life of Bajan, who enters history in 558, after he was elected *khagan* (great khan) of the Avars. His election came at a time of great crisis for the Avars, who had been evicted from several lands in central Asia and were now precariously hunkered down along the lower Danube.

Bajan saw his first task as establishing some security for his people, so he concluded a treaty with the Byzantine emperor Justinian I, who agreed to pay the Avars an annual tribute in exchange for their services as allies in defense of the northern frontier of Byzantium. Given this mandate, Bajan immediately expanded his defensive brief to lead aggressive raids during 558–63 into the territory now encompassed by Romania and Hungary. He also attacked the Franks, who managed to repel him at Thuringia in 562. During one of his Frankish raids, however, Bajan captured King Siegebert I of Austrasia, releasing him in 566 only after the payment of a heavy ransom. Following this, Bajan struck an alliance with the Lombards to defeat the Gepidae under King Cunimund in 568.

When Justinian II ascended the Byzantine throne, he called a halt to the annual payment of tribute to the Avars. In response, Bajan captured the Byzantine city of Sirmium, holding it as ransom until Tiberius II, who succeeded Justinian II in 578, resumed tribute payments.

Bajan proved as treacherous an ally as he was a ruthless adversary. In 581, Tiberius's forces were heavily engaged against the Persians when Slavs invaded Illyria. Tiberius called on his high-priced Avar troops for assistance. Perceiving that the Byzantine forces were weak and overextended, Bajan came to the emperor's aid only after demanding and obtaining the return of Sirmium in 582. That same year, however, Maurice became Byzantine emperor and refused Bajan's demand for another increase in tribute. Bajan then marched on Singidunum (modern Belgrade) and Viminacium (at the confluence of the Morava and Danube rivers), taking and occupying these cities. The Byzantine emperor could do nothing other than back down. He settled with Bajan in 584, but, later that same year, he again refused to render tribute, apparently believing that Bajan had instigated renewed Slavic raids along the frontier. In response, Bajan invaded the Byzantine empire proper, penetrating as far as Adrianople in Thrace. A strong counterattack from Maurice forced his withdrawal in 587. Bajan concluded a truce with Maurice, which bought the Byzantine emperor sufficient time to devote his full forces to defeating the Persians.

With the Persian threat disposed of, Maurice, in 592, made an alliance with the Franks to fight the Avars. By now perhaps 60 years old, Bajan nevertheless did not hesitate to meet the combined enemy head on and, in a series of brilliant campaigns, defeated the allies.

Maurice negotiated a new treaty with Bajan in 599, and Bajan wasted little time in abrogating it. He attacked Dalmatia, prompting Maurice to send a large army. Bajan was defeated in a series of battles that culminated in the 601 Battle of Viminacium, which pushed the Avars back to the Danube. Following this defeat, Bajan retreated into his realm. He had ended his reign not on a note of triumph, yet, nevertheless, the Avar holdings were ample, stretching from the Julian Alps to the Volga River, and from the Baltic Sea to the Danube, and the Avars themselves had evolved from tribal nomads to something resembling a unified nation.

LEADERSHIP LESSONS

✦

First things first. An effective leader's first objective is to create a secure
position for his enterprise.

✦

A dynamic leader is ruthless in acquiring new sources of revenue.

✦

Conclude effective alliances, but treat them with a degree of flexibility.

✦

A great leader gives his enterprise a viable collective identity.

Barton, Clara

Born: 1821   Died: 1912

**Character model   Improviser   Innovator   Mentor   Motivator
Problem solver   Rescuer   Systems creator   Visionary**

LEADERSHIP ACHIEVEMENTS

✦

Began by carving out a meaningful life in a society that offered few
opportunities to women

✦

Seized on immediate problems and set to work to address them

✦

By engaging local problems, developed programs with national and
international impact

✦

Put ideals into action, morals into deeds

✦

Led others by her example

LIFE

Most famous as the founder of the American Red Cross, Clara Barton was
also a pioneer in the field of military nursing. She was born Clarissa Harlowe
Barton in North Oxford, Massachusetts, to a socially liberal farming family.
Clara began her formal schooling at the age of three. She took naturally to
schoolwork, and when she was 11 years old, discovered another apparently
natural inclination. After one of her brothers was seriously injured in a fall,
Clara volunteered to nurse him, doing so faithfully for two years.

As a teenager, Barton volunteered as a tutor to the poor and as a nurse
to the sick. In the early 19th century, the profession of nursing did not exist
as such, so Barton took up school teaching. She carried her interest in education beyond the classroom by skillfully campaigning, at the local level, for
educational reform. Yet this field of endeavor did not fully engage her, so
she decided to pursue further education for herself. In 1850 she enrolled at
Clinton Liberal Institute, an academy in Clinton, New York, run by the
Universalist Church. Her education here was cut short, however, by the

death of her mother in 1851 and consequent family financial hardships. Moving to New Jersey, she taught school in Hightstown and then Bordentown, but, outraged when she discovered that she was being paid far less than a newly hired male teacher, she quit in 1854, returned home briefly, and then set out for Washington, D.C. Here she impressed the U.S. commissioner of patents, Charles Mason, who hired her as a recording clerk in the Patent Office—at the same salary as her male colleagues. After three years, Barton's career was interrupted by Mason's resignation; she did not return to her clerkship until Mason came back to the Patent Office in December 1860. In the interim, Barton struggled financially, but she also found time to nurse a nephew through a bout of tuberculosis.

The outbreak of the Civil War in the spring of 1861 prompted Barton to organize charitable drives to supply Union troops with badly needed provisions. When the Union suffered its initial stunning defeat at the First Battle of Bull Run in July 1861, one of the many shocks was the almost total unpreparedness of the army to cope with a high volume of wounded troops. In the capital, makeshift hospitals were quickly set up, including one at the Patent Office. Barton nursed the wounded here. Then, at the suggestion of a former landlady, she resolved to nurse the wounded on the battlefield itself. Skeptical officials hardly welcomed her at first, believing that any woman would be more of a hindrance than a help on the field of battle. Barton recruited the support of Massachusetts governor John Andrew, who aided her efforts to prevail upon the Union army quartermaster to allow her to aid the troops. Soon, Barton recruited others to serve as volunteer nurses. After the Second Battle of Bull Run in late August 1862, her reputation began to spread throughout the Union forces. But it was at the Battle of Antietam, Maryland, in September 1862, that Barton truly came into her own and won grateful praise as "the angel of the battlefield."

While Barton's efforts in aid of the wounded were deeply appreciated by the soldiers, she came into conflict with certain army officers and with such figures as Dorothea Dix, who was the organizer of a more or less official Union army nursing corps. At this point in her work, Barton preferred to labor alone rather than to organize and lead others, and her independence did not sit well with bureaucrats and even with some well-meaning officials. Rather than persist in her maverick ways and risk being barred from the battlefield, Barton selflessly compromised and cooperated—at least to some degree—with the Christian Commission and other officially sanctioned organizations.

As the war drew to a close in the spring of 1865, Barton secured permission from President Abraham Lincoln to organize searches for missing soldiers. Barton also led a project to identify and bury thousands of anonymous Union dead at the horrific Andersonville prisoner-of-war camp in Georgia. Leading 40 workers, Barton succeeded in transforming the miserable burial yard at Andersonville into a national cemetery.

In the fall of 1866, at the suggestion of a friend, Barton toured the United States to lecture on her Civil War experiences. She then brought her lecture programs to Europe, where, in 1869, she was visited by Dr. Louis Appia of the International Convention of Geneva, popularly known as the Red Cross. Appia had heard of her work during the Civil War, and he hoped that Barton could use her influence to persuade the U.S. government, always wary of "foreign entanglements," to sign on to the articles of the Geneva Convention, which legally bound signatory nations to provide impartial relief to the wounded, sick, and homeless during times of war.

But Clara Barton did not immediately return to the United States. In July 1870, the Franco–Prussian War broke out, and by the end of the month Barton volunteered to do relief work with the Red Cross. After the war, Barton was befriended by the Grand Duchess Louise, daughter of Kaiser Wilhelm I and the founder of the German branch of the Red Cross. Barton worked for a time at the German Red Cross Hospital in Baden.

The critical illness of her sister Sally brought Barton back to the United States at the end of 1873, and Sally's death early the next year sent Barton into a severe depression, for which she was briefly hospitalized. In 1877, however, the outbreak of war between Russia and Turkey prompted Barton to work toward creating an American Red Cross Society, which would provide international war relief. When the federal government persisted in refusing to recognize the Geneva Convention, Barton did not give up on the idea of an American Red Cross. If such an organization could not be sent to the relief of foreign populations ravaged by war, it could still be of great benefit at home, as an aid to Americans during natural and other disasters. Barton embarked on a campaign to educate the American public on the international Red Cross movement, and she led a growing campaign to win acceptance for an American branch of the organization.

It was formed, at long last, on May 21, 1881. In 1882, working with Susan B. Anthony, Barton was able to help win Senate approval of the Geneva Convention, which was signed by President Chester A. Arthur. In the meantime, American Red Cross chapters opened throughout the United States, with Barton serving as the organization's national president.

In September 1884, when Barton attended the Third International Conference of the Red Cross in Geneva, Switzerland—thereby becoming the first female diplomat to represent the United States—she persuaded the conference to adopt the principles of the American Red Cross, so that the international organization would now serve during peacetime to assist victims of natural and other disasters. Under Barton's leadership, the American Red Cross grew into a large and respected organization that rendered aid not only at home but also internationally.

Although Barton received scores of national and international accolades and medals, her uncompromising hands-on leadership—and micromanagement—of what had now become a vast organization brought serious criticism as she continued to advance in years. Barton, 82, resigned as Red Cross president on May 14, 1904.

LEADERSHIP LESSONS

◆

The most important qualification for leadership is a simple and immediate willingness to do whatever work is necessary.

◆

Worthwhile goals are an almost limitless source of energy and as certain a guarantee of success as any that can be hoped for.

◆

Open your eyes to the work before you. Then do the work and do it well.

◆

Leadership is comprised, in large part, of an intense need to help others.

◆

Actions do indeed speak louder than words. Lead by example. Lead through action.

◆

The great problem of the hands-on leader is allowing the productive presence of other hands.

◆

Great work may be local in scope.

Bismarck, Otto von

Born: 1815   Died: 1898

Conqueror   Innovator   Motivator   Strategist   Systems creator   Visionary

LEADERSHIP ACHIEVEMENTS

✦

Created policies that made Prussia dominant among the German states

✦

Fashioned Prussia into the nucleus around which a united German Empire
was created

✦

Reshaped European politics to suit the needs and desires of Germany

✦

Was, for better or worse, a principal architect of Europe on the brink of the
20th century

LIFE

The son of a Prussian landowner of modest means, Otto von Bismarck
became prime minister of Prussia (an eastern German state on the Baltic
Sea), which his military and diplomatic policies elevated to preeminence
among the German states. Prussia thus became the nucleus around which
those states fused into a nation destined to become one of the greatest
powers in Europe.

Young Bismarck was a restless youth who, for lack of anything more
appealing, took up the study of law—though, from all reports, he spent
more time drinking with his classmates than working toward his degree.
He left the university without graduating to enter the Prussian civil service. No sooner had he landed a position than he found it intolerably dull.
This sent him packing back to his father's farm to help manage the estate.
During this time, Bismarck became interested in local politics and, in 1849,
won election as a representative in the Prussian Chamber of Deputies. At
last, he found something he could be passionate about. Bismarck became
an eloquent and avid advocate of German nationalism.

Bismarck's intelligence and nationalist ideas soon caught the attention
of Kaiser Wilhelm I, who, in 1859, appointed him Prussian ambassador to

Russia, and then, in 1862, ambassador to France. Later that same year, the kaiser recalled him to Berlin, where he was named prime minister as well as foreign minister.

Bismarck's dual appointment enabled him to manage domestic as well as foreign policy. With single-minded focus, he maneuvered adroitly to unite the disparate German states under the unwavering leadership of Prussia. He declared that the great issues of the day would not be settled by "speeches and majority resolutions," but by "iron and blood." In 1866, he provoked war with Austria to wrestle from it dominion over the long-contested Schleswig–Holstein region. Having devoted Prussian resources to improving the kingdom's already formidable army, Bismarck was confident of victory over Austria, although even he was delighted by the speed with which it came: a mere seven weeks. As a result of the Austro–Prussian, or Seven-Weeks, War, Prussia not only acquired new territory, but replaced Austria as the dominant force among the German states. Prussia now became the center of a new North German Confederation.

Having all but united Germany around Prussia, Bismarck next goaded Napoleon III into the Franco–Prussian War of 1870–71. Again, Bismarck entered the war confident of victory, and, indeed, the Prussian forces made short work of the French army. The kingdom gained Alsace and Lorraine, but, even more important, acquired sufficient prestige to attract all of the German states, except for Austria, under the Prussian-held umbrella of a new German Empire.

Wilhelm I, now the first kaiser (emperor) of the German empire, gratefully appointed Bismarck his chancellor. Having used the Franco–Prussian war to reshape Europe by creating a unified Germany, Bismarck realized that steps were urgently required to maintain and protect the great structure he had created.

In terms of territory, the greatest boon Bismarck had brought the new Germany was the Alsace–Lorraine region, which was rich in one of the most important resources of the 19th century, coal. This territory had been the eastern frontier of France, and Bismarck understood that German possession of it now created an eternal enmity between France and Germany. Bismarck had shown that he was anything but averse to war, but he was not willing to embark on a war in which he was not absolutely confident of victory. He believed that German military might could deal with whatever France might hurl against it in the future, provided that France acted alone. Bismarck observed that, during the 1870s, Britain had pursued a policy British statesmen themselves described as "splendid isolation." As long as Britain maintained this policy of noninterference in continental affairs, Bismarck believed he had little to fear from that nation. Russia and Austria–Hungary, on the other hand, posed a serious threat. Bismarck decided to forestall any possible alliance between those countries and France by tying both Russia and Austria–Hungary to Germany, thereby freezing out the French. Accordingly, in 1873, he negotiated the Three Emperors' League, binding the three powers to assist one another in time of war.

It was a brilliant stroke of diplomacy; however, in 1878, Russia withdrew from the league, and Bismarck decided to further strengthen German ties to Austria–Hungary by creating the Dual Alliance in 1879. This agreement bound the two nations to aid one another if either was attacked by Russia. Next, in 1881, came the Triple Alliance, which included Germany, Austria–Hungary, and Italy. By this document, Germany and Austria–Hungary agreed to aid Italy if it were attacked by France, while Italy would aid Germany if it was attacked by France. If one of the signatories became involved with two or more powers, the others would come to its aid. Perhaps most provocative was a provision that, if one of the signatories launched a "preventive attack" on another power (that is, *started* a war), the others would remain benevolently neutral.

Even more alliances followed: in 1883, one between Austria–Hungary and Romania, with Germany as an adherent, and in 1887, a secret "Reinsurance Treaty" between Germany and Russia, by which the two nations agreed to remain neutral if either became involved in a war with a third power (unless Germany attacked France, or Russia attacked Austria–Hungary). This secret treaty, Bismarck believed, would prevent Germany from ever having to face a two-front war against both France and Russia. The secret treaty lapsed in 1890, however.

Bismarck's diplomacy shaped European politics around the needs and desires of Germany. Bismarck hoped to avoid war—or, at least, what he deemed *unnecessary* war—by means of the system of alliances he had engineered. Tragically, however, these very alliances prompted France, Britain, and Russia to make alliances of their own. By the end of the 19th century, Europe was a complex network of alliances and counteralliances, which ultimately entangled the great powers and dragged them, almost helplessly, into the great cataclysm of World War I.

As for Bismarck, his day came to an end with the ascension of Kaiser Wilhelm II to the German throne in 1888. Unlike Wilhelm I, the new kaiser, a vain and ignorant man, had no desire to share power with the "Iron Chancellor." He brought about Bismarck's dismissal in 1890. Bismarck retired an honored figure in Germany, and he died eight years later.

IN HIS OWN WORDS

"The right people in the right jobs."
—Speech, 1875

"Politics is the art of the possible."
—Remark recorded on August 11, 1867

LEADERSHIP LESSONS

Leadership is not about the power of the leader, but about the power of the relationships the leader creates.

Alliances should be forged proactively, to advance the enterprise and to forestall future conflict.

♦

One of a leader's principal purposes is to create a powerful sense of common cause among those he leads.

Blake, Robert

Born: 1599   Died: 1657

Leverager   Motivator   Strategist   Tactician

LEADERSHIP ACHIEVEMENTS

✦

Boldly leveraged modest naval resources to achieve great ends

✦

Inspired others by his example

✦

Was self-taught as a master commander at sea

✦

Made the most of his instinctive grasp of strategy and tactics

✦

Drew inspiration from his loyalty to Cromwell

✦

Except when the odds were impossible, adopted a resolutely aggressive approach

LIFE

Blake was a leader both audacious and innovative, who is justly called one of the fathers of the British navy. Born and raised in Bridgewater, Somerset, he was the eldest of 12 children and was by no means initially trained for a career at sea. He took a bachelor of arts degree from Wadham College in 1618 and probably attended the Inns of Court, which suggests his intention to become a lawyer. Although he did not enter the law, he did prosper in business and politics. From 1625 to 1640, he worked in his father's thriving trading firm and was sent to Parliament as the member for Bridgewater. He never took his seat, however. Instead, an enthusiastic supporter of Oliver Cromwell, he joined the Parliamentary army, in which he distinguished himself at the failed defense of Bristol during July 15–26, 1643. Promoted to lieutenant colonel, he held Lyme Regis against Royalist forces in 1644, a feat for which he was promoted to a full colonelcy. Late in 1644, Blake captured Taunton and held it against repeated Royalist assaults through July 1645. Appointed governor of Taunton, he was again elected to Parliament from Bridgewater in 1645, but did not take his seat until the following year.

When the Second English Civil War broke out in 1648, Blake organized forces in Somerset, but was then named one of three "generals at sea," along with Richard Deane and Edward Popham, in February 1649. His first naval command was a squadron sent to blockade the ships of Royalist ally Prince Rupert at Kinsale, Ireland, in April 1649. When Rupert managed to break through the blockade, Blake pursued him to the River Tagus in Portugal during September and October. Denied permission by Portuguese authorities to press the attack, Blake retaliated against Portugal's Brazil fleet by capturing six ships and burning another three. He then returned to England and once again set out after Rupert, sinking most of the Royalist flotilla off Cartagena, Spain, in November 1650. Blake went on to capture the Scilly Isles, an important base out of which Royalist privateers operated. He also participated in the siege and capture of Jersey. After this, he was made a member of the Council of State for the Commonwealth.

The next conflict the Commonwealth faced was war with the Dutch (1652–54), and Blake assumed command of the fleet in the English Channel. He boldly surprised a superior squadron at Goodwin Sands by attacking it, taking two ships as prizes on May 29, 1652. When the formal declaration of war on the Netherlands came on July 17, Blake set off to capture the Dutch North Sea herring fleet. A storm on August 3 prevented battle with the Dutch admiral Tromp, but, with William Penn (father of the founder of Pennsylvania, also named William), he defeated the famed Dutch admirals Michael de Ruyter and Cornelius de Witt off the Kentish Knock on October 8. Tromp regrouped his forces, however, and defeated Blake on December 10 at Dungeness, driving him into the Thames River. Not one to be beaten, Blake suddenly assumed the offensive and engaged Tromp in a three-day battle off Portland during February 28–March 2, 1653. His objective was the fleet of Dutch merchantmen Tromp was escorting. The desperate battle ended inconclusively, and Blake was severely wounded. He recovered, and, on June 12, 1653, joined George Monck on the Gabbard Bank (off North Foreland), where the two decisively defeated Tromp.

In addition to battle command, always stressing aggressive tactics, even when outgunned, Blake was instrumental in the extensive reform and reorganization of the Parliamentary navy during 1652–53. He collaborated with others in writing the *Fighting Instructions* issued in March 1653, and, always loyal to Cromwell, he served briefly in the Lord Protector's Barebones Parliament during 1653–54 before he took command of 24 ships in the Mediterranean for operations against state-sanctioned pirates and corsairs operating there. He succeeded in intimidating the Duke of Tuscany into paying England an indemnity, but he was unable to negotiate the release of English prisoners held in Tunis by the Tunisian bey. Blake decided to force the issue by attacking the Tunisian fleet at Porto Farina and by bombarding and destroying the fortresses there early in 1655. The bey released the prisoners.

When war broke out with Spain in 1656, Blake conducted operations off the coast of Cadiz. His policy of aggressive response dictated that he take the offensive and seize Gibraltar; however, he sorely lacked for forces sufficient to accomplish this. Blake was daring, but neither suicidal nor prodigal with the lives of others. He settled for the lesser objective of capturing the Spanish treasure fleet, in September 1656, and, the next year, bagging another, which lay at anchor in the fortified harbor at Santa Cruz de Tenerife in the Canaries. For this April 20, 1657, attack, Blake deployed his forces so skillfully that he not only took the treasure fleet, but demolished the harbor forts as well.

Unfortunately, at the moment of this triumph, Blake fell gravely ill and returned with his fleet to England. He died less than an hour before his vessel entered Portsmouth harbor on August 7.

LEADERSHIP LESSONS

✦

Do not dwell on the resources you lack, but rather make effective use of the resources at your command.

✦

Whenever possible, take the initiative, be aggressive, assume the offensive.

✦

Recognize your natural talents and give them full rein.

✦

Let boldness be your watchword, but retain sense enough to avoid suicidal—or simply futile—actions.

✦

Cherish loyalty and character.

Bolívar, Simón

Born: 1783 Died: 1830

Character model   Motivator   Problem solver   Rescuer
Strategist   Systems creator   Tactician   Visionary

LEADERSHIP ACHIEVEMENTS

✦

Repeatedly won key military victories in the struggle for Latin American
independence

✦

Refused to surrender to discouragement

✦

Expanded the scope of revolution beyond local and national boundaries

✦

Did much to unify disparate peoples of different classes

✦

Created an enduring legacy of the politics of liberty and liberation

LIFE

Remembered as "the Liberator," Bolívar was the key revolutionary leader of
19th-century Latin America, being instrumental in securing independence for
Venezuela, Colombia, Ecuador, Peru, and Bolivia. He had been born into a
privileged Creole family in Caracas, where he was educated by private tutors.
Following the death of Bolívar's father in 1789, these same tutors assumed
almost total responsibility for raising him. Among the youth's teachers was
Simón Rodriguez, who instilled in Bolívar a passionate interest in
Enlightenment thought, particularly the writings of Jean Jacques Rousseau. A
desire to see for himself the seat of the philosophy he had learned sent young
Bolívar on a journey through Europe during 1799–1802. In the course of his
tour, he met a Spanish noblewoman, married her, and returned to Venezuela,
where, almost immediately, the young woman contracted yellow fever and
died. In search of solace, the heartbroken Bolívar made a second trip to
Europe in 1804, and it was during this sojourn that he moved ever closer to
revolutionary activism. He witnessed the self-coronation of Napoleon, and
then voyaged to America, touring the eastern United States in 1807.

Everywhere Bolívar traveled, he opened his eyes and ears to themes of revolution and liberty. As he learned, he also bided his time, awaiting the proper moment for action. That came when Emperor Napoleon deposed the Bourbon monarchs of Spain, thereby creating a wave of change that roared through not only Europe, but Latin America as well. Spain's colonies were now ripe for rebellion.

In Venezuela, independence began in Caracas with a *cabildo abierto*—a town meeting—on April 19, 1810, which ousted the royal Spanish governor Vicente Emparán and, shortly afterward, proclaimed itself a junta governing in the name of Ferdinand VII, the emperor Napoleon had deposed. In the meantime, Bolívar met Francisco de Miranda, a Venezuelan revolutionary living in exile in England, and persuaded him to return to Venezuela to help bring about independence. He and Bolívar returned in time to play key roles in a congress convened by the junta. Led by Miranda, the congress declared independence from Spain on July 5, 1811. Miranda headed the ruling junta and the army, with Bolívar his chief lieutenant.

A constitution was adopted on December 21, 1811, inaugurating Venezuela's First Republic—christened derisively by Venezuelan historians *La Patria Boba,* the Silly Republic. Bolívar identified the republic's major flaws. The Caracas *cabildo* had failed to create unity. Worst of all, Bolívar recognized, the elite, the Caracas intelligentsia who had led the revolution, haughtily failed to secure popular support for the cause of independence. Venezuela's masses saw no advantage in being governed by the white elite of Caracas and so remained loyal to the Spanish crown.

In March 1812, an earthquake rocked Venezuela, devastating strongholds of independence while sparing just about every place commanded by royalist forces. Shortly after this, one of Bolívar's trusted subordinates betrayed him to the royalists, and he was captured. On July 25, 1812, Miranda surrendered his troops to the Spanish commander. Miranda was destined to die in a Spanish prison in 1816, but Bolívar, refusing to abandon the cause, managed to escape to New Granada (present-day Colombia). There, in exile, he assumed the leadership of Venezuela's independence struggle. Proclaiming the Second Venezuelan Republic, Bolívar led an army of invasion into Venezuela during May 1813 and defeated the Spanish forces in a series of six brilliantly planned and executed, albeit bloody, battles. On August 6, Bolívar took Caracas, where he was hailed as *El Libertador*. The new government faced opposition from royalist factions among the Venezuelans, and a bitter civil war commenced. Once again, Bolívar assumed military command and defeated the counterrevolutionaries. His luck ran out, however, in July 1814, at La Puerta, where he was badly outnumbered and severely defeated. Once again, Bolívar was forced to seek refuge in New Granada. And here, yet again, he raised an army.

But his vision of revolution had changed as a result of his defeat in Venezuela. Now he understood that effective revolution had to be even more than national. It had to involve as much of Latin America as possible. Accordingly, he did not immediately reinvade Venezuela, but set about the liberation of Bogotá, New Granada. At the Battle of Santa Maria, however, his forces were defeated by Spanish troops under General Pablo Morillo and Bolívar was forced to flee yet again, this time to Jamaica, in 1815.

Holed up in exile, Bolívar wrote a dynamic manifesto, *La carta de Jamaica (Letter from Jamaica)* and then returned to Venezuela in December 1816. Meeting Morillo's forces once again, near Barcelona, on February 16, 1817, he defeated them, only to be defeated in turn at the Second Battle of La Puerta one year later, on March 15, 1818. After this setback, Bolívar regrouped in the remote Orinoco region, where, during 1818–19, he built an entirely new army, which was augmented by several thousand British and Irish veterans of the Napoleonic Wars. He united this force with those of other revolutionaries. Bolívar decided not to turn immediately to the liberation of Venezuela, but to New Granada first.

Leaving the headquarters he had established at the place named for him, Ciudad Bolívar, on June 11, 1819, Bolívar led 2,500 men in an epic march, at remarkable speed, across the vast and forbidding wilderness of Venezuela. On July 6, Bolívar and his army achieved total surprise, which enabled them to defeat superior Spanish forces at the Battle of Boyaca on August 7, 1819. Bogatá fell three days later, and Bolívar established a republic. From his new position as president, Bolívar convened the Angostura Congress, which created Gran Colombia, a federation encompassing present-day Venezuela, Colombia, Panama, and Ecuador. The union was formalized at Cucuta in July 1821, and Bolívar became its president.

In 1822, President Bolívar met with the Argentine patriot José de San Martin at Guayaquil, Ecuador, hoping to bring Argentina into the union. This failed to materialize, but, during this time, Antonio José de Sucre liberated Ecuador (following victory at the Battle of Pichincha in May 1822), and subsequent victories in Peru—at Junin (August 1824) and Ayacucho (December 1824)—drove the remaining Spanish forces out of what were now being called the Bolívarian states: Venezuela, Colombia, Ecuador, Peru, and Bolivia.

Bolívar personally wrote a republican constitution for the state of Bolivia—as the liberated population of northern Peru decided to call their new nation—but defiance of his authority was so intense that, in 1828, Bolívar assumed dictatorial powers over Gran Colombia. This failed to bring an end to the instability, and, in the spring of 1830, discouraged, weary, and ill with tuberculosis, Bolívar stepped down as president of the nation. He died that winter, in the belief that he had failed to bring genuine liberty to Latin America. In fact, he had left an enduring legacy of progressive political thought that ultimately led to enduring independence.

LEADERSHIP LESSONS

✦

Think beyond the comfortable and familiar boundaries.

✦

Nurture enormous ambitions, and embrace boldness—the bolder the better.

✦

Give up parochial prejudices.

✦

Never surrender.

Bradley, Omar Nelson

Born: 1893   Died: 1981

Character model   Mentor   Motivator   Strategist   Tactician

LEADERSHIP ACHIEVEMENTS

✦

Rose rapidly to a position of great responsibility

✦

Combined a thorough grounding in strategy with a genius for leading men
in the field

✦

Tempered an impressive command presence with a common touch that
appealed to soldiers and the American public alike

✦

Was instrumental in the success of the Normandy (D-Day) invasion

✦

Planned and executed the initial breakout from the Normandy beachheads

✦

Led the largest military force that any U.S. general had ever commanded

LIFE

A planner and the field commander of the Normandy (D-Day) invasion during World War II and commander of U.S. 12th Army Group in the battle for Germany, Omar Nelson Bradley went on to become the first permanent chairman of the U.S. Joint Chiefs of Staff. Throughout his rise, Bradley retained his plainspoken leadership style and abiding, overriding concern for the welfare of his men, which earned him the affectionate nickname of the "G.I. general."

A native of Clark, Missouri, Bradley was educated at West Point, graduating in 1915 as a second lieutenant in the infantry. He did not see service overseas during World War I, but was instead posted in the American West, in Washington state and in Arizona, rising rapidly through the grades to major by June 1918. In 1919, he was appointed military instructor at South Dakota State College and the following year became an instructor at his alma mater, West Point, where he served through 1924.

Bradley was sent to the Infantry School at Fort Benning, Georgia, and after his graduation in 1925 was posted to Hawaii during 1925–28. Marked as a promising senior officer, he was sent to the Command and General Staff School at Fort Leavenworth, Kansas, graduated in 1929, and was assigned as an instructor at the Infantry School during 1929–33. From this assignment, he went on to the Army War College, the training institution for those responsible for doctrine and strategy. After graduating in 1934, Bradley was assigned as a tactical officer at West Point. He served in this senior teaching and planning role through 1938, having been promoted to lieutenant colonel in June 1936. From his West Point position, in 1938, Bradley was sent to the U.S. Army General Staff, and in February 1941 he was promoted to brigadier general. In March, he became commandant of the Infantry School, taking a large responsibility in readying a generation of officers for wartime command.

Bradley was transferred from the Infantry School in February 1942 to serve as commander of the 82nd Division (during March–June) and then of the 28th Division (from June 1942 to January 1943). Briefly, from January to March 1943, he was assigned as deputy to General Dwight D. Eisenhower, the supreme Allied commander, then was sent to replace Major General George S. Patton as commander of II Corps in North Africa as Patton prepared to take command of forces about to invade Sicily. It was Bradley who led II Corps during the final stages of the Tunisian campaign. He captured Bizerto on May 8 and then led the corps during the Sicilian campaign, from July 10 to August 17. At this point, Bradley was transferred from field command to Allied headquarters in England to participate in the planning of the D-Day invasion of France.

Promoted to lieutenant general, Bradley was named commander of the First Army in January 1944, the organization assigned to the right-wing position in the Allied landing at Normandy. After the landing, Bradley planned and then personally directed the breakout from the beaches to Saint-Lô in July. The following month, he was assigned even greater responsibility as commander of the Twelfth Army Group, consisting of the First Army (under Courtney L. Hodges) and the Third Army (under Patton). He now directed the vast southern wing of the great Allied advance across northern France, which spanned August to December 1944. Numbering 1.3 million men, the Twelfth Army Group was the biggest and most powerful military force ever commanded by an American general. In March 1945, Bradley was promoted to four-star general and continued to command the Twelfth Army Group during its concluding operations in Germany, through May 1945.

Bradley had earned a reputation not only as a fine strategist, but as a results-oriented field commander, who enjoyed a compelling rapport with men of all grades and ranks. In contrast to Patton, who reveled in ornate uniforms and spit-and-polish ceremony, Bradley wore the battle dress of the common soldier and was always informal in manner. Like Patton, however, he frequently toured the front lines, ensuring that he never lost touch with the men who were doing the actual fighting. Homely and plainspoken, Bradley did not look like a four-star general, and he was loved and respected all the more for that fact. Journalists dubbed him the "G.I. general," so it made sense, after the war, that he would be appointed to head the Veterans Administration. He served in this post through December 1947, when he was appointed to succeed Dwight Eisenhower as U.S. Army chief of staff. In February 1948, Bradley became the first chairman of the Joint Chiefs of Staff under the newly organized Department of Defense.

In recognition of his service, Bradley was promoted to general of the army—five-star general—in September 1950. The following year, he published his memoirs, titled simply (and revealingly) *A Soldier's Story*. He retired from the army in August 1953.

Although Omar Bradley was an able strategist and agile tactician, his was not among history's very greatest military minds. Where he truly excelled was in leadership itself—in particular, the leadership of an army marching in defense of a great democracy. Combining great command presence with a charismatic common touch, Bradley emerged as perhaps the single most widely admired commander of World War II.

IN HIS OWN WORDS

"Throughout the war I deliberately avoided intervening in a subordinate's duties. When an officer performed as I expected him to, I gave him a free hand. When he hesitated, I tried to help him. And when he failed, I relieved him."
—*A Soldier's Story*, 1951

"Far from being a handicap to command, compassion is the measure of it."
—*A Soldier's Story*, 1951

"However desperate the situation, a senior commander must always exude confidence in the presence of his subordinates. For anxiety, topside, can spread like cancer down through the command."
—*A Soldier's Story*, 1951

"In war there is no prize for the runner up."
—*A Soldier's Story*, 1951

"You may have heard this story about General Pershing in World War I. While inspecting a certain area, he found a project that was not going too well, even though the second lieutenant in charge seemed to have a pretty good plan. General Pershing asked the lieutenant how much pay he received, and when the lieutenant replied: '$147.67 per month, Sir,' General Pershing said, 'Just remember that you get $1.67 for making your plan and issuing the order, and $140.00 for seeing that it is carried out.'"
—"Leadership," in *Parameters,* Winter 1972

"There is still another ingredient in this formula for a great leader . . . and that is *luck*. He must have opportunity. Then, of course, when opportunity knocks, he must be able to rise and open the door."
—"Leadership," in *Parameters,* Winter 1972

LEADERSHIP LESSONS

✦

Put your people first. Whatever the nature of your business, remember that, first and foremost, you are in the people business.

✦

Identify with those you lead—and allow them to identify with you.

✦

Create balanced leadership by tempering your "command presence" with a common touch. Make and maintain contact with those you lead.

✦

Create balanced leadership by combining theoretical knowledge and clear, big-picture planning with your frequent presence in the field and front lines.

✦

Never let the perks and trappings of leadership get in the way of leadership.

Caesar, Gaius Julius

Born: 100 B.C.   Died: 44 B.C.

Conqueror   Motivator   Strategist   Systems creator   Tactician   Visionary

LEADERSHIP ACHIEVEMENTS

✦

Through a combination of political acumen and military achievement, rose
to the most powerful position in the world

✦

Greatly expanded the Roman Empire

✦

As a consummate strategist, compiled perhaps the greatest record of
military success the world has ever known

✦

Created a truly benevolent dictatorship, which, to a significant degree,
democratized Rome

LIFE

Julius Caesar may be the single most famous name in history. Certainly, Caesar was one of the greatest military commanders of all times, as well as a consummately skillful politician. He was born on July 13, 100 B.C., to a patrician family that claimed direct descent from Venus through Aeneas's son Iulus (Ascanius). Their pedigree notwithstanding, Caesar's family was not in the inner circles of power. Caesar's father was the brother-in-law of Gaius Marius and was married to Aurelia, a member of the prominent Aurelii family. Despite these connections, he died, about 85 B.C., before attaining a consulship. In 84, his son Caesar entered the priesthood of Jupiter and married Cornelia, daughter of Marius's former partner, Lucius Cornelius Cinna. When Lucius Cornelius Sulla, the enemy of Marius, ordered Caesar to divorce her, the young man refused and was compelled to endure a brief period of exile.

Caesar did not waste his time of exile, but used it to serve in the Roman Legion in Asia, making himself conspicuous for bravery at the siege of Mytilene in 80 B.C. Returning to Rome after the death of Sulla in 78, he unsuccessfully attempted during 77–76 to prosecute two of his family's enemies, Gnaeus Cornelius Dolabella and Gaius Antonius Hibrida, both partisans of Sulla. Departing Rome for study in Rhodes, Caesar was captured en route by pirates, from whom he was ransomed. After assembling a small private army, he succeeded in capturing the pirates in turn and brought about their execution in 75–74.

War with Mithradates VI of Pontus in 74 drew Caesar away from Rhodes when he was asked to serve in Lucullus's campaign against this ruler during 74–73. Caesar was made a pontiff at Rome in 73 B.C. and was elected military tribune. He then saw service, possibly against the rebellious slave Spartacus in 72 or 71, and he supported Pompey, chief architect of the downfall of the Sullan political system.

As a result of a series of triumphs gained and influential connections made, Caesar was elected quaestor in 69 and then earned popularity among the Transpadane Gauls by supporting their bid for Roman citizenship in 68. Following the death in 69 of his wife Cornelia, Caesar married Pompeia, granddaughter of Sulla and relative of Pompey, in 68. After this union, Caesar apparently carried out high-level military assignments for Pompey in 67 and 66 and then became aedile in 65, achieving great popularity by personally financing elaborate public games. In 65, he probably participated with Marcus Licinius Crassus in a scheme to annex Egypt to the Roman Empire. He also promoted the popular land-distribution bill of Publius Servilius Rullus. In 64 he presided over trials of persons who had committed murder during Sulla's proscriptions against the partisans of Marius, and in 63, Caesar employed bribery on a large scale to purchase elevation to the office of pontifex maximus, head of the Roman state religion.

Although Caesar did not participate in the infamous Catiline conspiracy to overthrow the Roman Senate, he did oppose the execution of Catiline's accomplices, which gained him much public favor, leading to his election as praetor in 62. Shortly after this, he divorced Pompeia on suspicion of infidelity and married Calpurnia in 58. In the meantime, he became governor of Further Spain in 61 and was elected, in 60, to the consulate. That same year, Caesar formed the First Triumvirate with Pompey and Crassus to consolidate power and influence. Caesar became proconsul of Illyricum, Cisalpine Gaul, and Transalpine Gaul. Using a large army that was put at his disposal, he fought the Gallic Wars from 58 to 51 B.C., subjugating the rebellious Gauls and thereby gaining tremendous political prestige and leverage.

Caesar's daughter Julia married Pompey in 59, a union Caesar hoped would cement relations with this triumvir; however, friction soon developed between Caesar and Pompey, which Crassus, maneuvering for increased power, did his best to exacerbate. The Triumvirate was renegotiated in 56, but the death of Julia in 54 and of Crassus the next year combined with the reputation Caesar had earned by his Gallic triumphs to destroy the relationship with Pompey once and for all. In 50, Pompey opposed Caesar's bid for a second consulate. On January 10, 49 B.C., Caesar responded by starting a civil war when he committed the illegal act of leading his army across the Rubicon to oppose Pompey in Italy. (To "cross the Rubicon" entered into popular speech as a synonym for taking a momentous and irreversible step.) Pompey's army disintegrated before Caesar's advance, and Pompey fled to Greece.

In August 49, Caesar defeated Pompeiian forces in Spain and was named dictator. Unwilling to tolerate the continued presence of Pompey, he pursued him into Greece. There Caesar was defeated at the Battle of Dyrrhachium, but he quickly recovered by destroying Pompey's larger army at Pharsalus on August 9, 48. Pompey now fled to Egypt, and Caesar followed. In Egypt, Caesar became involved in the civil war between Cleopatra and her brother Ptolemy XIII. Caesar took Cleopatra as his mistress and made her queen of Egypt.

The next year, Caesar went to Anatolia, where he crushed Pompey's ally Pharnaces, king of Bosporus, in a brief campaign at Zela. So swift was this victory that Caesar was able to report it in a single memorable phrase: *"Veni, vidi, vici"* ("I came, I saw, I conquered").

After returning briefly to Rome later in 47, Caesar was obliged to set off for North Africa in December to block yet another threat from forces loyal to Pompey. Caesar won the Battle of Thapsus in April 46, and was thereafter named dictator for 10 more years. Pompey having been murdered in Egypt, his sons now mounted a fresh resistance in Spain. Caesar intercepted them at Munda and, on March 17, 45, defeated them there. The next year Julius Caesar was appointed dictator for life and showered with additional honors.

As dictator, Caesar ushered in a host of reforms, including the representative expansion of the Senate, the revision of the system of taxation, and the extension of Roman citizenship to all subjects of the empire.

Caesar sought to balance these popular measures with gestures meant to placate those powerful nobles who still opposed him. Toward this end, he granted unheard-of clemency to his enemies. However, when Caesar dared to compare himself to Alexander the Great and proposed, like him, to conquer Parthia, fear of his boundless ambition spread through an aristocratic clique that included those to whom he had granted pardons. A band of conspirators led by Marcus Junius Brutus and Gaius Cassius Longinus approached him at a meeting of the Senate in Pompey's theater on the Ides of March—March 15, 44 B.C. Each conspirator stabbed him in turn, and Caesar, as he collapsed at the feet of Pompey's statue, spoke to Brutus not in Shakespeare's Latin—*"Et tu, Brute"*—but in Greek: *"Kai su, teknon?"* ("Even you, lad?").

IN HIS OWN WORDS

"I would rather be the first man here [in a small village] than second in Rome."
—Plutarch, *Lives,* A.D. 125

"Why lose men, even for victory? Why expose soldiers who deserved so well of him to wounds? Why even tempt fortune? Victory through policy is as much a mark of the good general as victory by the sword."
—*The Civil War,* 45 B.C.

LEADERSHIP LESSONS

✦
A leader is a builder of alliances as well as logically ordered conquests.
✦
The more authority and power you earn, the more imperative it becomes to share that authority and power, to give others a stake in the enterprise.
✦
Liberal reform tends to increase the leader's power by giving more people an interest in his administration.
✦
Immoderate expressions of personal ambition invite popular anxiety and, ultimately, ruin.

Castro Ruz, Fidel

Born: 1926 or 1927

Innovator Leverager Motivator Strategist Tactician

LEADERSHIP ACHIEVEMENTS

✦

Organized and led a grassroots revolution

✦

Successfully applied the principles of guerrilla warfare

✦

Leveraged a tiny group of followers into a momentous revolutionary movement

✦

Created solidarity among a demoralized people

✦

Transformed a revolution into a stable government

LIFE

With few exceptions, this book avoids modern political leaders who attained or maintained their power through primarily totalitarian means; however, the rise of Fidel Castro is an instructive example of the exercise of leadership to create dramatic change.

Fidel Castro Ruz was born on August 13, 1926 (some sources say 1927), on a farm in Mayan municipality, Oriente province. He was raised in a strict Catholic environment and given a rigorous Catholic education, which included training at the Jesuit boarding school, Colegio de Belén. The austere routine of this institution helped instill in Castro the habit of creating spartan order and discipline. After graduating from the Colegio, he enrolled in the University of Havana, from which he earned a law degree in 1950. At the time, the university was a hotbed of reform and radical politics. Young Castro became active in the social-democratic Ortodoxo Party, and he soon drew notice for his eloquent, even electrifying speeches in opposition to the corrupt, U.S.-backed right-wing dictatorship of Fulgencio Batista.

Not satisfied with mere words of opposition, Castro led an assault on the Moncada army barracks, a government armory, on July 26, 1953. The assault failed to take the armory, but it suddenly propelled the young radical into national prominence. Arrested, Castro was tried for his action, found guilty, and sentenced to 15 years of imprisonment. An amnesty in 1955—part of Batista's attempt to reconcile with the left wing—brought Castro's release after he had served two years.

Castro had not abandoned the idea of leading a revolution, but he had no interest in being arrested again for some futile act. After his release, therefore, he left Cuba for Mexico, where, in self-imposed exile, he founded the 26th of July Movement, an organization dedicated to creating revolution in Cuba.

Castro well understood that, while he was in Mexico, Batista's Cuba seethed with insurrection, culminating in a major uprising at Matanzas, which was, with difficulty, suppressed by government forces on April 29, 1956. In November of that year, Castro and 81 others, including the charismatic guerrilla leader Che Guevara, stealthily returned to Cuba, landing in Oriente province on November 30. The small guerrilla band was met by Batista's forces and was apparently routed. On December 2, it was reported that Castro had been killed. In reality, he and his followers had set up a secret base camp in the remote Sierra Maestra Mountains. From here, Castro planned and directed a highly coordinated and extraordinarily successful guerrilla war. His tactic of hit-and-run attacks applied continual pressure to the increasingly unpopular Batista government from 1957 through October 1958, when Castro and his followers emerged from hiding and transformed the hit-and-run raids into a fully coordinated offensive.

Castro was nothing if not a master of timing. He did not emerge until it was clear to him that Batista was on the ropes. Having lost ground steadily, the dictator fled the country on New Year's Day, 1959, and Fidel Castro occupied Havana on January 8.

By this point in the history of U.S.–Cuban relations, the administration of President Dwight D. Eisenhower was persuaded that the Batista regime was no longer viable, and the United States recognized the Castro government on January 7, the day before he occupied Havana. Indeed, Castro had not declared himself a Communist and had conducted his revolution on no ideological basis other than one of anti-imperialism, nationalism, and general reform of an inefficient and corrupt government. Once he took up the reins of government, he was careful to include in his inner circle moderates and democratic reformers in addition to left-wing radicals. Nevertheless, within a short time, the Castro government did become increasingly radical as well as defiant, particularly where the influence of the United States was concerned.

With the support of the people, whose living conditions had dramatically improved within the first few months of the new regime, Castro summarily nationalized foreign-owned properties and industries—most of which were American-owned. Against those who opposed this action Castro waged quick and ruthless war. Some opponents were executed, others exiled, jailed, or generally persecuted into submission. Realizing that Castro had become more than a benevolent reformer, but was, in fact, a full-blown Marxist, many of Cuba's professionals, technicians, and businesspeople fled the island, most of them seeking refuge in the United States. From this time forward, relations between Cuba and the United States deteriorated rapidly.

On May 7, 1960, Castro announced the resumption of diplomatic relations with the Soviet Union—with the blessing of the United States, Batista had broken off relations—and by the middle of the year, Castro went a step further by explicitly aligning Cuba with the USSR. For his part, Soviet premier Nikita Khrushchev warned the Western world that he would defend Cuba against aggression—especially U.S. aggression—even if doing so meant thermonuclear war. Emboldened by Soviet support, Castro threatened to take over the U.S. naval and marine base at Guantánamo Bay. To these threats, on November 1, 1960, President Eisenhower responded by declaring that the United States would take "whatever steps are necessary to defend" the base. On January 3, 1961, days before he left office, Eisenhower severed diplomatic relations with Cuba.

The new U.S. president, John F. Kennedy, responded to the threat of a bellicose Communist regime just 90 miles from the U.S. mainland by authorizing a covert invasion of Cuba by some 1,400 anti-Castro Cuban revolutionaries supported by the Central Intelligence Agency. The resulting Bay of Pigs operation, conducted during April 15–20, 1961, collapsed in total failure, largely because the CIA had blundered in its confident assumption that support for Castro was thin. Castro had, in fact, balanced popular enthusiasm for national sovereignty—real independence from the United States—with his own dedication to Marxism. This made him, at least for a time, perhaps the most popular Communist leader in the world.

The Bay of Pigs invasion proved such a fiasco that the United States sustained serious damage to its prestige, and Castro was emboldened to consolidate his power further. In December 1961, he declared Cuba's outright alliance with the Soviet Union, which, seizing an opportunity to gain a military and political outpost deep in the West, granted Cuba the extensive economic, technical, and military assistance it desperately needed, especially after so many of its most skilled people had fled.

Tension between Cuba and the United States soon reached a dangerous flash point. On October 22, 1962, Kennedy publicly announced that U.S. surveillance had "established the fact that a series of offensive missile sites is now in preparation" in Cuba. Thus the Cuban Missile Crisis began, which brought the world to the brink of thermonuclear war, but which ultimately resulted in the Soviets' removal of the Cuban missiles. Despite President Kennedy's victory over Cuba's chief ally, Castro remained defiant. On February 6, 1964, he cut off the water supply to Guantánamo Naval Base—a gesture of harassment rather than a serious military threat, since (as Castro well knew) the base was equipped with a self-contained desalinization plant.

Castro's regime endured another blow in July 1964, when the Organization of American States instituted sanctions against the island. This prompted Castro to permit refugees to fly to the United States. Between November 1965 and August 1971, about 250,000 Cubans deserted the island. Through all of this, the dictator maintained close ties to the Soviets, but did break with the Chinese Communists in 1966 because of their failure to deliver promised support. From 1959 to 1976, Castro was officially prime minister of Cuba. In 1976, he became president as well, and continues to govern the island nation.

LEADERSHIP LESSONS

✦

Change begins with a single committed person.

✦

Guerrilla tactics employ the principles of leveraged resources, efficiency, passion, and stealth.

✦

Never allow ideology to eclipse passion embodied in a personal leadership style.

✦

A leader shapes and then mirrors the collective identity of the group he leads.

Catherine the Great

Born: 1729   Died: 1796

Innovator   Mentor   Motivator   Systems creator   Visionary

LEADERSHIP ACHIEVEMENTS

✦

Worked behind the scenes to create a network that elevated her to power

✦

Used the great power she had achieved to benefit her nation

✦

Recognized the value of the work of Peter the Great and extended and improved it

✦

Continued to lead Russia into the modern world

✦

Recognizing the limitations of her reforms, devised means of extending them further

✦

Chose extraordinary subordinates

LIFE

Catherine II, better known as Catherine the Great, followed up on the reforms introduced by Peter the Great (Peter I) to further the transformation of Russia from a backward, feudal realm into a modern European nation. She accomplished this, moreover, within a strongly patriarchal society in which women were held in low esteem.

Catherine was not a Russian by birth, but had been born Sophie Fredericke Augusta in the Prussian town of Stettin (present-day Szczecin, Poland) on May 2, 1729, to the prince of Anhalt-Zerbst. When she was only 15, she was sent to Moscow for an arranged marriage to Peter, the uncouth, mentally retarded, and somewhat deranged nephew and heir of the Russian empress Elizabeth. Arriving in Moscow, Catherine was married in 1744 and accepted the Russian name of Ekatarina (Catherine).

Although Catherine found her husband repellent, she made her loveless marriage tolerable by creating a vibrant court, into which she introduced a liberal measure of cultivation and learning. She also took a series of highly placed lovers, including Gregor Orlov, whose brother Aleksei was an influential army officer. In this way, she developed a network of power parallel to that of the throne.

With the death of Empress Elizabeth on December 25, 1761, Catherine's husband succeeded to the throne as Peter III. As Catherine knew he would, the dim-witted Peter III quickly alienated his court, including Aleksei Orlov, who, with Catherine's conniving, led a coup d'etat in June 1762. Peter was deposed and later assassinated. This cleared the way for the immensely popular Catherine to take the throne.

Catherine was anxious to introduce good, sound, honest, and modern government into Russian life, and she was especially determined to bring the country out of its provincial backwardness and into the Age of Enlightenment. Catherine was Russia's most cultivated and Western-oriented monarch since Peter the Great, and she enthusiastically set about continuing Peter's work of modernization and Westernization. If anything, she meant to improve on Peter by appointing a distinguished corps of advisers, including the progressive Nikita Panin, as minister of foreign affairs; Aleksandr Suvorov, an extraordinary military commander; and Prince Gregori Potemkin, a remarkable statesman and administrator, who became the architect of a navy that was an essential adjunct to the creation of Russia as a world power.

If Catherine meant to be more efficient than Peter I, she was also more liberal—at least during the early years of her reign. Peter had approached the transformation of Russia as a kind of crash program. He issued decrees, proclamations, and orders compelling people—including his court—to adopt modern European ways. Catherine understood that the more effective approach was to institute reforms by example and incentive, rather than by dictatorial fiat. She had the patience and talent to recognize and nurture individual initiative. In 1765, for example, she established the Free Economic Society to promote the modernization of agriculture and industry. Moreover—again in contrast to Peter the Great—Catherine did not rely exclusively on her own perceptions to determine what needed to be done to reform Russian society. She set about assessing the needs and wants of her people. In 1767, she convened an assembly of deputies representing all regions of Russia and tasked the body with creating a new code of laws. Thus she restructured Russia's legal code from the perspective of the local level—yet she did not simply relinquish central control. Catherine personally drafted the *Nakaz* ("Instruction"), a set of guidelines to govern the creation of legislation.

Peter I had made great strides toward opening Russia culturally and economically to the rest of the world, but Catherine took the process even further. She encouraged the wider development of her nation by inviting foreign settlers into Russia and establishing new port cities, most notably Odessa on the Black Sea. These were intended to open up intercourse with other nations and people. To augment the opening of commerce, Catherine relaxed Russia's stringent censorship laws and encouraged a flowering of the arts, the spread of literacy, and the establishment of many printing presses throughout her empire. Catherine authorized the founding of numerous state and private schools, and she funded the University of Moscow in order to make the city a genuinely international center of learning.

Impressive as Catherine's reforms were, they met with only limited success. While the court and the upper classes certainly attained new levels of sophistication and enlightenment, fairly little changed for the peasant masses. Catherine's reforms did not reach the vast class of serfs who made up the largest part of the Russian population. The Assembly of Deputies did not stave off an insurrection in 1774–75, led by Yemelian Pugachev, whose following consisted of Cossacks, peasants, and other disaffected minorities. After much of eastern Russia rose in revolt, Catherine could do nothing but send an army to crush her opposition. After she had reasserted control, Catherine realized that military action, while effective now, was insufficient to prevent further revolt. She therefore embarked on a program to reform local government administration, and she made the central government wholly responsible for the administration and welfare of those serfs who had belonged to the Orthodox Church. Catherine took the wise step of integrating the Cossacks into the regular army, thereby bringing this formidable force under her direct control. Within the next 10 years, Catherine extended her reform effort by issuing royal charters to Russian towns and the Russian nobility. These charters made the towns and nobles responsible for local administration while guaranteeing them the support and protection of the central government. Thus Catherine co-opted the old feudalism, but did not introduce the tyranny of absolute central control.

Toward the close of the 1780s, Catherine began to doubt the wisdom of her liberal policies and began a kind of counterrevolution to her own revolution, reinstating many of the repressive measures she had earlier overthrown.

Still, Catherine could not retract the spirit of enlightenment she had introduced. Nor could she take back the successful wars she prosecuted against Turkey, which resulted in the establishment of Russian sovereignty over the Crimea, thereby giving Russia a vital Black Sea port. This fact alone opened the nation to the rest of the world and thrust it onto the world stage as a player in international affairs. The Ukraine and parts of Poland also came under Russian domination during Catherine's reign.

LEADERSHIP LESSONS
✦

Build networks to establish and extend your influence.
✦
The ultimate good of power is to improve the lives of those you lead.
✦
Choose subordinates wisely. Then empower them in their positions.
✦
Recognize the value contributed by your predecessors. Build on their work.
✦
Give first priority to evolutionary change. Revolution is a last resort.
✦
Avoid tyranny by sharing power without relinquishing control.
✦
Beware of second-guessing your major decisions.
✦
Avoid the fears that prompt you to undo your boldest actions.

Chandragupta Maurya

Reigned: ca. 321–ca. 297 B.C.

Conqueror Motivator Strategist Tactician

LEADERSHIP ACHIEVEMENTS

✦

Rose to power—somehow—from humble beginnings

✦

Understood how to take advantage of disorder to create a new order

✦

Raised and commanded vast forces, whose energy he focused on achieving specific goals

✦

Turned a defense against Greek invasion into an opportunity for further conquest

LIFE

The founder of India's Maurya dynasty, Chandragupta Maurya seized power from the last king of the Nanda dynasty and established a reign during which he vastly expanded his Indian empire.

It is believed that Chandragupta was the bastard son of a Nanda king and a maidservant. He seems early on to have been driven by a restless energy that prompted him to seek adventure, and he traveled far and wide throughout India. Little is known about these early years, but one account portrays him as having met Alexander the Great in the Punjab, during the conqueror's invasion of the region. It is said that Chandragupta offended Alexander "through boldness of speech" and had to flee for his life. While hiding from Alexander's men, Chandragupta met a Taxilian Brahman named Chanakya, or Kautilya, who helped him raise an army of mercenaries to overthrow the Nanda king. So goes one account of Chandragupta's rise to power. Another relates that he was sold as a servant to Chanakya, who then educated him and, later, directed him to overthrow the king.

However Chandragupta Maurya acquired his first followers, it is known that he won a decisive battle against the king and thereby seized control of the empire in Magadha. At this time, Alexander the Great died, leaving the Punjab in great disarray. Chandragupta took advantage of the chaos to attack Alexander's key outpost in the region. After taking the outpost, he amassed, sometime between 324 and 321 B.C., a very large army, which is traditionally put at 30,000 cavalry, 9,000 elephants, and 600,000 infantry. With this force, he overran all of northern India and established himself as absolute ruler over most of India.

For some 20 years following his major conquests, Chandragupta Maurya seems to have ruled without challenge and without major incident. Then, about 304 B.C., the Greek general Seleucos, who had inherited the eastern portion of Alexander's empire, attacked. Chandragupta led an army to meet him, defeated him decisively, and, in 303 B.C., compelled him to accept humiliating peace terms, which included forced marriage into the Maurya royal family. In return, Seleucos received the paltry payment of 500 elephants. Chandragupta's victory over Seleucos brought to the Maurya dynasty all the lands in northwest India as far as the Hindu Kush mountains.

In the final years of his life, Chandragupta Maurya renounced military conquest and, finally, the throne itself. He became an ascetic devotee of the Jam sage Bhadrahahu. When a prolonged drought devastated his vast empire, Chandragupta became convinced that his own failings had brought about the disaster as some form of divine retribution. Tradition records that, by way of penance, Chandragupta fasted, ultimately starving himself to death. Whatever the precise nature of his death, he was succeeded by his son Bindusara, and the Maurya dynasty continued to rule India until A.D. 186.

LEADERSHIP LESSONS

✦

Do not shun chaos. Regard it as an opportunity for creating effective order, a new reality you shape and control.

✦

Defend yourself and your enterprise, but beware of defining defense so narrowly that you fail to gain by it.

✦

External threats can be opportunities for conquest.

Charlemagne

Born: 742 or 743   Died: 814

Conqueror   Innovator   Strategist   Systems creator   Tactician

LEADERSHIP ACHIEVEMENTS

✦

Vastly enlarged the Frankish kingdom

✦

Transformed the Frankish kingdom into the nucleus of a partially united
Europe

✦

Offered hope (mostly unrealized) for the restoration of classical Roman
greatness

✦

Brought learning to much of Europe

✦

Brought a rational system of justice to his realm

LIFE

Charlemagne, king of the Franks and Holy Roman Emperor, managed
briefly to unite much of western Europe, creating a short-lived period of
order and enlightenment during the waning days of the Dark Ages. He was
born on April 2, 742 (or 743), to the Frankish king Pepin the Short and his
wife Berta. Pope Stephen III anointed him king, along with his brother
Carloman, in 754. After Pepin died on September 24, 768, Charlemagne
took possession of the western part—his assigned portion—of the kingdom
on October 9. Carloman, who ruled the eastern portion of the Frankish
realm, died in December 771, prompting Charlemagne to annex his portion of the kingdom. The following year, Charlemagne embarked on the
first of some 40 military campaigns that would occupy most of his 43-year
reign. This initial expedition was a punitive action against Saxon raiders.
Invited next by the pope to invade Italy and there fight the Lombards
under Desiderius, Charlemagne prevailed in 773–74 and then crushed a
Lombard revolt the next year.

Charlemagne's next major campaign was carried out against the Moors in Spain. The emperor was defeated when he failed to breach the fortress of Saragossa in 778. Hroudland—better known to us as Roland—margrave of the Breton *marchi,* fought a rearguard action to cover Charlemagne's withdrawal from Saragossa but was ambushed by Basques in the Pyrenees valley of Roncesvalles. The story of this defeat spread—and, with it, the further fame of Charlemagne—becoming a favorite subject of the troubadors. Thus, even in defeat, Charlemagne found glory. (Some 300 years after the emperor's death, the story assumed its final form as the 12th-century chanson known as *The Song of Roland.*)

Returning to the north, Charlemagne encountered stiff resistance from Saxon tribes. Hoping to deal with the Saxons once and for all, Charlemagne launched a long series of hard-fought campaigns in Saxony, establishing the bishopric of Bremen in 781, then defeating the Saxons at Detmold and Hase in 773 and triumphing over the Saxon leader Widukind in 785. He mounted additional campaigns against the Saxons throughout the 790s, including the suppression of a Saxon revolt in 793. In one campaign, it is said that Charlemagne ordered the execution by beheading of some 4,000 Saxon prisoners.

While he fought the Saxons, Charlemagne expelled Duke Tossila III from Bavaria during 787–88 and annexed his domain. No sooner was this accomplished than he turned against the Avars, who were raiding the Danube region. Victory against this tribe expanded Charlemagne's holdings to Lake Balaton and northern Croatia between 791 and 803. The indefatigable campaigner next mounted a second invasion of Spain during 796–801. In 801, he captured Barcelona.

Pope Leo III recognized Charlemagne as the greatest of European monarchs by crowning him emperor of the Holy Roman Empire in 800. His ascension spread great hope throughout educated Europe. There was talk of a restoration of classical Roman greatness. The fact is that Charlemagne had brought much of western Europe under the control of the Holy Roman Empire; however, his campaigns against the Byzantines for control of Venezia and the Dalmatian coast, during 802–12, were less successful than what he had accomplished in the west, although he did secure Byzantine recognition of his title as Holy Roman Emperor.

In victory, Charlemagne proved to be much more than a conqueror. While he was ruthless in actual combat, he also introduced a significant degree of humanity throughout much of Europe. He created an extensive system of justice administered by the *missi dominici*—a monk or bishop together with a count or military commander, who traveled under royal commission through the provinces in the capacity of circuit judges, hearing criminal and other cases. In this way, the multitude of petty tyrannies and corruption of local lords was effectively subdued. Although he was at best semiliterate himself, Charlemagne had great respect for learning, and he brought scholars from all over Europe to his court at Aachen (Aix-la-Chappelle), including Alcuin and Theodulf, the foremost thinkers of their day. Thanks to Charlemagne, the spark of classical learning was cherished and kept alive in the waning of the Dark Ages.

The final years of the emperor's reign over his vast realm were relatively peaceful. Unfortunately, however, his momentous reforms did not long endure after him. Certainly, nothing remotely approaching a revival of the Roman Empire took place. After Charlemagne sickened and died at Aachen on January 28, 814, his empire was carved up among his heirs, and, throughout the Middle Ages, the vast stretch of Europe he had brought together was once again fragmented.

LEADERSHIP LESSONS

✦

Leadership is hard work; a great leader continually advances, and is rarely satisfied merely to hold a position.

✦

Acquire territory by rapid conquest. Hold territory by improving the lives of those who live there.

✦

The greatest benefits a leader can bestow are learning and justice.

Churchill, Sir Winston Spencer

Born: 1874 Died: 1965

Character model   Mentor   Motivator   Problem solver   Rescuer   Strategist

LEADERSHIP ACHIEVEMENTS

✦

Mastered a wide variety of professions: soldier, journalist, politician, statesman, world leader, author

✦

As prime minister, led Britain through its time of greatest danger

✦

Was master of the great speech

✦

Provided a beacon in the darkest days of World War II

✦

Was an architect of Allied strategy in World War II

✦

Created great, Nobel-caliber histories of World War II and other subjects

LIFE

One of the giants of the 20th century, Winston Churchill led England in its time of greatest crisis, transforming the nation's darkest days into what he himself called its "finest hour." He was instrumental not only in saving England from defeat at the hands of the Nazis, but in directing the nation's role in defending the world against totalitarianism of the most brutal kind.

The son of Lord Randolph Churchill (who was descended from the First Duke of Marlborough) and Jennie Jerome (an American), Winston Churchill was packed off to Harrow School, where he compiled a poor academic record and, after graduation, rejected the university education that befitted his aristocratic station. Instead of enrolling at Oxford or Cambridge, he chose Sandhurst, the great British military academy, from which he graduated in 1894 with a commission in the 4th Hussars. Young Churchill took a two-month leave in 1895 to cover unrest in Cuba as a war correspondent, then returned to his regiment and was dispatched to India, where he served in the Malakand expedition to the Northwest Frontier during 1897. While on active duty, he continued to write as a correspondent and published the first of his many distinguished books, *The Malakand Field Force.*

In 1898, while serving in Lord Horatio Kitchener's expedition into the Sudan, Churchill rode in the charge of the 21st Lancers at the Battle of Omdurman and, afterward, published a two-volume account of the British army's Sudanese experience in *The River War* (1899). Early in 1899, Churchill resigned his army commission to enter politics. When he lost his first bid for Parliament, he sailed to South Africa on assignment from *The Morning Post* to cover the Second (Great) Boer War. Taken captive by the Boers, he managed a daring escape that catapulted him to world celebrity and greatly improved his popular political standing, so that, in 1900, he was elected to Parliament as a Conservative.

Churchill quickly earned a reputation as an eloquent debater. He did not remain long with the Conservatives, however. In 1904, he bolted, declaring himself a Liberal. It proved a timely transition. His new party came to power the following year, and Churchill was named undersecretary of state for the colonies. He was made a member of the cabinet in 1908, as president of the Board of Trade, and, two years later, was appointed home secretary. In 1911, he was elevated to first lord of the admiralty. This post gave Churchill his first truly significant opportunity to excel. Collaborating with First Sea Lord Admiral Lord Fisher of Kilverstone, he directed an ambitious program to modernize the Royal Navy and prepare it for what Churchill correctly saw as the coming world war.

At the commencement of World War I, Churchill's confidence in the navy he had been instrumental in creating knew no bounds. In 1915, he planned a daring amphibious assault on the Turkish-held Dardanelles, control of which would open a supply line to Britain's ally, Russia. While bold in conception, the assault was poorly conceived and even more ineptly executed. The result was a disastrous and tragically bloody failure, which only became worse as the associated land campaign at Gallipoli developed. Disgraced, Churchill was removed as first lord of the admiralty and relegated to a minor Cabinet post.

Churchill did not remain out of the war long. He accepted command of the 6th Royal Scots Fusiliers and fought with them in France until May 1916, when he returned to England. In July 1917, his friend, political ally, and new prime minister, David Lloyd George, named him to the cabinet post of minister of munitions. Churchill dedicated himself to this work with great energy and succeeded in increasing munitions production so dramatically that a shell surplus was achieved before the war ended.

After leaving the post at munitions, Churchill became secretary of state for war and air during 1918–21. In 1921–22, he was secretary of state for the colonies and negotiated key treaties in the Middle East. He also hammered out the 1921 agreement creating the Irish Free State and signaling the end of centuries of conflict between England and Ireland. These triumphs notwithstanding, Churchill lost his office as well as his seat in Parliament after Lloyd George's government fell in 1922.

After the collapse of the Liberal government, Churchill once again realigned himself with the Conservatives and was returned to Parliament in 1924, joining the cabinet of Prime Minister Stanley Baldwin in the most important role of chancellor of the exchequer. His tenure, from 1924 to 1929, proved disastrous. In 1925, he returned the nation to the gold standard, an action that deepened the depression that followed the end of the Great War. When economic hardship triggered the General Strike of 1926, Churchill vigorously condemned the strikers, creating a breach with labor that was never healed.

For 10 years from 1929, after he stepped down as exchequer, Churchill held no government office. He remained very much in the public eye, however, as a vehement critic of Baldwin's pro-independence policy for India. He was equally adamant during this period about the developing situation in Nazi Germany, warning that "Hitlerism" would once again bring the world to war. Churchill became the leading opponent of Prime Minister Neville Chamberlain's policy of "appeasing" Adolf Hitler's aggressive expansionism. To avoid war, Chamberlain connived at Germany's annexation of the Sudetenland in Czechoslovakia. Churchill argued that a dictator could not be appeased. When Chamberlain returned from the Munich Conference (September 29–30, 1938), having reached the agreement on the Sudetenland and claiming to have achieved "peace for our time," Churchill bluntly labeled the act of appeasement a "total and unmitigated defeat." Events, of course, would prove him right.

After Hitler invaded Poland in September 1939, bringing general war to Europe, Chamberlain offered Churchill his former post of first lord of the admiralty. With his characteristic aggressiveness, Churchill proposed an immediate assault on Norway to dislodge the Germans there. Like the Gallipoli campaign of World War I, the invasion was a fiasco and had to be quickly aborted. This time, however, it was Chamberlain who took the fall. He resigned, and Churchill replaced him as prime minister during the very darkest period of the war. Such was Churchill's character in a crisis that he did not for a moment brood on the Norway disaster, but set about saving England—and defending the free world.

With Europe rapidly falling to the Germans, Churchill turned to the United States, a neutral nation reluctant to involve itself in yet another "European" war. Churchill established an intensely personal relationship with President Franklin D. Roosevelt, whom he readily persuaded to drift away from neutrality, first by developing the policy of lend-lease. This provided England (and, soon, other Allies, most notably the Soviet Union) with arms, materiel, aircraft, and ships.

Lend-lease was a great step forward in Britain's war effort, but, in 1940, the German juggernaut seemed unstoppable. In June, the British army was beaten back—and very nearly annihilated—at Dunkirk, on the North Sea coast of France. Only a well-executed evacuation saved the mass of the army. Later in the summer, the Battle of Britain commenced as the German *Luftwaffe* (air force) did what Churchill had predicted years earlier: conducted a massive bombing campaign in English skies. Britons prepared to be invaded—or, more accurately, Churchill prepared his people to resist invasion with everything they had. On June 4, 1940, in one of many great and immeasurably effective speeches delivered to Parliament, Churchill declared: "We shall fight in the fields and in the streets, we shall fight in the hills; we shall never surrender. . . ."

Churchill possessed the personal character and rhetorical skill to maintain his courage and to fire the courage and determination of his people. To the stunned surprise of Nazi Germany—and the world—it was the British who emerged victorious in the Battle of Britain, the Royal Air Force (RAF) defeating the *Luftwaffe* and staving off invasion.

Nor was Churchill merely a cheerleader. He engaged fully in every aspect of the conduct of the war. In contrast to Hitler and Mussolini, who dominated their military commanders, typically to the detriment of strategy, Churchill formed a partnership with the military. What he did insist on, however, was that British forces not allow themselves to be tied down in a defensive posture. Churchill believed that the best defense was a vigorous offense, and he boldly diverted an entire armored division—one of two in Britain—to take the offensive against the armies of Hitler and Mussolini in the Middle East.

With the entry of the United States into the war following the Japanese attack on Pearl Harbor on December 7, 1941, Churchill stepped in to hammer out a three-way alliance among the U.S., the USSR, and Britain. His war strategy for the Allies was controversial, and its wisdom is still debated by historians. Churchill proposed avoiding an invasion of the European mainland until what he called the "soft underbelly of Europe" had been breached by clearing North Africa and the Mediterranean of the enemy. He did not want to face another Dunkirk, but did want to institute vigorous offensive operations. Roosevelt ultimately agreed with Churchill, and it was not until the summer of 1943 that the Allies invaded Sicily and then the Italian mainland, having fought the first part of the "European" war in North Africa. A year later, Churchill was instrumental in planning and supporting the Normandy D-Day invasion, which began on June 6, 1944.

Although Churchill's "soft underbelly" strategy governed much of the war, his influence somewhat diminished once the Normandy campaign was under way. With victory in sight, Churchill now saw the Soviets as a postwar threat. It was not only that he hated Communism, but that the hard lessons of two world wars had taught him to oppose *all* totalitarian regimes. He therefore advocated a drive by the Western Allies directly into Berlin specifically to prevent the city's occupation by Soviets. He was overruled by Allied Commander in Chief Dwight D. Eisenhower, who believed it necessary first to crush the last German resistance in the West. For immediate tactical purposes, Eisenhower's was, indeed, the soundest plan; but Churchill typically looked beyond the tactical range to see the overall strategic consequences of an action. In this case, he looked beyond World War II itself. Later, in a speech delivered at a small college in Missouri, Churchill would coin the phrase *Iron Curtain* to describe the hard pall of Soviet influence and tyranny that had descended across eastern Europe, thanks to the inroads made as a result of the Allies' war strategy.

In some ways, Churchill was disappointed by the final conditions of the Allied victory in Europe. He then received what any other man would have felt to be a crushing blow in July 1945, when a general election failed to return him to office following the unconditional surrender of Germany but just before the capitulation of Japan. Churchill, as usual, simply refused to be crushed. He received the first dismal election returns while taking a bath: "There may well be a landslide and they have a perfect right to kick us out," he calmly observed. "That is democracy. That is what we have been fighting for. Hand me my towel."

Churchill was returned to office in 1951, and he was knighted in recognition of his great service to the nation and the world. In July 1953, he suffered a stroke. Weakened and ailing, he nevertheless fought back to partial recovery and continued in office until April 1955, when he was succeeded by his handpicked successor, Anthony Eden.

Churchill spent his final decade pursuing his favorite recreation, painting, and seeing to the publication of the last of his great literary works, the four-volume *History of the English-Speaking Peoples* (1956–58). A man of prodigious achievement, Churchill would be remembered as a great journalist and historian, even if he had not been a leader of the free world. His major body of biographical and historical writings, including a monumental six-volume history of World War II published during 1948–54, earned him the Nobel prize for literature in 1953. He treasured even more the honorary U.S. citizenship conferred on him in 1963 by President John F. Kennedy and the Congress—the first and, thus far, only such honor ever rendered by this country.

IN HIS OWN WORDS

"I would say to the House, as I said to those who have joined this government: I have nothing to offer but blood, toil, tears, and sweat."
—Speech made to House of Commons, May 13, 1940

"We shall fight on the beaches; we shall fight on the landing grounds; we shall fight in the fields and in the streets, we shall fight in the hills; we shall never surrender. . . ."
—Speech to the House of Commons, June 4, 1940

"Today we may say aloud before an awe-struck world: 'We are still masters of our fate. We are still captain of our souls.'"
—Speech on the war situation, House of Commons, September 9, 1941

"Never give in—never, never, never, never, in nothing great or small, large or petty, never give in except to convictions of honour and good sense. Never yield to force; never yield to the apparently overwhelming might of the enemy."
—Speech to the boys of Harrow, October 29, 1941

"When I warned them that Britain would fight on alone, whatever they did, their Generals told their Prime Minister and his divided cabinet that in three weeks, England would have her neck wrung like a chicken.— Some chicken! Some neck!"
—Speech to the Canadian Parliament, December 30, 1941

"We have not journeyed across the centuries, across the oceans, across the mountains, across the prairies, because we are made of sugar candy."
—Speech to the Canadian Parliament, December 30, 1941

"Let us therefore brace ourselves to our duties, and so bear ourselves that if the British Empire and Commonwealth last for a thousand years, men will still say, 'This was their finest hour.'"
—Speech to the House of Commons, June 18, 1940, after the collapse of France

Lady Astor: "Winston, if I were your wife I'd put poison in your coffee."
Churchill: "Nancy, if I were your husband, I'd drink it."
—Exchange attributed to Churchill

LEADERSHIP LESSONS
✦
Never give up. Never yield to tyranny.
✦
Character and integrity are the greatest assets of any leader.
✦
A great leader is almost always a great communicator.
✦
The leadership image you develop is as important to the enterprise you lead as the plans, strategies, and policies you create.
✦
Optimism does not mean fostering delusions. Present all difficulties and dangers frankly and fully.
✦
Explain objectives and goals. Create common cause with those you lead. Present a clear picture of the benefits and consequences of proposed actions.

Cincinnatus, Lucius Quinctius

Born: 519? B.C.   Died: 430? B.C

Character model   Rescuer

LEADERSHIP ACHIEVEMENTS

✦

Rescued his nation from invaders

✦

Selflessly bowed out after his mission was accomplished

LIFE

Very little is known about the life of Cincinnatus, yet he endures as an emblem of selfless leadership. Tradition holds that Cincinnatus was a simple farmer who was appointed dictator of Rome in 458 B.C. for the purpose of rescuing a Roman consular army that was surrounded on Mount Algidus by rebellious Aequi. Summoned to leadership, Cincinnatus defeated the Aequi invaders, thereby saving the army and Rome itself. Having done his duty, Cincinnatus renounced his dictatorship and returned to the farm.

The name of Cincinnatus was revived to describe George Washington, the "Cincinnatus of the West" who left his farm to rescue his people and then, eschewing further glory, wanted nothing more than to return to it.

LEADERSHIP LESSONS

✦

The great lesson of Cincinnatus is leadership at its most efficient: The leader steps down when the job is finished.

✦

Know what you want in life.

✦

Values truly count; the rest is excess baggage.

Clark, Mark Wayne

Born: 1896   Died: 1984

Character model   Mentor   Strategist

LEADERSHIP ACHIEVEMENTS

◆

Devoted his life to becoming the consummate soldier

◆

Developed a bold leadership style based on a willingness to take
calculated risks

◆

Excelled in leadership of especially difficult and frustrating tasks

◆

Won the respect of all colleagues

LIFE

No less a figure than Winston Churchill dubbed Mark Clark the
"American Eagle" for his steadfast leadership in the heartbreakingly difficult Allied campaign in Italy during World War II.

The son of a career officer, Clark was born, quite literally, into the
army, at Madison Barracks, Sackets Harbor, New York. He graduated
from West Point and entered the infantry as a second lieutenant in 1917. In
April of the following year, Clark was sent to France with the 5th Infantry
Division, where he immediately found himself in the midst of the great
Aisne–Marne offensive. After suffering a serious wound in June, Clark was
assigned to the First Army staff during the Saint-Mihiel offensive
(September 12–16) and the Meuse–Argonne campaign (September
26–November 11), which closed the war. Clark remained on active duty in
Germany, serving on the Third Army staff during the Allied occupation of
the Rhineland.

On his return to the United States in November 1919, Clark was promoted to captain and served in a variety of posts in the Midwest until he
was transferred to the General Staff in Washington, D.C., during 1921–24.
He graduated from the Infantry School at Fort Benning, Georgia, in 1925

and in January 1933 was promoted to major. Two years later, he graduated from the Command and General Staff School at Fort Leavenworth, Kansas. During the Depression, he was assigned command of a unit of the Civilian Conservation Corps (CCC) in Omaha, Nebraska (1935–36).

In 1937, Clark graduated from the Army War College and was posted to a staff position with the Third Infantry Division until 1940. Then he became an instructor at the Army War College, where he was instrumental in efforts to expand and prepare the army for war. At the college, he mentored the generation of young officers who would lead American forces in World War II. Promoted to brigadier general in August 1941 and major general in April 1942, Clark was made chief of staff of Army Ground Forces in May. In July, he was named commander of U.S. ground forces in Britain and immediately set about organizing II Corps there.

Clark was never content to serve behind a desk. He planned and participated in an extremely hazardous espionage operation to obtain intelligence on Vichy French forces in North Africa in preparation for Operation TORCH, the Allied North African landings. Promoted to lieutenant general in November 1942, Clark was assigned command of Allied forces in North Africa under Dwight D. Eisenhower. In this capacity, he was among the chief planners of the invasion of Sicily and mainland Italy, which was launched from North Africa. At the head of the Fifth Army, Clark landed at Salerno, Italy, on September 9, where his forces held out against heavy defenses until Allied reinforcements and naval action checked German counterattacks during September 10–18.

Clark had the extraordinarily thankless task of commanding the Fifth Army in its painful advance up the Italian peninsula between October 1943 and June 1944. On January 22, 1944, elements of the Fifth Army landed at Anzio and fought grimly through to Rome on June 4. This action showed Clark at his boldest. Acting with great initiative, he deliberately defied the directives of the Fifteenth Army Group (combined U.S. Fifth and British Eighth armies) commander, British general Sir Harold Alexander. What Clark gained was a sure way for the American army to conquer Rome, but Clark's strategy also permitted the Germans to effect a strategic withdrawal, which kept the enemy army intact and meant that Allied forces would continue to encounter stiff resistance in Italy throughout the war. It was a daring leadership decision that carried a heavy price.

Clark commanded the Allied advance across the Arno River and north to the Gothic Line between July and December 1944. In December, he was named to replace Alexander as commander of the Fifteenth Army Group. In his new command position, he directed the Allied offensive through the Gothic Line, into the Po Valley, and finally into Austria from April 9 to May 2, 1945.

After Germany surrendered and the Fifteenth Army Group was deactivated, Clark was named Allied high commissioner for Austria and served in this capacity from June 1945 to May 1947, when he was made commander of the Sixth Army (1947–49). From this position, he was elevated to chief of Army Field Forces. He served in this post during 1949–52, the year he was named the third overall U.S. commander during the Korean War, succeeding Matthew B. Ridgway. Clark saw the Korean War through to its uneasy conclusion.

Clark found time during the latter part of his career to write two very popular memoirs: *Calculated Risk* (1950) and *From the Danube to the Yalu,* published in 1954, the year of his retirement from active duty. He then accepted the post of commandant of the Citadel, South Carolina's prestigious military academy, where he served until 1960. He lived the remaining 15 years of his long life in quiet retirement outside Washington, D.C.

LEADERSHIP LESSONS

✦

Get out from behind your desk and into the front lines whenever possible.

✦

Develop the ability to calculate risks, and cultivate a commensurate
willingness to act upon your calculations.

✦

Understand when and under what circumstances to defy authority.

✦

A leader must lead through victory, through defeat, and through the dark
and difficult region between these two extremes.

Cleopatra VII
(Thea Philopator)

Born: 69 B.C.   Died: 30 B.C.

Improviser   Leverager   Motivator   Rescuer   Strategist

LEADERSHIP ACHIEVEMENTS

✦

Understood the nature of power and the means of acquiring it

✦

Set out to rescue Egypt in its extremity

✦

Leveraged to great effect her most powerful resource: herself

✦

Had an unparalleled grasp of world politics

✦

Nearly succeeded not only in saving the Egyptian kingdom, but in
extending her power over much of the world

LIFE

Cleopatra is one of the most famous women of all time, and, as far as can
be discerned at this remove in history, one of the most misunderstood and
underestimated. Although she ruled Egypt during a period of desperate difficulty, and did so with great political savvy, she is remembered far more
for her liaisons with Julius Caesar and Marc Antony. Quite unjustly and
inaccurately, she is often regarded as little more than a regal courtesan.

Cleopatra was born in Alexandria, Egypt, after two older sisters,
Cleopatra VI and Berenice IV. It is believed that Cleopatra VI died as a
child and that Cleopatra's father, Ptolemy Auletes, had Berenice IV
beheaded, although it is not known why. Later, other children were born:
a sister, Arsinoe IV, and two brothers, Ptolemy XIII and Ptolemy XIV.
Nominal reign over Egypt fell to 18-year-old Cleopatra and her 12-year-old
brother, Ptolemy XIII, in the spring of 51 B.C., when Ptolemy Auletes died.
However, at Auletes' death, the Roman leader Pompey served as regent
over the children. The Ptolemies and Romans had been allied for some two
centuries, during which time the power of the Ptolemies diminished as that
of the Romans increased. By the reign of Auletes, Rome ruled Egypt as a

puppet state, extracting from it large tributes. With the death of Auletes, it seemed that even this arrangement would come to an end, and Rome would effectively annex Egypt altogether.

Egyptian law dictated that Cleopatra have a consort, either a brother or a son, of any age; therefore, she was married to Ptolemy XIII, but she took care to subordinate his position to hers. She did not include his name in official documents, and she authorized the use of her portrait and name, not his, on all coinage. These gestures were hardly sufficient to halt the disintegration of the empire around her. Cyprus, Coele-Syria, and Cyrenaica, long parts of Ptolemaic Egypt, slipped to the Romans. Anarchy reigned in other outlying regions and, at home, there was famine.

Cleopatra began to take aggressive action to save Egypt and preserve her power. By 48 B.C., she had alarmed the more powerful court officials of Alexandria by some of her actions. After she directed her mercenaries to kill the sons of the Roman governor of Syria when they came asking for Egyptian aid against the Parthians, a court cabal led by Theodotus, the eunuch Pothinus, and a half-Greek general, Achillas, staged a coup that overthrew Cleopatra in favor of her younger brother.

It is believed that Cleopatra fled to Thebaid. In the meantime, between 51 and 49 B.C., Egypt was gripped by drought and failed harvests. This prompted Ptolemy XIII to decree, on October 27, 50 B.C., a ban on shipments of grain to anywhere but Alexandria. Whatever conservation purposes this might serve, it also deprived Cleopatra and her remaining supporters of sustenance. This, however, did not stop the determined woman. She recruited an army from among the Arab tribes east of Pelusium and, with her sister Arsinoe, moved to Syria and then set up a temporary base at Ascalon. In the meantime, the Roman general Pompey, having been defeated by Julius Caesar at Pharsalus, Thessaly, in August 48 B.C., headed for Alexandria in the hope of finding refuge with Ptolemy XIII, his senate-appointed ward. But Pompey did not realize that his defeat at Pharsalus had destroyed more than his army. His credibility and reputation were ruined, and he was assassinated as soon as he landed at Alexandria, on September 28, 48 B.C. The treacherous Ptolemy XIII stood nearby and looked on. Four days later, Caesar arrived in Alexandria, bringing with him 3,200 infantrymen and 800 cavalry. Caesar also made it clear that he intended to assert the authority of Rome over

Egypt, and, amid riots in Alexandria and after Ptolemy XIII fled to Pelusium, he installed himself in the royal palace. The eunuch Pothinus fetched Ptolemy back to Alexandria to negotiate with Caesar. Hearing this, Cleopatra resolved not to be left out. She rolled herself in a carpet and had herself smuggled into the palace and delivered to Caesar, as if she were a gift. The next morning, both Cleopatra and Ptolemy were summoned before Caesar—but, by this time, Cleopatra had already seduced the Roman. Ptolemy had been beaten.

Almost certainly, Caesar intended to make Cleopatra sole ruler of Alexandria, believing that she would be his puppet. However, Pothinus began the Alexandrine War when he mustered Ptolemy XIII's soldiers—20,000 men—in November and deployed them around Caesar in Alexandria. During the war, portions of the great library of Alexandria were destroyed, as were some warehouses, but Caesar captured the Pharos lighthouse, which allowed him to maintain control of the harbor. During the siege, Cleopatra's sister, Arsinoe, escaped from the palace and ran to Achillas. She was proclaimed the queen by the Macedonian mob and the army—a betrayal for which Cleopatra never forgave her.

In the course of the war, Caesar executed Pothinus, and Achillas was murdered by Ganymede. More important, Ptolemy XIII drowned in the Nile while he was trying to flee, making Cleopatra sole ruler of Egypt, as Caesar had intended. Yet again, however, to satisfy Egyptian law, she had to marry her younger brother, 11-year-old Ptolemy XIV. But she also ensured that she quickly became pregnant by Caesar, hoping to give him a son to carry the throne and thereby sustain her dynasty. Their son, Caesarion (Ptolemy Caesar), was born on June 23, 47 B.C. A year later, in July 46 B.C., Caesar returned to Rome. Showered with honors and granted a 10-year dictatorship, he summoned Cleopatra to Rome, where she received an icy reception. Great resistance developed at the prospect of Caesar's marrying Cleopatra; but this was all made moot by Caesar's assassination on the Ides of March, 44 B.C.

Following Caesar's murder, Cleopatra fled from Rome and returned home to Alexandria. Because Caesar had failed to mention Cleopatra and Caesarion in his will, she felt that her life, as well as that of her child, was in danger. Accordingly, she had her consort, Ptolemy XIV, assassinated and established in his stead four-year-old Caesarion as her co-regent.

The Egypt to which she returned was groaning under plague and famine. Cleopatra had to focus on stabilizing Egyptian government by securing recognition for Caesarion with Caesar's former lieutenant, Dolabella. She sent him the four legions that Caesar had left in Egypt, but Cassius captured them, prompting Dolabella to commit suicide at Laodicea during the summer of 43 B.C.

Cleopatra keenly and calmly observed the developing situation, waiting to see who would emerge as the next power in Rome. After the chief conspirators against Caesar—Brutus and Cassius—had been killed, and after the triumvirate of Marc Antony, Octavian (Gaius Julius Caesar Octavianus Augustus), and Lepidus emerged triumphant in the civil war that followed Caesar's death, the picture became clearer to Cleopatra. Taken ill, Octavian returned to Rome, leaving Antony as the emergent power. In the meantime, Cleopatra's son had gained his right to become king when Caesar was officially declared a divinity in Rome on January 1, 42 B.C., so she was in an excellent position to secure her dynasty.

In 41 B.C., Antony invited her (and other Eastern leaders) to Tarsus for a conference. She had made it her business to learn all she could about Antony: about his weak strategic and tactical skills, his fondness for liquor, his uncontrollable womanizing, and his limitless ambition. Cleopatra seduced Antony with a show of sensual opulence. Her seduction of him was a brilliant political move, the best of the limited alternatives available to her.

In the spring of 40 B.C., Antony left Cleopatra for Rome and his wife, Fulvia. In the course of Antony's four-year absence from Cleopatra, Fulvia died, and Antony mended fences with the powerful Octavian by marrying his sister, Octavia, who had three children from her first marriage. In the meantime, Cleopatra had given birth to twins, one boy and one girl, in Alexandria. Antony's own first child by Octavia was a girl. Had Octavia given him a son and heir, he might well have remained in Rome and never approached Cleopatra again. But Cleopatra and, probably even more, the treasures of the Ptolemies beckoned him back to Egypt. Seeking to sell the treasures at the highest rate, he went to deal with the Parthians. Reaching Antioch, he sent for Cleopatra, who brought the twins with her. These Antony officially recognized, giving them the names Alexander Helios and Cleopatra Selene. Antony presented Cleopatra with much arable land, which was essential to drought-gripped Egypt. He gave her Cyprus, the Cilician coast, Phoenicia, Coele-Syria, Judea, and Arabia.

Egypt could now build ships with the lumber from the Cilician coast. At Antony's behest, Egypt constructed a large fleet, which Antony planned to use against the Parthians. But in 36 B.C., Antony was defeated, and he became increasingly indebted to Cleopatra, with whom he had a third child. On their return to Syria, she met him and what was left of his army with food, clothing, and money.

Early in 35 B.C., Antony returned to Egypt with Cleopatra. Octavia was in Athens with supplies and reinforcements; Antony sent her a letter telling her to come no farther. Her brother, Octavian, understood what was going on and tried to provoke Antony into a fight. Antony could have made peace with Octavian and Octavia even now, if he had only returned to Rome. But Cleopatra kept him in Alexandria.

In 34 B.C., Antony campaigned in Armenia and enjoyed success and profit. Cleopatra was named the Queen of Kings—a higher position than that of Caesarion. Alexander Helios was proclaimed Great King of the Seleucid empire, and Cleopatra Selene was called Queen of Cyrenaica and Crete. Cleopatra and Antony's son Ptolemy Philadelphos, age two, was named King of Syria and Asia Minor. Cleopatra now saw herself as becoming empress of the world.

In 32–31 B.C., Antony at last divorced Octavia, thereby compelling the western part of the ancient world to acknowledge his relationship with Cleopatra. He had already put her name and face on a Roman coin, the silver denarii, which was widely circulated throughout the Mediterranean. This act alienated Rome, and Octavian waged war against Antony and Cleopatra, defeating them at the naval Battle of Actium on September 2, 31. Less than a year later, Antony halfheartedly defended Alexandria against the advancing army of Octavian. The pragmatic Cleopatra, always looking to protect Egypt, now attempted to win the support of Octavian. She dispatched her messengers to tell Antony that she was dead, and she retired to her mausoleum. Pledging his undying love for her, Antony committed suicide.

Octavian regarded Cleopatra as nothing more or less than a military prize, and she learned that she was to be paraded through the streets of Rome as a war trophy. Rather than live as a slave, Cleopatra had an asp—

an Egyptian cobra—brought to her, smuggled past her guards in a basket of figs. She died, by her own hand, on August 12, 30 B.C., at the age of 39.

After Cleopatra's death, Caesarion was strangled, and the other children of Cleopatra were raised by Antony's former wife, Octavia. But Cleopatra's death ended the long line of Egyptian monarchs as the Roman emperors came to rule Egypt.

LEADERSHIP LESSONS

✦

Know your assets, and leverage them to the maximum.

✦

Study your opponents and allies. Learn their strengths and weaknesses.
Understand their motivations. See the world through their eyes.
Act accordingly.

✦

Do not underestimate the power of a strong leadership image.

✦

Use whatever you have. If image is your chief asset, build on it.
Properly managed, image may acquire enduring substance.

✦

Build alliances, but do not allow emotional attachments to color those
alliances.

✦

Above all, "know thyself." Understand your motives. Analyze and deal with
any ambivalence or doubt you may feel.

Clovis I

Born: ca. 466 Died: 511

Conqueror   Motivator   Visionary

LEADERSHIP ACHIEVEMENTS

✦

Founded and expanded the Frankish kingdom

✦

Understood the value of the dramatic gesture as an instrument of motivation

✦

Worked well with peoples of divergent beliefs

✦

Valued the spiritual life and imparted that value to others

✦

Synthesized barbarian ruthlessness and cunning with Christian spiritual direction

LIFE

Clovis I founded the Frankish kingdom that dominated much of Europe during the early Middle Ages. He had been born to the Salian Frank king Childeric I, whom he succeeded to the throne in 481. Five years later, he defeated the last of Gaul's Roman rulers, Syagrius, at the Battle of Soissons. This victory triggered the fall of most of Roman Gaul, although some individual cities continued to resist, as did the Armoricans in western Gaul and various groups along the Rhine. By 494, Clovis I was in control of the regions of the Somme and Seine.

Most of what is known of Clovis I comes via an account by Bishop Gregory of Tours, who portrays him as combining Christian piety and zeal with barbarian ruthlessness. For example, when one of Clovis's unruly Frankish followers appropriated a magnificent vase from a church, Clovis demanded that it be returned to the bishop. One of the Franks, incensed at this demand, smashed the precious object with his ax. Clovis restored the fragments to the bishop, saying nothing to the Frank. One year later, while Clovis was reviewing his troops, he recognized the warrior who had smashed the vase. He inspected the man's weapons and scolded him for maintaining them poorly. With that, Clovis seized the man's battle axe and threw it to the ground. When the Frank bent to retrieve it, the king split his skull with his own ax. "Thus," he declared, "you treated the vase at Soissons." Clovis understood the value of a dramatic leadership gesture.

Although he was raised a pagan, Clovis came to dominate a realm controlled on the local level by Catholic bishops. He got on well with these clerics, even though he himself did not convert until about 493, when he married the Burgundian princess Clotilda. At the time, his conversion was merely a matter of convenience; however, three years later, at the Battle of Zülpich against the Alamanni in the Middle Rhine region, Clovis turned to Christianity in earnest. Facing imminent defeat, he prayed to Christ for victory, which was indeed given him. It was another two years before this battlefield conversion moved Clovis to accept baptism, but once he did, his interest in Catholicism and its theology became intense. In about 510, he convened an important church council at Orléans, in which he personally participated.

Clovis's reign was punctuated by frequent conflict with the Alamanni, Thuringians, and Visigoths, all barbarian tribes. His 507 victory against the Visigoths at Vouillé he attributed to the intervention and patronage of St. Martin of Tours. Clovis penetrated into southern Gaul as far as Bordeaux. He did not, however, succeed in pushing the Goths out of the region and he ended by withdrawing from it, settling in Paris, from which he administered what had become a vast Frankish empire. Clovis I died in Paris on November 27, 511.

LEADERSHIP LESSONS

✦

Value the well-chosen, well-executed dramatic gesture of leadership.

✦

Do not demand lockstep thinking. Learn to work effectively with people whose beliefs diverge from yours.

✦

Remain open to "conversion" to more effective ways of achieving common goals.

✦

Know when to withdraw from no-win situations, to cut your losses and consolidate your gains.

Cortés, Hérnan

Born: 1485   Died: 1547

Conqueror   Leverager   Motivator   Profit maker   Strategist   Tactician

LEADERSHIP ACHIEVEMENTS

✦

Conquered one of the two great Native American empires

✦

Leveraged a small force to achieve a great end

✦

Created opportunity

✦

Opened a vast territory to Spain and amassed great wealth for himself

LIFE

Cortés was the most famous of the Spanish conquistadors. With a small body of men, he conquered the Mexican empire of the Aztecs.

Cortés was a son of the lower Spanish nobility. Born and raised in Medellín, Extremadura, he was sent at age 14 to the University of Salamanca, where he was a very intelligent student, but also wild and, according to a contemporary, "much given to women." Cortés left the university after two years and drifted about Europe until he heard accounts of the early transoceanic voyages of exploration and colonial expansion. These stories suddenly focused his ambitions and gave him purpose. The youth sailed in 1504 to Santo Domingo, in the Caribbean, to seek fame and fortune in the New World.

Cortés served with Diego de Velázquez de Cuellar in the Spanish conquest of Cuba and became *alcalde* (mayor) of the colonial capital of Santiago. By 1519, he had become a man of importance and influence in the Spanish New World, and he wasted little time in wresting from Velázquez command of an expedition to conquer Mexico from the Aztecs. It was a bold, ambitious, exhausting, and extremely hazardous undertaking. Cortés began by exploring the Mexican coastal region as far as modern Veracruz, where he established a city. He took great pains to gather sound intelligence concerning the political situation in the highlands. This information secured, he marched inland. Encountering the Indians of Tlaxcala, whom he had learned were traditional enemies of the dominant Aztec tribe, Cortés first fought them and then struck an anti-Aztec alliance with them.

Backed by the Tlaxcalas, Cortés marched on the Aztec capital of Tenochtitlan (modern Mexico City). He was met by the Aztec ruler Moctezuma (Montezuma) II, who not only offered no resistance to the invaders, but even welcomed them. Historians speculate that the Aztec emperor believed Cortés to be an incarnation of the deity Quetzalcoatl, an impression the conquistador did nothing to dispel. He and his conquistador band entered the capital, entirely unopposed, in November 1519.

The invaders collected vast quantities of gold and other treasure for several months until Cortés was compelled to take an expedition to the coast in order to counter a threat from a rival Spanish army under Panfilo de Narvaez. Easily defeating Narvaez, he returned to Tenochtitlan only to discover that the Aztecs, who had been sadistically brutalized by Cortés's second-in-command, Pedro de Alvarado, were now in full revolt. After incurring heavy losses, Cortés and his men fled the capital during what they called the *Noche Triste* ("sad night") of June 30, 1520. In this melee, Moctezuma II was slain—according to Aztec chroniclers, by the Spanish, and, in the Spanish version, by the outraged Aztecs themselves.

Evicted from Tenochtitlan, Cortés nevertheless refused to acknowledge defeat. He regrouped and resupplied his forces, and then led them back to the capital in a well-planned and thorough siege in 1521. Cortés controlled the great aqueducts leading to the city, thereby cutting off the Aztecs' supply of fresh water. His stranglehold prevented food and other supplies from reaching Tenochtitlan as well. After three months, starvation and disease had decimated the defenders of the Aztec capital. They surrendered to the Spanish on August 13, 1521.

In this way, Cortés acquired a great New World empire for his country and, as for himself, became a fabulously wealthy and powerful man. The Spanish conquest of the New World was driven largely by visions of gold. The conquistador class was made up primarily of the younger sons of nobility and minor nobility, who had little opportunity in Spain. The feudal system of primogeniture, in which first sons inherited all of a family's wealth, left subsequent offspring to fend for themselves. The New World presented a vast field of wealth and power. Yet, of all the conquistadors, Cortés was by far the most successful, the only one who actually realized the Spanish dream of fantastic wealth in America. For most of the others, privation, suffering, and, often, death were the only rewards of conquest.

Cortés returned to Spain several times and subsequently led expeditions to Honduras in 1524 and to Baja California in 1536. He participated in the unsuccessful Spanish attack on Algiers in 1541. He died near Seville on December 2, 1547.

IN HIS OWN WORDS

"There is no retreat . . . which does not bring an infinity of woes to those who make it, to wit: shame, hunger, loss of friends, goods, and arms, and death, which is the worst of them, but not the last, for infamy endures forever."
—Address to his army, 1520

LEADERSHIP LESSONS

✦

Confronted by a dearth of available opportunities, the effective leader makes his own.

✦

Knowledge truly is power. Devote time and resources to acquiring significant information before embarking on any enterprise.

✦

Forge strategic alliances to achieve desired goals.

✦

A self-confident image—even a bluff—is often essential to achieving your objectives.

Cromwell, Oliver

Born: 1599   Died: 1658

**Conqueror   Innovator   Motivator   Profit maker   Rescuer   Strategist
Systems creator   Tactician   Visionary**

LEADERSHIP ACHIEVEMENTS

◆

Provided leadership in three British civil wars

◆

Brought a (temporary) end to the monarchy in England

◆

Created a radically new form of parliamentary government

◆

Advanced Britain as a world power

◆

Laid the foundations of the British Empire

◆

Remodeled the British army into a large and formidable force

LIFE

Violently hated and extravagantly admired, Oliver Cromwell was the chief architect of the English civil wars of the 17th century that replaced the monarchy with parliamentary rule under the Commonwealth, over which he presided as lord protector. Cromwell was born at Huntingdon on April 25, 1599, the second son in a family whose members had a long tradition of service in Parliament. Educated at Sidney Sussex College, Cambridge, during 1615–17, Cromwell married in 1620 and soon became a convert to Puritanism.

In 1628, Cromwell was elected the member of Parliament for Huntingdon and rapidly earned notoriety for his unrelenting attacks on the bishops of the Church of England. In 1640, as the nation moved closer to civil war, Cromwell was chosen to represent Cambridge in the so-called Long Parliament. Again directing his fire against the bishops—this time calling for their total abolition and a general purification of the Church— Cromwell sided with those members of Parliament who advocated the overthrow of Charles I. As civil war became inevitable, Cromwell blocked the transfer of silver from Cambridge University to the king's coffers. He secured Cambridgeshire for Parliament and raised a troop of cavalry from his native Huntingdon. Late in October 1642, Parliament commissioned him commander of a military association of six counties, a double regiment of 14 troops later dubbed "the Ironsides."

Cromwell soon proved himself an extraordinary commander. He defeated Loyalist forces at Grantham on May 13, 1643, and at Gainsborough on July 28. Appointed governor of Ely, he led his troops to victory at Winceby on October 11, 1643, and then at Marston Moor on July 2, 1644. Unfavorable terrain prevented him from effectively employing his superior numbers in pursuit of Charles at the second Battle of Newbury on October 27, 1644, and, early in 1645, the Treaty of Uxbridge brought a brief truce, from January to March, during which Cromwell successfully argued in Parliament for vast military reforms. The result was the New Model Army, a standing military force raised by conscription and supported by a tax levy. Compared to the old militia system, it was an exceptionally stable and professional fighting force. Cromwell would use it well.

On June 14, 1645, Cromwell was one of the principal commanders responsible for the decisive victory at the Battle of Naseby, and, as second in command to Sir Thomas Fairfax, Cromwell helped take Oxford in 1646, which resulted in Charles's surrender and concluded the First Civil War.

Cromwell attempted unsuccessfully to reach an accord with Charles I, and he also found himself embroiled in a schismatic dispute between Presbyterians in Parliament and Puritans in the New Model Army. Early in 1647, Parliament voted effectively to disband the army, which, however, resisted. Cromwell, siding with the soldiers, took command of the forces, seized Charles I, and occupied London. The king conducted secret negotiations with Scots Presbyterians from August through October of 1647, and in November fled to the Isle of Wight. He promised the Scots to impose Presbyterianism as the English state religion for a period of three years in return for military support of his effort to regain his kingdom. On January 15, 1648, Parliament formally renounced its allegiance to the king, and the Second Civil War commenced.

Cromwell besieged and captured Pembroke in south Wales during June and early July 1648, and then met and defeated an invading Scots army at the Battle of Preston on August 17–19, 1648. With northern England secured, he returned to London on December 7, where, backed by his New Model Army, he pushed for a trial of King Charles. Late in January 1649, as one of 135 commissioners appointed to sit in judgment of the king, he succeeded in securing the monarch's execution, which was carried out on January 30.

Cromwell was chosen chairman of the new republic's Council of State. He moved swiftly to put down a mutiny within the ranks of the army during the spring of 1649, and then led his forces into Ireland, which, by virtue of a Royalist–Catholic alliance, defied the new Commonwealth's authority. The Irish campaign showed Cromwell at his most ruthless. He unleashed upon Ireland a period of terror that stretched from September 1649 to May of the next year. He besieged and took one Royalist–Catholic stronghold after another, including Drogheda, Wexford, and Clonmel. At the fall of each of these fortresses, Cromwell slaughtered the defending garrisons, including women and children, creating the worst internal military atrocity in British history.

No sooner did Cromwell return to England in 1650 than a general uprising commenced in Scotland. This episode is sometimes called the Third Civil War. Scottish Presbyterians proclaimed Charles II, son of the executed monarch, the new and rightful king of Great Britain. On January 1, 1651, Charles II was crowned in Scotland. In the meantime, from July through September 1650, Cromwell launched an invasion of Scotland. At first, the campaign went badly for Cromwell's forces, which were hampered by disease and the Scottish people's scorched-earth policy. Cromwell's troops were unable to forage, and some 5,000 of Cromwell's 16,000-man force died of disease and starvation. At Dunbar, a Scottish army of about 18,000 surrounded Cromwell's 11,000 remaining troops, but on September 3, 1650, the Puritan leader staged a surprise cavalry counterattack and scored a decisive victory, entirely routing the Scots. The victorious Cromwell was stricken by malaria during this campaign. His illness, combined with an internecine dispute among the Scots, stalemated the war for nearly a year. But, early in the summer of 1651, Cromwell, who had recovered his health, attempted to negotiate peace with the Scots. When peace talks collapsed, he led a lightning campaign in Scotland, taking Perth on August 2, 1651, and marching swiftly back down to England, where, at Worcester on

September 3, he trapped and destroyed Royalist forces led by Charles II. The Scottish uprising—or Third Civil War—had ended.

Cromwell prosecuted another war, this time with the Dutch, largely over the East India trade, during 1652–54. While he fought the Dutch, he was even more immediately concerned over the "Rump Parliament"— what remained of the Long Parliament after the Royalists and Presbyterians had been purged from it—which continued to be antagonistic toward the army and which was failing to enact the sweeping reforms of church and state called for by the Puritan program. In April 1653, Cromwell had had enough and forcibly dissolved the Rump Parliament. In its place, he then established the Little, or Barebones, Parliament. He charged this body with reforming English government and society. The legislators took their commission seriously and set to work with great speed, enacting reforms too radical for Cromwell, who dissolved the Barebones Parliament in December 1653.

With Parliament inactivated, a cadre of New Model army officers drew up the so-called Instrument of Government, a constitution that named Cromwell lord protector, empowering him to govern with the aid of a council of state and a single-chamber Parliament. But it was Cromwell and his council, not the new Parliament, that enacted the most significant governmental and legal reforms of the protectorate. The lord protector dissolved his first Parliament on January 22, 1655, setting up a regionally based system of government led by his trusted generals. War with Spain, fought during 1656–59 in an attempt to end the Spanish monopoly in the West Indies, nevertheless required a new Parliament to raise funds. That body offered to make Cromwell king in 1657, which he angrily refused. From this point onward, Cromwell increasingly fell to disputing with Parliament, which he again dissolved in February 1658. Later that year, his malarial infection flared, and on September 3, 1658, he died in London.

As a leader, Oliver Cromwell was entirely unyielding. He was willing to act on his beliefs, even if this meant killing the king and perpetrating, against the Irish, something very nearly approaching genocide. At the same time, Cromwell practiced a high degree of religious toleration, allowing (for example) Jews to settle in England for the first time since 1290. As prickly as he was with Parliament, Cromwell hammered Britain into shape as a formidable world power. He created a great army and navy, and he acquired the first of many British imperial possessions by winning Jamaica and Dunkirk as a result of victory in his war with Spain and its ally, France. For all that he achieved, however, his republican government did not long endure. His son, Richard Cromwell, became lord protector on September 3, 1658, but soon proved able to control neither Parliament nor the army. On May 7, 1659, Richard Cromwell resigned as lord protector, and in May 1660, Charles II was restored to the throne. Even though the republic collapsed, Cromwell's reforms lingered and have since remained a strong influence on British government and society.

IN HIS OWN WORDS

"Not only strike while the iron is hot, but make it hot by striking."
—Attributed

"Put your trust in God, but be sure to see that your powder is dry."
—To troops about to cross a river

LEADERSHIP LESSONS

✦

Begin by working within the system to create change, even radical change.

✦

Never underestimate the spiritual dimension of any enterprise.

✦

Combine spiritual inspiration with practical skills; Cromwell was intensely religious, but he never let faith substitute for a well-led, well-equipped army.

✦

Nothing succeeds like success. Cromwell strengthened his fledgling republic with an aggressive approach to international trade and imperial expansion.

Cyrus the Great

Born: 590–80 B.C. Died: ca. 529

Character model   Conqueror   Problem solver   Rescuer
Strategist   Systems creator   Tactician

LEADERSHIP ACHIEVEMENTS

✦

Founded the Persian (Achaemenid) Empire, The greatest empire of its time

✦

Exercised great energy in conquest, but administered conquered territories
with leniency, toleration, and justice

✦

Created a vast and remarkably stable empire

LIFE

Cyrus II, known as Cyrus the Great, founded the Achaemenid, or Persian, Empire, the greatest empire of its time. Cyrus was born in Media, also known as Persis—modern-day Iran—and was apparently one in a long succession of ruling chiefs. The realm Cyrus inherited, called Anshan, was itself quite small, which makes the more remarkable his expansion of it. By the end of his reign, Cyrus ruled over much of the Near East, from the Aegean Sea to the Indus River. He conquered the Babylonian empire and became master of the greatest city of his time, Babylon. As a conqueror in the ancient world, Cyrus was second only to Alexander the Great.

The outlines of his childhood were passed down to us through the histories of Herodotus and Xenophon. As with all founding figures, however, Cyrus's early years are shrouded in myth. Astyages, king of the Medes, married his daughter to his vassal, a noble of Persis called Cambyses. This union produced Cyrus; however, shortly after the birth of his grandson, Astyages dreamed that the infant would grow up to overthrow him. In a parallel with Sophocles's *Oedipus Rex,* Astyages is said to have immediately ordered the child's death; unwilling to carry out this cruel command, Astyages's chief adviser instead secretly gave the baby to a shepherd to raise. Ten years later, after Cyrus had already earned a degree of renown,

124

his survival became known to Astyages, who, at last, allowed himself to be persuaded to spare the boy. Grown to manhood, however, Cyrus did indeed revolt against and overthrow his grandfather. In 550 B.C., Astyages moved to suppress the rebellion, but Cyrus exercised such personal magnetism that the army of Astyages deserted him and joined Cyrus.

As a conqueror, Cyrus was both aggressive and endlessly energetic. After subjugating the Iranian tribes in the vicinity of the Medes, he turned west, to confront Croesus. The powerful ruler of Lydia in Asia Minor, Croesus was a foe of the Medes, and now hoped to exploit the overthrow of Astyages by carving out from the Medes a vaster empire for himself. He assumed that, in the absence of Astyages, he would meet with little resistance. Cyrus, however, responded by attacking Lydia and capturing its capital city of Sardis in 547 or 546. In this battle, Croesus either was killed, committed suicide by self-immolation, or was taken captive. Those accounts that claim he was made a prisoner of war note that Cyrus was at pains to treat Croesus well. Whether or not Croesus ever became Cyrus's prisoner, it is a fact that the conqueror is celebrated for the great toleration and generosity with which he treated those over whom he triumphed.

With the defeat of Croesus, the Greek cities of the Aegean fell to Cyrus, who periodically was called upon to suppress revolts, though, for the most part, the Ionian Greeks submitted peacefully, welcoming Cyrus's hegemony as an improvement over life under Croesus.

After his triumphs in Greece, Cyrus marched against Babylonia. He had decided to exploit the instability of that great kingdom, whose populace suffered under the corrupt rule of Nabonidus. Cyrus engineered the support of many Babylonians, whose cooperation and compliance allowed him to conclude a rapid conquest. The great city of Babylon fell in October 539.

Cyrus's conquest of Babylon occasioned the most celebrated instance of his toleration. The Bible credits him with delivering the Jews from their long Babylonian captivity and permitting a return to their homeland. With equal magnanimity, Cyrus allowed the Babylonians to retain their traditional gods and customs of worship. Thus he acquired a great empire without feeling the necessity to possess as well the souls of its inhabitants. His policy of liberal toleration meant that Cyrus gave the conquered people little reason to resist his rule. Indeed, typically, life under Cyrus was welcomed as a kind of deliverance.

Having conquered Babylonia, Cyrus also acquired dominion over that nation's conquests: Syria and Palestine. Other kingdoms, most notably Cilicia, submitted to Cyrus out of diplomatic necessity, and the evidence is always that Cyrus treated his allies and his acquisitions well.

Herodotus reports that the death of Cyrus came at the hands of an aggrieved mother. One of the nomadic tribes Cyrus conquered shortly after his overthrow of Astyages was the Massagetai, whose chieftain was female. Her son, whom Cyrus had taken prisoner, years later committed suicide while languishing in captivity. Vowing vengeance, his mother met Cyrus in battle and killed him. Cyrus left two sons, Bardiya and Cambyses, the second of whom succeeded him. According to Darius I of Persia, Cambyses murdered Bardiya, to ensure the absence of any rival; however, most historians believe Bardiya was killed by conspirators that included Darius. Doubtless, Cambyses approved. Cambyses was married to his sister Atossa. Under Cambyses and the rulers of his line during the next two centuries, the empire Cyrus had created continued to expand and prosper.

LEADERSHIP LESSONS

✦

For a great leader, strength and benevolence are by no means incompatible.

✦

Justice is the firmest foundation of any enterprise.

✦

Identify a power vacuum and act swiftly to fill it.

✦

Balance short-term gains against long-term goals. Build with an eye toward the future.

Darius I

Born: 550 B.C.   Died: 486 B.C.

**Conqueror   Improviser   Leverager   Problem solver   Profit maker
Strategist   Systems creator**

LEADERSHIP ACHIEVEMENTS

✦

Used guile to achieve a trusted position of power, becoming the
ultimate insider

✦

Refused to be intimidated by daunting odds and obstacles

✦

Combined ruthless energy with methodical organization

✦

Leveraged his resources by creating an elaborate system of border
fortifications both to defend and to aggressively expand his empire

✦

Brought efficient and beneficial administration to those territories
he conquered

LIFE

Darius I of Persia combined wit, bold cunning, ruthless energy, and a methodical doggedness to augment the greatness of Persia as one of the most important empires of the ancient world. He was the son of Hystaspes, satrap (governor) of Parthia. The Greek historian Herodotus records that Cyrus the Great, emperor of Persia, suspected the youthful Darius of plotting against him. This notwithstanding, Darius operated in such a way that he retained the trust of the royal family, even serving Cambyses II, the son of Cyrus, as a bodyguard. When Cambyses died in Egypt during the summer of 522, Darius traveled to Media, where he and six fellow conspirators successfully plotted the murder of Bardiya, another son of Cyrus, who had assumed the throne in March 522. Darius invented an elaborate story to justify the murder, claiming that the man he had killed was one Gaumata, a Magian impersonating Bardiya. Bardiya, Darius said, had actually been murdered by his own brother Cambyses. Darius went on to explain that he had acted against the "imposter" to restore the Persian throne to the rightful Achaemenid dynasty. Some believed him, but he also met with opposition in the form of widespread revolt in Susiana, Babylonia, Media, Sagartia, and Margiana. Even in Persia proper, a man named Vahyazdata, claiming to be Bardiya, staged a revolt. Darius refused to be intimidated, but mustered forces to suppress the rebellions one after the other. He fought no fewer than 19 battles against nine rebel leaders.

After Darius I had secured control of the empire, he methodically set about an unprecedentedly ambitious program of fortifying his frontiers. These fortifications performed double duty as defensive bastions and as staging areas from which Darius, with dogged precision, conducted campaigns to extend his borders. He defeated the Scythians in 519 and soon was in possession of the entire Indus Valley. He conquered eastern Thrace and the Getae, and then, in 513, crossed the Danube into Europe, where he pursued bands of Scythian nomads.

While Darius chased the nomads, his carefully chosen satraps in Asia Minor completed the subjugation of Thrace and Macedonia and secured the Aegean islands of Lemnos and Imbros. In 490, Darius engaged the Athenians at the Battle of Marathon, where he suffered a famous and stunning defeat. He never gave up, however, and was planning a third attempt against Greece in 486 when he died.

Although he failed to conquer Greece, Darius was one of the great empire builders of the ancient world. Part of his leadership genius was his ability to combine ruthless guile, an energetic military policy, a methodical approach, and a spirit of tolerance. Darius was a brilliant administrator, who organized an efficient government of satrapies and a system of equitable and efficiently collected provincial tributes (taxes). Darius generally improved the lot of those he conquered, greatly expanding trade and commerce to the benefit of all.

LEADERSHIP LESSONS

✦

Darius demonstrated that a conqueror can be ruthless in the acquisition of territory and power, and yet work as a builder and not a mere destroyer.

✦

Darius was never wasteful. He husbanded and leveraged his resources thoroughly.

✦

Darius devoted great care to appointing skilled and trustworthy subordinates.

David

Died: ca. 962 B.C.

Character model   Conqueror   Leverager   Mentor   Motivator
Strategist   Systems creator   Tactician   Visionary

LEADERSHIP ACHIEVEMENTS

✦

Developed a powerful personal leadership style, winning the loyalty
of his people

✦

Acquired power not through violence, but by building a following among
the most influential people

✦

Effectively built coalitions for the common good

✦

Showed great military and administrative skill

✦

United secular and spiritual dimensions to create a great empire

✦

Established the spiritual dimension of his empire so powerfully that it has
assumed a quality of timelessness

LIFE

As the second—and greatest—king of Israel, David not only brought
together and united loosely constituted tribes into a single empire, he transformed himself into the central and enduring symbol of the bond between
God and the Jewish people. He was born in Bethlehem, Judah, the
youngest son of Jesse and the grandson of Boaz and Ruth. Biblical tradition portrays David as a simple shepherd boy who became his people's
champion in single combat against the "giant" Philistine warrior Goliath,
slaying him with a slingshot stone. Whatever the historical basis of this
story, young David began his political career as an aide in the court of King
Saul, who came to regard the youth as a second son. David lived as a
brother to Saul's son and heir, Jonathan, and he married Saul's daughter
Michal. The idyllic life of Saul's court might have continued undisturbed
had not David's prowess as a warrior earned him the admiration of the

people, which made Saul increasingly jealous. Driven to a paranoid frenzy, Saul plotted to kill David. In the nick of time, David fled into southern Judah and Philistia, where he quickly built a popular following by taking up the life of a kind of biblical Robin Hood on the desert frontier of Judah. David gathered about him other bandits and refugees, forming them into an organized guerrilla force that defended the frontier populace against the depredations of various bands of raiders. In this way, David won the loyalty of increasing numbers of people.

David was a guerrilla leader, who, in contrast to the typical guerrilla, had no designs to overthrow King Saul. His growing popularity won over influential Judaean elders, who invited him first to become king of Judah in Hebron and then to succeed Saul himself, after Saul and Jonathan were killed by Philistine warriors at the Battle of Mount Gilboa in about 1000 B.C. Although he had come to power through peaceful consensus, David did not hesitate in the vigorous prosecution of a civil war with factions loyal to Saul's surviving son, Ishbaal. The struggle ended when Ishbaal was slain by his own courtiers, after which David was universally accepted as king of Israel—even by the remote tribes beyond Judah.

Having built a solid power base, David turned to Jerusalem, to which he carefully laid siege, ultimately taking it from the Jebusites, whom he expelled. This, the greatest city of Judah, David established as the capital of the empire. With a consummate understanding of the importance of vision, the spiritual dimension of leadership, David endowed his secular triumph at Jerusalem with great spiritual significance by transporting the ark of the covenant, central symbol of the presence of Yahweh (God), into the new capital. He thus transformed Jerusalem into a holy city.

Having secured and anointed his capital, King David campaigned against the Philistines, defeating them decisively, and then went on to annex surrounding tribal kingdoms, including Edom, Moab, and Ammon, creating a great empire, over which he ruled for about 40 years. David succeeded in neutralizing the greatest threat against Israel, the Philistines; he united the fractious tribes of Israel—something Saul had been unable to do; he greatly expanded his territorial holdings; and he established his empire as both a secular and spiritual realm—a place as well as the embodiment of a religion. Nevertheless, David's reign was also plagued by family dissension and rebellion. To unite the diverse tribes from which he forged his nation, David took many wives, raising a family made up of strangers who had little in common. David's third son, Absalom, killed his first son, Amnon, because Amnon had raped Tamar, sister of Absalom and half-sister of Amnon. As punishment, David exiled Absalom—only later to recall him. During the period of his exile, Absalom organized a rebellion against David. When Absalom returned to Jerusalem, he staged a revolt that sent David fleeing from the throne until he could organize a force of his own to retake his empire. Absalom was killed in battle by Joab, one of David's loyal commanders.

Yet David did manage to recover from internecine and familial strife to pass down his empire intact to Solomon, his son by Bathsheba. Although the kingdom was at last divided after Solomon's death, the religious dimension of the empire David created has endured through many millennia of Judaism.

LEADERSHIP LESSONS

✦

Striving for excellence and demonstrating skill and courage are often rewarded.

✦

Spiritual vision should never be sacrificed to immediate gain; such vision is a powerful driver of enterprise and achievement.

✦

An effective leader marries the spiritual to the temporal, creating systems in which the one serves the other.

✦

Great leaders are typically unifiers, people who forge common cause, even among the most diverse and jarring elements.

✦

Work to unite, not to divide.

✦

Leaders learn to separate issues from personalities. They do not let personal conflicts destroy the enterprise they lead.

Dayan, Moshe

Born: 1915   Died: 1981

Innovator Leverager Mentor Motivator Rescuer Strategist Tactician

LEADERSHIP ACHIEVEMENT

✦

Was a successful guerrilla leader and independence fighter

✦

Competently led a highly effective army

✦

Was a leader of great efficiency and boldness

✦

Commanded the Israeli army in the Six-Day War, achieving one of the most
spectacular victories in modern military history

✦

Projected an image of leadership and victory

✦

Developed an intensely personal style of command

LIFE

The leadership style of Moshe Dayan, flamboyant, dashing, courageous, and determined, was magnificently suited to his role as a frontline general in the Israeli army, an organization built on a high level of individual performance and dedication.

Dayan was born in the first *kibbutz*—farm collective—the Zionists established in Palestine. When he was a teenager, he joined the Haganah, the Jewish underground army dedicated to establishing Israel as a nation independent from British rule. In the Haganah, Dayan also received his first experience of frontline combat. The *kibbutz* was always vulnerable to Arab attack, and the Haganah served as its perimeter patrol. The young man saw his first significant action during the Arab revolt of 1936–39, when he served with Yizhak Sadeh's guerrilla units. During the revolt, the Jewish settlers frequently found it advantageous to cooperate with the British, which gave Dayan the opportunity for training under the fine British general Orde Wingate. However, Dayan's continued activity in the independence movement brought about his arrest at the outbreak of World War II. British authorities imprisoned him at Acre in October 1939, and he was not released until February 16, 1941, when, once again, the exigencies of war in the Middle East made cooperation between the Haganah and the British a necessity.

During the war, Dayan served as a scout operating in advance of the British invasion of Syria and Lebanon, held by the Vichy French, during June 1941. In combat on June 8, Dayan lost his left eye and from that point on wore a black eye patch that became his trademark.

Dayan was appointed to the general staff of the Haganah prior to the United Nations' partition of Palestine in November 1947. In the Israeli War of Independence that followed partition, he fought against the Syrians in Galilee, successfully defending the Deganya settlements during May 19–21, 1948. Drawing on his Haganah training, as well as his experience with Wingate, he organized the 89th Commando Battalion, a highly mobile mechanized strike force, which staged a series of devastating lightning raids against Arab-held positions at Lod and Ramallah between July 9 and July 19. These successes earned Dayan promotion to command of the Jerusalem sector during 1948–49, and, in this capacity, he was instrumental in early settlement negotiations with King Abdullah of Jordan in 1949.

After Israeli independence had been secured, Dayan traveled to England in 1953 for study at the Camberley Staff College. He returned to Israel later that year as chief of staff of the Israeli Defense Forces—the Israeli army. When the Sinai War erupted in 1956, Dayan took charge of planning and directing the Israeli campaign. Two years later, the war having been successfully concluded, he resigned his commission to enter politics. He was elected to the Knesset (Israeli parliament) on the Mapai (Labor) ticket in 1959 and served as minister of agriculture from December 1959 to November 1964. In 1964, he broke with his party to join David Ben-Gurion in founding the Rafi (Labor List) party and once again won election to the Knesset.

In June 1967, Dayan was appointed defense minister under prime minister Levi Eshkol. In this post, he directed operations during the Arab–Israeli Six-Day War of 1967, which resulted in a stunning and decisive Israeli victory.

Dayan stepped down from the Defense Ministry after Yitzhak Rabin succeeded Golda Meir as prime minister in May 1974, but he returned to government in 1977 to serve as foreign minister in the government of Menachem Begin through 1979. The general who had earned a reputation as a ruthlessly efficient and aggressive military commander was now instrumental in creating the Camp David peace settlement U.S. president Jimmy Carter mediated between Israel and Egypt.

Growing differences with Prime Minister Begin over policy toward the Palestinian Arabs prompted Dayan's resignation as foreign minister in 1979. He died two years later.

IN HIS OWN WORDS

"I paid a lot of surprise visits at night, mostly driving alone. I wanted to check whether units were in a constant state of readiness . . . and talk to the soldiers. . . . I wanted to hear things . . . at first hand, without intermediaries, and I believed that the young officers should hear what I had to say directly from me, in my own words, and in my own style."
—*The Story of My Life,* 1976

LEADERSHIP LESSONS

✦

Create effective small teams to leverage your resources most effectively.

✦

Develop a personal leadership style.

✦

Project a strong leadership image—and one perfectly suited to your enterprise.

✦

Gather as much information as possible firsthand. Talk to the people who work out front.

✦

Fight every battle as if your survival—and the survival of your enterprise—hangs in the balance.

Decatur, Stephen

Born: 1779   Died: 1820

Character model   Leverager   Motivator   Systems creator   Tactician

LEADERSHIP ACHIEVEMENTS

✦

Led by consistently heroic example

✦

Through the skillful application of aggressive tactics, leveraged the tiny
U.S. Navy into a highly potent military force

✦

Became the youngest man in U.S. naval history to hold the rank of captain

LIFE

Decatur's heroic leadership against the Barbary pirates and in the War of 1812 set an enduring and inspiring standard for U.S. naval gallantry and excellence of achievement. Born on Maryland's Eastern Shore, Decatur was raised in Philadelphia and enrolled at the University of Pennsylvania there. He left the university in April 1798 to join the navy as a midshipman and, within a year, was promoted to lieutenant. Aboard the U.S.S. *Essex*, he saw action during 1799–1800 in the undeclared naval war against France known as the Quasi-War. This was followed in 1801 by the outbreak of the Tripolitan War, in which President Thomas Jefferson ordered U.S. naval forces against Muslim state-sanctioned pirates who had been preying upon U.S. (and other) shipping in waters adjacent to the Barbary states (present-day Morocco, Algeria, Tunisia, and Libya). Rulers in this region demanded from all non-Muslim nations payment of tribute in exchange for protection against piracy. Jefferson decided to fight instead.

Decatur is best known for leading a daring and stealthy mission to deprive Tripoli's Pasha Yusuf Qaramanli of a U.S. frigate, the *Philadelphia,* which the pasha's forces had captured when it ran aground in October 1803. On the night of February 16, 1804, Decatur sailed the captured ketch *Mastico* (which he renamed *Intrepid*) into Tripoli Harbor and led a small band of sailors who set fire to the 36-gun *Philadelphia*—all under the noses of the pasha's troops. No less a figure than the great British admiral Horatio Nelson called this the "most bold and daring act of the age." It earned Decatur promotion to captain in May—at age 25, the youngest American ever promoted to this naval rank. Congress also ceremonially presented him with a sword of honor. Decatur was among the principal negotiators who hammered out a treaty with the Bey of Tunis, which ended the war triumphantly.

In 1808, Decatur served on the court-martial that suspended Captain James Barron for negligence in the infamous *Chesapeake–Leopard* incident of June 22, 1807, in which the U.S. warship *Chesapeake* was stopped by the British frigate *Leopard* off Norfolk, Virginia, and four seamen were "impressed" (forcibly removed) into the British service and others killed in an exchange of gunfire. The incident foreshadowed the War of 1812, in which Decatur was initially assigned to command the 44-gun frigate *United States*. He captured the 38-gun British frigate *Macedonian* in a spectacular battle on October 25, 1812, and was promoted to commodore.

The Algerine War, new trouble with the Barbary pirates, broke out in 1815. In May, Decatur was dispatched to the Mediterranean to fight in the war. On June 17, he captured the 46-gun *Mashouda,* flagship of the Algerian fleet, after which four vessels of his squadron ran the 22-gun *Estedio* aground off Cabo de Gata. This accomplished, Decatur personally dictated—"at the mouths of cannon"—highly favorable peace terms.

Decatur's return to the United States was triumphant. He was appointed to the Board of Naval Commissioners in November 1815. Five years later, however, James Barron resurfaced, embittered by the disgrace he had suffered in the *Cheasapeake–Leopard* court-martial. He challenged Decatur to a duel, mortally wounding him on March 22, 1820, in Bladensburg, Maryland.

LEADERSHIP LESSONS
✦
Expand your mission and leverage your resources.
✦
Consider proactive, aggressive action as preferable to reactive, defensive response.
✦
True heroism is the strongest form of leadership.

de Gaulle, Charles (-André-Marie-Joseph)

Born: 1890   Died: 1970

Character model   Improviser   Leverager   Motivator   Rescuer   Strategist

LEADERSHIP ACHIEVEMENTS

✦

Inspired and led the Free French resistance against Naziism

✦

Made himself the symbol of French dignity and liberty when the official government was in disgrace

✦

Was the architect of the Fifth French Republic

✦

Became one of the major leaders of World War II and the postwar world

LIFE

Charles de Gaulle came to world prominence as the military and political leader of the Free French, anti-Nazi military forces and of the government-in-exile during World War II. After the war, he was the moving force behind France's Fifth Republic. He was educated at the Military Academy of Saint-Cyr, the French equivalent of West Point, and joined an infantry regiment under Colonel Philippe Henri Pétain, as a second lieutenant, in 1913. He immediately impressed his commander and others with his quick intelligence, with his boundless initiative, and, after World War I began in August 1914, with his consistent courage. He fought at the do-or-die defense of Verdun, was wounded in combat three times, and was held as a P.O.W. for two years and eight months. During his captivity, he made five valiant—unsuccessful—attempts to escape.

After the Armistice, de Gaulle served briefly as a member of a military mission to Poland, and then taught at Saint-Cyr. He was selected to receive two years of special training in strategy and tactics at the École Supérieure de la Guerre (the French War College). Upon de Gaulle's graduation in 1925, Marshal Pétain promoted him to the Staff of the Conseil Supérieur de la Guerre, the Supreme War Council. As a major, de Gaulle served during 1927–29 in the army occupying the German Rhineland. Always an acute observer of politics and society, de Gaulle became alarmed during his Rhineland service by what he saw as the continued danger of German aggression. After his Rhineland assignment, he spent two years in the Middle East, and then, as a lieutenant colonel, served for four years as a member of the secretariat of the Conseil Supérieur de la Défense Nationale, the National Defense Council, where he attempted to prepare a policy capable of resisting renewed German aggression.

De Gaulle was a master of the military art. A consummate field and staff officer, he was also a formidable military theorist, who, in 1924, wrote a study of the relation of the civil and military powers in Germany, "Discord among the Enemy." He was also an avid student of the subject of leadership and even lectured on the subject, collecting and publishing his lectures in 1932 as *The Edge of the Sword*. While much of the military and political world was consumed in thinking about mass movements and the impact of technology on warfare, de Gaulle emphasized the role of the individual leader directing an army of leaders. He developed this theory further in his 1934 *The Army of the Future,* in which he detailed the concept of a small professional army based on a high degree of mechanization for maximum flexibility and mobility. Such a theory flew in the face of the wholly defensive, passive, and static strategy represented most dramatically in the Maginot Line, the hardened line of fortifications then nearing completion along France's frontier with Germany. De Gaulle vigorously appealed to political leaders and worked to persuade them to his point of view. The result was growing discord between de Gaulle and his commanders.

With the outbreak of World War II, de Gaulle was put in command of a tank brigade of the French 5th Army. He was quickly promoted to the temporary rank of brigadier general in the 4th Armored Division (the highest military rank he was to hold), then was named undersecretary of state for defense and war on June 6, 1940. French premier Paul Reynaud sent him on several missions to England to explore ways in which France might continue the war against Germany.

De Gaulle's posting to England was indeed fortunate. In his absence, the Reynaud government fell and was replaced by the collaborationist government of Marshal Pétain, who immediately set about seeking an armistice with Germany and, in effect, enslaved France to the Nazi regime. De Gaulle elected to remain in England, from which, on June 18, 1940, he broadcast his first appeal to those French people willing to resist Germany to continue, under his leadership, the war against the Nazis. As a result of this and repeated broadcasts, a French military court tried de Gaulle in absentia, found him guilty of treason, and, on August 2, 1940, sentenced him to death, loss of military rank, and confiscation of property. With the die irretrievably cast, de Gaulle threw himself into organizing the Free French Forces and a shadow Free French government. The scope of this task was enormous, especially inasmuch as de Gaulle was virtually unknown outside of French military circles. The ordinary French citizen had no reason to recognize him as a political figure, let alone a political leader. In this most desperate hour, all that sustained Charles de Gaulle was boundless self-confidence, strength of character, and an innate ability to lead.

Throughout the war, until the day France was liberated, de Gaulle continued to broadcast—from London and then from North Africa, when he moved his headquarters to liberated Algiers in 1943. From his head-quarters in exile, de Gaulle also directed the action of the Free French Forces and other resistance groups ("the underground") in France.

De Gaulle was an inspiring but unbending leader. He worked closely, but often not smoothly, with the British secret service, and when his relations with the British government and military became strained, he moved his headquarters to Algiers. There he became president of the French Committee of National Liberation. De Gaulle believed that only one man could lead Free France to victory, and that man was himself. While he served at first with General Henri Giraud in Algiers, de Gaulle skillfully engineered Giraud's ouster and his own elevation to the position of sole leader of the committee. In this capacity, he not only became the final authority and decision maker for the Free French war effort, but also the symbol of Free French leadership. In the space of a few months, he had risen from political obscurity to heroic prominence on the world stage. It was de Gaulle, at the head of the government-in-exile, who marched into Paris on September 9, 1944, after its liberation.

In the closing years of the war and just after its conclusion, de Gaulle led two successive provisional governments. He resigned on January 20, 1946, over a dispute with the political parties that formed the coalition government. He opposed the Fourth French Republic on the grounds that it was all too likely to repeat the errors of the Third Republic, and, in 1947, formed a party of his own, the Rally of the French People (Rassemblement du Peuple Français), which won 120 seats in the National Assembly in the 1951 elections. Becoming dissatisfied with the RPF, he severed his connection with it in 1953, and it disbanded in 1955. De Gaulle then retired for a brief period, 1955–56, and, in this short space, wrote three volumes of memoirs.

When insurrection broke out in Algiers in 1958 and threatened to bring civil war to France, de Gaulle was brought back as prime minister designate. On December 21, 1958, he was elected president of the Fifth French Republic, an office in which he served for the next decade. He died of a heart attack only one year after leaving office.

IN HIS OWN WORDS

"Since those whose duty it was to hold the sword of France have let it fall, I have picked up its broken point."
—Broadcast from London to the French people, July 13, 1940

LEADERSHIP LESSONS

✦

Leadership requires moral and physical courage.

✦

As a leader, be prepared to accept total and absolute responsibility.

✦

Acquire self-confidence, exercise boldness.

✦

Do not hesitate to inspire.

Dimitry Donskoy

Born: 1350   Died: 1389

Conqueror   Motivator   Rescuer   Strategist

LEADERSHIP ACHIEVEMENTS

✦

Rescued Russia (however briefly) from domination by the Golden Horde

✦

Formed an alliance among the disparate princes of Russia—a precursor to
eventual Russian unity as a nation

✦

Motivated decisive victories against the powerful Mongol armies

LIFE

A prince of Moscow and grand prince of Vladimir, Dimitry Donskoy skillfully exploited internal instability to deliver Russia from domination by the
mighty Golden Horde (the Mongol army that conquered eastern Europe
during the 13th century). He was born on October 12, 1350, in Moscow,
the son of Ivan II the Meek, whom he succeeded as prince of Moscow at
the age of nine, when his father died. Just three years later, ruling in his
own right, 12-year-old Dimitry persuaded the Great Khan of the Golden
Horde to transfer to him the title grand prince of Vladimir, which had been
held by Dimitry of Suzdal. This greatly added to his prestige and authority, providing a political base from which he went on to subdue the princes
of Rostov and Ryazan and to depose outright the princes of Galich and
Starodub. In this way, Dimitry Donskoy vastly enlarged the territorial
holdings of Muscovy.

Once he had broadened his power base, Dimitry exploited internal
dissension within the Golden Horde to make a move against it. He began
by cutting off tribute payments to the Great Khan, and then reached out to
his fellow Russian princes, persuading them, by his example, to do the
same and also to resist Mongol invasion. This led, in 1378, to the defeat of
a Mongol army at the Vozha River. When the Mongol general Mamai,
who held sway over the western portion of the Golden Horde, amassed his

own alliances to put down the Russian rebellion, Dimitry responded by leading a force to the Don River. There he defeated Mamai at the Battle of Kulikovo Pole, taking the name Donskoy ("of the Don") in commemoration of the victory.

Dimitry's triumph proved to be short-lived. The renegade Mongol leader Tokhtamysh overthrew Mamai in 1381 and, the following year, marched on Moscow, which he sacked, thereby reinstating Mongol suzerainty over the Russian lands.

LEADERSHIP LESSONS

✦

Proceed systematically in building a foundation of power.

✦

Negotiate even with your adversary.

✦

Use personal reputation and prestige to build coalitions to achieve your goals.

✦

Create strategic alliances to achieve well-defined objectives.

✦

Find common cause by defining common enemies or problems.

✦

Capitalize on victories; do not fall back on the comfortable status quo.

Diocletian (Gaius Aurelius Vaerius Diocletianus)

Born: ca. 250   Died: ca. 313

Innovator   Problem solver   Rescuer   Strategist   Systems creator

LEADERSHIP ACHIEVEMENTS
✦
Rose from unpromising origins to great power
✦
Effectively staved off the ultimate disintegration of Rome
✦
Efficiently managed the affairs of a vast empire long in decline
✦
Introduced bold reforms in government organization

LIFE

Diocletian's rise from humble origins to become the greatest of the emperors of Rome's late period was remarkable. He was born in Dalmatia, a commoner of most humble stock, and enlisted in the Roman army as an ordinary soldier. His exemplary performance propelled him rapidly through the ranks until he was named commander of the personal bodyguard of Emperor Numerian in 283. When Numerian was murdered on November 20, 284, Diocletian moved with great efficiency to arrest and execute the man he identified as the emperor's assassin, the praetorian prefect Aper—who also happened to be the archrival of Diocletian. Such was Diocletian's popularity with the army and those in power that he was elected emperor after Numerian's death. Immediately on assuming the throne, he led an army against Numerian's brother Carinus, who ruled the Western Empire. He defeated Carinus at the Battle of Margus River, in 285.

Thus, Diocletian united East and West under his own rule. This, however, did not last long. With Rome generally in decline, menaced on virtually every frontier, Diocletian soon realized that a single ruler could not successfully defend and maintain the empire. He therefore elevated his trusted friend Maximian to the office of caesar, in effect assistant emperor, in 285. Subsequently, he elevated Maximian to the office of augustus,

143

thereby giving him full co-emperor status. Next, in a series of sweeping administrative reforms designed to combat the ongoing disintegration of the empire, Diocletian appointed two additional caesars: Gaius Valerius Galerius and Flavius Valerius Constantius. Thus Diocletian created the Tetrarchy, rule by four.

Diocletian decreed centralized wage and price controls to retard ruinous inflation, and he instituted a general restructuring of the imperial administration. He separated military from civil authority, and apportioned the empire into smaller, more manageable provinces, gathered in groups of 12 to form larger administrative units or *dioceses*. In the military, his reforms were even more momentous. First, he doubled the size of the Roman army, and then he totally reorganized it for greater strategic and tactical flexibility.

Diocletian's remodeled army was tested in combat in 294–96, when a Roman usurper named Domitius Domitianus—or Achilleus—declared himself emperor in Alexandria, Egypt. Diocletian personally led the army to Alexandria and defeated Achilleus. After this, he provided aid to the Upper Egyptians and Nubians in their efforts to repel incursions by a barbarian tribe known as the Blemmyes.

Back in Rome proper, Diocletian ordered the last mass persecution of Roman Christians during 303–04. He did this in the belief that the Christian cults were eroding the empire from the inside. Soon after this episode of persecution, in 305, Diocletian abdicated, as did Maximian Augustus, leaving the empire to the two caesars. Diocletian retired to his palace in Spalatum—modern Split—on the Dalmatian coast and died about seven years later.

LEADERSHIP LESSONS

✦

Recognize the importance of delegating responsibility; few enterprises are so simple that they can be led by one person.

✦

Divide labor in rational, manageable ways.

✦

Devote time and effort to creating efficient and manageable administrative systems.

Dix, Dorothea

Born: 1802   Died: 1887

**Character model   Innovator   Mentor   Motivator   Problem solver
Systems creator   Visionary**

LEADERSHIP ACHIEVEMENTS

◆

Recognized a serious social problem and devised the means for attacking it

◆

Confronted by indifference and resistance, refused to give up

◆

Communicated her moral passion in ways that moved others to "do the
right thing"

LIFE

Dorothea Lynde Dix was a pioneer and leader in the humanitarian reform
of the treatment afforded convicts and the institutionalized mentally ill. She
also led a groundbreaking international crusade for the rights of prisoners
and the mentally ill.

Born in Hampden, Maine, Dix left her schoolteacher's position in
1836 to travel abroad for reasons of health. While visiting England, she
encountered the British prison reform advocate Henry Tuke, whose ideas
she found intensely inspirational. She returned to the United States in
1841, determined to work toward the improvement of prison conditions.
She began in a modest way, as a volunteer Sunday school instructor at the
East Cambridge, Massachusetts, jail. In this decrepit prison—all too typical
of American prisons of the day—Dorothea Dix found her calling. It was
apparent to her that primitive, brutal prison conditions hardened rather
than reformed criminals. It was also apparent that those suffering from
mental illness did not belong in prison, where conditions tended only to
exacerbate their illness.

The Sunday school teacher embarked on a mission of reform, beginning by writing eloquent letters to newspapers and legislatures throughout
the country. Her 1844 "Memorial to the Legislature of Massachusetts," a

comprehensive report on the treatment of the mentally ill in that state, motivated legislation to enlarge the Worcester insane asylum.

The early efforts of Dorothea Dix resulted in modernization and expansion of facilities in Massachusetts and Rhode Island and the construction of new institutions in Pennsylvania, New Jersey, and Canada. Ten other states passed reform legislation in response to Dix's campaign. Her work was instrumental in the founding of 32 mental hospitals, and her writings on reform of therapeutic treatment as well as criminal incarceration furnished models for other institutions in the United States, Canada, Russia, and Turkey. Most spectacularly, in 1854, Dix successfully petitioned the U.S. Congress to authorize $12 million for care of the insane; regrettably, the legislation was subsequently vetoed by President Franklin Pierce.

With the outbreak of the Civil War in 1861, Dix's reputation earned her an appointment as Superintendent of Women Nurses for the Union army. In this position, she created the foundation of what would become the Army Nursing Corps.

When the Civil War ended in 1865, Dix resumed her work on behalf of penal inmates and the insane. She spent her final days in retirement at the Trenton (New Jersey) Hospital, one of the institutions she had founded.

LEADERSHIP LESSONS

✦

Never doubt that a single person can make a difference in the world.

✦

Neither resist nor ignore passion; use it to drive worthwhile enterprises and achieve important goals.

✦

A leader's first decision is, quite simply, to lead.

Doolittle,
James ("Jimmy") Harold

Born: 1896   Died: 1993

**Character model Improviser Innovator Leverager Motivator
Problem solver Rescuer Tactician**

LEADERSHIP ACHIEVEMENTS

✦

Pioneered civil and military aviation

✦

Conceived, planned, and led the daring Tokyo Raid early in World War II

✦

Provided a critically needed example of leadership, courage, and success
at a low point in World War II

✦

Led important elements of the air war in World War II

LIFE

Jimmy Doolittle was a U.S. Army Air Forces general who planned and led a bold and unconventional air raid on Tokyo early in World War II, flying bombers from the deck of an aircraft carrier.

Born in Alameda, California, Doolittle was educated at Los Angeles Junior College and at the University of California. He joined the Army Reserve Corps in October 1917 after the United States entered World War I and was assigned to the Signal Corps, in which he served as a flight instructor through 1919. The following year, Doolittle was commissioned a first lieutenant in the Army Air Service and gained national attention by making the first transcontinental flight in less than 14 hours, on September 4, 1922.

Doolittle was not content merely to fly planes. He wanted to master the science of aeronautics, and, supported by the Army Air Corps, he enrolled in the aeronautical science program at Massachusetts Institute of Technology, earning an Sc.D. degree in 1925. After this education, Doolittle was assigned to several military aviation testing stations. At this time, one of the best places to test innovative aircraft design was in the sport of air racing. During 1925–30, Doolittle participated in many races, with the objective of promoting aviation generally and military aviation in particular. In September 1929, he dramatically demonstrated the great potential of instrument flying by becoming the first pilot ever to land a plane using instruments only.

Jimmy Doolittle resigned his commission in February 1930 to take an executive position as aviation manager for Shell Oil, where he worked on the development of new high-efficiency aviation fuels. He also continued to race, claiming victories in a number of prestigious competitions, including those for the Harmon (1930) and Bendix (1931) trophies. In 1932, he set a world speed record.

But as a new war loomed, Doolittle returned to active duty as a major in the Army Air Corps in July 1940. For the United States, war came, of course, on December 7, 1941, with the Japanese surprise attack on Pearl Harbor. The early months of the war in the Pacific were bleak for U.S. and Allied forces. Doolittle was confident that, given time, the United States would mount an irresistible counteroffensive against the Japanese. What was of immediate critical importance, however, was morale—the morale of U.S. forces that had met defeat at Pearl Harbor and the Philippines, and the morale of the American home front. Doolittle formulated a bold, innovative, daring, yet feasible plan for a mission that would not only lift morale, but would force the Japanese to divert a portion of their air forces to defense of their homeland. His idea was to make a bombing raid on the Japanese capital city of Tokyo. The bombers of the day lacked the range to carry out such a mission from any friendly air base; Japanese conquest in the Pacific had ensured that no airfields were anywhere near the Japanese homeland. Aircraft carriers of World War II vintage were capable of launching and recovering relatively short-range, single-engine fighters and dive bombers only. Doolittle proposed to lead 16 twin-engine B-25 "Mitchell" bombers from the aircraft carrier *Hornet*, which could be positioned close enough to the Japanese mainland to be within striking distance of Tokyo.

The problems were these: The aircraft were not designed to take off from an aircraft carrier, and doing so would demand the utmost skill from the pilots, especially because the planes would be loaded down with extra fuel and a full complement of bombs. Even if enough fuel could somehow be carried to permit a return flight to the *Hornet,* it was impossible for the B-25s to land on the short carrier deck. In any case, the planes could not carry sufficient fuel for such a round-trip. Doolittle and his men would have to land in China, which was largely occupied by the Japanese and subject to continual attack, and to depend on local anti-Japanese guerrillas to help them evade capture and find their way back to Allied lines. In short, what Doolittle proposed was as close to a suicide mission as any ever undertaken by American fighting men.

Doolittle proved an effective recruiter of volunteers, and, on April 18, 1942, the 16 bombers flew off the *Hornet*'s deck. All made it to their target and dropped their bombs on Tokyo.

Strictly in military terms, the physical damage caused by the Doolittle raiders was slight. However, the raid on the Japanese homeland was, for the Allies, a morale boost of incalculable proportions and did much to spur the American war effort. For the Japanese, the raid came as a great shock, and it did serve the strategically valuable purpose of tying down for home defense a portion of the Japanese air force that would otherwise have been employed in the Pacific war.

Perhaps most remarkable of all was the fact that Doolittle and the majority of his raiders survived the action. Most landed in China and were soon repatriated. Colonel Doolittle was promoted to brigadier general and was sent to England to organize the Twelfth U.S. Air Force in September 1942. Promoted to the temporary rank of major general, he commanded the Twelfth Air Force in Operation Torch, the Allied invasion of French North Africa, which was the first step in a counteroffensive campaign against the Nazis. From March 1943 to January 1944, Doolittle commanded strategic air operations in the Mediterranean theater and was promoted to the temporary rank of lieutenant general in March 1944. He was given command of the British-based Eighth Air Force's bombing operations against Germany from January 1944 to May 1945. After the war ended in Europe, Doolittle returned to the Pacific theater, where, with the Eighth Air Force, he provided support in the Battle of Okinawa (April–July 1945) and the massive bombardment of the Japanese home islands.

Following the war, in May 1946, Doolittle left active duty—he remained in the reserves—and took a new senior executive position with Shell Oil. During 1948–57, he served the government frequently as an adviser on scientific, technological, and aeronautical projects. After his retirement from Shell and the Air Force Reserve in 1959, he continued to work as a consultant, not only in matters of science and aeronautics, but on national security policy issues as well.

Doolittle was a great leader, executive, and innovator, whose courage was matched by his skill as an aviator and by his thorough understanding of the science of aeronautics. In addition to lifting the American spirit in the nation's hour of great need, Doolittle led military aviation to preeminence among the armed services.

LEADERSHIP LESSONS

✦

Courage is strengthened by knowledge. A courageous leader studies the enterprise thoroughly.

✦

Acquire the knowledge, skill, and courage to lead by example.

✦

Think outside the box. Push the envelope to achieve results. Innovate.

✦

Take calculated risks to achieve worthwhile goals.

✦

Never underestimate the power of morale and motivation.

✦

Achievement is measured by spiritual as well as physical yardsticks.

Eisenhower, Dwight David

Born: 1890   Died: 1969

Character model   Motivator   Problem solver   Strategist   Tactician

LEADERSHIP ACHIEVEMENTS

✦

Maintained and directed the greatest multinational alliance in
military history

✦

Directed history's largest and most important military operation, the Allied
invasion of Europe

✦

Provided a leadership environment in which subordinates excelled

✦

Effectively assumed personal responsibility for high-risk,
high-stakes leadership

✦

Created an extraordinarily effective leadership image

LIFE

Dwight Eisenhower was the 34th president of the United States, but he
made perhaps his greatest leadership impact as Supreme Allied
Commander in the European theater of World War II.

Dwight David—"Ike"—Eisenhower was born in Denison, Texas, and
raised in Abilene, Kansas. Enrolled in West Point, he graduated in 1915,
two years before the United States entered World War I. Second
Lieutenant Eisenhower was not given an overseas assignment, however,
but was put in command of a variety of stateside training missions. Even
in these posts, his strategic and administrative skills were quickly recognized, and by 1920 he had achieved promotion to major, a rapid rise
unusual for an officer who had not seen combat duty.

In 1922, Eisenhower was posted to Panama, returning to the United
States two years later to attend the prestigious Command and General Staff

School, from which he graduated at the top his class in 1926. In 1928, he graduated from the Army War College.

From 1933 to 1935, Eisenhower served under General Douglas MacArthur in the office of the chief of staff, and then accompanied MacArthur to the Philippines, serving with him there until 1939. Following his exemplary performance in massive prewar maneuvers during the summer of 1941, Eisenhower was promoted to temporary brigadier general (September 1941), and when the United States entered World War II, he was appointed assistant chief of the Army War Plans Division, serving in this capacity from December 1941 to June 1942. Again distinguishing himself, Eisenhower was promoted to major general in April 1942 and was named to command the European Theater of Operations on June 25. This extraordinary promotion, over other more senior commanders and of an officer who had yet to see combat, is evidence not only of Eisenhower's mastery of strategy—the "big picture"—but of his administrative and leadership ability. In the upper echelons of any military organization, egos often run wild, and the stakes of decision making are never higher. Eisenhower subordinated ego to the good of the enterprise and took a kind of selfless approach that facilitated the genius of others, yet kept jarring factionalism to a minimum. He made it possible for brilliant and difficult people to work effectively together. He recognized, without prejudice, where individual strengths and weaknesses lay, and he integrated operations in ways that maximized strengths while compensating for weaknesses.

Eisenhower served as Allied commander for Operation Torch, the invasion of French North Africa, in November. Next, he directed the invasion and conquest of Tunisia from November 17, 1942, to May 13, 1943. He led the next phase of Allied operations in Europe with his direction of the conquest of Sicily during July 9–August 17, 1944, followed by the invasion of the Italian mainland, which got under way during September 3–October 8.

After the landings in Italy, Eisenhower transferred his headquarters to London, where he took charge of plans for the principal Allied invasion of Europe, Operation Overlord—the Normandy invasion, or D-Day. He was appointed supreme commander of the Allied Expeditionary Force (as the invaders were dubbed) in December. From June 6 to July 24, 1944, he directed Operation Overlord, the invasion that penetrated Adolf Hitler's vaunted "Fortress Europa."

The invasion played for the highest stakes any military commander in history had ever contended with. To maintain the crucial element of surprise, time was of the essence, yet poor weather on the eve of the invasion posed a grave threat. Eisenhower made the monumentally difficult decision to proceed with the invasion, despite the weather. For this operation—the biggest, most complex operation in all of recorded military history—Eisenhower assumed direct personal responsibility. The invasion force consisted of some 4,000 ships, 11,000 planes, and nearly 3,000,000 soldiers, marines, airmen, and sailors. In addition to the weather, Eisenhower understood what it meant to face, even with massive resources, a highly defended and extremely well-prepared enemy. He resolved that, if the Allies failed to secure a strong foothold on D-Day, he would order a full retreat, and, accordingly, he prepared an extraordinary message to make public if this occurred: "Our landings in the Cherbourg–Havre area have failed to gain a satisfactory foothold and I have withdrawn the troops. My decision to attack at this time and place was based on the best information available. The troops, the air [force] and the navy did all that bravery and devotion to duty could do. If any blame or fault attaches to the attempt, it is mine alone." Such was the essence of Eisenhower's leadership: first and foremost, a shouldering of complete responsibility.

Fortunately for the world, Eisenhower never had to use the dispatch he composed. The Normandy beachheads were secured, and Eisenhower then assumed overall command of the advance across northern France, which spanned July 25 through September 14.

In December 1944, Eisenhower was promoted to general of the army and continued the masterly orchestration of huge and disparate forces under a wide variety of U.S. commanders—ranging from the popular and unassuming workhorse Omar Bradley to the flamboyant and unpredictable genius that was George S. Patton—and sharply differing Allies, including Britain, the Free French, and the Soviet Union. By addressing the needs of his varied constituency while keeping all focused on attaining their common objectives, Eisenhower maintained the greatest and perhaps the most difficult military alliance in history.

Although progress through France and beyond was generally rapid, from December 16, 1944, to January 19, 1945, the all-but-defeated Germans launched a desperate surprise offensive in the Ardennes, touching off the so-called Battle of the Bulge. Eisenhower effectively met this last-minute threat to the Allied advance across Europe by ordering the vastly outnumbered 101st Airborne Division to hold the key Belgian village of Bastogne while he ordered Patton's Third Army to rush to the relief of the Airborne. Thanks to Eisenhower's resolve and the extraordinary performance of the 101st and the Third Army, the final German offensive of the war was crushed, and the Allied advance resumed.

Eisenhower pushed his forces into Germany during March 28–May 8, and then made the courageous but controversial political and strategic decision to relinquish occupation of eastern Germany and Berlin to the Soviet troops of the Red Army, in part to ensure the continuation of the always-delicate alliance with the Soviets, and in part to ensure that no sizable portion of the surviving German army would escape Allied attack.

After the unconditional surrender of Germany on May 7–8, 1945, Eisenhower continued to command Allied occupation forces until November, when he returned to the United States, received a hero's welcome, and took up a post as army chief of staff (November 1945–February 1948). Eisenhower retired from the army in February 1948 and accepted the office of president of Columbia University, serving for two years during a time in which the great university expanded and grew in prestige.

In December 1950, as the Cold War heated up, President Harry S Truman recalled Eisenhower to active duty as supreme Allied commander Europe (SACEUR) and commander of NATO forces. Two years later, Eisenhower again retired to run for president on the Republican ticket. He served two terms (1953–61), presiding over a period of great international turbulence, yet, for the United States, a time of optimism and economic prosperity. As president, Eisenhower did not project the same powerful but genial leadership image he had created as supreme Allied commander in World War II. He cultivated instead the benign presence of a leader who refused to micromanage, and he was both widely admired and widely criticized for his unflappable, easygoing approach to government.

Eisenhower helped bring about an end to the Korean War, recovered from a serious heart attack, and continued President Truman's Cold War policy of "containing" Communism when he ordered intervention in Lebanon (June 15–August 21, 1958) and introduced American "military advisers" into war-torn Vietnam. After serving two terms, and following the inauguration of John F. Kennedy in January 1961, Dwight D. Eisenhower entered quiet retirement.

IN HIS OWN WORDS

"The troops, the air [force] and the navy did all that bravery and devotion to duty could do. If any blame or fault attaches to the attempt, it is mine alone."
—Statement prepared in case of the failure of the D-Day invasion, composed June 5, 1944

"Humility must always be the portion of any man who receives acclaim earned in blood of his followers and sacrifices of his friends."
—*Guildhall Address,* London, June 12, 1945

LEADERSHIP LESSONS
✦
The most effective leaders have a sufficiently strong sense of self to enable a selfless approach to leadership, one in which the enterprise assumes primary importance.
✦
Effective leaders are facilitators, who recognize, exploit, and balance the strengths and weaknesses of their subordinates.
✦
A great leader assumes responsibility for failure while sharing with others responsibility for triumph.
✦
An effective leader does not merely resolve problems created by diversity—diversity of background, needs, and objectives—but develops diversity for its strength.

Elizabeth I

Born: 1533   Died: 1603

Character model   Innovator   Leverager   Motivator   Problem solver
Profit maker   Rescuer   Visionary

LEADERSHIP ACHIEVEMENTS

✦

First achievement: survival—against all odds

✦

Combined innovation with continuity of leadership

✦

Resumed the Protestant Reformation in England

✦

Restored a significant degree of religious harmony in England

✦

Took effective steps to revive and build the English economy

✦

Developed a powerful leadership image that united the nation

✦

Led England from backward isolation to progressive expansion

✦

Emphasized freedom of individual conscience

✦

Kept England independent of French and Spanish domination

LIFE

Elizabeth was the daughter of Henry VIII and his second wife, Anne Boleyn. Henry had divorced his first wife, Catherine of Aragon, in part because she had failed to bear a surviving son. Anne too did not succeed in giving Henry the son he so ardently desired. Even if everything else had gone well, Elizabeth would have been at a disadvantage as a female monarch in a male-oriented, patriarchal society. But things did not go well. Henry arrested her mother, Anne Boleyn, on May 2, 1536, on a trumped-up charge of adultery with an unlikely roster of men. He also accused her of incest with her brother. Tried by a court of peers, Anne was unanimously convicted, and was sent to the block on May 19.

Eleven days later, Henry married Jane Seymour. She gave Henry a son, Edward, who, however, was sickly from birth and not expected to live long. As for poor Jane, she died 11 days after her confinement. Elizabeth was declared a bastard by Parliament and spent her early childhood not in the royal palace, but at Hatfield, well away from the court. Yet she was not mistreated, but, rather, given all the advantages of an excellent education. From the age of 10 onward, she was well cared for by her latest stepmother, Henry's last wife, Catherine Parr, who, almost immediately after Henry's death in 1547, married Thomas Seymour, England's lord high admiral. With King Henry out of the way, Seymour began scheming against his own brother, Edward Seymour, regent ("Protector") to the 10-year-old Edward VI. But in January 1549, shortly after Catherine Parr died, Edward Seymour moved against Thomas, charging him with many acts of treason, including plotting to marry young Elizabeth in order to assume control of the kingdom. Thomas Seymour was executed, and Elizabeth fell under a blanket of suspicion, accused of having slept with Seymour and of having participated in his plot. She was kept under close watch, and in these difficult circumstances learned how to conceal her feelings and how to act with crafty stealth.

When Edward VI died in 1553 at the age of 16, Elizabeth's half-sister, Mary I, a zealous Catholic intent on returning England to the Roman fold, ascended the throne. Now Elizabeth was in even greater danger, for she was closely identified with her father's break with the Roman Catholic church. Elizabeth conformed outwardly to the Catholic rituals of worship, and she earnestly professed loyalty and love to Mary. Despite this, she was continually under suspicion of plotting against Mary. In January 1554, when Thomas Wyatt led a Protestant rebellion in Kent, Elizabeth was seized and taken, a prisoner, to the Tower of London. She was held for two months, and then released to house arrest at Woodstock. After about a year, Elizabeth was freed—although she was always closely watched. Elizabeth not only endured the stress of this difficult time, she used the experience as an opportunity to learn, practice, and perfect the skills of political, spiritual, and physical survival.

Her own ascension to the throne came with the death of Mary I on November 17, 1558. Torn by religious strife and burdened by economic depression, England was on the verge of civil war. Few were happy to see another queen—another woman—assume the troubled throne. But Elizabeth presented herself in a way that worked immediately to dispel the doubts. In contrast to her sour and dumpy half-sister, Elizabeth was tall and beautiful, pale of complexion and possessed of silken, reddish blonde hair. She quickly established a charismatic rapport with the crowds that clogged the streets of London in celebration of the coronation.

Elizabeth made it clear that she meant to return England not only to the path of the Protestant Reformation, but to greatness in trade and among the nations. However, she created change slowly and carefully, so as not to stir rebellion. She always retained enough of the old and established ways to give many of her subjects a measure of comfort and confidence. Soon to be celebrated for her strong will, Elizabeth nevertheless gathered about herself the best and brightest political and economic minds of England to serve as her advisers. This group included holdovers from Mary's reign—even some Catholics—as well as new people handpicked by Elizabeth. The new queen meant to gather all perspectives. She invited dispute, but she demanded loyalty—bestowing her loyalty in return.

Elizabeth ruled in an era when most people believed women to be intellectually and temperamentally unsuited to leadership. Male leadership was consistent with the rule of God, whereas female leadership ran counter to this. Elizabeth confronted these objections with a combination of prudence, boldness, and genius.

Her prudence consisted of surrounding herself with excellent advisers. Her boldness was embodied in decisive commands and a resolve to shoulder ultimate responsibility for everything that occurred in her realm. Her genius lay in her deep understanding of the culture she shared with her people. As far as women were concerned, this culture favored two convergent ideals. The glamorous lore of chivalry and the courtly tradition painted the feminine ideal as a virgin, pale, fair of hair, and of willowy, ethereal figure. Concurrently, the religion of Roman Catholicism worshiped the Blessed Virgin not only as the mother of God, but as a kind of goddess herself, a being who could intercede for those who prayed to her, and a proper object of worship. Elizabeth recognized that a weakness of Protestantism, as far as the emotional life of the people was concerned, was its diminishment of the role of the Blessed Virgin. To be sure, she was still to be venerated as Christ's mother, but she was not to be set between the faithful and God as a kind of intermediate object of worship. Grasping that this "removal" of the Virgin had left a void in the Protestant heart, Elizabeth began to develop about herself—in her appearance, her conduct, her every pronouncement—the image of a virgin queen, at once a blend of the courtly ideal and the religious one. If the absence of the Blessed Virgin had created an empty place in Protestant England's emotions, Elizabeth herself would fill it.

This self-created virgin image was doubtless one of the factors that dissuaded Elizabeth from marriage. Additionally, realizing that placing a husband above her would diminish her power to lead, she saw marriage as more of a liability than a benefit. Still, the absence of marriage left the matter of succession unresolved. With great aplomb, Elizabeth purposely evaded the issue of the royal succession throughout a reign that spanned more than four decades.

For Elizabeth, then, leadership involved a combination of wise and competent administration based on the advice of able counselors, a bold personal style, a culturally savvy and intensely spiritual image, a cult of personal and patriotic loyalty, and an ability to act decisively and definitively when such action was called for.

During most of Elizabeth's reign, strife between Spain and England curtailed the free movement of English ships between the North Sea and the Strait of Gibraltar. Elizabeth encouraged exploration to open up new markets for English goods, and she thereby began the transformation of England from an insular island realm to an expansive world power. As tensions between Britain and Spain escalated, she encouraged the construction of more ships, and England grew into a great sea power.

Another persistent problem Elizabeth faced was the matter of religion. On the one hand, militant Protestants—especially the Puritans—demanded a rigorously Calvinist state religion, while, on the other hand, more liberal Protestants preferred less stringent Anglicanism, which was also more palatable to practicing Catholics. Elizabeth steered a middle course between the extremes. She ardently supported the Church of England, but made it clear that the souls of her subjects were their own affair. She did not really care what her subjects believed, as long as they kept controversial and anti-Anglican views to themselves. This attitude certainly prevented civil war, but it did not quell all religious strife. Rumors circulated that Catholics were going to attempt to assassinate Elizabeth, and when an assassination plot was actually discovered in 1586, Protestants in Parliament insisted that Elizabeth's Catholic cousin—and rival for the throne—Mary Queen of Scots suffer execution once she was implicated in the plot. For many years, Elizabeth had kept her rival in prison, but in doing so, had also protected Mary from a vengeful Parliament. By 1586–87, Elizabeth decided that Mary's involvement in a plan of assassination could not be overlooked. Mary was beheaded in 1587.

While managing personal rivals and rival religions at home, Elizabeth navigated a difficult foreign policy. She strove to avoid full-scale war with Spain, but she authorized privateering raids on Spanish shipping and ports, making great use of the brilliant sea dog, Sir Francis Drake. Privateering netted Elizabeth great treasures of Spanish gold and silver—all to the detriment of the Spanish economy.

By the mid-1580s, it had become apparent that a war between England and Spain was inevitable. It was believed that the great Spanish Armada would sail to the Spanish-controlled Netherlands, pick up the large Spanish army that was fighting there, and transport it to England. Invasion would depose Elizabeth and restore Catholicism to the country. In 1588, as the Armada approached England, Elizabeth delivered one of history's greatest speeches to the troops who stood ready to defend her realm. Her advisers warned that, by addressing the troops in their camp, Elizabeth was exposing herself to grave danger of assassination. With her typical courage, she declared that she would not distrust her "faithful and loving people," and, attired in a pure white gown and a silver officer's breastplate, she rode through the camp and gave the speech. "I know I have the body of a weak and feeble woman," she declared, "but I have the heart and stomach of a king—and a king of England, too." She further motivated her troops by promising them full recognition and ample monetary reward.

Elizabeth was a wise leader, who also created an effectively histrionic leadership image, celebrated by poets and painters alike—many of whom Elizabeth actively supported.

Thanks in part to military and naval skill, and in part to a terrible storm in the English Channel, the Spanish Armada was destroyed. But Elizabeth's reign after this period was afflicted by numerous troubles. Bad harvests, continued inflation—despite Elizabeth's brilliant efforts to counter it—and widespread unemployment eroded public morale to some degree. Yet, whereas England had been on the verge of economic ruin and civil war when Elizabeth assumed the throne, it was, despite difficulties, the most prosperous nation in Europe by the time of her death. Moreover, during Elizabeth's reign, English men and women developed the strong national identity that would become part of the British heritage for centuries to come.

IN HER OWN WORDS

"Be ye ensured that I will be as good unto you as ever Queen was unto her people. No will in me can lack, neither do I trust there lack any power. And persuade yourselves that for the safety and quietness of you all I will not spare if need be to spend my blood."
—Coronation eve address

"I will never be by violence constrained to do anything."
—Speech to Parliament, 1566

LEADERSHIP LESSONS

✦

A leader never stops learning.

✦

Create a strong leadership image. If you fail to do so, others will project images on you.

✦

Get into the front lines. Gather information firsthand. Show yourself to those you lead. Share their risks.

✦

Establish clear priorities. Do not neglect immediate issues, but never sacrifice long-term values to them.

✦

Demand as little obedience as possible. Lead by creating a common cause. Create cooperation instead of mere compliance.

✦

Favor evolution over revolution. Leaven innovation with continuity.

Fabius Cunctator (Quintus Fabius Maximus Cunctator)

Died: 203 B.C.

Problem solver   Rescuer   Tactician

LEADERSHIP ACHIEVEMENTS

✦

Employed delaying tactics to achieve victory

✦

Exercised leadership through restraint and patience

✦

Placed effective prudence above glorious futility

LIFE

The name of the Roman dictator Fabius became a byword for cautious change—hence the term *Fabianism* used in late-19th-century England to describe political and social reformers (most famously George Bernard Shaw) who advocated change, but not at a radical or revolutionary pace. Historically, Fabius is best remembered for his effective use of delaying tactics against Hannibal's invasion of Rome. His success in employing these tactics earned him the epithet "Cunctator" (delayer).

Fabius served Rome as a statesman as well as a military commander. He was consul in 233 and 228 B.C. and censor in 230, and then was elected dictator in 217 after Hannibal's devastating victory over Roman forces at Lake Trasimene. Fabius's strategy was to wage a war of attrition against the invaders rather than attempt to annihilate them by direct military action. The decision to employ such a strategy was a courageous one, for it went very much against the Roman grain. Rome traditionally favored aggressive action. Beyond the affront to Roman pride, Roman frontier regions suffered great devastation at the hands of Hannibal. Nevertheless, Fabius was able to draw Hannibal's forces into hill country, where cavalry attack was impossible. He then cut off the invaders' lines of supply and sniped at Hannibal's army piecemeal.

Despite the success of Fabius's strategy, the people voted to divide command of the Roman forces between the more conventionally aggressive general Minucius and Fabius. Fabius allowed Hannibal to wreak havoc on Compania, believing that a scorched-earth policy would eventually exhaust him. This policy enraged many Romans, however, who allowed Fabius's term as dictator to lapse and then staged an all-out attack against Hannibal. That attack, in the Battle of Cannae (216), was one of the great disasters in military history. Hannibal enveloped and annihilated the Roman legions that were thrown against him. After this defeat, Rome adopted the Fabian approach once again, and Fabius was elected consul for a third and fourth term, in 215 and 214. By 209, Fabius had succeeded in retaking Tarentum (Taranto) from Hannibal, whose forces had held it for three years. Again, despite his success in defending Rome, Fabius failed in his opposition of Publius Cornelius Scipio's (Scipio Africanus Major's) plan to invade Africa and thus take the war to Hannibal.

IN HIS OWN WORDS

Upon being urged by his son to seize an advantageous position at the expense of a few men: "Do you want to be one of those few?"
—Quoted in Frontinus, *Stratagems*, A.D. 84–96

LEADERSHIP LESSONS

✦

A leader must sometimes restrain rather than initiate action.

✦

A leader may have to enact unpopular policies.

✦

Prudence may be more effective than bold action taken merely for the sake of taking bold action.

✦

A great leader recognizes when to act from passion—and when to allow intellect and caution to rein in passion.

Farragut, David Glasgow

Born: 1801   Died: 1870

Character model   Conqueror   Motivator   Rescuer   Tactician

LEADERSHIP ACHIEVEMENTS

✦

Developed to the highest possible degree his natural talent for seamanship

✦

Led by courageous example

✦

Acting on bold initiative, captured New Orleans early in the Civil War—
thereby giving the North a great victory and a great advantage

✦

Conducted Mississippi River operations of great value in supporting the
land battles in the western theater of the Civil War

✦

Through action against Mobile Bay, deprived the Confederacy of its
remaining Gulf port

LIFE

The most important, daring, and skilled Union naval leader during the Civil War, Farragut was born, the son of a naval officer, near Knoxville, Tennessee, and christened James Glasgow Farragut. In 1810, three years after his father moved the family to New Orleans, Farragut's mother died and the boy was adopted by the distinguished U.S. naval commander David Dixon Porter.

Clearly destined for a naval career, the nine-year-old Farragut joined the navy as a midshipman in December 1810 and served under his foster father aboard the 32-gun frigate U.S.S. *Essex*. He took naturally to the sea, and, in 1813, when the *Essex* captured a British vessel in the Pacific during the War of 1812, Porter put Farragut (who was only 12) in command of the prize, with responsibility of bringing it into port. Midshipman Farragut also acquitted himself with distinction in a celebrated battle between the *Essex* and H.M.S. *Phoebe* off Valparaiso, Chile, on February 28, 1814. Thrilled by his experience in the War of 1812, when he returned to the United States at the conclusion of the war, Farragut changed his first name from James to David in honor of his foster father and captain. Back in the States, Farragut alternated additional schooling with periods of service aboard a series of ships during 1814–22. Farragut was not only a great sailor, but a brilliant student, who quickly mastered Arabic, French, and Italian under the tutelage of the U.S. consul in Tunis. These were the languages he felt would be most useful to a world-hopping U.S. naval officer.

Farragut was promoted to lieutenant in 1823 and served between February 1823 and December 1824 in a campaign against Caribbean pirates, again under Porter. While in command of a shore party at Cape Cruz, Cuba, on July 22, 1823, he led a brief battle with local pirates, which earned him a reputation as a courageous and highly capable scrapper.

Back ashore in the United States, Farragut returned to more routine duties, but he used the period of relative calm to study the emerging technology of steam propulsion. In September 1841, Farragut was promoted to commander and, a year later, was given command of the sloop *Decatur*, which patrolled off the coast of Brazil. From 1854 to 1858, he served in California, where he established the Mare Island Navy Yard, the U.S. Navy's first permanent Pacific facility.

At the outbreak of the Civil War, Farragut was called to command the West Gulf Blockade Squadron as part of the navy's ambitious effort to impose a general blockade around the Confederacy. Never content with passive duty, however, Farragut used his blockade assignment to mount an offensive against Confederate-held New Orleans. Steaming up the Mississippi by night, he slipped under the Confederate guns of Forts St. Philip and Jackson in the delta country below New Orleans. He attacked and destroyed a small Confederate river flotilla during April 23–24, 1862, and then went on to capture the city on April 25, also forcing the surrender of Forts St. Philip and Jackson three days later.

Farragut's triumph was brilliant, extraordinary, and carried out entirely on his own initiative. The early months of the Civil War were generally very bleak for the Union, which was burdened by a surfeit of timid and conventional commanders. Farragut was a singularly bold exception. Not only did the capture of New Orleans deprive the Confederacy of a key port, the feat greatly buoyed sinking Union morale.

After the victory at New Orleans, Farragut conducted additional operations upriver, successfully running past the formidable Confederate batteries at Vicksburg, Mississippi, on June 28. His promotion to rear admiral on July 16 made him the first officer to hold admiral's rank in the U.S. Navy. Admiral Farragut continued to operate on the Mississippi River, withdrawing again past Vicksburg to Baton Rouge, Louisiana, during July 22–25, 1862, and past Port Hudson on March 14, 1863, to blockade the Red River, a vital supply and transportation link in the war for the West.

Farragut returned to New Orleans after Porter arrived there on May 4, 1863. Together, they provided naval support to General Nathaniel Banks for the successful siege of Port Hudson during May 27–July 8, 1863. After this, Farragut led an assault against the defenses of Mobile, Alabama. On August 5, 1864, he sailed with a squadron of four monitors—the newly developed ironclad steamships—and 14 conventional wooden ships, including his flagship, the *Hartford*. One of the monitors, the *Tecumseh,* struck a mine, which, during the Civil War, was called a "torpedo" because of its elongated shape. The *Tecumseh* sank, sending a shockwave of confused panic through the rest of the federal squadron. It was all too apparent that the bay was thoroughly mined by torpedoes. Farragut, who had physically lashed himself to the *Hartford*'s rigging so that he could better observe and direct the battle, quelled the growing panic by ordering his flag captain to take the lead: "Damn the torpedoes!" he shouted. "Full speed ahead, Drayton!" After successfully sailing through the minefield, Farragut engaged and defeated the Confederate ironclad *Tennessee,* which brought about the surrender of Forts Gaines and Morgan at the mouth of Mobile Bay.

With the collapse of these forts, Mobile Bay, although not captured, was neutralized. Following this triumph, Farragut was promoted to vice admiral on December 23, 1864—again, the first U.S. naval officer to hold this rank. However, ill health forced Farragut reluctantly to retire from active service. On July 25, 1866 (shortly after the war's end), he was promoted to admiral, again the very first in the U.S. Navy. He was among the handful of Civil War military commanders who may be counted among the saviors of the Union.

IN HIS OWN WORDS

"I believe in celerity. Five minutes may make the difference between victory and defeat."
—quoted in Christopher Martin, *Damn the Torpedoes!,* 1970

"No man can tell how he will act in a responsible position, till he finds himself in it."
—Quoted in Loyall Farragut, *The Life of David Glasgow Farragut,* 1879

"I hope for the best results as I am always hopeful; put my shoulder to the wheel with my best judgment, and trust to God for the rest."
—Before the Battle of Mobile Bay, July 1864

"I always said I was the proper man to fight [the Confederate warship *Tennessee*] because I was one of those who believed that I could do it successfully. I was certainly honest in my convictions and determined in my will."
—August 8, 1864, quoted in Loyall Farragut, *The Life of David Glasgow Farragut,* 1879

"Men are easily elated or depressed by victory. As to being prepared for defeat, I certainly am not. Any man who was prepared for defeat would be half-defeated before he commenced. I hope for success; shall do all in my power to secure it, and trust to God for the rest."
—Letter to his wife, April 11, 1862

"The more you hurt the enemy, the less he will hurt you."
—Quoted in Christopher Martin, *Damn the Torepedoes!,* 1970

L E A D E R S H I P   L E S S O N S

✦

In leadership, there are no substitutes for knowing your job thoroughly and for exercising and exhibiting confidence and courage at all times.

✦

Be highly visible as a leader, and lead always by example.

✦

Develop the courage and confidence to act on bold initiative.

✦

Look for ways to transform passivity and reactiveness into bold and proactive initiative.

✦

Practice determined and aggressive leadership.

✦

Defiance of obstacles is a required first step to overcoming them.

Foch, Ferdinand

Born: 1851   Died: 1929

**Innovator   Mentor   Motivator   Problem solver
Rescuer   Strategist   Tactician**

LEADERSHIP ACHIEVEMENTS

✦

Worked his way up the ranks, from private to France's senior commander

✦

Combined theoretical acumen with practical military skill

✦

Combined the passions of mentor and commander

✦

Drove strategy and tactics with reliance on the force of morale

✦

Combined planning with a consistently aggressive spirit

✦

Injected new confidence into a faltering French military

✦

Preserved calm and order in the face of defeat and disaster

✦

Leveraged resources with supreme skill and to great effect

LIFE

Foch emerged as France's single most capable, intelligent, and inspiring commander of World War I. He was born at Tarbes, in the Pyrenees region, a civil servant's son. Sent to a Jesuit school for his primary and secondary education, Foch enlisted in the infantry as a private at the start of the Franco-Prussian War. Although the conflict ended before he saw any action, Foch was persuaded that the military life suited him well, and he enrolled in the military course at the École Polytechnique at Nancy in 1871. After graduation in 1873, he was commissioned a second lieutenant and the following year joined the 24th Artillery Regiment.

Foch served in a wide variety of largely routine garrison and staff posts before he enrolled in the École Supérieure de la Guerre in 1885, the French war college. After serving on the general staff, Foch returned to the

École Supérieure as a professor. He lectured dramatically and eloquently on such issues as flexibility, the massing of firepower, and the role of will and morale. In connection with the latter topic, he developed the concept of the "mystique of the attack," a doctrine that fitted well with such favorite French battle doctrines as *élan vital*—the "vital force" that many French military planners believed both indispensable to victory and a defining characteristic of the French army.

Foch published two important and highly influential collections of his lectures: *De la Conduite de le Guerre (On the Conduct of War,* 1897) and *Des Principes de la Guerre (Principles of War,* 1899). Foch always bolstered his broad theoretical statements—including his reliance on spirit, will, morale, and élan—with highly specific strategic and tactical doctrine. He was a brilliant and subtle military theorist, whose dramatic presentation not only made his work popular among his colleagues, but, unfortunately, frequently tempted them to oversimplify it. He was one of a small handful of French frontline military commanders who also made a dramatic impact as a theoretician.

In 1907, Georges Clemenceau, at the time a commissioner of military affairs, made Foch director of the École Supérieure, promoting him to the rank of general of brigade. In 1913, on the eve of World War I, Foch left the École to assume command of XX Corps at Nancy, near the German border. When war broke out, Foch's sector fell under very heavy attack. He rallied his forces for a fierce counterattack during August 14–18, 1914, but was surprised by a powerful drive from Crown Prince Rupprecht's Sixth Army at Morhange. Foch fell back with heavy losses during August 20–21. Lesser commanders would have allowed this defeat to become a rout, but Foch maintained his forces intact and was able to conduct an orderly withdrawal, which he punctuated with very damaging counterthrusts against the enemy.

On August 28, Foch was assigned command of three corps designated the "Foch Detachment" and subsequently renamed the Ninth Army. These he led at the make-or-break First Battle of the Marne during September 5–10, 1914. When the French situation rapidly deteriorated, Foch sent a message to the general-in-chief, Joseph Joffre, declaring: "My center is giving way, my right is falling back, situation excellent, I attack." It is possible that this message is apocryphal, but it accurately describes

Foch's aggressive approach to adversity. Indeed, thanks in large part to Foch, the Battle of the Marne arrested the German juggernaut, saved Paris from invasion, and rescued France from early defeat in the Great War.

Following the Battle of the Marne, Joffre appointed Foch his deputy during the so-called Race to the Sea (October–November 1914), as the opposing armies jockeyed for position in northwestern France. Foch was charged with coordinating Allied operations among the British, French, and Belgians. His ability to work with diverse allies and diverse command personalities made Foch a highly effective coordinator and leverager of forces and led to his eventual appointment as supreme allied commander.

Foch took overall charge at the First Battle of Ypres (October 19–November 22) and remained in command of the combined forces through 1915. At the Somme (July 1–November 13, 1916), he fiercely struggled to punch through the German lines, but, short of men and supplies, failed.

When Joffre was replaced by General Robert Georges Nivelle as French commander in chief on December 12, 1916, Foch, closely identified with the discredited Joffre, was also temporarily benched. After the shattering collapse of Nivelle's monumentally ill-advised offensive early in 1917, General Philippe Henri Pétain replaced Nivelle on May 11, 1917, and immediately appointed Foch chief of the general staff.

Foch acted decisively in his new post, rushing aid to Italy to bolster the faltering Italian front, hoping that progress there would offset the deadly stalemate on the Western Front. While Foch believed in concentrating intensely violent attacks, he also believed in exploring alternative options instead of stubbornly beating against immovable objects. Because he did enjoy a significant degree of success on the Italian front, he was promoted to a position on the Provisional Allied Supreme War Council and was charged with coordinating Allied offensive efforts in November 1917. Foch brought a new balance and optimism to the French forces and was given extraordinary authority as Allied generalissimo in the west on March 26, 1918.

His first task was to counter the new German Somme offensive of March 21–April 4, one of General Erich Ludendorff's desperate, all-out offensive pushes. Through the final spring of the war, Foch coordinated the Allied response to each of Ludendorff's punishing offensives, always managing his forces with great skill, looking for weak points to mass against instead of squandering resources piecemeal, as earlier French commanders had done. Foch had the courageous patience to allow General John Pershing to train and consolidate an effective American force when other Allied commanders clamored for Foch to compel Pershing to commit troops immediately, ready or not.

Uncharacteristically, Foch was taken by surprise at Aisne and Chemin des Dames during May 27–June 4. He had anticipated that this offensive would come farther north, at Amiens. Despite imminent disaster, Foch, as always, remained calm and was able to recover quickly, rushing his forces into position where they were most needed to parry the blow.

On August 6, 1918, Foch was promoted to marshal of France and, two days later, launched the major Allied counteroffensive that would bring the war to its conclusion on November 11. When that armistice came, it was Foch who dictated its terms, and it was also he who served as president of the Allied military committee at the Versailles treaty conference in January 1920. Finally, Foch was charged with overseeing and enforcing the terms of the armistice and the subsequent peace. Upon his death in 1929, Foch was accorded the supreme honor of interment beneath the dome of Les Invalides, with the viscount of Turenne and Napoleon.

IN HIS OWN WORDS

"One does simply what one can in order to apply what one knows."
—*Principles of War,* 1899

"Every attack, once undertaken, must be fought to the finish; every defense, once begun, must be carried on with the utmost energy."
—*Precepts and Judgments,* 1919

"War . . . permits only of positive answers: there is no result without cause; if you seek the result, develop the cause, employ force. If you wish your opponent to withdraw, beat him; otherwise nothing is accomplished, and there is only one means to that end: the battle."
—*Principles of War,* 1899

"Your greatness does not depend on the size of your command, but on the manner in which you exercise it."
—Quoted in Aston, *Biography of Foch,* 1929

"No victory is possible unless the commander be energetic, eager for responsibilities and bold undertakings; unless he possess and can impart to all the resolute will of seeing the thing through; unless he be capable of exerting a personal action composed of will, judgment, and freedom of mind in the midst of danger."

—*Precepts and Judgments,* 1919

"The principle of economy of force consists in throwing all one's forces at a given time on one point, in using there all one's troops, and, in order to render such a thing possible, having them always in communication among themselves instead of splitting them and of giving to each a fixed and unchangeable purpose."

—*Principles of War,* 1899

LEADERSHIP LESSONS

✦

Master all aspects of the enterprise you lead, from broad theory to practical implementation and execution.

✦

Inspire and inspirit through sound mentoring.

✦

Resist the temptation to throw resources at a problem. Always husband and leverage resources to concentrate them on areas of greatest need and greatest opportunity.

✦

The best defense is often an aggressive offense.

✦

You are not defeated until you give up. The lesson? Don't give up.

✦

Resist the impulse to act prematurely. For a leader, careful thought and planning are not the same as inaction.

Frederick Barbarossa (Frederick I)

Born: ca. 1123   Died: 1190

Conqueror   Innovator   Rescuer   Strategist   Systems Creator

LEADERSHIP ACHIEVEMENTS

✦

Unified Germany to an unprecedented degree

✦

Expanded the German states into Italy and eastern Europe

✦

Extricated Germany from subservience to papal authority

LIFE

His flaming red beard—a *barbarossa*—earned this most important Germanic emperor after Charlemagne his sobriquet, Frederick Barbarossa. Officially, however, he was Frederick I, who managed to unite under his imperial rule the diverse and contentious collection of dukedoms and principalities that made up early medieval Germany. He was the eldest son of Frederick II of Hohenstaufen, duke of Swabia. Swabia was just one of many competitive, often warring, realms ruled by dukes and princes who did elect a common emperor, but actually accorded him little authority. Germany was less a nation than a collection of disparate states.

The election of Frederick as emperor on March 4, 1152, was an important step for the dukes and princes of Germany, indicating that many of them now believed a disunited Germany was vulnerable to threats posed by Danes, Norsemen, Poles, Magyars, and others. The Hohenstaufens—also known as the Waiblingen—and the Welfs were the most powerful families in Germany, and they were perpetually at each other's throats. Frederick was a Hohenstaufen (Waiblingen), but he was related on his mother's side to the Welfs. Thus his election brought to the imperial throne a union of the two hostile bloodlines. Frederick fully exploited his dual heritage, but he was determined to do more than passively rely on his bloodline. He recognized that Germany was plagued not only by internecine warfare, but also by an ongoing conflict between the papal and the German thrones. Since the time of Charlemagne, whom the pope had named Holy Roman Emperor, a succession of popes had asserted their domination over the German monarchs. Frederick resolved to end Germany's subservience to Rome by advancing the doctrine of the divine right of kings. He articulated the radical proposition that it was not the pope who conferred imperial power, but God himself, directly. The pope's function was merely to *confirm* God's will.

Armed with this new doctrine and backed by what was at least the beginning of German unity, Frederick decided to augment German imperial power by expanding Germany's imperial holdings into Italy and Burgundy. In 1154, he invaded Italy in the first of six expeditions by which he subjugated many of the northern Italian cities, installing in each of them a royal governor, or *podesta*.

In 1155, Frederick rescued Pope Eugenius from a mob stirred to riot by the religious fanatic Arnold of Brescia. Frederick immediately ordered Arnold's execution, which pleased Eugenius. What did not please the pope, however, was Frederick's refusal to perform the traditional act of royal submission to papal authority—holding the pope's stirrup as he dismounted his horse. From the moment of this gesture, tension increased between emperor and pope, reaching a critical point after Hadrian (Adrian) IV succeeded to the papacy and proclaimed, in direct contradiction to Frederick's doctrine, that it was indeed the pontiff who had conferred the crown upon Frederick. Frederick responded by publishing a circular in which he claimed rule by divine right and election of the princes.

In 1158, before launching the second of his six invasions of Italy, Frederick decided it was prudent to consolidate his position on the home front by improving relations with his powerful and influential Welf kinsman, Duke Henry the Lion. Frederick restored to him Bavaria, which Frederick's uncle Conrad had seized. At the same time, to keep Henry from becoming too strong, he saw to the reinforcement of the armies of Henry's rival, Albert the Bear, margrave of Brandenberg. With two of Germany's most powerful leaders effectively placated, Frederick set about ruthlessly suppressing feuds among lesser rival lords throughout the German realm.

Having strengthened his position at home, during June of 1158, Frederick advanced into Italy and took Milan as well as other northern

Italian cities. In November, he convened the *diet* of Roncaglia at which he asserted his imperial authority over all of Italy and appointed a roster of imperial officers to administer the country. The following year, Pope Hadrian IV died and was replaced by Alexander III, whom Frederick greatly mistrusted. To oppose Alexander, Frederick secured the election of an antipope, Victor IV, an action that resulted in Frederick's excommunication in March 1160. At this, Milan rebelled against German rule, and Frederick responded by virtually wiping out the city.

Frederick returned to Germany in 1162, but Alexander III, having taken refuge from him in France, encouraged the Lombards to rebel against the German administration as well as the antipope. When Victor IV died in 1164, Frederick secured the election of another antipope, Paschel III. Frederick then entered Italy again in October 1166 and attacked Rome itself, to which Alexander had returned. When the city fell, Alexander fled to Sicily, and Frederick ceremoniously enthroned his elected antipope. At the moment of this triumph, however, Frederick's army was suddenly swept by plague. The oppressed cities of Lombardy exploited the vulnerability of Frederick's now sickly army by forming the Lombard League to oppose German dominion. With much of his army sick, dying, or dead, Frederick could not oppose the league and was forced to withdraw to Germany in the spring of 1168.

During the next six years, Frederick concentrated operations in Germany and on the eastern frontiers, installing German governments in Bohemia, Hungary, and part of Poland. Simultaneously, Frederick made significant diplomatic advances, formalizing friendly relations with the Byzantine Empire, France, and England. At last, by 1174, he believed he was ready to mount another invasion of Italy with the objective of defeating the Lombard League. The Lombard League dealt Frederick a terrible defeat at Legnano on May 29, 1176.

After Legnano, Frederick decided that the time was right to make peace with Alexander. A treaty was concluded in June 1177, and a six-year truce with the Lombard League followed shortly afterward. In 1183, Frederick concluded a lasting peace with the Lombard League, relinquishing certain of his Italian holdings to achieve this. To further solemnize the new peace, he betrothed his eldest son, Henry, to Constance, heiress to the Norman kingdom of Sicily, in 1184. This alliance greatly alarmed the papacy, and a dispute over the Tuscan lands of Countess Matilda created additional friction. Yet Pope Clement III recognized that Frederick, who reigned over a Germany united to an unprecedented degree, was not going to submit to papal supremacy so readily. Clement decided not to wage war against Frederick, but instead he prevailed upon the aging monarch to lead a new Crusade to Palestine. The aging Frederick agreed, and, in May 1189, advanced into Byzantine territory, en route to the Holy Land held by Saladin, although Byzantine guerrillas continually harried his soldiers' camps. Even worse, the populace fled before Frederick's advance, stripping the land of all food and provisions. At length, Frederick negotiated the balance of his passage through Byzantine territory, and he reached the empire of the Seljuk Turks in May of 1190.

The Seljuk sultan, Kilidsh Arslan, pledged Frederick his support, only to go back on his pledge and attack. By this point, Frederick's army had been greatly reduced by disease and starvation. Only 600 weakened knights reached the Seljuk capital of Iconium. Their poor condition and small numbers notwithstanding, Frederick led his knights in the rapid conquest of the capital in June. Forced to surrender, the sultan supplied Frederick's army. Shortly after this triumph, however, on June 10, 1190, while he either attempted to cross the River Saleph or sought in it relief from the intense heat, Frederick Barbarossa drowned. Leaderless, the Crusaders returned to Germany.

LEADERSHIP LESSONS

✦

Leadership pivots upon identity, creating an identity as a leader and creating a collective identity among those who are led.

✦

Balance external expansion with internal consolidation; to some degree, these two tasks can be carried out simultaneously.

✦

Make allies, but do not empower them to the point that they overpower you.

Frederick the Great

Born: 1712   Died: 1786

Character model   Conqueror   Innovator   Strategist   Visionary

LEADERSHIP ACHIEVEMENTS

✦

Ensured Prussia's dominance among north German states

✦

Transformed Prussia into a major European power

✦

Brought great culture and enlightenment to Prussia

✦

Served Europe and the world as a model of enlightened autocratic rule

LIFE

Frederick II, known as Frederick the Great, defined the "enlightened despot" of the 18th century. As king of Prussia from 1740 until 1786, he created the modern state of Germany out of disparate and fractious principalities and, in so doing, profoundly transformed European politics and history. Frederick was born in Berlin on January 24, 1712, the son of the Prussian King Frederick William I and Sophia Dorothea of Hanover, daughter of England's King George I. Frederick was a precocious and sensitive child who loved art and music and who early on conceived a passion for the cultural influence of the French. Frederick William did not approve of his son's cultural and artistic bent, which he considered effeminate, and he sought to counteract these influences by imposing on Frederick an austere military discipline. At 18, Frederick tried to escape his father's domineering by fleeing to England. Frederick William responded by ordering his son's arrest and imprisonment, going so far as to threaten the youth with execution. With no choice other than to yield to his father's will, Frederick decided to make the best of it. He cast off sullen rebellion and struggled successfully to ingratiate himself with Frederick William. For the next several years, Frederick lived happily enough, especially during a protracted period of study at Rheinsberg, where he managed to pursue his literary and artistic interests.

When his father died on May 21, 1740, Frederick inherited the crown, an event that prompted sneers from observers all across Europe. They believed Frederick would make a weak show after the sternly authoritative rule of his father. The Austrian ambassador went so far as to report that Frederick had confided in him that he was "a poet and can write a hundred lines in two hours. He could also be a musician, a philosopher, a physicist, or a mechanician. What he never will be is a general or warrior."

To say the least, Frederick's many critics were very wrong. Just seven months after assuming the throne, Frederick led a Prussian army in an invasion of Silesia, thus firing the opening round of the War of the Austrian Succession. Although his army was routed in this initial foray, Frederick eventually prevailed, acquiring Silesia by treaty in 1742. His reign thus began auspiciously with the augmentation of the Prussian kingdom.

In the course of his career, Frederick would not only show himself to be an able military commander and, at times, a brilliant strategist, but also the model of the "benevolent despot." In contrast to his father, Frederick instituted many liberal reforms throughout his realm. Among his first was the general lifting of censorship of the press and the abolition of penal torture. He next decreed a policy of broad religious toleration. In economic policy, Frederick managed to balance the Prussian budget and then produce a surplus. A brilliant man, whose interests apparently knew no bounds, Frederick encouraged and fostered major improvements in Prussian agriculture and manufacturing. Finally, he created an army that was by far the best equipped, best trained, and most highly disciplined in all of Europe. For better or worse, and despite Frederick's liberalism, this laid the foundation of militarism, which would mark Prussian and, indeed, German government and culture well into the 20th century.

When Russia, France, and Austria became allies in 1756, Frederick invaded Saxony and started the Seven Years' War. The death of Russia's czarina, Elizabeth, took that country out of the war and thereby allowed Frederick to make peace with the other powers. On the surface, this long and costly war had resulted in no positive gains for any of the belligerents. Yet Frederick had succeeded in demonstrating to the world that he was a military genius and that Prussia was a power to be reckoned with.

Frederick governed Prussia as an autocratic yet enlightened monarch. He also continued to preside over the expansion of Prussia, as it became the dominant state in northern Germany and the strongest unifying influence in the region. In 1772, Frederick was instrumental in the partition of Poland among Russia, Austria, and Prussia, an action that further enlarged Frederick's holdings.

While Frederick consolidated Prussia's influence and his own position as the political and spiritual leader of the hitherto disparate German people, Frederick also immersed himself in the arts and literature. Under the tutelage of no less a figure than Johann Sebastian Bach, he composed music of considerable merit. Although married, he sired no children and looked to his nephew as heir-apparent. In August 1786, Frederick reviewed his troops in Potsdam during a downpour. Drenched, he caught a chill, sickened, and died several days later on August 17. In later centuries, leaders from Napoleon to Hitler would pay their respects at the grave of Frederick the Great.

IN HIS OWN WORDS

"I believe that a general who receives good advice from a subordinate officer should profit by it. . . . Ideas of others can be as valuable as his own and should be judged only by the results they are likely to produce."
—*Principles of War,* 1748

"Gentlemen, the enemy stands behind his entrenchments armed to the teeth. We must attack him and win, or else perish. Nobody must think of getting through any other way. If you don't like this, you may resign and go home."
—To his officers at the Battle of Leuthen, December 5, 1757

"If you wish to be loved by your soldiers, husband their blood and do not lead them to slaughter."
—*The Instruction of Frederick the Great for His Generals,* 1747

"One of the falsest notions in war is to remain on the defensive and let the enemy act offensively. In the long run it is inevitable that the party which stays on the defensive will lose."
—Letter, January 8, 1779

"Never be ashamed of making alliances, and of being yourself the only party that draws advantage from them. Do not commit that stupid fault of not abandoning them whenever it is in your interest to do so."
—Quoted in *The Confessions of Frederick the Great,* edited by Douglas Sladen, 1915

"When I find any officer that answers me with firmness, intelligence, and clearness, I set him down in my list for making use of his service on proper occasions."
—Quoted in *The Confessions of Frederick the Great,* edited by Douglas Sladen, 1915

"Diplomacy without arms is music without instruments."
—Date unknown

"It is absolutely necessary to change your methods often and imagine new decoys. If you always act in the same manner, you soon will be interpreted."
—*The Instruction of Frederick the Great for His Generals,* 1747

LEADERSHIP LESSONS

✦

Strong leadership and liberal politics are not incompatible.

✦

A strong leader need not be a tyrant.

✦

An effective leader fosters excellence within his enterprise.

✦

Develop breadth as well as depth of knowledge and interests.

✦

Few great leaders are narrowly focused.

✦

Carefully acquire and prepare the tools by which power is enlarged
and developed; Frederick built a great army.

✦

Where your enterprise is concerned, settle for nothing less than the best.

Gandhi, Mohandas

Born: 1869   Died: 1948

**Character model   Leverager   Mentor   Motivator   Rescuer
Strategist   Tactician   Visionary**

LEADERSHIP ACHIEVEMENTS

✦

Developed nonviolent protest as a means of social change

✦

Organized a social revolution from the grass roots

✦

Led India to independence

✦

Awakened the conscience and social consciousness of the world

✦

Lived, in the fullest sense, an exemplary life

✦

Led purely by example

LIFE

Called affectionately by the Indian people *Mahatma* (Great Soul) or *Bapu* (father), Mohandas Gandhi was the father of India's independence from Britain and, on the world stage, the leading exemplar in the 20th century of nonviolent resistance and nonviolent social change. His great lesson was that people struggling for their rights must not forget their own obligation to respect life. Gandhi was a leader in no official sense. He never held a military or government post, other than the presidency of the upstart and unsanctioned Indian National Congress. And yet he was the supreme political and spiritual leader of India and a moral leader for the rest of the world.

He was born on October 2, 1869, in the Gujarat province of India, into a family of the Hindu Bania, or merchant caste. His father was a *diwan* (prime minister) of a small Indian state, and his mother—fourth wife of his father—was a profoundly religious Hindu. From his mother, Gandhi imbibed the religious traditions of Jainism, with its principal tenets of nonviolence and the belief that all in the universe is eternal. From the beginning, then, Gandhi believed in the Hindu concept of *ahimsa* (the necessity of doing no harm to any living being), vegetarianism, fasting as a means of self-purification, and religious tolerance.

As tradition prescribed, Gandhi was betrothed at an early age—to Kasturbai Makanji at the age of seven—and was married at 13. He was given a good education in India, but proved an unspectacular student. In 1888, when he was 19, he was sent to study law at London's Inner Temple. Returning to India in 1891, he took up the practice of law, but, finding it difficult to earn a living, moved to South Africa (like India, part of the British Empire during this period) in 1893 to work for an Indian firm.

In South Africa, Gandhi later wrote: "I discovered that as a man and as an Indian I had no rights." As a result of this revelation, and with the encouragement of the Indian community, Gandhi embarked on his career as an activist and moral reformer. He began by establishing for himself and those who would follow him three rules: First was a faith in *satyagraha* (truth-force). As Gandhi explained, this "term denotes the method of securing rights by personal suffering; it is the reverse of resistance by arms." Second was *ahimsa*, the doctrine of nonviolence he had learned from childhood. Third was *brahmacharya* (sexual abstinence). "A man or woman completely practicing brahmacharya," Gandhi believed, "is absolutely free from passion. Such a one therefore lives nigh unto God, is Godlike."

In South Africa, Gandhi became a successful lawyer and politician. He established a number of *ashrams*—spiritually based communities—including Phoenix Farm, near Durban, and Tolstoy Farm, near Johannesburg. In 1894, he organized the Natal Indian Congress and in 1904 founded *The Indian Opinion*, a weekly newspaper. On these foundations, he built his first campaign of nonviolent resistance or civil disobedience in 1906, aimed at overcoming discrimination against Indians in South Africa. He was imprisoned and sometimes beaten in the course of leading protest campaigns.

In July 1914, Gandhi, aged 45, left South Africa and returned to India. He founded another ashram, which he intended to serve as a model community, in which caste no longer played a part. Most dramatically, he invited a family of "untouchables"—the lowest caste in Hindu society, considered a source of spiritual pollution—to live alongside the caste Hindus. Gandhi understood that a major source of Hindu prejudice against Muslims in India was that many Muslims were the descendants of untouchable converts. In Hindu society, untouchables performed work no Hindu would defile himself with, such as disposing of human excrement. If no untouchables were available for this work, the excrement remained undisposed of and was a source of filth and disease. "If we approach any village, the very first thing we encounter is the dunghill," Gandhi observed, and, in the ashram, he insisted that everyone, himself included, take turns raking the latrines.

While living in the ashram, Gandhi aided the cause of local Indian peasants and mill workers, first using a fast (or hunger strike) to draw attention to social grievances in 1918. The following year, he organized the first all-India nonviolent protest campaign. Tragically, the campaign was sabotaged by mob violence, to which British administrators responded with the so-called Amritsar massacre, in which 379 Indians were slain.

At first, the horror of the Amritsar massacre caused Gandhi to doubt the wisdom of his nonviolent methods, but, soon, it served only to make him more determined to use such methods relentlessly against the British. Through nonviolence, the essential illegitimacy of British rule by force would be exposed; then British power would begin to dissolve. Gandhi now organized a boycott of British cloth by encouraging Indians to weave on their hand looms. The boycott was highly effective and had a substantial impact on British cloth exports. It was extended to a boycott of all British goods in a massive campaign of what Gandhi termed "noncooperation" with the British. Beyond halting the consumption of British goods, British institutions were shunned. Indian lawyers quit practicing in the British-run courts, and students stopped attending British-run universities.

The British government sought to silence Gandhi by imprisoning him in 1922 for sedition. Sentenced to six years, he served only two and, on his release in 1924, became president of the Indian National Congress. His goal was home rule for India—and, ultimately, independence—but he also led campaigns for the rights of untouchables and women. He promoted education, the development of village industries, and the improvement of hygiene.

In 1930, Gandhi led a 200-mile march to protest the British monopoly on salt, a staple item in India's climate. He proposed to lead the march to the sea and illegally extract salt from the seawater. He began at his ashram with few marchers, but, as he continued, the procession gathered more and more people, including, not coincidentally, foreign newspaper reporters and newsreel crews. The march was seen all over the world, and the Salt Campaign triggered peaceful and highly effective civil disobedience throughout India.

Again imprisoned in 1932, Gandhi fasted for six days in protest of the treatment of the untouchables. In 1933, he fasted for 21 days, an action that secured his release from prison by British officials who feared an insurrection if he should die in custody. This was a major victory for nonviolence over the coercive methods of the mighty British Empire.

World War II introduced an intermediate set of priorities for Gandhi. He was resolutely anti-Nazi, yet he nevertheless led a final civil disobedience campaign against British rule in India—the "Quit India" campaign—for which he and his wife were imprisoned at Poona. In February 1943 he undertook another 21-day fast, and, early in 1944, his wife, Kasturbai, contracted acute bronchitis. British authorities had a shipment of penicillin flown in to the prison for her. Gandhi decided that the injection of penicillin would be an act of violence and he insisted on nursing her himself using natural medicines. Kasturbai died. Broken in health, Gandhi was released in May 1944.

Gandhi saw that independence would inevitably come, and he now focused on bringing about Hindu–Muslim harmony in preparation for that independence. But, revered as he was, even he was unable to prevent massive riots, and partition of India into a separate predominantly Hindu India and predominantly Muslim Pakistan took place on August 15, 1947. In response, Gandhi fasted for five days to protest the partition and to stop the rioting. On January 20, 1948, a bomb exploded in the midst of his daily prayer meeting in the garden outside Birla House, New Delhi. Ten days later, on January 30, Gandhi, walking to prayers, was assassinated by a Hindu extremist. His final act was to bless his assassin.

IN HIS OWN WORDS

"If I were to know, after my death, what I stood for had degenerated into sectarianism, I should be deeply pained."

—quoted in www.gandhiinstitute.org, compiled by Sunanda Gandhi

"The noblest act of the British nation."

—On Britain's decision to grant India's independence; quoted in www.gandhiinstitute.org, compiled by Sunanda Gandhi

"Persons in power should be very careful how they deal with a man who cares nothing for sensual pleasure, nothing for riches, nothing for comfort or praise, or promotion, but is simply determined to do what he believes to be right. He is a dangerous and uncomfortable enemy, because his body which you can always conquer gives you so little purchase on his soul."

—Quoted by Gilbert Murray, 1918

"My writings should be cremated with my body. What I have done will endure, not what I have said or written."

—quoted in www.gandhiinstitute.org, compiled by Sunanda Gandhi

"Even if I am alone, I swear by nonviolence and truth."

—Letter to Lord Mountbatten, 1947

"No man, if he is pure, has anything more precious to give than his life."

—Speech, January 12, 1948

LEADERSHIP LESSONS

✦

Right is a leader's most powerful resource.

✦

Ends cannot be divorced from means. Forced change breeds
violent resistance.

✦

Lead by example.

✦

Demonstrate the rightness, the value, the benefit of your cause. This is the
essence of motivation toward a goal.

✦

A first step in leadership: simplify and focus.

✦

Look for alternatives that bring some good to all.

Genghis Khan

Born: between 1155 and 1167 Died: 1227

Conqueror Innovator Strategist Tactician

LEADERSHIP ACHIEVEMENTS

✦

Recovered from an early reversal of fortune to become one of history's
greatest leaders and conquerors

✦

Combined ruthless energy and resolve with the wisdom to provide efficient
and just government

✦

Commanded absolute loyalty

✦

Led by example

✦

Built his following on the basis of his achievements

✦

Became master of Mongolia and most of China—a conqueror second only
to Alexander the Great, yet a far more efficient and successful
administrator than Alexander ever was

LIFE

Rising from the status of social outcast, Genghis Khan not only unified the
Mongol state, but led it to dominance over central Asia. With Alexander
the Great, he was perhaps the greatest conqueror in history, who, despite
his reputation for ruthless destruction, typically improved the lot of the
peoples he conquered by bringing to them greater prosperity and a degree
of justice and human rights coupled with efficient administration.

He was born Temujin into the Borjigin clan in the middle of the 12th
century; the year of his birth is highly uncertain and typically assigned
somewhere between 1155 and 1167. When Temujin was eight or nine, his
father, Yesukai the Strong, a prominent member of the royal clan, was poisoned by Tartars, a nomad band that acted against Yesukai to settle an old
score. With Yesukai out of the way, a rival family took over leadership of
the clan and cast out Yesukai's heirs, including Temujin and his mother.

Temujin's mother responded to this reversal of fortune with extraordinary resolve. She was determined that her son would become a Mongol chief, as was his birthright. She began by teaching him to surround himself with a loyal band of men—a lesson Temujin never forgot and endeavored always to implement. Under his mother's tutelage, he next developed his prodigious natural talent for the hunt and for combat.

Temujin found opportunity to exercise power when his new bride was abducted and ravished by the Merkit clan. The young man struck a sly alliance with an acquaintance of his father's and was thereby able to borrow from him an entire army, which he led against the Merkit in 1180. Not only did Temujin redeem his bride, he annihilated the Merkit in the process. This deed of gallant arms won him a very large following, including a private army of some 20,000.

While Temujin fought the Merkit, the Jurkin clan took advantage of his absence to plunder his treasure. On his return, Temujin used this reverse to establish his reputation for utter ruthlessness. He responded to the assault on his property with no halfway measure, but swiftly exterminated all the Jurkin nobility. Not only did this make him a feared and respected figure, the experience with the Jurkin taught him a valuable strategic lesson that informed all of his subsequent career. Simply put, it was this: Always watch your back. Destroy or neutralize all enemies at your rear before advancing to the next conquest. Thus Temujin never settled for halfway measures in his methodical military progress. He took on enemies serially, one at a time, ensuring that he had thoroughly and absolutely defeated one foe before taking on the next.

After a series of conquests, Temujin decided to maneuver for a showdown with the Tartars, who were the chief obstacle to further conquest, and who had become more formidable than ever because of an alliance with the eastern Mongols. In a brilliantly orchestrated battle, Temujin routed the Tartars in 1201. Having destroyed the Tartar army, he systematically slaughtered every adult taller than the height of a cart axle. His belief was that adults, being already set in their ways, were difficult or impossible to convert to loyal subjects. Because it was futile to try to coerce or convert them, he killed them, so that they could not pass on their enmities to their children. In this way, Genghis Khan believed he could cultivate a generation completely loyal to himself.

In 1203, Temujin conquered the Naiman and Karait tribes, and by 1204 he built a capital city at Karakorum and was acknowledged master of Mongolia. It was during this period, during a grand assembly of clans by the River Onon, that Temujin took the name by which he is best known to history: Genghis Khan (Universal Ruler).

Having unified under his rule all of the Mongolian clans, Genghis Khan had followed through on one of his earliest lessons: Secure what is behind you before you advance to new conquests. With a vast home base secured, he led the Mongols to conquests beyond even the steppes of central Asia. As effective as Genghis Khan had been in conquering Mongolia, it was only now that the full extent of his military genius manifested itself. When fighting tribal wars, he had relied exclusively on swift but lightly armed cavalry, riding tough Mongolian ponies against nomadic peoples. Genghis Khan instantly recognized that such cavalry tactics were of little use in assaulting cities, such as those of China. So he quickly mastered the art of the siege—learning the use of works, catapults, ladders, and burning oil—and even accomplishing such engineering feats as diverting rivers. Genghis Khan used siege tactics in his invasions of the Western Hsia Empire in 1205, 1207, and 1209. He recruited Chinese engineers to help him breach city walls. In April 1211, he crossed the Great Wall of China itself to begin his conquest of the realm of the Chin Dynasty of northern China. By 1215, Beijing (Peking) fell to him, and within the space of two more years, the last Chin resistance was neutralized.

Genghis Khan turned next to the south, to Khwarezm, where a local official had massacred a Mongol trading envoy. This minor act of brutality was ample pretext for battle, and Genghis Khan promptly made war on Khwarezm, bringing 200,000 troops to overwhelm the country. They consumed everything in their path. Transoxiana (Bukhara and Samarkand), Khorasan, Afghanistan, and northwestern India fell in quick succession, and the campaign culminated in the defeat of Shah Mohammed's son Jellaluddin on the Indus River in a battle on November 24, 1221.

During 1221–23, Genghis Khan sent his generals into southern Russia, and, in 1225, personally led an invasion of northwestern China to crush a rebellion of the Chin and Hsi-Hsia. This he did by winning a great battle on the Yellow River in December 1226. A new Chin rebellion broke out in 1227, but Genghis Khan fell ill and died on August 18. He was secretly buried on Mount Burkan-Kaldan, the place to which he and his mother had been exiled.

LEADERSHIP LESSONS

✦

Do not allow yourself to be defined by your history, your misfortune, or your "fate." You are the creator of your destiny.

✦

Secure your rear before advancing.

✦

Whenever possible, fight one war at a time.

✦

Build on earlier conquests. Develop a policy of constructive aggression.

✦

Be thorough in conquest. Attend to details.

✦

Avoid halfway measures. Deal with problems—and opportunities—definitively.

✦

Be flexible. Adapt your tactics to the situation at hand. Precedent must be modified by immediate circumstances.

✦

Develop a loyal staff of high excellence.

✦

Lead by example.

✦

Conquest is fleeting without follow-up. Enhance the lives of those you lead. Give others a stake in your leadership.

Geronimo

Born: 1829   Died: 1909

Character model   Improviser   Leverager   Tactician

LEADERSHIP ACHIEVEMENTS

✦

Earned a legendary reputation early in life, which endured through and
even beyond his lifetime

✦

Harnessed destructive emotions to energize a campaign of
freedom fighting

✦

Was a great leverager of resources, defying with fewer than 100 men some
5,000 well-equipped soldiers

LIFE

This Chiricahua Apache war leader succeeded brilliantly in eluding vastly
superior American and Mexican forces during the Apache Wars of the late
19th century and became an enduring symbol of the spirit of Native
American resistance to conquest and oppression. His native name,
Goyahkla (He Who Yawns), hardly suggests the reputation he acquired
among those who knew him, for he earned early and lifelong renown as a
warrior and (in the admiring words of one Chiricahua) as a "wild man."

Born on the upper Gila River in present-day Arizona or New Mexico,
he served Chief Juh and later Chief Naiche (last chief of the Chiricahuas)
as a fearless warrior and military leader of great skill. Married seven, perhaps nine, times, Geronimo lived with several Chiricahua bands, depending on the origin of his current wife.

Following Chief Mangas Coloradas, young Geronimo and his family
settled in Chihuahua, Mexico. There, in a surprise raid on March 5, 1851,
Mexican federal troops killed 21 Apaches, including Geronimo's mother,
wife, and three children. This horrific event incited Geronimo to exact
vengeance on the Mexicans, and he began an intensive campaign of raiding along the U.S.–Mexican border. During this period, Geronimo became

a guerrilla leader, deriving from his anger and despair the energy to drive a campaign of liberation against Mexican oppression of his people.

From 1865 until his surrender in 1886, Geronimo alternated periods of raiding with a relatively quiet existence on the San Carlos (Arizona) reservation. From about 1881 to 1886, during the late phase of the Apache Wars, Geronimo's activities were so intensive that he became the focus of a major military operation in a conflict often referred to as Geronimo's Resistance. Typically, Geronimo led no more than 100 warriors, often fewer. With these men, he raided both in the American Southwest and in Mexico, always eluding army task forces that numbered as many as 5,000 men broadcast in a wide dragnet across the border region.

Only after leading his pursuers on a 2,000-mile, four-month chase did Geronimo finally surrender on September 4, 1886, to General Nelson A. Miles. Geronimo and the other Chiricahuas captured were sent to prisons in the East. Geronimo was jailed in Florida and then Alabama before he was finally transferred to a reservation attached to Fort Sill, Oklahoma. Yet he was often treated more as a venerated icon of the American experience than as a military prisoner. He was a living legend among whites as well as Indians, and President Theodore Roosevelt invited him to appear in his 1905 inaugural parade along with five other Indian leaders. He died on the reservation, in 1909, of pneumonia.

LEADERSHIP LESSONS

✦

Well-led, small-unit teams often outperform larger, more cumbersome forces.

✦

Emotion need not get in the way of the enterprise at hand. Feelings, provided they are well understood, may be used productively to drive achievement.

✦

Emphasize speed and efficiency.

✦

The essence of leadership is agility, especially where resources are limited. The more limited the resources, the more agility is required.

Gordon, Charles George

Born: 1833   Died: 1885

Character model   Leverager   Motivator   Rescuer

LEADERSHIP ACHIEVEMENTS

◆

Embodied the most respected values of the British officer corps

◆

Provided an inspiring example of courage under fire

◆

Used personal leadership to leverage small forces to great effect

◆

Transmitted determination and commitment to those he led

LIFE

"Chinese Gordon" won renown for his leadership of an extraordinary, valiant, determined, but doomed defense of Khartoum against Sudanese rebels led by the much-feared Mahdi. Born at Woolwich, Gordon was the fourth son of a prominent general, who, in 1848, enrolled the boy as an officer-cadet in the military academy there. After graduating in June 1852, Gordon was commissioned a second lieutenant of Royal Engineers and was dispatched to the Crimea. After arriving at Balaclava on January 1, 1855, he fought in every engagement through the collapse of Sevastopol on September 9, 1855.

Gordon made a strong impression on his commanders, who took note of his remarkable intelligence and exceptional coolness under fire. He was appointed to the international commission responsible for surveying the Russo-Turkish frontier during April 1856–November 1858, and then volunteered for service in China during the Second Opium War (1859–60). In this conflict, Gordon participated in major actions, including the landing at Beitang on August 1, 1860, and the attack on the forts of Dagu on August 21. He was present when British forces took Beijing on October 6, and then remained in China after the conclusion of the war to accept appointment, during April 1863, by the Chinese government to command of the grandiosely misnamed Ever Victorious Army against the Taiping rebels in a two-decade-long civil war that resulted in 20 million Chinese dead. Gordon stepped into the chaos to transform a small, ineffectual rabble into a well-disciplined, efficient army of modest proportions. After Gordon led the force to several victories over the numerically superior Taipings, his fame became legendary in China as well as in Europe, where he was dubbed "Chinese Gordon." Gordon developed a consummately understated leadership image, always marching at the head of his army, armed with nothing more imposing than a walking stick.

After participating in the capture of Suzhou in November 1863, Gordon returned to England, where he was appointed to command the Royal Engineer post at Gravesend in September 1865. In September 1871, he served on the Danubian commission in Galati, Romania, and then shipped out to Africa as governor of Equatoria—southern Sudan—in late 1873. Gordon landed in Cairo on February 6, 1874, and then traveled overland to Gondokoro, Sudan, where he set up his capital by mid-March. Gordon was a product of the best of Victorian England's policy of imperialism, which combined political domination and economic exploitation with a heartfelt (albeit high-handed and often misguided) passion for bringing what the English liked to call the "light of civilization to the dark corners of the world." Gordon traveled the Sudan tirelessly, building a system of military outposts and forts aimed at choking off the slave trade. In the process of his travels, Gordon also found time to make the first accurate map of the Nile and its associated lakes.

Gordon returned to England briefly in December 1876, and then went back to Sudan in late March 1877 as governor-general, now officially in the service of the khedive of Egypt. He was confronted with one local uprising after another and twice subdued Walad-el-Michael, brother of Ethiopian emperor John, in April 1877 and again in the fall of 1878. To suppress a rebellion in the Daffur province of western Sudan, in May 1877, Gordon relied more on the force of his personality than the force of arms. He persuaded the rebels to trust him. While putting down rebellion, Gordon continued the vigorous interdiction of the slave trade throughout Sudan during January–August 1879.

At the end of 1879, Gordon grew restless and resigned his post in Sudan to return to England, where he joined the staff of the Viceroy of

India designate, the Earl of Ripon, in May 1880. This post quickly proved insufficiently challenging, and Gordon gave it up to return to China, where he succeeded in dissuading the political leader Li Hung-chang from rebellion while also convincing the Chinese government not to declare war on Russia over the Ili River border dispute during June and July 1880. Having achieved these minor but important diplomatic triumphs, Gordon once again returned to England, spending a year there before assuming command of the engineer post on Mauritius (from April 1881 to April 1882). From this assignment, he went to the Cape Colony to train, reform, and reorganize the local militia forces during the summer of 1882.

Gordon made another return trip to England for a brief stay after completing his assignment in Cape Colony, and then set sail for Palestine, where this man of military action surprised everyone who knew him personally or by reputation by throwing himself into an intensive study of the Bible and biblical history during the entire year of 1883.

Early in 1884, Gordon was in Brussels, where he accepted an appointment from King Leopold I to govern the Congo. However, British prime minister Gladstone intervened with a request that Gordon travel to Khartoum, Sudan, to restore order in the midst of the Mahdist Revolt, which had begun in 1881. If he found that order could not be restored, Gordon was directed to see to the safe evacuation of the province.

Gordon arrived in Khartoum on February 18, 1884, and, seeing that the situation was indeed desperate, he made his first priority the evacuation of 2,000 women and children. On March 13, 1884, forces of the Sudanese rebel leader Muhammad Ahmad Ibn As-Sayyid 'Abd Allah, called al-Mahdi after the messianic figure of the Koran, blockaded Khartoum. British colonial authorities advised Gordon to relinquish Khartoum, but Gordon, believing this fortress at the junction of the White Nile and Blue Nile vital to the interests of the British Empire and the well-being of the Sudanese, was determined to hold it against the Mahdi. He repeatedly appealed to the government to send reinforcements, but was met with refusal. Gordon held out under siege through August, when British popular pressure and the urging of Queen Victoria at last moved the government to mount a relief expedition under General Garnet Joseph Wolseley. It was October before the expedition set out from Wadi Halfa. Along the way, Wolseley defeated two Mahdist forces, and news of these

British victories almost drove the Mahdi to lift the siege. But Wolseley was delayed, and this ultimately emboldened the Mahdi's forces to make a final assault through a gap in Khartoum's ramparts caused by the falling of the Nile's waters. After withstanding a siege for 10 months, Gordon and his small garrison were slaughtered to a man.

Already legendary in life, Chinese Gordon assumed near mythic proportions upon his death. He symbolized the highest Victorian notions of selfless leadership and British imperial valor: steady, determined bravery and limitless resourcefulness in the name of civilization, opposing the unthinking force of "primitive" peoples. To be sure, the imperialist project of which Gordon was an agent and product is distasteful to modern sensibilities. Nevertheless, Gordon remains an example of ultimate commitment, integrity, and courage in leadership.

IN HIS OWN WORDS

"Indecision is our bane. A bad plan, in my mind, followed out without wavering, is better than three or four good ones not so dealt with."
—Quoted in Paul Charrier, *Gordon of Khartoum*, 1965

LEADERSHIP LESSONS

✦

A leader's most important asset is his own integrity and commitment.

✦

Panic is a contagion. Uncontained, it will quickly destroy any enterprise.
Therefore, contain it.

✦

Never be embarrassed to trade on the strength of your good character.

Grant, Ulysses Simpson

Born: 1822   Died: 1885

Leverager   Motivator   Rescuer   Strategist   Tactician

LEADERSHIP ACHIEVEMENTS

✦

During the Civil War, achieved key victories that turned the tide of the war in the West

✦

Understood—as no previous commander had—the nature of the Civil War and exploited that understanding strategically to achieve victory

✦

Embodied and inculcated the will to fight, which was previously lacking in Union commanders

✦

Formulated and executed the "total war" strategy that brought victory in the Civil War

LIFE

Recognizing his fighting will and military skill, President Abraham Lincoln appointed Ulysses S. Grant to chief command of the Union Army, which had languished under a series of inadequate commanders. Grant led the North to victory in the Civil War.

He was born at Point Pleasant, Ohio, Hiram Ulysses Grant, the son of Jesse B. Grant, a farmer with some local political influence. The youth received an appointment to West Point in 1839, and when he discovered that he had been listed on the academy's rolls by his middle name, "Ulysses," and "Simpson," his mother's maiden name, he accepted Ulysses Simpson Grant as his name henceforth. He was, however, a mediocre cadet, who graduated in 1843, 21st of out of a class of 39. Upon receiving his second lieutenant's commission, Grant was assigned to the 4th Infantry and, two years later, during September 1845, was sent as part of Zachary Taylor's command to Texas as Mexico and the United States faced off on the brink of war.

In the U.S.–Mexican War (1846–48), Grant served with distinction, fighting in every major battle. After the war, he married Julia T. Dent (in

August 1848) and, between 1848 and 1854, was assigned to posts in New York, Michigan, California, and Oregon. At length, Grant grew impatient with the army's tortoise-paced system of advancement. He resigned his commission and returned to his family in Missouri in July 1854.

In civilian life, Grant discovered that he had little aptitude for anything other than soldiering. From whatever he tried, he enjoyed little success and was soon plagued by financial problems and failed business ventures, compounded by an overfondness for hard liquor. Profoundly discouraged, in 1860, he moved to Galena, Illinois, where he joined his father and brothers in the family leather-tanning business and was working as a clerk when the Civil War began in April 1861.

Grant had ample military experience, but no political connections. Instead of gaining a high-level assignment, he was tapped to train the Galena militia company. This completed, he went to the Illinois state capital, Springfield, where he worked in the state adjutant general's office until June 1861, when he finally received an appointment as colonel of the 21st Illinois Volunteer Infantry regiment. In August, he was promoted to brigadier general of volunteers and given command of the District of Southeast Missouri, headquartered at Cairo, at the southern tip of Illinois. In this command, Grant immediately exhibited the fighting initiative for which he would become famous. Without orders from higher command, he attacked and seized Paducah, Kentucky, on September 6, 1861, but was forced to retreat from Belmont, Missouri, on November 7. The aggressive Grant found himself at odds with his superior, the plodding, overly cautious General Henry Wager Halleck, known derisively throughout the army as "Old Brains." After much cajolery and persuasion, Grant successfully appealed to Halleck to allow him to attack Fort Henry on the Tennessee River, which fell to him on February 6, 1862.

After Fort Henry, Grant's next objective was Fort Donelson on the Cumberland River, which he invested on February 14. On the 15th, the Confederate garrison manning the fort made a concerted breakout attempt, which Grant barely managed to check, and, the next day, the battered garrison surrendered to him. To the fort's commander, Grant calmly stated that he would accept nothing less than "unconditional surrender," and from that point on, Grant acquired a new name among his admiring subordinates. He was no longer Ulysses Simpson, but "Unconditional

Surrender" Grant. Yet, even now, there was nothing unconditional about General Halleck's response to Grant's victories. Instead of recognizing and rewarding his achievement, Halleck believed that Grant's actions verged on insubordination. Accordingly, Halleck temporarily relieved him from command—though, fortunately, restored him to his position late in March.

At the Battle of Shiloh (April 6–7, 1862), Confederate general Albert Sidney Johnston surprised Grant, who nevertheless recovered, regrouped, and rallied his forces. Aided by the timely arrival of reinforcements, Grant saved the day. Although the Union army incurred very heavy losses, the Confederates had been driven back. Politicians and Grant's superiors were less impressed by the fact that Grant had, in strategic terms, won Shiloh than they were appalled by the casualties he had incurred. The nation was not yet accustomed to warfare on a brutal, massive scale. Halleck was assigned direct command of western forces after Shiloh, and Grant, never in his favor, was cast into the background. But when Halleck was promoted to general in chief of the Union army in July, Grant assumed command over not only his own army but that of William Starke Rosecrans as well. Rosecrans was certainly not a brilliant commander, but he was often highly competent, and he had achieved victories at the Mississippi towns of Iuka (September 19) and Corinth (October 3–4). Unlike Halleck before him, Grant recognized the importance of capitalizing on the victories of his subordinate commanders. Iuka and Corinth allowed Grant to launch his great campaign against Vicksburg in November 1862. The massively fortified Mississippi River town, perched on an unapproachable and commanding bluff, was the key to the entire river. Grant, a great tactician and a savvy strategist, recognized that controlling this river would break the back of the Confederacy, severing East from West, and would seriously impede the flow of supplies to the rebels. He therefore resolved to devote every effort possible to capturing Vicksburg.

From December 1862 through March 1863, Grant doggedly attempted various tactics to lay siege against the fortress town. That all of them failed did not discourage Grant, whose hapless civilian life had more than accustomed him to failure. In a brilliant tactical move, Grant took his army south of Vicksburg and, under covering fire furnished by Union gunboats plying the river, he was able to cross back to the east bank of the Mississippi during April 30–May 1. From this position, Grant took Grand

Gulf, just below Vicksburg, on May 3, and then captured Jackson, Mississippi, on the 14th. These actions split the armies of Confederate generals John C. Pemberton and Joseph E. Johnston. Grant fought and defeated Pemberton at Champion's Hill (May 16, 1863), driving Pemberton's forces back upon Vicksburg. With that army bottled up in town, Grant at last besieged the city. The citizens and soldiers of Vicksburg gallantly withstood the siege until July 4, 1863. Together with the Union victory at Gettysburg, Pennsylvania, which came on the same day, Vicksburg was the turning point of the Civil War. As Grant had predicted, control of the Mississippi River spelled the doom of the Confederate cause.

Grant was promoted to major general in the regular army and was assigned command of the Military Division of the Mississippi on October 4. His first task was to break the Confederate siege of Union-held Chattanooga, Tennessee. Arriving outside of the city on October 23, he and his subordinates, General George Thomas and General William Tecumseh Sherman, conducted operations that broke the siege during October 25–28, and then went on to defeat the army of Braxton Bragg in the Battle of Lookout Mountain and Missionary Ridge—called the Battle above the Clouds, because so much of the action took place on the fog-enshrouded mountain—during November 24–25.

The string of successes since the fall of Vicksburg brought Grant, hitherto an obscure commander, to the attention of Abraham Lincoln. Since 1861, Lincoln had appointed one commander after another to lead the Union armies, and each general proved a disappointment. In Grant, at last, Lincoln saw a general who had the will to fight, to endure casualties, and to fight some more. Early in 1864, then, Grant was promoted to lieutenant general and named the new general in chief of all the federal armies.

Grant had the qualities of a leader suited to desperate times. As a strategist, he grasped the overall picture of the war, understanding as no commander before him had understood that his objective had to be the destruction of the armies of the Confederacy. This, and not the capture and occupation of towns—the objective of more conventional military planning—was the key to victory. Grant understood that the people of the South were willing to absorb great losses and keep fighting. But if the instrument of war was destroyed, there could be no more war. It was that brutally simple.

So Grant set about destroying Robert E. Lee's Army of Northern Virginia, the principal force of the Confederacy. Against Lee he attempted an outflanking maneuver at the Battle of the Wilderness during May 4–7, 1864. As a result of the battle, Grant gained position and advanced farther south, but Union casualties were so heavy that some began calling the general "Butcher Grant." In this term of derision may be found one of the sources of Grant's grim greatness as a leader. He was willing to trade casualties for strategic objectives because he understood the mathematics of the Civil War. The North, with a massive population, could lose far more men than the South and still press the battle. As Grant saw it, unremitting aggression would win the war, aggression that was fueled by Union lives, but that would take a far costlier toll on the dwindling human resources of the South.

Grant fought Lee again at Spotsylvania on May 8–17, driving him back to the North Anna River during May 23–26. But the Union Army's advance southward was checked by Lee at the Battle of Cold Harbor on June 3. Instead of retreating to the north, however, Grant withdrew from in front of Cold Harbor, only to move farther south across the James River to attack the important port town of Petersburg during June 12–17. Grant knew that if Petersburg fell, the Confederate capital of Richmond would also fall. Grant doggedly invested Petersburg from August 1864 through March of the next year. In the meantime, he was victorious at Five Forks (March 29–31), and, from here, invaded Richmond—from which Confederate president Jefferson Davis and his cabinet fled—as Petersburg fell.

The fall of Richmond did not bring an immediate end to the war. Robert E. Lee's Army of Northern Virginia, though greatly diminished, remained intact. Lee hoped to keep fighting in order to wrest from the North the most favorable peace terms possible. But "Unconditional Surrender" Grant pressed his pursuit of the Army of Northern Virginia through early April, finally accepting Lee's surrender of the army at Appomattox Court House on April 9, 1865. The remainder of the Confederate forces capitulated soon after this.

After the war, Grant oversaw the military governments installed in the southern states during Reconstruction. In recognition of his great service to the nation, Grant was promoted to the newly created rank of general of the army in July 1866. Although still in uniform, he served briefly as interim secretary of war under President Andrew Johnson during 1867–68, but his insistence on measures to protect the army of occupation in the South caused a permanent rift with Johnson, a Tennessean, who favored highly lenient Reconstruction policies. Grant increasingly embraced the opposite extreme, advocating the harsh and often punitive Reconstruction policies of the Radical Republicans. Grant easily achieved the Republican nomination for president in 1868 and had little trouble defeating Democrat candidate Horatio Seymour.

Grant, a great military leader, proved inept in civilian office. Although he himself was an honorable man, his administration was engulfed in corruption and scandal. His personal popularity gained him reelection (over Democrat Horace Greeley) to a second term, but all eight years of the Grant presidency were rife with political chicanery and scandal. After the close of his second term, he returned to private life, settling in New York City in 1881. There began a new cycle of failed enterprises after he left office, and the hero of the Civil War, savior of his country, went bankrupt by 1884. At the urging of the great humorist Mark Twain, who owned a controlling share of a highly successful publishing company, the impoverished Grant, now terminally ill with cancer of the throat, wrote his *Memoirs*. He lived long enough to correct galley proofs of the work, completing his corrections just four days before his death. Grant's work is a literary masterpiece, and its popular success saved his widow from penury and did much to rescue her husband's reputation from the taint of his corrupt presidency.

IN HIS OWN WORDS

"No terms except an unconditional and immediate surrender can be accepted."
—To Confederate general Simon Bolivar Buckner at Fort Donelson, February 16, 1862

"Find out where your enemy is, get at him as soon as you can and strike him as hard as you can, and keep moving on."
—Quoted in Bruce Catton, *This Hallowed Ground*, 1956

LEADERSHIP LESSONS

◆

Identify your objective and pursue it at all costs.

◆

Be aggressive when your resources warrant it.

◆

Eschew crippling caution.

◆

Always formulate tactics in the context of strategy.

◆

Be willing to accept the costs of the enterprise.

◆

Understand your resources versus the resources of your adversaries.

◆

Never attempt to evade reality in formulating and executing strategy.

◆

Fight.

Haile Selassie

Born: 1892   Died: 1975

Character model   Innovator

LEADERSHIP ACHIEVEMENTS

✦

Introduced important reforms into backward and impoverished Ethiopia

✦

Rose to heights of great nobility in his attempt to preserve Ethiopia
from Italian conquest

LIFE

By Western standards, Haile Selassie's autocratic style made him a flawed
leader as emperor of Ethiopia from 1930 to 1974. However, he is also
remembered for introducing a series of enlightened reforms and, most of
all, for his vigorous and dignified resistance against Benito Mussolini's
1935–36 invasion.

Haile Selassie was born Tafari Makonnen on July 23, 1892, the
cousin of Emperor Menelik II. Menelik was succeeded in 1913 by his
grandson Lij Yasu, who had been converted to Islam and was now a zealous Muslim. In 1916, when Lij Yasu attempted to change the state religion
of Ethiopia from Coptic Christianity to Islam, Tafari Makonnen saw his
opportunity to seize power. He drove Lij Yasu from the throne, and
installed his aunt as Empress Zauditu while assuming for himself the
regency as Ras Tafari. He was not only the power behind the throne, but
he had positioned himself to succeed Zauditu. Crowned King Ras Tafari in
1928, he became Emperor Haile Selassie I two years later when Zaudita
died under mysterious circumstances.

An absolute ruler, Haile Selassie aggressively centralized Ethiopian
government while instituting various important reforms, including the abolition of slavery. His growing reputation as a reformer suited well his noble
and dignified figure. He came to be regarded as an early anti-Fascist hero
when he appeared before the League of Nations to seek aid against the
Italian invasion of Ethiopia led by Benito Mussolini. Although it was pow-

erful and moving, Haile Selassie's plea for assistance was in vain, since the League lacked both the resolve and the military authority to intervene in the Italian aggression. After Italy annexed Ethiopia, the emperor was forced into exile.

Ethiopia was liberated very early in World War II, so that Haile Selassie was restored to his throne by 1941. His record after the war can best be characterized as enlightened despotism. Haile Selassie refused to relinquish any authority to any governing body, but he did formulate and put into operation long-range plans to modernize his nation. This effort notwithstanding, postwar Ethiopia experienced increased resistance against the emperor's arbitrary autocracy. Haile Selassie survived and crushed a number of attempted coups d'etat during the 1960s before he was finally deposed by the army in 1974. He died in the Ethiopian capital of Addis Ababa on August 27, 1975.

LEADERSHIP LESSONS

✦

Even in failure, the preservation of character and integrity can be counted
a victory.

✦

Benevolent despotism is still despotism and tends, therefore,
to incite rebellion.

Halsey, William Frederick, Jr.

Born: 1882 Died: 1959

**Improviser Innovator Leverager Motivator
Rescuer Strategist Tactician**

LEADERSHIP ACHIEVEMENTS

◆

Put the U.S. Pacific Fleet on an aggressive, offensive footing—even at the lowest point of World War II

◆

With charismatic leadership, restored U.S. fighting morale amid many early defeats

◆

Instilled and maintained an aggressive policy of hitting the enemy hard, fast, and often

LIFE

His salty demeanor, along with his philosophy of hitting the enemy "hard, fast, and often," made William "Bull" Halsey the most famous naval commander of World War II, daring, controversial, but effective. He was born and raised in Elizabeth, New Jersey, the son of a naval officer. Destined for a naval career, he graduated from the Naval Academy at Annapolis in 1904 and was commissioned ensign in 1906, serving first under Admiral George Dewey. Halsey attended torpedo school at Charleston, South Carolina, and then was assigned duty aboard several destroyers and torpedo boats before he was given command of the destroyer U.S.S. *Flusser* (DD-20), serving aboard her from August 1912 to February 1913, and of U.S.S. *Jervis* (DD-38), serving from 1913 to 1915.

From 1915 to 1917, Halsey was attached to the Executive Department at the Naval Academy and was promoted to lieutenant commander during August 1916. With America's entry into World War I, Halsey was assigned command of two destroyers, U.S.S. *Duncan* (DD-46) and U.S.S. *Benham* (DD-49), performing demanding, arduous, and hazardous convoy escort duty. After the war, Halsey was transferred to the Office of Naval Intelligence in

1921. In 1922, the destroyer commander was appointed to the prestigious post of naval attaché in Berlin, as well as Norway, Denmark, and Sweden (1922–24). He returned to sea duty aboard destroyers in the Atlantic, and then transferred to the battleship U.S.S. *Wyoming* (BB-32) as executive officer during 1926–27. Promoted to captain in February 1927, he was given command of the U.S.S. *Reina Mercedes* (IX-25), the post ship at Annapolis, which had been captured from the Spaniards in 1898.

Halsey obtained his first unit command in 1930, when he was made commander of Destroyer Squadron 14. In 1932, he moved on to course work in the Naval War College (graduating in 1933) and the Army War College (graduating in 1934). This marked Halsey as a candidate for major command. His experience at sea, as an attaché, and in the service strategic schools persuaded Halsey that the future of naval warfare was not in great battleships—then considered the naval weapon par excellence—but in carrier-based aviation. He foresaw the use of carrier-based aircraft to fight sea battles between fleets in which ships never even came close enough to see one another. This was a highly controversial and unpopular point of view for any U.S. naval officer to entertain in the 1930s, but Halsey was a patriot and military strategist first, a careerist second. At the age of 52, in May 1935, he qualified as a naval aviator, completing flight training at Pensacola, Florida. Immediately after this, in July, he assumed command of the aircraft carrier *Saratoga* (CV-3). Two years later, he was assigned command of the Pensacola Naval Air Station, serving during 1937–38.

Halsey was promoted to rear admiral in March 1938, and was assigned command of Carrier Division 2 (1938–39), followed by Carrier Division 1 (1939–40). In June 1940, Halsey became vice admiral and was assigned to command the Aircraft Carrier Battle Force as well as Carrier Division 2.

The events of December 7, 1941, would thrust the carriers into a preeminence even Halsey had not foreseen. On that quiet Sunday morning, the Japanese made a devastating attack on the U.S. Pacific fleet at Pearl Harbor, sinking or badly damaging the great battleships there. By a stroke of good fortune, Halsey, at the time, was at sea with the carriers *Enterprise* (CV-6) and *Yorktown* (CV-5). In part by default, the carrier fleet became the backbone of the early U.S. war effort in the Pacific. Halsey used his carriers in the months that followed Pearl Harbor to strike back at the Japanese by raiding outlying Japanese-held islands in the Central Pacific from January to May 1942. He enthusiastically collaborated with Army Air Forces colonel James H. Doolittle in planning and executing Doolittle's daring, morale-boosting air raid on Tokyo, using 16 B-25 bombers launched from the carrier *Hornet*.

Late in May 1942, Halsey was stricken with a serious illness and turned over command to the brilliant Raymond Ames Spruance. His illness kept Halsey out of the Battle of Midway (June 4, 1942), which, more than any other single naval engagement, must be identified as the turning point of the Pacific war. By October, however, Halsey was returned to active duty and replaced Admiral Robert L. Ghormley as commander of the South Pacific Force and Area. He suffered a narrow defeat at the Battle of Santa Cruz during October 26–28, but he nevertheless turned his tactical loss into an important strategic victory by maintaining station—standing fast—off Guadalcanal, which land forces were in the process of invading. In a battle of November 12–15, 1943, Halsey decisively defeated the Japanese off the island of Guadalcanal, and then assumed command of naval support for the capture of the rest of the Solomon Islands from June to October 1943. The fall of Bougainville, toward the end of 1943 and beginning of 1944, isolated the key Japanese base at Rabaul, rendering it ripe for attack.

In June 1944, Halsey was named to command the Third Fleet. He took the battleship U.S.S. *New Jersey* (BB-62) as his flagship in August and, that autumn, directed landings at Leyte (October 17–20) in the campaign to recapture the Philippines. Here, however, he learned the consequences of his high-stakes, bold leadership style. His leading principle had always been to hit the enemy "hard, fast, and often." To this point, this tactic had proved highly effective against an enemy whose offensive doctrine was precisely the same. The Japanese had made their initial gains in Asia and the Pacific by hitting hard, fast, and often. Accordingly, Halsey set off in pursuit of the Japanese carrier force off Luzon, Philippines, on October 25, 1944. This emphasis on offense left the critical San Bernardino Strait covered only by a weak force of escort carriers and destroyers. These were set upon by Admiral Takeo Kurita's substantially superior Central Force of the Japanese fleet. The greatly outnumbered and outclassed Americans skillfully managed to repulse the Japanese attack in the Battle of Samar (October 25). Had Kurita achieved victory, the landing forces on the Philippines would have been dangerously vulnerable. As for Halsey, he had succeeded in sinking four Japanese vessels, but, receiving word of Samar, broke off pursuit to reinforce the beleaguered American forces in a full-speed sailing operation that was dubbed "Bull's Run."

Although Halsey's response helped save the day, the feeling throughout the navy was that he should never have allowed the San Bernardino Strait to become so vulnerable. The incident stained Halsey's otherwise spotless reputation, and he suffered a further, nearly catastrophic reverse when his Third Fleet, supporting amphibious operations in the Philippines, was struck by a typhoon—called by navy weathermen Typhoon Cobra—that sunk three destroyer escorts in December. Some criticized Halsey for not taking more timely action to protect the fleet in the typhoon. Nevertheless, he went on to sweep through the South China Sea, destroying massive amounts of Japanese tonnage during January 10–20, 1945.

Halsey turned over command to Spruance, and then returned to seagoing command during the last stages of the Okinawa campaign (May–June 22) and the raids against the Japanese home islands during July and August. Japan's official surrender took place aboard Halsey's new flagship, U.S.S. *Missouri* (BB-64), in Tokyo Bay on September 2.

Halsey was promoted to fleet admiral in December 1945 and was assigned to special duty to the office of Secretary of the Navy until he retired in April 1947. As James E. Merrill writes in his biography, *Fleet Admiral William F. Halsey, Jr.*: "Halsey had the knack of appointing extremely intelligent officers to his staff, on whom he relied for decision making. On only rare occasions did he overrule them. 'Admiral Halsey's strongest point,' wrote a staff officer, 'was his superb leadership. While always the true professional and exacting professional performance from all subordinates, he had a charismatic effect on them which was like being touched by a magic wand. Anyone so touched was determined to excel.'"

IN HIS OWN WORDS

"Hit hard, hit fast, hit often."

—Formula for winning war, frequently quoted

"You've told me all the reasons why the project is not feasible. This meeting is now adjourned and will reconvene in 15 minutes. When you return I want to hear from you the action you propose to take in order to get the job done."

—To his staff, 1943

"There are no great men, only great challenges that ordinary men are forced by circumstances to meet."

—Quoted in Thomas A. Bailey, *Presidential Greatness: The Image and the Man from George Washington to the Present,* 1966

LEADERSHIP LESSONS

✦

Embrace change and innovation.

✦

Know when to violate convention—then violate it.

✦

Command from practical knowledge. A middle-aged Halsey learned to fly before he assumed command of aircraft carriers.

✦

Be aggressive.

✦

Speak plainly and forcefully. Motivate others through communication they can understand.

✦

Accept responsibility for the hard decisions.

Hammurabi

Died: 1750 B.C.

Conqueror Innovator Problem solver Systems creator Tactician

LEADERSHIP ACHIEVEMENTS

◆

Created the world's first great body of law

◆

Created a highly efficient administration

◆

Used innovative techniques to achieve military victory

LIFE

The sixth ruler of the First Dynasty of Babylon, Hammurabi is remembered as the world's first giver of law. Born in Babylon, he was a member of the Amorite tribe, the son of the ruler Sin-muballit, whom he succeeded to the throne in 1792 B.C. In the year of Hammurabi's accession to the throne, Rim-Sin of Larsa, ruler of southern Babylonia, conquered Isin, a traditional buffer zone between Babylon and Larsa. From this point forward, Rim-Sin became Hammurabi's principal rival, against whom he struggled for control of the waters of the Euphrates River. In 1787 B.C., Hammurabi conquered the city of Uruk and took it from Rim-Sin, whom he fought a second time in 1786 B.C. Following this was an interval of some 20 years of peace, during which Hammurabi built great temples and other public works. Most likely it was also during this time that Hammurabi developed his code of law, 282 instances of case law encompassing economic rules (prices, tariffs, and the like), marriage and divorce, and criminal as well as civil matters. While the Code of Hammurabi includes many features typical of tribal society—such as trial by ordeal and *lex talionis* (the "law of the claw" with its attendant principle of retributive punishment), it is also remarkably forward-looking in barring such brutal "primitive" customs as the blood feud, private retribution, and marriage by capture.

Despite the degree of peace he brought and the order created by the Code of Hammurabi, the last 14 years of Hammurabi's reign were engulfed by ultimately ruinous warfare. In 1764, Hammurabi moved against an alliance among Ashur, Eshunna, and Elam—principal powers along the Tigris—who blocked access to the all-important metal-producing regions of the territory corresponding to modern-day Iran. The next year, he fought Rim-Sin again, employing the grandly innovative tactic of damming up a principal watercourse (probably a canal flowing out of the Euphrates) to flood Larsa or to deprive it of water. In either case, after a siege of many months, Larsa fell to Hammurabi.

In 1762, Hammurabi fought his eastern neighbors, and the following year he turned against a longtime ally, King Zimrilim of Mari. Why he did so is not known. During 1755–57, Hammurabi turned to the east once again, this time destroying Eshunna, again by damming the waters. This, however, was a pyrrhic victory, which exposed Babylon to aggression from the Kassite people. During the last two years of his reign, Hammurabi neglected all other public works to build elaborate fortifications in an effort to protect his realm against invasions from the Kassites.

LEADERSHIP LESSONS

✦

A leader's most enduring work often consists of the systems he creates.

✦

Create systems that draw on the best of the historical and current thought, but that are not shackled to these. Innovate when possible.

✦

Try to view familiar problems with innovative solutions in mind.

✦

Look beyond direct action. Sometimes the best solutions are indirect, as when Hammurabi dammed the waters around Larsa instead of acting directly against the military forces defending that city.

Hannibal Barca

Born: 237 B.C.   Died: 183 B.C.

Conqueror   Improviser   Innovator   Problem solver   Strategist   Tactician

LEADERSHIP ACHIEVEMENTS

✦

Consistently defeated superior forces through bold strategy and tactics

✦

Was a consummate problem solver, who innovated military strategy to overcome all obstacles

✦

Introduced the element of unstoppable mobility into military strategy and tactics

✦

At Cannae, achieved one of the greatest military victories in history: the double envelopment of a superior force

✦

Was one of the great captains who transformed war from mayhem to the skilled application of strategy and tactics

LIFE

The most celebrated of the three Carthaginian military leaders called Hannibal, Hannibal Barca has been dubbed the "Father of Strategy." His father was Hamilcar Barca, the Carthaginian general who had acquitted himself admirably against the Romans during the First Punic War. Hannibal traveled to Spain during his father's campaign there in 237, and then returned to Carthage to finish his education after his father's death in 228. In 224, he returned to Spain at the head of a cavalry unit in an army under the command of his elder brother Hasdrubal. After the assassination of Hasdrubal in 221, Hannibal became overall commander of the army and immediately led his force across northwest Iberia (modern Spain) on a campaign of pacification during 221 and 220.

After achieving victory in Iberia, Hannibal set his sights on Rome, determined to get vengeance for the defeat Carthage had suffered in the

First Punic War. Hannibal's plan was to attack Italy itself, but he had to do so while avoiding the Roman-controlled Mediterranean. The strategic alternative to an attack across the sea was an epic overland campaign, which Hannibal embarked upon brilliantly. First, he took Saguntum, an Iberian city-state allied to Rome. It fell late in 219 only after a painful siege of eight months. The next year, Hannibal left Iberia and invaded Gaul during July 218, all the while moving swiftly and stealthily to evade and outmaneuver a Roman legion led by Publius Cornelius Scipio (Scipio Africanus Major) the Elder at Massilia (modern Marseille). In August, Hannibal crossed the Rhone River and, by the fall, was confronted with the one natural obstacle Rome had every right to believe would protect it from northern invasion: the Alps. Hannibal sized up the problem and planned and executed a spectacular Alpine crossing that included, most famously, his train of elephants. After this extraordinary tactical feat, Hannibal was in Italy by September–October 218. He engaged and defeated Roman cavalry and *velite* units (lightly armed, highly mobile troops) at the Battle of the Ticinus in November, and then won a major victory against the main Roman force commanded by T. Sempronius Longus at the River Trebbia in December. Next to offer battle was the army of G. Flaminius. Hannibal at first assumed an effective defensive posture, against which Flaminius beat in vain, spending his troops in the process. At what he deemed just the right moment, Hannibal counterattacked in a devastating surprise move at Lake Trasimene in April 217.

The culmination of Hannibal's triumphs came at his most famous battle—indeed, among military historians, perhaps the most important example of brilliant strategy and execution in ancient military history: Cannae, on August 2, 216. Hannibal lured the substantially superior forces of G. Terentius Varro and L. Aemilius Paulus to attack his center, only to enfold the attackers in the left and right wings of his army, thereby achieving a double envelopment, which hit the Romans in their vulnerable flanks. In this, the worst defeat the Legions ever suffered, some 55,000 Roman soldiers died.

Hannibal's campaign against M. Claudius Marcellus in southern Italy, during November 216–June 214, ended inconclusively, and his assault against the citadel fortress of Tarentum (modern Taranto) in 213 was an outright failure. Nevertheless, he marched next on Rome itself during the summer of 211, brushing aside two legions under Gnaeus Fulvius Centumalus at Herdonea during the following summer. However, even Hannibal could not long sustain what he had gained. It was one thing to achieve quick, decisive victories, but quite another to occupy and hold the territory won. Little by little, Hannibal lost support among Roman colonial possessions in southern Italy, and he then found himself the victim of the patient strategy of attrition employed by Quintus Fabius Maximus Cunctator (Fabius Cunctator), who earned the epithet of "The Delayer." Fabius understood that Hannibal was all but impossible to defeat in open battle, but, like any occupying force far from home, his army was vulnerable to attrition. Time was on Rome's side, and Fabius kept Hannibal at bay as his supplies and support dwindled.

Hannibal's situation became critical when his younger brother Hasdrubal, coming to him with reinforcements, died in 207. At last, Carthage itself withdrew its support for Hannibal's extended campaigning, and the general had no choice but to return to Africa to defend against the invasion there of Scipio Africanus during the fall of 203. Scipio and Masinissa defeated Hannibal at the Battle of Zama in the spring of 202, and, following this, he negotiated peace with Rome. Elected *suffete* (magistrate) in 196, Hannibal instituted a series of reforms, for which he earned many enemies. Denounced to Rome by a group of his adversaries, Hannibal fled to Antiochus III the Great of Syria and made an offer of his military services. Hannibal raised and commanded a Phoenician fleet against Rhodes in 190, but was defeated there by Eudamus of Rhodes and L. Aemilius Regilus at the Eurymedon. Once again, Hannibal was forced to flee, landing first at Crete and then at Bithynia (in modern Turkey). His situation hopeless, he took his own life by swallowing poison.

While Hannibal's fame is legendary, Hannibal the man is a shadowy figure, for no Carthaginian chronicler recorded his accomplishments, which are known only from the records of his Roman enemies. Despite the paucity of hard fact, it is clear that he was one of history's greatest generals, a master of grand strategy and innovative tactics. He was also apparently at his best when confronting a superior force.

IN HIS OWN WORDS

"What do we do with a man who refuses to accept either good fortune or bad? This is the only general who gives his enemy no rest when he is victorious, nor takes any himself when he is defeated. We shall never have done with fighting him, it seems, because he attacks out of confidence when he is winning, and out of shame when he is beaten."
—Of the Roman consul Marcellus, 210 B.C.

"We will either find a way or make one."
—Attributed

"We have nothing left in the world but what we can win with our swords. Timidity and cowardice are for men who can see safety at their backs— who can retreat without molestation along some easy road and find refuge in the familiar fields of their native land; but they are not for you: you must be brave; for you there is no middle way between victory or death—put all hope of it from you, and either conquer, or, should fortune hesitate to favor you, meet death in battle rather than in flight."
—Address to troops after crossing the Alps into Italy, 218 B.C.

"Take away the blinding brilliance of the name, and in what can the Romans be compared to you?"
—Address before the Battle of the Ticinus, 218 B.C.

LEADERSHIP LESSONS

✦

Value mobility and surprise.

✦

Leverage your forces through the application of well-formulated strategy.

✦

Treat obstacles as an opportunity for the innovation of strategy and tactics.

✦

Stop at nothing.

✦

The path of least resistance may not be the most feasible or economical route to success.

✦

Think beyond the paths others have worn.

Harald I Fairhair (or Finehair)

Born: ca. 860 Died: ca. 940

Conqueror Innovator Leverager Motivator Strategist Systems creator

LEADERSHIP ACHIEVEMENTS

✦

Expanded his empire, and then unified it under his rule

✦

Combined the spirit of ruthless conquest with a willingness to share power
effectively

✦

Delegated authority effectively

✦

Enfranchised subordinates, creating loyalty by giving them a stake in the
enterprise

✦

Created a system of central administration and government unprecedented
in tribal Norway

LIFE

Most of what very little is known of Harald I Fairhair comes from legendary and literary sources, most notably the *Heimskringla*, a poetic history
of Norway's kings by the Icelandic author of the great *Prose Edda*, Snorri
Sturluson (1179–1241). We learn from this that Harald I was one of the
most important of Scandinavia's great warrior chiefs. He was the first ruler
to claim sovereignty over all of Norway.

Harald was the son of Halvdan the Black. At age 10, Harald was
given rule of a portion of southeastern Norway and soon, still at a tender
age, directed the suppression of a revolt in the Uplands. He made a pact
with Haakon, Earl of Lade, which allowed him to focus exclusively on a
campaign of conquest throughout western Norway. The decisive Battle of
Hafrsfjord, dated in contemporary sources to 872 but placed by most modern historians some 10 to 20 years later, won for Harald personal control
of Norway's western coastal districts. By developing a network of semi-
tributary chieftains, Harald expanded this victory to acquire indirect

dominion over other parts of the country as well. This was typical of Harald: What he could control directly, he seized; more remote holdings he controlled through others whom he made beholden to him. Those chieftains who refused to submit to Harald either perished in conquest or fled to Britain or Iceland. (Iceland was discovered during Harald's reign.)

Harald was undeniably ruthless in his aggression, yet he was also careful to establish enduring authority not through mere intimidation and conquest, but by developing relations with local chieftains. These he did not merely subjugate—although he did dominate them—but endeavored always to give them a share and a stake in the enterprise. In this way, Harald created a system of provincial administrations called *lagtings*, by which he introduced an unprecedented degree of central authority over a most unruly realm.

LEADERSHIP LESSONS

✦

Leaven ruthless conquest with an openness to shared power and strategic alliances.

✦

Distinguish between areas in which you can assert personal, direct control and those in which delegation of authority is more effective.

✦

Create effective loyalty by giving key personnel a stake in the enterprise.

✦

Follow through on victories by devising systems to sustain and maintain whatever gains have been made.

Henry II

Born: 1133   Died: 1189

Conqueror   Innovator   Systems creator   Tactician

LEADERSHIP ACHIEVEMENTS

✦

Centralized power in England, thereby increasing national identity

✦

Introduced equitable taxation in lieu of feudal service to the king

✦

Greatly reformed the English system of justice

✦

Unmistakably elevated the law above the power of individual monarchs

✦

Reduced the power of the church and increased that of the crown

LIFE

Considered by most historians as among the very greatest of English monarchs, Henry II became, at least for a time, the most powerful ruler in Europe. His enduring contribution to English government was to transfer power from the nobles to the crown, which became the central power of the realm.

Henry was born on March 5, 1133, at Le Mans, France, the son of Geoffrey Plantagenet, Count of Anjou, and Matilda, daughter of King Henry I of England. Henry I was a capable ruler, who had taken the first important steps toward transforming the Anglo-Saxon and Norman identity of his kingdom into something genuinely English. He granted royal charters to many English towns, thereby delivering the emerging merchant classes from domination by capricious and rapacious barons. He also promoted learning in his realm. But Henry I failed to establish an enduring legacy of reform and good government, which resulted in much discontent throughout the realm. Henry I's only son, William the Atheling, died before his father, whereupon the nobles pledged to accept Henry's daughter, Matilda, as their queen. When Henry I died in 1135, however, Stephen,

Count of Blois, stepped up to claim the throne. This claimant did not enjoy universal acceptance, and Matilda was encouraged to invade England to claim her right of rule. The result was a civil war, during which young Henry was taken to England to be educated; he then went to Normandy in 1144, which Geoffrey Plantagenet had just captured from Stephen. In 1147, Henry campaigned against Stephen in England, but suffered serious defeat. Two years later, he struck an alliance with King David of Scotland and launched a new campaign against Stephen, once again enduring a defeat, which nearly cost him his life.

Henry became Duke of Normandy in 1150 and succeeded his father as Count of Anjou the next year. He married Eleanor of Aquitaine, former wife of France's Louis VII, in 1152, a union that gave him dominion over vast realms in southern France. This gave Henry a much stronger base from which to invade England yet again, in January 1153. The fight against Stephen at the Battle of Wallingford in July 1153 was tactically inconclusive, but it did gain popular support for Henry, who, aided by Theobald, Archbishop of Canterbury, was able to negotiate a favorable, if tenuous, peace. It was now agreed that Stephen would rule until his death, at which time Henry was to succeed him.

As it turned out, Henry did not have long to wait. Stephen died in October 1154, and Henry was crowned Henry II on December 19. He ruled not only England, but the entire Angevin Empire, which included much of present-day France. In extent, the Angevin Empire was second only to the Holy Roman Empire among European realms. But it was upon England proper that Henry's rule left its most enduring mark. Early in his reign, during 1157, Henry set about recovering the northern regions of Northumberland, Cumberland, and Westmoreland from Scottish domination. Next, from 1159 to 1165, he campaigned in Wales, which he succeeded, for a time, in subjugating. In 1171, he annexed Ireland. Simultaneously with these conquests, from 1159 through 1174, Henry II also battled his continental rival, Louis VII of France.

In domestic affairs, Henry II led important reforms. He replaced the tradition of feudal service, which created much friction and resentment between the nobles and the crown, with a more flexible and equitable system of scutage, "shield money" paid to the crown in lieu of service. He also profoundly reformed the system of English justice, concentrating all

authority in the hands of royal circuit judges, thereby making the administration of law solely the responsibility of the crown. As the basis of English
law, Henry firmly established the primacy of English common law traditions, enriched by Norman refinements, thereby guaranteeing that the
administration of justice would be governed by enduring principles rather
than be subject to the whim of the current monarch. In effect, Henry put
the law above the king. Finally, Henry II guaranteed trial by a jury of one's
peers, and he established the right of appeal.

Henry's judicial reforms brought him into sharp conflict with his
longtime friend Thomas à Becket, archbishop of Canterbury. Henry
asserted the precedence of royal courts over ecclesiastical (church) courts.
Becket objected, and the conflict escalated, with brief periods of reconciliation, during 1162–70. In 1164, at the Council of Clarendon, Henry II summoned the bishops to sign an agreement essentially pledging their
allegiance and obedience to the king. Becket, believing his ultimate allegiance was to God and the Church, went into exile for six years rather than
sign. This created a leadership crisis for Henry II, because many of the
bishops rallied to Becket's side. Worse for Henry, many ordinary English
citizens felt greater allegiance to the Church than to the king. To them, the
Church represented local government and was a bulwark against royal
tyranny. When Becket returned to England in 1170, he delivered an inflammatory Christmas Day sermon, in which he excommunicated certain
knights loyal to Henry. He also predicted his own martyrdom. Henry, who
was in France at this time, exclaimed to his knights in exasperation: "Will
no one rid me of this turbulent priest?" Four knights interpreted this as a
command to assassinate Becket, which they did in 1171. Henry, in fact, had
been ambivalent about what to do with his friend, but he fully accepted
responsibility for his former friend's murder, made a public act of contri-
tion, and performed various other acts of penance prescribed by the pope.

While Henry retained his power following the death of Becket, parts
of England, which had simmered with revolt, now boiled over. Henry II
was faced with simultaneous wars against France, the Scots, and rebellious
English barons in 1173. Henry hurried to France, where he successfully
fought off attacks on Normandy and Anjou during the summer and fall.
He then had to rush back to England, to counter the threat of a Scots inva-

sion. At the Battle of Alnwick, July 13, 1174, he captured the Scots King William the Lion.

While Henry fought with great energy and success to impose and maintain order in his realms, he apparently ignored the anarchy and rebellion developing within his own family. He endowed his sons Richard (later, as Richard I, called the Lion-Hearted), Geoffrey, and John (later King John) with lands and titles, but he withheld funds from them. To avoid the kind of strife that had followed the death of Henry I, he crowned his eldest son, Henry, king. Young Henry repaid this act by rebelling against his father in 1183. The revolt was put down, and young Henry died of a fever soon afterward. Following his son's death, Henry II stirred further family discord by formally recognizing the right of his next son, Richard, to succeed him, yet he openly exhibited favor to his sons Geoffrey and John. Eleanor of Aquitaine incited Richard and Geoffrey to act against their father, and Richard allied himself with the new king of France, Philip II Augustus. The two allies began a war of rebellion against Henry II, which was secretly joined by John. In 1189, Henry II was forced to retreat at the Battle of Le Mans, where he fell ill and called for a truce. He agreed to peace terms generally unfavorable to him, and he retired to his castle in Chinon, where his illness worsened. On his deathbed, he was informed that John—his favorite son—had participated in the rebellion against him. He died, on July 6, 1189, in the arms of his youngest son, Geoffrey, muttering his last words: "Shame, shame on a conquered king."

LEADERSHIP LESSONS

✦

Henry II made a great effort to mold himself in the image of a great king.
Leaders need to project substantial character.

✦

Henry II was a military leader of skill, but, even more, of exemplary
courage. A leader must serve as a model of courage.

✦

Elevate fairness and justice over individual will and whim.

Henry III the Sufferer

Born: 1379   Died: 1406

Conqueror   Motivator   Systems creator

LEADERSHIP ACHIEVEMENTS

✦

Despite severe personal hardships—lifelong debilitating illness—created a
stable and efficient government

✦

Through a system of administrators and military commanders, effectively
led Castile, neutralizing its chief enemies and expanding its territory

✦

Reintroduced the rule of law to Castile, thereby suppressing persecution
of the Jews

LIFE

Henry III, king of Castile (a region of Spain), was chronically ill and disabled and was therefore dubbed Henry the Sufferer. Despite his disability, he created a system of administration that allowed him to lead Castile effectively and to institute valuable reforms. He was born in Burgos, Castile, on October 4, 1379, the son of John I, and he assumed the throne at age 11, when his father died. Before he began to rule in his own right at age 14, Henry's early reign was directed by regents, who actively encouraged the fanatical anti-Semitic preaching that resulted in a reign of terror against Castile's Jews. When Henry took over from his regents, he did not venture to decree a stop to the persecution of the Jews, but he acted to restore order and the rule of law, reinvigorating the royal council and courts. This effectively halted the wholesale persecution and improved the administration of justice generally.

Henry's chronic ill health prevented his personally leading an army in the field; nevertheless, he established a strongly autocratic rule through a royal council, the *Audencia* (equivalent to a supreme court), and a network of loyal *corregidores*, or magistrates. These officials were handpicked for their demonstrated loyalty, ability, and incorruptibility. They served as the king's eyes and ears. Beyond this, Henry made a politically strategic marriage to Catherine of Lancaster, which ended a dynastic rift that had long plagued Castile. So far as military campaigning was concerned, Henry appointed his younger brother Ferdinand to do battle against Granada. From 1396 to 1398, Henry also directed, through subordinates, an ongoing war with Portugal, ultimately forcing that nation to a favorable truce. He next commissioned Jean de Béthencourt to conquer and colonize the Canary Islands, thereby securing a rich prize for his kingdom.

LEADERSHIP LESSONS

✦

Direct control is not always necessary for effective leadership.

✦

Devote maximum effort and thought to the selection of subordinates, who
not only execute your policies, but serve as your eyes and ears.

✦

Establish efficient and effective rules and systems of procedure;
subordinate personalities and individual conduct to these.

✦

Do not surrender to hardship and handicap.

Henry V

Born: 1387   Died: 1422

Character model   Conqueror   Leverager   Motivator   Tactician   Visionary

LEADERSHIP ACHIEVEMENTS

✦

Brought England to a height of prestige in Europe

✦

Nearly brought about the union of England and France

✦

Became one of the great examples of leadership—for his people and for
much of Europe

✦

Built his leadership on character and courage

✦

For a time, became the most powerful leader in Europe

✦

Brought unprecedented stability and pride to England

LIFE

If Henry II was among England's greatest kings, Henry V was probably
the realm's most universally loved. He brought an unprecedented degree
of stability to the nation, even as he enlarged its French domains, coming
close to uniting England and France under a single crown. He was born at
Monmouth on or about September 16, 1387, the first son of King Henry
IV. At the time of his birth, Henry's father was in the field, combating
rebellions in England, Wales, and Ireland, while simultaneously defending
against an invasion from Scotland. In his father's absence, young Henry
was raised in the household of Richard II. Grown to manhood, he was
knighted for his services during his father's Irish campaign in the spring of
1399, and he was made Prince of Wales on October 15, upon the coronation of his father. From 1402 to 1409, Henry V fought against Welsh rebel
followers of Owen Glendowner.

Although Henry V was of great service to his father, he did not follow Henry IV's policies blindly. After 1408, Henry V began increasingly

to assert himself, often in opposition to his father and his ministers. On the death of Henry IV, on March 20, 1413, Henry V assumed the throne and immediately set about the suppression of a rebellion among the Lollards, a radical Christian sect. Advocates of the supremacy of individual conscience, the Lollards collaborated with others in a political revolt and were greatly feared as agents of anarchy. Henry IV had actively persecuted them, and Henry V took up the campaign, ruthlessly crushing armed revolts from December 1413 to January 1414. Henry captured and put to death the Lollard leader, Sir John Oldcastle. No sooner were the Lollards suppressed than Henry was faced with a revolt among nobles who wanted to place Edmund Mortimer, Earl of Monmouth, on the throne. This rebellion was quelled—again, without mercy—in July 1415.

Even while he was intensely occupied with these domestic affairs, Henry kept his eye on the international scene. Perceiving political chaos in France, he decided that the time was ripe for a declaration of war on that country. Claiming that Normandy was, by absolute right, an English possession, Henry sailed to the continent on August 10, 1415, and laid siege against the fortress of Harfleur from August 13 to September 22. The army he commanded consisted of professional soldiers rather than the usual conglomeration yielded by medieval levies. This was an advantage, but these professionals were also men of mixed background and loyalties, including among their number Welshmen, Irishmen, Gascons, and others. As a precaution, Henry enforced rigid discipline among them.

Harfleur surrendered on September 22, and Henry installed an English garrison, allowing most of the town's inhabitants to remain in place— although he demanded a ransom from the well-to-do, and he exiled the aged, infirm, and very young, all of whom he deemed useless mouths to feed. In the context of Henry's time, this was not judged an act of brutality, but a necessity of conquest. From Harfleur, Henry marched with 900 men-at-arms and some 5,000 archers to Calais in an effort to enlarge the area under his control. By October 1515, Henry's force was just south of the River Somme. Constable Charles d'Albret assembled a vastly superior army of 35,000 and brought Henry's 5,900 to battle at Agincourt on October 25.

The situation seemed hopeless, but the Battle of Agincourt was to prove Henry's finest hour. The king provided an example of courage and calm resolve, as well as of absolute faith in God's intention to bring the

English a victory. For their part, the French managed their forces with disastrous ineptitude, even as Henry employed his longbowmen with consummate skill. They took a heavy toll on the slow-moving French artillery and on mounted knights, who were arrayed in ranks so tightly packed that they had little room in which to maneuver and do battle effectively. Estimates of French killed at Agincourt vary from some 3,000 to as many as 8,000, with English losses put at a mere 250. The battle not only marked the high point of Henry's reign, but spelled the end of the heavily armored medieval knight as an effective agent of warfare. In his use of archers, Henry had introduced a great innovation in warfare as well as in society, for the triumph of the common archer also seemed to mark the ascendency of the common man over the noble.

At the height of battle, the French had lost two of the three cavalry waves at their disposal when a band of raiders attacked the English baggage train at Henry's rear. The king realized that, thus distracted, his forces were now vulnerable to attack by the third wave of French cavalry, which might act in concert with the many French prisoners the English now held within their ranks. Henry moved with terrible decisiveness, ordering that all prisoners be put to death. At this, the remainder of the French forces—the third wave—withdrew from the field.

From Agincourt, Henry went on to conquer all of Normandy during 1417–19. He captured Rouen after a siege that lasted from September 1418 to January 1419, marching on Paris in May 1420, and concluding an alliance with the Burgundy faction that ultimately resulted in the Treaty of Troyes, by which the weak French king, Charles VI, acknowledged Henry V heir to the throne of France, making him, for the present, regent. Thus empowered, Henry went on to subdue northern France, laying siege to and capturing Meaux from October 1421 to May 1422.

At this high point in his reign, Henry's great plan and ambition were to unite and lead all of western Europe in one mammoth Crusade against the heathen in the Holy Land. He had become, in the words of Sir Winston Churchill, "the supreme figure in Europe." But Henry V did not long remain on the heights. Exhausted by his campaigning in northern France, he fell ill with dysentery and died at Bois de Vincennes on August 31, 1422. The king's successors proved unable to hold France for long, and England failed to capitalize on most of what Henry had gained.

LEADERSHIP LESSONS

✦

Nothing substitutes for character. It is a leader's most valuable—and most
fragile—asset.

✦

Personal example is a leader's most powerful tool.

✦

An effective leader plays to the strengths of his enterprise, leveraging his
best resources, as Henry did in deploying his archers at Agincourt.

✦

Decisive, even ruthless, action is effective but risky. It is, however,
sometimes necessary.

Henry VIII

Born: 1491   Died: 1547

Innovator   Motivator   Visionary

LEADERSHIP ACHIEVEMENTS

✦

Did much to unify England and to centralize its government

✦

Won significant military victories that enhanced the prestige of England

✦

Triumphed over the English barons and other feudal lords as a genuine
sovereign

✦

Was successful in imposing his vision and will on those who served him

✦

Began the transformation of England from a backward feudal island nation
to a powerful force among the nations of the world

✦

Transformed the English court into one of the great royal courts of Europe

✦

Created the Church of England

LIFE

Henry VIII is England's most celebrated king, one who brought about the reformation of the English Church and made great strides in elevating the power of the throne over that of a welter of barons and other feudal figures. Henry VIII transformed the English court from a provincial backwater to a place of exquisite cultural sophistication, and he began the metamorphosis of England itself from an insular realm of the Dark Ages to a world power—a process his daughter, Elizabeth I, would continue.

The future king was born at Greenwich on June 28, 1491, the son of the first Tudor king, Henry VII. The boy avidly consumed the superb Renaissance education offered him, and he became adept at philosophical discourse, languages, and literature. He particularly loved music, and he became a performer as well as a composer of considerable contemporary renown. The popular image of Henry VIII, from his later years, is of an enormously fat monarch, but, in fact, as a young man, Henry was a fine athlete, who reveled in the hunt as well as the joust.

As a child, Henry VIII had little expectation of becoming king. The succession by right belonged to his older brother, Prince Arthur, but when Arthur died prematurely in 1502, Henry became the heir apparent. He succeeded to the throne on the death of his father on April 22, 1509. Prior to his coronation, teenaged Henry married Arthur's widow, Catherine of Aragon, the daughter of Ferdinand II and Isabella I of Spain.

Contemporary accounts suggest that, for almost 20 years, the marriage was a happy one. During this period, Henry personally commanded several creditable—though not spectacularly successful—military expeditions against the French. But by 1527, he was increasingly obsessed by what he saw as Catherine's failure to produce a surviving male heir. He voiced his concern that this failure was a judgment of God against him for his having violated a biblical injunction, in Leviticus 20:21, against marriage to the widow of a brother. Moreover, Henry had by this time become smitten with the youthful and vivacious Anne Boleyn, a lady of the royal court. He used the text from Leviticus as a basis on which to divorce Catherine, and he ordered his chief minister, Cardinal Wolsey, to petition Pope Clement VII for a decree proclaiming the marriage invalid, thereby leaving him free to marry Anne Boleyn. For her part, Catherine vigorously opposed the annulment, and in this she was supported by her nephew Charles V, Holy Roman emperor and king of Spain. Because Clement VII relied on the military might of Spain for protection, he rejected Henry's petition, even though, on strictly scriptural grounds, he was inclined to grant it.

Even in the absence of a papal decree, Henry VIII pressed ahead with a divorce trial, which was conducted in London in 1529. The lack of papal sanction, however, prompted the adjournment of the trial without a decision. Enraged and frustrated by this result, Henry dismissed Wolsey and replaced him in 1532 with the crafty Thomas Cromwell. The solution Cromwell proposed to the king's marital problem was bold and sweeping. He advised Henry to break with the Roman church and to create an independent Church of England. This would enable the archbishop of Canterbury, as head of the English church, to grant the divorce. Henry eagerly accepted the recommendation and pushed the legislation through Parliament in 1533. He established the Church of England as an independent national church, prevailed on the archbishop to grant his divorce from Catherine, and quickly married Anne Boleyn.

That Henry's object in breaking with Rome was chiefly to secure a divorce and not really to reform religion tempered the king's zeal. The reformation of religious practice moved ahead slowly at first, but, within a few years, Henry became increasingly enthusiastic about exploiting the advantages of a truly national church. In consequence, the reformation process accelerated, and, between 1536 and 1540, Henry ordered the dissolution of all the monasteries and nunneries in England. He confiscated for the government their considerable wealth and property. To enforce his actions, Henry commanded his subjects to swear an oath of supremacy, pledging loyalty to the king as head of the church. This greatly enhanced the roles of king and of the central government, but not everyone was compliant. The great theologian and philosopher Sir Thomas More, whom Henry VIII himself admired deeply, was nevertheless put to death because he refused to take the oath.

In September 1533, Anne Boleyn bore Henry a daughter, Elizabeth, who was proclaimed heir to the throne in place of Catherine's daughter, Mary, now deemed a bastard. Henry, of course, remained unsatisfied in having no male heir to the throne, and, in consequence, became increasingly discontent with Anne. As they drifted apart, Henry persuaded himself that Anne Boleyn had been unfaithful to him—almost certainly an unfounded charge—and she was tried for infidelity, which, because it was infidelity to a king, was tantamount to treason. Convicted, Anne Boleyn was sentenced to death and speedily executed in 1536.

Once again, Henry was free to marry, and he took as his third wife Jane Seymour, who quickly become pregnant and did produce a son, Edward. Henry's joy at this event was dampened by the child's frail and sickly condition. Edward was not expected to survive beyond infancy. In fact, Edward would survive to reign for six years, although he remained in poor health and died at 15. As for his mother, she never recovered from a difficult labor and birth. Jane Seymour died 11 days after Edward was born.

Disconsolate over the precarious health of his son and the death of Jane Seymour, Henry took as his fourth wife Anne of Cleves, a German noblewoman, in 1540. Unlike his previous marriages, this one was founded neither on love nor sexual attraction, but was negotiated by

Thomas Cromwell as a prudent political move. Fearing that the Catholic nations would align themselves against renegade England, Cromwell reasoned that the union of Henry and the Lutheran Anne would attract the diplomatic support of continental Lutherans. Henry, whose legendary girth attested to his fondness for the pleasures of the flesh, was repelled by the frankly plain Anne. He divorced her almost immediately and then turned on Cromwell, whom he charged with treason. The hapless minister was quickly tried and executed.

Henry's fifth wife was the young and beautiful Catherine Howard, niece of Cromwell's ambitious enemy Thomas Howard, duke of Norfolk. She was a spirited, headstrong, and romantic girl, who must have found little enough to cherish in her aging and obese royal spouse. When she was discovered in a liaison with her former fiancé (a distant cousin), she was charged with treason, tried, and sent to the block in 1542. Henry's last wife, Catherine Parr, achieved what none of the other five had: She became Henry's widow.

It is understandable that Henry VIII is remembered so vividly for his monumentally dysfunctional marriages; yet it is regrettable. On balance, he was a successful military commander, who earned his most significant military renown at the Battle of the Spurs (so called because of the haste with which the French cavalry beat their retreat) on August 16, 1513. In 1520, Henry met the French king Francis I in a ceremonial demonstration of friendship on the Field of the Cloth of Gold, near Calais, but from 1522 to 1527 he allied with Charles V against Francis, and he again fought the French with some success in 1544–46. Closer to home, Henry also subdued the always troublesome Scots at Flodden (1513) and Solway Moss (1542). Although these campaigns, though predominantly successful, greatly strained the English coffers while gaining England no foreign territories, they did earn the kingdom badly needed international prestige and a firm standing among the nations of the continent. Certainly, these ventures helped to position the small island nation for the role it would play in world affairs during the reign of Elizabeth I.

It must be acknowledged that Henry was deeply flawed as a leader. He was despotic, moody, and vengeful. Yet he also led England from backward and fractious feudalism to something approaching genuine nationhood. In the process, he transformed the English royal court from a backwater to a center of sophistication, art, and learning, and he created the conditions that enabled his most important successor, Elizabeth I (who followed to the throne her short-lived half-brother Edward and her unpopular half-sister "Bloody Mary"), to build a truly great empire.

LEADERSHIP LESSONS
✦

Recognize which trappings of authority are important, and cultivate them as elements of a leadership image.

✦

Understand the severe limitations of leadership by intimidation.

✦

Assess goals carefully. Some victories are important to enhance prestige and credibility, even if they do not return immediate, tangible profit.

✦

Be prepared to consider innovative and radical solutions to problems. If circumstances present difficulties, assess the feasibility of altering the circumstances themselves.

Heraclius

Born: ca. A.D. 575 Died: 641

**Conqueror Motivator Problem solver Rescuer Strategist
Systems creator Tactician Visionary**

LEADERSHIP ACHIEVEMENTS

✦

Rescued a rapidly failing enterprise—the Eastern Roman Empire

✦

Reformed and improved the infrastructure of the enterprise—the
government and military of the Eastern Roman Empire

✦

Attempted to reconcile opposing points of view for the common good

LIFE

Heraclius is an example of a leader working in a situation of chronic crisis.
He deposed Phocas to become emperor of the Eastern Roman Empire,
which was then in the throes of rapid disintegration.

Heraclius was born of Armenian lineage in eastern Anatolia (now part
of Turkey). His father was governor of the Roman province of Africa during
the reign of Emperor Phocas when influential elements in Constantinople
appealed to him to rescue the empire from misrule. Accordingly, the governor dispatched his son with an army to overthrow Phocus. Heraclius landed
in Constantinople in October 610, deposed the emperor, and was crowned
emperor in his place. The realm he nominally ruled was internally torn by
civil war even as it was menaced from the outside by Slavic, Persian, and
Turkish raiders. The frontiers of the Eastern Empire were continually
attacked, and exorbitant tributes were extorted by various invaders, which
greatly undermined the economy.

In an effort to rescue his empire, Heraclius embarked on a vigorous
reorganization of the corrupt and unwieldy imperial bureaucracy. He also
devoted all available resources to building up the deteriorating armies.
Despite his efforts, however, the Persians took Syria and Palestine in 614,
even capturing Jerusalem and appropriating the holiest of holy Christian

relics, what was believed to be Christ's cross. Five years later, Egypt and Libya fell to a Persian army of occupation. In the meantime, Heraclius negotiated with the barbarian Avar tribe in 617 or 619. He concluded a truce, which was, however, immediately broken, and Heraclius evaded capture only by outriding the Avar pursuers all the way back to Constantinople. It was not until 622 that Heraclius was able to come successfully to terms with the Avars. This accomplished, he was able to direct his resources against the Persians.

Heraclius launched an expedition against invading Persian armies with the principal object of recovering Jerusalem and the Cross; in effect, he started the first Crusade. Heraclius fought brilliantly, pushing the Persians out of Anatolia. This put him into a strong negotiating position, from which he offered a truce to the Persian emperor Khosrow II. The Persian ruler rejected Heraclius's terms and publicly denigrated Christ and Christianity. Seizing on this affront, Heraclius was able to inspirit and motivate a vast number of troops for an extended two-year campaign against Persia, which was a substantial success.

An inspiring leader, Heraclius took personal command of his troops. In 625, while camped on the west bank of the Sarus River in Anatolia, his men, catching sight of Persian forces on the east bank, made an unauthorized charge across the bridge. Persians emerged from ambush and were on the verge of annihilating Heraclius's forces when the emperor took up his sword, advanced to the bridge, struck down the leader of the Persian troops, and rallied his men in a well-organized and devastating assault. The next year, the Persians counterattacked at the Bosporus, intending to join the Avars in an assault on Constantinople itself. Heraclius's forces sunk the Persian fleet, leaving the Persian troops without transport. Unsupported, the Avar assault also failed.

Late in 627, Heraclius finally took the war into Persia. In a grand battle near Nineveh, he met the Persians, killing three generals in one-on-one combat and then leading his troops into the thick of the Persian lines. There he personally killed the chief commander of the Persian forces, which, leaderless, scattered. Early in 628, Heraclius entered the capital city of Dastagird. At his approach, Khosrow II was overthrown by his son, who eagerly concluded a peace with Heraclius. The emperor demanded the redemption of all captives, the return of captured Roman lands, and the return of the Holy Cross, which, in 630, he bore to Jerusalem and reinstalled in the Church of the Holy Sepulchre.

Unlike many conquerors, Heraclius believed in following up on his victories in order to sustain what they had gained. He was convinced that to retain what had been won he had to unite the Christian world by conciliating the diverse Christian theologies of Egypt, Syria, and Armenia, whose practitioners had long been persecuted by Christianized Roman emperors. Heraclius endeavored to bring about reconciliation, but to no avail, and he was near physical collapse in 634 when Arab forces invaded Syria. No longer fit to take personal command of his army, the emperor entrusted the Byzantine forces to other commanders, who suffered a decisive defeat at the Battle of Yarmuk in 636. The result was the loss of all Heraclius had won in Syria and Egypt. The emperor had to remove the hard-won Cross from the Church of the Holy Sepulchre and evacuate it northward.

Although he was fearless in battle, Heraclius was phobic where water was concerned. Enslaved to his phobia, he waited an entire year on the Asian side of the Bosporus before venturing across. At last, his men fashioned a pontoon bridge screened with leaves to hide the water from view. This Heraclius crossed into Constantinople, but there he fell ill. He died, apparently of prostate cancer, on February 11, 641.

LEADERSHIP LESSONS

✦

Analyze the status quo; discover ways to make existing systems more efficient or, where necessary, to replace them with innovative systems that work more successfully.

✦

Fight one war at a time.

✦

Define emotionally powerful, compelling goals; communicate these effectively.

✦

Whenever possible, favor negotiation over battle.

Ho Chi Minh

Born: 1890   Died: 1969

**Character model   Innovator   Leverager   Mentor   Motivator
Strategist   Systems creator   Tactician**

LEADERSHIP ACHIEVEMENTS

✦

Led the Vietnamese independence movement

✦

Inspired followers to make tremendous sacrifices

✦

Through personal leadership, held a beleaguered revolution together

✦

Leveraged very limited resources to enable his forces to outlast those of
his enemies

LIFE

Although his espousal of communism antagonized the Free World, most
notably the United States, Ho Chi Minh was a dynamic and inspiring
anticolonial leader. He became the first president of the Democratic
Republic of Vietnam (North Vietnam), serving from 1945 until his death
in 1969.

Born Nguyen That Thanh (and also called Nguyen Al Quoc), Ho
Chi Minh was the son of a poor country scholar in the village of Kim Lien.
The boy grew up in great poverty, yet nevertheless succeeded in gaining
an education at the grammar school in Hue, going on to become, for a
time, a schoolmaster himself. Later, he was apprenticed at a technical institute in Saigon. Ho left Vietnam (then called French Indochina) in 1911 to
work as a cook on a French luxury liner and then at a London hotel, where
he was employed through the period of World War I. As that conflict drew
to a close, Ho moved to France and there became active in the Socialist
Party. At the 1919 Paris Peace Conference, he unsuccessfully lobbied on
behalf of civil rights in Indochina. The frustration created by this experience radicalized the young man, who then became a founding member of

the French Communist Party, which sent him to the Soviet Union, where he studied revolutionary methods. Inducted into the Comintern—the international Communist organization controlled from Moscow—he was given the task of installing Communism throughout East Asia. Pursuant to this brief, Ho founded the Indochinese Communist Party in 1930 and, throughout the 1930s, lived in the Soviet Union and China.

With the outbreak of World War II, Ho returned to Vietnam, where, in 1941, he organized the Communist-controlled League for the Independence of Vietnam, or Viet Minh. This group led the resistance against the occupying forces of Japan. As leader of the Viet Minh, Ho worked with the Allies, including the United States OSS (precursor to the CIA), to undermine the Japanese occupying forces. At war's end, on September 2, 1945, Ho Chi Minh proclaimed the independence of the Democratic Republic of Vietnam and became its first president.

For the next 24 years, Ho Chi Minh served as president of a divided, perpetually warring people. He first led the Viet Minh in eight years of brutal—but highly effective—guerrilla warfare against France colonial forces from 1946 to 1954. After this, he vigorously supported the Viet Cong, successor to the Viet Minh, in another 15 years of costly battle against the anti-Communist South Vietnamese regime, which was established in Saigon pursuant to a 1954 United Nations conference in Geneva. Against overwhelming odds in a long war of attrition that spanned more than a generation, Ho Chi Minh guided the North Vietnamese spiritually as well as strategically. He leveraged very limited resources in a war that proved costly to all involved. In the end, however, it was the North Vietnamese who both lost the most and yet were the most willing to endure their losses. Largely through his personal leadership, the North Vietnamese made huge sacrifices, enduring massive loss of life, for the purpose of achieving independence within a communist context.

From 1959 to 1975, the United States became increasingly involved in the Vietnam War on the side of the anti-Communist South Vietnamese, committing more than half a million men to the effort by the end of the 1960s. Throughout the bitter struggle, Ho Chi Minh served as a symbol of unity under Communism for the two Vietnams, no matter what the cost—although his active role in the Vietnam War was steadily reduced beginning in 1959, when he began to suffer from ill health.

Ho Chi Minh did not live to see the Communist victory in 1975, which followed the U.S. withdrawal from South Vietnam, and which resulted in the unification of the country. Although Ho Chi Minh died on September 2, 1969, his official date of death was shifted to September 3 so that it would not coincide with Vietnam's National Day. His remains are enshrined in a mausoleum in Hanoi.

LEADERSHIP LESSONS

✦

Never underestimate the power of personal leadership; work to create inspiration.

✦

Never underestimate the compelling force of collective self-sacrifice toward a common goal.

✦

A leader cannot hesitate to identify himself entirely with his enterprise.

✦

Sometimes a leader must lead for endurance, not a quick, decisive action or attack. This is typically the most difficult kind of leadership.

Houston, Sam

Born: 1793   Died: 1863

Character model   Leverager   Motivator   Tactician   Visionary

LEADERSHIP ACHIEVEMENTS

◆

Led the Texas independence movement

◆

Leveraged a very small army to achieve a single great and decisive victory

◆

Provided an example of toleration and integrity in government

LIFE

More than any other individual, Houston was the architect of Texas independence from Mexico. He was a courageous and eminently practical visionary, a leader of a revolution that was both bold and moderate.

Houston was born near Lexington, Virginia, and spent his early childhood there before his family moved to Tennessee. The boy was given little formal schooling and grew up something of a wild child. As a youth, confronted with an "opportunity" to apprentice as a clerk in a local store, Houston ran off to live among the Cherokees. His sojourn among the Indians spanned 1808–11, when, incredibly enough, he set up briefly as a schoolteacher. In 1813, Houston was commissioned an ensign in the army and saw action under Andrew Jackson in combat against the Red Stick Creek Indians during the War of 1812. He participated in Jackson's major victory at the Battle of Horseshoe Bend on March 28, 1814.

The hitherto rebellious Houston took readily to army life. He served as a military subagent during the first phase of the grim removal of the Cherokees to Indian Territory (present-day Oklahoma) in 1817. The following year, Houston was promoted to first lieutenant, only to have his career cut short by a run-in with Secretary of War John C. Calhoun. Calhoun disciplined Houston for appearing before him in Indian dress and, more importantly, for having made an inquiry that called into question Calhoun's integrity in office. Offended by his treatment at the hands of the secretary of war, Houston abruptly resigned his commission in May 1818 and turned to the study of law. After the rough-and-ready preparation common on the frontier of his day, Houston was admitted to the bar in Nashville, Tennessee, late in 1818, just a few months after he had begun his studies. At about this time, he became increasingly interested in Tennessee politics, for which he seemed to have a natural inclination. He was chosen to serve as major general of the state militia in 1821 and, two years later, was elected to Congress. Houston served in the House until 1827, when he was elected governor of Tennessee. Reelected in 1829, he resigned in April of that year after his bride of three months deserted him, sending him into a profound depression.

Houston sought solace in the West, where, as he had done in youth, he took up residence among the Cherokees, who formally adopted him into their tribe in October 1829. Houston served the tribe as their representative to Washington, D.C., and became an advocate for the more equitable treatment not only of the Cherokees, but other tribes as well. President Jackson commissioned Houston to negotiate with several tribes in Texas during 1832. While Houston was in Texas as Jackson's envoy, he became increasingly involved in local politics and participated in the San Felipe Convention in April 1833, which drew up a constitution as well as a petition to the Mexican government for Mexican statehood. At this point, Houston decided to settle in Texas and, because of his military experience, was named to command the colony's small army in November 1835.

In the meantime, the Texas petition for full Mexican statehood was rejected, prompting Texans to meet in another convention, which declared independence on March 2, 1836. Houston, a leader of the convention, mobilized his army—all 740 men—after the fall of the Alamo to Mexican forces under Antonio Lopez de Santa Anna and the capture and massacre of Texas forces at Goliad. In one of the most astounding feats in American military history, Houston led his tiny army to victory over Santa Anna's vastly superior force of 1,600 well-equipped professional soldiers at the Battle of San Jacinto on April 21, 1836. The battle consumed a mere 18 minutes, in which Santa Anna and his men were completely routed. Houston's forces pursued, unleashing upon the Mexicans all the brutality Santa Anna had earlier directed against the Alamo defenders and the troops at Goliad. When the battle and its aftermath had ended, 630

Mexicans lay dead, a far greater number than all of the Texans who fell in the entire brief war. Texas casualties at San Jacinto were light, although Houston himself had been seriously wounded in the leg.

Houston did not exact revenge on Santa Anna, who had been captured after having ignominiously disguised himself as a private soldier. The Texas commander offered Santa Anna his life in exchange for his signature on the Treaty of Velasco, by which the Mexican leader agreed to recognize the former province as an independent republic.

Twice, Sam Houston was elected president of the Republic of Texas. When Texas was finally admitted as a state, Houston was elected senator in 1846 and was reappointed in 1852. Houston, a Democrat, did not vote with his party on issues relating to slavery and, as the Civil War drew near, he opposed secession. His support of the Union, unwavering, ensured that Texans would not return him to the Senate in 1858. Yet even the unpopularity of his views did not prevent his being elected governor in 1859. In 1861, he exercised all of his leadership influence in an attempt to block his state's secession from the Union. But it was to no avail. When Texas voted to secede, its governor refused to swear allegiance to the Confederacy. In March 1861, Houston was removed from office, and he retired to Huntsville, Texas, where he died two years later.

LEADERSHIP LESSONS

✦

Nothing is more valuable to a leader than integrity.

✦

Develop a personal leadership style that embodies the shared values of the enterprise.

✦

Act boldly and leverage your resources.

✦

Do not underestimate the motivating power of a great idea.

Ivan the Great

Born: 1440   Died: 1505

Conqueror   Rescuer   Strategist   Systems creator   Tactician   Visionary

LEADERSHIP ACHIEVEMENTS

✦

Learned lessons of leadership in a treacherous environment

✦

Conceived a vision of unifying Russia, and then dedicated his reign to realizing that vision

✦

Combined military prowess, diplomacy, and political maneuvering to acquire and consolidate territories

✦

Laid the foundation of the "modern" Russian nation

LIFE

Czar Ivan III, better known as Ivan the Great, led a series of remarkable military conquests and initiated a program of skillful diplomacy to free Russia from the feudal yoke of the Tatars of the Golden Horde and unite the disparate Russian principalities into a single kingdom. In Ivan is the beginning of the Russian nation.

He was born on January 22, 1440, in Moscow, in the heat of a great power struggle between his father, Vasily II, and his uncles. Ivan's earliest accomplishment as a leader was simply surviving this murderous environment. After his father was captured and blinded by Mongols in 1446, Ivan was hidden in a monastery—only to be betrayed to his father's enemies. Through a strange series of circumstances, however, Vasily's captors suddenly repented of their act and renewed their allegiance to Vasily, releasing him, blinded as he was, to rule again. This, of course, was also young Ivan's salvation. As heir to the throne, he was now given nominal command of a military unit and was always present when his father made policy decisions. The bright youngster kept his eyes and ears open, and thus learned the business of government in the treacherous world of feudal Russia.

When he was 18, in 1458, Ivan led a successful campaign against the Tatars. Following the death of his father in 1462, Ivan succeeded him as grand prince of Moscow. He was determined to break free of the web of feudal obligations that had bound his father and that had nearly resulted in his own death. The answer, Ivan concluded, was to unite all Russian lands under his sole control. With this vision in mind, he began a series of successful campaigns against the Golden Horde during 1467–69. Using his natural skill as a military commander, Ivan managed to free Russia of subservience to the Tatars in the east. This accomplished, he focused next on the powerful city-state of Novgorod. He led several unsuccessful attempts to take Novgorod by storm. When these failed, he laid siege against the city, which finally fell to him in 1478. Immediately, Ivan stripped Novgorod of all political autonomy, then annexed its possessions and colonized it with people who were loyal to him. Ivan understood that true conquest required more than merely capturing a place. The conquered people had to be absorbed into the very fabric of the nation.

Ivan also had no love for military conquest for its own sake. Whenever possible, he used diplomacy to acquire new realms, as when he took control of Yaroslavi and Rostov in 1474. By manipulating the Lithuanians, he attempted to take the city of Tver peacefully, but he finally had to resort to a show of force. The city capitulated in 1485. Ivan was also a master at manipulating the interests of others. He recognized the nature of conflicts between various groups within the realms he wished to acquire, and he exploited his understanding to play one tribe against another. For example, when Khan Ahmed of the Golden Horde allied himself with Poland-Lithuania, Ivan concluded an alliance with Khan Girei of the Crimea, and then led troops against Ahmed and crushed him, thereby freeing Moscow from any Tatar influence.

Ivan's singleminded focus on unification did take its toll. Following his great territorial gains, Ivan failed to distribute any land to his brothers. Worse, when his brother Yurii died, Ivan promptly seized all his possessions without apportioning any to his surviving brothers. Yet another brother voluntarily ceded all his lands to Ivan, which left two disaffected brothers, Boris and Andrei, aligned against Ivan. A willingness to compromise and share power with his brothers would have avoided much familial strife. As it was, Boris and Andrei approached King Casimir IV of Poland with a proposal for an alliance. Casimir turned them down, and they reconciled with Ivan. However, Andrei renewed his dispute with Ivan, who, at last, had his brother arrested in 1491. With Andrei confined, Ivan seized all his land. Three years later, on the death of Boris in 1494, half of his land fell to Ivan's control, the rest going to one of Boris's sons. Still, by the turn of the century, through a combination of conquest, diplomacy, and patience, Ivan had successfully acquired and united almost all of the Russian lands.

As successful as Ivan was in unifying Russia, he encountered great difficulty in designating an heir to the mighty throne he had created. The son of his first wife, Maria, vied for power with the son of his second wife, Zoë (or Sophia), causing great friction during the czar's final years. In the end, upon Ivan's death in 1505, it was the second wife's son, Vasily, who succeeded to the throne. He ruled a Russia that his father had set on a course to dominate the international politics of eastern Europe well into the 20th century.

LEADERSHIP LESSONS

✦

Value eclecticism. Master a variety of means to achieve your goals, and then use whatever works in a particular case.

✦

Never underestimate the power and value of vision to drive and focus action over the long term.

✦

Provide for your successor. Mentor your replacement. Failure to do so threatens the enterprise with dissent and dissolution.

Jackson, Andrew

Born: 1767   Died: 1845

Character model   Conqueror   Innovator   Problem solver   Visionary

LEADERSHIP ACHIEVEMENTS

✦

Achieved victory against the Red Stick Creek Indians in the War of 1812

✦

Acquired Spanish Florida for the United States

✦

Won a stunning victory at the Battle of New Orleans

✦

As an effective leader of mixed volunteer, militia, and regular army forces, proved he could forge diverse coalitions

✦

Imprinted his personality on the American political scene in ways that endure to this day

✦

Refocused American government on the needs of the "common man"

✦

Adopted policies that (for the most part) promoted the expansion of the American West

✦

Imprinted his leadership image on the "American character"

✦

Asserted and defended the supremacy of the Union over states' rights

LIFE

Jackson, a frontier commander and the seventh president of the United States, was hailed in his own day as the champion of the "common man." Although his role in the development of American democracy has been subject to critical historical review, his importance and effectiveness as a popular military and political leader are beyond question. Less clear, however, is whether Jackson was born in South or North Carolina, since his native Waxhaws settlement straddles the two. Most, but not all, authorities believe his parents, humble Scotch-Irish immigrants, lived on the South Carolina side. Jackson's father died before he was born, and the boy was given little formal education before his young life was shattered in 1780 by the brutal British invasion of the Carolinas during the American Revolution. His brothers, fighting in the Revolution, were captured at the Battle of Hanging Rock on August 1, 1780; one of them, Robert, died in captivity.

Although Andrew himself was too young to join the militia or the Continental Army, he became a patriot partisan and was subsequently captured, and then was severely wounded when an officer struck him with the flat of his sword after he refused an order to black the man's boots. In the meantime, Jackson's mother had volunteered to minister to American prisoners of war confined in miserable conditions on a ship anchored in Charleston Harbor. She contracted a disease then called prison fever, from which she died, leaving Andrew Jackson an orphan at age 14. The physical and emotional wounds Jackson suffered during the American Revolution planted within him an abiding hatred of the British and of political conservatism, which he associated with British notions of government by aristocracy.

Jackson's family was sufficiently well off to have left the boy with a modest inheritance—which, however, he quickly dissipated. Having sown his wild oats, Jackson settled down to the study of law and soon gained admission to the North Carolina bar. He then moved to Nashville, Tennessee, where, in 1791, he became attorney general for the Southwest Territory and, subsequently, circuit-riding solicitor in the area surrounding Nashville. Simultaneously, he served a number of private clients, many of whom were merchants who had suffered ruinous financial losses as a result of the extension of federal authority over the Tennessee territory. Based on this experience, Jackson began acquiring a reputation not only as a fighter against British imperial tyranny, but also against what he deemed federal tyranny. His stand against the growing power of the federal government made him very popular in Tennessee.

In 1791, Jackson married Rachel Donelson Robards. Robards made no secret of having been married before, but both she and Jackson believed that she and her first husband had been legally divorced. When this proved not to be the case, the couple remarried in 1794, but the implication of dishonor would haunt Jackson's private and political life for many years, ultimately becoming the subject of a duel. In the meantime, however, the political career of the popular Jackson developed apace. He was named a delegate to the Tennessee constitutional convention in 1796 and was elected to Congress from the newly formed state, serving from 1796 to 1797. He rapidly earned a fearsome reputation as an opponent of the Washington administration's conciliatory stance toward Great Britain and the Indian tribes that had sided with the British during the Revolution. In 1797, Jackson was appointed to serve out the senatorial term of his political mentor, William Blount, who had been expelled from the Senate as a result of his involvement in a British plan to seize Florida and Louisiana from Spain.

Despite the rise of his political star, Jackson was burdened by serious financial problems, and, in 1798, on the verge of bankruptcy, he decided that he had no choice but to resign from the Senate. He returned to Tennessee in order to set about rebuilding his fortune. For a number of years, from 1798 to 1804, he tried to combine private practice and other enterprises with public service as a Tennessee superior court judge, but he finally stepped down to devote himself full-time to private business. It was during this period that he built his famous plantation, the Hermitage, now a great national landmark outside of Nashville.

Although Jackson had become locally prosperous, his political career seemed to be over. And there was worse trouble, for in 1805, Jackson voiced support for Aaron Burr's illegal, hyperambitious, even traitorous scheme to create an empire stretching from the Ohio River to Mexico. To a slight degree, Jackson even became involved in the scheme. Although he subsequently repudiated Burr, Jackson was soundly rebuffed by President Thomas Jefferson when he sought office as governor of the newly purchased Louisiana Territory.

In 1806, one Charles Dickinson, a Nashville resident, insulted Rachel Jackson (basing his insults on her marital status) and published personal attacks on Jackson in the local newspaper. In a mood of general frustration and discouragement, Jackson challenged Dickinson to a duel, in which the young man was killed on May 30 and Jackson himself seriously wounded. Although "men of honor" still dueled in the United States, the practice was illegal and, in most circles, deemed barbaric. Now it seemed as if Andrew Jackson had definitively disqualified himself from politics.

Indeed, the public heard little more of Jackson until William Blount, by then governor of Tennessee, commissioned him major general of volunteers in the War of 1812. He proved a remarkably bold and effective commander, whose men were fiercely loyal to him. Toward the end of the war, in 1814, he marched against the pro-British Red Stick Creek Indians, defeating them in the decisive Battle of Horseshoe Bend on March 27. In itself, Horseshoe Bend was an important military victory. Jackson leveraged it into a major territorial acquisition by compelling all of the Indians of the region—hostiles, friendlies, neutrals, and even allies—to cede enormous tracts of land throughout Alabama and Georgia. Most of the War of 1812 had been a disastrous disappointment for the United States, a series of defeats, but Jackson had won a major territory and was hailed not only as a backwoods military genius, but as a man who knew how to handle Indians.

Following his success against the Red Sticks, Jackson was appointed to command the defense of New Orleans, the key Mississippi River and gulf port, which was now imperiled by British forces. Jackson pulled together disparate groups of volunteers, militiamen, regular army troops, and even the forces of the gulf pirate Jean Lafitte to mount a brilliant defense, which he used as the basis for a fierce counteroffensive against the attackers. The British were severely defeated on January 8, 1815, in one of the few formal, set-piece battles in the War of 1812 in which Americans could claim a clear-cut victory. As fate would have it, by the time the Battle of New Orleans was fought, representatives of the belligerents had already concluded the Treaty of Ghent (Belgium), which formally ended hostilities on December 24, 1814. Word of the treaty did not reach either Jackson or the British commander before the battle. That the Battle of New Orleans was fought after the war had ended hardly mattered to most Americans. Jackson's signal victory was greeted as a vindication of national honor in a war that had rarely gone well for the United States. Overnight, Jackson became a popular hero—indeed, a popular icon of American courage, military skill, and conviction of righteousness.

Jackson might have entered politics at this point, but chose instead to continue his military career. In 1817, he led the nation's first war against the Seminole Indians, mercilessly evicting them from their tribal homelands and pursuing them deep into Spanish Florida through the spring of 1818. Acting on his own initiative, Jackson freely expanded his mandate and mission as nothing less than the conquest of Florida, at the time a

Spanish possession. Thus he not only campaigned against the Indians, but audaciously deposed Spanish colonial authorities and others. In the name of national conquest, Jackson acted with ruthless zeal. He captured one Lieutenant Robert Armbrister of the British Royal Marines and an elderly Scots trader named Alexander Arbuthnot, charged both with aiding and abetting the Indians, convened a drumhead court, convicted both men, and hanged them. Following this summary action, he seized Spanish-held Pensacola on May 26, 1818.

Jackson's peremptory action precipitated diplomatic action in the form of the Adams-Onis treaty of 1819, by which Spain formally ceded Florida to the United States. Once again, thanks to Jackson, the United States had gained a vast territory; however, Jackson's high-handed and ultimately lawless conduct provoked conservative elements in Congress to seek his censure. Their failure proved that the advocate of the "common man" had become too popular to stop.

In 1821, Jackson resigned his army commission to become provisional territorial governor of Florida. The following year, the Tennessee legislature nominated him for the presidency, and then, in 1823, elected him to the U.S. Senate. In 1824, Jackson did run for president, only to be defeated by John Quincy Adams in a narrow election that, bitterly contested, had to be decided by the House of Representatives. When Jackson ran again in 1828, he won by a comfortable margin.

President Jackson capitalized on his popular image as a leader risen from the ranks of the common man. He disdained the traditional carriage ride to the White House and instead made the trip on horseback. Instead of the patrician inaugural ball, he planned a quiet celebration in the executive mansion. "The people"—the masses who had put Jackson in the White House—made the event anything but quiet, however. Crowds thronging the streets to cheer their new president now invited themselves to the private reception and nearly wrecked the White House in the process.

No one can dispute that Andrew Jackson's two terms as president—from 1829 to 1837—introduced an unprecedented degree of democracy to American government. Jackson's contemporaries, as well as subsequent generations of historians, have hotly debated whether the *kind* of democracy his administration fostered was always a good thing. Thanks directly to Jackson's leadership, during his administration most states abandoned property ownership as a prerequisite for eligibility to vote. Even as this movement expanded the electorate, making elected officials more fully representative of the people, it also encouraged a high degree of demagoguery. Similarly, although Jackson introduced a policy of equitable rotation in federal jobs—an important reform that was the forerunner of the modern civil service system—he also brought with him the so-called "spoils system," political patronage, whereby political supporters were rewarded with lucrative government employment. Jackson also opposed the program of internal improvements that had been sponsored by Henry Clay and John Quincy Adams, arguing passionately that the plan favored the wealthy. This may well have been the case, yet, in defeating federally funded roads and canals, Jackson retarded the development of commerce in the West—the very region of his constituency.

Jackson was a firm believer in the paramount importance of preserving the Union. This led to his vigorous and uncompromising response to the Nullification Crisis of 1832. The crisis came about over tariffs imposed on imports. Jackson's Southern constituents opposed such tariffs, whereas supporters in other regions—where manufacturing was struggling to establish itself—favored the protection tariffs would provide. Southerners had protested the tariffs established by Jackson's predecessor, John Quincy Adams, and they were profoundly disappointed when Jackson lowered them only slightly in 1832. Accordingly, on November 24, 1832, South Carolina acted on the doctrine of nullification espoused by one of its favorite sons, John C. Calhoun, who, in turn, based the doctrine on Thomas Jefferson. Nullification held that an individual state had the right to nullify within its borders any federal act the state judged to be unconstitutional. South Carolina declared both the tariffs of 1828 and 1832 null and void and prohibited the collection of tariffs in South Carolina after February 1, 1833.

Jackson rose to this unprecedented challenge to the authority of the federal government. On December 10, 1832, he issued the Nullification Proclamation, announcing his intention to enforce the law—although he also pledged to come up with a compromise tariff. South Carolina backed down, and civil war was postponed for almost 30 years.

In modern eyes, Jackson's response to the Nullification Crisis seems noble, even heroic. Yet his commitment to preserving the Union also moved him to take steps to silence the growing abolitionist movement, fearing that those who wanted to end slavery would tear the nation apart. In this, he seems less like a great moral leader.

Another key leadership stand Jackson took was against the Second Bank of the United States, which Missouri senator Thomas Hart Benton dubbed "the Monster." The purpose of the bank was to stabilize the economy by tightening credit and recentering U.S. currency on gold and silver. However, the bank undoubtedly created hardship for small merchants, farmers, and anyone struggling for a financial start in life. All three of these groups were prevalent in the West. When the bank's charter came up for renewal, Jackson opposed it by vetoing a recharter bill. After he won election to a second term in 1832, Jackson issued an executive order withdrawing all federal deposits from the bank. This was a fatal blow, and the bank closed its doors when its charter expired in 1836. Thanks to Jackson, credit became more plentiful and westward settlement proceeded more rapidly. The cost, however, was economic instability throughout the rest of the 19th century—especially in the West, which was plagued by a boom-and-bust economy.

Certainly the most troubling action of Jackson's presidency was his endorsement and enforcement of the 1830 Indian Removal Act, by which most of the eastern Indian tribes were ordered removed—at the point of a bayonet—to Indian Territory west of the Mississippi River, an area encompassing modern Oklahoma and parts of other states. Yet however we judge the achievements of Jackson's two terms as president, his leadership brought about such profound changes in American government that the era became known as the Age of Jackson.

Jackson's later years, including his final years as president, were plagued by ill health. He retired to the Hermitage after his second term ended, but remained a powerful force in the Democratic party until his death in 1845.

IN HIS OWN WORDS

"By the Eternal, they shall not sleep on our soil!"

—On learning that the British army had landed near New Orleans, December 23, 1814

"I will smash them, so help me God!"

—At the Battle of New Orleans, 1815

"Our federal union: it must be preserved."
—Toast at Thomas Jefferson's birthday celebration, 1830

"As long as our Government is administered for the good of the people, and is regulated by their will; as long as it secures to us the rights of person and of property, liberty of conscience and of the press, it will be worth defending."
—First Inaugural Address, March 4, 1829

". . . If I have mistaken the interests and wishes of the people the Constitution affords the means of soon redressing the error by selecting . . . a citizen whose opinions may accord with their own."
—Message to Congress, December 6, 1830

"There are no necessary evils in government. Its evils exist only in its abuses. If it would confine itself to equal protection, and, as Heaven does its rains, shower its favors alike on the high and the low, the rich and the poor, it would be an unqualified blessing."
—Message to Congress vetoing the renewal of the charter of the Second Bank of the United States, July 10, 1832

"Without union our independence and liberty would never have been achieved; without union they never can be maintained."
—Second Inaugural Address, March 4, 1833

LEADERSHIP LESSONS

Develop a personal leadership style that commands, rewards, and reciprocates loyalty.

Effective leaders typically possess and exploit the "common touch."

Consider the power of a leadership philosophy of maximum inclusiveness.

Be aware of the potential power of the leader's personality. It can percolate throughout the entire enterprise, which may become, for better or worse, a collective projection of the leader's attitudes and expressed personality.

Jackson, Thomas "Stonewall"

Born: 1824 Died: 1863

Character model   Leverager   Motivator   Tactician

LEADERSHIP ACHIEVEMENTS

✦

Was one the greatest examples in all military history of effective
personal leadership

✦

Possessed and exhibited boundless personal courage

✦

Used minimal resources to maximum advantage, always exploiting the
fighting spirit of his men, even against numerically superior forces

✦

Mastered tactics and was able to execute them smartly and efficiently

✦

Combined mastery of tactics with a spirit of ceaseless aggression

✦

Built absolute loyalty among his command

LIFE

As a Confederate general of the Civil War, Stonewall Jackson is second in
fame only to Robert E. Lee. His leadership was founded on a combination
of personal intensity, which commanded willing obedience, and tremendous tactical skill, which extracted victory against all odds. He was born in
Clarksburg, Virginia (now West Virginia), and graduated from West Point
in 1846 with a commission in the artillery. Immediately upon graduation,
Jackson saw combat in the U.S.–Mexican War under the command of
General Winfield Scott. He distinguished himself for his steely calm and
conspicuous gallantry at the Battle of Veracruz (March 27, 1847), at Cerro
Gordo (April 18), and the culminating Battle of Chapultepec (September
13). This last action occasioned his brevet promotion (a promotion for
bravery) to major.

Jackson left the army in February 1851 and took a position as professor of artillery tactics and natural philosophy at Virginia Military

Institute, serving from 1851 to April 1861, when he was commissioned colonel of Confederate volunteers. Promoted to brigadier general on June 17, he turned the tide at the First Battle of Bull Run on July 21. The forces of Union general Irvin McDowell at first drove the Confederates from their defensive positions and even managed to turn the Confederate left flank. That is when Jackson suddenly materialized with his brigade of utterly unwavering Virginians. Confederate general Barnard Bee (destined to sustain a mortal wound later in this battle and die the next day) saw Jackson and his men press the attack. He called out to all within hearing: "There's Jackson standing like a stone wall!" Then Bee gallantly gestured with his sword, calling out: "Rally behind the Virginians!"

And that is what the Confederates did, in an action that began to turn the tide of battle against the Union. As for Jackson, Bee's remark became his nickname. He was known as "Stonewall" from that day on, and his command was dubbed the "Stonewall Brigade."

For the rest of that afternoon, the First Battle of Bull Run seesawed. At last, Jackson decided that it was time to stop fighting a defensive battle and seize the initiative. His forces massed for a decisive counterthrust. "Yell like Furies," Jackson ordered his men as they charged. In this moment of inspiration, Jackson invented the fabled "rebel yell"—a high-pitched keening that was otherworldly and utterly terrifying on the battlefield. Combined with the ferocity of the attack, its effect was galvanic. The Union lines instantly crumbled, and terror-stricken soldiers fled before the pursuing enemy.

In October, Jackson was promoted to major general and, the next month, was appointed commander of all forces in the Shenandoah Valley. In this capacity, he conducted a masterful campaign against far superior Union numbers, successfully blocking reinforcement of Union general George B. McClellan's advance on Richmond during 1862. Although Jackson was defeated at Kernstown (near Winchester, Virginia) on March 23, even in defeat he did not falter, but managed a comeback by outmaneuvering and then whipping Union forces at Front Royal on May 23. This was followed by stunning victories at Winchester (May 24–25), Cross Keys (June 8), and Port Republic (June 9), by which he drove the Union forces out of the Shenandoah Valley.

After his triumphs in the valley, Jackson was ordered to Richmond, where he supported Lee's efforts to drive McClellan from the Peninsula during the series of bloody battles known as the Seven Days (June 26–July 2). After this, on August 27, Jackson engaged General John Pope's army in northern Virginia, first destroying its depot at Manassas Junction and then beating back its attack at the Battle of Groveton (August 28). During the next two days, Jackson was instrumental in the Confederate victory at the Second Battle of Bull Run. He was also a central commander in the Confederate invasion of Maryland, earning distinction at the Battle of Antietam on September 17. By October, Jackson had been promoted to lieutenant general and was made commander of II Corps. In this capacity, he commanded the right flank at Fredericksburg, Virginia, on December 13, and dealt Union commander Ambrose Burnside a terrible defeat. At Chancellorsville, during May 2–4, 1863, Jackson trapped the forces of Union general Joseph Hooker, who, like Burnside before him, led his forces to a disastrously costly defeat. During this battle, however, Jackson, as always, did not hesitate to expose himself to danger. He fell victim to friendly fire, mistakenly shot by one of his own troops. His left arm, badly mangled, had to be amputated. Visiting Jackson, Robert E. Lee remarked: "You have lost your left [arm]. I have lost my right arm." But there was worse to come. Like many grievously wounded in an era before antiseptics and antibiotics, Jackson developed a fatal infection and succumbed to pneumonia within a week of his injury.

The Confederate cause never recovered from the loss of this inspired and inspiring commander, who was not only a consummate tactician, but a personally fearless and ever-aggressive example to his subordinates. He was regarded as a peculiar man, religious to the point of fanaticism and a disciplinarian of unsparing sternness. Yet his men thoroughly identified with him, gave him absolute loyalty, and even loved him. They would have followed him anywhere.

IN HIS OWN WORDS

"Always mystify, mislead, and surprise the enemy if possible."
  —Attributed

"I like liquor—its taste and its effects—and that is just the reason why I never drink it."
  —Attributed

"Resolve to perform what you ought; perform without fail what you resolve."

—Attributed

"If officers desire to have control over their commands, they must remain habitually with them, industriously attend to their instruction and comfort, and in battle lead them well."

—Attributed

LEADERSHIP LESSONS

✦

Do not underestimate the power of morale among the members of your enterprise.

✦

Build confidence in your leadership.

✦

Do not hesitate to develop a personal leadership style and project a personal leadership image.

✦

Identify with your cause or your enterprise. You are the symbol of purpose for those you lead.

✦

There is no substitute for physical and moral courage.

✦

Master your art, your field, your profession. Perform from a level of high mastery.

Jefferson, Thomas

Born: 1743   Died: 1826

Character model   Innovator   Mentor   Motivator   Strategist   Visionary

LEADERSHIP ACHIEVEMENTS

✦

Was a prime intellectual leader of the American Revolution

✦

Wrote the Declaration of Independence

✦

Was governor of Virginia during the Revolution

✦

Drafted groundbreaking legislation on freedom of religion

✦

Served as ambassador to France

✦

Served as the first U.S. secretary of state

✦

Was the second U.S. vice president

✦

Created the Democratic–Republican party, which successfully opposed
autocratic Federalism

✦

Was the third president of the United States

✦

Made the Louisiana Purchase and commissioned
the Lewis and Clark Expedition

✦

Triumphed over international gangsterism in the Barbary wars

✦

Was an early cultural and scientific leader in the United States

✦

Became an author of international renown

✦

Was an architect of great distinction

✦

Was the father of the University of Virginia

L I F E

Author of the Declaration of Independence, third president of the United States, far-seeing purchaser of the vast Louisiana Territory, Thomas Jefferson was, like many of the other founding fathers, a man of many parts. However, the range of his interests and accomplishments is astounding even among that remarkable group. Born in the Virginia Piedmont, on his father's Albemarle County plantation, Jefferson received a classical education from local worthies, attended the College of William and Mary in the Virginia colonial capital of Williamsburg, and then apprenticed in law and became a brilliant attorney. He began his political career as a member of Virginia's House of Burgesses, the most venerable legislative body in colonial America.

In school and college, Jefferson was attracted to the great writers and thinkers of classical Greece and Rome as well as the architects of the Age of Enlightenment, the likes of Descartes, Voltaire, and Rousseau, and, among the English philosophers, Hume and Locke. The combination of his classical grounding and willingness to embrace the cutting-edge thought of his day helped propel Jefferson to a position at the intellectual forefront of the growing independence movement in America. In 1774, at the age of 41, he wrote and published *A Summary View of the Rights of British America,* a radical but well-reasoned and utterly unflinching indictment of the British crown and a key statement of the motives for revolution. Two years later, Jefferson's colleagues in the Continental Congress persuaded him to draft the Declaration of Independence. In this document, Jefferson defined and expressed the controlling ideas and ideals of the struggle for American liberty. He justified the Revolution to Americans, to the world, and to history itself. It was, perhaps, his single most momentous act of ideological leadership.

In the same year as the Declaration, 1776, Jefferson served in Virginia's House of Delegates and, almost single-handedly, undertook the staggering task of revising Virginia's outworn body of archaic British law into a set of modern statutes better suited to a new republic built on the rule of reason.

While others fought the military battles of the American Revolution, Jefferson led that struggle on its ideological front. In 1777, he drafted the Virginia Statute for Religious Freedom, a model for universal tolerance and the separation of church and state. In 1778, he drew up a Bill for the

More General Diffusion of Knowledge, embodying a complete plan for universal public education. Jefferson believed that only through widespread education could a free people intelligently govern themselves. As Jefferson saw it, knowledge was the firmest foundation of liberty.

From 1779 to 1781, Jefferson served as the first governor of revolutionary Virginia; in 1783, he was a delegate to the Continental Congress, and from 1784 to 1789, he served as the U.S. minister plenipotentiary— effectively, ambassador—to France. While there he secretly advised those who were planning the French Revolution. He also used his time in Europe to complete work on *Notes on the State of Virginia,* an extraordinary, comprehensive natural history of what was then the nation's largest state. Both lyrical and scientific, the book presented American nature at its most impressive and earned Jefferson worldwide acclaim as a naturalist and author. First published in the United States in 1788, it has never since been out of print.

As with the other founding fathers, Jefferson's leadership in the Revolution required great personal courage and commitment. Yet there was always an intellectual direction in Jefferson's contribution to the early life of the American republic. He was equally interested in American politics and American science. From 1797 to 1815, he served as president of the American Philosophical Society—the nation's most prestigious scientific association—even when he was in the thick of early American politics.

Jefferson served in the cabinet of George Washington as the nation's first secretary of state from 1790 to 1793. Dissatisfied with the conservative politics of the Federalists (who, as Jefferson saw it, invested too much power in the central government and had too little trust in the American people), Jefferson collaborated with his protégé, friend, and fellow Virginian James Madison to create a liberal party to oppose the Federalists. Under the banner of the still-embryonic Democratic–Republican party, Jefferson challenged John Adams, an old friend but now a political rival, for the presidency. Under the Constitution as it then was, Jefferson, who came in a close second behind Adams, served as vice president in the Adams administration from 1797 to 1801. The vice-president–elect arrived in Philadelphia (then the capital of the United States) carrying in his baggage the fossilized bones of a prehistoric creature to add to the collection of the American Philosophical Society headquartered in that city.

Jefferson successfully led the liberal opposition to the sometimes oppressive Federalist policies of Adams and his even more autocratic secretary of the treasury, Alexander Hamilton. In 1800 his opposition culminated in his landslide election to the presidency over the incumbent Adams. During his two terms, from 1801 to 1809, Jefferson redefined the presidency, shifting it markedly from what it had been under Washington and Adams. He liberalized the office, and he reconceived the president less as a head of state, a solo ruler, than as a genuine chief executive who worked collaboratively with a cabinet entrusted with more authority than either Washington or Adams had been willing to give.

In his effort to democratize American government, Jefferson saw to the complete dismantling of the Alien and Sedition Acts passed under the Adams administration. The Alien Act was overturned: No longer would newcomers have to wait 14 years before applying for citizenship; 5 years of residence would secure this privilege—and no longer did resident aliens have to fear instant deportation at the whim of the president. As for the Sedition Act, it would no longer be a federal crime for persons to assemble "with intent to oppose any measure of government" or to print, utter, or publish anything "false, scandalous, and malicious" against the government. Jefferson positively invited criticism, and he even voiced his belief that periodic revolution in government was good for a nation.

During his presidency, Jefferson successfully conducted a war with the Barbary States, North African countries whose state-sponsored piracy preyed on U.S. as well as European shipping. This triumph greatly enhanced the international prestige of the United States and affirmed its ability to enforce its sovereignty. Jefferson was not a warlike leader, but he was willing to commit the nation to armed conflict to achieve a worthwhile and enduring goal.

History honors the Jefferson administration most for the Louisiana Purchase, by which Jefferson more than doubled the extent of the new nation—and did so peacefully. Both Washington and Adams rose to greatness in office, but more than either of his predecessors, Jefferson led toward the future, a future he conceived as tied to the nation's western expansion. The Louisiana Purchase also excited Jefferson's scientific curiosity, of course. Even before the purchase had been finalized, he commissioned the great Lewis and Clark Expedition, which brought back a trove of scientific discoveries from the great West.

The Jefferson presidency was intensely personal, reflecting a leadership style quite different from that of Washington and the even more aloof Adams. Using his own funds, Jefferson hosted weekly dinners at the White House, which were attended by personally invited guests from Jefferson's own party, from the opposition, and from every important profession, as well as by foreign diplomats and dignitaries. Jefferson believed that, in leadership, there was no substitute for personal contact—for people explaining themselves to each other in person.

Jefferson emerged from his first term an extraordinarily popular man. His second term proved less successful. Confronted by interference in international trade from Great Britain, Jefferson sought a means of chastising that nation without precipitating war. He instituted an embargo on all British goods, hoping thereby to punish Britain where it was most vulnerable: the pocketbook. Instead, the embargo created economic hardship and discontent at home, while causing further deterioration in Anglo–American relations. It was the one great failure of Jefferson's presidency.

Like Washington before him, Jefferson declined to stand for a third term. He returned to Monticello, where he could pursue such passions as architecture, literature, music, and gardening. At age 80, Jefferson designed the campus and buildings of the University of Virginia. Moreover, he became the institution's father, drafting the state legislation that created it, drawing up its curriculum, articulating its forward-looking academic philosophy, and even directing the recruitment of its first faculty. In addition to working on the university, Jefferson spent his "retirement" improving Monticello and its associated plantation. He continued his scientific studies, and he wrote voluminous correspondence, the most impressive being with his former political rival, John Adams, with whom he was now reconciled in affectionate and respectful friendship. The two men, great leaders representing opposite ends of what was, after all, the same democratic spectrum, died on the same day in 1826: July 4, the 50th anniversary of the Declaration of Independence.

IN HIS OWN WORDS

"I would rather be exposed to the inconveniences attending too much liberty than to those attending too small a degree of it."
—Letter to Archibald Stuart, 1791

"All power is inherent in the people."
—Letter to John Cartwright, 1824

"I hold it that a little rebellion, now and then, is a good thing, and as necessary in the political world as storms are in the physical."
—Letter to James Madison, 1787

"Governments are instituted among men, deriving their just powers from the consent of the governed."
—Declaration of Independence, 1776

LEADERSHIP LESSONS

✦

A great leader has faith and confidence in those he leads.

✦

Great leaders are guided by great principles.

✦

Mentor those you lead. The more they know, the more successful your enterprise is likely to become.

✦

Curiosity is one appetite you should never seek to suppress.

✦

There is no substitute for personal leadership based on personal contact.

✦

Explain yourself and invite others to explain themselves.

✦

Refuse to stop learning.

✦

Consider the virtues of collaborative leadership. Surround yourself with able advisers. Listen to them. Remain open to them. Then make your decision.

✦

Always lead with an eye toward the future.

Joan of Arc

Born: ca. 1412   Died: 1431

Character model   Motivator   Rescuer   Tactician   Visionary

LEADERSHIP ACHIEVEMENTS

✦

Translated personal faith into action on a national scale

✦

Infused others with her own deepest beliefs

✦

Transformed a lost cause into the foundation of victory

✦

United disparate and discouraged officers and soldiers under
her leadership

✦

Created a powerful group identity that created a French nation

✦

Achieved important victories against the English occupiers of France

LIFE

Joan of Arc—Jeanne d'Arc or, in medieval French, Jehanne Darc, and, later, Saint Joan—was a French village girl who, claiming divine inspiration, led the French army against the English during the Hundred Years' War. She entered history not only as the French national heroine, but also as a beloved national saint.

Joan was born in the village of Domrémy, between Champagne and Lorraine, a quiet, pious child, who, by all reports, was well loved in her tranquil village. While all was harmonious in Domrémy, France at this time was in turmoil and distress. The throne was occupied by Charles VI de Valois, called Charles the Mad because of the mental illness that rendered him unable to govern. The actual government was in the hands of the dukes of Orléans, Burgundy, Berri, and Bourbon, as well as Queen Isabel. When Duke Louis of Orléans was assassinated on the orders of his cousin Duke Jean-sans-Peur de Burgundy in 1407, civil war broke out, with the result that France became divided between the Orléanist (or

Armagnac) faction and the partisans of Burgundy. While civil violence raged periodically in France, war with England was renewed in 1415 after the collapse of the Truce of Leulinghen. English king Henry V invaded Normandy in August 1415, taking the port city of Harfleur and then spectacularly defeating the French royal army at the Battle of Agincourt on October 25. For the French, defeat was humiliating and total. The English, outnumbered eight to one, nevertheless inflicted some 10,000 French casualties out of an army of 40,000. Among the nobility, losses were especially great, and the French government was thrown into chaos. Particularly hard hit was the Orléanist aristocracy. The principal Orléanist, and probably the ablest leader in France, Duke Charles d'Orléans, was captured and was destined to languish for 25 years as a prisoner of war.

In 1419, Duke Jean-sans-Peur de Burgundy was assassinated by partisans of Charles de Ponthieu, the dauphin (who would later become Charles VII). This propelled Jean's successor, Philippe-le-Bon, into the arms of the English with a full alliance. He signed the Treaty of Troyes in 1420, granting England's Henry V eventual title to the kingdom of France and presenting to him the hand in marriage of Catherine, daughter of Charles the Mad. The treaty thus disowned the dauphin, and France was effectively divided between Henry V and the Duke of Burgundy. One of the principal negotiators of the treaty was Pierre Cauchon, whom the Duke of Burgundy repaid by securing for him a profitable seat as bishop. From this position, Cauchon would later prosecute Joan, on behalf of the English, for heresy.

In 1422, both Henry V and Charles VI died, leaving the infant Henry VI as the king of both England and France. In France, the Duke of Bedford served as his regent and devoted much effort to creating alliances with the Dukes of Brittany and Burgundy while fighting forces of the dauphin—and generally defeating them. After Bedford's victories at Cravant (July 31, 1423) and Verneuil (August 17, 1424), the dauphinists became thoroughly demoralized.

It was at about this time, probably during the summer of 1424, that Joan, aged 13, began to have visions and to hear voices, which she later identified as those of Saint Catherine, Saint Margaret, and Saint Michael. The voices told her to raise an army to lift the English siege against Orléans and to embark on a mission to liberate France from English domination. Joan kept her voices secret for some five years, and then, in 1429, finally left Domrémy and, under escort, traveled to the court of the dauphin. In an audience, Joan attempted to persuade the dauphin to organize renewed resistance against the English and the Burgundians. The dauphin responded by subjecting Joan to tests administered by a body of clerics. The skeptical men of religion, persuaded by this guileless girl, issued a report to the dauphin, which prompted him to assemble his troops and place them under Joan's direct command. Thus she came to lead an expedition sent to the relief of Orléans, which had been under English siege for eight months.

In an eight-day battle in May 1429, Joan—aided by the experienced military commander Etienne de Vignolles, called La Hire—lifted the siege. Having achieved this victory, Joan next persuaded the dauphin to take the offensive, break through to Reims, and there accept coronation as the rightful king of France. Again Joan was given command, and she led French forces to victory over the English army of Sir John Fastolf and John Talbot, Earl of Shrewsbury, at the Battle of Patay (June 15, 1429). She not only took Shrewsbury prisoner, but decimated the English army, and thus the dauphin broke through to Reims by July 16 and was crowned.

After the coronation, Joan continued to lead the French army during July and August, gaining the submission of several towns to Charles VII, including Senlis, Beauvais, and Compiègne. She next marched on Paris, but failed to take that city and was wounded in battle on September 8. On September 22, the army disbanded at Gien, and Joan wintered with Charles VII from October until April 1430, when she set out to defend Compiègne from Burgundian attack. Arriving at Compiègne on May 14, she began the defense, but John of Luxembourg's Burgundian army was quick to lay down a massive siege on May 22. In a sortie out of the town, Joan was unhorsed and became John's prisoner on May 23.

At Rouen, during March 25–May 24, 1431, the Burgundians tried and convicted her of heresy. Sentenced to death, she recanted her visions on the scaffold on May 24 and was thereupon released to the justice of secular authority. An English court then sentenced her to life imprisonment. On May 29, however, judges who visited her in her cell determined that she had abjured her recantation. Some authorities believe that she did indeed deliberately abjure her recantation and asserted the truthfulness of her voices. Others conclude that the English judges were merely looking for a way of executing her—permanently removing her as a threat. In either case, she was burned at the stake as a heretic on May 30, 1431.

In 1456, a "trial of rehabilitation" officially reversed the verdict of the 1431 court, and Joan was generally revered as a great political and spiritual heroine. In 1903, she was formally proposed for canonization and, after a long process, was made a Roman Catholic saint on May 16, 1920.

Whether or not Joan was divinely inspired is a matter of faith. Beyond question is that she was an extraordinary leader, possessed of a powerful ability to inspire and persuade and, moreover, possessed of prodigious natural talent as a military commander with a sound intuitive grasp of tactics. In his *Birth of Britain,* Winston Churchill wrote: "Joan was a being so uplifted from the ordinary run of mankind that she finds no equal in a thousand years."

LEADERSHIP LESSONS

✦

Faith moves mountains—provided that you can convey your faith to others.

✦

A visionary single-mindedness makes for powerful leadership.

✦

Become receptive to your own best beliefs. Act on them.

✦

When you know what is right, do right.

✦

Moral courage attracts a following.

Jones, John Paul

Born: 1747 Died: 1792

Character model   Improviser   Innovator   Leverager   Motivator   Tactician

LEADERSHIP ACHIEVEMENTS

✦

Through personal courage, charismatic leadership, and consummate and innovative seamanship, leveraged the tiny Continental Navy into a highly effective weapon against vastly superior British forces

✦

Continually defied the odds to achieve outstanding results

✦

Through his victories, gave the often-flagging American Revolution a much-needed injection of morale

✦

Created a great founding tradition for the U.S. Navy

LIFE

John Paul Jones served the cause of independence in the American Revolution as a virtual one-man navy. His seamanship was extraordinary, his courage was boundless, and his men followed him unquestioningly.

The son of a gardener, he was born John Paul, near Kirkbean, Kirkcudbrightshire, on Solway Firth, Scotland. As a youth, John Paul went to sea as a cabin boy aboard a merchant vessel. On his first voyage, in 1759, he visited an elder brother living in Fredericksburg, Virginia, and so came to an early familiarity with America. In 1766, the bankruptcy of his employer ended Paul's stint as a cabin boy, and he was thrust into the post of chief mate on a Jamaican slave-trading vessel. It did not take long for the young man to become disgusted with the slave trade. In 1768, he left the slaver and took ship for Scotland in what proved a most fateful voyage. After the captain and the first mate died en route, Paul assumed command and took the ship safely home. The vessel's owners were so grateful that they rewarded Paul with command of another of their ships, the merchantman *John,* out of Dumfries, Scotland.

This appointment likewise proved fateful. During a voyage to Tobago, West Indies, Jones disciplined a sailor by flogging—the accepted disciplinary practice of the era. The sailor, however, deserted, jumped ship, and soon died, presumably of his wounds, aboard another vessel in April 1770. On his return to Scotland in November, Jones was arrested and jailed for murder, but was released on bail to obtain evidence that would exonerate him. Incredibly, while voyaging to Tobago to obtain witness accounts, Paul unintentionally killed a mutinous sailor in December 1773. Fearing now that he would stand no chance in a trial, John Paul disguised his name by adding Jones to the end of it and fled to America, where he participated in the settlement of his late brother's Fredericksburg estate in 1774.

With the outbreak of the American Revolution, Jones was hired by the Continental Congress to fit out the 20-gun *Alfred,* the first ship purchased by the new government. Four days after hoisting the new nation's colors over the vessel on December 3, 1775, Jones was commissioned senior lieutenant in the Continental Navy. He then sailed with the fleet to the Bahamas, where he participated in the capture of New Providence during March 1776.

On April 6, 1776, Esek Hopkins, the senior commander of the Continental Navy, led five U.S. ships back from the West Indies when the 20-gun British frigate *Glasgow* attacked the flotilla around midnight, off Block Island, New York. The *Glasgow* inflicted 24 casualties among the American sailors and severely disabled the *Alfred.* This done, the *Glasgow* handily escaped. Jones, commanding the *Alfred*'s main battery, distinguished himself in this battle while Hopkins earned the censure of Congress. Almost immediately, discipline in the fledgling navy began to fall apart. The small American fleet was blockaded by the British in December 1776, and a cry was raised to relieve Hopkins of command.

As Hopkins fell, Jones rose. He was given command of the *Providence,* and although he was the most junior of the new navy's captains, he quickly compiled a record that no other commander could approach. In command of the *Providence* and leading a small flotilla, Jones captured or sunk 21 British warships, transports, and commercial vessels as well as one Loyalist privateer by the end of 1776. In recognition of his remarkable achievement, he was jumped over 17 other captains and, on June 14, 1777, received command of the sloop *Ranger.* He was ordered to sail to France in this vessel, where he would take command of the frigate *Indien,* which was being built in Amsterdam expressly for the Continental Navy. When he arrived in December, however, he found that the ship had been given to France by the American treaty commissioners in Paris, so he continued to sail in the *Ranger,* leaving Brest on April 10, 1778, with a crew of 140.

During April 27–28, 1778, Jones raided Whitehaven on the Solway Firth in Scotland, spiking the guns of two forts and burning three British ships. Jones's far more ambitious plan was to burn all of the ships in the harbor. Circumstances prevented this, but he had succeeded in carrying out the only American operation on British soil. Next, he aimed to kidnap the earl of Selkirk and hold him hostage to ensure good treatment for American prisoners of war. The scheme failed only because Selkirk was not at home when Captain Jones called.

Undiscouraged, Jones crossed the Irish Sea to Carrickfergus, where he captured the British sloop *Drake* in an hour-long battle in which eight of his men were killed or wounded, while he inflicted 40 casualties on the British. By the time he returned to Brest on May 8, he had collected seven prize ships and a substantial number of prisoners of war. In the summer of 1779, the French, now formally allied with the American cause, prepared five men-o'war and two privateers for Jones to lead. His flagship was a refitted East Indiaman, the *Duras.* Jones rechristened the vessel after Benjamin Franklin's *Poor Richard's Almanac,* calling it *Bonhomme Richard.*

Jones faced the opposition not only of the enemy, but of jealous French naval officers, who resented the authority conferred on the American upstart. Jones understood that the only way to win the loyalty of his subordinates was to prove himself, and that is what he set out to do. Making a sweeping voyage clockwise around the British Isles, Jones captured 17 vessels.

His most famous encounter came on September 23, 1779, off Flamborough Head, along the York coast, in the North Sea. Jones's flotilla sighted two warships, the 44-gun *Serapis* and the 20-gun *Countess of Scarborough,* escorting a convoy of 40 British merchant vessels. Jones was aware that his converted merchantman was slow, not very maneuverable, and, with only 42 cannon, outgunned. Nevertheless, he was determined to carry out his mission and decided to pursue the *Serapis* while his three other vessels, the *Vengeance,* the *Pallas,* and the *Alliance,* chased the *Countess.*

At the very commencement of this battle fought by the light of the moon, two of Jones's biggest guns exploded. A lesser leader would have aborted the mission, but Jones found a way around their loss. He outmaneuvered the *Serapis* and rammed her stern. This, however, put *Bonhomme Richard* in a position from which none of her guns, all mounted broadside, could be brought to bear. Recognizing this, the captain of the *Serapis* called out: "Has your ship struck?"—meaning "struck its colors," lowered its flag, surrendered. Jones replied with perhaps the most famous utterance in American military history: "I have not yet begun to fight."

With this, Jones backed off from the *Serapis,* which then collided anew with the *Bonhomme Richard.* Jones took advantage of this accident and grappled onto the British vessel, pulling it toward the *Bonhomme Richard* and then pounding it, at point-blank range, with those of his cannon that still functioned. After a two-hour pounding, the *Serapis* struck *its* colors.

After this fight, which became one of the most celebrated naval engagements in history, Jones made it to Texel in the Netherlands, having had to leave the badly crippled *Bonhomme Richard* at sea. It sunk on September 25. Jones was obliged to turn over his remaining vessels, except the *Alliance,* to the French. As captain of the *Alliance,* he continued to harass British shipping. In December 1780, as skipper of the *Ariel,* a French military transport, he returned to America, capturing the British ship *Triumph* along the way. (It subsequently escaped.)

On his return to the States, jealous Continental Navy officers blocked Jones's promotion to rear admiral, but they were unable to prevent his being assigned to command the biggest ship in the fleet, the *America.* No sooner was it completed, however, than Jones learned that it was to be turned over to the French. It was with the French fleet that Jones sailed until the end of the war.

After the Revolution, Jones worked briefly in France and then returned to the United States, where Congress presented him with a gold medal on October 16, 1787. The following year, restless for action, Jones accepted an appointment in the Russian navy as a rear admiral and, in this capacity, defeated the Turks at the battle of Liman in the Black Sea during June 17–27. Once again, however, he fell afoul of jealous colleagues. Jones left Russia for Paris in 1789, dejected and broken in health. He died in 1793.

Jones was one of history's great naval commanders, who combined boundless courage with, equally important, an inexhaustible reserve of resourcefulness. While his victories were a great contribution to the American cause in the Revolution, perhaps even more important was the example of gallantry—the refusal to yield to adversity—that he set for the U.S. Navy. The impact of his leadership has extended through time.

IN HIS OWN WORDS

"It seems to be a law inflexible and inexorable that he who will not risk cannot win."
—Letter to Vice Admiral Kersaint, 1791

"I have not yet begun to fight."
—On being asked to surrender to the H.M.S. *Serapis*, September 23, 1779

LEADERSHIP LESSONS

✦

There is no substitute for the leader's courage, skill, and self-confidence.

✦

Speed, cunning, and determined energy, skillfully employed, can compensate for a shortage of other resources.

✦

Develop an ability to improvise. Look for alternatives. Be determined but flexible.

✦

You are not defeated until you surrender. The lesson here? Don't surrender.

✦

An outstanding performer must learn to deal effectively with the envy of those around him.

Joseph, Chief

Born: ca. 1840   Died: 1904

Character model   Improviser   Motivator   Tactician

LEADERSHIP ACHIEVEMENTS

◆

Led a magnificent evasion of vastly superior forces

◆

Preserved his people's pride and identity even in defeat

◆

Transformed a military defeat into an enduring moral victory

◆

Earned the respect and admiration of his adversaries

LIFE

Heroic, stalwart, and a tower of dignified strength, Joseph was not only an inspiring and resourceful leader of the Nez Perce resistance against the U.S. Army, he won the absolute loyalty of those he led as well as the supreme respect of those he fought.

Chief Joseph is sometimes called Young Joseph to distinguish him from his father, variously known as Joseph the Elder, Old Joseph, or even, confusingly, Chief Joseph. The younger Joseph was born in the Wallowa Valley of Oregon and given a Nez Perce name variously transliterated as Heinmot Tooyalaket, In-mut-too-yah-lat-lat, Hinmah-too-yah-lat-kekt, and Hinmaton-yalatkit. The name may be translated as "thunder coming from water over land." Old Joseph, himself a Christianized Indian, baptized his son Ephraim.

Old Joseph was among a group of Nez Perces and Yakimas who, in 1855, had agreed to a treaty with Washington's ambitious and land-hungry young territorial governor Isaac Stevens. The treaty clearly specified certain Nez Perce and Yakima lands that would be ceded to Washington Territory at a specified time; it further stipulated certain lands that the Nez Perce and Yakima would forever retain. The ink was scarcely dry on the treaty when Stevens violated it, prematurely opening the ceded territory to settlement and usurping certain lands explicitly excluded by the treaty. This touched off the Yakima War of 1855–56, but Old Joseph, believing warfare with the powerful whites was fruitless, managed to keep the Nez Perces out of the conflict.

Then, in 1861, gold was discovered in the region, and prospectors pushed settlement into the Wallowa Valley. In response to the gold rush, the government, in 1863, proposed to Indian representatives at the Lapwai Council to revise the treaty of 1855, drastically reducing the Nez Perce reservation. Those Nez Perces who still lived within the revised boundaries willingly signed the new treaty and agreed to the sale of the excluded land. Understandably, however, those whose land was to be appropriated refused to sign. Among the latter were Old Joseph and four other chiefs, whose bands thus became known collectively as the Non-Treaty Nez Perces.

White authorities were slow to act against Old Joseph's defiance and his refusal to lead his people to a reservation. Years went by without violence, and Old Joseph died in 1871 with the Wallowa Valley still peaceful. Young Joseph, who inherited his father's position as chief, continued his father's policy of passively refusing to move. But, at last, the tide of white settlement reached the Wallowa Valley. As homesteaders rushed in, Joseph protested and, surprisingly enough, the Indian Bureau proved responsive. After investigating the land situation, the bureau reported to President Ulysses S. Grant, who established the Wallowa Valley as a reservation in 1873. Joseph had achieved a bloodless victory.

Or so he thought. As frequently happened in white–Indian relations, eager settlers simply chose to ignore all federal attempts to regulate them. They settled wherever they wished, and, once having settled, became a political constituency determined to compel the government to change the very rules they had violated. Pressured by the political interests behind the new settlers, Grant, in 1875, reversed his 1873 decision and suddenly declared the entire Wallowa Valley open to settlement.

General Oliver O. Howard was sent to "negotiate" with Joseph and the other Non-Treaty Nez Perces; however, inasmuch as Howard was authorized to yield nothing, the meeting was more a showdown than a negotiation. Like his father before him, Joseph believed that war with the whites could end only in Indian defeat and destruction; therefore, he counseled peaceful compliance with Howard's demands. Many others in the tribe, however, led by Joseph's brother, the warrior Ollikut, pressed for war. However, the eloquent Joseph presented an unassailable argument for peace, and even the most warlike among the Nez Perces were brought to the verge of resigned compliance.

But just as federal policy often had distressingly little effect on stubborn individual settlers, so the word of a chief often failed to direct the actions of all his people. On June 12, 1877, a youthful warrior named Wahlitits avenged the earlier death of his father at the hands of whites by killing four settlers. This act provoked other warriors, all young, who were enraged at having to leave their land, to kill 15 more. Joseph saw that the die was cast, that the fate of the Nez Perces had been sealed by these rash acts. He decided that there was now no other choice than to support his warriors.

Thus what the army called "the pursuit of the Nez Perce" began. Before it was over, it would cover some 1,700 miles and last through four grueling months—at great cost to the army as well as to the Indians—until October 5, 1877, at the Battle of Bear Paw Mountain, where Chief Joseph surrendered to Nelson A. Miles (to whom Apache chief Geronimo would surrender nine years later).

The skill with which Joseph led his people, traversing some of the most rugged terrain on the continent, was extraordinary. But Joseph understood that, sooner or later, the army would prevail. On October 5, he met with the commander of his pursuers, Nelson Miles. Chief Joseph began:

> I am tired of fighting. Our chiefs are killed. Looking Glass is dead. Toohoolhoolzote is dead. The old men are all dead. It is the young men who say yes or no. He who led on the young men [Joseph's brother, Ollikut] is dead. It is cold and we have no blankets. The little children are freezing to death. My people, some of them, have run away to the hills, and have no blankets, no food; no one knows where they are—perhaps freezing to death. I want to have time to look for my children and see how many of them I can find. Maybe I shall find them among the dead. Hear me, my chiefs! I am tired; my heart is sick and sad. From where the sun now stands I will fight no more forever.

This remarkable speech, facing reality with dignified emotion, seemed to summarize the entire tragic history of white–Indian conflict in North America.

Having surrendered, Joseph and 150 followers were sent to the Colville Reservation in Washington. So profound was the respect of the chief's military adversaries, Oliver O. Howard and Nelson A. Miles, that they petitioned the government on his behalf to regain for the Nez Perces the Wallowa Valley reservation. Their efforts were to no avail, however, and Joseph died in 1904, among his people on the much-despised reservation.

LEADERSHIP LESSONS

✦

When the odds are hopelessly stacked against your enterprise, it is always best to lead toward peaceful compromise and accommodation.

✦

An effective leader defines, reflects, and maintains the pride and identity of the group he leads.

✦

Know when the game is up, when further effort becomes costly waste. Know when to quit—and how to do so without sacrificing character, identity, and hope.

✦

An effective leader is strong in defeat and disappointment as well as in triumph and fulfillment.

Juárez, Benito (Pablo)

Born: 1806 Died: 1872

**Character model   Innovator   Mentor   Motivator
Rescuer   Systems creator   Visionary**

LEADERSHIP ACHIEVEMENTS

✦

Earned the respect and confidence not only of Mexicans,
but of world leaders

✦

Built a revolution by building consensus;
understood how to bide his time constructively

✦

Worked for radical change through law rather than violence

✦

Led by example of personal selflessness and integrity

✦

Brought about fundamental changes in Mexican government, society,
and the economy

✦

Refused to give up

LIFE

Benito Juárez, president of Mexico from 1861 to 1872 and leader of the resistance against French occupation from 1864 to 1867, was the founder of modern Mexico. He was born on March 21, 1806, to Zapotec Indian parents in the mountains of Oaxaca and did not learn to speak Spanish until he was 12, when he moved to the city of Oaxaca to work as a household servant. His employer apparently recognized his servant's intelligence and sent him to school as a full-time student. At first, Juárez thought of training for the priesthood, but, in 1828, he decided to study law instead, and he enrolled in the Oaxaca Institute of Arts and Sciences. He received his law degree in 1831 and set up a practice first in Oaxaca and then in Mexico City. While living in the capital, Juárez became increasingly interested in public affairs and entered politics, winning a seat on the municipal council.

Over the decade of the 1830s, Juárez served with unimpeachable honesty and integrity in the state and national legislatures. His sterling record earned him an appointment as a judge in 1841 and then election as governor of Oaxaca in 1846. That state was on the verge of bankruptcy when Juárez took office. Through honest, vigorous leadership and the introduction of efficient systems of administration, Juárez rescued the state's economy. By the end of his term, the treasury of Oaxaca showed a surplus for the first time since 1821.

During his early political life, Juárez began developing a liberal ideology of leadership and social reform. It became clear to him that Mexico's problems were fundamental. Two well-entrenched institutions, the church and the landed aristocracy, held far too much power. Until a strong middle class was allowed to grow, Mexico's chronically poor economy would never improve, and the vast majority of Mexicans would be doomed to live in poverty. He believed that the main power of government needed to reside in a federal system. However, the elections of 1853 returned the Conservative party of General Antonio Lopez de Santa Anna to office, and the outspoken Juárez was forced to leave Mexico. He took up residence in New Orleans, where the brilliant Mexican politician and jurist made his living by rolling cigarettes. In 1855, however, a Liberal government under Juan Alvarez was elected, and Juárez returned to Mexico City, where he was appointed minister of justice and minister of public instruction.

Juárez took advantage of his appointments in the Liberal government to write and see through to passage a landmark law that abolished the special courts that tried cases involving the military and the clergy. No longer would these groups be given preferential treatment in Mexican law. Juárez believed that judicial equality was the absolutely necessary basis for building social equality. In 1857, Mexico adopted a new liberal constitution and elected Ignacio Comonfort president. The Mexican Congress appointed Juárez to preside over the Supreme Court, a post that made him ex-officio vice president of the nation.

The next year, 1858, the Conservatives rebelled and, in a coup d'etat, ousted Comonfort from office. Vice President Juárez had a sound constitutional claim to the presidency, but he knew that he lacked the support to make good on that claim. Idealistic in his political philosophy, Juárez was nevertheless a realist in politics. He saw that no good would come from asserting a claim he could not back. Therefore, he left Mexico City for Veracruz, where he set up an opposition government. He prepared to fight a civil war.

Juárez, essentially a jurist, was now faced with the task of raising and directing an army to defeat the Conservatives and enforce the constitution. He began by securing passage of a law to nationalize all church property except those buildings actually used for worship. He decreed the permanent separation of church and state, even putting under civil service control the registration of births and deaths. At the same time, he promulgated legislation to guarantee religious freedom to all Mexicans. With his government now unified behind a strong military force, Juárez was able to overcome Conservative resistance by 1861. He returned to Mexico City and was elected president of a reunified Mexico.

Juárez immediately faced a new crisis. The brief civil war had drained the already hard-pressed Mexican treasury. Juárez sought financial relief by suspending repayment of the national debt for two years. This act, essential to the economic survival of his nation, alarmed creditor nations, including England, Spain, and France. Largely at the instigation of Napoleon III, emperor of France, an invasion force was sent to Veracruz. England and Spain quickly realized that Napoleon III intended not only to secure Mexico's debts, but to make Mexico effectively a colony of France. Accordingly, both nations withdrew from the expedition. Napoleon III, however, enlarged his forces, and by June 1863 the French captured Mexico City.

Having taken Mexico City, Napoleon III abrogated the Mexican republic by high-handedly installing Archduke Maximilian of Austria as emperor of Mexico. Juárez and his government retreated to the U.S. border, setting up their headquarters in the city today named Ciudad Juárez. As the Civil War drew to a close in the United States, President Abraham Lincoln began sending supplies and other aid to Juárez, who was a popular figure in the States. When the Civil War ended, Lincoln's successor, President Andrew Johnson, invoked the Monroe Doctrine, the 1823 foreign policy statement of President James Monroe, which declared that any imperialist attack on any nation of the Americas would be regarded as an attack on the United States itself. Johnson warned the French to leave the continent, and General Ulysses S. Grant raised troops to aid a Mexican army in fighting the French. Thus threatened, the French forces withdrew, and Juárez attacked the remaining forces loyal to Maximilian. Without the backing of French troops, the Maximilian regime quickly collapsed, and the "emperor" was captured and executed.

In 1867, Juárez ran for reelection to the presidency of all Mexico and proposed a series of five constitutional amendments to strengthen the office of chief executive. Although Juárez was reelected, the issue of the amendments ignited bitter controversy and brought about a popular crisis of confidence, as many people felt that he was betraying democracy and replacing it with dictatorship. Afflicted by the doubts of his countrymen and now plagued by ill health (he suffered a stroke in October 1870) as well as personal loss (his wife died in January 1871), Juárez ran for reelection again, securing another victory, yet clearly losing more of his popular support. He died in office.

LEADERSHIP LESSONS

✦

Devise ways to attain your goals by using rules that are in place.
Avoid introducing anarchy.

✦

A leader understands the value of timing and of biding his time,
when necessary.

✦

Do not act out of panic.

✦

Premature action typically achieves nothing and may destroy hope
and possibility.

✦

Build consensus before pushing for change.

✦

Sometimes the road to unity is the path of conscientious opposition.

✦

Retain faith in those you lead.

✦

Avoid the impulse to dictatorship, even if your motives are pure.

Justinian I

Born: ca. 482   Died: 565

Innovator   Problem solver   Rescuer   Systems creator

LEADERSHIP ACHIEVEMENTS

✦

Made the most of educational opportunities to groom himself
for a leadership role

✦

Held the Byzantine (Eastern Roman) Empire together against tremendous
pressures from outside and in

✦

Was willing to make unpopular, even brutal decisions for what he saw as
the good of the empire

✦

Juggled multiple objectives and dealt with multiple crises vigorously and,
on balance, effectively

✦

Codified Roman law and developed enduring principles of justice in law as
well as enforcement

✦

Never backed down from a difficult problem

LIFE

Justinian was emperor of Byzantium (or the Eastern Roman Empire) from
527 to 565, a time of great menace to Roman civilization. He led with a
strong hand, codified Roman law, and took steps to bring an end to the discord that plagued early Christianity in the Byzantine Empire.

Born Flavius Petrus Sabbatius in the Macedonian Balkans to parents
of Latin-speaking peasant background, he was nephew to the future
emperor Justin I, who took the boy with him to Constantinople (present-
day Instanbul). There young Flavius received as fine an education as any
available at the time. In gratitude to his uncle, he took the name Justinian.

When Anastasius I died in 518, Justin succeeded him as emperor, and
he bestowed upon his very able nephew a series of positions of increasing
responsibility. At last, on April 1, 527, Justinian was named co-emperor

and, during this period, married the remarkable Theodora. On August 1, 527, Justin I died, leaving Justinian sole emperor.

Persia staged major campaigns against the Eastern Empire during this period, and Justinian responded vigorously, but his military efforts proved very costly. In the early years of his reign, Justinian was censured by the Senate as autocratic and oppressive. Yet he persevered and refused to yield to popular pressure, understanding that to do so in the face of internal and external threats to the empire would mean political dissolution. The dissension within the empire culminated during January 13–18, 532, in the Nika Riots, which began as a mob disturbance in the Constantinople Hippodrome and rapidly escalated into an uprising of angry people calling for radical governmental reform. The aristocracy took advantage of the chaos to attempt a coup against Justinian, who responded harshly but decisively by deploying loyal troops to massacre the rioters.

Having dealt with the internal dissidents, Justinian seized the moment later in 532 to conclude a "Perpetual Peace" with the empire's archrival, Persia. Justinian rightly judged that the new Persian king, Chosroes I, would be amenable to peace, and he saw that bringing an end to a chronic and costly war would free up Byzantine military resources for the liberation of Roman territories in the West that had been taken by barbarians. Justinian aimed first to recover lost territory in North Africa. He sent his best general, Belisarius, to fight the Vandals, who were defeated in 533–34. Next, Justinian turned to Italy, which was held in thrall by the Ostrogoths. By 540, Belisarius was in a position to negotiate a favorable peace with them. However, that peace proved little more than a truce, as the Ostrogoths rebelled once again, only to be put down by another Byzantine commander, Narses, in 552.

In 540, the same year as the first victory against the Ostrogoths, Chosroes I broke the Perpetual Peace by invading the region now encompassed by Syria and Palestine. Thus, from 540 to 562, Justinian was faced with the difficult task of shuttling his armies back and forth between two distant theaters of war. Only after Justinian negotiated a treaty supported by tribute payments was a stable peace finally secured between the Eastern Empire and Persia.

The harsh justice meted out to the Nika rioters and the final decision to placate Persia with tribute money were difficult and controversial acts

of leadership. What no historians dispute, however, is the value of
Justinian's codification of Roman law. The work was begun, at Justinian's
direction, in 528 by the lawyer Tribonian and ultimately encompassed all
valid existing laws, opinions by Roman jurists, a textbook for students,
and new laws. In contrast to most rulers, Justinian applied and enforced
the law with stern evenhandedness, upon aristocrat and commoner alike.
The aristocracy objected to his codification and strict enforcement of laws
against tax evasion and the abuse of power, but Justinian was never afraid
of being unpopular, and he administered the laws narrowly in the service
of justice. His systematization of the body of law, his proportioning pun-
ishments to crimes, his equitable enforcement practices, and his insistence
on the prevailing concept of no person being above the law had enormous
positive influence on the future development of European and, ultimately,
American law.

Religious affairs occupied Justinian at least as much as legal matters
did. The early Christian Church in the Eastern Empire was beset by great
discord. Sects fought over the divinity of Christ, the separation of religious
and secular authority, and other matters. Justinian sought to reconcile these
differences by convening the Fifth Ecumenical Council. While he did establish the important leadership principle of the supremacy of his authority, as
caesar, over that of the Church, the emperor was unable to resolve the theological disputes. Ultimately, the Eastern dissidents—chief among them the
Monophysites—formed a church separate from the mainstream that dominated Christianity in Syria and Egypt.

Justinian never enjoyed easy times during his troubled reign. The
Byzantine economy faltered during his closing years, religious differences
intensified, and, worst of all, the empire was swept by a pandemic of
bubonic plague (542–43). Justinian faced mounting opposition from within
the empire and repeated barbarian attacks out of the Balkans, some of
which came perilously close to the capital. The death of Justinian on
November 14, 565, was to many of the people of Constantinople an occasion for celebration. They did not understand what history has learned to
appreciate: that Justinian's willingness to make difficult decisions, hammer
out painful compromises, and create whatever he could of enduring order
staved off the final dissolution of the Eastern Empire and preserved
Byzantine culture and influence.

LEADERSHIP LESSONS

✦

Find a mentor or recognize when one finds you—as Justinian did in the case of his uncle Justin.

✦

Learn all that you can. Never cut yourself off from knowledge. Preparation for leadership is learning, and learning remains the driving force behind leadership.

✦

Recognize priorities beyond immediate popularity.

✦

Do not be blinded to internal threats by external ones—and vice versa.

✦

Create rules and policies in conformity with enduring and worthwhile principles.

✦

A leader leads in the present, but also creates the precedents that guide the future.

✦

Know when to compromise, and be willing to make difficult concessions for the good of the enterprise.

✦

Adversity is the absolute test of leadership.

Kamehameha I the Great

Born: 1758? Died: 1819

Conqueror Innovator Profit maker Systems creator

LEADERSHIP ACHIEVEMENTS

✦

Unified the Hawaiian Islands under a single king

✦

Brought peace and stability to the islands by synthesizing tradition
and innovation

✦

Humanized and liberalized harsh Hawaiian tribal law without sacrificing
his own authority

✦

Introduced a new, modern body of law

✦

Created an efficient government staffed by able officials

✦

Balanced autonomy with an openness to international trade,
which greatly enriched the Islands

LIFE

Kamehameha I was the first king of Hawaii, the leader who united the Hawaiian Islands and founded a dynasty extending through five kings. He was born in the Kohala district on the island of Hawaii, probably in November 1758. His given name was Paiea—"Soft-Shelled Crab"—and he was the son of Keoua, a tribal chief, and his wife, Kekuiapoiwa, daughter of a former Hawaiian chief named Alapai. Kamehameha is so revered that Hawaiian tradition relates that his birth was heralded by a portentous sign: Koloiki, a brilliant star, appeared in the heavens just before the boy's birth. Indeed, it is a fact that Halley's comet appeared in November 1758. When Paiea was an infant, various Hawaiian priests and mystics predicted that he would become a fearless conqueror who would defeat all rivals. Hearing this, his jealous grandfather Alapai ordered the infant killed, but others spirited him secretly away, and he grew to manhood in seclusion, for which reason he took the name Kamehameha, "The Very Lonely One" or "The One Set Apart." Whether this is true or a self-created Moses-like myth is unknown.

During the period of Kamehameha's coming of age, the Hawaiian Islands were not unified, but the principal island of Hawaii was ruled by a single king, Kalaniopuu. On his death in 1782, the island was divided between his son, Kiwalao, and his nephew, Kamehameha. For a few months, this arrangement promised to be a peaceful one, but in July 1782, conflict broke out between chiefs loyal to Kiwalao and those whose allegiance was to Kamehameha. The dispute rapidly escalated into a brief war, and in a battle at Mokuohai, Kiwalao was killed. Thus Kamehameha emerged as sole ruler of the island of Hawaii. In 1795, he set about subduing the other islands of the Hawaiian group, conquering all but Kauai and Niihau. These were peacefully ceded to him by a treaty in 1810, and from this point forward, Kamehameha ruled a unified Hawaii.

Kamehameha was a king, not a democratically elected president, but he ruled wisely, taking care to appoint highly qualified governors to administer each of the islands and look after the needs of his subjects. He united not only the Hawaiian Islands, but also joined tradition with innovation. He perpetuated the *kapu,* Hawaii's traditional strict code of tribal laws, but he also introduced the *mamalahoe kanawai*—"The Splintered Paddle"— which mitigated and humanized the absolute, often arbitrary authority of tribal chieftains to punish offenders at will. Kamehameha I also brought to an end the ages-old practice of human sacrifice. In addition to bringing a greater degree of humanity to the conduct of government in Hawaii, Kamehameha ushered in an era of limited intercourse with the world at large, thereby ending centuries of Hawaiian isolation. This action enriched Hawaii by bringing substantial revenues from the trade in sandalwood and by collecting a port duty from visiting vessels.

Opening up the islands to the world carried a risk, of course. But Kamehameha managed to maintain the islands' independence during a period of intense European activity in the Pacific. Following his death (on May 8, 1819, at Kailua), however, the autonomy of Hawaii steadily eroded under assault from imperialist European powers and, later, the United States.

LEADERSHIP LESSONS

A leader must put the needs of his people first.

Consider fostering—or creating—a strong image to develop a mythic presence that enhances leadership status.

An effective leader devotes much time, effort, and thought to appointing loyal, efficient, selfless subordinates.

◆

Leadership is often a matter of synthesizing comfortable tradition and sharp innovation.

◆

Engaging in intercourse with powers outside of the enterprise is a necessary risk.

◆

Do not sacrifice autonomy for the sake of quick profits.

Kanishka

Active: 1st century A.D.

Conqueror Innovator Visionary

LEADERSHIP ACHIEVEMENTS

✦

Expanded the great Kushan Empire

✦

Used religion to unify a vast and diverse empire, but embraced religious
and cultural diversity

LIFE

Only a few key facts are known about Kanishka, the greatest of the kings
of the Kushan empire, a vast realm encompassing the northern Indian subcontinent, Afghanistan, and (probably) much of Central Asia. Historians
do not know when, precisely, Kanishka ascended the throne. It may have
been as early as A.D. 78 or as late as 225, although the range 78 to 144
seems most likely. Since the year 78 marks the beginning of the Saka era—
a dating system some scholars believe Kanishka introduced—78 may well
mark the beginning of his reign. It is believed that Kanishka ruled for 23
years. Kanishka's realm extended from Bukhara (in the modern Uzbek) in
the west to Patna in the east, and from Pamirs (in the modern Tadzhik
Republic) in the north to central India in the south, truly a vast territory.
There is also good evidence that he subjugated the important city-states of
Khotan, Kashgar, and Yarkand, all of which are in modern Chinese
Turkestan.

Kanishka used religion to unify this far-flung empire. He convened a
great Buddhist council—only the fourth such of its kind—at Kashmir,
which resulted in the founding of Mahayana Buddhism and the production
of learned religious texts and commentaries. Even as he advocated
Buddhism, supporting it as a state religion, Kanishka freely tolerated
within his realm Zoroastrian, Brahman, and other beliefs. Moreover, he
developed an active trade with the Roman Empire, which not only

enriched his realm, but provided a measure of cross-cultural fertilization, as evidenced in the Gandhara school of art, incorporating Greek and Roman classicism into Buddhist religious imagery.

LEADERSHIP LESSONS

Shared beliefs, values, and goals can be important to unifying diverse members of an enterprise; however, diversity can also add strength to any organization.

Karageorge
(George Petrovich)

Born: 1762   Died: 1817

Improviser   Leverager   Mentor   Motivator

LEADERSHIP ACHIEVEMENTS

◆

Transformed oppressed peasants into a highly effective army of liberation

◆

Consistently achieved victory against larger, better-equipped, better-trained forces

◆

Channeled popular outrage into effective action

◆

Made several effective attempts at diplomacy, but was betrayed by his ally

LIFE

The nickname by which the fierce Serbian nationalist George Petrovich was known from youth, Karageorge—Black George—was inspired by his dark eyes, black hair, and swarthy complexion. It might also have described his disposition and character. Morose and moody, Karageorge could be a terrifying man. He was subject to fits of sudden violence, and personally killed some 125 people, including his father. An iron disciplinarian, he typically punished transgressions among his troops with summary execution. Yet he was a thoroughly remarkable military leader, who organized and led an extraordinarily effective peasant army that defeated a far-better-equipped and better-trained professional force.

He was born in Visevac, Serbia, to a peasant family and earned his living as a youth working as a swineherd and a stable groom. In 1786, he killed some Turks—Serbia was dominated by the Ottoman Empire at this time—in a scuffle, and he was forced to flee to Urbica to evade prosecution. Here he settled just long enough to marry before moving on to Austria in 1787. In Austria, he found work as a forest ranger, and then, in 1788, enlisted in the Austrian Freikorps, an unofficial nationalist army, which appealed to Karageorge because it afforded an opportunity to fight the hated Turks. The young man fought in Italy and in the Austro-Russo-Turkish War. After Austria concluded an armistice with Turkey in 1790, Karageorge returned to Serbia, where he led small groups in a guerrilla campaign against local Turks.

Karageorge called off his campaigning after the conclusion of the Treaty of Sistova on August 4, 1791. He moved to the village of Topola, where he started to trade in cattle, and, by the beginning of the 19th century, Karageorge had become a wealthy trader and the father of seven children—the third of whom would later became prince of Serbia. He rose to political prominence when the Serb peasantry resolved to renew its chronic rising against the Turks. Karageorge was elected *vozhd*—leader—of the independence movement.

The target of the independence movement was the Janissaries, an elite and politically powerful legion of mercenary soldiers, nominally in service to the Ottoman Sultan, but so powerful that they were never really under his orders. The Janissaries exercised tyrannical and arbitrary control over Serbia. Through a combination of natural military talent, a commanding leadership presence, and an ability to transform the peasants' hatred of the Janissaries into effective action, Karageorge successfully waged war, but even after the Janissary leader had been killed, Karageorge refused to stop fighting. He was loath to lose the momentum of a grassroots rebellion. Feeling it insufficient merely to have rid Serbia of the Janissaries, Karageorge wanted the Ottoman sultan to grant Serbia independence or, at least, full autonomy. What he offered in exchange was his proven record of effectiveness against the Janissaries. He would help the sultan suppress the rebellious mercenaries.

It was a sound proposal, but the sultan arrogantly rebuffed it. In response, Karageorge whipped his peasant army to a new level of discipline and effectiveness, launching them against highly trained Turkish regulars at the Battle of Ivankovac in 1805. His victory was decisive, propelling Karageorge to political leadership of a Serbian State Council, the first step toward establishing complete independence. When the Turks attacked at Misar in 1806, Karageorge was there to meet them. Victorious in this battle, he invaded and occupied Belgrade, the principal city of the region. With the ejection of the Turks from this capital, Serbian independence had been achieved.

An extremely effective guerrilla leader, Karageorge also proved capable of following through diplomatically. In 1807, he bolstered Serbia's independent status by concluding an alliance with Russia in one of its many wars against Turkey. However, when Russia excluded Serbia from the armistice of Slobodzen later in 1807, Karageorge believed himself and his country betrayed. He transmitted his rage to his army and other followers, and he persuaded the Serbian State Council to break with Russia and express its full independence by promulgating the first-ever Serbian Constitution. The constitution included a provision naming Karageorge the "first and supreme hereditary leader."

In 1809, when war broke out again between Turkey and Russia, Karageorge decided to give a Russian alliance another chance. He led a mixed Serbo-Russian army to victory over the Turks at the Battle of Varvarin in 1810. This not only suppressed the Turkish menace against Serbia, but created temporarily cordial Serbo-Russian relations as well. However, the Treaty of Bucharest, which ended the Russo-Turkish War, specified nothing more than a vague amnesty and autonomy for Serbia, leaving the question of outright independence open and stipulating that it was to be settled between the Turks and Serbs.

Yet again Russia had betrayed Serbia by denying the country an opportunity to certify its independence. The Turks took the ambiguous treaty as a signal that Russia would not defend Serbia against an attempt to retake it. In 1812–13, the Turks threw all of their forces against the Serbs, who were ultimately defeated. Karageorge fled to Austria, where authorities interned him for a year before he was permitted to go on to Bessarabia in 1814. The Russians refused to allow Karageorge to return to Serbia during the revolt that took place the following year there. The exiled leader traveled to St. Petersburg to argue on behalf of his cause. This prompted Russian authorities to intern him in the Ukraine, and it wasn't until 1817 that he managed to travel secretly through Bessarabia back to Serbia. There, in his sleep, he was assassinated by agents of the pro-Turkish Serbian leader Milosh Obrenovich and the Turkish vizier of Belgrade.

LEADERSHIP LESSONS
✦

Identify, define, and articulate the dominant common cause of
those you lead. Develop methods of transforming this common cause
into effective action.
✦

Become the voice of those you lead.
✦

Leadership by fear and intimidation is often temporarily effective—even
highly effective—however, such leadership is almost impossible to sustain.
✦

Monitor all alliances. Never become complacent about your partners.

Kearny, Stephen Watts

Born: 1794   Died: 1848

**Character model   Conqueror   Leverager   Mentor
Motivator   Systems creator**

LEADERSHIP ACHIEVEMENTS

✦

Combined a military career with exploration

✦

Tempered military conquest with the administration of wise,
evenhanded civil government

✦

Created an army suited to the special demands of the frontier

✦

Successfully combined a vigorous approach to military objectives with a
policy of using minimum force

✦

Consistently subordinated personal objectives to the mission at hand

✦

Followed what he conceived of as right, even at the risk of his personal
advancement

LIFE

Popularly called "The Pathfinder," Stephen Watts Kearny was one of the most admirable military figures on the American western frontier. He was not only a capable and courageous soldier and a fine leader, but his firm belief in creating sound civil government motivated his peaceful capture and occupation of Santa Fe during the U.S.–Mexican War.

Kearny was born in Newark, New Jersey, and studied at Columbia College (today's Columbia University) across the Hudson in Manhattan from 1808 to 1810. He enlisted in the army just before the outbreak of the War of 1812 and was commissioned a first lieutenant in March 1812. Kearny fought at the Battle of Queenston Heights with the 13th Infantry, suffering a wound and capture on October 13. In those days, POWs were typically exchanged or discharged on parole. Released by the British, Kearny was promoted to captain on April 1, 1813, and served at Sacket's Harbor, Long Island, and Plattsburgh, New York, through the end of the war. Unlike many other officers, he remained with the army after the war, transferring to the 2nd Infantry, with which he was dispatched west in 1819. In 1820, he pioneered a route from Council Bluffs, Iowa, to the St. Peter's River in Minnesota. In 1821, he was assigned to duty at Fort Smith, Arkansas, as paymaster and inspector, and then, in June, joined the 3rd Infantry in Detroit. Two years later, he was given a brevet promotion—a field promotion in rank, without a step up in pay—to major. Considering the notoriously glacial pace of promotion in the United States Army of the time, Kearny's progress up the ranks was rapid, an acknowledgment of his competence and efficiency.

Kearny was next attached to the 1st Infantry, based at Baton Rouge, Louisiana, and was assigned to the Second Yellowstone Expedition up the Missouri River during 1824–25. After returning from the Far West, he built Jefferson Barracks in St. Louis as the headquarters of the army's Great Plains region, and then, in 1828, was sent to Prairie du Chien, Wisconsin, as commander of Fort Crawford. While serving there, he played a key role in negotiating the 1830 Treaty of Prairie du Chien with the Indians, which opened up local territories to settlement.

During 1831–32, Kearny reestablished Fort Towson in Indian Territory (present-day Oklahoma), and then returned to the East to serve as superintendent of recruiting in New York City (1832–33). Appointed lieutenant colonel of the newly created 1st Dragoons on March 4, 1833, he returned to Jefferson Barracks and set out under General Leavenworth on an expedition into Pawnee and Comanche country during 1834. The expedition did not meet with Indian hostility, but it was plagued by disease. Accompanying Kearny on the this assignment was his nephew, Philip (Phil) Kearny, who became his uncle's protégé and was destined to serve as a soldier of great distinction in the U.S.–Mexican War and the Civil War.

Stephen Watts Kearny was promoted to colonel of his regiment on June 4, 1836, and took the unit to Fort Leavenworth, Kansas, where he built it into an elite frontier regiment. Kearny applied his experience of the frontier to formulate a training program for well-disciplined, highly effective frontier troops. His *Carbine Manual, or Rules for the Exercise and Maneuvers for the U.S. Dragoons,* which he wrote during this period (it was published in 1837), served for decades as *the* textbook of frontier warfare.

In 1837, Kearny laid out a military road from Fort Leavenworth to the Arkansas River and, two years later, successfully intervened to prevent a war between the Potowatomies and the Otoes. In 1840, he was instrumental in heading off civil disturbances among the Cherokee, and in 1842 prevented the Indians from participating in a Texas–Mexico border clash. Such achievements were typical of this most atypical military leader. Armies are created primarily to kill people and break things; but Kearny was a builder and peacemaker first, a soldier—an excellent soldier—second. He earned a reputation as an able, energetic, and incorruptible administrator who was committed to peaceful resolution of conflict wherever possible. All interests honored him as a man of integrity, dedicated to justice and fair play.

In July 1842, Kearny returned to Jefferson Barracks to command the newly created Third Military District, which encompassed all of the Great Plains. He led an expedition over the Oregon Trail to Wyoming and back by way of Colorado and the Santa Fe Trail in 1845. The following year, with the outbreak of the U.S.–Mexican War, he was called on to mount an expedition to capture New Mexico and then to occupy California. Organizing his dragoons as well as a force of Missouri mounted riflemen (under Alexander Doniphan), he led his 1,700-man army to the conquest of Santa Fe on August 18. The mere presence of his force, which, though small, he had made impressive, brought about surrender of this major trading center. Kearny realized that capturing Santa Fe was one thing, however, and holding it peacefully and effectively was another. Exercising his skill, respect, and generosity as an administrator, he quickly won the confidence and cooperation of the native Mexican population.

Receiving intelligence that Commodore R. E. Stockton and Lieutenant Colonel John Charles Frémont had taken California, Kearny set out for the Pacific Coast with a detachment of 120 dragoons. When he reached the vicinity of San Diego on December 2, he found that a rebellion against U.S. occupation was under way. Encountering a force of Mexicans at San Pasqual, he fought a sharp but inconclusive engagement on December 5, and then pressed onward to join Stockton just outside San Diego. Kearny had been given authority as U.S. commander in California, but Stockton, who had already proclaimed himself governor, challenged him. Focusing on the mission, Kearny set aside ego and even official authority. He recognized that it was Stockton's men who constituted the bulk of U.S. forces locally available, so he decided to bow to Stockton's authority. This done, he was able to secure Stockton's full cooperation in a combined army and navy assault on Los Angeles. With Stockton's aid, Kearny defeated the Mexicans at San Gabriel on January 8, 1847, and at Mesa on January 9. This achieved, U.S. authority in California was reestablished and the rebellion suppressed.

At this point, however, a new dispute erupted with Stockton, and his arrogant ally John Charles Frémont—this time over who should command land forces. Although Kearny secured confirmation of his authority from Washington, Stockton remained uncooperative and unyielding. At last, Stockton was relieved by Commodore W. Brandford Shubrick, but, as a parting gesture, he appointed Frémont governor. Prudently, Kearny waited until reinforcements arrived before he himself, acting on the president's orders, replaced Frémont as governor. The transfer of power was peaceful and respectful.

As military governor of California, Kearny quickly set about creating a stable government for the nation's new territory. As soon as he had accomplished this, he returned to Fort Leavenworth, with Frémont in tow. Only after arrival at Fort Leavenworth, far from California, did he turn to the matter of Frémont's insubordination. Despite the efforts of Frémont's father-in-law, the powerful Missouri senator Thomas Hart Benton, a court-martial convicted Frémont of having willfully exceeded his authority. Kearny could have dropped the matter, for he was well aware that Frémont's powerful connections put his own career at risk. But he proceeded as he thought best for the interests of the nation and the army. Indeed, in retaliation for his action against his son-in-law, Benton tried unsuccessfully to block Kearny's assignment in Mexico as commander of Veracruz in April 1848.

In Mexico, Kearny was stricken with yellow fever and was sent to Mexico City to recuperate. After partially recovering, he took command of 2nd Division and was appointed military governor of Mexico City. He returned to Veracruz, and then sailed for the United States on July 11, broken in health, reaching Jefferson Barracks on July 30. Just before his death three months later, Kearny was breveted major general—despite a two-week filibuster from Benton opposing the promotion.

LEADERSHIP LESSONS

✦

A leader is a mentor.

✦

Tailor principles to operating conditions. A parade-ground army may not be very effective on the frontier.

✦

Leverage training and discipline so that a minimum of force or other costly assets need be used to achieve your objectives.

✦

Lead by the least coercive means possible.

✦

Be a pioneer.

✦

A leader can find no adequate substitute for personal integrity.

✦

Do the right thing, even if—especially if—it is inconvenient, difficult, and even dangerous.

Kennedy, John F.

Born: 1917   Died: 1963

**Character model   Innovator   Motivator   Rescuer
Systems creator   Visionary**

LEADERSHIP ACHIEVEMENTS

✦

Valiantly rescued members of the crew of PT-109

✦

Understood and aspired to courage

✦

Became a distinguished popular author

✦

Defeated Richard M. Nixon to become the youngest elected U.S. president

✦

Created triumph from potential world-ending catastrophe in the Cuban
Missile Crisis

✦

Outlined a bold new social agenda for America

✦

Led the nation in advancements in the arts and sciences—paramountly the
space race

✦

Created a foreign policy based on strength and a commitment to
international humanitarian goals

✦

Led the nation to idealism and an aspiration to excellence

LIFE

At 43, John Fitzgerald Kennedy was the nation's youngest elected president, and, when he was assassinated on November 22, 1963, he became the youngest to die. These facts say much about Kennedy as a leader: He brought to the White House the powerful magic of youth and vigor, made the more compelling for its fleeting nature. But what transformed this quality into the material of true leadership was Kennedy's eloquence and intelligence as well as his ability to direct his energy toward high ideals and noble aspirations and to inspire the nation to forge along that road with him. The Kennedy presidency was, in many ways, troubled. JFK was rarely able to create an effective consensus with Congress. Yet no other administration was as inspiring as his. He taught the nation to dream large and to aspire to the most difficult goals, from genuine equality among all citizens to landing a human being on the moon.

He was born in Brookline, Massachusetts, the son of a political family of Irish descent. His father, Joseph P. Kennedy, was a political power broker and, in the years leading up to World War II, ambassador to England. The Kennedy family—nine children in all, presided over by the matriarchal Rose Kennedy—enjoyed wealth and privilege, but both parents made it clear that great things were expected of the children. John Kennedy was educated at Harvard, graduated in 1940, and joined the navy during World War II.

Because he had experience handling small sailing craft—the family compound was located seaside at Hyannis Port, Massachusetts—he volunteered to skipper PT boats, a most hazardous duty. On the night of August 2, 1943, while in command of PT-109 in the Pacific, Kennedy was hunting for targets. Suddenly, a Japanese destroyer bore down on the plywood-hulled PT boat, rammed the vessel, and split it in two. The collision instantly killed two of Lieutenant Kennedy's men. The others leaped off the boat as it exploded into flame. Kennedy, who had severely injured his back playing football at Harvard, reinjured it in the collision, but nevertheless endured terrible pain to rescue his men, including badly burned and now helpless crewman Patrick McMahon. Through the night, Kennedy and his crew clung to floating wreckage. At daybreak, Kennedy led his men toward a small island visible a few miles off. Although injured himself, Kennedy towed McMahon ashore, clenching the burned man's life jacket strap between his teeth as he swam. Six days later, two islanders found Kennedy and his crew. The skipper scratched out a message on a piece of coconut shell, gave it to the islanders, and sent them for help. Kennedy was awarded the Navy and Marine Corps Medal for leadership and courage.

Before the war, Kennedy had considered becoming a teacher and a writer. It was always planned that his older brother, Joseph P. Kennedy, Jr., would be the Kennedy to enter politics. However, Joe, a bomber pilot, died during a perilous mission over Europe in 1944. Kennedy's father persuaded John to pursue his brother's destiny, and he successfully ran for

Congress on the Democratic ticket in 1946. After serving three terms, the instantly popular Kennedy advanced to the Senate in 1953, marrying Jacqueline Bouvier on September 12 of the same year. Intelligent, elegant, and beautiful, "Jackie" Kennedy would prove a great political asset to the rising young senator. However, in 1955, Kennedy's back injuries became cripplingly painful and even life-threatening. He endured two major surgeries and, while recuperating, wrote *Profiles in Courage,* a book of biographies of American political leaders who had risked—and sometimes sacrificed—their careers to fight for their beliefs. The book, enormously successful, was awarded the Pulitzer Prize in history.

In 1956, Kennedy was considered as the Democratic nominee for vice president. His failure to win the nomination only prompted him to set his sights higher. He decided to run for president, and, four years later, he won the nomination on the first ballot and found himself up against Richard M. Nixon, two-term vice president under the very popular Dwight David Eisenhower. In an era gripped by the Cold War, with the nation in deep fear of Soviet world domination, Nixon had the advantage of a reputation as an uncompromising anti-Communist, whose eight years by Eisenhower's side made him a veteran Cold Warrior. Some saw Kennedy as inexperienced, an upstart rich kid; others were leery of his Roman Catholicism, even suspecting that he would owe allegiance to the pope. Still others recalled his father's record as ambassador to Great Britain and how he had too long advocated a fatal policy of appeasement of Hitler and Mussolini; these voters now feared that son John would show a similar softness, this time toward Communism. Despite these liabilities, however, JFK—as he was already called—was an irresistible campaigner, who projected an image of youthful vigor, intelligence, idealism, integrity, and boyish charm that Nixon sorely lacked. Millions watched Kennedy's televised debates with Nixon, and while some felt that Nixon outperformed Kennedy in discussing issues, there was no question as to who was more personally appealing. JFK went on to win election by a very narrow margin in the popular vote.

His inaugural address set the leadership tone for his administration. It was, characteristically, a challenge to the American people: "Ask not," he proclaimed, "what your country can do for you—ask what you can do for your country." He also threw down the gauntlet to those who would oppose America, announcing, in effect, that his administration would be anything but "soft" on Communism.

President Kennedy introduced a number of economic initiatives that, doubtless, helped spur the country to what was its longest sustained expansion since World War II. He faced grave international crises, badly faltering in the conduct of the botched Bay of Pigs invasion of Fidel Castro's Cuba, but subsequently triumphing during the Cuban Missile Crisis, forcing the Soviet Union to remove nuclear missiles it had secretly established in Cuba. The crisis brought the world to the brink of thermonuclear war; however, Kennedy's courageous, balanced, and sage management of the crisis not only averted disaster but won America prestige in the eyes of the world and, ultimately, set U.S.–Soviet relations on a far more open, if hardly cordial, course. The successful outcome of the Cuban Missile Crisis gave Kennedy the credibility he needed to render meaningful his pledge to continue to support and defend West Berlin. When he visited that city—engulfed by Soviet-controlled East Germany, and divided from East Berlin by a wall that symbolized Soviet tyranny itself—Kennedy declared to his audience, *"Ich bin ein Berliner"* (I am a Berliner)—a statement that rang with moving symbolic significance. It was nothing less than a promise to stand with all people who were threatened by totalitarianism.

But Kennedy's foreign policy was not all about threat, a show of military muscle, and a willingness to go to war. Under his administration, an Alliance for Progress extended economic and humanitarian assistance to the impoverished nations of Latin America, greatly strengthening the democratic integrity of the Western Hemisphere. With Kennedy's personal participation and encouragement, the Peace Corps was founded as a means of putting the idealism of America's young men and women into action in programs designed to aid the world's poorest, most desperate peoples. The Kennedy administration also supported excellence in American science and technology, focusing on the space program with the goal of landing astronauts on the moon before the end of the 1960s.

On the home front, Kennedy backed comprehensive initiatives against poverty and to promote the cause of civil rights. However, opposed by a reluctant Congress, he made frustratingly little progress on these fronts. It was Lyndon Johnson—Kennedy's vice president succeeding him after the assassination—who effectively exploited the young president's "martyrdom" to push through the legislative branch the social programs that had been conceived during the Kennedy years, including the momentous Civil Rights Act of 1964.

The Kennedy leadership extended to the tone and quality of American national culture. The White House became a focal point for performances by great American musicians and dancers, and for visits by literary giants and artists. Under Mrs. Kennedy's direction, the White House itself was restored to new grandeur as a showplace of the best of American decorative and fine arts. People looked to the administration and all that surrounded it as a kind of Camelot, an awakening to the magnificent possibilities of a newly youthful American civilization.

In the years since President Kennedy's assassination—which occurred during a visit to Dallas on November 22, 1963, at a point just beyond his first thousand days in office—the Kennedy legacy has been subject to much scrutiny and reevaluation. Revelations about his personal life, especially his prodigious and reckless womanizing, have tarnished his image, at least in some eyes. Even more controversial is his role in beginning the escalation of U.S. involvement in the Vietnam War. Some blame Kennedy for leading the nation deeper into the quagmire, while others suggest that, had Kennedy lived, he would have avoided further involvement in what he saw as a war that had to be won not by outside intervention, but by the South Vietnamese themselves. This, of course, we cannot know. With more certain justification, many historians have pointed out that President Kennedy, for all his popular magic, never succeeded in fashioning a productive relationship with Congress. Yet, regardless of the reassessment and rethinking, few would deny the enduring impact John F. Kennedy has had on American politics, political philosophy, and life. In this sense, above all else, he must be regarded as an extraordinarily powerful leader.

IN HIS OWN WORDS

"The stories of past courage . . . can teach, they can offer hope, they can provide inspiration. But they cannot supply courage itself. For this each man must look into his own soul."
—*Profiles in Courage*, 1956

"[T]here is always inequity in life. Some men are killed in a war and some men are wounded, and some men never leave the country, and some men are stationed in the Antarctic and some men are stationed in San Francisco. It is very hard in the military or personal life to assure complete equality. Life is unfair."
—Press conference, March 21, 1962

LEADERSHIP LESSONS

✦

The greatest courage is selfless, a strong urge to help others and to do what is right, regardless of the risk and the cost to oneself.

✦

The most inspiring leadership is compounded of eloquent instruction and inspiration, reinforced by personal example.

✦

Direct the energy of youth and optimism toward the achievement of worthwhile objectives.

✦

Do not hesitate to inspire those you lead.

✦

Embrace idealism, which has the potential for great things. Avoid cynicism, which is almost always destructive.

✦

Do not make the mistake of assuming that cynicism is synonymous with realism.

✦

Challenge those you lead. Invite them to aspire to excellence.

✦

Set the bar high and then even higher. Provide the support and inspiration to make each successively higher goal a realistic one.

✦

Expect the best. Anticipate the best. Encourage the best. Support the best.

✦

Encourage restlessness.

King, Ernest Joseph

Born: 1878   Died: 1956

**Character model   Innovator   Mentor   Motivator   Problem solver
Rescuer   Strategist   Tactician**

LEADERSHIP ACHIEVEMENTS

✦

Respected naval history, experience, and tradition while
continually innovating

✦

Successfully challenged himself to master new technologies,
from a practical level up to command

✦

Mentored a generation of naval officers

✦

Assumed major command after a crippling crisis and motivated
recovery and success

✦

Directed strategy for the overwhelmingly successful U.S. Pacific campaign
in World War II

LIFE

Admiral Ernest King was not a leader beloved by his men. He was, however, a sound naval strategist and a man with a solid reputation for getting things done. As he said when he was appointed chief of naval operations after Pearl Harbor: "When they get into trouble, they always call for the sons of bitches." He is remembered chiefly as an example of a straight-ahead, no-nonsense, mission-focused approach to leadership; however, King was also an able mentor, who was instrumental in training many of the naval officers who fought in World War II.

Born in Lorain, Ohio, King served as a midshipman during the Spanish–American War aboard the U.S.S. *San Francisco,* on patrol off the East Coast during April–December 1898. He saw no combat during the conflict, but, after the war, returned to the U.S. Naval Academy, from which he graduated near the top of the class of 1901. As an ensign in 1903, he served aboard the U.S.S. *Cincinnati,* which was dispatched to observe naval action during the Russo–Japanese War (February 1904–September 1905). This made a powerful impression on King, who saw firsthand the destructive force of modern naval guns.

Promoted to lieutenant in June 1906, King served as an ordnance instructor at the Naval Academy until 1909. At his request, in 1909, he was assigned sea duty aboard battleships of the Atlantic Fleet. After promotion to lieutenant commander in July 1913, he transferred to a shore post with the Engineering Experimental Station at Annapolis, and then, in 1914, was given command of the destroyer U.S.S. *Terry* (DD-25) off Veracruz during the April–November Mexican crisis.

King was promoted to commander in 1917 and to the temporary rank of captain in September 1918. He served in the Atlantic Fleet during the United States' participation in World War I. After the war, he was named to head the postgraduate department of the Naval Academy, and then, in 1921, chose sea duty again, as commander of a refrigerator ship off the East Coast. Never a man to shy away from technologies he believed crucial to combat, in 1922 he began submarine training at New London, Connecticut, and afterward assumed command of Submarine Division II. In 1923, he became commandant of the Submarine Base at New London, until he was appointed senior aide to Captain H. E. Yarnell, commander of Aircraft Squadrons Scouting Fleet (1926–27). This assignment exposed him to yet another developing technology, naval aviation. Many old-line commanders were resistant to aviation in a naval context. King, in contrast, embraced it. While serving with Yarnell, the 48-year-old King enrolled in aviator training and received his pilot's wings in May 1927.

King approached all of his commands from a basis of practical knowledge. Before accepting a submarine command, he became a submariner. After achieving proficiency in naval aviation, he accepted appointment as assistant chief of the Bureau of Aeronautics during 1928–29, and then became commander of the naval air base at Hampton Roads, Virginia. From 1930 to 1932, he skippered the aircraft carrier U.S.S. *Lexington* (CV-3). King graduated from the Naval War College senior course in 1933 and was promoted to rear admiral in April of that year, securing an appointment as chief of the Bureau of Aeronautics.

In 1938, King was promoted to vice admiral as commander of the five-carrier Aircraft Battle Force. He soon left this post to join the General Board in August 1939, and then assumed command of the Fleet Patrol Force in the Atlantic in December 1940. Promoted on February 1, 1941, to admiral and commander in chief of the Atlantic Fleet, he directed the undeclared antisubmarine war with Germany off the U.S. East Coast.

Following the Japanese attack on Pearl Harbor on December 7, 1941, King was named chief of naval operations and, on March 13, 1942, commander in chief of the U.S. Fleet. In this post, he played a critical role in formulating Allied strategy and was present at all of the major Allied conferences. Promoted to fleet admiral on December 17, 1944, he retired after the war, in December 1945.

IN HIS OWN WORDS

"Any man facing a major decision acts, consciously or otherwise, upon training and beliefs of a lifetime. This is no less true of a military commander than of a surgeon who, while operating, suddenly encounters an unsuspected complication. In both instances, the men must act immediately, with little time for reflection, and if they are successful in dealing with the unexpected it is upon the basis of past experience and training."

—*Fleet Admiral Ernest J. King, A Naval Record,* 1952

LEADERSHIP LESSONS

✦

Learn from history, from mentors, and from tradition,
but never fear to innovate.

✦

Do not arbitrarily break with the experience of the past, but never let
precedent retard useful innovation.

✦

Separate the timeless principles from time-bound technologies.

Kinkaid, Thomas Cassin

Born: 1888   Died: 1972

Leverager   Motivator   Problem solver   Systems creator   Tactician

LEADERSHIP ACHIEVEMENTS

✦

Built a vast base of practical command experience

✦

Combined command presence with great charm, a talent that facilitated
the work of coordinating large operations with other commanders and
other service branches

✦

By empowering subordinates with a high degree of autonomy, developed
extraordinary flexibility and efficiency, which were critical in fending off a
counterattack at Leyte, Philippines

✦

Was adept at leveraging lesser forces against greater

LIFE

The major American commanders of World War II were a varied lot, not
in terms of their abilities—which were uniformly quite high—but in their
approach to command. Admiral Ernest J. King was a no-nonsense commander, whose blunt approach produced many sore toes. Thomas Cassin
Kinkaid, in contrast, was a military diplomat who excelled at forging a
coordinated effort among the often overly competitive service branches.

He was born in Hanover, New Hampshire, and graduated from the
Naval Academy in 1908, in time to sail with the navy's Great White Fleet
aboard the battleships *Nebraska* (BB-14) and *Minnesota* (BB-22) during
1908–11. Kinkaid resolved to become expert in naval gunnery and attended
the ordnance course at the Naval Postgraduate School in Annapolis in 1913.
Promoted to lieutenant in June 1916, Kinkaid served patrol duty off the
East Coast as the United States prepared to enter World War I. Promoted
to lieutenant in November 1917, he was sent overseas as gunnery officer of
U.S.S. *Arizona* (BB-39) in April 1918.

After the war ended, Kinkaid returned to the States as an officer in the Bureau of Ordnance, where he served until 1922, when he was promoted to lieutenant commander and assigned as aide to Admiral Mark Bristol. Kinkaid received his own sea command, as skipper of the destroyer U.S.S. *Isherwood* (DD-284), in 1924, and then returned to shore duty in 1925 as an officer at the Naval Gun Factory in Washington, D.C. He returned to sea as commander and gunnery officer with the U.S. fleet from 1927 to 1929, when he enrolled in the Naval War College, graduating in 1930.

From 1933 to 1934, Kinkaid served as executive officer on the battleship *Colorado* (BB-45). Next, from 1934 to 1937, he commanded the Bureau of Navigation's Officer Detail Section. Promoted to captain, he was assigned command of the cruiser *Indianapolis* (CA-35), leaving this command in 1938 to become naval attaché and naval air attaché in Rome (November 1938) and naval attaché in Belgrade, Yugoslavia. In March 1941, Kinkaid returned to the United States, where he was promoted to rear admiral and assigned to command Cruiser Division 6 just one month before Pearl Harbor.

In March 1942, after the attack on Pearl Harbor, Kinkaid's division was assigned to support raids against the major Japanese bases at Rabaul and New Guinea. He fought in the battle of Coral Sea (May 4–8) and at Midway, during June 2–5, which, together, formed the turning point of the naval war in the Pacific. Following victory at Midway, Kinkaid assumed command of Task Force 16, built around the aircraft carrier U.S.S. *Enterprise* (CV-6). In this role, he supported the crucial landings on Guadalcanal (August 7) and fought in the carrier battles of the Eastern Solomons (August 22–25) and off the Santa Cruz Islands (October 25–28). During November 12–15, he fought Japanese surface ships near Guadalcanal.

Named to command the North Pacific Task Force, Kinkaid directed the recapture of the Aleutian Islands, retaking Amchitka on February 12, 1943, and Attu on May 11–30. He landed troops unopposed at Kiska on August 15, the final action of the Aleutian campaign.

Promoted to vice admiral in June, Kinkaid was transferred to command of Allied Naval Forces in the Southwest Pacific Area and, on November 26, the U.S. Seventh Fleet as well. He coordinated naval effort with General Douglas MacArthur's amphibious advance along the New

Guinea coast toward the Philippines. He also worked closely with Admiral William F. "Bull" Halsey's Third Fleet to cover the American landings (October 20, 1944) on Leyte in the Philippines. A critical juncture of this campaign came when Kinkaid responded to reports of a massive Japanese counterattack by deploying his outmoded battleships under Admiral Jesse B. Oldendorf to blockade the southern entrance to Leyte Gulf at Surigao Strait. Despite being outnumbered and outgunned, Oldendorf checked the advance of the Japanese southern force and, during a spectacular night battle on October 25, destroyed it. The main Japanese attack force, which arrived off the east coast of Samar, was met only by a small group of escort carriers under Admiral Clifton E. Sprague. Fortunately, Sprague was quickly joined by a detachment of Oldendorf's battleships on October 25, and the Japanese withdrew. The action was a classic example of leverage, using a smaller force of older ships to block an action that might have succeeded in cutting off the U.S. landing force on Leyte.

Kinkaid next directed additional Philippine amphibious operations against Mindoro (December 15) and at Lingayen Gulf on Luzon (January 9, 1945). After promotion to admiral in April 1945, he directed the landing of American occupation forces in China and Korea during September.

Following the end of the Pacific war, Kinkaid left the Seventh Fleet to take command of the Eastern Sea Frontier, headquartered at New York. After serving in this post from January to June 1946, he was named commander of the Atlantic Reserve Fleet in January 1947, in which post he served until he retired on May 1, 1950.

Personally warm and genial, Kinkaid made a sharp contrast with both Ernest Joseph King and Bull Halsey, neither of whom was celebrated as a master of tact. Kinkaid made effective use of his people skills to secure highly effective cooperation from Army, Navy, and Army Air Force units. His commanders recognized this talent and exploited it, giving Kinkaid command of some of the Pacific war's most important amphibious efforts, from the Aleutians to the Philippines, all of which required precise coordination among the service branches. Kinkaid's own subordinates loved working with him. Kinkaid believed in empowering his officers with a high degree of autonomy, and they, in turn, made it their business to avoid disappointing him.

IN HIS OWN WORDS

"It is highly desirable that a military man speak and write the English language clearly and forcibly. It is essential that he be articulate in the formation of orders and directives."
—Quoted from 1959 in Peter G. Tsouras, *The Greenhill Dictionary of Military Quotations*, 2000.

LEADERSHIP LESSONS

◆

Negotiated coordination is always more effective than forced compliance.

◆

Personal charm is a highly desirable quality in a leader.

◆

Leadership is conferred from the top, but it is earned from the bottom up.

◆

Select subordinates carefully, mentor them conscientiously, and then empower them extensively.

◆

Empowerment of trusted subordinates is the surest means of producing flexibility, speed, and efficiency.

Lafayette, Marie Joseph Paul Yves Roch Gilbert du Motier, Marquis de

Born: 1757   Died: 1834

Character model   Leverager   Motivator   Tactician   Visionary

LEADERSHIP ACHIEVEMENTS

◆

Nurtured his passion for liberty and turned it to account by embracing the American cause

◆

Helped George Washington create a disciplined and effective Continental Army

◆

Reinforced the leadership of Washington

◆

Was instrumental in the survival of the Continental Army through the winter of Valley Forge

◆

Proved highly effective in Virginia against Lord Cornwallis

◆

Combined a passion for liberty with a sense of political moderation

LIFE

The Marquis de Lafayette was born at Chavaniac in the French Auvergne. His father, a French officer, fell at the Battle of Minden on August 1, 1759, when his son was only two years old. Eleven years later, in 1770, Lafayette's mother died, leaving him an orphan but also a wealthy youth. At age 14, in 1771, Lafayette joined an infantry regiment, and then, after two years, transferred to the dragoons and was promoted to captain in 1774.

In 1776, Lafayette was approached by Silas Deane, the U.S. minister to France. By December, Deane had negotiated an agreement by which Lafayette would serve as a military adviser to the colonies in the American Revolution. The young officer arrived in America in company with another European champion of American liberty, the Prussian officer Baron de Kalb, in April 1777. Lafayette's service was motivated by a long-nurtured passion for liberty. In all of their negotiation, he and Deane had never settled upon his salary or rank.

Lafayette's first American action was at the Battle of Brandywine, where he fought with distinction and suffered a wound on September 11. Although Brandywine was a defeat for the Continental Army—and, indeed, revealed certain weaknesses of George Washington as a military tactician—Lafayette quickly conceived a great admiration for Washington and became a loyal supporter. During the trial that was the winter in Valley Forge, a time in which faltering support for the Continental Army threatened the troops not merely with disbandment, but with starvation, Lafayette's steadfast resolve, his willingness to undergo the same privations as his men, and his unwavering support of Washington helped see the army through this most difficult period. Lafayette's loyalty, military skill, courage, and character also persuaded Washington to put him in charge of an invasion of Canada during March–April 1778. That plan soon had to be abandoned, however, but Lafayette continued to distinguish himself in every battle he fought: at Barren Hill (May 18); at Monmouth Court House (June 28), where he led a division; and at Newport (July–August).

Lafayette returned briefly to France on leave. He was promoted to colonel while he was there, and, in April 1779, he drew up the initial plans for a full-scale French expeditionary force to aid the colonies. After he returned to America in April 1780, he was given command of the Virginia light troops and, during March 1781, worked feverishly to counter the highly effective Virginia raids led by the turncoat Benedict Arnold. Lafayette also successfully evaded British general Charles Cornwallis's attempts to draw his badly outnumbered force into battle during April–June. Cornwallis's determination to crush Lafayette amounted virtually to a personal vendetta.

Early in June 1781, Lafayette received reinforcements and rushed with them to coordinate action with General Anthony Wayne. Together, on July 6, 1781, the two commanders fought a fierce battle against Cornwallis at Green Spring, Virginia. Believing that a commander had to lead from the front, Lafayette, as usual, put himself in harm's way, and had two horses shot from under him. By August, it was Cornwallis who was on the run, and Lafayette was among those who pursued him to Yorktown. There Lafayette played a key role in the siege of that peninsula during

September 14–October 19, 1781, which culminated in the surrender of Cornwallis and brought about the successful conclusion of the American Revolution.

Upon his return to France, Lafayette was promoted to major general in December 1781. Three years later, during July–December 1784, he toured the United States, where he was welcomed as a hero. Lafayette was named a member of the French Assembly of Notables in 1787 and represented his native Auvergne in the Estates General of 1789. He was appointed commander of the newly established National Guard on July 26, 1789. In this capacity, in October, he saved the royal family from the Paris mob as the French Revolution got under way.

Lafayette sided with the republicans during the French Revolution and, promoted to lieutenant general in 1791, he was given command of the Army of the Center. Always a man of reason, his moderate views were clearly out of step with the bloody radicalism of the architects of the Reign of Terror. Jacobin leaders brought about his relief from command, and Lafayette, understandably fearing the guillotine, fled to Belgium in 1792. There he was arrested by Austrian authorities and imprisoned, released, and then imprisoned a second time by the Prussians, first at Magdeburg and then at Olmutz. He was not released until September 23, 1797, whereupon he returned to what was now the France of Napoleon Bonaparte.

In Napoleon, Lafayette saw a great captain, but he profoundly distrusted his boundless ambition. He declined to accept a role in the military or the government and retired from public life, taking up quiet residence on his wife's estate at La Grange Bleneau. When a defeated Napoleon was compelled to approve the liberal constitution of 1815, Lafayette reemerged, accepting the position of vice president of the Chamber of Deputies. In this capacity, he was instrumental in securing Napoleon's second, and final, abdication.

Lafayette served during the Bourbon restoration as a deputy, but soon became a leader of the liberal opposition. With the tide turned against liberalism, however, he was defeated in his 1824 bid for reelection to the Chamber of Deputies. He took time to tour the United States, where he was accorded an ecstatic welcome. Returning to France, he was at last reelected to the Chamber in 1827 and was given command of the National Guard during the revolution against Charles X in July 1830. Always seeking a way to combine order with liberty, Lafayette at first supported Louis Philippe. In 1832, however, he denounced the emperor because of his failure to uphold the liberal pledges he had made. Lafayette died two years later.

Lafayette could have lived a life of idle privilege, but he chose to dedicate himself to the cause of liberty. Although he had had little experience as a commander when he joined the American cause, he quickly proved an excellent officer, not only a capable tactician, but an inspiring leader of men, who commanded loyalty and gave it in return.

LEADERSHIP LESSONS

✦

Recognize, nurture, and channel your passionate beliefs.

✦

Demand loyalty, and render loyalty in return.

✦

Convey confidence—confidence in yourself, in those you lead, and in those you follow.

✦

Treat adversity as an opportunity for outstanding achievement.

✦

Leverage your resources. Make the most of what you have.
Typically outnumbered, Lafayette learned to exploit to advantage
the mobility of his smaller forces.

Lawrence, T. E.
(Lawrence of Arabia)

Born: 1888   Died: 1935

**Character model   Improviser   Innovator   Leverager   Mentor   Motivator
Problem solver   Rescuer   Strategist   Tactician   Visionary**

LEADERSHIP ACHIEVEMENTS

◆

Raised unconventional leadership to a spectacular height

◆

Synthesized European and Arab tactics to create an extraordinarily
effective guerrilla force in World War I

◆

Led by combining a thorough understanding of two vastly different cultures

◆

Earned the confidence of his British superiors as well as
the Arab forces he led

◆

Combined military genius with the highest possible degree of
emotional intelligence

◆

Leveraged a small group of warriors so that they proved effective against a
major, well-equipped army

◆

Mastered the demanding tactics of hit-and-run desert warfare, greatly
extending the scope and flexibility of the British war effort

◆

Led without compromise, always maintaining the highest personal integrity

LIFE

Destined to legendary renown as Lawrence of Arabia, T. E. Lawrence, the
British organizer of Arab guerrilla forces in World War I, was a most
unlikely leader. He was born at Tremadoc, Caernarvonshire, Wales, the
illegitimate son of Sir Robert Chapman by his daughters' governess, Sara
Maden. Intelligent and sensitive, he eagerly devoured a superb education
at Jesus College, Oxford, and embarked on what promised to be a life of
quiet and arcane archaeological scholarship. In 1909, he traveled to the
Middle East to study Crusader castles, and he wrote his first-class honors

thesis on the subject in 1910. From 1911 to 1914, he enjoyed a traveling endowment from Oxford's Magdalen College, which allowed him to join an archaeological expedition excavating Carchemish (Barak) on the Euphrates River.

Early in 1914, Lawrence set out on his own to explore the northern Sinai. With his scholarly credentials firmly established, local government authorities naturally assumed that Lawrence's interest in the region was strictly archaeological. In fact, he was operating in the service of his majesty's government. As Britain and all Europe stood at the brink of a world war, Lawrence volunteered to reconnoiter the situation in the strategically critical region of Turkish Palestine. He was a spy.

Just before World War I began in the summer of 1914, Lawrence returned to England and was given an officer's commission in the British army. When war broke out in August, he was assigned as a cartographer to the War Office's map department. The apparently bookish Lawrence did not take well to desk work, and he was thrilled when, after German-allied Turkey declared war on England, he was dispatched to Cairo in December 1914 as an intelligence officer attached to the Arab section.

During the fall of 1915, British and French generals and diplomats negotiated an agreement with Hussein, the grand sherif of Mecca, pledging—if quite vaguely—to help him gain territory and, more important, to support Arab independence from the Ottoman Turks. In return, Hussein agreed to cooperate with the Allies in operations against the Turks. Accordingly, on June 5, 1916, Hussein attacked the Turkish garrison at Medina, then boldly proclaimed independence for the Arabs and went on to storm the Turkish garrison at Mecca, which surrendered to him on June 10. Hussein's next attack, on Turkish forces at Medina, failed, but Hussein's actions hampered the Turkish war effort in the region, and it was clear that his participation in the war was of significant benefit to the Allies.

Lawrence, at this point an army captain, studied the unsuccessful Arab operations at Medina and drew a conclusion that had escaped his more conventional military superiors. Lawrence reasoned that the Arab cavalry could not be expected to challenge well-defended Turkish positions. Siege work was not the kind of fighting the highly mobile Arabs were suited to. They were best at small-group, hit-and-run raids. Securing the permission of his commanders, Lawrence called on Hussein's third son,

Faisal, who served as field commander of the Arab army, to break off the direct attack against Medina and instead to use his forces first to dissemi- nate pro-independence propaganda among the Arabs, in order to unite them, and then to raid the overextended Turkish lines of communications.

The military genius of Lawrence lay in his understanding of what modern tacticians call "force multiplying," knowing how to leverage mod- est resources to exploit their strongest assets and thereby to leverage them, to multiply their effectiveness. That was Lawrence's military genius. His even greater power lay in his ability and willingness to lead the Arabs not as a British officer leading natives, but as a man who had come to identify with the Arabs and their cause. Lawrence effectively adopted an Arab per- sona, an Arab approach to war, and, indeed, an Arab mind-set. He even shed his British uniform and wore the dress of an Arab warrior. Yet he brought to those he led the best that the British military had to offer: dis- cipline, organization, coordination, and focus.

The combination of Arab and British military tactics proved highly effective. Continually struck by hit-and-run raids, coming seemingly out of nowhere, the Turks had no choice but to halt their offensive operations south of Medina, and they also had to assign valuable troops—troops who would otherwise be committed against the main British forces—to defend long stretches of the strategically vital Hejaz railway. With about 6,000 men, Lawrence succeeded in tying down some 25,000 Turks.

Lawrence's success earned him the grudging admiration of his British colleagues and superiors, who nevertheless also resented his unconventional approach to combat and to what they perceived as the natural order of things—that is, European dominance over "native" peo- ples. Faisal appointed Lawrence his chief adviser, which meant that he assumed strategic leadership of Faisal's forces. Lawrence led Faisal's army in the capture of Wejh, a critical port on the Red Sea coast. After he took this objective on January 24, 1917, he organized guerrilla strikes against the Hejaz railway between March and April. Later, after an important vic- tory at Tafila during January 21–27, 1918, Lawrence was promoted to lieu- tenant colonel.

In the early fall of 1918, Lawrence approached the commander in chief of British forces in the Middle East, General Sir Edmund Allenby, with a plan for Arab participation in the major offensive that Allenby intended as the decisive, culminating campaign of the war in the Middle East. Lawrence proposed that the Arabs form the right flank of the British army's advance through Palestine to its objective, Damascus, Syria.

Allenby liked Lawrence's plan and concurred with it. What he did not know was that Lawrence had an ulterior motive. The British high command made vague promises to the Arabs that Britain would support their bid for independence. Lawrence understood that the British government had no intention of honoring its promise, but he meant not only to use the Arabs as allies in the war, but to lead them to genuine and enduring independence from the Ottoman Empire. Secretly, Lawrence proposed to Faisal that he would lead the Arab contingent in advance of Allenby and capture Damascus before the main body of British troops arrived. This would give Faisal a claim on the city as the new capital of an independent Arabia.

As Allenby's main force advanced on Damascus, Lawrence led 3,000 camel-mounted Arabs against Deraa. This attack drew off Turkish forces from Allenby's principal objectives, and greatly aided his advance. Allenby also realized, however, that the attack brought Lawrence and his Arabs closer to Damascus, and he ordered Lawrence not to continue the advance. It was an order Lawrence ignored.

By September 30, 1918, the Turks had evacuated Damascus, and Lawrence, at the head of his small army, entered the city about three hours before Allenby reached it. Although he had disobeyed orders, Lawrence had used 3,000 men to tie down more than 15,000 Turks, and a bemused Allenby chose not to court-martial him but to promote him from lieutenant colonel to colonel.

For his part, with the war all but over, Colonel T. E. Lawrence had had enough. He did not relish official military glory, and at the moment of his greatest triumph and recognition, he resigned his commission.

Lawrence returned to Britain on the very day of the armistice, November 11, 1918, and vigorously sought to make good on his promise to the Arabs to support their independence. He tried tirelessly, but without success, to intercede at the highest levels of government, in England as well as France, on behalf of the Arab cause. Although he was chosen to be a member of the British delegation to the Versailles peace conference, which would determine the disposition of nations and colonial possessions in the wake of Allied victory, Lawrence was unable to prevent the colonial dis-memberment of Arabia. He agreed to serve the British government, during 1921–22, as adviser on Arab affairs in the Middle Eastern Division of the Colonial Office, but he was quickly disillusioned with government policy and resigned.

After he left the government service in 1922, Lawrence found it impossible to escape the celebrity status his exploits had earned him, and, in August 1922, he enlisted in the Royal Air Force (RAF) under a pseudonym. When a newspaper revealed his secret in January 1923, he resigned and enlisted in the Royal Tank Corps in March, calling himself T. E. Shaw—a name he would legally adopt in 1927. Lawrence transferred back to the RAF in 1925 and then privately published his wartime memoirs, a monumental literary masterpiece entitled *The Seven Pillars of Wisdom,* in a limited edition of only 150 copies. In 1927, he abridged the book as *Revolt in the Desert* and allowed its commercial publication to a wide audience. Lawrence left the RAF in 1935 and, shortly afterward, was fatally injured in a motorcycle accident near his home, Cloud Hill, in Dorset. *The Seven Pillars of Wisdom* was commercially published in its original version posthumously and to great acclaim. It remains a widely read classic and has reached perhaps its broadest audience as the basis of David Lean's great 1962 film *Lawrence of Arabia.*

IN HIS OWN WORDS

"Our tactics were always tip and run, not pushes, but strokes. We never tried to maintain or improve an advantage, but to move off and strike somewhere else. We used the smallest force, in the quickest time, at the farthest place."

—On guerrilla tactics, in "The Evolution of a Revolt," *Army Quarterly,* 1920

"Nine-tenths of tactics were certain enough to be teachable in schools; but the irrational tenth was like the kingfisher flashing across the pool, and in it lay the test of generals. It could be ensued only by instinct (sharpened by thought practicing the stroke) until at the crisis it came naturally, a reflex."

—On military genius, in *The Seven Pillars of Wisdom,* 1925

LEADERSHIP LESSONS

✦

Refuse to be pigeonholed or typecast. Surprise people with your initiative and your hunger for excellence.

✦

Think—and act—outside of the box. Do not be shackled by prejudice and preconception.

✦

Adapt your tactics and your objectives to circumstances and to available assets.

✦

Be willing to shift objectives when advantage in alternatives is found.

✦

Learn to multiply the forces at hand. Never neglect an opportunity for leverage.

✦

Earn the loyalty of those you lead by identifying with their needs, their weaknesses, and their strengths.

✦

Dare to be unconventional. Achievement will vindicate you.

✦

In the interests of the enterprise, defy authority.

✦

Embrace responsibility. Take initiative. Decide that everything depends on you, on who you are, and on what you do.

✦

Bigger is not necessarily better. Consider the effectiveness of small, tightly integrated teams tackling well-defined tasks quickly and efficiently.

✦

Presented with a risk, calculate the risk. All else being equal, take the risk.

Lee, Robert Edward

Born: 1807   Died: 1870

**Character model   Improviser   Leverager   Mentor   Motivator
Problem solver   Strategist   Tactician**

LEADERSHIP ACHIEVEMENTS

◆

Developed and exercised great intelligence, graduating second in his
West Point class

◆

Earned a reputation as a problem solver and a great planner and engineer

◆

Combined every skill of a great commander: an ability to lead,
tactical brilliance, an instinctive grasp of battlefield psychology,
and an appreciation of overall strategic goals

◆

Was a model of integrity, respected by friend and foe alike

◆

Effectively emphasized flexibility, speed, and surprise

◆

Commanded extraordinary loyalty and devotion

LIFE

Commander of the Confederate Army of Northern Virginia during the
Civil War, Robert Edward Lee is probably the most universally respected,
admired, and beloved military officer in U.S. history. He was born at
Stratford, Virginia, the third son of Revolutionary War hero Henry
"Lighthorse Harry" Lee and his second wife, Ann Hill Carter. After graduating from West Point, second in the class of 1829, Lee was commissioned
in the Corps of Engineers. Stationed along the southeast coast, he met and
married another illustrious ancestor of the Revolution, Mary Custis, great-
granddaughter of Martha Washington.

In his early career, Lee showed himself to be a brilliant military engineer, whose work on the Mississippi River at St. Louis and on the New
York Harbor defenses during 1836–46 earned him glowing praise. During

the U.S.–Mexican War, he served as chief engineer under General John E. Wool. For Wool's expedition to Saltillo, between September 26 and December 21, 1846, Lee built bridges and selected routes. He then joined General Winfield Scott at the Brazos River during January 1847 and served with distinction as a staff officer at the capture of Veracruz on March 27 and at Cerro Gordo on April 18. Lee's extraordinary reconnaissance efforts located the route Scott used for his outflanking force at Cerro Gordo. His reconnaissance was also critical to the victories at Contreras, Churubusco, and, on September 13, 1847, Chapultepec Castle, the last step before the invasion of Mexico City itself.

After the U.S.–Mexican War, Lee was appointed superintendent of West Point, serving there from 1852 to 1855, and was then promoted to colonel, commanding the 2nd Cavalry, headquartered in St. Louis. From 1855 to 1857, Lee served in Texas and the Southwest before he was recalled to Virginia in 1857 to serve as executor of his father-in-law's estate. Lee was still in Virginia when he was ordered to Harpers Ferry to put down the raid on the federal arsenal there by the abolitionist John Brown. He commanded a contingent of U.S. Marines in the successful operation against Brown, who was captured on October 18, 1859.

From February 1860 to February 1861, Lee commanded the Department of Texas and was recalled to Washington on February 4 as the secession crisis deepened. On April 20, 1861, Abraham Lincoln personally offered Lee command of all federal forces. Like many other U.S. Army officers at this time, Lee was unwilling to take arms against his home state. He declined Lincoln's offer, and he resigned his commission. He then accepted command of Virginia's military and naval forces. Unlike Lincoln, Confederate president Jefferson Davis did not fully recognize Lee's abilities as a field commander. He assigned Lee to the somewhat secondary role of his personal military adviser.

Indeed, Lee did not enjoy success with his first field command in western Virginia. Here, the locals were hostile to Tidewater Virginia and broke with the state to unite with the Union. Lee was also hampered by uncooperative subordinates. He was beaten at the Battle of Cheat Mountain (in present-day West Virginia) during September 12–13, 1861, and was then driven out of the mountains. Following this, Davis withdrew Lee from West Virginia to use his engineering expertise in strengthening the defenses of the southeast coast at Charleston, South Carolina, Port Royal, Virginia, and Savannah, Georgia. Lee was occupied with this work from October 1861 to March 1862. He carried out his assignment to the best of his ability, but was disappointed that he was not serving in a frontline combat capacity.

In March 1862, Lee was recalled to Richmond once again to advise Davis as Union forces bore down on General Joseph E. Johnston's army, pushing it back toward the Confederate capital. It was Lee who urged Major General Thomas ("Stonewall") Jackson to embark on the devastatingly effective Shenandoah Valley Campaign during May 1–June 9, 1862. After General Johnston was seriously wounded at Seven Pines (May 31–June 1), Lee was summoned to replace him. He immediately created the Army of Northern Virginia and led it in a successful defense against Union commander George B. McClellan in the battles known collectively as the Seven Days (June 26–July 2). Lee also spectacularly outgeneraled John Pope, humiliating him at the Second Battle of Bull Run during August 29–30.

Lee stood apart from most of his contemporaries for his formidable combination of leadership qualities. He was, first and foremost, a man of extraordinary character, whose very presence commanded respect. His leadership style was not dictatorial, but collegial. He empowered his subordinates to a high degree, often eliciting from them top performance and unswerving loyalty. He was a tactical commander of great skill and imagination. In most situations, he possessed an uncanny faculty for putting himself in the place of his opponent and thereby deducing the enemy's likely moves. Not only was Lee a great tactician, however, he was also a superb strategist. He quickly grasped the nature of the task facing the Confederacy. He understood the realities of southern resources, which were inferior to those of the North in terms of available manpower, available finance and credit, and an available manufacturing base. He accepted this reality and devised a strategy to minimize its impact. As Lee saw it, the South did not have to win a decisive victory over the North. It had merely to win battles, to keep the North fighting fruitlessly until the northern popular will to fight faded and a favorable peace could be concluded.

In accordance with Lee's understanding of the best southern strategy, he was determined to fight a primarily defensive war, one in which he forced the northern armies to beat themselves against unattainable objectives. Defensive wars are never popular with generals, who believe that no army ever won a war by a defensive strategy. Yet Lee saw costly attrition as his most powerful ally and was willing to go against accepted military doctrine.

Lee was also eminently flexible. When General McClellan proved a consistently overcautious opponent, Lee decided to exploit a psychological advantage by taking an offensive stance with an invasion of Maryland. McClellan responded on September 17, 1862, by attacking Lee at Antietam. The result was either a very narrow Union victory or a bloody draw. Although Lee successfully repulsed McClellan, he himself was forced to withdraw into Virginia. There he confronted General Ambrose Burnside, whom he defeated at the Battle of Fredericksburg on December 13, 1862. Because of the inept Burnside's determination to move against Fredericksburg with a series of ill-judged frontal attacks, the Union defeat was particularly costly. Next, at Chancellorsville, during May 2–4, 1863, Lee scored a brilliant victory over Joseph Hooker, bringing about a Union disaster on a scale similar to Fredericksburg.

The decisive victories at Fredericksburg and Chancellorsville emboldened Lee to invade the North again. With the northern public reeling from two terrible defeats, Lee hoped that a bold raid into Pennsylvania would greatly dishearten the North.

At the Battle of Gettysburg (July 1–3, 1863), however, Lee's hallmark command style, his habit of dealing with subordinates as colleagues, his absolute faith in them, and his empowerment of them, failed him. Poor reconnaissance and Lee's own failure to issue consistently clear orders contributed to a Confederate defeat at the hands of Union general George G. Meade in the battle regarded as the turning point of the war. Lee withdrew into Virginia, and the North was secure from invasion. Lee would never conduct an offensive campaign again.

Indeed, Lee conducted no further major campaigns until General Ulysses S. Grant became Union general in chief on March 9, 1864. Lee then employed a brilliantly successful defense against Grant at the Battle of the Wilderness during May 5–6, 1864, and bested Grant again at Spotsylvania (May 8–12). But, like Lee, Grant fully grasped the strategy appropriate to the army he commanded. What Grant understood was that the North had vast resources and the South few—with those few dwindling. As long as the North's will to fight could be maintained, it would be the North and not the South that would win a war of attrition. Grant understood and, even more important, accepted the grim calculus of this war: The North could afford to lose many more men than the South.

On May 23, Grant enveloped Lee, forcing him out of his entrenchments at the North Anna River. However, Lee, in turn, repulsed Grant's assault at Cold Harbor on June 3, inflicting heavy Union losses, but then suffered an envelopment that forced him back across the James River. Grant crossed this river during June 12–16 and mounted an assault against Petersburg, Virginia. Thanks to Lee's skilled deployment of men behind extremely well-prepared defenses, the Petersburg campaign became a long siege. This, however, served only to put off the inevitable. As the Union army could absorb more losses than the Confederate army, so it could outsit the Confederates in a siege. Lee's army continued to dwindle.

In the meantime, an increasingly desperate Jefferson Davis named Lee general in chief of the Confederate armies on February 3, 1865. On March 27, 1865, Confederate commander John Brown Gordon made a surprise assault on Fort Stedman, a Union position on the Petersburg front, which Grant readily parried. Now Lee once again found himself outflanked by Grant, at Five Forks, during March 29–31. Lee withdrew from Richmond and Petersburg during April 2–3, 1865, but Grant pursued, always applying pressure. With his route of escape through the Carolinas blocked, Lee surrendered the Army of Northern Virginia to Grant at Appomattox Court House on April 9, 1865. For all intents and purposes, this act ended the Civil War.

Lee was made a prisoner of war for only a brief period before he was paroled. In September 1865, he accepted the presidency of Washington College (later renamed Washington and Lee University) in Lexington, Virginia. The hardships—and heartbreak—of the war had prematurely aged the general, however, and he died just five years later.

IN HIS OWN WORDS

"How can I trust a man to command others who cannot command himself?"
—Quoted in Douglas Southall Freeman, *Douglas Southall Freeman on Leadership,* 1993

"No matter what may be the ability of the officer, if he loses the confidence of his troops, disaster must sooner or later ensue."
—Letter to Jefferson Davis, August 8, 1863

"We usually think and act from our local surroundings. The better rule is to judge our adversaries from their standpoint, not from our own."
—Notes found in Lee's desk, 1870

"I begin to fear that the enemy will not attack us. We shall therefore have to attack him."
—Letter to John B. Floyd, September 30, 1861

LEADERSHIP LESSONS

✦

Analyze and accept reality. Do not deny it. Work within it. Leverage it.

✦

Imagination is an underrated leadership quality. A leader who can put himself in the mind of his opponent has an immeasurable advantage.

✦

Play to your strengths, yes, but, equally important, play to the opponent's weaknesses.

✦

Absolute victory is not always the only option for winning. Sometimes the only feasible goal is to avoid defeat and thereby maneuver the opponent into a favorable settlement.

LeMay, Curtis Emerson

Born: 1906   Died: 1990

Innovator   Motivator   Problem solver   Systems creator   Tactician

LEADERSHIP ACHIEVEMENTS

✦

Developed the doctrine and tactics of strategic bombing

✦

Innovated tactics

✦

Elicited maximum performance from air crews and their machines

✦

Created daring tactics that proved highly effective

✦

Was key commander of the Berlin Airlift

✦

Was chief architect of the Cold War era air force and the
Strategic Air Command

LIFE

Brash and often intolerant, Curtis Emerson LeMay was nevertheless a focused personality who was one of the key architects of the U.S. Air Force and led it into the nuclear age by creating the Strategic Air Command.

Born in Columbus, Ohio, LeMay knew disappointment early when he failed in his bid to obtain an appointment to West Point. He did not let this deter him from a military career, however, and attended Ohio State University, largely for its ROTC program. After he completed the program, he left the university and joined the army in September 1928 as a cadet in the Air Corps Flying School. LeMay earned his wings on October 12, 1929, and was commissioned a second lieutenant in January 1930.

While on active duty with the 27th Pursuit Squadron, LeMay completed the civil engineering degree he had begun at Ohio State. He graduated in 1932, worked for the depression-era CCC (Civilian Conservation Corps), and then flew the air mails when President Franklin D. Roosevelt assigned Army fliers to air mail operations in 1934. This was demanding, hazardous flying, which allowed LeMay to hone his skills and nerve as a pilot.

Promoted to first lieutenant in June 1935, LeMay attended an over-water navigation school in Hawaii, and then, in 1937, transferred from flying pursuit planes to the 305th Bombardment Group at Langley Field, Virginia. Here LeMay conducted exercises to demonstrate the ability of aircraft to find ships at sea. During this period, LeMay also became one of the first army pilots to fly the new B-17 bombers, the Flying Fortress, which would be the mainstay U.S. heavy bomber of World War II. LeMay was chosen to lead a flight of B-17s on a goodwill tour to Latin America during 1937–38, when President Roosevelt was promoting his Good Neighbor Policy with the nations south of the border. When LeMay returned from the tour, he attended the Air Corps Tactical School (1938–39) and, in January 1940, was promoted to captain and given command of a squadron in the 34th Bomb group.

As war loomed, LeMay was clearly on a fast track. Promoted early in 1941 to major, he was a lieutenant colonel by January 1942 and, three months later, a full colonel. At this time, in April 1942, he assumed command of the 305th Bombardment Group in California and brought that unit to Britain as part of the Eighth Air Force. Once his unit was in place overseas, LeMay set about perfecting precision bombing tactics by the risky means of abandoning evasive maneuvering over targets and by also introducing careful target studies prior to missions. These innovative techniques required strong leadership, since they involved a high degree of risk, rendering the bombers more vulnerable to fighter and antiaircraft artillery attack. However, the techniques soon doubled the number of bombs placed on target, making each mission much more effective.

In June 1943, LeMay was assigned command of the 3rd Bombardment Division, which he led on the so-called "shuttle raid" on Regensburg, Germany, in August. The following month, LeMay was promoted to temporary brigadier general, followed by promotion to temporary major general in March 1944. He was then sent to China to lead the 20th Bomber Command against the Japanese.

After LeMay took command of the 21st Bomber Group on Guam in January 1945, he stunned his air crews by modifying their B-29s to

carry more bombs. Once again, he had to instill in his command sufficient confidence to undertake missions in planes that, to save weight,
had been largely stripped of their defensive guns, including the guns,
gun crews, and ammunition. Furthermore, he ordered the aircraft to
attack targets singly, not in formation, and at low level. As in Europe,
the risk, though great, yielded a dramatic improvement in
effectiveness—and did not significantly increase casualties among air
crews. The 21st Bomber Group annihilated four major Japanese cities
with incendiary bombs in a campaign of destruction that was far more
devastating than the subsequent atomic bombing of Hiroshima and
Nagasaki. LeMay earned a reputation as an uncompromising leader
who demanded maximum effort from his men, but who produced outstanding results. Far from feeling demoralized, the members of his command were proud of their achievements.

As the war wound down, LeMay was named commander of the
Twentieth air force (20th and 21st Bomber Groups) in July 1945 and then
deputy chief of staff for research and development, a post he held through
1947. In that year, he was promoted to temporary lieutenant general in an
air force made independent of the army in 1947. He was assigned to command U.S. Air Forces in Europe on October 1, 1947, and, in this capacity,
was a key planner in the spectacular Berlin Airlift of 1948–49. This was
another high-risk, very demanding mission of monumental proportions. In
an effort to block the creation of an independent West Germany with a capital, West Berlin, deep within Soviet-controlled East Germany, the USSR
blockaded West Berlin. Fearing that the loss of West Berlin would ultimately mean the loss of all Germany to the Soviets, President Truman
ordered the air force to supply West Berlin by air. No city had ever been
supplied exclusively from the air before, but, over the course of 321 days,
LeMay directed more than 272,000 flights over Soviet-occupied territory to
provide West Berlin with thousands of tons of supplies each day. Failure
would have meant a Soviet triumph, and failure loomed as a real possibility. LeMay's aircraft were flying round the clock in all weather, over potentially hostile territory. Nevertheless, on May 12, 1949, the Soviets were
forced to concede that the blockade had failed, and they reopened Berlin
to Western traffic. East and West Germany were formally named separate
nations later in the month.

The air force recognized LeMay as a leader who achieved the difficult and the near impossible, and always on a grand scale. Accordingly, in October 1948, he was recalled to the United States as head of the newly created Strategic Air Command, which, until the development of ICBM (intercontinental ballistic missile) systems, functioned as the armed forces' sole delivery system for atomic and thermonuclear weapons. Always an innovator, LeMay recognized that the air force's inventory of B-29s was inadequate to serve as the nation's primary atomic-age bomber. He led the air force into the jet age with the hybrid B-36 and then the fully jet-driven B-47 and B-52 bombers. LeMay also fostered the development of midair refueling, using large jet tanker aircraft (KC-135s). This not only greatly extended the bombers' range, it allowed bomber patrols to fly 24 hours a day, seven days a week. LeMay pioneered the tactics of continual high readiness, in which nuclear-armed aircraft were always in flight, prepared to retaliate against attack. Nor was LeMay sentimental about manned aircraft. Many officers resisted the introduction of unmanned missiles, fearing that they would replace pilots and planes. By the 1950s, LeMay oversaw the introduction of ICBM weapons into the air force's inventory of nuclear and thermonuclear delivery systems.

Curtis LeMay was promoted to general in October 1951, the youngest four-star general since Ulysses S. Grant. In 1957, he was named vice chief of staff of the U.S. Air Force and became chief of staff in 1961. During the 1960s, his hard-nosed, unyielding, and at times racist conservatism brought him into conflict with the liberal administrations of John F. Kennedy and Lyndon Johnson. His relations with Secretary of Defense Robert S. McNamara were particularly strained and even bitter. As he met with resistance, LeMay became increasingly irascible, extreme, and outspoken. On February 1, 1965, he retired from the air force, and with his political conservatism hardening during the turbulent late 1960s, he became the running mate of the notorious segregationist George Wallace in his failed 1968 bid for the presidency. The association with Wallace, unfortunately, tarnished the image of this uncompromising commander, who demanded "maximum effort" from his air crews and from their aircraft, and who shaped the modern air force as the most strategic of the triad of services.

IN HIS OWN WORDS

"The Base commander wanted to mow the grass; the Group commander wanted to fly his airplanes. . . . Answer? They mowed the grass. Because why? Because the Base commander made out the efficiency report on the Group commander. He got rated whether his grass was cut or not, or whether his buildings were painted. By God, that's what he was going to do: mow grass."
—*Mission with LeMay,* 1965

"If you're going to fight, you're going to have some people killed. . . . While it tortured me to lose people in the ETO [European Theater of Operations] and the Pacific, I think that in most cases I would be willing to meet them, and I would say, 'Well, you were properly expended, Gus. It was part of the price.' "
—*Mission with LeMay,* 1965

LEADERSHIP LESSONS
✦
Leadership is not a popularity contest. Define the mission, and then motivate those you lead to accomplish the mission.
✦
Nothing builds confidence and credibility like results.
✦
Be willing to give and demand maximum effort.
✦
Decide what you need; then decide what you must do. Strip away all else.
✦
Innovate.
✦
Avoid sentimental attachments to tactics and procedures. Use what works. Discard what fails.
✦
Understand that there is no reward without risk.

Lettow-Vorbeck, Paul Emil von

Born: 1870   Died: 1964

Improviser   Leverager   Problem solver   Tactician

LEADERSHIP ACHIEVEMENTS

◆

Learned the lessons of guerrilla warfare—a complete reeducation

◆

Was a great leverager

LIFE

Little celebrated in history, Paul von Lettow-Vorbeck was an extraordinary leader of German colonial forces in Africa during World War I. His is an unparalleled example of resourcefulness and an ability to leverage minimal resources to achieve major results. He was born at Saarlouis, the son of a prominent Prussian army officer. From earliest childhood, Lettow-Vorbeck was groomed for a military career. After his graduation from the prestigious *Kriegsakademie* in 1899, his promise as an officer was apparent from very early on. He was chosen for service on the General Staff (1899–1900) and was then assigned the critical job of leading the German contingent of the international coalition dispatched to China to punish the so-called Boxers, Chinese nationalists who rebelled against European interests in their country. With the end of the Boxer Rebellion in 1901, Lettow-Vorbeck was sent to German Southwest Africa (present-day Namibia) to fight the Hottentots and Hereros during 1904–08. This was Lettow-Vorbeck's baptism of fire. He saw how inadequately his formal European training had prepared him to fight a guerrilla war, and he was determined to learn from the enemy. Seriously wounded in an ambush in 1906, he was sent to a hospital in South Africa, recovered, continued to command in the field, and then returned to Germany in 1908, where he was promoted to lieutenant colonel. Early in 1914, Lettow-Vorbeck was sent back to Africa as commander of forces in German East Africa (present-day Tanzania). His native troops, called *askaris,* were armed with obsolete weapons and, as

Lettow-Vorbeck knew, would be totally cut off once a world war commenced. With limited supplies and very limited manpower, he resolved to strike preemptively, to gain with surprise and speed what he lacked in manpower and equipment.

As soon as World War I began in August 1914, Lettow-Vorbeck raided British rail lines in Kenya and then launched an attempt to capture Mombasa. He was driven back by September, but even this defeat was a victory, since he had succeeded in forcing the British to commit valuable manpower that might have been used elsewhere. Moreover, Lettow-Vorbeck in turn successfully defended against a British amphibious attack on the port town of Tanga in northeastern Tanzania during November 2–3, 1914. His defense made the attack especially costly for the British. He not only inflicted heavy losses on them, but he acquired a large cache of badly needed arms and ammunition. Thus supplied, Lettow-Vorbeck continued to strike at the British, who were themselves poorly supplied and ordered to maintain a defensive posture only.

The British Royal Navy struck Lettow-Vorbeck a serious blow when it sank the German cruiser *Köningsberg* in the Rufiji River. It was the ship on which the Germans depended heavily for support and supply. With great resourcefulness, Lettow-Vorbeck set about salvaging most of the vessel's guns and commandeered her crew to use as land troops.

It was not until March 1916 that Lettow-Vorbeck faced a truly formidable offensive, led by South African general Jan Christian Smuts. Knowing that he would be greatly outnumbered and outgunned, Lettow-Vorbeck enlisted the climate and terrain as his allies. He avoided full-on engagements, fighting nothing more than delaying actions to wear down Smuts's troops. In the end, tropical diseases did far more damage than German bullets. Nevertheless, as the British poured more men into the African campaign, Lettow-Vorbeck gradually yielded to the invasion, always exacting from the invaders as high a price as he could. Periodically, he suddenly turned on his pursuers to counterattack. These jabs from a retreating army always came as a shock. At Mahiwa, during October 15–18, 1917, he cost the British forces—which outnumbered his four to one—1,500 casualties while he suffered no more than 100.

Despite his success, it was clear to Lettow-Vorbeck, always a realist, that the British would ultimately drive him out of German East Africa. A lesser commander would have given up or, perhaps, prepared for some hopeless stand. Lettow-Vorbeck took an entirely surprising route. He invaded the Portuguese colony of Mozambique in December and supplied his 4,000-man army by raiding Portuguese garrisons. He raided as far south as Quelimane on the coast during July 1–3, 1918, then turned north again, and reentered German East Africa during September–October. After this, he launched an invasion of British-held Rhodesia (present-day Zimbabwe) and took the principal city of Kasama (modern Zambia) on November 13—two days after the armistice was signed in Europe.

Isolated from the world at large in a forgotten corner of the war, Lettow-Vorbeck heard only vague rumors of the German surrender, but these were sufficient to prompt him to open negotiations with the British. He surrendered his undefeated army to the British at Abercorn (Mbala, Zambia) on November 23.

After World War I ended, Lettow-Vorbeck became an anti-Communist right-winger. Nevertheless, he was also an opponent of the Nazi regime, which he found loathsome. When it became apparent to him that opposition to the Nazi Party was a lost cause, he retired to private life.

LEADERSHIP LESSONS

✦

A leader can bemoan shortages and inadequacies or can take maximum advantage of whatever is available.

✦

The great lesson any leader can learn from guerrilla warfare is to make as many allies as possible. Make every circumstance work for you.

Difficult situations may require redefining achievement goals. Victory may consist of nothing more or less than avoiding defeat and inflicting maximum losses on your opponent.

✦

The value of tactics is bound to particular frames of reference. Be willing to learn and relearn, as the current situation suggests or dictates.

Lincoln, Abraham

Born: 1809   Died: 1865

**Character model   Leverager   Mentor   Motivator
Problem solver   Rescuer   Strategist   Visionary**

LEADERSHIP ACHIEVEMENTS

✦

Extensively educated himself

✦

Earned a local reputation for integrity and ability

✦

Nationalized his local reputation

✦

Applied lofty principles to practical problems

✦

Balanced pragmatism and idealism

✦

Led the nation through the Civil War

✦

Preserved the Union

✦

Began the process of freeing the slaves and abolishing slavery

LIFE

The 16th president of the United States, Abraham Lincoln led the nation through the Civil War, emancipated the slaves, and fought to restore and preserve the union. A leader of great personal integrity, intelligence, and humanity, seasoned by his frontier upbringing, Lincoln was, by consensus, among our greatest presidents.

Lincoln was born in a log cabin near Hodgenville, Kentucky, on February 12, 1809. From the beginning, he came to understand the hardships of the working poor. Lincoln's earliest education was catch-as-catch-can in a log schoolhouse about two miles from home; however, when he was seven, Lincoln's family moved west to Indiana. As Lincoln grew older, more and more difficult chores fell to him. He became handy with an axe and was often behind a plow. When his mother, Nancy Hanks Lincoln, succumbed to illness on October 5, 1818, however, life for the family became squalid. Within a year, Lincoln's father married Sarah Bush Johnston, thanks to whom the youth resumed his elementary education, learning to read, write, and work sums. Lincoln also became increasingly popular as the region developed and earned a reputation as a local athlete and a great storyteller. He continued to nurture a desire for learning, and he borrowed and devoured as many books as he could find in the backwoods. When Lincoln was 19, he moved with his family to Illinois, settling on the north bank of the Sangamon River, west of Decatur. Lincoln worked for a time on a flatboat and carried a cargo to New Orleans, where he first witnessed a slave auction. On his return to Illinois, Lincoln was hired as a store clerk in the little village of New Salem. Lincoln quickly acquired a fine reputation in the community as an athlete, a wrestler, and a young man intent on making something of himself. With a local schoolmaster, he improved his education, but broke this off in April 1832 to serve in the militia to fight a war against the Sac and Fox chief Black Hawk. Lincoln was immediately elected captain of his volunteer company.

After his term of enlistment expired, he returned to New Salem. Having tasted leadership as a militia captain, Lincoln decided to enter politics and sought election to the state legislature. Although he won virtually all of the votes in and around Salem, he lost the election because he was not well known throughout the county. After this disappointment, Lincoln and a partner bought a store on credit, which soon failed. He then worked as a surveyor, was appointed postmaster, and did odd jobs. He ran for the Illinois House of Representatives again in 1834 and was elected—and reelected in 1836, 1838, and 1840. His most important achievement in the state legislature was to move the capital from Vandalia to Springfield, his home district. During this period, Lincoln also studied law, obtaining a license to practice in 1836. The following year, Lincoln moved to Springfield and practiced law. He worked so earnestly to pay off the debts incurred by the failure of his store that he earned the nickname "Honest Abe," which would serve him in his later political career. He also became widely known throughout Illinois because his law practice made him a circuit rider over some 12,000 square miles of the Eighth Judicial Circuit. Over the years, Lincoln built up an impressive practice and earned a reputation as a shrewd, eloquent, and ingenious lawyer, often working on behalf of the major railroads.

On November 4, 1842, Lincoln married Mary Todd, a high-spirited and rather vain, but highly intelligent young woman. The couple would have four children, of whom only Robert Todd Lincoln (born in 1843) lived to adulthood.

Lincoln was elected to the U.S. Congress on the Whig ticket in 1846, but achieved little distinction. In 1848, after working in the election campaign of Zachary Taylor, Lincoln hoped to obtain the patronage office of commissioner of the General Land Office in Washington. Failing to capture this post, he returned to Springfield, discouraged with politics, but recommitted to his law practice. He emerged as one of the state's leading lawyers.

In 1854, Stephen A. Douglas, whom Lincoln had known as a young lawyer and legislator and who was now a Democratic leader in the U.S. Senate, engineered the repeal of the section of the Missouri Compromise that prohibited slavery in the Louisiana Purchase north of the line of 36 degrees, 30 minutes. As Douglas modified the compromise with the Kansas-Nebraska Act, the question of slavery was left to the people in the territories of Kansas and Nebraska. Lincoln, never a committed abolitionist, nonetheless believed that slavery was inherently unjust, and he opposed its extension. Thus motivated by a cause, he became a campaigner against slavery.

In 1856, the Republican Party was created from a collection of smaller antislavery parties, and, two years later, Lincoln opposed the incumbent Douglas in the race for the U.S. Senate. He opened his campaign with the profound declaration, " 'A house divided against itself cannot stand.' I believe this government cannot endure permanently half-slave and half-free," and he challenged Douglas to a series of seven debates. Whereas Douglas declined to take a position on the rightfulness or wrongfulness of slavery, Lincoln defined slavery as a moral issue and offered as his solution a return to the principles of the founding fathers: Tolerate slavery where it existed, but bring about its ultimate extinction by preventing its spread. Douglas defeated Lincoln by a narrow margin, but the brilliance of the debates had catapulted Lincoln to national attention, and Lincoln became the Republican candidate for the presidency. He faced a splintered Democratic party, which split the opposing vote and propelled Lincoln to victory by a plurality, but not a majority.

He well understood the gravity of the prospect before him. In his farewell speech at the Springfield railway station, he spoke of facing "a task . . . greater than that which rested upon [George] Washington." By the time of his election, seven southern states had seceded from the Union and had formed a breakaway government. Before Lincoln even reached the capital, Jefferson Davis had been inaugurated president of the Confederate States of America. More states were preparing to secede.

The leadership crisis Lincoln confronted had been made far worse by the inability of the outgoing administration of President James Buchanan to cope with it. Congress seemed likewise incapable of action, the national treasury was in crisis, the government bureaucracy included many secessionists, and, worst of all, the U.S. Army, a small body, had been further diminished by the defection of enlisted men and experienced officers—some of the best—to the southern cause. Lincoln was right. No president, Washington included, had ever assumed office at a more perilous moment.

Lincoln understood the importance of projecting to the American people a strong leadership image, but, en route to the capital, he yielded to warnings that he was in danger of assassination, and he permitted those responsible for his safety to usher him into Washington surreptitiously by night. Thus Lincoln, known nationally only for his performance in the debates with Douglas, made his entrance into power as a seeming coward.

Nor did he make an initial impression as a dynamic leader. As a lawyer, Lincoln was famous for "keeping his office in his hat"—filing away legal papers and memoranda in his stovepipe top hat—and he approached presidential administration much the same way. Moreover, he did not show great discernment in selecting his cabinet, some of whom were quite capable men, but they failed to coalesce into an effective team. Nor did Lincoln supervise them closely. Finally, Lincoln was not especially effective at working with Congress. Nevertheless, the new president was in all other respects a born leader. His commitment to preserve the Union never wavered and always guided and drove him. This determination was founded not on mere stubbornness, but a conviction, as he said, that the United States, a great experiment in democracy, was "the last, best hope of earth." Despite his own deficiencies as an administrator and politician, and despite the often poor quality of the Union army's leadership, through many military defeats and disappointments, Lincoln steadfastly drove the nation's war effort. In this, his focus was intense. At times, he assumed nearly dictatorial powers, overriding constitutional considerations, the objections of Congress, and the complaints of the public.

For all the controversy Lincoln's actions generated, his conviction and strength of character, his passionate and compassionate eloquence, his homespun honesty, and his fierce courage commanded, as time went on, the loyalty and confidence of the American people. In contrast to his immediate predecessor, James Buchanan, and many earlier presidents, Lincoln was accessible. He made it clear that he was the people's president. Like an ancient or mythological leader, he took upon himself the burdens of his people. He offered hope.

He also possessed a genius for consistently defining the greater purpose of the great sacrifices for which he asked. He elevated the Civil War to a high moral plane, yet made its purpose instantly and compellingly accessible to the people. His Gettysburg Address, spoken at the dedication of the war cemetery at the Gettysburg battlefield, consumed little more than two minutes, yet it crystallized the meaning of the war, making it comprehensible and, in the deepest sense, worthwhile.

And if Lincoln entered office a rather inept politician, he soon learned how to be a far more effective one. He used political patronage as a means of sealing loyalty and cooperation even as he undermined opponents. While he defined the war effort in moral terms and ultimately linked it explicitly to the slavery issue with the Emancipation Proclamation, he also refrained from creating unnecessary divisiveness by forcing issues. His paramount goal was to preserve the Union, and toward this great end, he was willing to be both flexible and pragmatic. "My policy," he sometimes said, "is to have no policy." He was adept at handling problems as they arose. He prioritized matters on the fly, as it were, never allowing himself to become overwhelmed. For example, when British shipyards and munitions manufacturers freely violated their government's policy of neutrality by supplying vessels and arms to the Confederacy, Lincoln resisted demands that the United States declare war on England. "One war at a time, gentlemen," he remarked.

A prime example of Lincoln's pragmatism was the Emancipation Proclamation. Issued in preliminary form on September 22, 1862, and in final form on January 1, 1863, the document did not free all slaves. It exempted from liberation those slaves in the border states—slave states still loyal to the Union—and in all Confederate territory already under the control of Union armies. His compromise came, in part, from his sense that to do more would invite the Supreme Court to declare the proclamation an unconstitutional seizure of property and also from his desire to avoid offending the border states, thereby pushing them to secede, and to avoid any cause for insurrection in Union-occupied southern territory.

The leadership steps Lincoln took were bold—and not always legal. Without congressional approval, he authorized an increase in the size of the regular army and navy. Because he doubted the loyalty of certain government officials, he turned over public funds to private agents in New York to purchase arms and supplies. He assumed fully the role of commander in chief and put himself at the head of the Union war effort. Perhaps the most daunting and discouraging task the commander in chief faced was finding capable commanders, especially an adequate general in chief. It was not until 1864 that Lincoln appointed Ulysses S. Grant to head the Union armies. Prior to this appointment had come a succession of well-meaning but woefully inadequate commanders. In the unassuming Grant, however, Lincoln found an officer willing to fight boldly, aggressively, and ceaselessly. He found an officer who understood the cruel calculus of this war: that the Union's superiority of numbers, superiority in terms of industry and resources, and superiority in terms of economics would inevitably win the war, provided that the will to fight was preserved and the Southern army destroyed. Grant's willingness to accept the costly realities of war caused some in the North to brand him "butcher," and others criticized his overfondness for strong drink. Lincoln, having found his general, threw the full weight of his loyalty behind him and steadfastly defended Grant.

With great dignity and self-confidence Lincoln endured much abuse, both from the Democrats and from the more zealous members of his own party. He was called many names: "political coward," "dictator," "ape," "ignorant," and "shattered, dazed, utterly foolish." Yet, thanks in large part to the tide of the war turning in favor of the North, Lincoln was elected to a second term. It was at this time that he looked increasingly forward to the peace he was confident would come. Amid cries for vengeance against the "traitors" of the South, he preached reconciliation and healing. In his second inaugural address, he pleaded with his countrymen to act "with malice toward none; with charity for all" in an effort to "bind up" the nation's wounds toward the end of achieving and cherishing "a just, and a lasting peace."

Through the terrible ordeal of the war, Lincoln also endured personal hardships. Early in 1862, his son Willie died of typhoid, precipitating a total nervous collapse in the always high-strung Mary Todd Lincoln. She never fully recovered from the loss, and Lincoln nursed her throughout the rest of his life. He himself was plagued by "melancholy"—what today would be called depression—and, weighted down by the horrors of war, was beset by frequent nightmares. Still, he bore up bravely and effectively. One of the most tragic aspects of his assassination, by John Wilkes Booth, on April 14, 1865, is that it came with total victory all but an accomplished fact. Thus Lincoln was deprived of the relief of realizing his goal, and the nation—especially the defeated South—was deprived of his gentle hand and equitable approach to postwar Reconstruction.

IN HIS OWN WORDS

"With malice toward none, with charity for all, with firmness in the right as God gives us to see the right, let us strive on to finish the work we are in; to bind up the nation's wounds; to care for him who shall have borne the battle, and for his widow and his orphan—to do all which may achieve and cherish a just and lasting peace, among ourselves, and with all nations."
—Second Inaugural Address, March 4, 1865

"I have not permitted myself, gentlemen, to conclude that I am the best man in the country; but I am reminded, in this connection, of a story of an old Dutch farmer who remarked to a companion once that 'it was not best to swap horses while crossing streams.'"
—Reply to Delegation from the National Union League, June 9, 1864

"The probability that we may fall in the struggle ought not to deter us from the support of a cause we believe to be just; it shall not deter me."
—Speech on the Sub-Treasury, in the Illinois House of Representatives, December 26, 1839

"Leave nothing for tomorrow which can be done today."
—Notes for a Law Lecture, July 1, 1850?

"In your hands, my dissatisfied fellow-countrymen, and not in mine, is the momentous issue of civil war. The Government will not assail you. You can have no conflict without being yourselves the aggressors. You have no oath registered in heaven to destroy the Government, while I shall have the most solemn one to 'preserve, protect, and defend it.'"
—First Inaugural Address, March 4, 1861

LEADERSHIP LESSONS

✦

"Honesty is the best policy." (Favorite saying of Lincoln)

✦

Have confidence in the power of lofty principles. Do not be afraid to inspire those you lead.

✦

Appeal to the best in people, not the lowest common denominator.

✦

Pragmatic compromise does not require the negation of idealism.

✦

A good solution now is far more valuable than a perfect solution when it is too late.

✦

Prioritize. It is often best to fight "one war at a time."

✦

Endure criticism, learn from criticism, and act in spite of criticism.

✦

Labor in the service of the highest goals.

Louis XIV

Born: 1638   Died: 1715

**Character model   Innovator   Motivator   Problem solver
Strategist   Systems creator   Visionary**

LEADERSHIP ACHIEVEMENTS

✦

Acquired absolute power as king of France

✦

Created a brilliant court with extremely able advisers, who were
nevertheless clearly subordinate to him

✦

Reformed government to a high degree of efficiency

✦

Introduced more equitable government for France

✦

Was instrumental in bringing French art and culture to their greatest height

✦

Expanded the French empire

✦

Made France the most influential and powerful nation in Europe

✦

Became so thoroughly identified with France as a force in the world
that he is regarded as no less than the architect of an entire epoch
of civilization

LIFE

Universally known as the Sun King because of the dazzling brilliance of his Versailles court as well as the ambitions he held for his empire, Louis XIV was the longest-reigning monarch in European history (1643–1715) and was the most spectacular example in modern times of an absolute monarch.

The first child of Louis XIII and Anne of Austria, Louis XIV was born late in his parents' lives, on September 5, 1638. When the boy was only four years old, his father died, and he assumed the throne under the regency of his mother. This was a time of great turbulence in France; from

1648 to 1653, the nobles and the judges of the French *Parlement* (Parliament) staged a violent but poorly coordinated rebellion known as the Fronde. At issue were the policies of Louis XIII's hyperambitious and ever-scheming minister, Cardinal Richelieu, and Richelieu's equally aggressive successor, Cardinal Giulio Mazarin. Both of these powers-behind-the-throne worked to centralize authority in the royal court, usurping authority from the nobility and other government officers. Twice during the Fronde, the royal family was driven out of Paris, and young Louis and his mother were even held prisoner for a time under house arrest in the royal palace.

When Mazarin at last succeeded in quelling the Fronde, thereby avoiding a full-blown revolution, France was positioned to become the dominant power in Europe. In 1648, it had emerged from the Thirty Years' War, having gained Alsace and most of Lorraine. War with Spain ended with the Peace of the Pyrenees in 1659, which was guaranteed the following year by the marriage of Louis XIV to Marie Therese, daughter of Spain's monarch, Philip IV.

During the early years of Louis XIV's reign, even after his mother's regency ended, the youthful king did little governing in his own right. Like Richelieu before him, Cardinal Mazarin ran the government, but upon Mazarin's death in 1661, Louis boldly took command, announcing that, henceforth, he would serve as his own chief minister. It was a radical act for a French king, and Louis took immediate steps to enforce his decision. He put on trial for corruption Nicholas Fouquet, the royal finance minister and the man who was next in line for the post of chief minister. The trial spanned 1661 to 1664, and, in the end, Fouquet was imprisoned for life. This action foreclosed any further questions about finding a chief minister for the king.

Although Louis ensured his supremacy as absolute leader of France, he was not foolish enough to believe that he could rule the nation without a highly select team of ministers. Louis possessed a genius for appointing skilled advisers and for retaining those who had shown ability during his father's reign, including Jean Baptiste Colbert (in domestic affairs) and the marquis de Louvois (in military affairs). Louis also retained the traditional *conseil d'en haut* (high council), but, in a radical departure from precedent, he excluded from the *conseil* members of his immediate family, great princes, and others of the *noblesse d'épée* (the "nobility of the sword," the old military nobility). Such entrenched figures always felt themselves entitled to power by the mere fact of their birth. As such, their competence and motives were always questionable—but their ambition, and, therefore, the treachery of their self-interest, could always be depended upon. So Louis purged them, and he put in their place the newer, younger, and more progressive *noblesse de robe* ("nobility of the robe," the judicial nobility). As for the day-to-day and local administration of government, Louis instituted a system of *intendants*, essentially subgovernors, who could be appointed, removed, and replaced, depending on royal assessment of their actual performance.

The leadership reforms Louis put in place were highly successful and greatly improved the efficiency of government, a fact that, in itself, addressed many long-held grievances of the French people. The political and social obstructionism of the old *Parlements* was eliminated, and the system of criminal justice was vastly improved and rendered far more equitable. Efficient, competent, far-seeing government fostered the development of commerce, industry, and, especially in North America, colonial expansion, all of which appreciably reduced the national debt. Another popular flashpoint, a burdensome and inequitable system of taxation, was also overhauled. Not only were many (though, as the hapless Louis XVI would discover, not all) tax inequities ameliorated, but the collection of taxes was rendered more efficient and was purged of corruption.

As noted as Louis XIV became for his governmental reforms, it is the brilliant age of art and culture he personally fostered that earned him greatest renown in his own time and through history. He regarded the arts as a means of celebrating the monarchy, as manifest evidence of the magnificence of French civilization under his leadership. Thus the Sun King became patron to the greatest French literary and artistic figures of the age, including the playwright Jean Baptiste Molière, the composer Jean Baptiste Lully, and many other notables. Under the personal patronage of Louis, great academies of art and learning were created. The Académie Française, founded by Cardinal Richelieu, came under formal royal patronage and control in 1671. Like the great emperors of the Roman classical age, Louis was anxious to create a legacy of beautiful monuments, and he directed the completion of the Louvre in Paris and the incomparable Palace of Versailles, which, under Louis XIII, had been nothing more than an elaborate hunting lodge.

Louis was almost as prolific in making war as he was in making culture. He launched the War of Devolution during 1667–68 against the Spanish Netherlands on the grounds that these Spanish-controlled provinces had "devolved" by succession to his Spanish wife rather than to her half-brother Charles II. Next, Louis opened hostilities against the United Provinces of the Netherlands in the Third Anglo–Dutch War of 1672–78. His object was to get revenge for Dutch intervention in the earlier War of Devolution and, even more important, to cripple Dutch trade, which competed with that of France. Louis prevailed in both of these wars, gaining significant territory in Flanders. He also acquired the formerly Spanish Franche-Comté region. Here Louis commissioned the foremost military architect of the age, Sébastien Le Prestre de Vauban, to design an impregnable fortress for this outpost of what was then France's eastern frontier.

Louis's will to power was a kind of dynamo, and with supreme arrogance he established "courts of reunion," which were elaborate legal rationales for annexing various towns along the Franco–German and Franco–Italian borders. In the Alsace, Louis seized the great city of Strasbourg; in Italy, he took Casale.

The Sun King's bold series of military and international adventures marked the zenith of his reign, however. In 1685, Louis XIV made the catastrophic move of revoking the 1598 Edict of Nantes, which he had earlier supported. The revocation deprived the right of the Huguenots (the French Protestant minority) to worship in freedom, and it unleashed a deadly campaign of persecution against them. The revocation had three disastrous effects: It revealed to the nation and the world Louis's religious intolerance. It sent many of the Huguenots, a highly productive and valuable segment of French society, fleeing from the country. And, worst of all, it united many of the Protestant powers of Europe against France.

Thus in September 1688, Louis found himself in a military confrontation with the member states of the Protestant League of Augsburg. This marked the beginning of nine years of costly and inconclusive warfare known as the War of the Grand Alliance. France emerged from the conflict still in possession of Strasbourg and its other "reunion" acquisitions, but with its coffers seriously drained. And no sooner was this war concluded than another, the War of the Spanish Succession, commenced in 1701. This war—to enforce the succession of Louis's grandson, Philip V, to the Spanish throne following the death of Charles II—dragged on for 14 bloody years, exacting a ruinous toll on the French economy. Again, however, it ended with most of Louis's former conquests intact. Moreover, Philip V did inherit Spain as well as its overseas colonies, but the Holy Roman Emperor Charles VI, who had been backed by France's opponents, acquired the Spanish Netherlands and Spain's Italian possessions. To avoid further warfare, Louis reluctantly agreed that the crowns of France and Spain would remain separate, notwithstanding their connection through the Bourbon dynasty.

Toward the end of his reign, Louis XIV also waged a bitter battle to suppress the theologically radical followers of Cornelius Jansen. In this struggle, the king successfully enlisted the aid of the pope, but had to sacrifice in return his claim to the semi-independence of the French Catholic church.

Louis XIV had lifted France to lofty heights of empire, of economy, and of civilization, but by the time of his death on September 1, 1715, while the French empire was very much intact and its cultural achievements unchallenged, the nation's economic foundation was badly weakened. Even worse, the aging and infirm monarch had, with his advancing years, gradually let slip the personal control he had exercised so relentlessly earlier in his reign. He had outlived his best administrators and, without his personal guidance, the administration of government slipped back into corruption and inefficiency, becoming an entrenched bureaucracy, arrogant and out of touch with the needs of the people. Under the next two monarchs, this situation would only become worse, and, before the end of the 18th century, it would give rise to a violent revolution and a chaotic reign of terror in its wake.

IN HIS OWN WORDS

"Every time I bestow a vacant office I make a hundred discontented persons and one ingrate."
—Quoted in Voltaire, *Le Siécle de Louis XIV,* 1751

"I am the state."
—To *Parlement,* 1651

"Has God forgotten all that I have done for Him?"
—Response to news of a military defeat at Malplaquet, 1709

LEADERSHIP LESSONS

Leadership is not given, but earned, won, or taken.

✦

Be judiciously jealous of your authority.

✦

Choose advisers and other subordinates wisely. Establish working
relationships unambiguously.

✦

Embrace vision.

✦

Understand your ambition. Then allow it to drive your achievement.

✦

Identify with the enterprise you lead. Invite those you lead to identify
with you.

✦

Present those you lead with value: with multiple opportunities for profit, a
guarantee of fair treatment, and an arena in which they can excel.

✦

The downside of absolute power is absolute failure. Be warned.

Mahmud of Ghazna

Born: 971   Died: 1030

Conqueror   Leverager   Motivator   Strategist   Tactician   Visionary

LEADERSHIP ACHIEVEMENTS

✦

Expanded a small city-state into a great empire

✦

Motivated typically outnumbered forces to high levels of aggressive
performance

✦

Combined ruthless aggression with a spirit of toleration

✦

Made maximum use of opportunities presented to him

✦

Sought to create spiritual unity, but always tolerated diversity

✦

Valued art, culture, and learning; did not merely conquer and destroy,
but always built

LIFE

Mahmud built a great empire in Afghanistan and Khorosan (part of Iran),
with territories also reaching into northern India. He transformed his capital, Ghazna, into the political, economic, and cultural center of Central Asia,
and, in the course of 17 successful invasions, drove Islam deep into India.

The son of Amir Sabuktigin, a Turkish slave who became ruler of the
small sultanate of Ghazna in 977, Mahmud was 27 years old in 998 when
he succeeded his father. He exercised great diplomatic skill, which he combined with personal fearlessness and military boldness to expand Ghazna
explosively, until it included Kashmir, Punjab, and most of Iran.

Mahmud started by forging a strategic alliance with the mighty
Abasid caliph in Baghdad, whose mere recognition would legitimate many
of Mahmud's conquests. Mahmud brought ruthless energy to strict
method and clear goals. Early in his reign, he resolved to invade India
annually, and from 1001 to 1026, he led 17 expeditions into that realm. On

349

his first invasion, Mahmud rode at the head of 15,000 cavalry troops. At Peshawar, he was met by 12,000 cavalrymen, 30,000 infantry soldiers, and 300 elephants commanded by Jaipal, ruler of the Punjab. Although he was vastly outnumbered, Mahmud refused to go on the defensive, but moved swiftly and aggressively, routing Jaipal's forces, killing some 15,000 of his men, and capturing Jaipal himself, together with 15 of his relatives and commanders. Aggressive as he was in conquest, Mahmud exercised prudent mercy. He released Jaipal, hoping to work with him in the conduct of Punjab affairs. Humiliated, however, the raja abdicated in favor of his son, Anandpal, and then ascended his own funeral pyre and immolated himself.

Anandpal had no intention of yielding to Mahmud and amassed an alliance of rajas from all over India, gradually assembling a huge army to counter the annual assaults against the subcontinent. By 1008, Anandpal fielded a tremendous force against Mahmud at a battlefield between Und and Peshawar. For 40 days and nights the rival armies faced one another. At last, Anandpal attacked, making extensive use of 30,000 fierce Khokar tribesmen, who fought Mahmud's army to the point of retreat. On the verge of defeat, however, the tide turned when Anandpal's elephant became frightened and fled from the battlefield. Seeing their leader in apparent retreat, the Indian forces panicked, broke ranks, and fled. Mahmud seized his good fortune and, instead of holding ground, advanced deep into India, formally annexing the Punjab and looting its riches.

With the bounty gained from his many invasions, Mahmud transformed the capital city of Ghazna into a wealthy metropolis of great magnificence, in which the arts and scholarship flourished. Moreover, while Mahmud did not hesitate to subjugate a substantial portion of Central Asia and India, he treated the people he conquered with great respect. It is true that, in 1024, when he sacked the city of Somnath, he defiled the Hindu temple there, breaking its sacred *lingam*. This, however, was an exception to his usual practice of tolerating non-Islamic faiths. Even as he sought to inculcate Islam throughout his conquests, he also maintained a large unit of Hindu troops under the command of Indians, and he never sanctioned religious persecution.

LEADERSHIP LESSONS

✦

Whenever even remotely possible, adopt a proactive, aggressive posture.
Always advance.

✦

Be prepared to recognize and seize opportunity. Do not rely on good
fortune, but do accept and exploit it.

✦

Emphasize building over tearing down.

✦

Promote solidarity, shared values, and common goals, but practice
toleration of diversity.

✦

Use all available resources, as when the Muslim Mahmud employed Hindu
troops in his predominantly Hindu realms.

✦

Endeavor to understand those you lead.

Maria Theresa

Born: 1717   Died: 1780

Innovator   Problem solver   Systems creator   Tactician

LEADERSHIP ACHIEVEMENTS

Earned admiration and respect as a woman leader in a
male-dominated world

Combined conservatism with a willingness to institute reform and change

◆

Inaugurated a progressive program of universal secular education

◆

Modernized and greatly improved her nation's army using direct evaluation
of performance

Instituted many domestic reforms that strengthened her nation and
bettered the lot of the disenfranchised and poor

LIFE

In the 650 years of the Hapsburg dynasty, Maria Theresa was the only woman to rule. Her 40-year reign in Austria, from 1740 to 1780, was marked by three major armed conflicts: the War of Austrian Succession (1740–48), which began almost immediately upon her ascent to the throne, the Seven Years' War (1756–63), and the War of the Bavarian Succession (1778–79). Her response to these, combined with her enlightened program of internal domestic reforms, prompted no less a figure than her archrival, Prussia's Frederick the Great, to call her "a credit to her throne and her sex."

She was born in Vienna and inherited the Hapsburg crown after her father, Charles VI, died in 1740 without male heirs. She was a proactive and highly engaged leader. A close observer of her army's performance during her reign's major wars moved her to undertake a bold and sweeping modernization of the military. On the civil front, Maria Theresa acknowledged the inequities and inefficiencies of an archaic system of taxation, so she completely revamped it, supervising the restructuring personally. A leader very much in touch with the Enlightenment overspreading Europe, she instituted a system of universal public education that was secular and completely separate from the Church. Finally, Maria Theresa created a program of economic relief for the always beleaguered peasant class.

In many ways a progressive monarch, especially in the context of the notoriously conservative, hidebound, and even backward Hapsburg line, Maria Theresa was also, in important respects, intolerant. Her strain of Catholicism was narrow. Fearing the growth of the Jesuits' political and cultural influence, she acted vigorously and brutally to suppress the order. And her policies toward Jews were at least as repressive as those of the most intolerant European monarchs of her day—and certainly out of step with the Enlightenment tone of much of her reign.

Maria Theresa was the mother of 16 children, the most famous of whom were Joseph II, emperor of the Holy Roman Empire from 1765 to 1790, and Marie Antoinette, the queen of France who fell victim with her husband, Louis XVI, to the French Revolution. As for Maria Theresa herself, she combined an essential conservatism with a forward-looking efficiency that did much to strengthen and sustain an Austrian empire whose varied and fractious elements always threatened to fall apart.

LEADERSHIP LESSONS

✦

Take nothing for granted. Assess the status quo unflinchingly. Determine where change is needed. Make necessary change happen.

✦

Emphasize education. The more those you lead know, the more successful your enterprise will be.

✦

Base decisions on performance and results. Face facts and accept the necessity of change.

✦

Ultimately, efficiency and fairness cannot be separated.

✦

Earn your identity as a leader by successfully addressing the needs of those you lead.

Marshall, George Catlett

Born: 1880   Died: 1959

**Character model   Innovator   Leverager   Mentor   Motivator   Problem solver
Rescuer   Strategist   Systems creator   Tactician   Visionary**

LEADERSHIP ACHIEVEMENTS

✦

A master logistician, was instrumental in creating efficient military systems
in two world wars

✦

Was an important military teacher between the wars

✦

Radically reorganized the army during World War II for greater
effectiveness

✦

Brilliantly managed the wartime growth of the army from 200,000 to
8,000,000 men

✦

Synthesized military and civilian leadership roles

✦

Synthesized military and diplomatic roles

✦

Developed the Marshall Plan, a political and humanitarian landmark
of the 20th century

✦

Won the Nobel Peace Prize

LIFE

George Catlett Marshall was one of those rare leaders who combine military brilliance with humane, far-seeing statesmanship. He served the United States as chief of the Joint Chiefs of Staff during World War II and, after the war, as secretary of state and, later, as secretary of defense. He was the architect of the Marshall Plan, perhaps the single most important "weapon" in the free world's Cold War arsenal and a program Winston Churchill called the "most unsordid political act in history."

Marshall was born in Uniontown, Pennsylvania, and, unlike so many military officers destined for greatness, he did not graduate from West Point, but from Virginia Military Institute, in 1901. Commissioned a second lieutenant of infantry on February 3, 1902, he was posted to the Philippines during the anti-American insurrection on Mindoro. Marshall served on Mindoro with the 30th Infantry Regiment during 1902–03, and then returned to the United States to attend Infantry and Cavalry School at Fort Leavenworth. He graduated at the top of the class of 1907 and stayed on at the Staff College during 1907–08. Promoted to first lieutenant in 1907, Marshall served as an instructor at both schools from 1908 to 1910.

From 1910 to 1913, Marshall was variously posted, and then returned to the Philippines for three years as aide to General Hunter Liggett. Promoted to captain in 1916, he once again returned to the United States and was assigned as aide to General James F. Bell. In June of 1917, after the United States entered World War I, Marshall shipped out to France as a staff officer with the 1st Division. As a talented young officer, he was assigned to the key position of division operations officer, tasked with helping to plan the first U.S. offensive of the war in May 1918.

Like many promising officers in the World War I U.S. Army, Marshall received rapid but temporary promotion. He was bumped to temporary colonel in July and, in August, attached to General Headquarters of the commander in chief of the American Expeditionary Force, General John J. Pershing. In this position, Marshall became the central member of the team that planned the massive—and highly successful—Saint-Mihiel offensive of September 12–16, 1918. After the offensive, he was directly charged with rapidly and efficiently transferring 500,000 men from the Saint-Mihiel salient to the next objective, the Meuse-Argonne front. If Marshall had demonstrated great leadership and strategic skill in planning the Saint-Mihiel operation, he showed, if anything, even greater flair for logistics. The troop movement was accomplished so swiftly and smoothly that Marshall was named chief of operations for the First Army in October, and then, the next month, was made chief of staff of VIII Corps.

At the conclusion of the war, Marshall was assigned to service with the Allied army of occupation in Germany. In this capacity, he saw firsthand the toll war took on civilian populations. It was a lesson he would never forget and one that would inform his work, following World War II, on the Marshall Plan to relieve an even more thoroughly devastated Europe.

In September 1919, Marshall returned to the States and reverted to his prewar rank of captain, but was appointed aide to Pershing, who was now army chief of staff. Marshall served Pershing through 1924 and collaborated with him on formulating key aspects of the National Defense Act. He also played an important role in writing the general's reports on the American Expeditionary Forces in the war.

In July 1920, Marshall was promoted to major, and, just three years later, to lieutenant colonel—by the standards of the sluggish army of the interwar years, a rapid climb. He left Pershing's staff to serve in Tientsin, China, as executive officer of the 15th Infantry, returning to the United States in 1927, where he was named assistant commandant of the Infantry School at Fort Benning, serving there through 1932. Promoted to colonel in 1933, Marshall worked with the Civilian Conservation Corps (CCC)—Franklin D. Roosevelt's New Deal civilian army to provide economic relief from the Great Depression while furnishing the nation with much-needed public works projects. Again, Marshall gained valuable experience with applying military thinking and logistics to the civil good. In 1933, he also became senior instructor to the Illinois National Guard, serving until 1936, when he was promoted to brigadier general and given command of 5th Infantry Brigade at Vancouver Barracks, Washington.

In 1938, Marshall left his assignment at the 5th Infantry to come to Washington, D.C., as head of the War Plans Division of the Army General Staff. Promoted to major general in July, he was appointed deputy chief of staff. On September 1, he was made a temporary general and appointed chief of staff. From this position, he launched a rapid expansion of the army preparatory to war. Under his direction, the army would grow from its prewar strength of 200,000 to 8,000,000. The job of managing this tremendous growth under the most urgent and critical of crisis conditions called for not only a powerful leader, but a supremely efficient one. Again, Marshall exercised his formidable prowess as a master logistician.

After Pearl Harbor thrust the United States into World War II, Marshall rapidly reorganized the General Staff and, by March 1942, completed the remodeling of the army into three superefficient major commands: Army Ground Forces, Army Service Forces, and Army Air Forces.

As one of the joint chiefs of staff, Marshall was the principal military adviser to President Franklin D. Roosevelt, and he was present at all the great Allied conferences of the war, first with Roosevelt and then with President Harry S Truman. In this capacity, Marshall became one of the key architects of American and Allied military strategy, as well U.S. political strategy bearing on the war.

In December 1944, Marshall was promoted to the rank of general of the army—five-star general—and concluded his service as chief of staff on November 20, 1945. Just five days after he resigned as chief of staff, however, President Truman sent him to China as his special envoy. For the next year, Marshall attempted to mediate a peace between Chiang Kai-shek (and his Nationalist Party) and Mao Tse-tung (and the Chinese Communist Party). It was an impossible task.

After his return to the United States, Marshall replaced James F. Byrnes as secretary of state in Truman's cabinet on January 1947. In June of that year, the secretary of state spoke at a Harvard University commencement ceremony and proposed a sweeping program of economic aid to rebuild war-ravaged Europe. His objective was not only to provide urgent humanitarian aid, but, in so doing, to block the spread of Communism in economically devastated areas. This was the core of what became the European Recovery Program, soon dubbed the Marshall Plan. In Europe, it was a stabilizing force of inestimable value, saving much of the continent not only from economic disintegration, but from unwilling absorption into the Soviet bloc. Almost certainly, the Marshall Plan was also instrumental in preventing another major war in Europe.

Marshall stepped down as secretary of state in January 1949, but returned in September of the next year as secretary of defense and served in that post during the opening months of the Korean War. During this period, the rabid red-baiting Wisconsin senator Joseph McCarthy targeted Marshall as "soft on Communism" and was unstinting in his attacks on the statesman, who, at this point in his life and career, began to suffer from ill health. He resigned as secretary of defense and retired from public life in September 1951. Three years later, in December 1953, Marshall was publicly vindicated when he was awarded the Nobel Peace Prize, chiefly in recognition of the Marshall Plan. Fittingly, Marshall was the first soldier ever honored with the prize.

IN HIS OWN WORDS

"Don't fight the problem, decide it."

—Quoted by Walter Isaacson and Evan Thomas in *The Wise Men,* 1986

"It is not enough to fight. It is the spirit which we bring to the fight that decides the issue. It is morale that wins the victory."

—*Military Review,* October 1948

"If man does find the solution for world peace it will be the most revolutionary reversal of his record we have ever known."

—*Biennial Report of the Chief of Staff, United States Army,* September 1, 1945

LEADERSHIP LESSONS

✦

Effective leadership is often a matter of creating effective systems.

✦

Never stop learning.

✦

Think beyond the straitjacket of your organization—as Marshall brilliantly synthesized military and civilian points of view, purposes, and methods.

✦

Do not be afraid to shake up and remodel the organization, if necessary.

✦

The greatest plans turn on the principle of leverage.
Marshall's European recovery program simultaneously served sweeping humanitarian and political ends.

✦

Persevere even in the face of unjust criticism.

Meiji (Mutsuhito)

Born: 1852 Died: 1912

Character model Innovator Mentor Motivator Systems creator

LEADERSHIP ACHIEVEMENTS

◆

Ushered Japan into the modern age

◆

Was perhaps the best loved of Japanese emperors in any age

◆

Centralized Japanese government, ending arbitrary feudalism

◆

Concentrated power in the emperor, yet also introduced constitutional
monarchy, thereby diminishing the emperor's actual political role within a
strong central government

◆

Presided over Japan's ascendency as a world power

LIFE

The emperor Meiji earned the love and loyalty of the Japanese people and
guided the ancient empire successfully into the industrial age, opening Japan
to commerce with the West. He had been born Mutsuhito into the imperial
family on November 3, 1852, in Kyoto, the second son of Emperor Komei.
In July 1860, when he was designated heir to the throne, Mutsuhito took
the royal name Meiji. He succeeded his father in December 1866 and was
formally crowned in a ceremony on January 9, 1867.

In January 1868, a year after Meiji took the throne, the forces
opposed to the Tokugawa military regime overthrew Yoshinobu
Tokugawa, the last shogun—hereditary military overlord—in Japan. After
almost a millennium of shogunate rule, this restored the ancient supreme
political authority solely to the emperor. Meiji was suddenly extremely
powerful and had a freer hand than any of his predecessors in determining
the future course of Japan.

He chose a path very different from that of his reactionary and tradition-bound father. Meiji looked far beyond Japan's borders and believed

that the traditionally xenophobic nation had much to learn from the West. Accordingly, he promulgated the Charter Oath on April 6, 1868, which proclaimed his commitment to modernization. In the spirit of change, he moved the court from the ancient capital of Kyoto to Edo, which he renamed Tokyo, meaning "Eastern Capital." In 1871, Meiji replaced the autonomous provincial rulers who had long administered Japanese government with centralized prefectural governments, each reporting directly to Tokyo. The next year, the Meiji government revised the ancient feudal land policies, allowing much more liberty of movement and settlement to the peasant class. Next, in 1873, came compulsory, universal national education and military service. Beyond these sweeping reforms, Meiji introduced even more profound changes. In a bold move that no previous emperor dared contemplate, Meiji banned the samurai class, which had always been a simultaneously tyrannical and anarchic element in Japanese society. He also made strides in the leveling of Japanese class structure by lifting many restrictions regarding caste and membership in the professions.

Understandably, Meiji's reforms triggered strong reactions. The emperor asserted the authority of his government by dealing swiftly and effectively with local rebellions during the 1870s. In the international community, he raised the stature of the imperial government by voluntarily changing it to a constitutional monarchy along the lines of similar Western governments; yet he balanced this reform against the maintenance of the doctrines of rule by divine right and of the inviolability of the crown.

Before the ascension of Meiji, European countries generally viewed Japan as a quaint, backward nation. Japan's victories in the Sino-Japanese War of 1894–95 and, even more dramatically, in the Russo-Japanese War of 1904–05, both of which used the most advanced tactics and weaponry, demonstrated that the nation had become a world power. Under Meiji, Japan annexed Korea and Taiwan and maintained tight control over Manchuria.

In transforming Japan into a modern state, Meiji effectively and progressively reduced his own role—the role of emperor—to that of a figurehead and spiritual guide. He did so willingly, for what he perceived as the good of the Japanese people. He conveyed to them the feeling that the profound changes he introduced were for their good. Well loved, Meiji was a figure with sufficient integrity to minimize formal opposition to the many reforms of his government.

LEADERSHIP LESSONS

✦

An capable leader manages change effectively. A great leader brings about change without destroying continuity.

✦

Effective leadership generally involves the creative centralization and sharing of power.

✦

A leader earns loyalty through the creation of justice.

✦

One of the modern leader's most important tasks is the opening up of the enterprise, the empowerment of diverse people capable of making diverse contributions to the attainment of common goals.

✦

A great leader makes sacrifice of power part of his program, if he believes that doing so serves those he leads.

✦

A great leader is not afraid to make changes that may put him out of a job.

Mitchell, William ("Billy")

Born: 1879   Died: 1936

Character model   Innovator   Mentor   Motivator   Visionary

LEADERSHIP ACHIEVEMENTS

◆

Pioneered military aviation, especially the role of ground support
and bombardment

◆

Advocated both land-based and carrier-based (naval) aviation

◆

Was willing to sacrifice his career for the sake of his nation's defense

◆

Channeled his passion into (ultimately) effective advocacy

LIFE

William "Billy" Mitchell was a passionate innovator, whose defiant advocacy of military aviation cost him his career, but ultimately transformed America's defense.

Mitchell was born, in Nice, France, the son of John Lendrum Mitchell, who was later elected U.S. senator from Wisconsin. When Mitchell was still a child, the family returned to the United States, where Billy grew up in Milwaukee and was educated at Racine and Columbian (later George Washington) universities. Mitchell enlisted in the First Wisconsin Infantry at the outbreak of the Spanish–American War in 1898 and saw action in Cuba, rising to the rank of lieutenant of volunteers and then receiving a commission as lieutenant in the regular army.

Mitchell was assigned to the Signal Corps and attended the Army Staff College at Fort Leavenworth, Kansas, during 1907–09. He served briefly on the Mexican border before he was transferred to the General Staff in 1912. For a young officer on the rise, no posting was more coveted than a position on the General Staff. However, in 1915, Mitchell eagerly gave up staff work to transfer to the aviation section of the Signal Corps. (At this time, there was no Army Air Corps; military aviation, very much in its infancy, was the province of the Signal Corps.)

Mitchell enrolled in flight school at Newport News, Virginia, and earned his wings in 1916. Shortly after graduating from flight school, he was sent to Europe, which was fighting the Great War, as an observer. In April 1917, when the United States entered the war, Mitchell, already in place abroad, was appointed air officer of the American Expeditionary Force and promoted to lieutenant colonel in June. In May 1918, he became air officer of I Corps with the rank of colonel. He became the first U.S. officer to fly over enemy lines.

Mitchell was chiefly interested in innovating aerial bombardment on a large scale. Using the primitive aircraft of the time, he organized and commanded a massive Franco-American bombing mission consisting of 1,500 aircraft—the greatest number of planes ever massed to that time. The mission flew successfully against the Saint-Mihiel salient in September and demonstrated just what air support of ground action could accomplish.

Promoted to brigadier general, Mitchell commanded the combined French and American air services for the Meuse-Argonne offensive. On October 9, he personally led another massive formation of bombers against targets behind enemy lines. French and German military aviation was far more advanced than anything the United States had at this time. That Mitchell, an American, conceived, planned, and led massive air forces in World War I is extraordinary evidence of his innovative leadership. He did not let the limitations of U.S. military policy restrict him, and his passion for military aviation persuaded the French command to yield leadership of major bombing missions to him.

After World War I, Mitchell was named assistant chief of the Air Service in 1919 and immediately embarked on a highly controversial, even inflammatory, campaign to create an air force separate from the army. Even more radical was his advocacy of unified control of military air power—that is, subjecting military aviation to the joint authority of the army and the navy. He reasoned that aviation transcended both the ground and the sea; therefore, its proper coordination and management required direction from both traditional services.

The military establishment vehemently resisted Mitchell's recommendations. Eager to communicate his vision of how air power had transformed the conduct of war, Mitchell boldly declared that the airplane had made the battleship obsolete. When outraged navy officials demanded that he back up this statement, Mitchell dramatically demonstrated his point by bombing the captured German dreadnought *Ostfriesland*. In 1921, he sunk this large battleship in 21½ minutes. Gratifyingly, Mitchell's demonstration spurred the navy to conduct further tests during 1923, which led to a program to develop the aircraft carrier as an offensive weapon. World War II, in which the aircraft carrier would displace the battleship as the primary naval surface weapon, revealed just how prescient Mitchell had been.

If the navy was willing to innovate, the army proved much more recalcitrant. Mitchell relentlessly pushed his campaign for enlargement of the Army Air Service and the ultimate creation of an independent air force. His superiors, frustrated, caused him to be demoted to colonel, and his responsibility as an air officer was reduced to command only of the VIII Corps Area in San Antonio, Texas (effective April 1925). Despite this, Mitchell kept the controversy alive, often going around his superiors and making statements directly to the press. When the navy dirigible *Shenandoah* crashed in a thunderstorm on September 3, 1925, Mitchell went to the papers with accusations of War and Navy Department "incompetency, criminal negligence, and almost treasonable administration of the National Defense."

This proved to be the last straw. Mitchell was court-martialed, convicted of insubordination in December 1925, and sentenced to five years suspension from duty without pay. Rather than accept the punishment, which he considered unjust, Mitchell resigned his commission on February 1, 1926, but continued to speak out from his Middleburg, Virginia, home until his death a decade later.

Billy Mitchell was a leader ahead of his time, and he was a man willing to sacrifice his career for the sake of his country's defense. Virtually all of his doctrinal theories about the role of aviation in warfare would prove true—including his assessment (much ridiculed) that the navy's fleet at Pearl Harbor in the Hawaiian Islands was vulnerable to a carrier-launched air attack, which, Mitchell predicted, would be made by Japan.

Mitchell refused to compromise. He was not an astute politician. Indeed, he was often deliberately caustic and certainly provocative. After his death, his major positions were vindicated, and he came to be considered the founding spirit of the U.S. Air Force. The U.S. Army Air Force named its lead medium bomber, the B-25, in his honor: the Mitchell Bomber.

LEADERSHIP LESSONS

✦

Do not deny your passionate beliefs; channel them into advocacy.

✦

Test your theories and be willing to demonstrate their validity to others.

✦

Know your business thoroughly.

✦

Innovation often requires reaching beyond, above, and outside the
institution in which you work.

✦

A leader must be an advocate.

✦

Determine and resolve the priority of your values. What are you willing to
sacrifice in order to achieve your goals?

✦

Being right is not always personally profitable.

Mitscher, Marc Andrew

Born: 1887   Died: 1947

Innovator   Mentor   Motivator   Tactician

LEADERSHIP ACHIEVEMENTS

◆

Was a leading architect of naval aviation

◆

Overcame diminutive size and frequent ill health to become a great pilot
and a great commander

◆

Was instrumental in developing the air arm into a great naval weapon, the
weapon that turned the tide in the Pacific during World War II

◆

Was an innovator, who skippered the U.S.S. *Hornet* to launch Doolittle's
daring raid on Tokyo early in the war

◆

Consistently achieved victory in the Pacific

◆

Mastered the doctrine of naval air power and employed it to
maximum effect

◆

Commanded great affection and loyalty among men who respected him as
a fellow pilot

LIFE

Of diminutive stature and mild-mannered appearance, Marc Andrew
Mitscher did not look like an admiral, much less a daredevil pilot who led
the development of the navy's early aviation programs and transformed
the airplane into a major naval weapon.

Mitscher was born far from the ocean, in Hillsboro, Wisconsin, and
raised in even drier country, Oklahoma City. Nevertheless, he developed a
passion for the sea early on and gained admission to the U.S. Naval
Academy, from which he graduated in 1910. He was serving on the U.S.S.
California during 1913–15, when he took part in the landings at Veracruz in

April 1914. The next year, he took flight training at the Pensacola Naval Air Station and earned his wings in June 1916. He stayed in Pensacola for advanced flight training and served aboard the attack cruiser *Huntington,* performing balloon and aircraft catapult experiments during April 1917.

Following a period of convoy escort duty in the Atlantic after the United States entered World War I, Mitscher was posted to Montauk Point Naval Air Station on Long Island, New York, and then was appointed to command the Rockaway, Long Island, Naval Air Station in February 1918. The following year, he was transferred to command of the Miami Naval Air Station. In May 1919, he attempted to fly across the Atlantic, but made it only as far as the Azores—a feat for which he received the Navy Cross.

In the winter of 1920, Mitscher transferred to the Pacific as commander of the Pacific Fleet's air unit based in San Diego, California. He then took charge of the Anacostia NAS in Washington, D.C., and also served with the Plans Division of the Bureau of Aeronautics from 1922 to 1926. He led the navy team at the international air races in Detroit in 1922 and St. Louis in 1923.

After leaving the Plans Division, Mitscher served aboard U.S.S. *Langley,* the navy's first aircraft carrier, in the Pacific from July to December 1926. He transferred to the newly built carrier U.S.S. *Saratoga* for precommissioning duty and was appointed the ship's air officer when it entered the fleet in November 1927. Promoted to commander in October 1930, Mitscher returned to shore duty in Washington at the Bureau of Aeronautics, serving until 1933, when he was named chief of staff to Base Force commander Admiral Alfred W. Johnson. He served aboard the seaplane tender *Wright* for a year before being appointed executive officer of the *Saratoga* in 1934. Once again, Mitscher returned to the Bureau of Aeronautics as leader of the Flight Division from 1935 to 1937.

Mitscher was given command of the U.S.S. *Wright* late in 1937 and was promoted to captain the following year. He then took command of Patrol Wing 1, operating out of San Diego. Then, during June 1939, Mitscher was appointed assistant chief of the Bureau of Aeronautics. He served in this post until the eve of World War II, when he was given command of the new aircraft carrier, U.S.S. *Hornet,* in July 1941. Mitscher brought the ship into commission in October, and he was in command when Army Air Corps colonel Jimmy Doolittle used the carrier as the base from which he launched 16 B-25 Mitchell bombers on his celebrated raid against Tokyo in April 1942. Mitscher was also skipper of the *Hornet* at the turning-point battle of Midway during June 3–6, 1942, and was promoted to rear admiral and commander of Patrol Wing 2 in July. In December, he was appointed commandant of Fleet Air, based at Noumea Island. When U.S. forces took Guadalcanal, he moved his base there in April 1943.

During the Solomons campaign, Mitscher directed combined operations of army, navy, marine, and New Zealand air units before he returned to sea duty as commander of the Fast Carrier Task Force, which operated against Japanese positions in the Marshall Islands, Truk, and New Guinea from January to June of 1944.

Promoted to vice admiral in March 1944, Mitscher took charge of carrier operations at the Battle of the Philippine Sea and succeeded in decimating the Japanese carrier force in the one-sided battle dubbed the Marianas Turkey Shoot of June 19–21. His next assignment was to support amphibious landings at the Bonins and Palau during August and September. He also commanded air operations to provide cover for the landings at Leyte, Philippines, in October. During the Battle for Leyte Gulf (October 24–26), Mitscher directed the carrier operations responsible for destroying most of the remaining Japanese carriers.

Mitscher played a supporting role at Iwo Jima in February 1945 and at Okinawa in April. In the Battle of the East China Sea, on April 7, his carriers sank the battleship Yamato—the biggest and mightiest battleship of World War II—and most of her escorts. In July, Mitscher returned to Washington, D.C., as deputy chief of Naval Operations (Air) and, shortly after the war, in March 1946, he was promoted to admiral. He commanded the Eighth Fleet briefly before his death, at age 60, from illness.

Colleagues remembered Mitscher's brilliance as a tactician, but, even more, they remembered his almost supernatural calm under fire and under the pressure of command. It was a quiet confidence that pervaded units under his charge. Although he demanded maximum effort from his fliers, he was zealous in finding ways to protect their safety without compromising combat effectiveness.

LEADERSHIP LESSONS
✦

An impressive height and physique are, without doubt, leadership assets;
but a demonstration of skill and heart overcomes the physical
disadvantage of short stature.
✦

Support bold action.
✦

Innovation is important in many leadership roles, provided that it is
accompanied by mastery.
✦

The convincing leader shares the risks of those he leads.
Their needs, wants, and problems are his.
✦

Project calm confidence. It is a contagious form of excellence.

Mountbatten, Louis Francis Albert Victor Nicholas

Born: 1900 Died: 1979

Character model   Improviser   Innovator   Leverager
Motivator   Problem solver   Tactician

LEADERSHIP ACHIEVEMENTS

◆

Combined thorough knowledge of his profession, a respect for tradition, and a willingness to innovate

◆

Developed an impressive command presence without losing the common touch that bonded him to his troops

◆

Used errors and defeats as opportunities to learn and improve

◆

Led the Allies to victory in the difficult and neglected Southeast Asian theater of World War II

◆

Was a great leverager of paltry resources

LIFE

Lord Louis Mountbatten was one of the last great men of the British Empire. Commander in Southeast Asia during World War II, he was an admiral, statesman, and the last viceroy of India, the man who managed the transfer of India from British control to independence.

He was born at Frogmore House, Windsor, to Prince Louis of Battenberg (later Lord of Milford Haven) and Princess Victoria of Hesse-Darmstadt (a granddaughter of Queen Victoria). During World War I, Mountbatten's father changed the family name because it sounded too Germanic. Young Mountbatten entered the Royal Navy as a cadet at the Osbourne Naval Training College, which he attended from May 1913 to November 1914, and then continued at the Royal Naval College, Devonport, graduating at the top of his class in June 1916. He entered active service during World War I as a midshipman aboard Admiral David Beatty's flagship H.M.S. *Lion* from July 1916 to January 1917 and aboard

H.M.S. *Queen Elizabeth* from February 1918 to July of that year. After promotion to lieutenant, Mountbatten transferred to P-boat (coastal torpedo boat) service in August and served aboard the small P-boats until the end of the war in November 1918.

After the armistice, Mountbatten spent a year at Cambridge University, and then toured Australia, Japan, and India with the Prince of Wales (later Edward VIII) beginning in 1920. He married Edwina Ashley on his return to Britain in 1922. The two formed a remarkable partnership, and, during World War II, Lady Edwina would become almost as famous as Mountbatten as she worked tirelessly to lift morale on the hard-pressed and often neglected Southeast Asian fronts.

In 1923, Mountbatten served on H.M.S. *Revenge* (1923), and then enrolled in an advanced signals course, graduating, once again, first in his class, in July 1925. Signals training qualified Mountbatten to serve as assistant fleet wireless officer in the Mediterranean during 1927–28, and in 1931 he was made fleet wireless officer. Promoted to captain in 1932, he continued to serve as Mediterranean Fleet wireless officer through 1933, when he was briefly assigned command of the destroyer H.M.S. *Daring*. From 1936 to 1938, Mountbatten served as naval aide-de-camp to Edward VIII and, after Edward's abdication, to George VI.

On the eve of World War II, in June 1939, Mountbatten was assigned command of the destroyer H.M.S. *Kelly,* then under construction. After overseeing the completion of the vessel, he sailed it as commander of the 5th Destroyer Flotilla, consisting of *Kelly* and *Kingston,* on September 20, 1939. Mountbatten performed with great distinction in the evacuation of Namsos following the ill-fated British offensive in Norway during June 1940. During the evacuation of Crete, however, *Kelly* was sunk by German dive bombers on May 23, 1941.

Following the loss of *Kelly,* Mountbatten was made captain of the aircraft carrier H.M.S. *Illustrious,* which was being repaired in a U.S. navy yard during October 1941. Mountbatten traveled to the States to oversee the work, and he used the opportunity to make many valuable contacts among American officers and political leaders. His own charm, competence, and quiet courage greatly impressed American naval leaders, and, in contrast to many other British military leaders, Mountbatten formed a highly respectful opinion of the American commanders.

In April 1942, Winston Churchill recalled Mountbatten from sea duty to serve as director of Combined Operations. In this role, Mountbatten acted on his eagerness for England to take offensive action in the war. He was among the principal planners of the raid on Dieppe (August 18, 1942), which resulted in a disastrous British defeat. Mountbatten remained unshaken by the loss, which made him determined to improve the British military's amphibious capabilities, being convinced that any offensive campaign would depend on amphibious operations. Mountbatten built up the amphibious-capable force, so that by April 1943, Combined Operations consisted of some 2,600 landing craft and 50,000 personnel. He also turned his attention to making technological improvements to amphibious operations. It was Mountbatten who pioneered the use of "mulberries" (towed harbors) and the PLUTO (Pipe-Line under the Ocean) system, both of which were important in the D-Day Normandy invasion of 1944.

In the August 1943 Quebec Conference among the Allies, Mountbatten was jumped above more senior officers to become supreme allied commander for Southeast Asia—a very difficult and unenviable assignment in an all but neglected corner of the war that was chronically undermanned and poorly supplied. As supreme allied commander of this theater, Mountbatten directed all Allied operations in Burma and the Indian Ocean, and immediately exhibited a genius for managing irregular and inadequate resources and conflicting command personalities toward a common goal. The job called for a leader of great flexibility and a willingness to improvise. Key to Mountbatten's success was the close working relationship he developed with British general Sir William Slim. Working as a team, the two commanders led the liberation of Burma from late 1944 through August 1945, waging war on a shoestring and against a fanatically dedicated enemy, always laboring in conditions of terrain and climate that could be more lethal than any human-made weapons.

After the war, Mountbatten faced another daunting task. He had to accept Japanese surrender and then reestablish colonial authority in places that were now increasingly determined to achieve independence. Mountbatten found himself executing his duties despite his growing conviction that the age of colonial rule had indeed passed, and that independence was the appropriate circumstance of the postwar world. He became politically active in advocating the peaceful transition from colonial to independent status. In the immediate aftermath of the war, Mountbatten was also zealous about locating and liberating Allied POWs, who had been abused and starved by their Japanese captors, as quickly and as humanely as possible.

Mountbatten's postwar authority extended to Indochina and Indonesia during September 1945–46, and from March 24 to August 15, 1947, he served as the last British viceroy of India. In this post, he led the extraordinarily difficult—and, for many Brits, emotionally wrenching—process of withdrawal from India and the inauguration of independence for India and Pakistan.

Named a viscount in 1946, Mountbatten was made an earl in 1947. In 1950, he was appointed fourth sea lord of the Royal Navy, serving in this capacity until 1952, when he became commander in chief of the Mediterranean Fleet. In 1954, he was made first sea lord and served in this post until 1959. Promoted to admiral of the fleet in this same year, he was also named chief of the United Kingdom Defence Staff and chairman of the Chiefs of Staff Committee. He served in these posts until July 1965, effectively directing the military resources of Great Britain.

In 1965, Mountbatten accepted appointment as governor and, in 1974, as lord lieutenant of the Isle of Wight. He fell victim to Irish Republican Army (IRA) terrorists on August 27, 1979. Mountbatten and his teenaged grandson Nicholas, along with a local Irish boy, were killed when an IRA bomb exploded aboard Mountbatten's yacht.

Mountbatten uniquely combined many of the qualities of traditional British imperial aristocracy with a forward-looking engagement with the realities of a changing world. He was among the Allies' most flexible, inventive, and innovative military thinkers, who reached out to all under his command, from senior generals and admirals of several nations to the private soldier.

IN HIS OWN WORDS

"Of the 240 men on board this ship, 239 behaved as they ought to have and as I expected them to. . . . One did not. I had him brought before me a couple of hours ago, and he himself informed me that he knew the punishment for desertion of his post could be death. You will therefore be surprised to know that I propose to let him off with a caution, one

caution to him and a second one to myself, for having failed in four months to impress my personality and doctrine on each and all of you to prevent such an incident from occurring. From now on I will try to make it clear that I expect every one of you to behave in the way that 239 did, and to stick to their post in action to the last. I will under no circumstances whatever again tolerate the slightest suspicion of cowardice or indiscipline, and I know from now on that none of you will present me with any such problems."
—*Address to the officers and men of H.M.S. Kelly, 1940*

LEADERSHIP LESSONS

✦

Use everything—tradition, education, instinct, an openness to innovation—
but do not become dominated by anything.

✦

Leverage your resources.

✦

Faced with shortages and other material disadvantages, your most
precious resource is morale. It is cheap but very difficult to maintain.

✦

A leader holds office by official authority, but his standing as a leader must
be earned from those he leads—and must be earned on a day-to-day,
project-by-project basis.

✦

The proper response to defeat is not discouragement, but a
determination to learn.

Napoleon I

Born: 1769   Died: 1821

**Conqueror   Innovator   Motivator   Strategist
Systems creator   Tactician   Visionary**

LEADERSHIP ACHIEVEMENTS

✦

Was the most prolific conqueror of modern times

✦

Rose from obscurity to become the world's most powerful leader

✦

Was one of history's great captains

✦

Was a visionary with a genius for realizing his vision

✦

Fired the world's imagination—and continues to do so

✦

Bequeathed to France a great body of law

LIFE

No figure in modern history is more famous than Napoleon I, a leader who rose from the margins of society to guide the destiny of France and redraw the map of Europe. In his own day, Napoleon drew both hatred and virtual idolatry; today, he continues to excite an almost mythic fascination. His name is synonymous with brilliant conquest, innovative leadership, military genius, absolute power, and, ultimately, abject defeat.

The early life of Napoleon Bonaparte hardly portended greatness. He was born on August 15, 1769, at Ajaccio, Corsica, the second surviving son of Carlo and Marie-Letizia Buonaparte. Although he was permitted to enroll in a French military school at Brienne-le-Chateau from April 1779 to October 1784, his classmates and instructors spurned him as a provincial and a foreigner. Young Bonaparte responded to this rejection by withdrawing into himself and devoting himself passionately to his studies. Despite his hard work, however, he did not excel academically, graduating 42nd in a class of 58. Nevertheless, he qualified for additional study at the

Military Academy in Paris, and he was commissioned a second lieutenant of artillery on September 1, 1785. Bonaparte was assigned to La Fère Artillery Regiment.

During his early years in the army, Napoleon came under the influence of the military theorist J. P. du Teil and, beginning in 1789, also became increasingly involved in a Corsican nationalist movement. He was transferred to the Artillery Régiment du Grenoble in February 1791, securing promotion to first lieutenant. At this time, he became active in the Jacobin Club of Grenoble, traveled to Corsica, and engineered his election as lieutenant colonel of the Ajaccio Volunteers on April 1, 1792. After participating in an unsuccessful action in Sardinia during February 21–26, 1793, Napoleon fell into a dispute with the anti-French Corsican nationalist Pasquale Paoli. This put the Bonapartes in danger, and, with his family, Napoleon fled to Marseilles on June 10, 1793.

When the Revolt of Midi (July) broke out, Napoleon joined the Republican cause and was commissioned commander of artillery in the Army of Carteaux. On September 16, 1793, he participated in the successful siege of Toulon, a royalist stronghold that had welcomed a counterrevolutionary British fleet. By December 17, the British had been driven out, and Toulon fell to the Republicans on December 22. Napoleon had so distinguished himself that he was promoted to brigadier general and subsequently given command of artillery in the French Army of Italy in February 1794. With the overthrow of Maximilien Robespierre in July 1794, however, Napoleon was imprisoned from August 6 to September 14, 1794.

Following his release, Napoleon declined a new artillery command in the Army of the West and was assigned instead to the Bureau Topographique. This led to appointment as second in command of the Army of the Interior. In this capacity, he ended the Parisian rebellion of 13 Vendémiaire (October 5, 1795), which protested the means of implementing the new constitution introduced by the National Convention. Napoleon dispersed the insurrectionists with what he called a "whiff of grapeshot," thereby saving the Convention. The Directory, as the new governing body was called, rewarded the young brigadier by giving him full command of the Army of the Interior. It was at this time, in March 1796, that Napoleon married Josephine de Beauharnais, the somewhat infamous widow of a republican general.

Napoleon led the Army of the Interior in a vigorous campaign against the armies of Piedmont and Austria, forcing an armistice with Piedmont by the end of April, after he defeated its army at Modovi on April 21. This triumph secured the cession of Savoy and Nice to France. From this victory, he moved swiftly against the Austrians, defeating them at Lodi on May 10, and then marching into Milan on May 15. He drove the Austrian forces out of Lombardy during May and June. Mantua, the last Austrian stronghold in the region, fell to Napoleon in February 1797 after a protracted siege. Napoleon next advanced on Vienna itself, a move that prompted the Austrians to sue for peace. Napoleon personally negotiated the Treaty of Campo Formio on October 17, 1797, by which the war of the First Coalition—the first of the French revolutionary wars—was ended.

In control of Italy, Napoleon wasted no time in reshaping Italian politics by creating the Cisalpine Republic and establishing various puppet governments throughout the peninsula. Napoleon also did not scruple to pillage Italian art collections in order to help finance French military operations.

The Directory hailed Napoleon as a hero of classical proportions. The next target the Directory chose for the young general was England, which the Directory proposed to invade. Napoleon, however, presented an alternative strategy: His idea was first to invade Egypt so as to obtain a staging area for an invasion of British India. He believed that the great powers were most vulnerable in their imperial holdings, and that these should be attacked and conquered before taking on the country directly. On May 19, 1798, therefore, Napoleon set off for Alexandria with about 35,000 troops. En route, he captured Malta, neatly evading the British fleet under the command of Horatio Nelson. From here he went on to occupy Alexandria and Cairo.

Napoleon had no desire to alienate the indigenous population and therefore guaranteed that Islam and Islamic law would be protected and respected. This notwithstanding, Napoleon also set about modernizing the secular government during September 1798–February 1799.

On August 1, 1798, Admiral Nelson's fleet destroyed the French fleet at Abukir Bay, cutting Napoleon off from France. Despite this blow, Napoleon continued operations in Egypt. When the Ottoman Turks declared war on France in February 1799, Napoleon sought to head off a Turkish invasion of Egypt by preemptively invading Syria. Turkish troops under British command halted his advance at Acre during March 15–May 17, and the French army was stricken with plague. Napoleon brought his army back to Cairo in June, and then, on July 25, defeated an Anglo-Turkish invasion attempt at Aboukir.

At this point, the French situation in Europe had reached a crisis, as French forces were suffering defeat at the hands of the Second Coalition. Napoleon embarked for France on August 24, 1799, arriving in Paris on October 14. There he participated in the coup d'etat of November 9 (18 Brumaire) against the Directory. Appointed commander of the Paris garrison, Napoleon secured appointment as one of three consuls in a new Consulate, which replaced the Directory. In February 1800, under the Constitution of the Year VIII, Napoleon was elected first consul, with power to appoint members of the council of state as well as government officials and judges.

In the position of consul, Napoleon was able to consolidate his power until he had effectively assumed dictatorial powers. Certainly Napoleon centralized government to an unheard-of degree. He centered all authority on himself, making sure that, soon, the French government would be under his personal control. Part of Napoleon's genius for the acquisition of power was his ability to read the mood of the French nation. Racked by years of revolutionary terror and anarchy, still menaced by royalists, the people, it was clear to Napoleon, were now ready to confer absolute authority on a strong leader. It was during this period that Napoleon was instrumental in creating the Napoleonic Code, a sweeping codification and rationalization of civil law. It remains to this day the basis of the French legal system.

The first consul concluded the 1801 Concordat with Pope Pius VII, which reestablished Roman Catholicism as the state religion and gained France important alliances based on religion. In addition, Napoleon, in another sweeping reform, radically restructured the French national debt, rescuing the French economy from revolution-borne ruin. Napoleon actively promoted the development of industry and the improvement of the educational system. He also launched a visionary program of public construction, which was inspired by examples of Roman imperial splendor.

While he pursued internal reform and improvements, Napoleon waged wars intended to establish France as the greatest of world powers.

He defeated the Austrians at the Battle of Marengo on June 14, 1800, bringing about the Treaty of Luneville (February 9, 1801) and initiating a brief interval of peace with all of Europe, including England, which signed the Treaty of Amiens (March 27, 1802). On August 2, 1802, a grateful France enacted a plebiscite creating Napoleon first consul for life—in effect, perpetual dictator.

The peace of Luneville and Amiens was short-lived as, once again, Napoleon embarked on redrawing the map of Europe. In the Netherlands he created the Batavian Republic and in Switzerland the Helvetic Republic. Savoy-Piedmont he annexed, and then took the first step toward abolishing the Holy Roman Empire by enacting the Imperial Recess of 1803, which consolidated free cities and minor states dominated by the Holy Roman Empire. He also attempted to recover the Caribbean island nation of Haiti, which had rebelled against French colonial domination. Napoleon's renewed aggression, coupled with his refusal to grant trade concessions to Britain, reignited war in May 1803. (Within a few months, Napoleon abandoned the Caribbean and essentially withdrew from the New World. He authorized his chief minister, Talleyrand, to negotiate the sale of the Louisiana Territory, the last French holding in North America, to the United States.)

As Napoleon prepared a massive army of 170,000 troops to invade England, an assassination plot, financed by the British, was discovered. Alarmed by this, the French Senate petitioned Napoleon to establish a hereditary dynasty. The first consul did not hesitate to seize the opportunity offered him and, on December 2, 1804, as Pope Pius VII looked on, he crowned himself emperor. In a single grand gesture, Napoleon abrogated the republic for which he had fought. He created a royal court populated by former republicans as well as by old-time royalists. As usual, however, Napoleon was not content with what had been offered him, no matter the grandeur of its scale. The Corsican outsider was now determined to create a dynasty for France as well as for other parts of Europe. Eventually, he installed family members on the thrones of Naples, the Netherlands, Westphalia, and Spain. In 1809, he divorced Josephine because she had failed to bear a male heir. On April 2, 1810, he married Marie-Louise, daughter of the Austrian emperor. A son was born to the couple within a year.

In the meantime, Napoleon formulated a grand strategy to draw the mighty British fleet away from England so that he might launch his long-contemplated invasion. The strategy was basically sound, but it failed because of the essential inferiority of the French navy. Napoleon was master of much of the continent, but Britain remained undisputed master of the seas. Worse, Austria now prepared to renew war, and Napoleon had no choice but to turn from England to attend to the Austrian threat. On May 26, 1805, he was crowned king of Italy, and during July through September he maneuvered against the Austrians led by General Karl Mack von Leiberich. In a tactical masterpiece, Napoleon enveloped and crushed Leiberich at Ulm during September 25–October 20, 1805. At sea, however, British admiral Lord Nelson sunk most of the French fleet at the Battle of Trafalgar on October 21. Despite the victory against Austria, invasion of England was now out of the question.

Undaunted, Napoleon advanced on Vienna, which fell to him on November 13. From here he continued into Moravia, where the Russian army under Marshal Mikhail Kutuzov offered battle at Austerlitz. Napoleon's total victory here, on December 2, was his greatest single military triumph. By the end of the month, Austria signed the Treaty of Pressburg, relinquishing Venice and Dalmatia to Napoleon's Kingdom of Italy, and on July 12, 1806, Napoleon achieved his dream of abolishing the Holy Roman Empire. It was replaced by the Confederation of the Rhine, a French protectorate of German states. Intent now on easing hostilities with England, Napoleon offered to return Hanover to British control, but, in the delicate game of Napoleonic international politics, this provoked war with Prussia in September.

Now under Prussian direction, a Fourth Coalition was organized against Napoleon. No sooner were its armies committed to battle, however, than they met with decisive defeat at the battles of Jena and Auerstadt (both on October 14, 1806). Following this, Napoleon fought the Russian army at Eylau on February 8, 1807, in a battle that ended in a draw. Next, he engaged the Russians at Friedland, on June 14, 1807. This battle, a solid victory for the emperor, forced Czar Alexander I to sign the Treaties of Tilsit in July 1807, which created the French-controlled Grand Duchies of Warsaw and the Kingdom of Westphalia. Napoleon I now enjoyed unprecedented hegemony throughout Europe.

Like Alexander the Great's, Napoleon's hunger for conquest was never satisfied. England still figured as his great rival. Unable to defeat it by military means, Napoleon took a different tack in 1806–07 by instituting the Continental System, essentially a broad blockade of British trade, which was intended to strangle the British economy. Although aimed against England, this unwise measure created great unrest throughout Europe. For its part, Portugal immediately announced that it would not participate in the blockade. In response, Napoleon launched the Peninsular War to compel Portugal's obedience. This, however, provoked unrest in Spain and the abdication of King Charles IV as well as his son Ferdinand VII during May 5–6, 1808. Next came a popular uprising against Napoleon's chosen successor to the Spanish throne, Joseph Bonaparte.

While Napoleon was embroiled on the peninsula, Austria formed the Fifth Coalition. At first, the new alliance against Napoleon produced several victories, but the War of the Fifth Coalition culminated in a decisive French victory at the Battle of Wagram on July 5–6, 1809. Napoleon married Marie-Louise following the July 12 armistice with Austria, which, by the Treaty of Schonbrunn (October 14, 1809), relinquished Illyria and Galicia.

Despite this major victory, Napoleon's insistence on the Continental System had greatly undermined his support throughout much of Europe, and it was clear that the emperor was losing his grasp on Spain and Portugal. Now Russia also withdrew from participation in the Continental System. This would prompt Napoleon to his greatest catastrophe. Militarily overextended, Napoleon nevertheless staged a full-scale invasion of Russia on June 23–24, 1812. The Russian armies used the mightiest weapon they had in their arsenal: the vast Russian land itself. The Russians retreated before the emperor's advance, pulling him deeper and deeper into the country. Napoleon was victorious at Borodino on September 7, 1812, and he arrived in Moscow within a week. Despite the fall of his capital, Czar Alexander I refused to surrender, and Russian partisans set fire to the city. Under attack by freshly reinforced Russian armies, and, even worse, confronting the Russian winter, Napoleon began an agonizing retreat that soon proved more costly than any battle. Through his personal leadership, Napoleon managed to preserve the core of his Grand Army, but he had suffered terrible losses nevertheless.

Once the French had been defeated in Russia, Prussia abandoned its short-lived alliance with the French to form a Sixth Coalition against Napoleon, consisting of Prussia, Russia, Britain, and Sweden. In Paris, in the meantime, Napoleon rebuilt his army and used it to defeat Coalition forces at Lutzen on May 2, 1813, and at Bautzen on May 20–21, forcing a brief armistice. In August, Austria joined the Sixth Coalition, and Napoleon defeated Austrian troops at Dresden during August 26–27 but, badly outnumbered, was in turn defeated at Leipzig on October 16–19, 1813. Napoleon retreated across the Rhine, but refused to surrender any conquered territory.

In 1814, Coalition armies invaded France itself, but the emperor successfully repelled each attempt to penetrate to Paris until repeated mauling of his dwindling forces prompted a mutiny of his marshals, which precipitated the fall of the capital on March 31, 1814. A few days after this catastrophe, on April 6, Napoleon abdicated in favor of his son. The Coalition allies rejected this, and Napoleon abdicated unconditionally on April 11. He was exiled to the British-controlled island of Elba. Astoundingly, in 1815, Napoleon returned to France, landing at Cannes on March 1. The Bourbon monarch, Louis XVIII, fled before his approach, and Napoleon occupied Paris on March 20. The allies, meeting at the Congress of Vienna, spurned Napoleon's claim of peaceful intentions. Seeking to forestall combined attack by Russian and Austrian armies, Napoleon decided to strike preemptively to divide and destroy Prussian and Anglo-Dutch armies in Belgium. Napoleon prevailed against the Austrians at Ligny on June 16 and, again, against the British at Quatre Bras on the same day. He was, however, defeated at Waterloo by the Duke of Wellington reinforced by Austrians under Gebhard von Blucher on June 18, 1815.

Following Waterloo, Napoleon returned to Paris, abdicated for the second time on June 23, and was prevented from fleeing to the United States. He surrendered to the captain of a British warship and was exiled, this time to the island of Saint Helena. There he composed his memoirs and grew increasingly ill. He died on May 5, 1821. For many years, it was believed that he had died of stomach cancer, although various historians and others theorized that he had been poisoned by his British captors. Recent evidence, including chemical analysis of strands of Napoleon's hair, reveal high doses of arsenic, and it is now generally believed that he was a victim of deliberate poisoning—probably by a member of his own trusted staff, however, and not his British jailors.

IN HIS OWN WORDS

"After making a mistake or suffering a misfortune, the man of genius always gets back on his feet."

"He who fears being conquered is sure of defeat."

"A leader is a dealer in hope."

"Never interrupt your enemy when he is making a mistake."

—All quotations are from the www.napoleonic-literature.com website

LEADERSHIP LESSONS

✦

Napoleon immersed himself in military history and devoted himself to the study of strategy and tactics. A great leader lives and breathes his work.

✦

Napoleon led by personal example, his presence always inspiring his subordinates to great deeds.

✦

Never give up; Napoleon repeatedly recovered from serious loss.

✦

Know when to abandon a foolish policy. Napoleon failed to do this in the case of the ill-fated Continental System.

✦

Never let personal resentment or prejudice influence leadership decisions. Napoleon's catastrophic adherence to the Continental System was motivated in large part by a personal hatred of England.

Nelson, Horatio, Viscount

Born: 1758   Died: 1805

Character model   Conqueror   Innovator   Leverager   Motivator   Tactician

LEADERSHIP ACHIEVEMENTS

◆

Compiled a record of victory unmatched in the Royal Navy

◆

During the French Revolutionary Wars and the Napoleonic Wars, won key
strategic victories, especially at Aboukir Bay and Trafalgar

◆

Combined absolute self-confidence with a flexible openness to
contributions from others

◆

Understood when to act independently and when to coordinate action
with others

◆

Combined boundless courage and daring with unerring good judgment

LIFE

Horatio Nelson is generally considered the greatest naval officer to sail for
Britain and, perhaps, for any nation. He combined daring and consummately skillful seamanship with charismatic leadership.

Nelson was born at Burnham Thorpe in Norfolk, England, into the
family of a clergyman. He was schooled at Norwich, Downham, and
North Walsham, and then joined the Royal Navy in 1770 as a midshipman,
serving aboard H.M.S. *Raissonable* under his uncle, Captain Maurice
Suckling. With Suckling, he transferred to H.M.S. *Triumph* in 1771 and set
sail for the West Indies and on an Arctic expedition. After returning to
England in 1774, he served aboard H.M.S. *Seahorse* on an East Indian cruise
during 1774–76, followed by a brief stint aboard the frigate H.M.S.
Worcester. Promoted to lieutenant, he was assigned to H.M.S. *Lowestoft* in
1777, cruising the West Indies.

Nelson's first command was H.M.S. *Badger,* followed by promotion to
captain, with command of the frigate *Hinchbrook* in 1779. During 1780,

while conducting operations off Central America, against San Juan del Norte, Nicaragua, Nelson contracted a jungle fever and, desperately ill, had to return to England. After his recovery, he was assigned convoy escort duty as captain of H.M.S. *Albemarle,* and then returned to the West Indies during the American Revolution. After that war, he commanded the frigate H.M.S. *Boreas,* again assigned to patrol West Indian waters.

On March 11, 1787, Nelson was married to Frances Nisbet—an unfortunate union punctuated by many bitter disputes, which made Nelson all the more eager to put out to sea after war broke out with France. He was made captain of the 64-gun H.M.S. *Agamemnon* on February 7, 1793, and while serving with this vessel in the Mediterranean, Nelson met the beautiful Emma, Lady Hamilton, wife of the British ambassador in Naples. He began a long and celebrated liaison with her.

It was against Napoleon's navy that Nelson earned his reputation as an inspired seaman and fearless commander. His leadership style was always to place himself in the thick of the action, sharing whatever dangers his men faced. Indeed, Nelson believed that a leader had to do more than merely share danger. He had to invite it, to demonstrate to his men utter fearlessness, thereby setting for them a compelling and inspiring example. During June–August 1794, while fighting on and near Corsica and around Calvi, this leadership principle cost him his right eye when he was grievously wounded in battle.

Nelson fought next under Admiral William Hotham at Genoa on March 14, 1795, and then sailed along the Italian Riviera, where he operated brilliantly in action to disrupt and destroy the French lines of communication. With the entry of Spain into the French Revolutionary Wars as an ally of France, Nelson was assigned to lead a two-frigate task force to evacuate the British garrison from Elba during December 1796–January 1797. This hazardous mission required him to make a close approach to the enemy in dangerous waters and to evacuate the troops quickly and quietly. Nelson proved that he was not merely a leader who relied on boldness and dash, but that he could also practice the utmost stealth.

After the Elba operation, Nelson was elevated to commodore by Admiral Sir John Jervis. Given this new responsibility, Nelson was determined not to disappoint. He was instrumental in Jervis's victory off Cape St. Vincent on February 14, 1797. Possessing an instinctive grasp of tactical situations at sea, Nelson acted decisively to cut off the escape route of a portion of the Spanish fleet and managed to capture two vessels in the process. For this, he was promoted to rear admiral and knighted.

During the spring of 1797, Nelson was assigned to blockade Cadiz, Spain, and on July 24, 1797, he attacked Santa Cruz de Tenerife. The attack went badly, and at the height of the battle, Nelson received a severe wound, resulting in the loss of his right arm.

Although physically battered, Nelson was by no means beaten. He recovered from his wound by April 1798 and rejoined Jervis off Gibraltar. The admiral sent him with a small squadron to probe French naval and land-based operations at Toulon on May 2. Unfortunately, a storm on May 20 damaged his flagship, H.M.S. *Vanguard*, and by the time repairs had been made, the French fleet had left Toulon. Joining Commodore Sir Ernest Charles Troubridge, who brought 10 additional ships of the line, Nelson determinedly scoured the Mediterranean until, on August 1, 1798, he located the French fleet at Aboukir Bay. The fleet had just finished convoying Napoleon's army to Egypt.

A more conventional commander than Nelson would have taken time to make extensive preparation for the attack. Nelson decided that surprise, in this case, was more important than preparation. The opportunity presented itself in the moment, and that moment had to be seized. He therefore made a surprise attack, which rapidly developed into a battle of mammoth proportions. Troubridge lost the H.M.S. *Culloden* when it ran aground, and 900 British sailors became casualties—including Nelson, who was again wounded. However, Nelson decimated the French Mediterranean fleet: Only two of 13 ships of the line and two of four frigates survived. This momentous victory, the product of Nelson's decisive timing, gave Britain control of the Mediterranean, and that, in turn, doomed Napoleon's army in Egypt. It was the first great reversal Napoleon suffered. After the victory at Aboukir Bay, Nelson was named Baron Nelson of the Nile.

On September 22, 1798, Nelson arrived off Naples to support Neapolitan operations against the French. When the land campaign faltered, Nelson evacuated the royal family to Palermo late in January 1799, and then returned to blockade Naples and Malta. This proved effective, and the French were ultimately forced to withdraw from Naples, whereupon Nelson restored the royal family to their city in June 1799.

In Nelson's judgment, nothing was more important than the operations in Naples. When Admiral Jervis's successor, Admiral Keith, ordered him to Minorca while he was in the midst of the evacuation, Nelson decided to ignore the order. He understood, as Keith did not, that the British base there was in no danger, whereas the Neapolitan royal family was in utmost peril. Nevertheless—and although Nelson was right—his initiative drew a reprimand from the admiralty, so that, shortly after he joined Keith at Livorno on January 20, 1800, he was ordered back to England. He traveled overland, in company with Lady Hamilton—and her husband.

The reprimand did not prevent Nelson's promotion to vice admiral on January 1, 1801, and his appointment as second in command in Admiral Sir Hyde Parker's Baltic Fleet. However, during the Battle of Copenhagen on April 2, he once again took it upon himself to ignore a superior's command when Parker ordered him to break off action. The relentlessly aggressive Nelson, in an instantly famous gesture, put the spyglass to his blind eye and announced that *he* could see no signal from Parker. This instance of disobedience brought an English victory against the Danes, who were compelled to conclude a much-desired armistice.

The admiralty recalled Parker in May and assigned Nelson to succeed him as commander of the Baltic Fleet; however, hostilities there ended in June, and Nelson, suffering from exhaustion, returned to England to recuperate.

Nelson set out to sea again in 1801 and met defeat at Boulogne when he attempted to destroy invasion barges there on August 15. After the Peace of Amiens, Nelson took up residence in Surrey with the Hamiltons from March 27, 1802, to May 16, 1803. In June, he was summoned again to duty when the war with France resumed. Assigned to command the Mediterranean Fleet, Nelson arrived off Toulon and set up a blockade. Under cover of foul weather, the French fleet under Admiral Pierre Charles Villeneuve eluded the blockade on March 30, 1805. Nelson gave chase, mistakenly concluding that Villeneuve had made for the West Indies. From April to August, he sailed to the West Indies and back, finally locating the French fleet at Cadiz in October. On August 18, Villeneuve entered the Mediterranean to support Napoleon's Italian campaign. Nelson was lying in wait for him. He engaged Villeneuve off Cape Trafalgar on October 21, 1805, and fought the most famous battle in modern naval history. Napoleon had proven impossible to defeat on land. Not only did Italy hang in the balance, but a defeat here would ultimately mean an invasion of England itself. As usual, Nelson understood what was at stake, and he effectively communicated this to his subordinate commanders and men. He led by a combination of skill, energy, and contagious courage.

Nelson directed the combat from his flagship H.M.S. *Victory.* He had determined to pursue a radically unorthodox and innovative departure from standard line-ahead attack tactics, whereby the attacker concentrates all his force upon a single vulnerable point in an effort to overwhelm the enemy by main force. Instead, Nelson led a column of 12 ships toward the center of the combined Franco-Spanish fleet while, to the south, Vice Admiral Cuthbert Collingwood led another 15 ships. Accepted naval tactics unconditionally proscribed dividing one's forces in the face of the enemy. To do so invited the enemy to divide and conquer, defeating one's forces in detail. But Nelson believed that the two-column approach would so bewilder the French that they would be too confused to respond effectively.

He was right. One of the French vessels was sunk outright, and eight French as well as nine Spanish ships were subsequently captured. Moreover, this monumental victory was achieved with very few British casualties—but among these few was Lord Horatio Nelson. As usual, he had made himself conspicuous on the deck of his flagship. He wore the full dress uniform of a British admiral—not from any motive of vainglory, but because he believed that the sight of him thus arrayed was profoundly inspiring to his men. Morale, he understood, was key to victory. He paid for this display with his life, cut down and mortally wounded by a sharpshooter's musket ball fired from Villeneuve's flagship *Bucentaure*. In agony, Nelson was taken below decks on the *Victory,* living just long enough to witness the British triumph. The Battle of Trafalgar effectively neutralized the French navy as a serious threat to the British mastery of the high seas, thereby ensuring that, whatever else Napoleon might achieve on land, he would not be able to invade England.

Few combat leaders have accomplished what Nelson achieved, and few possessed, as he did, the abundance of qualities that make for a great sailor and military leader. Although supremely confident—a quality that emanated from his every action—he was also flexible and receptive to contributions from his trusted officers, who were always selected for their proven abilities. Repeatedly, he showed himself capable of independent action, even to the point of outright insubordination. Yet, when close cooperation and coordination with superiors and subordinates were called for, Nelson instantly submerged his ego and became the most cooperative of team players. Most important, he knew when to follow orders and when to act on his own, and he had the courage to act on this knowledge.

IN HIS OWN WORDS

"I have only one eye, I have a right to be blind sometimes. . . . I really do not see the signal."
—Battle of Copenhagen, 1801

"In case signals can neither be seen or perfectly understood, no captain can do very wrong if he places his ship alongside that of the enemy."
—*Memorandum to the Fleet, off Cadiz,* October 9, 1805

"England expects every man will do his duty."
—Signal hoisted to the fleet before the Battle of Trafalgar, October 21, 1805

LEADERSHIP LESSONS

✦

Demonstrate courage.

✦

Share the dangers of those you lead.

✦

An effective leader is always conspicuous.

✦

An effective leader dramatizes risk to motivate performance.

✦

Know when to disobey orders. Then disobey them.

✦

Know when to depart from conventional wisdom. Then depart from it.

✦

Balance a vision of immediate tactics with a grasp of overall strategy.
Prioritize your operations accordingly.

✦

Create a compelling leadership image. Do not hesitate to exploit it.

✦

A large part of victory depends on strategy and tactics. An even larger part
depends on morale.

Nimitz, Chester William

Born: 1885   Died: 1966

**Conqueror   Innovator   Leverager   Mentor   Motivator   Problem solver
Rescuer   Strategist   Systems creator   Tactician**

LEADERSHIP ACHIEVEMENTS

◆

Was instrumental in modernizing the U.S. Navy

◆

Was a mentor to many World War II–era naval officers

◆

Transformed the Pacific war in World War II from a desperate defensive to
a triumphant offensive

◆

Was a key formulator of the island-hopping strategy that ultimately
confounded the Japanese in the Pacific

◆

Was a brilliant manager of subordinates

◆

Motivated his officers to extraordinary achievement

LIFE

Chester William Nimitz was commander of the entire U.S. Pacific Fleet during World War II and led the Navy from defeat and defense to victory. He was born in Fredericksburg, Texas, and enrolled in the U.S. Naval Academy at Annapolis in 1901, graduating in 1905. Two years later, Nimitz was commissioned an ensign while serving on China station; he then became one of the small corps of officers in the fledgling submarine service, serving aboard the submarine *Plunger*. Promoted to lieutenant in 1910, Nimitz was assigned to command the submarine *Skipjack*. Two years later, his command was expanded to the Atlantic Submarine Flotilla. Recognized by naval command as an innovative young officer, Nimitz was sent to Germany and Belgium in 1913 to study diesel engines. When he returned to the States, he undertook direction of construction of the U.S. Navy's first diesel ship engine.

In 1916, Nimitz was promoted to lieutenant commander and, after U.S. entry into World War I in April 1917, he was appointed chief of staff to the commander of the Atlantic Fleet's submarine division. After the war, in 1921, Nimitz was promoted to commander and, in 1922, was sent to the Naval War College. After completing the War College program in 1923, he was attached to the staff of the commander in chief, Battle Fleet, until 1925, when he was transferred to the staff of the commander in chief, U.S. Fleet.

In 1926, Nimitz was tasked to organize the first training division for naval reserve officers at the University of California, a program he administered until 1929, when, (having been promoted to captain in 1927) he was assigned command of Submarine Division 20. He commanded the division through 1931.

In 1933, Nimitz was given command of his first surface vessel, the cruiser U.S.S. *Augusta* (CA-31), sailing as its skipper until 1935, when he was named assistant chief of the Bureau of Navigation. After a 1938 promotion to rear admiral, Nimitz left his desk job to command a cruiser division and then a battleship division, returning to the Bureau of Navigation in June 1939 as its chief.

Following the resignation of Admiral Husband E. Kimmel on December 17, 1941, ten days after the disastrous Japanese surprise attack on Pearl Harbor, Nimitz was promoted to admiral and named as Kimmel's replacement on December 31. He was now commander in chief of the Pacific Fleet.

The task facing the new commander was overwhelming, but Nimitz took it up methodically and authoritatively. His subordinates found in him a combination of complete confidence, total competence, and a willingness to inspire, to instruct, and to learn. His first priority was to reorganize defenses in the Hawaiian Islands to prevent another Pearl Harbor; simultaneously, he set about rebuilding the badly shattered Pacific fleet. On March 30, 1942, he was given unified command of all U.S. naval, sea, and air forces in the Pacific Ocean Area.

Nimitz's primary objective was to turn the tide of the Pacific war by assuming the offensive as quickly as possible. But he did not intend merely to gamble with the fleet. He devoted major resources to developing a system of naval intelligence to give him the information he needed to put scant but growing resources precisely where they would do the most good. The first fruit of this intelligence was the defeat of Japanese invasion operations against Port Moresby, New Guinea, at the battle of the Coral Sea on May 7–8, 1942. Coral Sea may be viewed as a narrow tactical defeat for the U.S. Navy, but an important strategic victory, in that Port Moresby was saved. The next battle Nimitz directed was at Midway, June 2–6, 1942.

If the Japanese could take Midway Island, they would have a key link in a defensive perimeter that could make Japan virtually impregnable. Intending to dilute any American response, Japanese admiral Isoroku Yamamoto sent a diversionary force to the Aleutian Islands, while Admiral Chuichi Nagumo, who had led the Pearl Harbor attack, took a four-carrier strike force followed by an invasion fleet—some 88 ships in all—to Midway. Nimitz, who possessed a powerful imagination that often enabled him to think like his opponent, had anticipated just such a diversion and main attack. Accordingly, he brought together two task forces east of Midway, designated Number 16 (under Admiral Raymond Spruance) and Number 18 (under Admiral Frank Fletcher). The task forces included the carriers *Enterprise, Hornet,* and *Yorktown,* in addition to land-based aircraft on Midway itself. The planes attacked elements of the Japanese fleet on June 3, unfortunately inflicting only slight damage. The following day, 108 Japanese aircraft struck Midway. The damage was severe, including the destruction of 15 of 25 U.S. Marine aircraft based there. But Nimitz remained steadfast. He ordered U.S. torpedo bombers to attack the Japanese fleet. The first assault sunk no ships and resulted in the loss of seven planes. A second assault also failed, with the loss of eight more aircraft. A third attack, by Midway-based B-17 heavy bombers, again failed to damage or sink any of the enemy carriers. This was followed by a torpedo bomber attack launched from the U.S. carriers, in which 35 of the 41 aircraft engaged were lost—having inflicted little damage. Still, Nimitz remained determined to make a stand. The last sortie opened the way for a massive make-or-break attack by 54 dive bombers from *Enterprise* and *Yorktown,* which sunk three Japanese aircraft carriers, their planes unlaunched, in the space of five minutes. The fourth Japanese carrier, *Hiryu,* was sunk in a separate attack later in the day—though not before *Hiryu*'s planes had delivered a fatal blow against the *Yorktown.*

It was a catastrophe from which the Japanese navy would never recover. Japanese forces began withdrawing on June 5, 1942, and Midway was the unmistakable turning point of the Pacific war. From this point on, the U.S. strategy became unremittingly offensive. Nimitz was instrumental in formulating the offensive as a program of "island-hopping." He recognized that the Japanese had attempted to forge an unbreakable and vast defensive perimeter around their home islands. The flaw in this strategy is that the Japanese planners anticipated an American attempt to advance from one island to the next. Nimitz decided instead to hop over some islands, to attack only those necessary to draw closer to Japan itself. This would cut off and isolate Japanese forces on some islands, while simultaneously forcing the Japanese continually to contract their defensive perimeter closer and closer to the homeland.

Nimitz personally directed the campaign in the Gilbert Islands (November 20–23, 1943) and in the Marshalls (January 31–February 23, 1944), but he did not hesitate to delegate specific tactical authority to key subordinates. Never a micromanager, Nimitz worked brilliantly and harmoniously with other commanders. His steady calm and the confidence with which he relied on them were an inspiration. Officers were gratified to serve under him.

Nimitz oversaw the advance into the Marianas during June 14–August 10, 1944, and then into the Palaus during September 15–November 25. At this time, he also linked up with General Douglas MacArthur's forces from New Guinea and coordinated the invasion of Leyte, Philippines, in the U.S. return to the islands on October 20, 1944.

On December 15, 1944, Nimitz was promoted to the newly created rank of fleet admiral—the naval equivalent of general of the army—and then went on to direct the capture of Iwo Jima during February 19–March 24, 1945. As the best available air base between Saipan (some 700 miles to the south, which U.S. forces had already taken) and Tokyo, Iwo Jima was one of the most strategically critical objectives of the Pacific war. Its fall to the U.S. was followed by the campaign to take Okinawa from April 1 to June 21, 1945, which made possible massive operations against Japan itself. Fittingly, the formal surrender of Japan took place aboard Nimitz's flagship, the U.S.S. *Missouri,* on September 2, 1945.

After World War II, Nimitz served as chief of naval operations from December 15, 1945, to December 15, 1947, and was then appointed special assistant to the secretary of the navy during 1948–49. He was named the United Nations commissioner for Kashmir from 1949 to 1951 and wrote (with E. B. Potter) an important history of warfare at sea, *Sea Power: A Naval History,* published in 1960. But it was for the tremendous burden he so successfully shouldered in World War II that Nimitz was most remembered. He shared with Dwight David Eisenhower, supreme commander of the European theater, a calm competence and a remarkable ability to manage, motivate, and empower diverse subordinates and work harmoniously and effectively with a varied array of officers. Like Eisenhower, he avoided flash and impulsiveness, maintaining instead the steady hand so necessary in managing large, high-stakes projects in time of extreme emergency. Yet beneath his calm facade was a man driven by passion, willing to push resources to their limits, and willing as well to innovate whenever necessary.

LEADERSHIP LESSONS

✦

Genuine innovation does not require flamboyance.

✦

First think like your opponent, then outthink your opponent.

✦

Do not give up. Be willing to accept tactical defeat to achieve strategic victory.

✦

Be relentless in pursuit of make-or-break objectives.

✦

Do not let your opponent determine your strategy. Think beyond the conditions your foe has created. Remember Nimitz's island-hopping.

✦

Choose subordinates carefully, then inspire and empower them.

✦

Cultivate calm confidence and relaxed energy. Practice conveying these qualities to others.

Otto I the Great

Born: 912   Died: 973

Conqueror   Rescuer   Strategist   Tactician

LEADERSHIP ACHIEVEMENTS

◆

Rescued much of Europe from violent disintegration toward the end of
the Dark Ages

◆

Brought unprecedented security and unity to the German states, at least
for a time

◆

Personally rose to a position of great power

◆

Led a series of highly effective military campaigns

◆

Effectively combined military prowess with sage diplomacy

◆

Created sufficient tranquillity to foster a period of cultural renaissance

LIFE

Otto I is not very well known to the English-speaking world, yet he was
one of the most important leaders of the European Middle Ages. For all
practical purposes, Otto I created the medieval German monarchy and
rebuilt the Holy Roman Empire (Germany, Italy, Burgundy). The
Germany into which he was born, on October 23, 912, was in extreme
chaos. It was certainly no nation, but, rather, a loose collection of fractious
states. Otto was the son of Duke Henry, who later assumed the throne of
Saxony as King Henry I the Fowler. When he came of age, in 929, Otto
married Eadgyth, the daughter of England's King Edgar the Elder, and
Henry the Fowler nominated Otto as his heir, a choice confirmed by election among the German dukes convened at Aachen on August 7, 936, after
the death of Henry.

Immediately after his coronation by the bishops of Mainz and Cologne,
Otto asserted his authority over the German dukes, who included Otto's half-

brother Thankmar and younger brother Henry. Resentment and defiance ran high. Allying himself with Dukes Eberhard of Bavaria and Eberhard of Franconia, Thankmar led a revolt against Otto during 938–39, to which Otto responded with swift decision. The revolt was quickly crushed. Otto's younger brother, Henry, led a new revolt, however, in league with Eberhard of Franconia and Giselbert of Lorraine and supported by Otto's brother-in-law, King Louis IV of France. This threat was far stronger and more serious, and combat lasted from 939 to 941. Yet, once again, Otto proved himself a skillful and courageous commander. He won decisively at the battles of Xanten in 940 and Andernach in 941. Eberhard and Giselbert were both killed, and brother Henry agreed, at last, to submit to Otto's authority. Otto responded with great generosity, not only pardoning Henry for the revolt itself, but also forgiving him even after he discovered, in December 941, that Henry had plotted directly against his life. These magnanimous and well-timed acts of clemency solidly won the younger brother's loyalty and did so far more effectively than costly force of arms would have. However, Otto did not show Louis IV similar forgiveness, and he launched an invasion of France in 942. This action resulted in a peace favorable to Otto.

In 944, Otto faced a revolt in Bavaria and was defeated at the Battle of Wels by Duke Bertold; however, during 946–47, he used a combination of military pressure and diplomacy to regain control over the rebellious region. This achieved, Otto invaded France for a second time in 948, now marching to the aid of Louis IV, who had been imprisoned by the rebellious Hugh the Great, Count of Paris. After Otto defeated the forces of Hugh at Rheims, capturing that city, the count surrendered and restored Louis to the throne.

In 950, Otto turned east to invade Bohemia, forcing Duke Boleslav to accept his suzerainty. Next, in response to the plea of Princess Adelaide of Burgundy, who had been imprisoned by Berengar, margrave of Ivrea, Otto invaded Italy in 951. He rode to the rescue of Adelaide, who was the widow of Italy's King Lothair. This put him in position to challenge—and defeat—rival claimants to the throne of Lombardy in 952. He crowned himself king of the Lombards, freed Adelaide, and then took her as his second wife. Berengar was now subject to him.

Otto hardly had time to savor his Italian triumph before news reached him that his son Ludolf had launched a rebellion in league with

Duke Conrad the Red of Lorraine, Archbishop Frederick of Mainz, and others. Otto rushed back to Germany in 953, but was defeated and captured by the rebels. He managed an escape, however, and then embarked on a determined offensive against Mainz and Regensburg in 953–54. Neither of these stronghold cities yielded. Suddenly, at this time, some 50,000 to 100,000 Magyars (Hungarians) mounted the Great Magyar Raid into Bavaria and Franconia. In 954, Conrad treacherously allied himself with the Magyars, helping them to cross the Rhine at Worms, and then facilitating their entry into Lorraine. They crossed the Meuse River to ravage northeastern France, traveling through Rheims and Châlons into Burgundy, thence to Italy, through Lombardy, and then into the valleys of the Danube and the Drava. From here, a Magyar force moved against Bavaria. This menace assisted Otto, for Ludolf had no choice but to surrender Regensburg to his father early in 955, so that, together, they could fight the invasion.

Riding at the head of an army of 10,000, Otto arrived at Augsburg, which was under siege by some 50,000 Magyars. On August 10, 955, the Magyars lifted the siege and fought Otto at the Battle of Lechfeld. In the initial states of combat, the Magyars outmaneuvered Otto, captured his camp, and drove a third of his forces from the field. Otto stood firm, however, and Conrad, having been betrayed by the Magyars (who had overrun Lorraine), now sided with his former enemy Otto and helped him first to repel the enveloping Magyars, and then to turn the tide of battle against them. By the end of the day, Otto had captured the Magyar camp, inflicting heavy losses. At the moment of victory, Conrad was slain, and Otto pursued the retreating Magyars for three days. Thus the Great Magyar Raid was brought to an end.

Immediately after he had disposed of the Magyar threat, Otto marched to the north, where he joined forces with Gero, the margrave of Brandenburg, to drive the Slavic Wends out of Germany at the Battle of Recknitz in October 955. Five years later, in 960, Otto moved against Slavic tribes between the Middle Elbe and the Middle Oder. In response to a request of Pope John XII to fight Berengar, who was now Berengar II, king of Italy, Otto embarked for Italy. By the fall of 961, Otto had defeated Berengar, who submitted to vasselage. From this victory, Otto moved on to Rome, where Pope John XII crowned him Holy Roman Emperor on

February 2, 962. Now, however, Otto was shocked to learn that the pope had begun negotiating a treaty with Berengar. In response, Otto deposed John and saw to his replacement by Leo VIII. Otto captured Berengar and sent him, a prisoner, to Germany. Otto himself returned to Germany only after suppressing a Roman revolt against Leo, who was deposed by Benedict V. Since Leo died before the revolt had been put down, Otto appointed John XIII as his successor. This pontiff was driven out of Rome by yet another revolt in 965, which prompted Otto to invade Italy for a third time in 966.

Otto put down the Roman revolt, and then marched to southern Italy, where he fought victoriously against the Saracens and Byzantines. To cement the peace, Otto arranged a marriage between his son Otto II—his chosen successor—and the Byzantine princess Theophano on April 14, 972.

After this most exhausting series of conflicts, Otto returned to a Germany that was now secure and united to an unprecedented degree. He succeeded in strengthening not only the German states but the Holy Roman Empire, and the stability he brought to destructively turbulent times fostered a brief period of artistic and intellectual productivity known as the Ottonian Renaissance. Unfortunately, Otto's death on May 7, 973, ushered in a five-year period of violent civil war, as Bavaria's Henry the Wrangler and Boleslav of Bohemia rebelled against Otto II.

LEADERSHIP LESSONS

✦

Maintain maximum flexibility to combat threats and exploit opportunities from multiple directions.

✦

Generous treatment, from a position of strength, is an effective means of creating loyalty.

✦

A great leader acquires great power by bestowing great benefits. Otto I became powerful by improving the lives of the people he led.

✦

Never give up. Captured, Otto escaped. Outnumbered, he found allies.

Patton, George Smith, Jr.

Born: 1885   Died: 1945

Conqueror   Mentor   Motivator   Tactician

LEADERSHIP ACHIEVEMENTS

✦

In childhood, overcame severe dyslexia

✦

Major architect, builder, organizer, and master tactician of modern armored (tank) warfare

✦

Proved himself a master tactician during the largest, most ambitious military training maneuvers the U.S. Army had ever staged, on the eve of the nation's entry into World War II

✦

Transformed a defeated and thoroughly demoralized American force in North Africa into an army capable of defeating the Nazis' most brilliant general, Erwin Rommel, the feared "Desert Fox"

✦

Invaded Sicily with lightning speed that outstripped even the British general Sir Bernard Law Montgomery

✦

As commanding general of the Third Army, relentlessly drove across France and into Germany, destroying more of the enemy and liberating more towns than any other commander in the history of American arms

✦

Performed a tactical miracle at the Battle of the Bulge, turning his troops, exhausted from three months of forced march and continual battle, 90 degrees north to launch a bold counterattack into the southern flank of the German army to rescue encircled U.S. forces

LIFE

George Smith Patton, Jr., was born November 11, 1885, on his father's California ranch and vineyard, sprawling over what is today the city of Pasadena and much of the UCLA campus. He was a frail boy, greatly adored by his parents. With single-minded determination, he built up his strength and became a fine horseman and all-round athlete. He delighted in his father's stories about his Virginia ancestors, distinguished Confederate military men all.

Young George was clearly an intelligent boy, but he had an inordinate amount of trouble learning to read and write, and Patton's parents decided to educate him at home. At the time, there was no name for the learning disorder now called dyslexia, a complex of learning problems that includes reading, writing, and spelling reversals as well as difficulty concentrating, hyperactivity, mood swings, and feelings of inferiority. For George Patton, dyslexia became an early foe to vanquish. After struggling to learn to read, Patton became a voracious reader of history, especially military history.

Following his home schooling and some years in a private preparatory academy, Patton enrolled at the Virginia Military Institute for a year in preparation for an appointment to West Point. Patton studied at the U.S. Military Academy from 1904 to 1909. Failing math his first semester, he had to repeat part of his first year, but he persevered, becoming a good student, a star athlete, and adjutant of the Corps of Cadets.

After graduation, Patton served on a number of military posts, quickly acquiring a reputation for great energy and ability. He competed on the U.S. pentathlon team in the 1912 Olympics in Stockholm, Sweden, displaying singular prowess in the grueling competition that included a 300-meter swim, pistol shooting, a 4,000-meter run, fencing, and a 5,000-meter steeplechase. Although his fifth-place showing overall did not earn him a medal, Patton was praised by the Swedish newspapers, who noted that "his energy is incredible" and said of his fencing that it was "calm . . . and calculated. He was skillful in exploiting his opponent's every weakness."

Patton's swordsmanship was so expert that he was chosen by the Army to attend the French cavalry school at Saumur and was then sent back to the States to enroll in the Mounted Service School at Fort Riley, Kansas, in 1913. From 1914 to 1916, he served as an instructor at Fort Riley and was appointed master of the sword, with responsibility for writing the Army's new saber manual. He even worked with the Ordnance Department to design a new sword for the cavalry. Officially called U.S. Saber, M-1913, it soon came to be known informally and universally as the "Patton sword."

In 1916, Lieutenant Patton served with General John J. "Black Jack" Pershing in a "punitive expedition" against the Mexican revolutionary bandit Pancho Villa. Pershing was impressed with Patton, who was promoted to captain in 1917. For his part, Patton idolized Pershing as a mentor—his ideal of everything a commander should be.

In May 1917, just one month after the United States entered World War I, Patton was assigned to Pershing's staff and was sent to France with the first contingent of the American Expeditionary Force (AEF). Despite his great admiration for Pershing, Patton wanted a combat assignment rather than a staff job, and he became the first U.S. officer to receive tank training. At this time, tanks were essentially an experimental weapon, unreliable but promising, and it is a testament to Patton's vision that he embraced the new technology. Trained in the age-old traditions of a cavalryman, expert in the ancient art of swordsmanship, Patton now rushed to meet the future.

No sooner was Patton himself trained than he was asked to set up the AEF Tank School at Langres, France, in November 1917, to train others. Promoted to temporary lieutenant colonel and then colonel, he organized and led the 1st Tank Brigade in the key battle against the Saint-Mihiel salient (September 12–17, 1918), in which he was wounded. Patton also commanded tanks at Meuse-Argonne, the last Allied offensive of the war (September 26–November 11).

Returning to the United States in 1919, he reverted to the rank of captain but was quickly promoted to major and given command of the 304th Tank Brigade at Fort Meade, Maryland (1919–21). Unfortunately, the peacetime army had little interest in developing tanks, and Patton decided to return to the cavalry after he was offered a prestigious posting at Fort Myer, Virginia, where he served from 1921 to 1922. After graduating from the Command and General Staff School with honors in 1923, Patton was appointed to the army's General Staff, serving until 1927. Appointed chief of cavalry in 1928, he left that post to attend the Army War College in 1932. During the 1930s, Patton achieved promotion to lieutenant colonel (1934) and then colonel (1937) and, after a stint commanding cavalry, was tapped for command of the 2d Armored Brigade in 1940. Promoted to temporary brigadier general and then temporary major general, he was given command of the 2d Armored Division in April 1941.

With war looming, the United States had begun to mobilize, and, in June, massive maneuvers (war games) were organized in Tennessee. From

July through September, even more ambitious maneuvers were staged in Louisiana and Texas, followed by further exercises in the Carolinas during October and November. Patton emerged victorious from the war games and attracted the notice of his superiors, who, with the entry of the United States into World War II, assigned him to create the Desert Training Center near Indio, California. From March 26 to July 30, 1942, Patton undertook the task of training a first generation of U.S. Army desert fighters.

During August 1942, Patton participated in the planning of Operation TORCH, the U.S. landings in North Africa. He personally commanded the Western Task Force in these landings, which took place on November 8, 1942. In March of the following year, he was called on to replace General Lloyd R. Fredendall after the U.S. II Corps suffered a stunning defeat at Kasserine Pass.

The crisis brought on by the Kasserine debacle was grave. Defeat in the very first contest between the U.S. Army and the German Afrika Korps under General Erwin Rommel, the famed "Desert Fox," was a severe blow to American military confidence. Arriving at II Corps headquarters, Patton immediately sized up the problem as one of mismanagement and weak leadership. Patton instituted a tough regime aimed at achieving perfect discipline. In a remarkably short time, he managed to transform II Corps into a winning organization.

Patton's prickly personality resulted in conflict with British allies, and he was transferred from command of II Corps to command of I Armored Corps, which grew into the Seventh Army. From July 10 through August 17, Patton drove this organization through a difficult but triumphant invasion of Sicily. At the very height of his triumph came the incident for which he is still most notorious. On August 3, Patton visited wounded troops at the 15th Evacuation Hospital. Amid the gravely wounded men was Private Charles H. Kuhl, who, exhibiting no visible wounds, had been hospitalized for battle fatigue. Enraged by what he took as Kuhl's cowardice, Patton slapped the soldier's face with his glove, raised him to his feet by his shirt collar, and sent him out of the tent with a kick in the rear. While this incident passed without further consequence, during a visit to a different evac hospital on August 10, the general encountered another victim of battle fatigue. And there was another slap.

It was this second incident that ignited a firestorm of public and professional outrage, which very nearly ended Patton's career. Ordered by Dwight D. Eisenhower to make the rounds of every Seventh Army unit and apologize for the incident, Patton did so sincerely and with such conviction that he turned a career-breaking nightmare into a morale-building triumph.

Still, the "slapping incident" kept Patton out of the action until January 1944, when he was sent to England and given command of the newly formed Third Army. While in England, he was used as a decoy to deceive the Germans into thinking that he was to lead an invasion of France, not from the beaches of Normandy, but across the Pas de Calais. The ruse worked, and Hitler ordered most of the strength of the German forces concentrated at Calais rather than at Normandy, where the D-Day landings actually took place.

Patton arrived in France with the Third Army on July 6 and led it in the breakout from Normandy across France and into Germany. In the course of little more than nine months, Patton's army liberated or gained 81,522 square miles in France, 1,010 in Luxembourg, 156 in Belgium, 29,940 in Germany, 3,485 in Czechoslovakia, and 2,103 in Austria. An estimated 12,000 cites, towns, and villages were liberated or captured, 27 of which contained more than 50,000 people. Moreover, during the last-ditch German Ardennes offensive, the so-called Battle of the Bulge, when the 101st U.S. Airborne Division was cut off and the Allied advance threatened, Patton wheeled his entire weary army 90 degrees to the north and launched a devastatingly successful counterattack in record time.

The Third Army varied in strength from about a quarter-million personnel to 437,860 as its final campaign ended on May 8, 1945. During August 1, 1944, to April 30, 1945, a payroll of $240,539,569 was disbursed. During this same period, 1,234,529 long tons of supplies were brought into the Third Army area by rail, truck, and air. Within Third Army boundaries, 2,186,792 tons of supplies were transported a total distance of 141,081,336 miles. Third Army engineers built 2,498 bridges of all descriptions—about 8.5 miles of bridges, total. They repaired or reconstructed 2,240 miles of road and 2,092 miles of railroad. The organization's Signal Corps laid 3,747 miles of open wire and 36,338 miles of underground cable. Its telephone operators handled an average of 13,986 calls daily.

The Third Army captured 1,280,688 prisoners of war from August 1, 1944, to May 13, 1945. The enemy suffered 47,500 killed and 115,700 wounded—a total of 1,443,888 casualties—to the Third Army, which incurred 160,565 casualties, including 27,104 killed, 86,267 wounded, 18,957 injured, and 28,237 missing, of whom many were later reported captured.

Under General Patton, the Third Army went farther and faster than any other army in the history of warfare.

After the war in Europe was won, Patton hoped to be sent to the Pacific, but the supreme commander in that theater, General Douglas MacArthur, would never stand for "competition" from a general such as Patton. Instead, Patton was assigned as military governor of Bavaria, an assignment for which this combat commander was utterly unsuited. In October 1945, Patton was relieved as Third Army commander and given command of the Fifteenth Army, largely a "paper" organization, the chief duty of which was to compile a history of the war in Europe. Although greatly discouraged by this turn of events, Patton went about his new assignment diligently, until December 9, 1945, when he suffered a fatal injury in an otherwise minor car accident on a road near Mannheim. He died in a Heidelberg military hospital on December 21.

IN HIS OWN WORDS

"Always attack. Never surrender."

"When in doubt, attack."

"There can never be defeat if a man refuses to accept defeat. Wars are lost in the mind before they are lost on the ground."

"No decision is difficult to make if you will get all the facts."

"You have to pick your enemies with as much care as you do your friends."

"We will never let the enemy pick the battle site."

"The best is the enemy of the good. By this I mean that a good plan violently executed now is better than a perfect plan next week."

"Nothing is impossible, provided you use audacity."

LEADERSHIP LESSONS

✦

Lead from the front, not from behind.

✦

Always look and act like a leader in everything you do.

✦

Share the risks, the liabilities, and the credit with those you lead.

✦

Opportunities are easily lost. Better to act on a good plan than wait for perfection, which may never come.

✦

Know exactly what you are doing. Know what you know—and what you do not know.

✦

Leadership by remote control is bound to fail. Get out from behind your desk and into the world.

✦

When you see a problem, don't cast blame. Work the problem. Fix it now.

✦

Choose your battles. Don't waste resources on worthless fights.

Pericles

Born: 495 B.C.   Died: 429 B.C.

Conqueror   Innovator   Strategist   Systems creator   Visionary

LEADERSHIP ACHIEVEMENTS

✦

Brought democracy to Greece—and the world

✦

Brought Athenian culture and art to their height

✦

Created, briefly, an Athenian empire

LIFE

Pericles is one of history's great names, yet because he had no contemporary biographer to record his exploits, he is, despite his fame, somewhat obscure. Indeed, his career is marked throughout by paradox. He was an ardent champion of democracy, but he ruthlessly played the tyrant in order to force democratic government on the Greek city-states subordinate to Athens. Pericles brought Greece to the height of its greatness, which included the extension of Athenian democracy even to the humblest of citizens, as well as the building of the temples and statues of the Acropolis and the creation of the Athenian empire; however, his relentless effort to impose Athens' will on all other states sowed the seeds of a rebellion that eventually brought about the fall of Athens and, ultimately, the decline of Greece.

Pericles was the son of Zanthippus, a prominent statesman, and Agariste, a member of the influential Alcmaeonid family. He first came to public attention in 472, when he provided and trained the chorus for Aeschylus's play *The Persians*. Years later, in 458, he was elected *strategos* (effectively, commanding general), which was an important policy-setting office. The term of service was only one year, but, over a 30-year period, Pericles was very frequently reelected.

Pericles was of noble birth, yet he was an ardent supporter of democracy—a fact the more extraordinary when we consider that the period of Pericles' early career was marked by almost universal tyranny. Yet while he was democratic in his philosophy, Pericles was personally autocratic and imperious. This was reflected in the way he dealt with other city-states. The Delian League was a confederation of city-states formed to fight Xerxes and the Persians. Athens collected money from many of the member states to maintain an army and build a navy. These forces soon came to be dominated by Athenians, and the other states of the confederation grew to resent paying tribute to maintain forces that often served to impose the Athenian model of government on them. Moreover, a portion of the tribute money was diverted to finance Pericles' ambitious program of sculpture-raising and temple-building. Worse, under the system of *cleruchy,* Athenian colonists were granted lands abroad while retaining the rights and privileges of Athenian citizenship. It became clear to subordinate and neighboring city-states that Athens intended to build an empire of tributary states.

While Pericles realized his ambition to make Athens preeminent among Greek states, and while the oppression Athens brought down upon those states in the name of democracy did, among other things, bring a period of peace, stability, and the rule of law, his unbending insistence on the rightness of democracy for all states incited Sparta to lead the powers of the Peloponnesus in a revolt against Athens—the two Peloponnesian Wars.

While Athens lay under siege during the wars with Sparta, a plague swept the city. Amid the turmoil, Pericles was briefly deposed from office. A few weeks later, the Athenian people restored Pericles to office. However, Pericles had been stricken by the plague and died within a year.

LEADERSHIP LESSONS
✦
A great idea is a leader's most powerful weapon.
✦
Coercion may gain ground in the short term, but the tyrannical imposition of will tends ultimately to produce discontent and even rebellion.

Perry, Oliver Hazard

Born: 1785   Died: 1819

Character model   Improviser   Leverager   Motivator
Problem solver   Rescuer

LEADERSHIP ACHIEVEMENTS

✦

Identified a problem and improvised a daring solution

✦

Created an entire naval force from scratch

✦

Refused to be defeated

✦

Inspired his men to victory

✦

Implemented highly effective techniques of motivation and inspiration

LIFE

Oliver Hazard Perry is most famous for his extraordinary victory at the Battle of Lake Erie, which saved the United States from ignominious defeat in the War of 1812. A native of Rocky Brook, Rhode Island, and the older brother of another future naval hero, Matthew C. Perry, Oliver H. Perry joined the navy in early youth, sailing in 1799 as a midshipman under his father, Christopher R. Perry, captain of the 28-gun frigate, U.S.S. *General Greene*. Young Perry was promoted to lieutenant in 1802 and served through 1803 in the Mediterranean against the Tripolitan corsairs, state-sanctioned pirates who preyed upon European and U.S. merchant shipping.

During 1804–06, Perry served as captain of the 12-gun schooner *Nautilus* on Mediterranean duty. After he returned to the United States, he supervised the building of gunboats to augment the fledgling U.S. Navy. This experience prepared him for building the instant Lake Erie fleet, which would be instrumental in averting defeat during the War of 1812. Also during 1807–09, Perry sailed on patrols to enforce President Thomas Jefferson's Embargo Act.

Perry's career was nearly cut short in 1811 when his 12-gun U.S.S. *Revenge* ran aground in a dense fog in Newport Harbor. Court-martialed on a charge of negligence, he was duly acquitted and then assigned command of the Newport gunboat flotilla when the War of 1812 commenced.

On February 13, 1813, Perry was sent to Lake Erie to serve under Commodore Isaac Chauncey. He arrived at Presque Isle (modern Erie), Pennsylvania, only to discover that there were no American vessels on this strategically vital lake. Whoever controlled Lake Erie controlled a key means of transport and supply. Recognizing a grave crisis when he saw one, Perry came up with a radical solution. Although he had few supplies and a serious shortage of officers and sailors, Perry set to work rapidly building gunboats. By the early summer of 1813, he had completed nine vessels mounting 54 guns. It was an instant naval force ideally suited to inland waters.

On May 27, Perry and Chauncey assisted Colonel Winfield Scott in the capture of Fort George (Ontario). Perry then returned to his gunboats, slipping them out of Presque Isle harbor during August 1–4. On September 10, he engaged the British fleet blockading Lake Erie, leading the attack from his 20-gun flagship *Lawrence*. That vessel Perry personally had named for James Lawrence, a naval hero recently slain in battle, whose dying words—"Don't give up the ship"—were emblazoned on the banner of the ship. This leadership gesture was typical of the charismatic Perry, who combined a roll-up-your-sleeves approach to problem solving with an extraordinary talent for motivating great achievement.

In the Battle of Lake Erie, the *Lawrence* took a terrible beating. While the rest of the American Lake Erie flotilla lagged behind, the British vessels pounded Perry's flagship, finally damaging it so badly that Perry abandoned it, rowed back to the rest of the flotilla in a small boat, and, through personal leadership, roused the flotilla to action. The result was a stunning—and, to the enemy, profoundly shocking—defeat for the British fleet. Perry sent a message to General William Henry Harrison, who was waiting to commence the land attack: "We have met the enemy and they are ours. Two ships, two brigs, one schooner, one sloop." Perry then went ashore to serve under Harrison in the ensuing Battle of the Thames River. This sailor even personally led a charge on October 5.

Triumph on Lake Erie deprived the British land forces of supply and support and directly enabled the great land victory at the Battle of the

Thames. Up to this point, the War of 1812 had been a string of disasters for the United States. Perry saved the American cause.

Perry was promoted to captain and was given the thanks of Congress in January 1814. After the War of 1812, he commanded the 44-gun frigate *Java* in the Mediterranean during 1816–17. In 1819, he took command of a diplomatic mission to the new republic of Venezuela. While in South America, on the Orinoco River, he contracted yellow fever and died from it, at sea, off the coast of Trinidad.

LEADERSHIP LESSONS

✦

View problems not as traps, but as opportunities for triumph.

✦

Assume you can achieve the impossible.

✦

Do not look for solutions. Create them.

✦

Improvise, improvise, improvise.

✦

There is no substitute for personal courage.

✦

Never hesitate to inspire those you lead.

✦

Celebrate heroism and share achievement.

✦

Refuse to give up.

✦

Be reluctant to compromise when victory hangs in the balance.

Pershing, John Joseph

Born: 1860   Died: 1948

Motivator   Problem solver   Strategist   Systems creator   Tactician

LEADERSHIP ACHIEVEMENTS

✦

Combined the qualities of a military leader with the imagination and self-restraint of a consummate diplomat

✦

Personally advanced his career by impressing the highest level of authority

✦

Led the American Expeditionary Force (AEF) to victory in World War I

✦

Accomplished history's biggest and most complex troop movement and deployment up to that time

✦

Preserved the integrity and effectiveness of the AEF against Allied demands that he relinquish control

✦

Mentored another of the great American commanders, George S. Patton

LIFE

Pershing was given the greatest leadership task assigned to any American commander since Ulysses S. Grant. He led the American Expeditionary Force (AEF) overseas into World War I.

Pershing did not come from a military family, but was born and raised on a Laclede, Missouri, farm. From 1878 to 1882, he worked as a schoolteacher, and then obtained an appointment to West Point, graduating in 1886. The new second lieutenant was assigned to the 6th Cavalry, with which he served in the West during the late phase of the Indian Wars. Among his grimmest duties was rounding up fugitives following the massacre at Wounded Knee, Dakota Territory (December 28, 1890).

The army put his teaching experience to work from 1891 to 1895, when he was assigned as commandant of cadets at the University of Nebraska. During this period Pershing was promoted to first lieutenant (1892), and then took time out to earn a law degree, which was awarded in June 1898.

From October 1895 to October 1896, Pershing saw service as an officer with the 10th Cavalry, the famed African American regiment of
"Buffalo Soldiers," which, in the segregated military of the day, was commanded by white officers. It was from this assignment that Pershing earned
the nickname that would stay with him for life: "Black Jack" Pershing.

After service with the 10th, Pershing was appointed to the coveted
position of aide to General Nelson A. Miles, one of the army's most senior
commanders. He then returned to West Point as an instructor in tactics
from June 1897 to April 1898, after which he was again assigned to the
10th Cavalry, this time as its quartermaster. With the outbreak of the
Spanish–American War in 1898, Pershing was among the first to go to
Cuba, fighting at El Caney and San Juan Hill (July 1–3, 1898), the war's
centerpiece land engagements. Like many other soldiers in that conflict,
however, Pershing was hard hit by disease. Seriously ill with malaria, he
was invalided, sent home, and then briefly assigned quiet duty at the War
Department toward the end of his convalescence in August 1898. After
this, he received an appointment as chief of the Bureau of Insular Affairs,
serving from September 1898 to August 1899, when he requested service
in the field. Posted to the Philippines, he served on northern Mindanao,
and from December 1899 to May 1903, he was engaged in the pacification
of the Moros, the Islamic tribespeople living on Mindanao and the Sulu
Archipelago, who stubbornly resisted American authority.

In 1899, Brigader General John C. Bates had negotiated an agreement
with the Sultan of Sulu, nominal leader of the Moros, acknowledging U.S.
sovereignty. The sultan's control of the Moros, a proud warrior people,
proved tenuous, and their resistance to the Americans exploded into a religious war. In November 1901, Pershing led two troops of the 15th Cavalry
and three infantry companies to Mindanao, where he relied heavily on diplomatic skill—backed by a show of strength—to win over the Moros, one clan
at a time. Without firing a shot, he was soon able to reach an accommodation with those living on the north shore of Lake Lanao, but the clans on the
southern shore frequently skirmished with his troops as well as with the U.S.-
sponsored native Moro Constabulary. Pershing was instrumental in a successful battle to take the Moro stronghold at Pandapatan, where he
established Camp Vicars. From this base, between June 1902 and May 1903,
Pershing renewed his diplomatic offensive. When he failed to persuade the

Moros to cooperate, he conducted a series of carefully planned military expeditions, which he limited in order to avoid alienating the Moros of the northern shore. By the summer of 1903, when Pershing returned to the United States, the worst of the Moro violence had been quelled. Unfortunately, the new military governor of the Moro province, Major General Leonard Wood, disdained Pershing's diplomatic approach and was determined instead to beat the Moros into unquestioning submission to American authority. The result was a chronic state of guerrilla warfare.

From the Philippines, Pershing returned to Washington, D.C., and staff duty. He married Helen Francis Warren on January 25, 1905. Then, from March 5, 1905, to September of 1906, Pershing was stationed in Japan as a military attaché and observer in the Russo–Japanese War. The assignment turned out to be Pershing's great opportunity, because it brought him into personal contact with President Theodore Roosevelt. Pershing, with his quiet courage, confidence, and thoroughgoing competence, made an extraordinary impression on Roosevelt. Concluding that Pershing was just the kind of leader the United States Army needed, Roosevelt authorized his promotion, in a single leap, from captain to brigadier general on September 20, 1906.

From December 1906 to June 1908, Pershing was assigned command of a brigade at Fort McKinley, near Manila, Philippines, and then accepted an appointment as military commander of Moro Province in the Philippines in November 1909. He served in this post until early 1914, continually conducting small-scale operations against ever-recalcitrant Moro rebels. In April 1914, Pershing was assigned command of the 8th Brigade in San Francisco, but was almost immediately dispatched to the Mexican border during the civil war in Mexico. On August 27, 1915, while Pershing was in south Texas, a fire swept through his family's quarters in the Presidio at San Francisco. Pershing received the overwhemingly tragic news that his wife and three of their daughters had died in the fire.

The Mexican social bandit and revolutionary leader Francisco "Pancho" Villa was among the many prominent personages who wrote or wired their condolences to the general. On March 9, 1916, Villa, outraged at President Woodrow Wilson's support for Mexican president Venustiano Carranza, raided Columbus, New Mexico, leaving 17 U.S. citizens dead. Wilson ordered Pershing to invade Mexico and capture Villa. Commanding a force of 4,800, Pershing chased Villa and his men for 10 months, until he was ordered home on January 27, 1917. Some commentators have judged the so-called "Punitive Campaign" against Villa as fruitless. While it is true that Villa himself evaded capture, Pershing's relentless pursuit not only prevented further violent incursions into the United States, but eliminated Villa's leading commanders, greatly reducing the effectiveness of his army.

In April 1917, the United States joined France, Britain, and the other Allies in fighting Germany and Austria in World War I. On May 12, 1917, Pershing was named to command the American Expeditionary Force (AEF). The task he faced was monumental. Although the United States had been preparing for war for some months, the army was still building. In addition to recruiting, training, and equipping a massive force, Pershing had to see to its safe and efficient transportation overseas. And, once transported, the troops and their equipment had to be accommodated. As if the logistical problems were not sufficiently staggering, Pershing was facing an enemy that had three years of experience fighting the most destructive war the world had ever seen. At the moment of U.S. entry into the war, the enemy was, if anything, winning.

Pershing soon realized that he was not only fighting the common enemy of the Allies, but also the Allies themselves. The French in particular argued for ultimate control over the American forces. Desperate for men, French commanders wanted to send units to the front piecemeal, as they became available. Pershing believed that an American army had to be commanded by an American officer, namely himself. He had led American men to Europe, and, while he was willing to cooperate with the French and British and even to defer to them in most strategic matters, he was determined to shoulder the entire responsibility for how his men were employed. Most important, Pershing realized that to send green troops into combat a few at a time would result only in the needless deaths of those troops. He made the leadership decision that his forces had to be consolidated and molded into a real army with real working units before troops were committed to battle. This was a time-consuming process, but the alternative, Pershing believed, was simple slaughter.

Putting both the lives of his men and the good of the enterprise before all other considerations, Pershing first secured the backing of President Wilson and Secretary of War Newton Baker, and then combined a steadfast refusal to cave in to the demands of the Allies with his customary skill at diplomatic negotiation to reach a workable compromise. He would retain control of U.S. forces, but would release some units somewhat ahead of the schedule he thought ideal.

Once the working relationship between the AEF and the other Allies had been established, Pershing went on to conduct three major offensives, which culminated in Allied victory in World War I: Aisne-Marne (July 25–August 2, 1918), Saint-Mihiel (September 12–17), and the Meuse-Argonne (September 26–November 11). The performance of the American troops and their commander was extraordinary, and the U.S. presence turned the tide of the war. On Pershing's triumphal return to the United States, he was promoted to general of the armies—a *six*-star general, a rank unique in the history of the U.S. military.

Pershing declined all offers to enter politics, choosing instead to remain in the military he had served so well. Appointed army chief of staff on July 21, 1921, he held this post until his retirement on September 13, 1924. Pershing published his memoirs in 1931. In 1938, he nearly succumbed to a debilitating illness, from which he recovered only partially. By 1941, his health failing, Pershing took up permanent and final residence in Walter Reed Army Hospital.

Pershing presented to the world a cool, unsmiling, and rather remote surface, although no one who came into contact with him doubted for a moment his competence and confidence. General George S. Patton, who served as Pershing's aide during World War I, judged him the finest general the American military had ever produced.

IN HIS OWN WORDS

"We came American. We shall remain American and go into battle with Old Glory over our heads. I will not parcel out American boys."
—On maintaining control of the AEF, 1917

"We never really let the Germans know who won the war. They are being told that their army was stabbed in the back, betrayed, that their army had not been defeated. The Germans never believed they were beaten. It will have to be done all over again."
—On the prospects of another war, 1923

"Lafayette, we are here!"

—The most famous quotation widely attributed to Pershing; actually spoken by
   Charles E. Stanton, the AEF paymaster, at the tomb of Lafayette, July 4, 1917

LEADERSHIP LESSONS

Temper force with diplomacy.

Choose negotiation over force whenever possible, but always negotiate
from a position of visible strength.

Identify the people with the power to promote you and your enterprise.
Amaze them.

Understand your enterprise fully, then lead only in ways that
further the enterprise.

To resist pressure effectively, recruit support from all levels.

Decide on the core principles you cannot afford to compromise or
relinquish. Then hold to them.

Put the welfare of those you lead uppermost among your priorities.

Cooperation does not require relinquishing final control.

Shoulder the full burden of responsibility. Then exercise the full measure
of leadership.

Peter I the Great

Born: 1672   Died: 1725

Character model   Conqueror   Innovator   Mentor   Systems creator   Visionary

LEADERSHIP ACHIEVEMENTS

✦

Expanded his personal horizons and, by extension, those of his nation

✦

Created a powerful leadership image

✦

Was an innovator and visionary with the talent and determination to realize
his dreams on a vast scale

✦

Had tremendous self-confidence, but recruited others to do the jobs he
could not do himself

✦

Knew when to ask for help

✦

Sought to educate—and reeducate—his court and his country

✦

Redesigned the military and the administration of government

✦

Observed, analyzed, and learned from the best examples—a champion of
"best practices"

✦

Used his prodigious mind to lead his nation, not merely to satisfy
his own curiosity

✦

Acted with great energy after careful planning

LIFE

Considered the greatest of the Russian czars, Peter I was a model of the enlightened despot, an absolute monarch who devoted his energy to bringing his backward realm into the modern world for what he believed was the benefit of his people.

Peter was born on June 6, 1672, in Moscow, to Czar Feodor III Alakseevich and his second wife, Natalia Kirillovna Naryshkina. Feodor

III died in 1682, when Peter was only 10, and the boy was proclaimed czar. Before the end of the year, however, the *streltsi*—or "militia musketeers," a powerful military and political force—revolted, forcing Peter to share the throne with his mentally retarded brother Ivan V under the regency of their sister Sophia, who favored the interests of the *streltsi*. During this early period, Peter had virtually no power, but he did have ample opportunity to sharpen and exercise his prodigious mind and great curiosity. He became fascinated with the world that lay beyond Russia, and he developed a passion for European culture, learning, fashion, and military practices. He read all he could about western Europe, and he decided that Russia must have the benefit of modern civilization. Accordingly, as he grew into young manhood, Peter became impatient with serving as a figurehead in the shadow of his sister. Russia needed a real leader, and a progressive leader.

Peter had been assigned a residence outside of Moscow, in Prebrazhenskoye, isolated from the royal court. He now used this isolation to his advantage by quietly forming two elite regiments of guards. He plotted with his guardian, Prince Boris Golitsyn, as to how these men could be used to enforce a coup d'état against Sophia. After the two perfected their plan, Golitsyn moved successfully against Sophia in August 1689, and Peter took control of the government.

Peter I looked like a leader. He took advantage of his remarkable stature—six feet, six inches among a people who were typically a full foot shorter—to project a powerful leadership image. He moved with deliberate energy, not with the lethargic, stately steps expected of a czar, but by broad, swift strides. With commensurate energy, he set about consolidating his newly won power during the period from 1689 to 1696, not only installing highly qualified and completely loyal ministers in key government positions, but acting to establish control of Russia's disputed frontier. He led successful military expeditions to the White Sea during 1694–95 and wrested the Azov region from Turkish hands during 1695–96.

With his frontiers secured, Peter acted on his early dream of traveling to western Europe. From March 1697 to August 1698, he toured Germany, Britain, and the Netherlands, hungrily observing examples of the most advanced technology and science as well as examples of western European fashion, style, and mores. He took it all in systematically and in great detail. However, he was forced to cut short his tour when news reached him of another revolt by the *streltsi*. Rushing back home, he led a military response to the revolt that was savage in its intensity. By summer's end in 1698, the *streltsi* had been crushed.

With major external and internal political threats neutralized, Peter embarked on a program of vigorous social reform. He believed that it was important to symbolize these conceptual changes with an external transformation as well, and he commanded the court nobility—the boyars—to shave their traditional beards and to don European-style dress. He introduced European learning into Russia, and he even abandoned the traditional Julian calendar for the new Gregorian calendar, which was just then gaining currency in the nations of Europe. (It is a measure of the Russian reluctance to abandon tradition that the Gregorian calendar was not universally adopted until after the Russian revolutions of 1917.)

Peter also remodeled the army. He did not want to have to rely on politically dangerous military organizations such as the *streltsi* or make the army the exclusive reserve of the nobility. Accordingly, he introduced compulsory military service, conscripting some 32,000 commoners to create a force capable of going up against Russia's rival, Sweden. Peter struck an alliance with Augustus II of Poland and Saxony in November 1699 and, with him, attacked the Swedes at Livonia in August 1700. Unfortunately for Peter, he was going up against one of the great captains of Europe, Swedish king Charles XII, leading one of continent's great armies. Peter had some very advanced military ideas, but his imagination in military matters outstripped his practical grasp of strategy and tactics. Charles defeated him at the Battle of Narva on November 30, 1700.

The defeat did not long dishearten Peter, who resumed his transformation of Russia into a European-style industrial and military power. He founded factories, arms manufactures, and military schools. He developed a system of internal transport, as well as encouraged the growth of a shipbuilding industry in order to open up commerce with the rest of the world. Most of all, he learned from his defeat at Narva. Setting aside all considerations of ego, he decided to recruit and put his trust in the best military advisers he could find. Peter secured the leadership of Field Marshal Count Sheremetev in an invasion of Ingria, at the time a key Swedish possession. On January 9, 1702, Peter and Sheremetev defeated Swedish armies at Erestfer and then, on July 29, at Hummeishof in Livonia. Peter was quick to exploit what he had gained, sending a force to occupy the valley of the Neva River in December 1702.

He now had what he called a "window on the West." Here he founded the city of St. Petersburg on May 16, 1703. Built on a frozen marsh on the Gulf of Finland, it became for Peter the object of his greatest attention. He envisioned St. Petersburg as a model city for the new Russia, and he personally oversaw its design according to the latest examples of European neoclassicism. The city was not just a monument to Peter's imagination, it was intended to attract the best of European culture and learning and to lead Russia into the future, putting it on an equal footing with the rest of Europe.

From June 12 to August 21, 1704, Peter besieged Narva, this time successfully. His ally, Augustus II, had already surrendered to Charles XII of Sweden by the time Peter, now holding Narva, proposed a peace with the Swedish monarch. Charles angrily rejected the offer and invaded Russia during 1707–08, throwing Russia into crisis by pushing back the overextended Peter as far as the central Ukraine. There the czar holed up at Poltava during the winter and spring of 1708–09. But he did not give up. Using the time to assemble a counteroffensive, on July 8, 1709, he massed his forces against the Swedish army—which, deep in Russian territory, was now badly overextended—and he defeated Charles at the Battle of Poltava, virtually destroying the opposing army.

Having disposed of the northern threat for the time being, Peter turned next to the south, moving against Turkish Moldavia in March of 1711. Outmaneuvered by Turkish forces, Peter found himself hemmed in at the River Pruth, and he was compelled to negotiate a settlement with the Turks on July 21, 1711. Three years later, Peter again directed his efforts against the Swedes, planning with Admiral Feodor Apraskin a devastating attack on the Swedish fleet near Hango in the Baltic on July 7, 1714. It proved a master stroke. By it, Peter gained control of the Baltic Sea, including the prizes of Livonia, Estonia, Ingria, and southern Karelia, which were ceded to Russia by treaty on August 30, 1721. This threw open to Russia the great world beyond its borders.

Having greatly expanded his empire, modernized his court, and gained firm control over a fractious nobility, Peter I decided in 1721 to take the title of emperor of all the Russias, rejecting the traditional name of *czar*.

He spent the next two years campaigning against Persia on his empire's Asian frontier, and his forces occupied Derbent (in Dagestan), Rasht, and Baku during 1722–23.

That Peter the Great selflessly undertook all that he did for the sake of his country is suggested even by the manner of his death. He died on February 8, 1725, from complications arising from a cold he had caught while helping to rescue soldiers who had fallen into the frozen Neva River.

IN HIS OWN WORDS

"Not to follow regulations is the same as a blind man not following a wall."

—Quoted in Yevgeny Savkin, *Basic Principles of Operational Art and Tactics,* 1972

LEADERSHIP LESSONS

✦

Understand external as well as internal problems. Address both.

✦

Develop a strong and consistent leadership image.

✦

Never be afraid to dream, but always think in terms of realizing what you dream.

✦

Great leaders identify their dreams with the future of the enterprises they lead.

✦

Ask for help—and always from those best qualified to help.

✦

Invest in people—the best subordinates, the most capable allies.

✦

Emulate outstanding models of achievement.

✦

Realize your dreams on a doable but impressive scale.

✦

Lead for the short term as well as for the long term.

✦

Marshal and maintain your energy and that of the enterprise.

Philip II Augustus

Born: 1165   Died: 1223

Innovator   Rescuer   Strategist   Systems creator   Visionary

LEADERSHIP ACHIEVEMENTS

✦

Restored French sovereignty over French lands

✦

Exercised masterful and sophisticated diplomacy

✦

Conceived a vision of French destiny and implemented actions to attain
that vision

✦

Reformed French government and laid the foundation for the cultural
greatness of Paris

LIFE

King of France from 1179 to 1223, Philip II reclaimed local sovereignty over French lands formerly held by England. He was born in Paris on August 21, 1165, the son of King Louis VII. Louis relinquished the throne to his son when the youth turned 14, an act that touched off a power struggle among several French provinces and England, all of which strove to control the new monarch. Despite his youth, however, Philip was not about to be manipulated; on the contrary, he seized an opportunity to gain firmer control in France. When Henry II of England turned over all English territories in France (except Normandy) to his son John, the king's older son, Richard the Lion-Hearted, rebelled. Philip immediately exploited this dissension by striking an alliance with Richard, helping him to acquire the lands in question for himself. In turn, Richard appointed Philip as his feudal lord.

In the meantime, Jerusalem had fallen to the armies of Saladin in 1187, and Philip joined forces with Frederick Barbarossa and Richard the Lion-Hearted to launch the Third Crusade. After the combined forces captured the city of Acre, Philip returned home, leaving Richard to attempt to capture Jerusalem. Failing in this, Richard set out for England, but was captured in Austria and held for ransom. Once again, Philip seized opportunity. He now shifted his allegiance from the absent Richard and allied himself with his former foe, John, in a bid to wrest Normandy from Richard. But when Richard died in 1199 and John became king of England, Philip swiftly turned against his latest ally. Opposing John, Philip declared, in 1202, all English holdings in France to be void, and he decreed their return to the French crown. King John attempted to repossess his lost French real estate, fighting, with allies, the Battle of Bouvines on July 27, 1214. Philip defeated Otto IV of Germany and his combined army of English, German, and Flemish knights. After deft shifting of alliances, Philip resolved by a single make-or-break battle the long-disputed issue of English holdings in France.

Unlike many other monarchs of the time—most notably Richard the Lion-Hearted—Philip's attention to military success did not come at the expense of internal government. Philip introduced many key reforms, most notably awarding of high-ranking positions in the government only to those he judged eminently qualified to hold them. This criterion took precedence over any hereditary claims. Moreover, Philip conceived a great vision for Paris, planning that it should become the leader among European cities. Toward this end, he embarked on a major building program, which culminated in the construction of a defensive wall around the town, the paving of the city streets with stone, and the improvement of the University of Paris.

The closing years of Philip's reign were peaceful, and when the monarch died at Nantes, France, on July 14, 1223, he left behind a kingdom that was one of the most powerful in Europe.

LEADERSHIP LESSONS

✦

In strategic alliances, balance loyalty with pragmatism.

✦

Multitask; do not allow focus on one project to blind you to the ongoing needs of the rest of the enterprise.

✦

Devote maximum time, effort, and thought to choosing subordinates.

✦

Introduce innovation to increase the effectiveness of the organization.

✦

Develop a clear vision; use it to guide your actions.

✦

Set worthwhile goals only. Reject the questionable.

Piccolomini, Prince Ottavio

Born: 1599   Died: 1656

Conqueror   Strategist   Tactician

LEADERSHIP ACHIEVEMENTS

✦

Brought strategy and tactics to a new height in the 17th century

✦

Earned a legendary reputation as a great personal commander

✦

Led by direct inspiration and a willingness to endure great pain and danger

✦

Tempered his loyalty with a Machiavellian approach whereby he sold his services to those who would value them the most

✦

Combined military prowess with great diplomatic skill

✦

Preserved the integrity of the Holy Roman Empire in the peace negotiated at the conclusion of the Thirty Years' War

LIFE

Piccolomini was an Italian general in the service of the Holy Roman Empire. Courageous and skilled as a commander of cavalry in the field, he was also a brilliant strategist. Beyond this, Piccolomini was an adroit diplomat, whose negotiations preserved the Holy Roman Empire from having to endure very harsh treaty terms at the conclusion of the Thirty Years' War.

Piccolomini was a native of Florence, who first joined the Spanish army in 1616, and then moved to the Austrian Imperial army—the army of the Holy Roman Empire. He campaigned in Italy, Bohemia, Hungary, and northern Germany, becoming, after 1627, the leading lieutenant under the great Wallenstein, the overall commander of the Holy Roman armies. During the War of the Mantuan Succession, he commanded Wallenstein's bodyguard, but was soon given independent command during 1628–31.

Piccolomini fought at Lützen on November 16, 1632, earning nearly leg-endary fame for his almost superhuman endurance. He repeatedly charged the enemy, collecting seven wounds in the process. Although he refused to give up, the Imperial forces narrowly lost the contest. Nevertheless, Piccolomini's inspirational brilliance was rewarded by Wallenstein in 1633 when he gave Piccolomini to key commands in Bohemia and Silesia.

Wallenstein repeatedly assigned important commands to Piccolomini, but he also consistently promoted others above him. In the Machiavellian world of 17th-century European military politics, the rule was eat or be eaten, and Piccolomini chose to eat. He played a leading role, with the Austrian general Matthias von Gallas, in a conspiracy that overthrew and, ultimately, assassinated Wallenstein on February 25, 1634. This action earned the Holy Roman emperor's approbation. Piccolomini was rewarded with an estate in Bohemia, but he was denied what he most wanted: to suc-ceed to Wallenstein's command. When the emperor gave the command to Gallas, Piccolomini left the Imperial army and returned to the service of Spain in 1635.

On behalf of Spain, Piccolomini fought the French in the Netherlands, dealing a severe blow to the numerically superior army of the Marquis de Feuquiéres at the Battle of Thionville on June 7, 1639. For this, Spain's King Philip IV bestowed on Piccolomini the duchy of Amalfi. Then, in the early 1640s, Piccolomini returned to the Imperial army, hop-ing now to succeed Gallas. Again, Piccolomini was frustrated. He was assigned to serve under Archduke Leopold William, and was present at the Austrian defeat in the second battle of Breitenfeld on November 2, 1642. Discouraged, believing that victory would have been achieved under his command, Piccolomini transferred yet again to the Spanish army.

As before, the Spanish crown rewarded Piccolomini well for his serv-ice, but, when the Holy Roman emperor Ferdinand III at last named him commander in chief of Imperial forces, he returned to Austria and com-menced the final campaign of the Thirty Years' War, leading an army to the relief of Prague in May 1648. Before Piccolomini completed his campaign, however, the Peace of Westphalia ended the long and terrible conflict.

Piccolomini turned next to the diplomatic phase of his career, serving as head of the imperial delegation to the Congress of Nürnberg in 1649, which negotiated issues left unsettled by the Peace of Westphalia. His

diplomatic skill proved as remarkable as his military prowess, as he negotiated a peace that was not fully warranted by the scope of the empire's military achievement. In recognition of what he had accomplished, Ferdinand III
named Piccolomini a prince of the empire in 1650.

LEADERSHIP LESSONS

✦

A high-level leader must balance tactical ability with a vision of
grand strategy.

✦

There is no substitute for leadership by direct, inspirational example.

✦

Leadership is often, first and foremost, a demonstration of willing
endurance.

✦

Value yourself sufficiently to be ruthless when appropriate.

✦

Define the limits of mere loyalty.

Porus

Died: 317 B.C.

Character model   Rescuer   Strategist

LEADERSHIP ACHIEVEMENTS

✦

Valiantly defended his kingdom against superior forces, winning for himself
and his people a favorable negotiating position

✦

Refused to yield, but knew how to avoid fighting in vain

LIFE

A prince of India, Porus almost single-handedly stood up to the onslaught of Alexander the Great's army as it invaded the Punjab. We know little about the early life of this leader beyond the facts associated with Alexander's invasion of his realm. Alexander swept through India with little opposition until 326 B.C., when he approached the Hydaspes River, the frontier of Porus's domain. Here the Indian prince met the Greeks head-on with an army of his own. Porus made especially effective use of his elephant corps, which struck terror into the soldiers of Alexander as they faced the mighty animals across the swollen river. The result was a standoff. Alexander's forces refused to cross the river. At last, the conqueror was forced to outmaneuver Porus by moving upstream. Here he was able to cross, and then wheel around to attack Porus from the back. Even then, the Indian army fought long and valiantly, until the elephants panicked and turned on their handlers.

Meeting with the defeated Porus to discuss surrender terms, Alexander was moved by the prince's extraordinary valor on the field, as well as by his eloquence in negotiation. He therefore permitted Porus to maintain suzerainty over all of the conquered territory, ruling it as a Macedonian dependent. Unfortunately, shortly after Alexander's death, Porus was murdered by one of the conqueror's generals, Eudemus.

LEADERSHIP LESSONS

✦

A leader must lead in defeat and disappointment as well as in triumph.

✦

Leadership is sometimes about defending territory and cutting losses.

✦

A leader sets an example of valor.

✦

Personal character is a powerful bargaining tool.

✦

Defeat comes in degrees; in the worst case, a leader fights for the best
defeat possible.

Powell, Colin Luther

Born: 1937

**Character model   Motivator   Problem solver   Strategist
Systems creator   Tactician**

LEADERSHIP ACHIEVEMENTS

✦

Rose from humble surroundings in a tough New York neighborhood to
achieve top military command

✦

Was the first African American chairman of the Joint Chiefs of Staff

✦

Exercised overall responsibility for the successful completion of
Operation Just Cause, which required both diplomatic skill
and innovative military thinking

✦

Exercised overall responsibility for the Persian Gulf War,
which required the coordination and deployment of massive resources
and a large coalition of allied nations

✦

Became the first African American secretary of state

LIFE

A career military man, Colin Powell came to broad public attention as
chairman of the Joint Chiefs of Staff during the Persian Gulf War of
1990–91 and became sufficiently popular to contemplate a run for the
White House. In 2001, he became the nation's first African American secretary of state.

Powell was born in New York City to a family of Jamaican immigrants. In 1958, he became the first in his family to complete a college education, when he graduated from the City University of New York. Powell
had enrolled in the ROTC program at the university and, on graduation,
was commissioned a second lieutenant in the army. During 1959–62, he
was assigned as platoon leader and company commander in Germany, and
then was sent to South Vietnam during 1962–63 as one of a contingent of

U.S. military advisers to the Army of the Republic of Vietnam (ARVN). He returned to South Vietnam during 1968–70, as an infantry battalion executive officer and assistant chief of staff (G-3) with the 23rd (Americal) Infantry Division.

After his return to the United States in 1971, Powell earned an M.B.A. degree from George Washington University and was also honored by selection as a White House Fellow. He was made special assistant to the deputy director of the Office of the President, serving in that capacity during 1972–73. After promotion to lieutenant colonel, Powell returned to field command during 1973–75, as commander of the 1st Battalion, 32d Infantry in South Korea. Back in the States again, he attended the National War College, from which he graduated in June 1976.

After he was promoted to colonel, Powell was assigned command of the 2d Brigade, 101st Airborne Division (Air Assault) at Fort Campbell, Kentucky, during 1976–77, and then returned to Washington, D.C., where he served in the Office of the Secretary of Defense. For a brief time, he was executive assistant to the secretary of energy in 1979, and then was appointed senior military assistant to the deputy secretary of defense, a post he held from 1979 to 1981.

Powell consistently straddled the worlds of civilian and military policy, and, even after he attained high government appointments, he did not want to absent himself long from direct military command. In 1981 he was made assistant division commander of the 4th Mechanized Infantry Division, at Fort Carson, Colorado, and then returned to Washington in 1983 as senior military adviser to Secretary of Defense Caspar Weinberger until 1985. The following year, Powell was put in command of U.S. V Corps in West Germany. Two years later, he came back to Washington to serve as deputy assistant for national security affairs in the Reagan administration. After this he served as assistant for national security affairs to Presidents Reagan and George H. Bush from December 1987 to January 1989.

On October 1, 1989, President Bush selected Powell to serve as chairman of the Joint Chiefs of Staff as well as commander in chief, U.S. Army Forces Command. He was the first African American to hold this position, and his first major action was to direct, in December 1989, Operation Just

Cause, an invasion of Panama to apprehend the nation's dictator, Manuel Noriega, and bring him back to the United States to stand trial on drug trafficking charges. The mission was highly sensitive and, indeed, unique in U.S. military history. Never had a war operation been waged essentially against a single individual. Powell had to see to it that Noriega was secured, but also that collateral damage—especially civilian losses—was held to an absolute minimum. In this operation, Powell showed innovative military thought.

From August 1990 to March 1991, Powell directed U.S. participation in UN operations against Iraqi dictator Saddam Hussein, which culminated in the Persian Gulf (Kuwait) War of January 17–February 28, 1991. Powell had overall responsibility for a force of more than half a million troops and massive amounts of equipment, aircraft, and ships. He was at the center of an unprecedented coalition among 48 nations, of which 30 provided military forces. He was also under great public and political pressure to achieve the U.S. and UN objective of the war—the liberation of Kuwait from Iraqi domination—as rapidly as possible. The American public feared becoming mired in "another Vietnam."

Working closely with field commanders such as General H. Norman Schwarzkopf, Powell directed a lightning war, the ground phase of which was completed in about 100 hours. At the cost of 95 troops killed, 368 wounded, and 20 missing in action, the coalition inflicted about 160,000 Iraqi casualties, including 50,000 killed, 50,000 wounded, and some 60,000 taken prisoner. Vast quantities of Iraqi arms and equipment were destroyed.

The overwhelming coalition victory in the Persian Gulf gained Powell a great deal of favorable public exposure and approval. Soft-spoken but forthright, Powell communicated effectively with his military colleagues and subordinates as well as with the American people. The highest-ranking African American in the U.S. armed forces, Powell was seen as an intelligent and politically attractive figure. Many Americans hoped he would declare himself a candidate for president when he retired from the military in 1993, but he chose not to do so, pursuing instead various enterprises in education. In 2001, Powell accepted an appointment as secretary of state in the cabinet of President George W. Bush.

LEADERSHIP LESSONS

Do not waste time envying the early advantages of another—the "silver spoon"; make use of adversity as valuable experience. We develop through overcoming resistance and obstacles.

Ideally, try to balance theoretical knowledge with practical experience, desk work with work in the field.

The effective leader bridges different worlds and different cultures. Much of Powell's success came from his facility for moving between the civilian and the military realms.

✦

The effective leader accepts personal responsibility but recognizes the necessity of coordinating the efforts of a large number of individuals.

✦

Do not be afraid to innovate and, when necessary, to improvise.

Psamtik I

Died: 610 B.C.

Conqueror Improviser Innovator Strategist Visionary

LEADERSHIP ACHIEVEMENTS

✦

Took an innovative approach to achieving power

✦

Forged effective alliances to achieve well-defined objectives

✦

Created a vision for the restoration of Egyptian greatness, and then largely
executed that vision

LIFE

Psamtik I used Greek mercenaries to reunite Egypt and expel Assyrian
overlords from it. He was thereby able to found the 26th Dynasty.

Little is known about Psamtik I beyond what the Greek historian
Herodotus records about him. He was apparently one of 12 corulers of
Egypt, which, at the time, was subject to Assyrian rule. Psamtik looked far
beyond the system of which he was a part and hired an army of Greek mercenaries to wrest power from his 11 peers. This accomplished, he emerged
as Egypt's sole ruler—until his vassals rebelled against the Assyrians in 663
B.C. The Assyrians quickly reasserted control, and it was they who reinstalled Psamtik as governor of Athribis, a city on the Nile delta.

Psamtik did not rest content with the power doled out to him by
Assyrian masters. He forged an alliance with Gyges, king of Lydia, by
which he was able to subdue his fellow vassals and then attack and defeat
Assyrian princes throughout the delta during 658-51. With Assyrian
authority expunged from Egypt, Psamtik I established his capital at Sais,
the city of his birth. From here, he embarked on nothing less than the
remaking of Egypt. The Cushites—who inhabited a kingdom south of
Egypt—dominated Thebes. Psamtik persuaded the priestess of Amon (the
god worshiped by the Thebans) to adopt his daughter. Although the governor of Thebes remained a Cushite appointee, the adoption gave Psamtik

access to the great wealth of the Theban temples. Moreover, Psamtik was able to install his own administrators elsewhere in the south and in middle Egypt. Thus Psamtik peacefully but efficiently undermined Cushite domination of Thebes.

Psamtik showed similar political brilliance in dealing with the threat posed by the resident military classes throughout Egypt. As a permanent part of the Egyptian army, he created a corps of Greek mercenaries, answerable directly and exclusively to himself. He also forestalled the feudal fragmentation of authority by developing a policy of large property donations to temples. On a more directly cultural level, Psamtik counteracted the pressures of foreign influence by encouraging a revival of Old Kingdom notions of religion and art. He thereby reasserted a specifically Egyptian "national" identity.

Psamtik I managed to regain some of Egypt's former strength and cohesion, and the revived empire was maintained after his death by his son, Psamtik II, but succumbed to a Persian invasion in 525 B.C., which grandson Psamtik III failed to stop.

LEADERSHIP LESSONS
✦

Know when to "outsource," as Psamtik did in building an army of mercenaries.
✦

Beware of fragmentation of authority.
✦

Take steps to establish a group identity.

Rabin, Yitzhak

Born: 1922   Died: 1995

Character model   Innovator   Motivator   Problem solver   Rescuer   Visionary

LEADERSHIP ACHIEVEMENTS

✦

Was a valiant, skilled, and aggressive soldier and military commander in the service of his country

✦

Had overall direction of Israeli forces during the Six-Day War, a spectacular Israeli triumph

✦

Led Israel to increased rapport with the United States

✦

Pushed Israel to greater economic strength

✦

Used his reputation as a ruthless defender of Israel to endorse a groundbreaking independence initiative with the Palestine Liberation Organization in an effort to bring peace to the Middle East

✦

Was awarded the 1994 Nobel Peace Prize

LIFE

An Israeli military leader and statesman, Yitzhak Rabin spent most of his life and career as a hard-line foe of Palestinians and others who threatened the survival of Israel, but he went on to the extraordinarily heroic step of endorsing a reconciliation agreement with the Palestine Liberation Organization in an effort to bring peace to the Middle East. The price he paid was his life.

Rabin was born in Jerusalem and studied at the Kadoorie Agricultural College, from which he graduated with distinction. In 1940, he joined the Palmach, an elite unit of the Haganah, the outlawed Zionist army that fought for the creation of an independent Israeli state. In the 1948–49 War of Independence, Rabin commanded the Harel Brigade, which was deployed on the Jerusalem front, and for the first 20 years of Israel's existence as a nation he served with the Israel Defense Forces (IDF) as chief of operations of the Northern Command (1956–59), as chief of operations and deputy chief of staff (1959–64), and as chief of staff (1964–68). Rabin was in overall command of the IDF during the spectacularly successful Six-Day War against the combined forces of Egypt, Syria, and Jordan. Israel's swift victory in this conflict was among the most impressive achievements in modern military history.

Rabin retired from the military on January 1, 1968, and was soon appointed ambassador to the United States, enhancing a period of especially close relations between the two countries. He returned to Israel in the spring of 1973, became active in the Labor Party, and was elected to the Knesset—the Israeli parliament—in December 1973. In April 1974, Prime Minister Golda Meir appointed Rabin to the key post of minister of labor. Meir stepped down in May, however, and Rabin succeeded her as prime minister.

Rabin led Israel toward achieving three major goals: to broaden and strengthen the Israeli economy, to solve a growing number of internal social problems, and to reinforce the IDF against always looming threats. Even while he built up the army's strength, however, Rabin accepted American mediation to conclude "disengagement" agreements with Egypt and Syria in 1974 and a more extensive interim peace agreement with Egypt in 1975. Later in the year, Rabin signed the first Memorandum of Understanding between the governments of Israel and the United States, which simultaneously strengthened the alliance between the two nations and pledged Israel to a course of constructive reconciliation with its Arab neighbors.

In June 1976, Palestinian terrorists hijacked an Air France airliner, holding 103 Jews hostage at Entebbe, in Idi Amin's Uganda. Rabin authorized a daring Israeli commando raid, which, against formidable odds, succeeded in liberating the hostages.

When the Labor Party lost ground in 1977, Rabin resigned as prime minister and was succeeded as party leader by Shimon Peres. In 1984, Rabin reentered the government as defense minister in a coalition government of the Labor and Likud parties. Late in the 1980s, Rabin ordered a very harsh crackdown against an Arab uprising—*intifada*—in the West Bank. Although controversial, the crackdown was effective, and Rabin ousted Peres as Labor party leader in 1992. He then led his party to victory in the national elections, becoming prime minister as well as defense minister.

With his credentials as a tough military leader long and well established, Rabin next astounded the world by playing an active role in peace negotiations between Israel and its Arab neighbors. This culminated in 1993 with his endorsement of what many had thought unthinkable: a historic peace agreement with the Palestine Liberation Organization (PLO), which provided for mutual recognition and a transition to Palestinian self-rule in the Gaza Strip and West Bank. For this extraordinary act of far-seeing leadership, Rabin shared with Peres and PLO leader Yasir Arafat the Nobel Peace Prize in 1994. That same year, he went on to sign a peace treaty with Jordan, and the following year expanded the PLO agreement to further enhance Palestinian self-rule.

In all of this, Rabin was well aware that he took grave political and personal risks. Extremists exist in Israel as they do everywhere in the world. Rabin was assassinated on November 4, 1995, by an Israeli law student with ties to Israeli right-wing extremist groups.

LEADERSHIP LESSONS

✦

Negotiate from strength.

✦

Successful negotiation brings benefit and value to *all* parties involved.

✦

True vision requires the courage to see beyond long-held fears and long-cherished prejudices.

✦

As vision enhances courage, courage enables vision. The most difficult leadership decisions become possible when you truly believe in the good of what you do.

✦

Leadership and goodwill go hand in hand.

✦

Choose your enemies as wisely as you choose your allies. The greatest threats are often internal—and, therefore, most difficult to recognize.

Ramses II the Great

Born: ca. 1320 B.C.   Died: ca. 1225 B.C.

Problem solver   Visionary

LEADERSHIP ACHIEVEMENTS

✦

Led numerous military expeditions, which put him in position to negotiate
with longtime Hittite enemies

✦

Accepted a negotiated peace rather than needlessly expend resources

✦

Ruled Egypt from a position of great experience and knowledge

✦

Perceived military action as an opportunity not merely to destroy and
subdue, but also to build

LIFE

Ramses II, called Ramses the Great, pharaoh of the Nineteenth Dynasty,
ruled Egypt for 67 years, longer than any other pharaoh with the exception of Pepe II (Sixth Dynasty), who reigned for 90 years. But it was not
only the longevity of his reign that marked Ramses II as a remarkable
leader. He was a tireless warrior and a visionary builder, who became perhaps the most powerful king ever to rule Egypt.

Virtually from the cradle, Ramses II had been trained in governance.
The son of Pharaoh Seti, he was, by age 10, an army captain, who already
demonstrated a remarkable grasp of military strategy. Seti made Ramses his
coruler, so that, when Seti died around 1290, Ramses was amply prepared
to govern. One of his first projects was to tackle business his father had left
unfinished. For many years, Seti had tried in vain to defeat the formidable
Hittite forces that occupied lands claimed by Egypt along the eastern
Mediterranean coast. In his fourth year as pharaoh, Ramses led a magnificently equipped army out of the delta toward present-day Syria and eastern
Turkey with the purpose of ejecting the Hittites from the disputed territory.
As Ramses and his troops approached the Hittite town of Kadesh, two pris-
oners of war revealed to him that most of the Hittite army was actually miles

away at the city of Aleppo. Taking this intelligence at face value, Ramses confidently attacked Kadesh—only to discover that the prisoners had deceived him. The full force of the enemy was in hiding behind the town. Since a large portion of Ramses' army had yet to advance to the battle area, the Hittites, with 2,500 chariots and 7,500 men, greatly outnumbered the Egyptian army. The pharaoh and his vanguard were quickly surrounded. They were on the verge of surrender when, at last, the bulk of the Egyptian army arrived to avert disaster. Indeed, the battle was a tactical victory for Ramses, even though the Hittites remained in possession of the strategically critical town of Kadesh. Ramses II realized that he could not gain his objective at present, so he concluded a truce with the Hittites and then withdrew. Some years later, Ramses made another attempt to eject the Hittites from the Egyptian borderlands. When this failed, he negotiated a permanent truce with the Hittite emperor, which defined explicit boundaries between their two lands.

During his military campaigns, Ramses II was not content merely to attack and destroy. He was also determined to build, and he left in the border country many monuments to his achievements. At home, he built the great temples at Abu Simbel, the largest of which includes four statues of Ramses, each over 65 feet high. (When the Aswan Dam was completed in the 1960s, this massive temple, carved out of the live rock, was cut into sections and moved to the top of the cliff to protect it from the backed-up waters of the Nile River.) A smaller temple, memorializing Nefertari, Ramses' favorite wife, was built at the same time downstream.

The reign of Ramses II was the apogee of imperial Egypt. Following his death, Egypt declined, as newer powers around the Mediterranean assumed political and economic dominance.

LEADERSHIP LESSONS

✦

An effective leader is a thoroughly prepared leader; there is no substitute for knowing your enterprise thoroughly.

✦

Be persistent, but know when to compromise.

✦

Negotiate compromise definitively, as when Ramses established permanent boundaries, thereby resolving a long-standing dispute.

✦

Look for opportunities to build, to create enduring results.

Roosevelt, Eleanor

Born: 1884 Died: 1962

Character model   Innovator   Mentor   Motivator   Rescuer   Visionary

LEADERSHIP ACHIEVEMENTS

✦

Saw beyond the narrow world of her upbringing to create
a meaningful life and career

✦

As a wife, mother, and woman, created a life of useful independence

✦

Rescued her husband's political career when polio—and his
overbearing mother—threatened to end it

✦

Led many social reforms, both before and after her husband became
president of the United States

✦

Extended the outreach of the Roosevelt administration during a time of
grave national crisis

✦

Served her husband as his eyes and ears

✦

As U.S. representative to the United Nations, was instrumental in creating
the United Nations Declaration of Human Rights

✦

Became an example of leadership for a generation of women

✦

Became one of the most widely admired women in modern history

LIFE

The wife and political partner of President Franklin Delano Roosevelt, Eleanor Roosevelt was, in her own right, one of the nation's great leaders of reform. Arguably, the very first person she led was her husband, encouraging and guiding his own innovative programs of social change. Associated with the president, she was never in his shadow, but served as a leadership example to a generation of women. The policies she advocated, sponsored, and helped to develop have had an enduring impact on American national policy, especially with regard to racial equality, women's rights, and the poor. Her advocacy of the United Nations was instrumental in generating popular support for the institution in the United States, and she played a key role in the groundbreaking United Nations Declaration of Human Rights, which she considered the most important achievement of her career.

She was born Anna Eleanor Roosevelt in New York City, daughter of privilege and social prominence, and a niece of President Theodore Roosevelt. Despite the economic advantages of her upbringing, the childhood of Eleanor Roosevelt was troubled. Her mother, a woman of great physical beauty, spurned her daughter, who was a plain and rather awkward girl. When the early deaths of her parents left her an orphan, Eleanor was put into the care of her strict and ungiving grandmother. Privately tutored as a young girl, she went on in her early teens to Allenswood, an exclusive finishing school near London. Here she had the great good fortune to come under the wing of the school's headmistress, Marie Souvestre, who encouraged the painfully shy student to become a leader among the other girls. When she returned to New York in 1902, she dodged what she regarded as the stifling existence of the debutante by enthusiastically engaging in hands-on charity work at a slum settlement house. She quickly discovered that working with New York's poor gave her a deep sense of satisfaction.

In 1905, Eleanor married her fifth cousin, Franklin D. Roosevelt, and embarked with him on a journey that would be filled with great opportunity and profound hardship. During the first 11 years of marriage, Eleanor Roosevelt's life was consumed mainly with motherhood. She bore six children, one of whom died in infancy, and she continually coped with the interventions of her husband's domineering and unyielding mother. She reinforced and fostered Franklin Roosevelt's still-developing social conscience, but, for the most part, during his early career, she played the role of the dutiful political wife. During World War I, while Franklin Roosevelt served as assistant secretary of the navy, Eleanor devoted as much time as she could to strenuous volunteer work with the American Red Cross. The end of the war brought her breathing space—and the hard discovery that her husband was having an affair with another woman, her own social secretary, Lucy Mercer.

Although the couple reconciled, the discovery of the affair signaled a change in the direction of Eleanor Roosevelt's life. From this point on, she pursued a life of activism, in harmony with Franklin's political beliefs but ultimately quite independent of him and his career. She was a leader in the League of Women Voters, the Women's Trade Union League, and the women's division of the Democratic Party. When her husband was left a paraplegic as a result of a bout with polio, Eleanor Roosevelt became at once even more independent and yet more active as a partner in her husband's political life. Against the wishes of her mother-in-law, who wanted her stricken son to live a life of genteel invalidism at the family's Hyde Park, New York, estate, Eleanor Roosevelt not only encouraged her husband's fight for recovery, but also kept him in politics. Before he was sufficiently recovered to make extensive public appearances, she acted as his stand-in, and in this way fashioned herself into a very public figure.

Yet even as she became increasingly politically active on behalf of her husband, she expanded her own social activism. In 1926, she became a founder of a custom furniture factory established in Hyde Park to give work to the unemployed. The next year, she acquired an ownership interest in New York's Todhunter School, where she served as vice principal and as an instructor in history and government.

She was very much a social activist during her husband's terms as governor of New York, but it was when he entered the White House in 1933 that Eleanor Roosevelt came most fully into her own as a tremendously popular figure. Traditionally, first ladies had been quiet hostesses, receding demurely into the background. Eleanor Roosevelt, in contrast, held weekly press conferences with women reporters and embarked on nationwide lecture tours, promoting the New Deal social policies of her husband's administration. She had her own nationally broadcast radio program and a syndicated newspaper column, "My Day," which was widely read. Eleanor Roosevelt saw herself as her husband's eyes and ears, and as she traveled widely, she became keenly attuned to the needs and feelings of a nation gripped by the Great Depression. As always, hers was an important and eloquent voice for legislation to aid the poverty-stricken and racial minorities, whom the depression hit particularly hard.

America's entry into World War II made even greater demands on Mrs. Roosevelt. She frequently toured both the European and Pacific fronts as well as military bases throughout the United States and the Western Hemisphere. Franklin Roosevelt was renowned as a leader with a warm, human touch. Eleanor amplified and multiplied this personal outreach, which lifted the national morale during the depression and the war.

The sudden death of President Roosevelt, on April 12, 1945, from a cerebral hemorrhage early in his fourth term, did not end Eleanor Roosevelt's life of public leadership. In December 1945, Roosevelt's successor, Harry S Truman, appointed her a member of the U.S. delegation to the United Nations. In the UN, she became chairman of the Commission on Human Rights and took a leadership role in the drafting of the United Nations Declaration of Human Rights, a cornerstone document in the struggle to guarantee international human rights. In 1952, Mrs. Roosevelt resigned from her United Nations post, only to be reappointed by President John F. Kennedy in 1961.

Eleanor Roosevelt's continued social activism and her work with the UN did not keep her out of party politics. A staunch Democrat, she enthusiastically campaigned on behalf of Adlai Stevenson, who twice unsuccessfully challenged Dwight D. Eisenhower for the White House, in 1952 and 1956. She also unsuccessfully supported his nomination at the Democratic convention in 1960.

Somehow, she managed to cram into her busy life authorship of a number of books, the best known of which are the autobiographical works *This Is My Story* (1937), *This I Remember* (1949), and *On My Own* (1958).

IN HER OWN WORDS

"A little simplification would be the first step toward rational living, I think."

—"My Day," January 22, 1936

LEADERSHIP LESSONS

✦

Self-fulfilment is often a matter of selfless action.

✦

Worthwhile leadership aims to improve the world, even by some small degree.

✦

Solve the problems that are nearest to you.

✦

To lead well is to work hard.

Roosevelt, Franklin Delano

Born: 1882   Died: 1945

**Innovator   Motivator   Problem solver   Rescuer
Strategist   Systems creator   Tactician**

LEADERSHIP ACHIEVEMENTS

◆

Overcame the limited perspective of a privileged and sheltered upbringing
to develop an understanding and concern for the "common man"

◆

Overcame a major disability, polio, to carry on a strenuous political career

◆

As president, led the nation through its two greatest 20th-century
challenges: the Great Depression and World War II

◆

Offered bold and innovative measures to combat the depression

◆

Projected a strong, confident, optimistic, and thoroughly credible
leadership image

◆

Was one of history's great communicators

◆

Fostered unprecedented wartime productivity by balancing the best of
capitalism with values of selfless patriotism

◆

Oversaw U.S. and Allied strategy in World War II

LIFE

The four-term 32nd president of the United States, Franklin Delano
Roosevelt led the nation through two of its most challenging crises: the
Great Depression and World War II.

Roosevelt was born on January 30, 1882, into the privileged world of
a patrician New York family at their estate in Hyde Park. Raised mainly by
a loving but overbearing mother, Franklin came even more fully under her
influence after his father, James Roosevelt, died in 1900, when Franklin
was 17. Up to this time, Franklin's life had been both idyllic and sheltered.

Through age 14, he was schooled at home by governesses and tutors. From 1896 to 1900, he attended Groton School in Massachusetts, where he was particularly influenced by headmaster Reverend Endicott Peabody, who emphasized an ethic of public service, teaching that the privileged classes owed a duty of service to society. From Groton, Roosevelt went on to Harvard, graduating in 1904.

While he was at Harvard, Roosevelt fell in love with Anna Eleanor Roosevelt, his fifth cousin once removed and the niece of Theodore Roosevelt. On March 17, 1905, they were married, and over the next 11 years the Roosevelts had six children: Anna (1906), James (1907), Elliott (1910), Franklin D., Jr. (1914), John (1916), and a child who died in infancy. Outwardly satisfactory, their marriage was, in fact, often troubled. Eleanor had Franklin's overbearing mother to contend with, she was often ignored by her husband, and she later discovered that he was having an affair with her social secretary, Lucy Mercer. Nevertheless, on a profound level, the marriage was also a remarkable one. Husband and wife functioned as a team, and Eleanor would prove a great political asset to Franklin—as well as an extraordinary social activist in her own right. Her highly developed social conscience nurtured and guided Franklin's own.

Franklin Roosevelt attended Columbia University Law School until the spring of 1907, but chose not to continue to pursue his degree after he passed the New York state bar examination. He became a lawyer with a top Wall Street firm, but he soon found corporate law unfulfilling and devoted much of his time to pro bono work for indigent clients. In 1910, he decided to run for state senator on the Democratic ticket. He proved a tireless and highly charismatic campaigner, and he easily won election in a traditionally Republican district. In the state house, Roosevelt quickly made a name for himself as a Progressive reformer and opponent of the machine politics of New York's Tammany Hall. Roosevelt's reformist leadership attracted attention far beyond the state and laid the foundation of a national reputation. He continued to build this reputation by supporting, in 1912, the presidential candidacy of reform Democrat Woodrow Wilson. With Wilson safely nominated, Roosevelt ran for reelection to the state Senate. His campaign was severely curtailed when he contracted typhoid fever, but his new aide, Louis Howe, helped him to achieve reelection nevertheless. Howe would become Roosevelt's most trusted adviser.

Although he had been reelected to another state Senate term, Roosevelt accepted the offer of a subcabinet post in the administration of Woodrow Wilson. He became assistant secretary of the navy under navy secretary Josephus Daniels. Roosevelt was attracted to the post because it was national in scope, allowed him to deal with ships and naval matters (both of which he loved), and was the very job Theodore Roosevelt had held a decade and a half earlier. It ushered Franklin Roosevelt into the corridors of national power, and he quickly showed himself to be far more dynamic than his boss, Josephus Daniels. He advocated preparedness for war, the development of a big navy, and an active, engaged foreign policy. With the outbreak of World War I in 1914, Roosevelt became an early supporter of U.S. entry into the conflict (clashing mildly with the pacifist-leaning Daniels), and he personally visited the front in 1918. But his greatest talent was his ability to deal with people on all levels and of every class: admirals, department bureaucrats, and shipyard labor unions. He was highly effective in opposing the collusive bidding and price-fixing practices of defense contractors, and he became a kind of ramrod for the Navy Department, the administrator to whom everyone turned when they needed to get something done quickly and efficiently.

In 1920, Roosevelt was nominated as the Democratic vice-presidential candidate, running with the governor of Ohio, James M. Cox. In the isolationist political atmosphere of postwar America, Roosevelt knew that he and his running mate would not win, but he did not take a defeatist attitude. Rather, he looked upon the run as an opportunity to gain exposure, to express his ideas, and to hone his campaigning skills. He loved to campaign. After the inevitable defeat, Roosevelt returned to the practice of law, forming his own firm and becoming vice president of a financial firm.

In August 1921, Roosevelt was confronted with the greatest personal challenge of his life. While vacationing at the Roosevelt family compound in Campobello, Canada, he was stricken with polio, which left him a paraplegic. With the help of his wife, Roosevelt successfully fought off despair. She also supported him in resisting his mother's wishes that he retire to her care and an invalid's life at Hyde Park. Eleanor Roosevelt believed that Franklin was destined for greatness, and she deemed it essential to the nation and to his own well-being that he not abandon his political career. From the crucible of devastating disease, Franklin Roosevelt emerged stronger and, if anything, more optimistic and more energetic than ever.

In 1924, while fighting back to recovery, Roosevelt discovered the medicinal waters of Warm Springs, Georgia. Bathing in these waters gave him relief and, he hoped, might help him regain some use of his legs. In typical Roosevelt fashion, he wanted to extend this discovery to other polio victims and formed and financed the Warm Springs Foundation. Also in 1924, Roosevelt delivered an eloquent and attention-getting speech nominating Al Smith for the presidency. Four years later, Roosevelt successfully ran for governor of New York—a banner triumph in an otherwise Republican year. Roosevelt was elected to two terms as governor, battling a Republican legislature to push through many Progressive measures, including reforestation, state-supported old-age pensions and unemployment insurance, labor legislation, and the public development of electric power. With the deepening of the Great Depression in 1931, Roosevelt was the first governor to create an effective state relief administration. He put social worker Harry Hopkins in charge of the agency. Later, alongside Howe, Hopkins would become one of President Roosevelt's closest advisers.

During Roosevelt's tenure as governor, he created the "Fireside Chat," using the radio to broadcast informal addresses directly to the American people. It was an unprecedented and extraordinarily effective use of the relatively new medium, and it would become a mainstay of his presidency. The Fireside Chats also augmented the governor's tremendous popularity. He was reelected in 1930 by 750,000 votes, the largest margin in state history. During his gubernatorial administration, Roosevelt, in search of innovative solutions to problems associated with the depression, enlisted what he called a "brain trust" of Columbia University professors to help create programs to fight the hard times. These individuals he would carry over into his presidency, where they would be instrumental in formulating the New Deal.

Roosevelt was nominated by the Democrats as their presidential candidate in 1932, having broken precedent by flying to the convention to accept the nomination. He spoke: "I pledge you, I pledge myself, to a new deal for the American people." The New Deal Roosevelt proposed included federal spending for relief and public works, a plan to curb the agricultural overproduction that was depressing farm prices, a policy of conservation of environmental resources, a policy to generate public power, a policy to provide old-age pensions and unemployment insurance, a policy to regulate the stock exchange, and the repeal of Prohibition. By a wide margin, Roosevelt defeated Herbert Hoover, the Republican president many blamed (unjustly) for the depression and many others blamed (with some justification) for doing too little to alleviate the effects of the depression.

Roosevelt was inaugurated on March 4, 1933, at the very nadir of the depression, with the nation desperate as some 15 million Americans found themselves unemployed. The failure of banks and other financial institutions had created widespread panic, which, in turn, brought about the collapse of even more banks.

Roosevelt entered the picture by projecting an image of realistic confidence and optimism. His assertion in his inaugural address that "the only thing we have to fear is fear itself—nameless, unreasoning, unjustified terror," rung true, especially as he assured his fellow Americans that he would not stand by as the depression deepened. He would obtain from Congress "the one remaining instrument to meet the crisis—broad executive power to wage a war against the emergency, as great as the power that would be given to me if we were in fact invaded by a foreign foe."

Roosevelt took immediate action by declaring a "bank holiday" to prevent a panic run on still-functioning banks, and he called Congress into emergency session. During the first hundred days of his administration, FDR introduced a sweeping program of relief measures. He took the nation off the gold standard, a step that offered some relief to debtors and exporters. He prevailed on Congress to appropriate $500 million in federal relief grants to states and local agencies. Under Harry Hopkins, he created the Federal Emergency Relief Administration, the Civil Works Administration (CWA), the Civilian Conservation Corps (CCC), the Home Owners Loan Corporation (HOLC), and the Public Works Administration (PWA). The CCC employed more than 2.5 million young men on conservation work, the HOLC furnished emergency assistance to mortgagors and homeowners, enabling them to avoid foreclosure, and the PWA created great public works projects. These and other measures not only provided immediate relief to the desperate, but generally restored hope among those hardest hit by the depression. Without such measures, many believed the nation would have headed toward civil insurrection or even revolution.

The New Deal was structured on a vast and all-encompassing scale. In addition to emergency relief, it included a program of longer-range reform. The Federal Deposit Insurance Corporation (FDIC) insured bank deposits, an important safeguard against runs on banks. The Securities and Exchange Commission (SEC) inaugurated the regulation of the stock exchanges, a safeguard against the kinds of practices that contributed to the sudden fall of the markets in 1929. The Tennessee Valley Authority (TVA) built great multipurpose dams to control floods and generate cheap hydro-electric power. Two agencies of special importance were the National Recovery Administration (NRA) and the Agricultural Adjustment Administration (AAA). The NRA provided incentives to management as well as labor to establish codes of fair competition within each industry, codes that included equitable pricing and production policies, collective bargaining, minimum wages, and maximum hours. The AAA sought to raise farm prices by setting production quotas approved by farmers in referenda and then subsidizing farmers who stayed within the quotas.

The New Deal enjoyed limited success, but it did provide quick relief and longer-term hope. FDR revealed himself to be innovative, flexible, determined, and compassionate. He was outgoing and communicative, keeping the nation informed through frequent press conferences, speeches, and Fireside Chats. An overwhelming majority of Americans found his charisma irresistible and his optimism inspiring—and, more important, believable. Although true and enduring relief from the depression would not come until the approach of war increased demand for goods, Roosevelt's various interventions did halt the downward slide of the depression's darkest days.

Roosevelt had to navigate a perilous course between preserving capitalism and a free market economy, on the one hand, and providing appropriate intervention, support, and control, on the other. In 1935, FDR ushered through Congress three of his most sweeping initiatives: the Works Progress Administration (WPA), which employed millions in work relief programs; the Wagner Act, which set up the National Labor Relations Board (NLRB) and thereby guaranteed labor the right to bargain collectively on equal terms with management; and Social Security, which provided for federal payment of old-age pensions and for federal–state cooperation in support of unemployment compensation and relief of the needy blind, of the disabled, and of dependent children.

Roosevelt was reelected in 1936 by a landslide. He did not accept this victory as a cause for complacence, however, declaring in his second inaugural address that "I see one-third of a nation ill-housed, ill-clad, ill-nourished," and acknowledging the need to press on with reform, relief, and recovery. The second term proved, if anything, even more controversial than the first. His "court reform" plan amounted to an attempt to pack the Supreme Court with judges favorable to many of his constitutionally questionable programs. In some places, workers became increasingly militant—for which FDR was blamed. When the depression suddenly deepened in 1937, FDR was uncharacteristically slow to respond with increased federal spending. While national confidence in FDR himself remained largely unshaken, more conservatives were elected to Congress, making it difficult for the president to promote his new programs.

On the turbulent and ultimately cataclysmic international front during the Roosevelt presidency, FDR emphasized personal diplomacy. Important innovations in the 1930s included U.S. diplomatic recognition of the Soviet Union (still an outcast in much of the diplomatic community), the development of many reciprocal trade agreements, and the creation of a "good neighbor policy" with the nations of Latin America. By the end of FDR's first term, it was clear that the militaristic dictatorships of Germany, Japan, and Italy boded ill for world peace, and Roosevelt's 1936 speech accepting renomination would prove prophetic: "This generation of Americans," he declared, "has a rendezvous with destiny."

Up to 1938, FDR had agreed to accept the congressional Neutrality Act designed to keep the United States out of another world war, but he was no isolationist. At last, in 1939, the naked aggression of Germany compelled—or allowed—Roosevelt to take a tougher position. He tried to secure repeal of many of the provisions of the Neutrality Act, but did not succeed until September 1940, when World War II began in Europe with the German blitzkrieg invasion of Poland. After gaining reelection to an unprecedented third term in 1940, FDR initiated the "lend-lease" program to aid the anti-German allies. This innovative legislation provided an alternative to the restrictive cash-and-carry policy of supplying arms and materiel to Britain and other allies (including, in June 1941, the USSR), giving the president broad discretion in releasing war goods. FDR also authorized U.S. destroyers to escort convoys of Allied supply ships partway across the Atlantic. By December 1941, the United States and Germany were engaged in an undeclared war on the Atlantic.

With regard to Japan, Roosevelt had attempted to contain that nation's aggressive expansion by imposing an embargo of vital goods. Conceived as an alternative to war, this policy goaded Japanese militarists into attacking Pearl Harbor, Hawaii, on December 7, 1941, thereby propelling the United States into World War II.

Franklin Roosevelt was now a wartime president. In addition to taking a strong hand in directing U.S. prosecution of the war, FDR promoted the rapid mobilization of U.S. industry at home. Among many African Americans at this time a semimilitant movement to end employment discrimination had begun. To avert racial disorder, Roosevelt set up a Fair Employment Practices Committee (FEPC) to prevent discrimination in defense-related employment. It was a milestone in civil rights. FDR also brought business leaders into policy-making positions, offered corporations generous contracts and tax breaks, and downgraded progressive domestic reforms, all in the name of putting American industry on a war footing—albeit at the expense of many of the liberal reforms of the New Deal. This brought considerable criticism from liberal supporters who thought themselves betrayed, but, in a desperate war, FDR had to set priorities.

With the help of White House advisers, industrialists, and others, the president's wartime leadership innovations included an emphasis on competition. Instead of appointing a production "czar" to oversee the war effort, FDR harnessed capitalist principles, assuming that a competitive atmosphere would produce the best results. He did create a number of boards and agencies to control prices, develop manpower policy, and supervise the allocation of scarce materials, but, for the most part, it was a zeal to win the war that fostered a productive cooperation among workers, employers, and the government. By refusing to become a dictator, FDR transformed a war on behalf of democracy against totalitarianism into a triumph of democratic methods and ideology.

Militarily, Roosevelt accepted all responsibility and a great deal of criticism. He was accused of having left Pearl Harbor unprepared. He was criticized by some hard-line American politicians for "cooperating" with the enemy, Vichy French admiral Jean Darlan, by negotiating with

him in advance of the Allied invasion of North Africa. He was also criticized for holding to a policy of unconditional surrender, which may
have discouraged anti-Hitler resistance within Germany. Even today,
most military thinkers believe Roosevelt was mistaken to rely heavily on
strategic bombing, which never proved highly effective. Many within the
U.S. military community believed FDR should have opened up the "second front" against Hitler earlier than the Normandy invasion (D-Day) of
June 1944.

Right or wrong, FDR made all the necessary decisions, and what he
did ultimately resulted in victory by an alliance of disparate nations—
mainly the United States, Britain, and the Soviet Union. Victory was
achieved, and the alliance was held together. Moreover, the people of the
United States had sufficient confidence in FDR to elect him to a fourth
term in 1944. This represented a tremendous sacrifice for the aging and ailing leader, whose health had deteriorated dramatically under the strains of
war. In fact, he died early in his fourth term, on April 12, 1945, of a cerebral hemorrhage. He was 63.

Roosevelt is still regarded as one of the nation's most controversial
leaders. Conservatives continue to claim that he transformed the federal
government into a monster that destroyed states' rights and even compromised individual liberty. Many liberals criticized—and still criticize—him
for taking insufficiently radical action against the depression. On balance,
however, historians consider Roosevelt one of America's great leaders, a
savior and shaper of modern America.

IN HIS OWN WORDS

"It is common sense to take a method and try it. If it fails, admit it
frankly and try another. But above all, try something."

"I'm not the smartest fellow in the world, but I can sure pick smart
colleagues."

"It is a terrible thing to look over your shoulder when you are trying to
lead—and find no one there."

—Source for all of the Roosevelt quotations is www.usdreams.com/RooseveltFW25.html.

LEADERSHIP LESSONS

✦

Understand the dimensions of your background and how they shape your vision. Then endeavor to look beyond these limits.

✦

To lead others requires understanding others. To understand others requires imagination and a willingness to leave behind comfortable assumptions.

✦

Act decisively when action is called for. Often, a good solution now is far better than a perfect solution later.

✦

Project credible confidence and optimism. These are infectious.

✦

Communicate fully and often. Create common cause by clear explanation and definition of goals and values.

✦

Do not be afraid to inspire.

✦

Empower others. Allow people to achieve excellence.

✦

Build a team of the best available advisers.

✦

Foster creative competition among those you lead, but ensure that it is competition toward a common goal.

✦

An effective leader makes many difficult decisions regarding priority of objectives and goals.

✦

Keep plans flexible. Do not become emotionally attached to any particular course of action.

✦

Leadership is sacrifice.

Roosevelt, Theodore

Born: 1858   Died: 1919

Character model   Innovator   Mentor   Motivator
Problem solver   Rescuer   Visionary

LEADERSHIP ACHIEVEMENTS

✦

As a youthful New York state legislator, earned a reputation as an advocate
for child labor reform and safe working conditions for all

✦

As New York police commissioner, extensively reformed a corrupt and
ineffectual department

✦

As U.S. civil service commissioner, strove (in the words of
President Benjamin Harrison) "to put an end to all the evil in the world
between sunrise and sunset"

✦

Became a hero of the Spanish–American War

✦

As New York governor, introduced broad political and economic reforms

✦

As U.S. president, liberalized the office while amassing unprecedented
executive authority

✦

Transformed the presidency, bringing to the office great energy
and fresh vision

✦

Championed the creation of the modern U.S. Navy

✦

Introduced the concept of "big-stick" diplomacy

✦

Was chiefly responsible for building the Panama Canal

✦

Championed conservation, establishing great national parks
and other preserves

✦

In 1906, for his mediation in the Russo–Japanese War, became the first
American awarded the Nobel Peace Prize

L I F E

The 26th president of the United States (among other major achievements), Theodore Roosevelt guided the country to a position of leadership among nations and set for all Americans an example of continual striving for excellence, which he summed up in the phrase "the strenuous life." Roosevelt expanded the power of the chief executive and introduced the idea of the president as a social activist and reformer. He increased government regulation of business and fostered the development of labor unions, while introducing measures to conserve America's natural resources and natural heritage. Bigger than life, TR became an icon—sometimes beloved, sometimes disdained—of aggressive Americanism.

Theodore Roosevelt was born to privilege in an old New York family. An extraordinarily curious and intelligent child, he was also frail and sickly, afflicted with asthma and bad eyesight. He was educated at home by private tutors before entering Harvard College. Loathing his physical weakness, he drove himself hard, learning to ride, box, and shoot in order to build up his physique and restore his health. His physical activity did not eclipse his intellectual pursuits, however, and, at Harvard, he found himself absorbed by natural history, political history, and military history. While still an undergraduate, he began writing *The Naval War of 1812,* which was published in 1882, two years after he graduated.

Shortly after graduation, Roosevelt married Alice Hathaway Lee, who died on February 14, 1884, soon after the birth of the couple's daughter, Alice. On the very same day, Roosevelt's mother died. By this time, the politically precocious Roosevelt was already serving a third term in the New York State Assembly and was seen as a leader of a minority of reform-minded Republicans. While in the Assembly, Roosevelt initiated and led the fight to regulate New York City sweat shops and other practices that exploited labor.

In an effort to overcome his grief at the death of his wife, Roosevelt threw himself into his political work and the writing of history. He also purchased a cattle ranch in the Dakota Territory and then traveled there to work the land personally, largely in the hope that a strenuous outdoor life would hasten his emotional recovery. He returned to New York in 1886 and made an unsuccessful run for mayor. After this, he sailed to London, where he married his childhood sweetheart, Edith Kermit Carow. Together, they would have four sons and a daughter.

For more than two years following his second marriage, Roosevelt lived a vigorously leisured life as a sportsman and gentleman-scholar, publishing biographies of Gouverneur Morris and Thomas Hart Benton as well as books about the American West. Then, in 1889, he was appointed to head the U.S. Civil Service Commission, which he thoroughly reformed to bring an end to the corruption of political patronage and the spoils system.

In 1895, Roosevelt left Washington and returned to New York as president of the Police Commission of the City of New York, dedicating himself to modernizing and cleaning up the New York City Police Department. During his two years in office, bribery and other forms of corruption were greatly reduced. Although these stubbornly returned when he left the post, many of his administrative reforms were more enduring.

Roosevelt departed the Police Commission in 1897 to become assistant secretary of the navy in the administration of President William McKinley. Roosevelt used his position to maneuver the nation toward war against Spain in order to promote the independence of Cuba. Roosevelt wanted to see European influence eliminated from the hemisphere, and he wanted the United States to assert itself among the great powers of the world.

As soon as the Spanish–American War broke out in 1898, Roosevelt resigned as assistant secretary of the navy and became a lieutenant colonel of the 1st U.S. Volunteer Cavalry—better known as the Rough Riders. He was promoted to colonel in Puerto Rico and led the Rough Riders in their famous charge not up San Juan Hill (as popular memory records), but up Kettle Hill during the battle for San Juan. The romantic gallantry of his performance in what was, in fact, a make-or-break battle earned Roosevelt an instant reputation throughout the United States. He successfully ran for governor of New York in the summer of 1898 and performed so impressively in office that even the highly partisan, pro-Democrat *New York World* praised his administration as "high and good." Among his reforms were many measures to promote clean government, to support labor, to improve public education, to end racial discrimination in public schools, and to ameliorate the misery of the slums. Within New York, the governor also instituted a program of conservation, which foreshadowed the major environmental initiatives he would introduce as president.

Responding to pressure from big business, the Republican leadership, in the meantime, wanted to kick Roosevelt upstairs by taking him out of the governor's mansion and sending him to Washington as vice president on the ticket with McKinley, who was running for a second term in 1900. Feeling that the vice presidency could lead to the White House, Roosevelt accepted the nomination. Just six months after McKinley's reelection, the president was assassinated, and Roosevelt succeeded him—at 42, the youngest man ever to hold the office. (President John F. Kennedy, the youngest *elected* president, was 43 when he was inaugurated.)

Roosevelt liberalized the office McKinley had left him. He was committed to being the president of *all* the people, and he tried to reconcile the interests of big business and labor—but usually came down very much on the side of labor and earned a reputation as a "trust buster," breaking up monopolistic practices, especially among the railroads, which had an economic stranglehold on smaller businesses, the American consumer, and, above all, the American farmer, who was squeezed between high transportation costs and low commodity prices.

Internationally, Roosevelt significantly moderated the bellicosity that characterized his attitude toward the Spanish–American War. He promoted such precursors of the League of Nations and the United Nations as the international court of arbitration at The Hague, but he also practiced imperialism when he believed it was in the best interest of the United States to do so. In 1903, Roosevelt was poised to buy out a bankrupt French company's rights to build a canal through Panama, which was then part of Colombia. When the Colombian senate rejected Roosevelt's terms, he quietly supported a revolution to win Panamanian independence. He then concluded a treaty with the new Republic of Panama, which gave the United States sovereignty over the Panama Canal Zone, a strip 10 miles wide across the entire isthmus of Panama. Roosevelt was not literally an empire builder, but, with the so-called Roosevelt Corollary to the Monroe Doctrine, he did assert the United States' right to intervene, when necessary, in certain affairs of the Latin American states.

Roosevelt was swept into office in his own right in 1904 and ushered through Congress a package of social and economic reform legislation he called the Square Deal. Measures included the Hepburn Act of 1906, which gave the Interstate Commerce Commission power to fix railroad rates and to prohibit discrimination among shippers; the Pure Food and Drug Act, which organized the Food and Drug Administration; and an important employer's liability law, designed to protect the safety of workers. Ultimately, Roosevelt aspired to nothing less than fashioning government into a precisely scientific and always just instrument that was acutely responsive to the public needs. Often, Congress felt that the chief executive was encroaching on its turf, and relations between the legislative and executive branches became anything but cordial.

As boldly as Roosevelt acted in the economic, social, and international arenas, his initiatives to promote conservation of natural resources had the most innovative, sweeping, and enduring effect. The leadership task here was extremely demanding, for it called upon states, lawmakers, and people to set aside at least some portion of immediate profit and current private interest to preserve for the future what was in the public interest. Under TR, many conservation measures were enacted, including the reorganization of the U.S. Forest Service and the creation of great national parks and preserves.

Often criticized as warlike, Roosevelt earned the Nobel Peace Prize for successfully mediating, in 1905, an end to the horrifically destructive Russo–Japanese War. Shortly afterward, however, he sent the Great White Fleet of the American navy on a world cruise to demonstrate the potential of what was being termed "big-stick" diplomacy: "Speak softly," Roosevelt famously proclaimed, "and carry a big stick." Yet he was essentially moderate on the subject of anything resembling genuine imperialist expansion, and he accordingly made important compromises with Japan, which he recognized as the emerging economic powerhouse of Asia, whose future, Roosevelt believed, would be increasingly important to that of the United States.

Roosevelt declined to run for a second term in his own right, and was gratified by the victory of his handpicked successor, William Howard Taft, who was inaugurated in March 1909. Roosevelt went on a combination hunting and scientific expedition to Africa, then returned to the United States, and began calling for a program of public welfare and business regulation far more ambitious than what he had attempted during his presidency and certainly beyond what the ultimately conservative Taft was willing to advocate. In 1912, after he failed to win the Republican nomination as the party's candidate for president, Roosevelt participated in the creation of a third party, officially called the Progressive Party but better known as the Bull Moose Party. While campaigning, Roosevelt was wounded by an assassin's bullet in Milwaukee. The candidate was saved from death by his eyeglasses case and the multiply folded manuscript of the speech he was about to give, both of which were tucked into the breast pocket of his coat and absorbed much of the bullet's impact. Nevertheless, Roosevelt had been hit and was bleeding, yet he refused entreaties to proceed immediately to the hospital, and, declaring that it took "more than a bullet to stop a Bull Moose," he insisted on delivering his speech.

In a three-way race among Democrat Woodrow Wilson, Republican William Howard Taft, and Progressive Roosevelt, Wilson won, with 42 percent of the popular vote (and an overwhelming victory in the Electoral College), but Roosevelt earned 27 percent of the popular vote, whereas Taft carried only two states.

After this impressive showing, Roosevelt wrote an autobiography that he matter-of-factly titled *Autobiography,* led an expedition up an unmapped river in Brazil, and then agitated for early U.S. entry into World War I. After the nation finally entered the war in 1917, Roosevelt unsuccessfully appealed for command of an army division in France. He was so convinced of the justice of the cause that, when his son Quentin died in aerial combat over France, he commented that it was "very dreadful that [Quentin] should have been killed, [but] it would have been worse if he had not gone." The former president died a year after his son Quentin, albeit peacefully, at Sagamore, his home in Oyster Bay, Long Island. He had never fully recovered his health after a bout of malaria contracted during his expedition in Brazil.

IN HIS OWN WORDS

"Be practical as well as generous in your ideals. Keep your eyes on the stars, but remember to keep your feet on the ground."
—Address at the Groton School, Groton, Massachusetts, May 24, 1904

"Speak softly and carry a big stick; you will go far."
—West African proverb often used by Roosevelt

"Don't hit at all if you can help it; don't hit a man if you can possibly avoid it; but if you do hit him, put him to sleep."
—Speech, New York City, February 17, 1899

"It is true of the nation, as of the individual, that the greatest doer must also be a great dreamer."
—Speech, Berkeley, California, 1911

LEADERSHIP LESSONS

✦

Energy alone does not make a leader, but is indispensable to leadership.

✦

Leaders are fixers. They cannot be comfortable when things are wrong.

✦

Persuade yourself that the power to effect change is yours.

✦

Positive morale, high energy, and optimism are contagions an effective leader is eager to spread.

✦

Strength and health, products of a "strenuous life," create a strong platform from which to lead others.

✦

Give those you lead a "square deal."

✦

The most difficult thing a leader can do is persuade others to forgo immediate profit or private gain for the benefit of some greater future good. Yet such acts are often required for the prosperity, even the survival, of any enterprise.

✦

Take joy in what you do, and, as a leader, communicate that joy to others.

Saladin (Salah Ad-din Yusuf ibn Ayyub, "Righteous of the Faith")

Born: ca. 1138 Died: 1193

**Character model   Conqueror   Mentor   Motivator
Strategist   Tactician   Visionary**

LEADERSHIP ACHIEVEMENTS

✦

Used the force of religion to unify very disparate and geographically far-flung peoples

✦

Created an empire founded on commonality of religious faith

✦

Envisioned a unified Islamic Empire, which, to a large degree, he succeeded in creating

✦

Prioritized titanic tasks, first subduing rivals and then attacking a common enemy

✦

Achieved brilliant military victories, tempered by justice and mercy

✦

Promoted learning and culture, to the benefit both of his people and of civilization

LIFE

A brilliant leader, Saladin consolidated the Islamic Empire, which he ruled from 1171 to 1193. He was born in Takrit, Mesopotamia, the son of an influential Kurdish family. As a young man, he accompanied his uncle on a military expedition to liberate Egypt from the Frankish domination brought by the First Crusade. He served briefly as governor of Alexandria, and when his uncle died in about 1169, he became vizier of Egypt and the commander of Syrian troops. Within two years, he had established himself as the sole ruler of Egypt. For the next decade, Saladin set as his principal goal the union of the various countries of the Middle East under the standard of Islam. In this enterprise he enjoyed great success. At the time, the

461

Islamic Empire extended across thousands of square miles—from Gibraltar in the west to beyond the Indus River in the east, and from Turkey in the north to the tip of the Arabian Peninsula in the south. Saladin worked to reconcile the disparate factions of Islam, creating a force that tied together the peoples of this vast area.

To achieve unification, Saladin either negotiated with or fought against various Islamic rulers. As part of his effort, he transformed Islam into a haven for religious scholars and teachers, to whom he assigned responsibility for instilling in the masses the tenets of Mohammedism. What he achieved by the sword he always reinforced and extended by means of knowledge and learning.

By 1187, Saladin had so consolidated the vast Islamic Empire that he now felt prepared to turn from battle against his Islamic rivals to wage war on the Christian states established by the Crusaders over the preceding 100 years. Jerusalem itself had been occupied by Christians for 88 years, and one of Saladin's top priorities was to reestablish Islamic influence there. In northern Palestine, on July 4, 1187, Saladin and his magnificently trained army met a poorly equipped Frankish army near the city of Tiberius. Within hours, the Islamic forces had routed the Franks and, within the span of three months, Saladin had captured the cities of Acre, Toron, Beirut, Sidon, Nazareth, Caesarea, Nabulus, Jaffa, Ascalon, and Jerusalem.

In victory, Saladin declined to persecute the defeated Christians as the Crusaders had persecuted those whom they had conquered years before. Instead, he treated the vanquished with fairness, courtesy, and a degree of civility unknown to the Crusaders. Nevertheless, when news of the fall of the Kingdom of Jerusalem reached Europe, calls were issued for a new Crusade—the third—and Richard I the Lion-Hearted of England, Philip II of France, and Frederick I of Germany (Frederick Barbarossa) took their armies to the Holy Land in this latest attempt to "free" it once and for all. However, Frederick was drowned on the journey east, and after reoccupying Acre, Philip returned home, followed by Richard, who concluded a peace with Saladin. The Third Crusade, then, ended as a victory for Saladin in that most of the Islamic Empire stayed intact, and Jerusalem remained in his hands.

Throughout his reign, Saladin exercised great diplomatic and military skill. His unification of Islamic nations into a single military power strengthened the culture and religion of the Muslim world. Through his efforts, the influence of a century of Crusader activity in the Holy Land, while not totally eliminated, was dramatically reduced. Finally, all of this was accomplished with a high degree of humanity, mercy toward enemies, and a spirit of fairness to all concerned. Saladin died in Damascus on March 4, 1193, shortly after the end of the Third Crusade.

LEADERSHIP LESSONS

✦

Do not underestimate the power of vision to motivate action and to unify disparate elements of the enterprise.

✦

Try to fight one war at a time. Saladin subdued his Islamic rivals before he mounted an effort against the Christian invaders.

✦

Coercion and brute force may be effective in the short run, but they are not generally effective in maintaining an enterprise through the long run. Temper force with education, instruction, and demonstrations of fair, generous treatment.

Samudragupta

Reigned: ca. 330–80

Conqueror Mentor Strategist Systems creator Tactician

LEADERSHIP ACHIEVEMENTS

✦

Annexed to his empire much of the Indian subcontinent

✦

Improved the lands he conquered, thereby building loyalty

✦

Was responsible for much of the enduring spiritual character of India

✦

Treated opponents selectively, eliminating some and coopting others

✦

Planned his conquests systematically and progressively

LIFE

Modern scholars sometimes call Samudragupta the Indian Napoleon. At the risk of condescension, the comparison is appropriate in that it suggests the Indian ruler's skill at conquest as well as his desire to introduce the cultural and administrative benefits to those regions he conquered.

In his own time, this son of Chandragupta I was called the Exterminator of Kings for his conquests, between 330 and 380, gained for him a vast portion of the Indian subcontinent.

When his father died, Samudragupta inherited territory that extended from Magadha to Allahabab. He resolved to expand his inheritance greatly and, to this end, waged war on a host of lesser kings in the Upper Ganges Valley. The leaders, he ruthlessly killed; the people, he refused to oppress. Samudragupta reasoned that leaving a conquered nation better off than he had found it would build loyalty—especially in the absence of the original monarch.

From the base he established near present-day Delhi, Samudragupta operated across a vast area. Some kings he spared, reducing them to abject vassalage. In this way, he subjugated Samatata (eastern Bengal), Davaka

(Nowgong in Assam), Kamarupa (western Assam), Nepal, Kartripura (Garhwal and Jalandhar), and numerous tribal states in the eastern and central Punjab, Malwa, and western India. He also made vassals of the chiefs of the Kushans and Sakas. After he had completed these conquests, Samudragupta moved into the Deccan, where he defeated, captured, then reinstated (in return for heavy tribute) an impressive catalogue of rulers.

Samudragupta's many campaigns brought into his empire vast tracts extending south from the Himalayas to Narmada, and west from the Brahmaputra to the Jumna and Chambal. In addition, kings in east Bengal, Assam, Nepal, and the eastern portion of Punjab, and several tribes of Rajasthan paid tribute to him. During the course of his wars of expansion, he killed nine rulers and subjugated a dozen others, earning, in the bloody process, the gratitude of most of the peoples he conquered, for he brought to them cultural and economic improvements as well as more efficient systems of government. Samudragupta's conquests may well have been the chief means by which so much of Indian society adopted its long-enduring and characteristic Hindu theological system and code of social conduct.

LEADERSHIP LESSONS

✦

Build loyalty by improving the lives of those you lead. Give value.

✦

Consider conquest not as an opportunity for taking, but as an opportunity
for giving.

✦

Understand your opponents. Treat them according to your
understanding of them.

Sargon of Akkad

Reigned: ca. 2334–2279 B.C.

Conqueror Innovator Profit maker Strategist Tactician Visionary

LEADERSHIP ACHIEVEMENTS

✦

Rising from humble beginnings, attained great power

✦

In a world of fragmented city-states, conceived a vision of unified empire

✦

Acted to realize his vision on a grand scale

✦

Innovated a new system of government on an unprecedented scale

✦

Approached empire building from the point of view of self-sustaining trade

✦

Created a powerful empire fueled by trade

LIFE

The first Semitic king of Mesopotamia, Sargon of Akkad founded the great Akkadian dynasty. Operating from his capital, Agade—also known as Akkad—Sargon conquered and united many city-states into a vast, well-organized empire. This not only produced the ancient world's first great empire, it introduced central government into the world—a radically new form of political organization. In addition to the Akkadian empire proper, Sargon also became overlord of various petty states throughout Mesopotamia. Ultimately, Sargon conquered all of southern Mesopotamia and parts of Syria, Anatolia (modern Turkey), and Elam. His 56-year reign was highly stable.

Although Sargon is one of history's first rulers about whom anything of substance is known, it is not known how he became king of Mesopotamia in the first place. Legend tells that he was born about 2350 B.C. to a Semitic nomad father and a mother who was a temple votary. In a mythological motif familiar from the story of Moses, Sargon's mother was said to have put him in a basket and set him coursing down the river, where he was found by a gardener, who raised him as his own son.

It is known as historical fact that, as a young man, Sargon became a cupbearer to Ur-Zababa, the Sumerian king of Kish. This position put him close to the king and his court, so it may be that, somehow, Sargon managed a coup d'état and was able to claim Ur-Zababa's throne. This, however, is only speculative.

Once Sargon had attained power, probably around 2334 B.C., he set out on a series of military campaigns. Defeating Lugalzaggesi of Uruk, overlord of the city-states of Sumer, Sargon became ruler of all of southern Mesopotamia. Sargon was possessed of an impressive sense of strategy. He was a visionary; in a world made up of independent city-states, he saw the value of uniting in order to increase and control trade. Accordingly, he campaigned to conquer the cities along the middle Euphrates River, and, aware of the importance of controlling production of trade goods, he extended his reach to the silver region of southern Anatolia and captured Susa, the capital of the Elamites in the Zagros Mountains of present-day western Iran. He may even have reached Egypt, Ethiopia, and India. Following these conquests, Sargon had access to the cedar of Lebanon and the lapis lazuli mines of Badakhshantrade.

From the riches that flowed to him, Sargon built Agade—located somewhere along the Euphrates—into a magnificent capital, and his trade flourished throughout the Indus Valley, the coast of Oman, the islands and coastal towns of the Persian Gulf, the Taurus Mountains, Cappadocia, Crete, and possibly Greece.

LEADERSHIP LESSONS

✦

Drive innovation with vision.

✦

A great leader does not hesitate to imagine on a vast scale.

✦

Expansion must be self-sustaining to be both worthwhile and enduring.

✦

Think systemically. Sargon structured his conquests to attain control of
resources, production, and trade routes.

✦

A leader is essentially a builder.

Saul

Reigned: ca. 1020–1000 B.C.

Character model   Conqueror   Motivator   Rescuer   Strategist

LEADERSHIP ACHIEVEMENTS

✦

Achieved great renown as a military commander

✦

Unified the fractious Hebrew tribes into a formidable nation

✦

Reclaimed Israel from the Philistines

✦

Established a reign of wisdom and justice

LIFE

The first king of Israel, Saul created a nation out of disparate Hebrew tribes, and he effectively defended that nation against the military might of the Philistines. He was the son of Kish from the tribe of Benjamin. In youth, Saul earned a reputation for military prowess. What little that is known of him derives from the Bible, 1 Samuel 9–12, which does not furnish a single, unambiguous history of how he came into power. What is apparent, however, is that Samuel, an influential leader of what was at the time a very loosely constituted league of Hebrew tribes, advocated the elevation of Saul as supreme ruler of the tribes. At the same time, it is clear that Samuel sought to avoid creating a tyrannical, absolute monarchy. Whatever misgivings Samuel and others may have had concerning possible loss of freedom under a single powerful ruler, it seems to have been clear to them that chronic division and disunity constituted an even greater liability. Separately, the tribes stood little chance against the highly organized Philistines. Saul was the most famous warrior among all the tribes, and thus he emerged as the most promising candidate to govern and defend them.

King Saul did unify the Hebrews, and he led them in a successful campaign to evict the Philistines from the central hill country. Moreover,

Saul extended his rule into Judah and the northern Transjordan region, yet he did not become a despot. Indeed, he earned a reputation for his great justice and wisdom. Yet even he had human flaws. As Samuel relates the history, Saul became increasingly jealous of his charismatic protégé, the young warrior David. As time passed, his jealousy assumed the proportions of obsession, which clouded even this wise king's judgment. Focusing on David, he ignored the renewed threat posed by the Philistines. As a result, he was ill-prepared for battle against the Philistines at Mount Gilboa. Facing defeat and desperate to avoid capture, he committed suicide. David succeeded Saul as king of Israel.

LEADERSHIP LESSONS
✦

A leader builds on his reputation and never hesitates to capitalize on it.
✦

Creating common cause and defining common interests are prime leadership activities.
✦

Separate personal feelings from the leadership task at hand; failure to do so has brought down many leaders—and, too often, their enterprise as well.

Scharnhorst, Count Gerhard Johann David von

Born: 1755 Died: 1813

Innovator   Mentor   Systems creator   Tactician

LEADERSHIP ACHIEVEMENTS

✦

Combined practical military experience with theoretical brilliance

✦

Was a creative teacher

✦

Taught Clausewitz, the most influential military theorist of modern times

✦

Presented his lessons in an instantly accessible form

✦

Introduced systematic, sweeping reforms in the Prussian army

LIFE

This general led innovations that transformed the Prussian army into the most efficient and feared military organization in Europe. Scharnhorst was born at Bordenau, near Hannover, and was commissioned in the Hannoverian army in 1788. His talent as a mentor was immediately apparent, and he was appointed an artillery instructor. He also collaborated on an officers' handbook as well as a military pocketbook for use in the field. These volumes, the first of their kind, were published in 1792.

Scharnhorst fought under the Duke of York in the Netherlands at Hondschoote on September 8, 1793, and then at Menin during April 27–30, 1794. After the second battle, he wrote and published a study of the defense of Menin and another work that sought to answer why France had been so successful in its revolutionary wars.

Scharnhorst's scholarship and valor in the field made him a well-known figure in military circles. He was promoted to major and transferred to the staff of the Hannoverian army, on which he served from 1796 to 1801, the year he joined the Prussian army with the rank of lieutenant colonel. Ennobled by the king of Prussia, who was eager to retain his service, Scharnhorst was appointed instructor at the War Academy in Berlin. Among his most illustrious students was Karl von Clausewitz, perhaps the greatest and certainly the most influential of modern military theorists. Scharnhorst also served as tutor to the crown prince during 1802–04.

From March 1804 to 1805, Scharnhorst was deputy quartermaster general and commander of the 3rd Brigade, and from 1805 to 1806, he was chief of staff to the Duke of Brunswick. He fought at Auerstädt on October 14, 1806, and was wounded. The following month, he was captured at Ratkau, but was speedily exchanged in time to serve with the Prussians at Eylau during February 7–8, 1807. Promoted to major general in July, he was appointed minister of war and chief of the general staff on March 1, 1808. From these posts, he worked to reform and rebuild the Prussian army in order to make it a supremely efficient national force. However, pursuant to Napoleon's edict of September 26, 1810, barring foreigners from service in the Prussian army, the Hannoverian Scharnhorst had to step down and leave Prussia. He entered semirctirement, taking the time to write a manual on firearms.

In 1812, he was recalled to active duty as chief of staff to Napoleon's great nemesis, Gebhard Blücher. He fought at Lützen on May 2, 1813, and was wounded there. Subsequently, he was sent to Prague to negotiate for Austria's entry into the war, but he failed to recover from his wound. His health deteriorated, and he died on June 8, 1813.

LEADERSHIP LESSONS

✦

Practice and theory are not mutually exclusive, but complementary.

✦

Theory is dead without application. Application is wasteful without theory.

✦

A great leader is 90 percent mentor.

✦

Try to impart your wisdom and experience in readily accessible, instantly usable forms.

✦

Think in terms of recreating the entire organization.

Schwarzkopf, H(erbert) Norman

Born: 1934

Character model   Conqueror   Motivator   Strategist   Tactician

LEADERSHIP ACHIEVEMENTS

✦

Created a highly successful military career, balancing executive and field assignments

✦

As field commander, led the massive coalition forces to victory in the Persian Gulf War

✦

Succeeded not only in the efficient management of a monumental undertaking against Saddam Hussein, but also in presenting a strong leadership image to the American and international public

✦

Through leadership, restored American confidence in the U.S. military

LIFE

During the Persian Gulf War of 1990–91, H. Norman Schwarzkopf was one of the best-known men in America. He was the overall commander of the U.S.-led coalition forces assembled against the Iraq of Saddam Hussein.

A native of Trenton, New Jersey, Schwarzkopf was born on August 22, 1934, the son of a World War I army officer who went on to command the New Jersey State Police from 1921 to 1936 before he returned to the army during World War II. Norman Schwarzkopf enrolled in West Point, from which he graduated in 1956 and began a career marked by steady advancement. Although he held numerous high-level staff strategic and personnel management assignments, Schwarzkopf was never satisfied with a desk career and alternated his staff work with frontline field commands. He served two tours of duty in Vietnam—early in the war, as adviser to the Vietnamese Airborne (1965–66) and, later, as battalion commander in the Americal Division (1969–70). In 1974, Schwarzkopf enthusiastically accepted command of a brigade in Alaska, an assignment few coveted, in preference to manning a desk. He served in Alaska through 1976.

After Vietnam, Schwarzkopf's next combat command was as deputy commander of U.S. forces in the 1983 invasion of Grenada. Although that operation was quite successful, it revealed various logistical shortcomings, especially with regard to coordinating action among the services—army, navy, air force, and marines—which Schwarzkopf carefully analyzed. He was determined to learn from errors.

By August 1990, when the United States launched Operation Desert Shield, the preparatory response to Iraq's invasion of neighboring Kuwait, Schwarzkopf held the rank of general and was one of the most senior commanders in the U.S. military. He was assigned overall field command of a force that amounted to more than half a million men and included troops from an unprecedented coalition of 48 nations (30 of which provided military forces). On January 17, 1991, two days after the deadline set by the United Nations for Iraqi withdrawal from Kuwait, Operation Desert Shield became Operation Desert Storm, and the Persian Gulf War began.

Schwarzkopf, and his commanding officer in Washington, Joint Chiefs of Staff chairman Colin Powell, not only faced the task of commanding and coordinating a massive and diverse force, they also had to manage public fears that the United States would become mired in "another Vietnam." Since the end of that war in 1975, public attitude toward the military had often been skeptical. Many people had doubts as to the military's effectiveness and even basic competence.

Schwarzkopf directed the Gulf War to a rapid and overwhelmingly successful conclusion. After a month of sustained aerial bombardment operations, the ground phase of the war was completed in about 100 hours. Of 530,000 coalition troops engaged, 95 were killed, 368 were wounded, and 20 were reported missing in action. The coalition inflicted on the Iraqi army about 160,000 casualties, including some 50,000 killed, 50,000 wounded, and 60,000 taken prisoner.

During the entire period of the war, in both its air and ground phases, Schwarzkopf frequently briefed press conferences, projecting not only to the American public but to an international audience an image of forthrightness, determination, and consummate military competence leavened with a plain-spoken humanity. "Any soldier worth his salt," Schwarzkopf declared, "should be antiwar. And still there are things worth fighting for."

Schwarzkopf retired shortly after the conclusion of the Persian Gulf War and published a highly successful memoir, *It Doesn't Take a Hero.*

IN HIS OWN WORDS

"Leadership is a combination of strategy and character. If you must be without one, be without the strategy."

"You learn far more from negative leadership than from positive leadership. Because you learn how not to do it. And, therefore, you learn how to do it."

—Source for quotations: *It Doesn't Take a Hero: The Autobiography of H. Norman Schwarzkopf,* 1992

LEADERSHIP LESSONS
✦
Balance theory and practice.
✦
Do not allow yourself to get lost behind a desk.
✦
Share risks with those you lead.
✦
Lead from the front.
✦
Develop and project a positive leadership image.
✦
Develop effective communication with those you lead and with those to whom you report.
✦
Your single most valuable leadership asset is your *demonstrated* integrity.

Scipio Africanus Major (Publius Cornelius Scipio)

Born: 236 or 235 B.C.   Died: 184 or 183 B.C.

Conqueror   Motivator   Rescuer   Strategist   Tactician

LEADERSHIP ACHIEVEMENTS

✦

Used his family and social connections to build leadership

✦

Combined a brilliant grasp of strategy with a powerful personal command
presence and great courage

✦

Projected realistic optimism, even in the wake of disaster

✦

Refused to yield to defeat

✦

Anticipated his opponent's actions and prepared effective responses
in advance

✦

Did not allow himself to fear a legend, the mighty Hannibal

LIFE

Scipio's fame rests on his victory over the great Carthaginian commander Hannibal in the Second Punic War. It is in commemoration of this triumph that he was called Scipio Africanus.

Born into one of Rome's great patrician families, Publius Cornelius Scipio used his connections to achieve both military and political power. His father, also named Publius Cornelius Scipio, was a general and consul of 218. Young Scipio married into another prominent Roman family, taking as his bride Aemilia, daughter of Aemilius Paullus, the consul of 216, who fell at the Battle of Cannae (216).

Scipio was given his first command when he was just a teenager, a unit of cavalry at the Battle of Ticinus River (218). He accompanied his father, who had been sent to campaign against Hannibal in Spain while an army was being raised to invade Africa and attack Carthage itself. Hannibal moved so swiftly, however, that the senior Scipio had to fight a delaying action in Italy itself, along the tributaries of the River Po, until the army that was being assembled for use in Africa could join him there instead. According to possibly credible legend, at the Battle of Ticinus River, the junior Scipio saved his wounded father after he had been cut off by the enemy.

The next recorded appearance of Scipio Africanus was during the aftermath of the disastrous Battle of Cannae (216), in which Hannibal, whose forces numbered 42,000, killed some 60,000 Roman soldiers (including consul Aemilius Paullus) out of an army of 80,000. At Canusium, Scipio rallied the terror-stricken and entirely demoralized survivors of the battle, and, refusing to yield to defeat, managed to forge them into a new fighting force.

His salvage of the Cannae disaster made Scipio a very popular man, and he was elected *aedile* (magistrate) in 213. Restless in civilian life, he returned to military command when his father and his uncle, Gnaeus, were defeated and killed in Spain in 211. The Romans originally sent Gaius Claudius Nero, who had successfully retaken from Hannibal the key city of Capua, to replace the fallen brothers, but in 210, the people of Rome granted 25-year-old Scipio unprecedented proconsular powers and sent him to replace Nero.

Scipio's first priority was to reestablish Roman control north of the Ebro River. Commanding 27,500 men, he made a surprise attack on the capital city Carthago Nova (New Carthage, present-day Cartagena, Spain), laying siege to it by land as well as sea. The town fell to him in 209. Scipio next defeated Hannibal's brother Hasdrubal Barca at the Battle of Baecula, near present-day Cordova, Spain, in 208. By 206, after Scipio led a force of 48,000 to victory against 70,000 Carthaginians under Mago and Hasdrubal Gisco at the Battle of Ilipa (or Silpia), Spain was securely in Roman hands.

Returned to Rome, Scipio was elevated to consul for 205, and, despite political opposition from the ultraconservative Quintus Fabius Maximus Cunctator (Fabius Cunctator) and his adherents, he set about raising a magnificent volunteer army of 30,000 men. The force left the Sicilian port of Lilybaeum in 204, bound for an invasion of Africa and a strike at Carthage itself, for Scipio was not content to fight a defensive war. After landing near the North African city of Utica (near present-day Tunis),

Scipio fought the Battle of the Tower of Agathocles (204), pillaged the countryside, and then laid siege to Utica. At some time during the action preceding the siege, Hannibal's brother Hanno was killed. However, Hasdrubal Gisco and King Syphax of the Masaesyles approached with a large army, forcing Scipio to break off the 40-day-old siege and take up a fortified position near the coast. An armistice was agreed to, during which Scipio participated in peace negotiations—only to make a surprise nighttime attack on the Carthaginian camp, which he burned (203), butchering the enemy army as it ran, unarmed, from the flames.

Enraged by Scipio's treachery, Hasdrubal Gisco and Syphax raised another army and attacked Scipio at the Battle of Bagbrades (203). The Roman was well prepared for the onslaught, however, which he had fully anticipated. He achieved total victory and captured Syphax. The Carthaginian Senate, desperate, sued for peace—even as it summoned Hannibal and his brother Mago to return from Italy. Mago, who had been wounded in Liguria, died en route, but Hannibal was able to build an army around the 18,000 men he had brought with him from Italy. With 45,000 infantry and 3,000 cavalry, he marched from Carthage in an effort to draw the Roman forces away from that city. Scipio, who had been joined by forces under the command of the Numidian tribal leader Massinissa, pursued with 34,000 infantry and 9,000 cavalry. Following an inconclusive parley between Hannibal and Scipio, the Battle of Zama (202) commenced. Half of Hannibal's men were raw recruits, whereas Scipio commanded battle-tested veterans. He also deployed these men brilliantly, anticipating Hannibal's characteristic use of elephants. Scipio arranged his forces so that the animals could be diverted and then herded to slaughter.

As usual, Hannibal's cavalry performed valiantly, but Scipio commanded three times Hannibal's number, and, using massed force, swept Hannibal's horsemen from the field. The cost of the battle to Hannibal was 20,000 Carthaginian lives. The survivors, including Hannibal, fled to Carthage. Roman losses were trivial by comparison: 1,500 dead, 4,000 wounded. Carthage again sued for peace—this time in earnest—forfeiting its warships and elephants, agreeing to establish Massinissa as King of Numidia in place of the Carthaginian ally Syphax, and paying a heavy tribute to Rome.

Scipio Africanus returned to Rome in triumph and was elected censor (the official responsible for the census and for supervising public morals and behavior) for 199. He was also named *princeps senatus* (leader of the Senate). In 194, he was elected consul, but failed in his attempt to persuade Rome to maintain a presence in Greece so that it might curb the ambitions of Antiochus III of Syria. Scipio soon found himself the victim of his own charisma and popularity. Roman conservatives, including the powerful elder Cato, distrusted him as a potential demagogue. For his part, Scipio became disgusted with politics. Years of campaigning had taken a toll on his health, and he retired to his estate at Liternum, where he died.

LEADERSHIP LESSONS

✦

Use to the maximum whatever advantages are available to you.

✦

A leader is most valuable when circumstances are darkest. Develop permanent optimism tempered by realism.

✦

Project a winning attitude. Minimize any discussion of your doubts and misgivings. Success is an attitude.

✦

Know your opponents. Anticipate their moves. Reject plans that call for response. Act first.

✦

Do not content yourself with a defensive strategy. Identify the source of a problem, and make the source the objective of your strategy.

Seti I

Born: ca. 1339 B.C.   Died: ca. 1279 B.C.

Mentor   Rescuer   Visionary

LEADERSHIP ACHIEVEMENTS

✦

Recovered much of the territory lost by previous pharaohs

✦

Mentored his son, who became perhaps the greatest of the
Egyptian pharaohs

✦

Completed, restored, or built some of Egypt's greatest monuments

LIFE

Seti I was the son of Ramses I and the father of Ramses II. Pharaoh of the
Nineteenth Dynasty, Seti I ruled Egypt from 1290 to 1279 B.C. and is generally accepted as the true founder of the Ramessid pharaonic line. He
began his reign by recovering much of the territory lost by pharaohs of the
Eighteenth Dynasty.

In addition to restoring Egyptian glory and prosperity, Seti I was a
major advocate of the development of mines and wells. He built many fortifications to secure the Egyptian borderlands, and he set about erecting
new monuments as well as restoring and repairing existing ones, most
notably the temple at Karnak. Seti built his own funeral temple at Abydosm
and his grave site is the most impressive in the Valley of the Kings.

Seti I became one of the ancient world's great mentors by allowing his
son Ramses II to rule alongside him during the latter part of his reign.

LEADERSHIP LESSONS

✦

Emphasize creativity and productivity.

✦

Mentor your replacement.

Shaka

Born: ca. 1787   Died: 1828

Conqueror   Innovator   Motivator   Strategist   Systems creator   Tactician

LEADERSHIP ACHIEVEMENTS

◆

Combined training, motivation, and innovation to create a great
military machine

◆

Motivated a huge following

◆

Perfected the art of war in Africa

◆

Grew his realm from a small tribe to a formidable empire

◆

Let nothing stand in his way

LIFE

Shaka is probably the most celebrated of Africa's tribal rulers. He ruled
the Zulu Empire from 1816 until his death in 1828, elevating what was a
relatively minor African tribe to a position of great fame and importance.
Son of a Zulu chieftain and a princess, both of the Langeni clan, Shaka
was raised primarily by his mother. In Zulu culture, marriages were sel-
dom permanent, and Shaka's parents separated shortly after he was born.
When he was about 15 years old, Shaka was driven with his mother,
Nandi, out of the Langeni village. They found a new home among the
Dietsheni, a subclan of the Mtetwa. A few years later, Shaka was called to
render military service for his adopted clan and showed great courage and
brilliance as a soldier.

In 1816, Shaka's natural father died, and his adoptive father, a chief
among the Mtetwa, sent the young man back to the Zulus, so that he could
assume his birthright as chieftain. At this time, the Zulus were a small tribe,
with perhaps 1,500 members.

Upon taking the role of chieftain, Shaka immediately put his military
experience to work, transforming the Zulu army from a poorly armed and

inadequately trained mob into a disciplined, polished, and well-equipped professional fighting machine. Over the next several years, Zulu warriors would command respect and create fear throughout much of Africa. Shaka not only personally trained and disciplined his troops, he innovated among them. Traditionally, the warriors of southern Africa were armed with a rather small shield and a long spear made for throwing. Shaka rejected these and instead adopted a large shield that covered the entire front of the body and introduced a shorter spear that could be used for jabbing in hand-to-hand combat as well as for throwing. Shaka also examined and revised the methodology of war. Native troops in battle generally faced each other from a distance, threw their spears, jeered at each other, and then ended the fight. Typically, no clear-cut winner emerged in these contests, which partook more of ritual than of genuine warfare. In contrast to prevailing tradition, Shaka trained his men to get in close, to protect themselves with the large shield, and to slash with the short, powerful spear. He transformed ritual combat into frank warfare.

Shaka was a great systems creator. One of his most important military reforms was to introduce regimental and garrison concepts into his army. Men were domiciled, according to regiment, in separate *kraals,* or villages, which were distributed across the countryside. In this way, they formed unit identities and could also be most efficiently deployed. Beyond this, Shaka focused on offensive tactics. His most famous attack formation mimicked the shape of a bull. The army was divided into four elements: The central element, the bull's "chest," would directly engage the enemy, while the "horns" (the two elements on either side of the "chest") enveloped the foe with the object of attacking from behind. The "loins," a reserve element, backed up the "chest" and were deployed as needed.

The results of Shaka's military innovations were nothing short of overwhelming and immediate. His army conquered one clan and subclan after another. After each success, the size of the Zulu army grew, as members of the defeated clans joined Shaka. Within a very few years, the Zulu army had grown to the largest and most formidable native force in Africa. And Shaka did not hesitate to use his army. Generally, he killed any force or any person who stood in his way. In 1817, he eliminated Dingiswayo, the man directly responsible for having made him chief of the Zulus to begin with. With Dingiswayo out of the way, Shaka entirely took over leadership of the Zulus. Having achieved absolute power, he spent the next decade subduing tribe after tribe. By the 1820s, his forces had displaced or killed more than 2 million people. By the time the Boers made their Great Trek in the 1830s, much of the southern Africa they traversed had been largely depopulated.

The death of Shaka's mother, Nandi, in 1827 clearly unhinged the warrior chief, setting him off on a yearlong orgy of killing. He turned his wrath on his own people. More than 7,000 Zulus perished to appease Shaka's grief. Shaka banned the planting of crops and the drinking of milk, a staple food among the Zulus. Pregnant women were killed along with their husbands. Then Shaka once again turned to conquest. Beginning early in 1828, he committed his army to a series of hard campaigns, with no interval of rest between them. On September 22, 1828, his two half-brothers, Dingane and Mhlangana, weary of Shaka's relentless drive and the violent reprisals that had followed his mother's death, assassinated him.

LEADERSHIP LESSONS

◆

Use experience to create innovation.

◆

Think in big terms; if something needs reinventing, don't merely tinker with it.

◆

Think multidimensionally; Shaka innovated for his army in terms of equipment, training, and tactics.

Sheridan, Philip Henry

Born: 1831   Died: 1888

Character model   Mentor   Motivator   Tactician

LEADERSHIP ACHIEVEMENTS

◆

Injected into the Union military a badly needed spirit of aggression and a
will to victory

◆

Thoroughly inspired and motivated those he led

◆

Led by personal presence and direct example

◆

Embodied tremendous energy and daring

◆

Transformed the Union cavalry into a force to be reckoned with, one that
was agile, efficient, and always aggressive

◆

Was a superb subordinate commander, the tactical instrument for
accomplishing strategic ends

◆

With his Shenandoah campaign, dealt a crippling blow to the Confederacy
from which it never recovered

◆

Was a leader of blunt directness and absolute honesty, qualities that
helped earn the complete loyalty and dedication of his men

LIFE

Philip Henry Sheridan was an aggressive, highly successful, and enormously popular American military leader, whose dash and brilliance were
an inspiration to his command as well as to the nation.

He was born in Albany, New York, and graduated from West Point
in 1853, first seeing action against Indians when he served with the 1st
Infantry Regiment in Texas and the 4th Infantry in Oregon. Promoted to
first lieutenant in March 1861, Sheridan rose to captain in May of that year
and, during the Civil War, made his first serious impression on his superiors by his stellar performance in the Corinth (Mississippi) campaign of

1862. In May 1862, Sheridan was appointed colonel of the 2nd Michigan
Cavalry. An intense, direct, sometimes frankly profane man, he was especially effective at forging strong teams and leading small groups in quick,
aggressive, and efficient action. In short, he was the ideal cavalry commander—and the Union army, whose cavalry was generally far inferior to
that of the Confederates, sorely needed great cavalry commanders.

Sheridan's daring raid on Booneville, Mississippi, on July 1, 1862,
earned him promotion to brigadier general of volunteers. Next, in command of the 11th Division of the Army of the Ohio, he led with distinction
at Perryville (October 8) and at Stone's River (December 31, 1862–January
3, 1863). His aggressiveness—a willingness to fight—stood in welcome contrast to the overcaution that characterized many Union commanders, and
he was promoted to major general of volunteers in 1863.

Sheridan served with the Army of the Cumberland in the Tullahoma
campaign of 1863 and then led the XX Corps to support General George
Henry Thomas in the extraordinarily bloody Battle of Chickamauga during September 19–20. His aggressive rearguard action covering Thomas's
retreat was responsible for saving much of that general's command.

At the Battle of Chattanooga, during November 24–25, 1863,
Sheridan led a gallant—and highly effective—charge up Missionary Ridge.
By April 1864, his record of skillful aggression and boundless energy—and
his demonstrated ability to inoculate his men with these very qualities—
earned Sheridan appointment as commander of Cavalry Corps, Army of
the Potomac. In this capacity, Sheridan fought directly under Ulysses S.
Grant in the Battle of the Wilderness (May 5–6) and at Spotsylvania Court
House (May 8–18). His raid against rebel lines of supply and communications during Spotsylvania resulted directly in the defeat of J. E. B. Stuart at
Todd's Tavern on May 7 and, again, at Yellow Tavern on May 11. For
Union cavalry to hold its own, let alone defeat Confederate cavalry, was a
tremendous achievement—one not only of tactical and strategic value, but
of immeasurable value to Union morale.

Assigned to destroy rail lines near Charlottesville, Virginia, Sheridan
successfully engaged Confederate units at Haw's Shop on May 28 and at
Trevilian Station on June 11–12. After this, in August, he was assigned
command of Union forces in the Shenandoah Valley and conducted his
finest campaign of the war. The Shenandoah was the breadbasket of the

Confederacy and was also a back door to Washington, D.C. As long as the Confederates controlled the valley, they had a source of food and a means of menacing the Union capital. Sheridan's victories at the Battle of Winchester on September 19, 1864, and at Fisher's Hill on September 22 freed up his army to burn a swath of destruction through the Shenandoah, which rendered it useless to the Confederates. It was a tremendously crippling blow.

Sheridan was promoted to brigadier general of regulars in September 1864. Later that month, while he was absent from his army, it was hit by a surprise attack at Cedar Creek, Virginia. As soon as he got word of the attack, Sheridan galloped 20 miles to take personal command of the battle—an action immortalized as Sheridan's Ride. The general quickly rallied and regrouped his forces, then leading them in a counterattack that drove the Confederates off. It was an example of personal leadership in the tradition of no less a figure than George Washington.

In November 1864, Sheridan was promoted to major general of regulars and, in February 1865, ceremonially received the thanks of Congress. He went on to raid Petersburg, Virginia, during February 27–March 24. Linking up with Grant's main force, he turned Robert E. Lee's flank at the climactic Battle of Five Forks on April 1 and then engaged Lee's rear guard at Sayler's Creek on April 6. This blocked Lee's only avenue of retreat at Appomattox Court House, where, on April 9, the Confederate commander at long last surrendered his Army of Northern Virginia to General Grant, for all practical purposes bringing the Civil War to an end.

In May 1865, Sheridan was named to command the Military Division of the Gulf, and in March 1867 he was appointed commander of the Fifth Military District, to which was added the vast Department of the Missouri in September. In this capacity, Sheridan initiated a campaign against the Indian tribes of the Washita Valley in Oklahoma during 1868–69. In March 1869, Sheridan was promoted to lieutenant general with command of the Division of the Missouri. He was detached from this post during the Franco–Prussian War of 1870–71 and sent to Europe as an observer and as a liaison officer with the Prussians, bringing back to the United States a wealth of military information and advice.

During 1876–77, Sheridan directed the campaign against the Southern Plains Indians and then became commander of the Military Divisions of the West and Southwest in 1878. In November 1883, he replaced his former commander, mentor, and friend William Tecumseh Sherman as commanding general of the U.S. Army. He was promoted in rank to full general just two months before his death.

Sheridan was a great military leader, who combined boundless energy and a will to utmost aggressiveness with an ability to motivate and inspire his men. He was, moreover, a great tactician—indeed, a far more able tactician than strategist. Without question, he was a highly effective leader of small forces. Fortunately, when he was given command of larger units, his assignment, as in the Shenandoah Valley, was still tactical rather than strategic in nature. As such, he accomplished it brilliantly.

Like Sherman, for better or worse, he embraced war in all of its grim reality, which meant that, like Sherman, Sheridan advocated and was willing to carry out "total war"—that is, combat against civilian as well as military objectives. This was demonstrated in the destructiveness of the Shenandoah Campaign during the Civil War and in the ruthless policies by which he later conducted warfare against the Indians in the West. Sheridan was famous—or infamous—for his policy of fighting Indians in a series of winter campaigns precisely because combat was more brutal and effective against them during the hard winter months. And that combat was also hard on his own troops—yet, no matter what he called upon them to do, Sheridan's soldiers greatly loved him. A man of slight stature, he was affectionately dubbed "Little Phil" by his command, who appreciated his loyalty and his frank, blunt-spoken wit. Sheridan once summed up his service in Texas by quipping, "If I owned both Hell and Texas, I'd rent out Texas and live in Hell."

IN HIS OWN WORDS

"Men who march, scout, and fight, and suffer all the hardships that fall to the lot of soldiers in the field, in order to do vigorous work must have the best bodily sustenance, and every comfort that can be provided. I knew from practical experience on the frontier that my efforts in this direction would not only be appreciated, but requited by personal affection and gratitude; and, further, that such exertions would bring the best results to me."

—*Personal Memoirs,* 1888

"I do not advise rashness, but I do desire resolute and actual fighting, with necessary casualties."
—Official communication of September 23, 1864

"I already knew that even in the ordinary condition of mind enthusiasm is a potent element with soldiers, but what I saw that day [at the Battle of Cedar Creek] convinced me that if it can be excited from a state of despondency its power is almost irresistible. I said nothing except to remark, as I rode among those on the road: 'If I had been with you this morning this disaster would not have happened. We must face the other way; we will go back and recover our camp.'"
—*Personal Memoirs,* 1888

"Those who live at home in peace and plenty want the *duello* part of this war to go on; but when they have to bear the burden by loss of property or comforts, they will cry for peace."
—Telegram to Major General Henry W. Halleck during the Shenandoah
  Campaign, November 26, 1864

"A prompt and vigorous pursuit is the only means of ensuring complete success."
—Quoted in Peter G. Tsouras, *The Greenhill Dictionary of Military Quotations,* 2000

LEADERSHIP LESSONS

✦

There is no substitute for focused energy and an ability to communicate
that energy to those you lead.

✦

Aggression driving skill is a formula for victory.

✦

Understand the differences between strategy and tactics. Most leaders
overemphasize strategy at the sometimes fatal expense of tactics.

✦

Nothing is more compelling than leadership by direct personal example.

✦

Put the needs of those you lead first and foremost.

✦

Face the truth, and speak the truth. Evasion is often easier in the short
term, but it cannot sustain an enterprise.

Sherman, William Tecumseh

Born: 1820   Died: 1891

Conqueror   Innovator   Leverager   Mentor   Motivator   Strategist   Tactician

LEADERSHIP ACHIEVEMENTS

◆

Was a highly skilled, able, and courageous field commander

◆

Overcame serious failure to achieve military greatness

◆

Brought to combat an uncompromising vision of the realities of war

◆

Established goals and objectives with regard only for the mission
and none for sentiment

◆

Innovated a winning strategy for the late phase of the Civil War

LIFE

William Tecumseh Sherman's uncompromising view of war and combat made him a controversial figure in his day and still sparks debate among military historians. He is an example of a mission-oriented leader of ruthless efficiency in an age when many military men preferred to camouflage their profession in the glittering trappings and hollow rhetoric of glory.

Born in Lancaster, Ohio, Sherman was the son of an Ohio Supreme Court judge. His father's prominence enabled him to obtain an appointment to West Point, from which he graduated in 1840 as a second lieutenant of artillery. His efficient performance in Florida during action against the Seminoles earned him rapid promotion to first lieutenant in November 1841. With the outbreak of the U.S.–Mexican War, Sherman was posted to the staff of Stephen Watts Kearny, but was disappointed to see no combat during the conflict because he was assigned as an administrative officer in California until that territory joined the Union in 1848. Despite promotion to captain, his subsequent assignment, in September 1850, as a commissary (supply) officer, was equally unfulfilling. Like many other young men in the

19th-century peacetime U.S. Army, Sherman became sufficiently discouraged with his career that he resigned his commission.

In 1853, he started a building firm, but this business failed, and he moved to Leavenworth, Kansas, where he set up as a lawyer in 1857. Enjoying little success as an attorney, Sherman found great satisfaction as superintendent of the newly established Alexandria Military Academy in Baton Rouge, Louisiana. This institution would later become the Louisiana Military Academy, and, finally, Louisiana State University. Sherman served as its first superintendent from October 1859 until January 1861, when it became clear to him that the nation was about to fight a civil war. He resigned to go back to the North and, in May 1861, returned to active military duty as colonel of the 13th Infantry.

Sherman commanded a brigade at the First Battle of Bull Run on July 21, and in August became a brigadier general of volunteers. In October, he was assigned to command all Union forces in the border state of Kentucky. This duty brought on the most serious crisis of Sherman's military career. He faltered badly in this assignment and seemed on the verge of a nervous collapse. Many of his colleagues believed that he had become mentally unhinged and that, certainly, his military career was at an end. Sherman's emotional crisis seems to have been brought about by his penetrating insight into the Civil War. All around him, politicians and even military men who should have known better deluded themselves with the belief that the war would be brief and that the rebellion would, in fact, soon collapse. In contrast, Sherman faced the truth of what he saw as a new kind of war, a war in which troops were equipped with mass-produced weapons of unprecedented destructiveness, a war in which both sides were prepared to commit massive numbers of men. What convinced a number of Sherman's military colleagues that he was clearly insane was his assessment of the time and human resources the war would consume. Whereas others spoke of weeks or months and thousands of troops, Sherman talked in terms of years and tens, even hundreds of thousands of men. Time, of course, would prove him correct.

Fortunately for Sherman—and for the Union cause—his superiors maintained faith in him, and, in November, he was transferred to the Western Department, where he quickly pulled himself together. In February 1862, Sherman was assigned as a division commander in the

Army of the Tennessee, commanded by Ulysses S. Grant. At the horrific Battle of Shiloh, during April 6–7, Sherman's calm heroism and firm leadership in midst of a confusing and unprecedentedly destructive battle wholly redeemed him after his Kentucky difficulties. In May, he was promoted to major general of volunteers and fought under Grant in the Corinth (Mississippi) campaign during May–June, and then began operations against the fortified Mississippi River town of Vicksburg.

During the Vicksburg campaign, Sherman suffered a defeat at Chickasaw Bluffs on December 29, which stopped his advance. Transferred to command of XV Corps, Army of the Mississippi, he took Arkansas Post on January 11, 1863, then transferred with XV Corps to the Army of the Tennessee. With this army, he returned to the Vicksburg front to support Grant's siege of the town during January 1863–July 1864. He took Jackson, Mississippi, on May 14.

In July 1864, Sherman was promoted to brigadier general of regulars and rushed to the relief of William Rosecrans at Chattanooga. After Grant's promotion to general in chief of the Union armies, Sherman succeeded him as commander of the Army of the Tennessee in October. He brilliantly coordinated with George Henry Thomas's Army of the Cumberland and was in command of the Union left at the important Battle of Chattanooga during November 24–25. In December, he marched to the relief of Ambrose Burnside, who was besieged in Knoxville. It was characteristic of Sherman that he was, in his own right, a highly efficient and aggressive commander, but, in contrast to many other aggressive leaders, he was also very much a team player, who was willing to coordinate action with other commanders and, if necessary, play a subordinate role. His objective was always to accomplish the mission, never to achieve personal glory.

Named commander of the Military Division of the Mississippi in March 1864, Sherman now led three armies: those of the Cumberland, the Tennessee, and the Ohio. Previous commanders had made the strategic error of spreading their forces broadly and thinly in the belief that victory was proportional to the amount of territory controlled. Like Grant, Sherman embraced a radical revision of the doctrine of controlling territory. He reasoned that the war would be won not by taking land, but by destroying the enemy army. Accordingly, instead of dividing his forces, he consolidated them—some 100,000 men—and focused them in a spectacular drive toward the fortress city of Atlanta, coordinating this advance with Grant's ongoing advance against the Confederate capital, Richmond.

Sherman had a reputation for being a fierce warrior. But he also made use of his experience as a logistics officer, and emerged not only as a great combat leader, but as an extraordinary manager. He led his army in an unremitting 100-mile advance in the space of 74 days, pushing before him the army of Confederate general J. E. Johnston. During this time, he fought major battles at Dalton, Georgia, on May 8–12; at Resaca, on May 15–16; at New Hope Church, on May 24–28; and at Dallas, on May 25–28, as he closed in on Atlanta. Although he suffered a reverse at Kennesaw Mountain on June 27, he beat John Bell Hood at the Battle of Peachtree Creek, just outside of Atlanta, on July 20. Northwest of the city, he defeated the rebels at the Battle of Ezra Church on July 28, and, on September 2, occupied the city of Atlanta itself, a key military position and a major rail hub.

Sherman's attitude toward the citizens of Atlanta was typically uncompromising, yet not gratuitously brutal. He wrote an extraordinary reply to the city's mayor, who had begged him to rescind his order to evacuate the city:

> . . . I assert that our military plans make it necessary for the inhabitants to go away . . .
>
> You cannot qualify war in harsher terms than I will. War is cruelty, and you cannot refine it. And those who brought war into our country deserve all the curses and maledictions a people can pour out. I know I had no hand in making this war, and I know I will make more sacrifices today than any of you to secure peace. But you cannot have peace and a division of our country. . . .
>
> You might as well appeal against the thunderstorm as against the terrible hardships of war. They are inevitable, and the only way the people of Atlanta can hope once more to live in peace and quiet at home is to stop the war. . . .
>
> . . . I want peace, and I believe it can only be reached through union and war; and I will ever conduct war purely with a view to perfect an early success. But, my dear sirs, when peace does come, you may call on me for anything. Then will I share with you the last cracker, and watch with you to shield your homes and families against danger from every quarter.

Now you must go, and take with you the old and feeble, feed and
nurse them, and build for them in more quiet places proper habitations
to shield them against the weather until the mad passions of men cool
down and allow the Union and peace once more to settle over your
old homes at Atlanta.

Perhaps Sherman's greatest strength as a leader was his ability and willingness to face, without flinching, the bare truth of a situation.

Atlanta was, of course, subsequently destroyed by a fire, for which
Sherman's troops may or may not have been responsible. Whoever actually set the blaze—Union troops or Confederate soldiers or civilians—the
fire was an all too fitting prelude to the devastation that followed.

Sherman led his forces in what must be called a campaign of "total
war," carrying combat beyond the enemy army and to the civilian population. He decided to "march to the sea," cutting along the way a broad swath
of devastation. The purpose of this controversial strategy was multifold:
Sherman intended to destroy as much infrastructure and supply as possible; he hoped, too, to undermine the very will of the South to continue
fighting; he wanted to demonstrate to the people of the South that their
government was truly illegitimate, in that it was incapable of protecting its
citizens; and, finally, he wanted to force combat with, so that he could
destroy, whatever units came to defend against his destructive course.

The infamous March to the Sea commenced on November 16.
Sherman's soldiers looted and destroyed all that lay before them. His army
occupied Savannah on December 21, 1864, after which Sherman started
up the coast, to the Carolinas, beginning a drive on February 1, 1865, that
culminated in the capture and burning of Columbia, South Carolina, on
February 17. (Although this fire was blamed on Sherman's troops, it is more
likely that retreating rebel troops set the blaze.)

Sherman successfully repulsed a surprise attack by General Johnston
at Bentonville, North Carolina, during March 19–20, and then went on to
capture Raleigh on April 13. Two weeks later, on April 26, he received
Johnston's surrender near Durham Station, North Carolina. With Grant's
acceptance of Robert E. Lee's surrender at Appomattox (on April 9), this
victory marked the end of the Civil War.

After the war, in June 1865, Sherman was appointed commander of
the Division of the Missouri and was promoted to lieutenant general of reg-

ulars in July 1866. From his headquarters in Chicago, he directed much of the strategy and policy during the Indian Wars, although he personally participated in no battles. In November 1869, he became commanding general of the army and received a promotion to general. He retired in 1884.

Sherman published a frank and very well-written memoir in 1875, and, anxious to educate the officers of the American army in the realities of war, he created a still-important army officer training center at Fort Leavenworth, Kansas, in 1884. The Republican Party pressed Sherman to become their candidate for president in the 1884 election, but Sherman, who distrusted politics and politicians as inherently dishonest, declined the nomination. As a leader, Sherman combined intelligence, honesty, and insight with a will to ruthlessness. What he understood above all else is that the essence of war is destruction, and this was the basis of his conception of a professional soldier. In his duties after the war, he brought a large measure of reality to military training. While he remains a controversial figure, his men never doubted him, but were always intensely loyal to the man they called "Uncle Billy."

LEADERSHIP LESSONS

✦

A leader needs clear goals and a clear vision of them.

✦

Leadership requires a firm willingness to see, to accept, and to exploit the truth and its consequences.

✦

A great leader not only understands and accepts the reality of a given situation, but persuasively communicates his understanding to others.

Simeon I

Born: ca. 864   Died: 927

Conqueror   Mentor   Rescuer   Visionary

LEADERSHIP ACHIEVEMENTS

✦

Rescued Bulgaria from the tyranny and oppression created by his brother

✦

Asserted the power of the Bulgars against that of the more established
Byzantines

✦

Greatly expanded the Bulgar empire and its influence

✦

Introduced the best of Greek culture into Bulgarian culture,
thereby invigorating both

✦

Increased learning within his empire

LIFE

Little known in the West, Simeon I was the greatest of the Bulgar rulers. He challenged the vast Byzantine Empire and came to dominate the Balkans. His drive to conquer was founded on a powerful set of values acquired early in life. Although he was born and raised in Constantinople, capital of the Byzantine Empire, Simeon was irresistibly drawn to Greek culture and ideas, and he came to despise everything Byzantine. When Simeon's father, Boris I, abdicated the Bulgar throne in 889 in favor of his eldest son, Vladimir, Bulgaria found itself under the heel of a ruthless tyrant, whose cruelty was gratuitous and who forcibly imposed paganism on the Bulgars. Appalled, Boris returned from monastic retirement and overthrew Vladimir in 893, and then installed Simeon in his place.

The new emperor did not disappoint his father. He rescinded his brother's oppressive edicts, and then set about extending the Bulgar Empire, ultimately raising it to its zenith. To the west, he conquered territory on the Adriatic Sea, defeating the Serbs and taking possession of the southern regions of Macedonia and Albania. This accomplished, he decided to pursue his most-cherished ambition: the conquest of the Byzantine Empire.

Beginning in 894, Simeon led at least five—perhaps more—separate campaigns against the Hungarian Magyars and the Byzantines, more than once defeating both. Despite his victories, he never succeeded in wholly subjugating the Byzantines, and he failed to capture Constantinople. Simeon also suffered a serious setback in losing Bulgaria's prosperous lands north of the Danube River. At last, after he had invested huge sums of money, men, and materiel on his Byzantine campaigns, Simeon acknowledged their failure. Determined as he had been to conquer Byzantium, he had no desire to ruin Bulgaria. He turned instead to the Turks, enjoying moderate success against them, by which he acquired some eastern territory by a treaty of 924. This compensated Bulgaria for some of its losses, and it allowed Simeon to save face. Thus bolstered, he solidified his leadership image by declaring himself czar—emperor—of all the Bulgarians and Greeks.

As czar, Simeon elevated the archbishop of Bulgaria to the rank of patriarch, thereby asserting Bulgarian dominance over the Greek Orthodox Church, but also promoting Greek culture throughout the Balkans. Simeon did not use force to inculcate the values he cherished, but did use his authority to commission and support scholars in producing translations of Greek works into Slavonic. Simeon's wish was to borrow the best from Greek culture to invigorate Bulgar culture. Accordingly, he also helped to establish a Bulgarian literature and culture independent from Greek models.

Simeon died on May 27, 927, and was succeeded by his second son, Peter I.

LEADERSHIP LESSONS

✦

Embody personal values creatively in leadership policies and goals.

✦

Know when to cut your losses. Determination is valuable in a leader, but even a determined effort should cease before irreparable damage is done.

✦

Observe the law of compensation. Errors and losses in one area may be counterbalanced by gains in other areas.

✦

Minds and hearts are far more effectively influenced by intellectual and emotional means than by force. Educate those you lead.

Sitting Bull
(Tatanka Yotanka)

Born: ca. 1831   Died: 1890

Character model   Mentor   Visionary

LEADERSHIP ACHIEVEMENTS

◆

Was one of a group of Indian leaders responsible for the Sioux's reputation
as mighty warriors

◆

Inspired those he led to maintain tribal identity and pride

◆

Won the respect of Indians and whites alike

◆

Came to symbolize the dignity of the Plains Indian

◆

Led his people through tragic times

LIFE

The dignity, courage, spiritual presence, and moral force of this Hunkpapa
Sioux chief and medicine man made him the most famous Indian warrior-
leader in American history. A member of the Hunkpapa tribe, a branch of
the Teton Sioux, Sitting Bull was born on the Grand River in South
Dakota, the son of a renowned chief. He showed leadership qualities from
an early age. He was famed as a hunter by the time he was 10 years old,
and he had distinguished himself on the field of battle by 14. By 1856, he
was a prominent member of the Strong Heart warrior lodge. But his first
major engagement against white settlers came in the Minnesota Sioux
Uprising of 1862–63, which began with an attack against settlers in New
Ulm. On July 28, 1864, Sitting Bull led the Battle of Killdear Mountain
(North Dakota), fighting troops under General Alfred Sully. It was Sitting
Bull who represented Indian interests in concluding the generally favorable
Treaty of Fort Laramie in 1868.

Unfortunately, like most Indian–white agreements during the period
of the western Indian Wars, the Fort Laramie peace did not long endure.

When prospectors began to invade the Black Hills—country sacred to the Sioux—after gold was discovered there in 1874, Sitting Bull was elevated to chief of the war council of combined Sioux, Cheyenne, and Arapaho in Montana. He did not participate in combat against George Armstrong Custer at the Battle of the Little Bighorn on June 25, 1876, but, as medicine man, he "made the medicine" that made the triumph possible.

To avoid reprisals after the Little Bighorn, Sitting Bull led most of the Hunkpapa to Canada in May 1877. Life there was hard on the Hunkpapa, who suffered greatly from hunger and disease; however, the people remained loyal to their leader, who kept them together. At length, Sitting Bull brought the Hunkpapa back to the United States, where he and 170 followers surrendered at Fort Buford, North Dakota, in July 1881 and submitted to life on a reservation. As for Sitting Bull, he was held at Fort Randall, South Dakota, from 1881 to 1883 before he was placed at Standing Rock Reservation, North Dakota. During this period, Sitting Bull became an advocate of traditional Sioux culture, which he struggled to maintain against the inexorable incursions of the whites. He did befriend and respect at least one white man—William "Buffalo Bill" Cody—who recruited him as a performer in his Wild West Show during 1885–86.

Back on the reservation after his stint with Buffalo Bill, Sitting Bull supported the Native religious revival called the Ghost Dance movement during 1889–90. Sitting Bull believed that the Ghost Dance would give back to the Indians some of the dignity, identity, and hope they had lost. The U.S. government, however, feared the Ghost Dance as a threat to order and anticipated an uprising. When it was decided to arrest Sitting Bull, Native American reservation police officers were dispatched to his home on the Grand River, South Dakota. A scuffle and something approaching a riot broke out during the arrest, and the Hunkpapa leader was slain with two of his sons on December 15, 1890.

Sitting Bull commanded the respect and even awe not only of the Sioux he led, but of other Indians and many whites. He acquired his reputation through courageous and wise performance, and then maintained his leadership position by offering a continual example of steadfast courage and a refusal to yield. The values of Native American identity he held were never compromised.

LEADERSHIP LESSONS

✦

The most powerful leadership technique is personal example.

✦

A leader resolves to be a leader in everything he says and does.

✦

A great leader identifies completely with those he leads.

✦

An effective leader never attempts to divorce personal destiny from the
collective destiny of the enterprise.

✦

Integrity is the single most valuable leadership asset.

✦

A great leader mirrors and models the collective identity of the group.

Solomon

Reigned: ca. 965 B.C.–ca. 925 B.C.

Conqueror   Problem solver   Profit maker   Strategist   Systems creator

LEADERSHIP ACHIEVEMENTS

◆

Vastly expanded the kingdom of Israel, largely through nonmilitary means

◆

Created a rational government for his kingdom

◆

Left an enduring poetic, philosophical, and spiritual legacy preserved
in the Old Testament

LIFE

Solomon was the son of King David and Bathsheba. In an effort to unite the disparate tribes of Israel, David had married wives of varied clans. This did help to unify the kingdom, but it also created a great deal of dissension and intrigue within the palace. As David's other children vied for succession to the throne, David sought to preempt strife by abdicating in favor of Solomon, thereby eliminating any question of succession.

Immediately after he became king, Solomon embarked on a campaign to enlarge an empire his father had already made great. The program of expansion was largely nonmilitary; instead, Solomon vigorously made marital arrangements with the daughters of kings and leaders of other nations. King Solomon is said to have had 700 wives and 300 concubines. For him, as for his father, marriage was largely an instrument of power and the acquisition of territory. For example, through his alliance with the daughter of the pharaoh, Solomon was able to acquire the seaport of Eziongeber on the Gulf of Aqaba, which gave him direct access to the Red Sea and the Indian Ocean beyond. Among the great powers of the day, only Egypt itself had access to both the Indian Ocean and the Mediterranean Sea. This advantageous trade location, at the junction of Africa and Asia, put Israel in a powerful position among the world's leading nations.

The rapid growth of Solomon's empire called for the erection of strong defenses, which prompted the king to embark on a massive building program that, in time, severely taxed his kingdom's resources. He built a new wall around the capital city of Jerusalem, he built fortified cities at Hazor, Megiddo, and Gazer, and he expanded the armed forces. Solomon's building program also included nonmilitary projects, such as the great Temple at Jerusalem, a structure that would become a central shrine in both Judaism and, centuries later, early Christianity.

Solomon, whose very name would become a byword for wisdom, was one of history's great designers of systems. He divided his empire into 12 districts (these were in no way related to the historic 12 tribes of Israel), and then set up a schedule whereby, for one month per year, each district was required to finance the cost of running the government. This arrangement brought an unprecedented degree of administrative order to the empire. The great empire endured through the reign of Solomon, but, on his death, his son and successor, Rehoboam, proved unable to maintain the unity of the empire. A northern nation of Israel was organized by the most disaffected elements, leaving only the southern portion, henceforth called Judah, for Solomon's descendants.

If Solomon's empire failed to outlive him, the king's verse and parables were immortalized in the Old Testament. Some biblical scholars believe that Solomon wrote at least 4,500 poems and parables.

LEADERSHIP LESSONS

✦

Look for opportunities to make strategic alliances.

✦

Devote time and effort to the creation of workable systems to maintain the enterprise.

✦

Protect and defend the enterprise.

✦

Beware of growing the enterprise beyond its financial means.

Solon

Born: ca. 638 B.C. Died: ca. 559 B.C.

**Character model   Innovator   Motivator   Problem solver
Systems creator   Visionary**

LEADERSHIP ACHIEVEMENTS

✦

Democratized ancient Athens

✦

Transformed society by redistributing land in Athens

✦

Created a body of wise, equitable law

✦

Created an innovative and visionary government

✦

Employed a persuasive personal leadership style based on character and
eloquence

✦

Was a mentor to his people

LIFE

The Athenian lawgiver, political reformer, and poet Solon has been called
the father of democracy. His ancestors were nobles and he himself claimed
descent from the last king of Athens, yet his own parents were of modest
means and station. Solon first made a name for himself when Athens
warred with Megara in about 600 B.C., in a contest to determine which
state would rule Salamis. When most Athenians were ready to give up the
fight, Solon persuaded them, through eloquently patriotic poetry, to persevere. After a long struggle, Athens did prevail. Throughout his political
career, Solon would use verse to persuade, instruct, and guide. Long after
his death and even after the demise of some of his political innovations,
Solon's poetry survived, and Greek schoolchildren often memorized the
more popular verses.

The Salamis episode catapulted Solon to the post of chief archon of
Athens. From this powerful political position, he immediately set about

reforming the Athenian constitution, working to devise a democracy that would treat the poorer classes more equitably. In Solon's day, Greek society was divided between wealthy landowners and poor peasants, many of whom had sold themselves into slavery. Debt among these peasants was rampant and crushing. The situation of the poor was all but hopeless, as few could expect ever to work themselves out of poverty. Solon attacked this problem first by canceling all debts that had enslavement as collateral. He also set limits on the amount of land that any one owner could possess, thereby effecting a land distribution program, which allowed the poorer classes an opportunity to acquire property.

The great wealth of many landowners had been built on the massive exportation of grain, even though the poorer people were faced with a food shortage at home. To remedy this situation, Solon banned export of all Athenian products except olive oil, which was produced in abundance. He then divided all Athenian citizens into four classes, according to wealth, and directed that members of each group would be qualified to serve in the government; furthermore, they would all pay taxes based on their ability to contribute.

Many of Solon's constitutional changes were indeed revolutionary. He enfranchised the peasants, allowed representatives of all four classes to serve in the judiciary system, reduced the autocratic power of the council of former rulers, and instituted a method of selection of officials by election and by lot. Unfortunately, Solon's new regulations and constitutional changes were not welcomed by the elite, a class unwilling to relinquish any of its privileges. Solon boldly decided to withdraw from political life for a period, in order to allow time for his innovations to gain acceptance. For the next decade, he absented himself from Athens entirely, touring Egypt, Cyprus, and many countries in Asia Minor. By the time he returned, the Athenian populace was more or less reconciled to his reforms.

In 561 B.C., at an advanced age, Solon once again took up politics in an unsuccessful effort to block a new tyranny instituted by his friend Pisistratus. Nevertheless, after his death, Solon was honored as one of the Seven Sages of Greece, and his ashes were scattered over Salamis. In modern times, Solon's name became a byword for a wise lawgiver.

LEADERSHIP LESSONS

✦

Communication and expression are critical to leadership; a leader must explain and persuade.

✦

A leader is a mentor—in the case of Solon, a mentor to the masses.

✦

Persuasion in leadership sometimes includes knowing when to withdraw, to allow people to evaluate your proposals and directions.

✦

Leadership in democracy requires informed empowerment of people.

✦

Design for the "big picture." Solon recognized that he could change Athenian politics and society only by radically reshaping land ownership in the nation.

Stilwell, Joseph Warren

Born: 1883   Died: 1946

**Character model   Improviser   Leverager   Mentor   Motivator
Problem solver   Strategist   Tactician**

LEADERSHIP ACHIEVEMENTS

◆

Mentored a generation of West Point cadets

◆

Studied China before World War II, thereby providing a rare and valuable
advantage in the China-Burma-India (CBI) theater when war broke out

◆

Learned from failure

◆

Was a magnificent leverager of inadequate resources in the CBI

LIFE

Dubbed "Vinegar Joe" because of his acidic, tell-it-like-it-is approach to difficult situations, Joseph Warren Stilwell was the American commander of the
always hard-pressed and under-supplied China-Burma-India front in World
War II. Born in Palatka, Florida, Stilwell was raised in Yonkers, New York,
and graduated from West Point in June 1904. Commissioned a second lieutenant in the infantry, he asked to be posted to the Philippines, where he
served with the 12th Infantry Regiment there. He saw his first combat on the
island of Samar against the rebel Puljanes during February–April 1905.

Stilwell returned to West Point as a foreign language instructor in
February 1906 and soon discovered his natural talent for teaching. From
March 1906 to January 1911, in addition to teaching languages, he taught
history and tactics and he coached athletics. On January 11, 1911, he trans-
ferred back to the Philippines, where he was promoted to first lieutenant.
It was during November–December that he visited China for the first time.

From 1913 to 1916, Stilwell was back at West Point as a language
instructor. He was promoted to captain in September 1916 and in July
1917 was made brigade adjutant in the 80th Division, an assignment that

carried a promotion to temporary major. After the United States entered World War I, Stilwell shipped out to France in January 1918 as a staff intelligence officer. During March 20–April 28, he was attached to the French XVII Corps near Verdun, and then received an assignment as deputy chief of staff for intelligence under General Joseph T. Dickman in IV Corps during the Meuse-Argonne campaign (September 26–November 11). He was promoted to temporary lieutenant colonel on September 11, 1918, and then to temporary colonel in October. After the armistice, he served in occupation duties until May 1919.

Stilwell loved active service abroad, and while most of his colleagues were aching to return to the States, Stilwell requested an assignment to China as a language officer. He served there from August 6, 1919, to July of 1923, using this time to make an ally of the influential warlord Feng Yu-hsiang.

When he returned to the United States in 1923, Stilwell enrolled in Infantry School at Fort Benning, graduating in 1924, and then took the advanced course at the Command and General Staff School at Fort Leavenworth from 1925 to 1926. With this preparation, he was returned to China to command a battalion of the 15th Infantry at Tientsin in August 1926. During this period, he met George C. Marshall, who was also serving in China and destined to become the U.S. Army chief of staff during World War II. Promoted to lieutenant colonel in March 1928, Stilwell became head of the tactical section of the Infantry School in July 1929, largely because of Marshall's recommendation.

Stilwell left the Infantry School in 1933 to become training officer for the IX Corps reserves from 1933 to 1935. After this, he was appointed military attaché to China and was promoted to colonel on August 1, 1935. Stilwell understood the strategic importance of China, and he used his assignments there to make himself intimately familiar with vast regions of the country. Of particular concern to him was the Sino–Japanese War, in which Stilwell correctly saw the development of Japanese imperialism—as well as the awesome capabilities of the Japanese army.

Stilwell returned to the United States in 1939 and received his promotion to brigadier general while en route on May 4, 1939. He was assigned command of the 3d Brigade, 2nd Division in September 1939. He played a major role in the Third Army's maneuvers of January 1940, and then commanded the "red" forces in the massive Louisiana-Texas maneuvers of May 1940. Stilwell distinguished himself in these prewar maneuvers, gaining attention for his ability to move troops quickly and in unexpected ways. On the strength of his performance, he was assigned to command, on July 1, 1940, the newly created 7th Division stationed at Fort Ord, California. Promoted to temporary major general in September 1940, he was moved up to command of III Corps in July 1941.

After the Japanese attack on Pearl Harbor brought the United States into World War II, Stilwell was promoted to lieutenant general and, in January 1942, was appointed to command U.S. Army forces in the China-Burma-India (CBI) theater. Given the rapid and overwhelming Japanese advances in this theater and the paucity of Allied men and supplies, it was a highly unenviable but crucially important assignment. Stilwell possessed the unique combination of thorough familiarity with the region, fluency in Chinese, and a flair for leveraging resources and moving troops with great efficiency and imagination.

He set up a headquarters at Chungking (Chongqing), China, where he quickly made an ally of Chiang Kai-shek, the Chinese nationalist generalissimo. Chiang Kai-shek turned over to Stilwell command of Chinese forces in Burma on March 6, 1942. A few days later, on March 11, Stilwell arrived in Burma with a single Chinese division. Subsequently, with great energy and initiative, he raised eight more divisions.

Like his British counterpart in the CBI theater, General Sir William Slim, Stilwell suffered from chronic shortages of supplies and reinforcements. He also had to contend with conflicting directives from Chiang Kai-shek. Ultimately, he was forced to withdraw from Burma to India during May 11–30. In talking to politicians, fellow commanders, and the press about this defeat, he pulled no punches—and thereby earned his "Vinegar Joe" moniker. He emerged from the experience determined to make the most of what he had, which required carefully training and equipping three Chinese divisions in India and then creating "the Hump," a stupendously hazardous airlift chain over the Himalayas to supply Kunming during January–February 1943. He was determined not to allow the Japanese to cut off Burma or China. But he needed time to prepare a credible force, lest the Allies suffer further defeats.

In July 1943, Stilwell was appointed deputy supreme Allied commander in the CBI theater under Lord Louis Mountbatten. The common-man background and "vinegar" personality of Joe Stilwell differed sharply from the patrician charm of Mountbatten, but the two greatly respected one another and worked brilliantly together. Mountbatten endorsed Stilwell's plan for the Salween-Myitkyina-Mogaung offensive of March–August 1944, aimed at retaking Burma. It proved a hard-won success, ending in the capture of Myitkyina on August 3 and the subsequent liberation of all northern Burma.

Following this major breakthrough in the CBI theater, Stilwell was promoted to temporary general. However, he found it impossible to maintain a productive working relationship with the supremely difficult Chiang Kai-shek. At Chiang's request, President Franklin D. Roosevelt regretfully recalled Stilwell to the States on October 19, 1944. Here he was named commander of Army Ground Forces on January 23, 1945, and was decorated with the Legion of Merit and the Oak Leaf cluster of the Distinguished Service Medal (DSM) on February 10, 1945. Dispatched to Okinawa, Stilwell took command of the Tenth Army there on June 23 and was among those present at the Japanese surrender ceremony in Tokyo Bay on September 2, 1945.

After V-J Day, Stilwell became president of the War Equipment Board and then commander of the Sixth Army and the Western Defense Command in January 1946. His career and life were cut short, later in the year, when he succumbed to cancer of the stomach.

Before his recall to the United States, Vinegar Joe Stilwell performed miracles on a shoestring in the CBI theater. His assessment of the difficult situation there was always supremely realistic—which led to his difficulties with Chiang Kai-shek—yet his response to these difficulties was always positive: He found a way to deal with the problems he faced, and he never backed down. Lord Louis Mountbatten, supreme allied commander of the CBI theater, always attributed his ultimate success in the theater to his immediate subordinates: William Slim and Joe Stilwell.

IN HIS OWN WORDS

"I claim we got a hell of a beating. We got run out of Burma and it is as humiliating as hell. I think we ought to find what caused it, and go back and retake it."

—In *New York Times,* May 26, 1942

"The average general envies the buck private; when things go wrong, the private can blame the general, but the general can blame only himself."
—Quoted in Anton Myrer, *Once an Eagle*, 1968

"[The general] must act so that he can face those fathers and mothers [of the men he commands] without shame or remorse. How can he do this? By constant care, by meticulous thought and preparation, by worry, by insistence on high standards in everything, by reward and punishment, by impartiality, by an example of calm and confidence. It all adds up to character."
—Quoted in Anton Myrer, *Once an Eagle*, 1968

"Q: If a man has enough character to be a good commander, does he ever doubt himself? He should not. In my case, I doubt myself. Therefore, I am probably not a good commander."
—Quoted in Anton Myrer, *Once an Eagle*, 1968

LEADERSHIP LESSONS

Facing difficult realities does not require pessimism.

✦

Even the grimmest of situations leave room for positive action; it is up to the leader to find that room.

✦

Given inadequate resources, you can choose to grumble and give up, or you can work to acquire more resources while making the most of what you have.

✦

An effective leader assesses situations honestly, realistically, and accurately.

Suleiman the Magnificent

Born: ca. 1494   Died: 1566

Conqueror   Leverager   Strategist   Systems creator   Tactician   Visionary

LEADERSHIP ACHIEVEMENTS

✦

Greatly expanded the Ottoman Empire in the east as well as the west

✦

Built a mighty navy that significantly extended the reach of the Ottomans

✦

Used the spoils of conquest to build a magnificent Islamic civilization

✦

Had a keen appreciation of international politics and used "foreign"
religious issues to his strategic advantage

LIFE

Suleiman I, known as "the Magnificent," ruled the Ottoman Empire from 1520 until his death in 1566. He not only greatly expanded the empire, he fostered extraordinary advances in Turkish art, architecture, and learning.

He grew up in government, the only son of Sultan Selim I, who, early on, gave the youth administrative responsibilities. During the reign of his grandfather, Sultan Bayezid II, Suleiman was appointed governor of Kaffa in the Crimea. Later, during his father's reign, Suleiman became governor of Manisa in Asia Minor. When his father died in 1520, Suleiman became sultan. Almost immediately, he embarked on a series of campaigns against the Christian nations that surrounded the Mediterranean Sea. He took Belgrade in 1521 and Rhodes in 1522, and then defeated the Hungarian king Louis II at the Battle of Mohacs in August 1526. Suleiman installed a vassal, John, in his place, and when John died in 1540, Suleiman committed vast resources to the final conquest of the country. By 1562, after years of fighting, no progress had been made, and Suleiman agreed to a compromise peace. In the meantime, as early as 1534, Suleiman also focused on the east in a series of wars against Persia. Following up on his father's earlier efforts, Suleiman captured eastern Asia Minor and Iraq, but two protracted eastern campaigns failed to gain for Suleiman all of the territory that he wanted.

509

Suleiman was a skilled army commander, but he did not neglect the navy. Indeed, he built a great fleet, which he used successfully in 1538 against the combined fleets of Venice and Spain. In 1551, his navy bombarded and captured the city of Tripoli. Suleiman's navy became his long imperial arm, sailing as far as India.

Suleiman was not only a gifted military strategist, he was also a sophisticated diplomat and international politician. During his wars against European powers, he exhibited great cunning in the way he pitted Protestant factions against the pope and his followers. Although he had no great interest in Western religion, Suleiman understood that it was in his interest to keep Europe divided in matters of religion. He fostered conflict between Protestant nations and the rulers of the Ottoman's arch-rival, the Catholic Hapsburg Empire. In Hungary, for example, Suleiman allowed Calvinism to flourish in the areas he controlled. So liberal was his treatment of Hungary's Protestants that clergymen looked upon this Muslim sultan as their protector.

Suleiman greatly strengthened the Ottoman Empire, raising it to a position of leadership in Eastern Europe, the Mediterranean basin, and the Near East. He also brought Ottoman culture to a height that eclipsed most of what Europe had achieved at the time. In addition to Suleiman's massive building programs, which produced scores of mosques, bridges, fortresses, and other public works, his administrative efforts included the conversion of Constantinople into Istanbul, making it the center of Ottoman government.

As Suleiman advanced in years, his empire was torn between his two covetous sons. Thus, after Suleiman died in battle during a September 1566 assault against a Hungarian fortress, the Ottoman Empire fell into a long period of decline under a series of weak, even degenerate sultans.

LEADERSHIP LESSONS

✦

Nothing succeeds like success; build on your earlier conquests.

✦

Understand the culture of your adversaries; discover the weaknesses in others by which they will ultimately defeat themselves.

✦

Divide and conquer is a time-honored, highly effective tactic.

✦

Reinvest in your enterprise; become known as a builder, not a quick profit taker.

Tecumseh

Born: ca. 1768   Died: 1813

Character model   Conqueror   Motivator   Strategist   Tactician   Visionary

LEADERSHIP ACHIEVEMENTS

✦

Achieved personal greatness as a warrior

✦

Achieved prominence within the Shawnee tribe and worked to unite the
tribe with others

✦

Came as close as any Indian leader to forging a genuine union among
disparate tribes

✦

Navigated a diplomatically sound course for the Shawnees and others
during the American Revolution and the War of 1812

LIFE

Through a combination of charisma and persuasive reasoning, the
Shawnee chief Tecumseh was able to unite several tribes and thereby
mount a powerful resistance to white settlement during the American
Revolution, the Indian Wars of the Northwest, and the War of 1812. He
was the child of a Shawnee father and a Creek mother, and it is believed
that he was born in the Shawnee village of Old Piqua—present-day
Springfield, Ohio. After his father was killed in Lord Dunmore's War on
October 10, 1774, Tecumseh was adopted by the prominent Shawnee chief
Blackfish, who raised him as his own son.

Under the tutelage of Blackfish, Tecumseh soon earned a reputation as
a prodigious young warrior. Not only was he personally courageous and
skilled at arms, he was a naturally sophisticated diplomat. Reasoning that a
British victory in the American Revolution would effectively block westward
settlement by white frontier people and therefore preserve Indian lands,
Tecumseh persuaded the Shawnees and other tribes to ally themselves with
the British. The alliance was effective from about 1780 to 1783, and while the
Americans were victorious in the Revolution, they never defeated Tecumseh

or his people. Indeed, following the Revolution, Tecumseh organized highly effective Shawnee resistance in what historians call the Indian Wars of the Old Northwest from September 1790 to August 1795.

General Anthony ("Mad Anthony") Wayne defeated Tecumseh decisively at the Battle of Fallen Timbers on August 20, 1794. Following this, Tecumseh remained at peace until the eve of the War of 1812. However, in August 1795, he refused to sign the Treaty of Greenville (Indiana), by which many of his fellow tribesmen ceded much Indian land to the federal government. Instead of agreeing with this, Tecumseh moved to uncontested Indian territory along the Wabash River. There, with his brother Tenskwatawa—who became known as "the Prophet"—he worked patiently and systematically for the next few years to organize a union among several tribes. It was a daunting task, for Indian society at the time was not at all conducive to unified action across tribal lines; moreover, the structure of Indian government was democratic to the point of anarchy. There was no central authority. Tribal chiefs did not rule so much as they guided and advised; their decisions were rarely binding on the tribe. Yet the message Tecumseh powerfully delivered to all those tribes he visited was that only through unified action would the Indians save Indian land and the Indian way of life. A brilliant orator, Tecumseh traveled with his message throughout much of the Midwest and into New York. He also trekked across the Southeast, but met with little success in this region.

While Tecumseh was absent from his Wabash River headquarters village, his brother violated the chief's injunction to refrain from violence. Tecumseh knew that uncoordinated action against white settlers would only invite reprisals. He did not want to strike until he could lead a massive, unified campaign. But the Prophet attacked a force under Ohio territorial governor William Henry Harrison at Tippecanoe on November 7, 1811. Not only was the Prophet defeated, he was disgraced: He had not personally participated in the fighting, and he had told his followers that his "medicine" would protect them and ensure victory. In fact, many Shawnees died, and the headquarters village was burned. Worst of all, the union Tecumseh had spent years creating was suddenly left in tatters.

When Tecumseh returned to his ruined village, he led the remnants of his followers to Canada, where they joined with British army forces at the outbreak of the War of 1812 in June 1812. As he had during the

American Revolution, Tecumseh reasoned that a British victory would arrest the rush of white settlement in Indian lands.

Tecumseh commanded a mixed force of British troops and Indians at the Battle of Detroit in August and scored a victory at nearby Maguada on August 9, 1812. In recognition of his triumph, he was commissioned a brigadier general of British troops and was assigned to fight under General Henry Proctor during the sieges of Fort Meigs (Maumee, Ohio) and Fort Stephenson (Fremont, Ohio) during April–August 1813. The problem was that Tecumseh was far bolder, far more imaginative, and a far better tactician than the cautious, marginally competent Proctor. Proctor did not use Tecumseh and his forces effectively.

Tecumseh performed well leading the rear guard that covered Proctor's withdrawal into Canada during September, and then he led his Indian warriors alongside Proctor's regulars against William Henry Harrison at the Battle of the Thames on October 5, 1813. As usual, though, Proctor made little effort to coordinate his actions with those of Tecumseh, and, in a hard-fought battle, Harrison, greatly benefiting from the destruction of the British inland fleet on Lake Erie at the hands of Oliver Hazard Perry, defeated the British and Indian forces. It was in this battle that Tecumseh himself fell.

With the death of Tecumseh died a great hope for the creation of a politically and militarily effective union of Indian tribes.

LEADERSHIP LESSONS

✦

Great leaders combine personal achievement with a selfless ability to create consensus.

✦

Vision drives achievement.

✦

Creating unity and common cause sometimes requires great patience and endurance.

✦

Effective leadership requires personal contact. Outreach is always preferable to an ivory tower.

✦

An effective leader plans carefully, but executes boldly.

Thatcher, Margaret

Born: 1925

Character model   Innovator   Motivator   Problem solver   Tactician

LEADERSHIP ACHIEVEMENTS

✦

In male-dominated British politics, rose through Parliament to become head of state

✦

Became the first woman prime minister in British history

✦

Became Britain's only 20th-century prime minister to win three successive terms

✦

Instituted difficult, aggressive programs to turn the faltering British economy around

✦

Greatly reduced the British welfare state

✦

Successfully prosecuted the Falkland Islands War

LIFE

Winning election as Great Britain's first woman prime minister would be reason enough for including Margaret Thatcher among history's most significant leaders, but her gender was perhaps the least distinguishing feature of her tenure. She served longer than any other British prime minister in the 20th century, and she led what was dubbed the Thatcher Revolution, a program of social and economic changes that dismantled many aspects of Britain's postwar welfare state. While some Britons found this an example of heartless conservatism, the majority saw Thatcher's policies as a means of restoring Britain to the fullness of economic health. On balance, she was a tremendously popular national leader, who also commanded great respect internationally, especially during the Falkland Islands War of 1982.

Margaret Thatcher was born Margaret Hilda Roberts in the town of Grantham, the daughter of a grocer who was also active in local politics, serving as borough councillor, alderman, and mayor of Grantham. After attending Kesteven and Grantham Girls' High School, Thatcher won a scholarship to Somerville College, Oxford, where she pursued an unconventional course of study for a young woman at the end of the 1940s, earning a degree in chemistry. She went on to earn a master of arts degree at Oxford and then worked in industry for four years as a research chemist. (In 1983, Thatcher's science credentials earned her election as a Fellow of the Royal Society.) While she worked as a chemist, Thatcher studied law and was called to the bar by Lincoln's Inn in 1954. She left chemistry to practice taxation law.

During her undergraduate years, Thatcher was president of the Oxford University Conservative Association. She ran unsuccessfully for a seat in the House of Commons in 1950 and 1951 and was elected in 1959 as member for Finchley. In 1961, Thatcher was appointed parliament secretary to the Ministry of Pensions and National Insurance, remaining in this position until the change of government in 1964. While the Conservatives were the opposition party, from 1964 to 1970, Thatcher rose to prominence as a leading spokesperson for the Conservative point of view. When the Conservatives were returned to office in June 1970, Thatcher was appointed secretary of state for education and science and was made a privy counselor. With the change of government in February 1974, she was once again appointed to the opposition's Shadow Cabinet and was a front-bench opposition spokesperson, focusing primarily on environmental issues and, later, on matters related to the Treasury.

For her ability to articulate the opposition position and to muster support for it, Thatcher was elected leader of the Conservative Party in February 1975. Following the success of the Conservative Party in the General Election of 1979, she was appointed prime minister, first lord of the treasury, and minister for the civil service on May 4. When the Conservative Party subsequently won the General Elections of June 9, 1983, and June 11, 1987, Thatcher, the first woman ever to serve as Britain's prime minister, also became the first British prime minister of the 20th century to contest successfully three consecutive General Elections.

Thatcher took the helm of a nation in the throes of a long economic decline, which had culminated in recession. She introduced measures intended to revive the economy by reducing the British welfare state and privatizing certain government-controlled functions and industries. Her reforms were vigorous, and some would say ruthless—ruthless enough to merit her being called the Iron Lady. She took a strong stand against the trade unions during the great miners' strike of 1984–85, and she moved the nation toward privatization by selling to private business minor interests in public utilities. Her policy of "rate capping" effectively took control of expenditures out of the hands of city councils and was part of a program of centralizing spending to reduce what she saw as the wasteful and destructive influence of local governments in fiscal matters. Perhaps the most controversial of her reforms was the 1989 community poll tax, a regressive tax levied without regard to socioeconomic status or income.

For all their controversy, Thatcher's economic policies, which some condemned as undemocratic and oppressive, did have a positive effect in reversing the long downward spiral of the national economy. By the close of the 1980s, Britain was steadily climbing toward a prosperity it had not witnessed for some two generations.

While the economic situation presented Thatcher with her most enduring and formidable crisis, the 1982 outbreak of the Falkland Islands War was an event that proved to the world her mettle as a leader. The Falklands, off the coast of Argentina in the south Atlantic, had been disputed territory since the 17th century. Britain formally occupied the Falklands in 1833 and expelled Argentines living there; however, Argentina persisted in asserting its claim to the islands. On February 27, 1982, negotiations between Argentina and Great Britain over Falkands sovereignty broke down and led to an Argentine military invasion of the islands. On April 2, 1982, the Argentine Navy landed thousands of troops, overwhelming the badly outnumbered detachment of Royal Marines defending the islands. The United Nations Security Council passed Resolution 502 calling for the withdrawal of Argentine troops, and backed by the resolution, Thatcher ordered major British forces to the scene. With a firm resolve to liberate the islands, Thatcher conducted a 72-day war, which cost 235 British killed and 777 wounded. Argentine casualties were much higher. In the end, British sovereignty over the Falklands was affirmed and control over the islands regained. Thatcher was propelled to even greater popularity among the British public and, indeed, internationally.

The end of the Thatcher era came in 1990, when her cabinet became deeply divided over a number of issues, paramountly the role of England in the European Community. She resigned as prime minister and, two years later, entered the House of Lords, as Baroness Thatcher of Kesteven. Largely retired from government, she began work on an extensive, multi-volume memoir.

IN HER OWN WORDS

"People think that at the top there isn't much room; they tend to think of it as an Everest. My message is that there is tons of room at the top."

"You may have to fight a battle more than once in order to win it."

"Thinking realistically never got anyone anywhere; be true to your heart and aim for your dreams!"

—Source for all the Thatcher quotations is www.thatcherweb.com.

LEADERSHIP LESSONS

✦

Do not allow yourself to be trapped by convention or conventional wisdom.

✦

Being a realist does not rule out dreaming or acting on what you dream.

✦

Making difficult decisions is easier if your goals are clear and worth achieving.

✦

Effective leaders are willing to sacrifice immediate popularity for the long-term good of the enterprise.

✦

A leader accepts the power and the burden of final accountability.

Themistocles

Born: ca. 528 B.C.   Died: ca. 462 B.C.

Motivator   Problem solver   Rescuer   Tactician

LEADERSHIP ACHIEVEMENTS

✦

Accurately "read" his adversary

✦

Recognized an urgent problem and devised a solution

✦

Created unified, effective action

✦

Rescued Athens from Persian conquest

LIFE

Themistocles saved Athens from Persian conquest by sea through his fore-sight and preparedness at the Battle of Salamis in 480 B.C.

He had been born into a wealthy Greek family. Although it is proba-ble that his mother was not a Greek, Themistocles was a citizen of Athens, who, in 493 B.C., was elected *archon* (chief magistrate). In 490, he fought at the Battle of Marathon, in which Athenian spearmen successfully repelled a Persian attempt to take and occupy their city. After the Persian defeat at Marathon, Themistocles' fellow Athenian officials almost to a man believed that the Persian menace had been eradicated. Themistocles rea-soned that the Persians would return and, having failed to take Athens by land, would next exploit its weakness at sea by a seaborne assault. Like any great leader, Themistocles reached these conclusions by putting himself, imaginatively, in the mind of the enemy. He asked of himself the critical question: *What would I do if I were in their place?*

Having drawn his conclusion, he set about persuading Athens of the necessity of immediately building a large naval force and sending it to the Mediterranean to meet head-on what he was sure would be an invasion fleet. Themistocles made his case confidently, with calm passion and solid reasoning. In short order, even the most reluctant members of the Athenian assembly were persuaded. They dedicated the entire proceeds of a new state-owned silver mine to financing the expansion of the puny Athenian navy. By 480 B.C., when Persia did indeed threaten Greece again, the Athenian navy boasted some 200 new warships.

Themistocles did not wait for the invasion fleet to come to Athens. He acted aggressively by luring the Persian fleet into the most vulnerable position he could think of: the narrow straits of Salamis. Consistently successful commanders choose their battlefields as carefully as they choose subordinates. They never let the enemy select the site. The Persian vessels, built for the open water, emerged clumsily from the straits, could not be readily maneuvered, and were ripe for destruction when the Athenian fleet intercepted them.

Themistocles had rescued Athens, but, on his return to the city, he was denied the hero's welcome he so highly merited, and the fickle populace did not reelect him *archon*. Dispirited, he retired to Asia Minor, where he died, possibly by suicide.

LEADERSHIP LESSONS

✦

Trust your instincts.

✦

"Read" people, especially your adversaries; empathize with them; put yourself into *their* place and work out *their* moves.

✦

Never let an adversary choose the field of battle; maneuver the adversary into a position most beneficial to you.

✦

Sell your ideas and solutions to a key constituency that has the power to put them into action.

Theodora

Born: ca. 500   Died: 548

Character model   Innovator   Rescuer

LEADERSHIP ACHIEVEMENTS

✦

Rose to a position of great power and excelled in it

✦

Demonstrated an extraordinary ability to adapt to new and demanding
circumstances

✦

Exercised great strength of character and a will to lead

✦

Advocated justice

✦

Worked to benefit her constituency

✦

Directed affairs with great decision

LIFE

Theodora, who rose to become the most powerful woman in the history of
the Byzantine Empire, used her influence to gain rights for women and religious tolerance for her Monophysite faith.

Theodora was not born to royalty, but, rather, was raised on the margins of society, the daughter of a bear keeper in the Constantinople
Hippodrome. At an early age, Theodora became an actress, and it is
known that she bore at least one child out of wedlock. In addition to acting, Theodora supported herself as a wool spinner. When Emperor
Justinian met her, his attraction to her was instantaneous and intense. She
quickly became his mistress, and he elevated her to the rank of patrician,
marrying her in 525. With Justinian's coronation in 527 as emperor of the
Byzantinium, Theodora became his queen.

Justinian recognized in this actress and wool spinner a woman of
great intelligence and good sense. He relied on her as his most trusted
adviser, and there were not a few courtiers who considered her to be the

power behind the throne. It is a fact that her name appears in nearly all important legislation of the time, and she regularly corresponded with and received foreign officials. When the two political parties of Byzantium rose against Justinian and attempted to overthrow him in the Nika Rebellion of January 532, Justinian's ministers were unanimous in their counsel to abdicate. Only Theodora believed he should not step down, and it was she who persuaded him not to yield. It was also Theodora who ordered the military to round up the rebels and confine them in the arena, where they were executed—en masse—for treason.

As a leader, Theodora was decisive, autocratic, and, at times, merciless. But she never forgot her origins, and she emerged as a remarkable champion of women's rights in an age and culture in which females were regarded as little more than chattel. Among the reforms she instigated and oversaw was a revision of the divorce laws, to give women greater legal protection. She also promoted legislation outlawing the employment of girls as prostitutes.

Theodora was somewhat less successful in her efforts to end Justinian's persecution of the Monophysites, believers not in the Trinity but in a single divine nature within the person of Jesus Christ. Although she never won true religious freedom for this sect, of which she herself must be counted a member, she did manage to curb most legislation against it.

Her death from cancer in early middle age not only left Justinian bereft, it robbed the Eastern Empire of a rare voice of toleration and an advocate for the rights of the disenfranchised.

LEADERSHIP LESSONS

◆

Be flexible. Do not allow yourself to be narrowly defined by your background or position in society.

◆

Do not forget where you came from. Use your background in the present and for the future.

◆

Make yourself valuable to the enterprise by contributing your best counsel to it.

◆

It is never a bad leadership choice to advocate what is right and what is just.

Thutmose I

Reigned: 1504–1492 B.C.

Conqueror   Innovator   Leverager   Motivator   Profit maker   Strategist

LEADERSHIP ACHIEVEMENTS

✦

Expanded Egypt to its greatest ancient extent

✦

Took Egyptians into entirely new territories

✦

Leveraged opportunities with his Nubian expedition, not only acquiring gold
mines, but also securing the Egyptian frontier by subduing hostile peoples

✦

Developed a strong leadership image through a program of
commemorative monuments

LIFE

Thutmose I was a pharaoh of the Eighteenth Dynasty who expanded the
Egyptian Empire to its greatest ancient extent. The son of a mother of common stock, Thutmose may have coruled Egypt for a time with his predecessor, Amenhotep I. It was his marriage to Amenhotep's daughter that
assured him of succession to the throne.

Once he had achieved solo rule, Thutmose launched a well-planned
invasion of Nubia, where rich gold deposits had been found. In addition to
a desire for profit, Thutmose's invasion was also motivated by the necessity of subduing hostile forces on Egypt's southern frontiers. The expedition beyond the Nile's Fourth Cataract went farther than any Egyptian
army had ever before penetrated. Shortly after the Nubian expedition had
been successfully concluded, Thutmose moved north to evict the barbarian Hyksos from the delta. Once this objective was achieved, the pharaoh
marched his army as far as the Euphrates River—another first for an
Egyptian force. Thutmose memorialized this feat with a stele, or monument,
that still survives to tell the story.

The triumphs of Thutmose I were not confined to conquest. He added significantly to the temple of Amon at Karnak and built a magnificent hypostyle hall of cedar wood, decorated with copper, gold, and electrum to memorialize his own victories.

LEADERSHIP LESSONS

✦

Explore new territory.

✦

Leverage opportunities; strive to make each objective serve multiple purposes.

✦

Devote careful attention to developing a leadership image.

✦

Recognize and commemorate achievement; encourage the entire organization to claim a stake in each triumph.

Timoleon

Died: ca. 337 B.C.

Conqueror   Rescuer   Tactician   Visionary

LEADERSHIP ACHIEVEMENTS

✦

Liberated Syracuse from tyranny and impending invasion

✦

Brilliantly outmaneuvered the Carthaginians at Syracuse,
achieving a definitive victory

✦

Envisioned greatness for Sicily and took effective steps to realize
that vision

LIFE

Timoleon was a Corinthian Greek who liberated Syracuse from military dictatorship. Not that Timoleon himself was a democratic ruler. In fact, the first of his deeds history records is the assassination, about 365 B.C., of a favorite brother who refused to support his despotic rule. For the two decades following this, Timoleon's activities are obscure. Nevertheless, in 345 B.C., the citizens of Syracuse appealed to him for rescue from the reign of terror they suffered under the administration of Dionysius the Younger. The Syracusan situation was made the more dire by the approach of a Carthaginian fleet intent on capturing Syracuse by exploiting the city's weakness under Dionysius.

Timoleon responded by assembling his fleet, and then stealthily maneuvering it around the Carthaginians, who were within the harbor awaiting him. In a brilliant offensive—the details of which are not recorded—the Corinthians defeated both the Carthaginians and the forces of Dionysius.

Following this signal victory, Timoleon embarked on a campaign to purge Sicily of all its tyrants. This accomplished, he opened the country to immigrants from mainland Greece and Italy with the object of transforming the land into a mighty power. Timoleon fought a second battle against the Carthaginian army about 341 B.C. This produced another decisive victory for Timoleon and put him in position to hammer out an enduring peace with Carthage.

Having brought greatness and stability to the realms of Sicily, Timoleon lived out his later years in Syracuse, much honored in his retirement.

LEADERSHIP LESSONS

✦

Value the element of surprise. Devise unexpected means to achieve expected ends.

✦

Follow through on major achievements to secure and extend them, as Timoleon did in purging Sicily of all tyrants. Be ambitious.

✦

Formulate and enact the steps necessary to realize your vision for the enterprise.

Tito, Josip Broz

Born: 1892   Died: 1980

Innovator   Rescuer   Strategist   Systems creator   Tactician   Visionary

LEADERSHIP ACHIEVEMENTS

◆

Was a self-made man within the Socialist and Communist hierarchy
of Yugoslavia

◆

Put the welfare of his nation and opposition to tyranny ahead of
Communist ideology

◆

Led a highly successful resistance against the Nazi occupation
of Yugoslavia

◆

Was the only Eastern European leader to make Communism work
effectively

◆

Steered a sane course between the Soviet bloc and the West

◆

Maintained Yugoslavia's identity and independence

◆

Brought stability to an inherently unstable nation

◆

Tempered authoritarian rule with genuine regard for those he led

◆

Although guided by ideology, never allowed ideology to take precedence
over the needs of his people

◆

Built a strong economy that was a hybrid of Communism and capitalism

LIFE

Dictators, especially Communist dictators, are rarely useful as examples of
effective leadership, but Josip Broz Tito was always an exception to the
usual run of Communist dictators. While he was certainly no democrat, he
was a great leader of resistance to the most terrible kind of tyranny, that of

Adolf Hitler in World War II, and, after the war, that of the Soviet Union's Josef Stalin. Moreover, Tito effectively maintained Yugoslavia against pressures from outside as well as from those within. Just how important his personal leadership was to preserving peace among the jarring ethnic factions of his country became tragically apparent after his death. With Tito out of the picture, Yugoslavia dissolved into ethnic warfare.

He was born Josip Broz in Kumrovec, near Zagreb, one of 15 children in a peasant family. When he was 13, Broz was sent to the town of Sisak to apprentice to a locksmith. He found general metalworking more to his liking, however, and was soon traveling throughout much of central Europe as a journeyman metalworker. He joined the metalworkers' trade union, which led him to membership in the Social Democratic Party of Croatia. Broz became a committed Socialist.

For Broz, nationalism took precedence over Socialism in 1914 at the outbreak of World War I. He enlisted in the 25th Regiment of Zagreb, which marched against the Serbs in August. Falsely accused of disseminating antiwar propaganda, Broz was soon imprisoned, and then released in January 1915 after the charges were dropped. Upon his release, he was sent back to his regiment on the Carpathian front, where he distinguished himself in combat and was decorated for bravery. The 25th was then transferred to the Bukovina front, where it saw heavy action. Here Broz was severely wounded in hand-to-hand combat and taken prisoner by the Russians. He was sent to a labor camp in the Ural Mountains and was there as the Bolshevik Revolution took place in October 1917. When the camp was disbanded, he made his way to Siberia, where he sided with the Bolsheviks and fought in the Red Guard during the Russian Civil War. When he returned home in 1920, Tito considered himself no longer a Socialist, but a Communist—albeit without the fanatic zeal typical of the Bolsheviks. Tito steered a moderate course.

He joined the Communist Party of Yugoslavia (CPY) and was promptly arrested by government agents in 1923 and tried for subversion, but acquitted. He found work in a shipyard in Croatia, but was arrested again in 1925 for political agitation, and, this time, he was sentenced to seven months' probation. Continual harassment from the government not only failed to discourage Tito, it strengthened his resolve. He became a more thoroughly committed Communist and quickly rose within the party hierarchy, gaining membership in the Zagreb Committee of the CPY in 1927. The following year, he was named deputy of the Politburo of the Central Committee of the CPY, as well as secretary general of the Croatian and Slavonian committees. In August of 1928, however, he was again arrested. When he defiantly declared that the tribunal had no right to judge him, Broz was sentenced to five years' imprisonment.

He served his full term and, released in 1934, he traveled throughout Europe on behalf of the party. For reasons of security on these trips, he adopted the code name Tito, which he used thereafter. In 1935, Tito went to Moscow, where he worked in the Balkan section of the Comintern, the organization of international Communism. In August 1936, he was named organizational secretary of the CPY Politburo, but the following year, Josef Stalin began his infamous party purges. Prominent Yugoslav Communists were among the first targeted for "liquidation," and some 800 Yugoslavs simply disappeared inside the Soviet Union. The CPY was saved from complete annihilation only by the intervention of a high-ranking Comintern official. Tito not only escaped the general bloodbath, but, by the end of 1937, was named secretary general of the CPY by the Executive Council of the Comintern. When he returned to Yugoslavia to reorganize the Communist party, the party itself formally appointed him secretary general in October 1940.

The international Communist movement was stunned when Stalin concluded a nonaggression pact with Adolf Hitler's Germany, betraying Communism's supposedly unshakable opposition to Fascism. At the beginning of World War II, Yugoslavia declared itself neutral, but when the pro-Nazi leader Prince Paul was overthrown in a coup d'état, Adolf Hitler invaded Yugoslavia by way of reprisal. Under German occupation, the Yugoslavs at first remained passive. Then, in June 1941, Hitler launched Operation Barbarossa, the invasion of the Soviet Union in total abrogation of the nonaggression pact. Tito now led his followers in a brilliantly orchestrated campaign of sabotage and resistance against the occupying Germans. His movement was so successful that, in the summer of 1942, he was able to organize much more than resistance. His partisans actually mounted an offensive into Bosnia and Croatia, forcing the Germans to commit substantial numbers of troops to stop them. Despite the German counteroffensive, the partisans held their own, and by December 1943,

Tito announced a provisional government in Yugoslavia, with himself as president, secretary of defense, and marshal of the armed forces.

With the final defeat of Nazi Germany in May 1945, Tito went about the business of establishing his government on a permanent basis. He formed a party oligarchy, the Politburo, and held Soviet-style elections in November. Emulating Lenin and Stalin, he promulgated a Five-Year Plan for economic recovery and development. In contrast to the Soviet plans, however, his actually worked, in large measure because of his own great popularity as a war hero and patriot. Moreover, unlike Stalin, Tito was a reasonable man who disdained paranoia and terror and who was genuinely committed to the welfare of his country.

The combination of popularity and rationality was something Stalin was not prepared to tolerate. He intended to make Tito a Soviet puppet, as he was in the process of doing to other Eastern European leaders. Despite threats and intimidation, Tito held firm in declaring himself a Yugoslav first and a Communist second. He did not embrace Western capitalism, to be sure, but neither did he submit to Stalinism. Ideologically a Communist, he nevertheless maintained Yugoslavia's independence, and his maverick style of Communist government soon came to be labeled "Titoism." It influenced other Soviet satellite nations to oppose Stalin.

As a leader, Tito was a modern example of what would have been called in the 18th century an "enlightened despot." He maintained an absolute and very personal grip on Yugoslavia. The government he created was totalitarian. Yet, within the totalitarian framework he had created, Tito entrusted his people with a large degree of constitutionally specified and guaranteed liberty. A Communist, he refused to align his nation with the Soviet bloc, and he even encouraged a substantial degree of free enterprise. This made Yugoslavia one of the richest of nations of Eastern Europe, and the prosperity he fostered brought three decades of stability to a country traditionally racked by violence, dissension, and civil war.

When Josip Broz Tito died—in office—just three days before his 88th birthday, he was a living legend, not only in Yugoslavia, but around the world. His courageous opposition to Stalin and to domination by the Soviet state were appealing to the democratic West. Hardly an insular ruler, he traveled widely in Eastern Europe and Asia, speaking on Titoism to the people of nonaligned countries. He was determined to bring to his people—and, if possible, to others in the world—what he deemed best about Communism, without adhering to the savagery of the Stalin regime and its Soviet successors.

LEADERSHIP LESSONS

✦

An effective leader does not fall victim to ideology or ideological stereotyping.

✦

Never allow policy—or ideology—to take precedence over common sense and the fulfillment of human needs.

✦

Avoid labels.

✦

Independence requires courage.

✦

Build a consensus that serves your constituents, not some outside force or power.

✦

Establish your values and embody them in all you do.

✦

Recognize wrong when you see it, and act to make it right.

✦

Compromise wisely. Principled pragmatism is always preferable to a blind allegiance to theory and doctrine.

✦

Above all, do not yield to intimidation.

✦

Build a loyal constituency. By your actions, earn its continued loyalty.

✦

At least consider striving for legendary status.

Tokugawa Ieyasu

Born: 1543   Died: 1616

Conqueror   Innovator   Leverager   Mentor   Strategist   Systems creator

LEADERSHIP ACHIEVEMENTS

✦

Established himself as a great *daimyo* (feudal lord)

✦

Expanded his holdings and influence

✦

Through alliances, skillful deployment of resources, and wise patience,
became shogun (supreme military ruler of Japan)

✦

Brought unprecedented unity—and, thereby, peace and prosperity—
to Japan

LIFE

Tokugawa founded the last of Japan's shogunates—hereditary military dictatorships—and brought to Japan, torn and ravaged by competing warlords, an unprecedented degree of unity.

Tokugawa was born in Okazaki, into a family of the feudal warrior caste. Much of his early life was spent in Sumpu, as a hostage in service to the Imagawa family, but during this period he was also trained for the military and for civil governance. In service to Imagawa, he led his first military expedition in the late 1550s and proved an excellent commander.

In 1560, Imagawa was killed in battle, and Tokugawa's service to the family ended. Tokugawa returned to his father's lands, where he took control of the family castle and vassals. He allied himself with the powerful Oda Nobunaga, the warlord who overthrew the Ashikaga shogunate and brought half of Japan under his control. Tokugawa also observed the dissolution of his former master's domain. As the Imagawa holdings disintegrated under weak leadership, Tokugawa moved in, encroaching eastward and taking land piece by piece. By the early 1580s, Tokugawa was a *daimyo*, a feudal lord, whose holdings extended from Okazaki to the mountains of Hakone, the western portion of Honshu Island.

In 1582, Oda Nobunaga committed suicide after he was grievously wounded by a rebellious vassal. Toyotomi Hideyoshi assumed control of Oda's holdings. At first, Tokugawa decided to move against Toyotomi, but a few battles with him convinced Tokugawa to strike an alliance instead. In 1589, Toyotomi and Tokugawa fought side by side against Hojo Ujimasa, the warlord who held eastern Honshu. After their victory over Hojo, Toyotomi turned on his ally, forcing Tokugawa to abandon his holdings west of the Hakone mountains and to take instead the old domain of the Hojo. Tokugawa established his new capital at Edo—modern Tokyo.

Working from Edo, Tokugawa patiently organized the resources of his holdings. He selected his most capable and trusted vassals, placing them closest to Edo—and to himself. Those Tokugawa thought capable of betraying him, he placed on outlying parcels of land. He also took care to protect Edo further by reserving a large tract near the town and placing it under the direct supervision of one of his most trusted court officials. This land was to be used exclusively for raising crops sufficient to support Edo in case of siege. Next, Tokugawa saw to the disarmament of villagers in the vicinity of Edo. With his capital thus insulated from rebellion and conquest, Tokugawa invested much time and money in attracting the foremost artisans and businessmen to Edo. Through systematic acquisition, planning, and patience, Tokugawa thus amassed both the largest army in 16th-century Japan and the most productive and richest lands.

When Toyotomi Hideyoshi died in 1598, the *daimyos* of Japan fell to fighting for possession of his lands. Tokugawa was ready for battle, and in 1600 led his army against rivals at the Battle of Sekigahara. Few leaders have ever been so well prepared for battle. Victorious, Tokugawa became, in effect, the most powerful man in Japan—its first virtually undisputed leader.

Tokugawa acted quickly to resettle the *daimyos* much as he had his own vassals. Those *daimyos* he considered valuable allies he placed in strategic positions—not close to himself, but adjacent to his enemies. In addition, Tokugawa centralized his power by appointing a substantial class of administrators. This bureaucracy supplanted much of the independent authority and influence of the *daimyos*.

During this period in Japanese history, the real power of the emperor paled beside that of the shoguns, and in 1603 the imperial court conferred on Tokugawa the title of *shogun*, supreme military commander. Having attained this goal—hereditary authority for his family—Tokugawa retired, leaving the shogunate to his third son, Hidetada.

"Retirement," for Tokugawa, meant a very active life indeed. He served effectively as the emperor's foreign minister, dealing with Dutch, Portuguese, and English traders, as well as Portuguese and Spanish missionaries. Initially, Tokugawa welcomed the introduction of Western influence into Japan, but by 1612 he acted to stem the proliferation of missionaries and even of trade. Tokugawa also used his later years to build Edo fortress, at the time the largest castle in the world. The imposing structure was intended as the center around which Edo would flourish and grow as a great trading city.

Tokugawa was not one to be lulled into complacency by the mere possession of a title and monumental buildings. He remained on the alert for threats to his shogunate. In 1615, he concluded that one of the sons of Toyotomi Hideyoshi, who was ensconced at Osaka Castle, posed a threat to his hegemony. Acting preemptively, Tokugawa mounted a major attack on the castle, destroying it and all who lived within its walls. Aside from this action, the shogunate founded by Tokugawa brought Japan an unprecedented span of peaceful prosperity.

LEADERSHIP LESSONS
◆
Choose your alliances wisely.
◆
If you can't beat 'em, join 'em. The trick is knowing when you can't beat 'em.
◆
Deploy your assets to maximum advantage.
◆
Establish a fortress—an impregnable core of power on which you can draw and from which you can operate.

Toussaint Louverture

Born: ca. 1744 Died: 1803

Character model Motivator Rescuer Tactician Visionary

LEADERSHIP ACHIEVEMENTS

♦

Led the fight to end slavery in the Carribean

♦

Led the fight to liberate Haiti from colonial rule

♦

Entirely self-taught, proved his charismatic organizational genius as a revolutionary leader

LIFE

Born a slave, Toussaint Louverture taught himself to read and write, and, acting on his genius for motivation and organization, led the movement for Haitian independence. His actions attracted admirers and supporters worldwide, and his example remains an inspiration today.

Little is known about Toussaint's early life, except that he was born a slave and was given his freedom shortly before the Haitian slave uprising of 1791. Early on, he joined the rebellion to liberate the slaves, and he rose very rapidly to prominence within the movement, becoming the primary force in organizing and expanding it. In 1793, he briefly united with the Spanish of Santo Domingo, and, in concert with Spanish colonial forces eager to act against French colonial authorities, he led a series of rapid armed campaigns during which he earned the epithet Louverture or L'Ouverture ("The Opening," "The Beginning"), a name he embraced.

Toussaint subsequently professed allegiance to France, first to the republic and then to the empire under Napoleon, but he did so pragmatically, only in the hope of achieving liberation for his people. Late in 1793, when the British occupied all of Haiti's coastal cities and joined forces with the Spanish in the eastern part of the island, Toussaint became leader of the forces resisting the invaders. By 1798, leading liberated slaves and working in concert with French generals, Toussaint drove the British out of many of the towns they held. The following year, however, the mulatto general André Rigaud, in league with Alexandre Pétion and Jean Pierre Boyer, asserted mulatto supremacy and suddenly led a rebellion against Toussaint, who managed to end the uprising when he defeated Pétion at the southern port of Jacmel.

With the mulatto uprising suppressed, Toussaint conquered Santo Domingo in 1801. Because Santo Domingo had been ceded by Spain to France in 1795, Toussaint's conquest of it put him in control of all Haiti. He then made new professions of allegiance to France in order to secure the breathing space necessary to begin a reorganization of the Haitian government. This he began, and he also instituted a program of public improvements in an effort to ameliorate desperate Haitian poverty. But in 1802, Napoleon acted to regain full control of the island and sent a large army against Toussaint.

Toussaint led the Haitians in a stout resistance, and forced the French to negotiate a peace. However, during negotiations, the French commander treacherously seized Toussaint, who was sent in chains to France, where he was imprisoned in a dungeon at Fort-de-Joux and there died.

Toussaint Louverture brought Haiti a fleeting measure of liberty, but more enduring was his role as a symbol of the fight against tyranny worldwide and through history.

LEADERSHIP LESSONS

✦

Distasteful alliances are sometimes necessary to achieve specific goals.
The key is never to lose sight of the goal.

✦

Great leaders allow others to discover and act on their own greatness.

✦

Lead from the most powerful principles you can define.

✦

Give those you lead a stake in the enterprise. Better yet, lead so that
everyone is keenly aware of the stake they already have.

Truman, Harry S.

Born: 1884   Died: 1972

Character model   Motivator   Problem solver   Rescuer   Strategist   Tactician

LEADERSHIP ACHIEVEMENTS

◆

Successfully blended politics with genuine public service

◆

As a reform-minded senator, significantly improved the performance of
defense contractors

◆

Rose to greatness in crisis—the death of FDR

◆

Made the difficult and momentous decision to use nuclear weapons
to end World War II

◆

Led the Cold War policy of "containment" of Communism, promulgating the
Truman Doctrine

◆

Championed the Marshall Plan, a milestone for humanity and democracy

◆

Successfully led the Berlin Airlift, a major Cold War triumph

◆

In the Korean War, succeeded in blocking the expansion of Communism
without triggering a larger conflict—World War III

◆

Made many unpopular (and necessary) decisions, but ultimately earned a
place in history as one of the century's greatest leaders

LIFE

Harry Truman had the staggering task of taking up the reins of government upon the sudden death of Franklin D. Roosevelt. The nation was
nearing the end of World War II and was faced with bringing that war to
a conclusion and then dealing with the Soviet Union, which was prepared
to gather up for itself as many pieces of the war-shattered world as it possibly could. Few Americans had much confidence in Truman, and, indeed,
FDR had kept him largely in the dark. Yet Truman would more than rise

to the occasion, lead the nation to victory—and into the nuclear age—champion the Marshall Plan to rescue a devastated Europe, and then navigate a most perilous course through the opening of the Cold War era and the Korean War, in the process earning international respect for his strength, his plain speaking, and his essential humanity.

Truman was born in Lamar, Missouri, the oldest of three children, and moved with his family to Independence in 1890. Plagued by poor eyesight requiring thick glasses, young Harry became rather bookish and was intensely fascinated by history. He also learned to play the piano and, at one point, even considered a career as a concert pianist. Although Truman would have loved a university education, family financial problems precluded his enrolling, and an ambition to enter West Point was foiled by his poor eyesight.

Truman worked for a railroad and two banks, and then, at age 22, took up farming for the next 11 years. During this period, he began to find that he had even more affinity for people than for his beloved books, and he became involved in local politics. When the United States entered World War I in 1917, Truman, already 33, received a commission in the National Guard, and, as an artillery captain, shipped off to France in command of Battery D of the 129th Field Artillery, 35th Division, American Expeditionary Force. Truman participated in the major late offensives and discovered that he had both a talent for and an attraction to leadership. His men were devoted to him.

After the war, Truman married his childhood sweetheart, Elizabeth (Bess) Wallace, and, with a partner, opened a haberdashery in Kansas City. The store fell victim to the depression that followed the end of the war, and Truman was left with heavy debts he was determined to pay in full. (Eventually, he did just that.) At this point, he was open to the invitation of Kansas City political boss Thomas Pendergast to enter politics. Managing to avoid the corrupt side of machine politics, but nevertheless using the machine to advance himself, Truman was elected judge of the Jackson County court in 1922. Although he failed to win reelection in 1924, he became presiding judge of the court two years later and was reelected in 1930. As judge, Truman did not hear legal cases, but rather administered the business of the county, and he earned local renown as a builder of roads, which were badly needed in this part of rural Missouri.

In 1934, Truman ran for the U.S. Senate, proving to be a vigorous and highly effective campaigner. He won and became an ardent partisan of President Roosevelt's New Deal. He earned a reputation as a selfless and hardworking senator, who, as a member of the Interstate Commerce Committee, was instrumental in creating the Civil Aeronautics Act of 1938 and the Transportation Act of 1940. Crippled by his association with Boss Pendergast, who had been imprisoned for tax evasion, Truman refused to renounce what he considered the debt of loyalty he owed to his early supporter and mentor. This nearly cost Truman reelection in 1940, but he was reelected nonetheless.

Truman now embarked on a series of hard-hitting Senate investigations into government and government contractor fraud and waste. As head of a Special Committee to Investigate the National Defense Program, he not only promoted economy and efficiency among defense contractors, he held them to a high standard of excellence in production. In this, his work was of great value to U.S. defense before Pearl Harbor and to the war effort after it. It is typical of Truman that he eloquently and mercilessly criticized prewar "pacifists" and "isolationists" as unrealistic and therefore destructive, but he never himself became a mindless militarist. With America on the brink of entry into the war, Truman worked for the creation of an international organization to preserve peace, and he advocated such measures as lend-lease (a policy of supplying Britian and its allies with war materiel on a noncash basis), economic aid, and economic sanctions as alternatives to U.S. entry into combat. The attack on Pearl Harbor on December 7, 1941, ended these options, of course, and Truman became a wholehearted supporter of the U.S. military and of the war effort.

Although Truman enjoyed being a senator and had no ambitions beyond the Senate, he accepted President Roosevelt's request that he run with him as vice presidential candidate in his bid for a fourth term in 1944. Once Truman was in office, however, Roosevelt rarely met with him and certainly made no effort to train, mentor, or even brief him. Thus, when Roosevelt succumbed to a cerebral hemorrhage on April 12, 1945, Truman was thrust into office as a rank novice. When he offered his condolences to Eleanor Roosevelt and asked her if there was anything he could do for her, the president's widow replied, "Do for me? What can we do for you? You're the one who is in trouble now."

Truman applied himself with extraordinary energy to learn the office and get up to speed on the current status of the war and relations with the Allies. He was determined to continue, seamlessly, FDR's and the Allies' policy of securing nothing less than the unconditional surrender of Germany. At the end of April, shortly before Germany surrendered the next month, Truman supported the start of the United Nations by attending its founding conference in San Francisco.

By far the most difficult wartime decision the death of FDR left to Truman was whether—and how—to use two atomic bombs that the immense Manhattan Project had produced. Reasoning that Japan's war culture precluded military surrender, and that an invasion of Japan, even at this late stage in the war, would cost more than a million American lives (and even more Japanese lives), Truman concluded that the bombs, horrible as they were, could end the war quickly, decisively, and unconditionally. Ultimately, he believed, the terrible weapon would save lives. Furthermore, if the war ended quickly, the Soviets, who were about to declare war on Japan, would not be able to gain a foothold and a claim on Japan and Japanese-occupied Manchuria. The bombs were dropped on Hiroshima (August 6) and Nagasaki (August 9), and Japan surrendered on August 14.

Truman's leadership immediately looked beyond the end of war. He was determined to avoid the errors the United States had made after World War I, in which it had won the war but lost the peace by rapidly weakening its military and by withdrawing from involvement in the politics of the world. Truman was determined to contain Soviet expansion and to prevent giving to Stalin the same political advantages that post–World War I appeasers had given men such as Hitler and Mussolini. Yet Truman could not fight demobilization, and he therefore lacked the military might to back up much of his hard line on Soviet expansion.

What he did do had very significant effect, however. He promulgated the so-called Truman Doctrine, which granted aid to Greece and Turkey and promised assistance to other nations threatened "by armed minorities or by outside pressure." As a result, neither Greece nor Turkey fell under the Soviet heel. He championed the vast program of economic aid developed by Secretary of State George C. Marshall—the Marshall Plan, which used America's vast economic resources to give immediate as well as long-term aid to European nations and economies still outside of the Soviet sphere. Called by Winston Churchill the "most unsordid political act in history," the Marshall Plan not only saved lives, it kept millions from falling under the domination of the Soviets. Another spectacular Cold War success was the Berlin Airlift of 1948–49, which kept West Berlin supplied with food and fuel after the Soviets blockaded the city in an effort to prevent the creation of an independent, democratic West Germany. The success of the airlift brought about the end of the Berlin blockade and was a major Cold War triumph. Under Truman's leadership, the North Atlantic Treaty Organization (NATO), America's first-ever peacetime military alliance, was created, to block the expansion of the Soviet sphere into Western Europe. It was Truman the statesman who developed or endorsed these policies, but it was Truman the politician who mustered the necessary bipartisan support to put them into action.

Most historians conclude that Truman was less successful on the domestic front than internationally. His efforts to continue and expand the New Deal as the Fair Deal were largely unsuccessful, with the notable exception of the important Housing Act of 1949, which included a provision for public housing. Truman was an early leader in civil rights—taking the struggle much further than his predecessors—but his most effective weapons were executive orders (including a groundbreaking order to desegregate the U.S. armed forces), rather than legislative initiatives. He was repeatedly foiled by a southern coalition that opposed executive-sponsored legislation mandating equal opportunity, an end to legally sanctioned racial discrimination, and such curbs on black suffrage as poll taxes. Truman's efforts in labor, both on behalf of labor unions and, in the case of nationwide railroad and coal industry strikes, against them, were largely unsuccessful.

By the election of 1948, Truman's domestic policies had made him unpopular, and it was generally assumed that he would lose his run for the White House to Republican Thomas E. Dewey, the popular governor of New York. In the face of the naysayers, Truman responded with a vigorous and highly upbeat campaign, in which he promised to "give 'em hell"—by which he meant that he would fight a complacent ("do-nothing") 80th Congress, dominated (he said) by men with "a dangerous lust for power and privilege." To the surprise of all—including Truman himself—his message got across, and he narrowly defeated Dewey.

Truman's second term was immediately marked by a deteriorating situation in Asia, beginning with the collapse of the Chinese Nationalists and the triumph of the Chinese Communists. Hard on the heels of the Chinese Communist revolution came the invasion of South Korea by Communist North Korea on June 25, 1950.

Truman understood only too well that the postwar American military, relying blindly on its nuclear monopoly, was undermanned and weak. Yet he decided to bluff by securing from the United Nations Security Council a resolution recommending that member states furnish aid to South Korea. Truman circumvented Congress by issuing an executive authorization of U.S. military intervention. This set a precedent for emergency executive action that, in the hands of President Lyndon Johnson a decade and a half later, would lead tragically to the escalation of the Vietnam War.

As aggressive as Truman was in Korea, he recognized the limits of U.S. power, especially after the Communist Chinese crossed the border into North Korea and joined the battle. When the supreme commander of the Far East, General Douglas MacArthur, called for an expansion of military operations to defeat the Chinese, even if nuclear weapons were required to do so, Truman pulled back from triggering a new world war. The rash MacArthur publicly criticized administration policies, trumpeting rank insubordination to the commander in chief, whereupon Truman relieved him of his command on April 11, 1951.

Truman's "firing" of one of the great heroes of World War II was a controversial and unpopular decision. Worst of all, it tended to obscure the success the United States had, in fact, achieved in Korea. True, the Asian nation was divided, but South Korea remained independent, the Communist expansion had been blocked, and—no small thing—World War III had been averted. Yet a climate of political panic had been created, which proved fertile ground for the red-baiting of Senator Joseph R. McCarthy and others.

Constitutionally, Truman could have run for another term—it would have been only his second *elected* term. Had he done so, it is quite possible that power would have remained in Democrat hands. But he decided that his usefulness in office had come to an end, and the Republican candidate, World War II supreme allied commander Dwight D. Eisenhower, sailed to an easy victory in 1952. Truman retired to Independence and spent his later years traveling, speaking, and writing.

IN HIS OWN WORDS

"I never give [the public] hell. I just tell the truth, and they think
it is hell."
—*Look* Magazine, April 3, 1956

"The buck stops here."
—Motto on Truman's Oval Office desk

LEADERSHIP LESSONS
✦
Effective leadership is founded on a demonstration of honesty and integrity.
✦
Plainspoken, direct, honest communication is a powerful instrument of
leadership.
✦
Presented with a problem, begin to work with the problem. Learn all you
can. Prioritize. Proceed step by step. Avoid panic and remain methodical,
even if you have to learn on the job.
✦
Be willing to make unpopular decisions.
✦
All leaders are campaigners for themselves, for their ideas, and ultimately
for the enterprises they lead.

Vespasian
(Titus Flavius Vespasianus)

Born: A.D. 9   Died: A.D. 79

**Character model   Conqueror   Innovator   Leverager   Mentor   Problem solver
Profit maker   Rescuer   Strategist   Systems creator   Tactician**

LEADERSHIP ACHIEVEMENTS

◆

Expanded the Roman Empire

◆

Rescued Rome from the economic, political, and moral bankruptcy
created by Nero and other poor leaders

◆

Brought unprecedented stability to Rome

◆

Redesigned Roman government for the public good

◆

Brought about an economic revival of Rome

◆

Increased tax revenues by broadening the tax base,
not by burdening taxpayers

◆

Created an enduring government

LIFE

Vespasian, reigning from 69 to 79, brought peace and prosperity to a Rome afflicted by war and internal strife. He was born on November 17 or 18, A.D. 9, near Reate (modern Rieti), Italy, and, in early youth, joined the Legions. He served first in Thrace, rising quickly to become *quaestor* (an official responsible for finance and administration) in Crete and Cyrenaica. As a leader, Vespasian was popular as well as capable, and he was soon named *aedile* (an official responsible for public works, games, and food and water supplies) and then *praetor* (an elected magistrate ranked just below consul). During the 30s, he served valiantly in the frontier wars of the German provinces, and then was given command of the Second Legion in Britain under Aulus Plautius. During 43–44, he conquered the Isle of

Wight and advanced into modern-day Somersetshire. Vespasian served briefly as consul in 51, and then was named governor of the African provinces in 63. He accompanied Nero on his Greek tour, before being sent, late in 66, to Palestine to put down the Jewish rebellion in Judaea. There he confronted determined, even fanatical resistance, but by 69 had laid siege to Jerusalem.

While Vespasian was fighting in the Middle East, the deranged Nero committed suicide in 68, and Servius Sulpicius Galba was proclaimed emperor. Although most of the empire recognized his sovereignty, the Praetorian Guard, always a volatile force, turned on him, and assassinated him so that they could bring to the throne, early in 69, their candidate of choice, Aulus Vitellius, who had served as commander of Roman forces in Germany. However, in July 69, the army in Egypt and his own forces in Judaea proclaimed Vespasian emperor.

In Rome, Vitellius enjoyed the support of the German legions, but Vespasian drew the allegiance not only of the Middle Eastern troops, but also of those in the Balkans and in Illyria. With loyalties thus aligned, Vespasian turned over command of the Middle Eastern forces to his son Titus and set off for Italy while another ally, Antonius Primus, used the legions of the Danube region to invade Italy in advance of his arrival and engage Vitellius. Antonius Primus was victorious at the second Battle of Bedriacum in October 69, so that when Vespasian arrived in Rome in December 69, his rival emperor was dead and the city itself was held by Primus's troops.

Vespasian assumed the throne just as his son Titus captured Jerusalem in 70. In this same year, Vespasian's forces successfully suppressed the Rhineland revolt of Claudius Civilis. Having triumphed on all fronts, Vespasian quickly turned to a program of badly needed domestic reform. Nero's corrupt and extravagant reign had drained the treasury. Vespasian attacked the debt through a combination of stringent economy measures and increased taxation. Instead of burdening present citizens with tax increases, however, he broadened Rome's tax base by granting Roman citizenship to selected towns and provinces. In this way, Vespasian leveraged the coveted boon of Roman citizenship.

After annexing portions of Anatolia and Germany, Vespasian reinforced garrisons in Great Britain, especially Wales and Scotland. While enforcing prudent economies, he also commenced an ambitious program of construction, the grandest product of which was the Roman Colosseum.

To Rome, Vespasian brought something it had long lacked—sound government conducted for the public good. Concerned to bring lasting stability to the empire, Vespasian established the Flavian dynasty by naming his son Titus as his successor. He gave him the strategic appointment of prefect of the notoriously dangerous Praetorian Guard. The strategy worked. When Vespasian died—of natural causes—on June 4, 79, having brought prosperity and peace to the empire, Titus succeeded him with the full support of the Praetorians and the acclamation of the Senate. Titus and, after him, Domitian had learned well from their father. Like him, they ruled wisely, honestly, and equitably.

LEADERSHIP LESSONS

✦

A leader must subordinate himself to the benefit of those he leads.

✦

Delegate key tasks wisely; do not try to go it alone.

✦

Solve problems by finding the opportunities within them, as Vespasian did in broadening his tax base by granting more people Roman citizenship.

✦

Recognize and leverage your assets, as Vespasian did with the benefit of Roman citizenship.

✦

Practicing good economy does not necessarily require a spending moratorium. Focus your resources.

✦

Take steps to perpetuate the enterprise beyond yourself. Mentor your replacement.

✦

Address the needs of all of your constituents.

Wainwright, Jonathan Mayhew, IV

Born: 1883   Died: 1953

Character model   Leverager   Motivator   Rescuer

LEADERSHIP ACHIEVEMENTS

✦

Defended the Philippines to the utmost

✦

Surrendered only when continued fighting would have sacrificed lives
without gaining any useful objective

✦

Through example, did much to sustain the morale and well-being of his
imprisoned command

✦

Was a leader in extreme adversity

LIFE

Usually, the leaders we most admire, wish to learn from, and emulate are
victorious. Wainwright, however, is best known for his valiant, but hopeless, defense of the Philippines against Japanese attack in World War II and
his subsequent leadership of American prisoners of war held by the
Japanese under the most inhumane of circumstances. Wainwright's leadership demonstrated that it is possible to be defeated without being beaten.

A native of Walla Walla, Washington, Wainwright attended West
Point, graduating in 1906 with a second lieutenant's commission in the cavalry. He saw service with the 1st Cavalry in Texas, and went with the 1st
to the Philippines, where he participated in the difficult campaign against
the Moro pirates on Job Island during 1908–10. Promoted to first lieutenant in 1912, Wainwright graduated from the Mounted Service School
four years later and was also promoted to captain.

When the United States entered World War I in April 1917,
Wainwright was promoted to temporary major of field artillery and was
assigned as an instructor at the officers' training camp in Plattsburgh, New
York. He shipped out for France with the 76th Division in February 1918,
where he was seconded to the British near Ypres, Belgium. After this, he

was made assistant chief of staff for operations (G-3) in the U.S. 82nd Division and served with the unit in the triumphant Saint-Mihiel offensive of September 12–16 and at Meuse-Argonne from September 26 to the armistice on November 11. Wainwright remained in Germany after the armistice, serving with the Third Army on occupation duty until October 1920, when he returned to the United States.

Like most officers given temporary wartime promotions, Wainwright reverted to his permanent rank, captain, but he was quickly promoted to major. Assigned as an instructor at the Cavalry School in Fort Riley, Kansas, he served there until 1921, when he became a general staff officer with the 3rd Infantry Division. From 1921 to 1923, Wainwright worked in the War Department as a strategic staff officer. He was assigned to the 3rd Cavalry until 1925, and then returned to the War Department. Promoted to lieutenant colonel in 1929, he graduated from the Command and General Staff School at Fort Leavenworth in 1931, and then attended the Army War College, graduating in 1934. While serving as commandant of the Cavalry School, he was promoted to colonel in 1935. Wainwright left the school in 1936 to assume command of the 3rd Cavalry.

In 1938, Wainwright was promoted to the temporary rank of brigadier general and was assigned to command the 1st Cavalry Brigade. He was promoted to major general in September 1940 and sent to the Philippines to command the Philippine Division as senior field commander under General Douglas MacArthur. When the Japanese attacked and invaded the Philippines at the start of World War II in the Pacific, the brunt of the defense fell squarely on Wainwright. He had no hope of reinforcement or resupply. He knew that it would be months—or more—before the United States could mount a counterattack. As commander of the Northern Luzon Force (11th, 21st, 71st, and 91st Filipino Divisions, and the U.S. 26th Cavalry Regiment), he nevertheless had a crucially important mission: to delay the Japanese, who had landed at Lingayen Gulf during December 22–31, so that the American and Filipino forces could fall back to Bataan and take a stand there. The longer Wainwright could delay the Japanese, and the costlier he could make their invasion, the more time he would buy for the Allies to begin to stem the tide of Japanese advance on all Pacific fronts. Few leaders have ever been put in a more desperate situation.

The defense of northern Bataan fell back under a first assault during January 10–25, and Wainwright and MacArthur repulsed a second assault during January 26–February 23. The Japanese were stunned that their strict timetable of conquest had been set back. As for Wainwright, he was promoted to lieutenant general and made commander of U.S. forces in the Philippines after President Franklin Roosevelt ordered MacArthur to flee to Australia in March 1942. Wainwright could be sacrificed; MacArthur could not be.

Astoundingly, without reinforcement or supply, Wainwright was able to conduct his defense through early April 1942. His obstinate, skillful, and heroic defense—his ability to elicit from his men the utmost effort—cost the Japanese many lives and, equally important, much time. The price of this delaying action, however, was a terrible one. The U.S.–Filipino forces on Bataan surrendered on April 9, and a massive Japanese assault on Corregidor forced Wainwright to surrender all forces on May 6. The general and his men were sent to POW camps in the Philippines, Taiwan, and finally Manchuria. Most infamous was the Bataan Death March, in which the defeated defenders of Corregidor were marched to camps in Bataan under conditions of starvation and exhaustion. Ten thousand POWs died en route. And the treatment only became worse throughout the course of the POWs' long captivity. Through it all, Wainwright made valiant efforts to sustain the morale and welfare of his men. He willingly shared their hardships, and he sustained their identity and conduct as soldiers.

Among the cruelest aspects of Wainwright's captivity was his feeling that, in surrender, he had failed to do his duty. He had surrendered only when he believed that further loss of life would serve no purpose, yet he feared that he would face disgrace after he and his command were liberated by Russian troops in Manchuria in August 1945. Wainwright's fears proved unfounded. He was properly hailed as a war hero, whose combat actions had greatly aided the Pacific campaign in its darkest hours and whose conduct in captivity had upheld the honor of the army and had saved many American and Filipino lives. The frail, shockingly emaciated Wainwright was accorded the honor of attending the Japanese surrender ceremonies in Tokyo Bay aboard the U.S.S. *Missouri* on September 2. He commented with characteristic reserve, good humor, and self-irony: "The last surrender I attended the shoe was on the other foot." He was awarded the Medal of Honor and assigned to command the Fourth Army in Texas in January 1946, but, broken in health, retired the following year.

Wainwright was an excellent soldier and fine commander, whose resourcefulness, skill, and courage made the Japanese victory in the Philippines extremely costly. Both as a leader in a desperate combat situation and as a prisoner of war, his example served as a symbol of the gallantry of which U.S. forces were capable.

IN HIS OWN WORDS

"It is with a broken heart and head bowed in sadness but not in shame, that I report to Your Excellency that I must go today to arrange terms for the surrender of the fortified islands of Manila Bay.

"There is a limit of human endurance, and that limit has long since been passed. Without prospect of relief I feel it is my duty to my country and to my gallant troops to end this useless effusion of blood and human sacrifice. If you agree, Mr. President, please say to the nation that my troops and I have accomplished all that is humanly possible and that we have upheld the best tradition of the United States and its Army. May God bless and preserve you and guide you and the nation in the effort to ultimate victory.

"With profound regret and with continued pride in my gallant troops, I go to meet the Japanese commander. Good-bye, Mr. President."
—Message to President Roosevelt, May 6, 1942

LEADERSHIP LESSONS
✦
Loss is not synonymous with defeat.
✦
Sacrifice must be useful. When it ceases to serve a purpose, it is not heroic, but merely wasteful.
✦
Great leaders share the fortunes of those they lead.
✦
Lead first and foremost by example.
✦
Leadership is built on character. There are no shortcuts or substitutes.

Walesa, Lech

Born: 1943

**Character model   Innovator   Mentor   Motivator   Problem solver
Rescuer   Tactician   Visionary**

LEADERSHIP ACHIEVEMENTS

✦

Organized a successful labor movement in Poland

✦

Was instrumental in freeing the Polish labor movement from
Communist control

✦

Was a principal founder of Solidarity, which combined labor concerns with
a drive toward democracy

✦

Was instrumental in the ultimate overthrow of Communist totalitarianism in
Poland and the rest of Eastern Europe as well as in the Soviet Union

✦

Earned an international reputation as a freedom leader

LIFE

A shipyard electrician in the Polish port of Gdansk, Lech Walesa earned international renown as the organizer and leader of Solidarity, the union that undermined Communist tyranny in Poland and, by its example, touched off the demise of Communism throughout Eastern Europe and the Soviet Union.

Born in Popowo, Poland, Walesa graduated from vocational school and then worked as an auto mechanic from 1961 to 1965. After two years in the Polish army, he began working in the Gdansk shipyards in 1967 as an electrician. Two years later, he married Danuta Golos, with whom he raised a family of eight children.

Walesa began his rise through the Polish labor movement in December 1970, when he was arrested as one of the leaders of a clash between the workers and the government. After this, he organized the shipyards extensively, and in 1976 was fired because of his activities as a shop steward. While continuing to work in the labor movement, Walesa supported his family with a series of temporary jobs. In 1978, he firmly broke with the Communist-sanctioned labor movement by organizing free, non-Communist trade unions. Government harassment during this period was frequent and often intense, yet he had achieved a sufficiently high profile that authorities did not dare act too aggressively against him.

In August 1980, Walesa led the massive Gdansk shipyard strike that inspired a tidal wave of strikes over most of Poland. Walesa now found himself not merely a local labor leader, but a leader of national prominence and, moreover, a leader of a movement not only in support of labor but opposed to the government of Poland. Walesa was eloquent in organizing workers as well as in communicating their grievances to those in authority. He hammered away at a set of primary demands for workers' rights, and when it became apparent that the workers would never back down, authorities surrendered and sat down with Walesa to negotiate the Gdansk Agreement of August 31, 1980. For the first time in the history of Communist totalitarianism, a government yielded substantial liberties to workers and citizens. The Gdansk Agreement gave workers the right to strike and to organize their own—independent—union. In a one-party state, this was a monumental concession and, in it, many throughout Poland and the rest of the world saw the beginning of the end of Soviet hegemony in Europe.

The Catholic Church supported the Solidarity movement, and in January 1981 Walesa was warmly received in the Vatican by Pope John Paul II, a Polish national. The papal reception only served to reinforce the international acclaim that was pouring down upon Walesa, who was seen as a leader for human rights and individual liberty. During 1980–81, he traveled to Italy, Japan, Sweden, France, and Switzerland as guest of the International Labor Organization. In September 1981, he was elected chairman of the Solidarity union at the First National Solidarity Congress in Gdansk.

At this high point of hope for Poland, in December 1981, Poland's premier, General Wojciech Jaruzelski, a Soviet puppet, feared that the USSR would soon send troops into Poland. To forestall this, Jaruzelski preemptively cracked down, declaring martial law and "suspending" Solidarity. He ordered the arrest of most Solidarity leaders, including

Walesa, who was held in a remote country house. Under mounting international pressure, however, Walesa was released in November 1982 and, moreover, was reinstated at the Gdansk shipyards. He was closely observed by the government, but he refused to break off his Solidarity connections or his continued work with the "suspended" organization.

In July 1983, Jaruzelski lifted martial law, although many restrictions on what few freedoms Poles enjoyed persisted. In October 1983, the Nobel committee announced that Walesa would receive the Peace Prize. Even as this created a sensation throughout Poland, the Jaruzelski regime denounced the award—an action that made the government an object of even more intense popular hatred and contempt. Worsening economic conditions drove the Jaruzelski government to open negotiations once again with Walesa and Solidarity. What resulted was a bloodless revolution in the form of an agreement to hold parliamentary elections. Despite limitations placed on the elections, the people put into place Poland's first non-Communist government since the end of World War II. Fortunately, this revolution took place in the context of a new Soviet regime. Under Mikhail Gorbachev, it was clear that the USSR would not employ military force to prop up the Polish Communist Party—or, in fact, to keep Communism in power in any Soviet satellite.

Walesa was now leader of the revived Solidarity labor union and, in effect, a national leader. As such, he began a series of meetings with world leaders, and, in November 1989, became only the third foreign national in history—after Lafayette and Winston Churchill—to address a joint session of the U.S. Congress. The following year, Walesa was elected chairman of Solidarity with a 77.5 percent majority, and in December 1990, he was elected president of the Republic of Poland. It was an acknowledgment that Walesa had been instrumental in leading the Polish state to democracy.

Walesa was defeated in the election of November 1995 and has since traveled and lectured worldwide. In addition to the Nobel Prize, he has been presented with honorary degrees from many universities and has been awarded the Medal of Freedom (U.S.), the Award of the Free World (Norway), and the European Award of Human Rights. He now heads the Lech Walesa Institute, which was established to advance the ideals of democracy and free market reform throughout Eastern Europe and the rest of the world.

IN HIS OWN WORDS

"You have riches and freedom here but I feel no sense of faith or direction. You have so many computers, why don't you use them in the search for love?"
—Quoted in *Daily Telegraph* (London), December 14, 1988

"The thing that lies at the foundation of positive change, the way I see it, is service to a fellow human being."
—Quoted at *www.cyber-nation.com/victory/quotations*

"Power is only important as an instrument for service to the powerless."
—Quoted at *www.zompist.com/quotes.html*

"I've never worked for prizes . . . I'm as ready to receive prizes as I am to be thrown into prison, not that I'm ungrateful for this honor; it's just that neither the one nor the other could ever divert me from the course I've set myself."
—Response to being awarded the Nobel Peace Prize, 1983

"The hungry hare has no frontiers and doesn't follow ideologies. The hungry hare goes where it finds the food. And the other hares don't block its passage with the tanks."
—Interview, 1981

"The supply of words in the world market is plentiful but the demand is falling. Let deeds follow words now."
—Quoted in *Newsweek* (New York), November 27, 1989

LEADERSHIP LESSONS

Discover and develop common cause with and among those you lead.

✦

Focus on achievable goals, which are also open-ended and can be enlarged in scope. For Solidarity, labor rights became the doorway to democratic government.

✦

Sometimes, high visibility is indispensable to leadership. Develop open and transparent policies and procedures.

Washington, George

Born: 1732 Died: 1799

Character model   Conqueror   Innovator   Leverager   Motivator
Problem solver   Rescuer   Systems creator   Tactician

LEADERSHIP ACHIEVEMENTS

✦

Served with bravery and distinction in the French and Indian War

✦

Trained and commanded an effective Virginia fighting force during the
French and Indian War, outperforming the British regulars

✦

Leveraged a small, inadequate army into victory in the American
Revolution

✦

Leveraged disadvantage and defeat into ultimate triumph

✦

Held the Continental Army together, often by the strength of
his character alone

✦

Led by personal example; consistently demonstrated courage

✦

Commanded great loyalty; squelched the Conway Cabal merely by
restrained personal appeal

✦

Strongly molded the office of president

✦

Introduced firm restraint into the office of chief executive

✦

Chose to become neither king nor dictator

✦

Was deemed father of his country

LIFE

No American leader is more revered than George Washington—and
rightly so. He not only led the military campaign that wrested American
independence from Britain, but, as the independent nation's first president,
guided the United States through its early years and, for all intents and

purposes, created the office of president. Washington's commitment to strong leadership, coupled with his refusal to be a king or dictator, put the American democracy on a firm footing. In the fullest sense possible, he deserves the Roman honor, accorded him even before his death, of being called "father of his country."

George Washington was born in Westmoreland County, Virginia, and, after the death of his father on April 12, 1743, he was raised by his eldest brother, Lawrence. His education was spotty, but he enthusiastically learned the surveyor's trade—a crucial profession in colonial America—and became an assistant surveyor in 1748 and from 1749 to 1751 served as surveyor for Culpeper County.

Washington's brother Lawrence died in July 1752, and Lawrence's daughter Sarah two months after him, leaving Washington a substantial inheritance, including Mount Vernon, a magnificent Virginia plantation estate. Now a member of the landed gentry, Washington was appointed adjutant for southern Virginia and given the militia rank of major in November 1752. In 1753, he was also named adjutant of Northern Neck (the territory between the Rappahannock and Potomac rivers) and the Eastern Shore. On the eve of the French and Indian war, Virginia governor Robert Dinwiddie sent Washington to assess French military activity in the Ohio Valley and to evict any French trespassers on British colonial ground. Washington set out from Williamsburg, Virginia's capital, on October 31, 1753, and delivered Dinwiddie's ultimatum to the commandant of Fort LeBoeuf (Waterford, Pennsylvania) on December 12, 1753: Get out or suffer attack. The French commandant, 30 years Washington's senior, politely but firmly declined to leave. Washington headed back to inform Governor Dinwiddie, who ordered the construction of a fort at the strategically critical "forks of the Ohio," the junction of the Monongahela and Allegheny rivers, the site of present-day Pittsburgh. The French quietly watched the construction of Dinwiddie's fort and, when it was completed, attacked. Badly outnumbered, the new outpost surrendered on April 17, 1754. The English stronghold was now christened Fort Duquesne and occupied by the French. Unaware of this—and on the very day that the fort fell—Dinwiddie once again sent Washington (now promoted to lieutenant colonel) with 150 men to reinforce the fort. En route, on May 28, the young commander surprised a 33-man French reconnaissance party. In the

ensuing combat, 10 of the Frenchmen were killed, including Ensign Joseph
Coulon de Villiers de Jumonville, a French ambassador. This was the first
battle of the French and Indian War.

Realizing that the French would soon retaliate, Washington sought
reinforcement from his Indian allies, but found few willing to help.
Washington determined that it was too late to retreat, so, at Great
Meadows, Pennsylvania, he built a makeshift stockade and dubbed it Fort
Necessity. On July 3, Major Coulon de Villiers, brother of the ambassador
Washington's small detachment had killed, led 900 French soldiers and
Indian allies against Fort Necessity. Hopelessly outnumbered, Washington
fought calmly and valiantly. When the outpost's defenders had been
reduced by half, on the fourth of July, Washington surrendered—and was
permitted to leave with the survivors.

Despite his defeat, Washington was greeted as a hero on his return to
Virginia and, promoted to the local rank of colonel in March 1755, was
assigned as aide-de-camp to British general Edward Braddock, who had
been dispatched from the mother country to defend the colonies. It was a
difficult assignment, because, while he was a courageous commander,
Braddock was a poor strategist and tactician, and, like many regular British
officers, he was thoroughly contemptuous of "provincial" troops and their
officers.

Washington had direct charge of the Virginia volunteers, and he
marched with Braddock on a full-scale mission to retake Fort Duquesne
during May–July. The force Braddock led out of Fort Cumberland,
Maryland, was an unwieldy one of 2,500 men loaded down with heavy
equipment. Along the way, French-allied Indians sniped at the slow train.
Washington advised Braddock to detach a "flying column" of 1,500 men,
light on supplies and other encumbrances, to make the initial attack on Fort
Duquesne, which Braddock believed was defended by 800 French and
Indians. By July 7, the flying column set up a camp 10 miles from their
objective. Actually, Fort Duquesne was held by only 72 regulars of the
French Marine, 146 Canadian militiamen, and 637 assorted Indians. On the
morning of July 9, these forces made a surprise attack against Braddock's
encampment, throwing the British troops into a panic. Soldiers fired
wildly—sometimes at each other. Many of the British regulars huddled in
the road like sheep. Braddock was mortally wounded. Of 1,459 officers and

men who had engaged in the Battle of the Wilderness, only 462 returned. But through it all, Washington led his Virginians calmly and effectively. Their survival rate was much higher than that of the British regulars, and they never panicked. Washington emerged unscathed, although he had had two horses shot from under him and his coat was pierced by four bullets. He demonstrated in this disastrous battle what he would repeatedly manifest later, in the American Revolution: unshakable courage.

The defeat outside of Fort Duquesne was recognized as Braddock's fault, not Washington's, and the young militia colonel was given command of all Virginia forces in August. He set about supervising the construction of a series of frontier forts during 1755–57 and, during July–November 1758, accompanied another British general, John Forbes, in an arduous but, this time, successful expedition to Fort Duquesne.

Washington was elected to the House of Burgesses in 1758. Upon his resignation from the militia, he was promoted to honorary brigadier general. During this period, on January 6, 1759, he married Martha Dandridge Custis, a wealthy widow, and he began his term of service as justice of the peace for Fairfax County in 1760. He would serve through 1774.

As the clouds of revolution gathered, Washington became a key member of the first Virginia provincial congress in August 1774. He was chosen as one of seven Virginia delegates to the First Continental Congress in September 1774 and served as a member of the Second Continental Congress in May 1775. Once war broke out in earnest, the Congress asked Washington to serve as general in chief of the Continental forces. He accepted the challenge with due humility, for he understood the odds of winning against the mightiest military power on the planet.

On June 15, 1775, Washington directed the blockade of Boston, and then formally took command of the army in Cambridge, Massachusetts, on July 3, 1775. Finding the army poorly disciplined, poorly equipped, and disorganized to the point of disintegration, Washington reshaped it and, even more, injected it with patriotic fervor. Washington was not always a great—or even good—tactician, but he was always an inspiring leader. During the siege of Boston, he did deploy his troops very effectively, forcing the British army under William Howe to withdraw from the city.

Washington was far less successful in his defense of New York City during August–November 1776. Yet he avoided total disaster. While he lost

New York, he kept his army intact. When he observed soldiers about to panic or make an unauthorized retreat, he galloped to the scene to take personal command. Troops found it impossible to behave as cowards in the presence of Washington. And even in losing New York, Washington proved himself a capable strategist, drawing the British far from their supply lines as he withdrew across the Hudson River, into New Jersey and, in November, Pennsylvania. Washington understood that his puny forces could not decisively defeat the British. What he could do, however, was endure and make each battle very costly for the redcoats. If he could keep his army together, if he could avoid disastrous losses, the cause of American independence, in time, might well prevail.

Yet Washington was not content with mere defense. Having relinquished New York and having retreated across New Jersey to Pennsylvania, Washington, on the stormy night of December 25–26, 1776, suddenly recrossed the Delaware and made a devastating surprise attack on the British-employed Hessian mercenaries encamped at Trenton, New Jersey. This triumph not only cost the British substantially, but greatly elevated the morale of the Continental Army and others involved in the rebellion. Washington followed this victory with success at the Battle of Princeton, where he managed to rout three British regiments on January 3, 1777, before retiring into winter quarters at Morristown, New Jersey, on January 6.

When he learned that British general John Burgoyne planned to cut off New England from the other colonies by means of a large-scale invasion of the Hudson Valley from Canada, Washington studied the situation and concluded—correctly—that the principal weakness of Burgoyne's plan was an absence of naval support. He therefore dispatched many of his best troops and ablest officers north, into the upper Hudson River Valley, to check Burgoyne's advance, while he remained in New Jersey to engage Howe. He was determined to keep Howe and Burgoyne separate. Washington's problem was that he lacked sufficient forces to prevail in a full-scale battle with Howe. He therefore played for time, parrying through May and July of 1777 each of Howe's attempts to force a battle. When a fight finally came, at Brandywine Creek, Pennsylvania, on September 11, 1777, Washington's lines caved in. As usual, however, Washington proved highly capable of managing defeat. He withdrew intact and regrouped for a surprise counterattack at Germantown, just north of Philadelphia, on October 4. Hobbled by bad weather and a plan too complex for relatively inexperienced soldiers to execute effectively, the Germantown campaign failed, at least in an immediate military sense. But French observers of the battle were so impressed by Washington's daring and audacity—a defeated commander responding with an attack—that the action motivated Louis XVI to conclude a formal alliance with the Americans. Washington's "defeat" had won America its most valuable ally.

Up north, the news was also good. The subordinates Washington had detailed to confront Burgoyne scored a magnificent victory against him at the Battle of Saratoga on October 17. Burgoyne surrendered his entire army.

In many ways, Washington's most formidable enemy was not the British, but the inefficiency and stinginess of the Continental Congress. His troops were poorly supplied, miserably fed, and inadequately clothed. They were rarely paid as promised. Thus, when the forces gathered around Washington went into winter quarters at Valley Forge, Pennsylvania, they were heavily demoralized. The winter was harsh—though not unusually so—but the ragged, threadbare condition of the troops' clothing and their meager supplies brought tremendous hardship. It is a measure of Washington's character and ability to lead that he managed to hold the army together during November 1777–April 1778. He not only held it together, but, thanks to the expertise of the Marquis de Lafayette and Baron von Steuben, both liberty-minded officers from Europe, he was able to improve training and thereby strengthen the beleaguered army.

During this period, however, Washington was faced with a critical challenge to his leadership: the so-called Conway Cabal, a conspiratorial scheme to replace him in command with General Horatio Gates, a politically savvy but thoroughly mediocre officer. Washington responded to the scheme with great dignity, appealing to his officers for their confidence and loyalty. This was sufficient to suppress the movement during November–December 1777.

On June 28, 1778, Washington engaged General Sir Henry Clinton in a battle at Monmouth, New Jersey, fighting him to a costly draw. Gates, in command of southern forces, was badly beaten at Camden, South Carolina, on August 16, 1780, and Congress appealed to Washington to save the South. On October 22, 1780, the commander in chief appointed General Nathanael Greene to take charge of the region, and the Americans enjoyed greater success. Washington was a skilled judge of his subordinates' performance, and he almost always put the right man in the right place.

Washington now collaborated with French general Jean Baptiste Rochambeau and Admiral François de Grasse to plan the Yorktown (Virginia) campaign, which was executed beginning in August 1781. By massing a large amphibious force against the army of General Charles Cornwallis, trapping it on the Yorktown peninsula, Washington and his allies forced the surrender of his army on October 19, 1781.

Although major cities and geographical areas remained under British control, the defeat of Cornwallis prompted liberal forces within the British government to push for a peace settlement, culminating in the Peace of Paris on September 3, 1783.

As the man most responsible for winning independence, Washington could have assumed virtually unlimited powers in the new nation. Instead, with an eloquent, heartfelt speech, he took leave of his troops at Fraunces Tavern, in Manhattan, on December 4, then returned to Mount Vernon and resigned his commission. He continued to work to unite the disparate colonies into a single government, and he was elected president of the Constitutional Convention in Philadelphia in 1787. Although he had not sought the office, he was, in February 1789, unanimously elected as the first president of the United States and was inaugurated on April 30. He was reelected to a second term in December 1792, but declined a third, thereby establishing a tradition of a two-term limit that was unbroken until the four-term tenure of Franklin D. Roosevelt in the mid-20th century. (The Twenty-Second Amendment to the Constitution, ratified on February 26, 1951, now limits presidential tenure to two terms.)

The two-term tradition was perhaps the least consequential of the many precedents Washington set. His nobility of character earned the admiration not only of his countrymen, but of the world, which quickly came to respect, honor, and even envy the new republic.

In addition to guiding the nation successfully through its first eight years under the Constitution that had replaced the woefully inadequate Articles of Confederation, Washington essentially created everything that the office of president would become. The Constitution is silent on many details of the executive branch; it was Washington who created the key executive departments, naming Thomas Jefferson as secretary of state, Henry Knox as secretary of war, Alexander Hamilton as secretary of the treasury, Samuel Osgood as head of the Post Office, and Edmund Randolph as attorney general. It was Washington who created the American form of the Cabinet. Most of all, however, it was George Washington himself who served as the model for the presidency, and the paramount quality he introduced into the office was restraint. He avoided conflict with Congress, believing it was not the chief executive's duty to propose legislation. He also opposed the formation of political parties— although, by the time of his second term, two opposing parties had been formed: the conservative Federalists, headed by John Adams and Alexander Hamilton, and the more liberal Democratic-Republicans, headed by Thomas Jefferson. In his handling of such crises as the Whiskey Rebellion, Washington firmly but fairly asserted the primacy of the federal government over local jurisdictions, and he successfully defended U.S. sovereignty in such matters as the XYZ Affair. The tempting course would have been to seize as much power as possible, but Washington's active restraint gave democracy the room it needed to establish itself.

Washington firmly decided against a third term as president. He could certainly have had the job for life, if he so desired. But such a tenure was fit for a king, not a president. In March 1797, he finally retired to his beloved Mount Vernon, although he briefly served as army commander in chief during a crisis with France, which looked as if it would flare into war in 1798. Unfortunately, Washington did not long enjoy his retirement. In December 1798, he took ill with severe laryngitis and died.

IN HIS OWN WORDS

"Labour to keep alive in your breast that little spark of celestial fire, conscience."
—From his schoolboy copybook

"Observe good faith and justice toward all nations. Cultivate peace and harmony with all."
—Quoted in Peter G. Tsouras, *The Greenhill Dictionary of Military Quotations,* 2000.

LEADERSHIP LESSONS

✦

There are no substitutes for character and courage.

✦

As panic is infectious, so is the competent calm of a courageous leader.

✦

Focus on keeping the enterprise together at all costs. Be an advocate for
the forces you lead.

✦

Leveraging scant resources requires defining attainable objectives that will
nevertheless lead to the achievement of the ultimate goals of the
enterprise. This typically requires patience, endurance, and the willingness
to tolerate a protracted period of great anxiety.

✦

Get into the front lines. Intervene in serious problems personally. Firsthand
information and personal presence are your most powerful leadership tools.

✦

Power is ultimately self-defeating if sought or employed without restraint.

✦

Democratic rule is about empowerment of the best; therefore, empower
the best.

✦

Demand absolute loyalty. Return nothing less than the same.

✦

A founder must be a leader in every sense.

✦

The best foundations are built of solid precedents.

Wayne, Anthony

Born: 1745   Died: 1796

Leverager   Mentor   Motivator   Rescuer   Strategist   Tactician

LEADERSHIP ACHIEVEMENTS

✦

Developed his natural military talent into the skills of a fine
commanding general

✦

Earned the loyalty of his men because his first regard was for his men

✦

Combined resolute bravery and bold action with careful planning
and preparation

✦

Embodied combat ferocity without dangerous impetuosity

✦

Refused to panic even under the most terrible circumstances

✦

Learned from his defeats as well as his victories

✦

Stressed mentoring, training, and preparation

LIFE

"Mad Anthony" Wayne was one of the most effective U.S. commanders during the American Revolution, and, in the Indian wars that followed it, the military campaign he led brought a significant degree of peace to the turbulent Old Northwest.

He was born in Waynesboro, Chester County, Pennsylvania, and, beginning in 1765, worked as a surveyor and land agent in Nova Scotia. Two years later, he returned to Pennsylvania to take over his father's prosperous tannery, which he ran until 1774, when he was elected to the Pennsylvania legislature. During this time he served on the Pennsylvania Committee of Public Safety, a revolutionary organization dedicated to resisting British tyranny. In September 1775, Wayne resigned his legislative seat to raise a regiment of volunteers. On January 3, 1776, he was formally commissioned colonel of the 4th Pennsylvania Battalion.

Wayne participated in the disastrous invasion of Canada early in the Revolution and was wounded at Trois Rivières on June 8, 1776. Assigned to command Fort Ticonderoga in upstate New York, he was promoted to brigadier general on February 21, 1777, and then was assigned command of the Pennsylvania Line at the Battle of the Brandywine on September 11. Although Wayne fought bravely and well, the Battle of the Brandywine was a bad defeat for the army of George Washington. Worse, on September 21, Wayne's encampment at Paoli, Pennsylvania, was hit by a surprise night attack, the British troops falling on the slumbering Americans with unaccustomed stealth. British commander William Howe claimed that his men had killed 500 of the 1,500 Americans camped at Paoli. Wayne, however, counted 150 bodies. To preserve stealth, the British had attacked with bayonets rather than bullets, and the bodies were so mangled that local residents dubbed the encounter the Paoli Massacre. Wayne did quickly recover from the shock and managed to rally his panic-stricken men, most of whom escaped to safety, taking recently captured British cannon with them. Nevertheless, the Paoli Massacre put Wayne under a cloud of suspicion of dereliction of duty. To clear his name, which he felt essential not only for his personal honor but to preserve his effectiveness as a commander, Wayne demanded a court-martial. Tried, he was acquitted of any wrongdoing.

Horrific as it was, Wayne quickly put Paoli behind him. He fought gallantly at the Battle of Germantown, just outside of Philadelphia, on October 4, sustaining a minor wound in this action. Although Washington's army lost Germantown, French observers were so impressed with the fighting spirit of Washington and commanders such as Wayne that King Louis XVI and his ministers made the long-delayed decision to ally France with the cause of American independence.

Wayne wintered with the army at Valley Forge during 1777–78, sharing with this force the hardships of that terrible winter. He then achieved victory in the Battle of Monmouth Court House on June 28, 1778, by leading the initial attack and then successfully defending the center against the British counterattack. But it was the stealthy and daring night attack on the British-held Hudson River fort at Stony Point, New York, on July 16, 1779, that earned Wayne his early reputation. With a force of 1,350 men, each handpicked, Wayne applied the hard lessons of Paoli. As the British had done in that assault, he ordered his men to use bayonets exclusively.

Except in one battalion, not a single musket was so much as loaded. Even after the British began to fire on the Americans with cannon as well as muskets, Wayne's troops returned not a single shot. Instead, they continually advanced, under fire, until they overran the fort. In this action, 63 British soldiers were killed, more than 70 were wounded, and 543 were taken prisoner. Wayne also captured precious artillery and other equipment. The cost to his forces was 15 killed and 80 wounded.

While Wayne's reputation was born with the action at Stony Point, his famous nickname, "Mad Anthony," although it came about at this time, had nothing to do with the Stony Point triumph. A neighbor of Wayne's, having deserted from the Continental Army, was arrested. He told the authorities that held him to contact Wayne, who would vouch for him. Not only did General Wayne refuse to help the deserter, he denied knowing him at all. "He must be mad," the deserter responded incredulously. The epithet stuck—to Wayne.

Wayne was in command of operations along the lower Hudson River in 1780 when he suffered defeat at Bull's Ferry during July 20–21. Early the following year, he responded immediately to news of Benedict Arnold's treachery by rushing to defend—successfully—imperiled West Point, New York.

During January 1–10, 1781, a general mutiny swept through the ranks of the Pennsylvania Line, which a stingy and impecunious Continental Congress had failed not only to pay, but to equip and feed. Through sheer force of reputation and integrity, Wayne personally suppressed the mutiny and saved the Pennsylvania Line for the cause.

Early in the Revolution, George Washington learned that victory was as much a matter of outlasting the British will to continue to fight as it was a matter of defeating the British army. His principal task became the preservation of his army as a fighting force. Wayne absorbed this lesson as well. He was defeated at Green Spring, Virginia, on July 6, 1781, by a greatly superior British force, which threatened to annihilate his army. With great skill, Wayne preserved his army, not only managing its escape from the British, but holding it together and preventing discipline-destroying panic.

Wayne participated in the decisive Franco-American victory at Yorktown during May–October 17, 1781, which brought about the surrender of Lord Cornwallis's army. Then, fighting under General Nathanael

Greene, he led a devastatingly effective expedition into Georgia against British-allied Creek and Cherokee Indians during January–July 1782.

Although Wayne was breveted (promoted for bravery) to the rank of major general on September 30, 1783, he resolved to seek no further military glory, but retired from the army at the end of the Revolution in the hope of taking up a quiet life as a farmer. He was also active in politics as Chester County's representative to the Pennsylvania General Assembly during 1784–85, and then was elected by Georgians—grateful for his action against the Creeks and Cherokees—as their representative to Congress on March 4, 1791. The election, however, was declared void because of charges of election fraud and, more importantly, the fact that Wayne, a Pennsylvanian, failed to meet Georgia residency requirements.

Wayne returned to the farm—but he did not last long as a farmer. On March 5, 1792, he was appointed major general and commander in chief of U.S. Army forces in the Old Northwest—Ohio and the upper Midwest—and tasked with the mission of fighting the Indians of that region. The Shawnee chiefs Little Turtle and Blue Jacket had triumphed over two previous commanders: Joshua Harmar and Arthur St. Clair. Indeed, on November 4, 1791, St. Clair lost 623 officers and men out of a force of about 1,400. In proportion to the number of men fielded in battle, the defeat still stands as the worst the U.S. Army had ever sustained.

Asked to command an army very much shaken in its confidence and morale, Wayne was determined not to lead his men into a new disaster. Although settlers pressured him to attack immediately, Wayne, always a bold officer, was never an impetuous one. Instead, he patiently and thoroughly prepared his troops, training them and also maneuvering them into the most advantageous position possible. Finally, on August 20, 1794, he met Little Turtle on a field of combat he himself had chosen. The Battle of Fallen Timbers resulted in the decisive defeat of Little Turtle and the Shawnees, who signed the Treaty of Greenville, by which the tribe ceded vast tracts of land to the government. This opened most of the Ohio country to settlement and brought to the Old Northwest an unprecedented 14 years of relative calm, which would not be broken until the onset of the War of 1812. As a further result of Wayne's victory over the Indians, British traders in the Ohio region lost their Indian allies and were compelled in 1796 to surrender to Wayne the forts, which, in violation of the Treaty of

Paris that had ended the American Revolution, the British had continued to man along the Great Lakes. Unfortunately, Wayne had little time to enjoy the adulation and gratitude of his government and its citizens. He succumbed suddenly to illness at the end of 1796.

The nickname "Mad Anthony" has helped to preserve the general's fame, even though the name was not earned in battle. It does suggest his ferocity in combat, which was a spectacle of awe and wonder to his men, but it does not do justice to even more important aspects of his leadership. His regard was always first and foremost for his men, and he was determined to lead into battle only an army that had been well prepared and trained and that was positioned for greatest effect and advantage. Bold in combat, Wayne was also a careful and patient planner, who bequeathed to the fledgling U.S. Army a tradition of thorough professionalism.

LEADERSHIP LESSONS

✦

Careful planning is not necessarily incompatible with bold action.

✦

Bold action does not require impetuosity and recklessness.

✦

The courage to take risks does not require disregard for personal safety or the well-being of those you lead.

✦

Invest time in training and mentoring.

✦

Integrity is a leader's single most valuable asset. Its exercise can work wonders, but, once lost, it can never be fully regained.

✦

Panic ratifies defeat; therefore, avoid panic.

Wellington, Arthur Wellesley, 1st Duke of

Born: 1769   Died: 1852

Character model   Conqueror   Motivator   Strategist   Tactician

LEADERSHIP ACHIEVEMENTS

◆

As a military commander, amassed an extraordinary record of victory

◆

Turned the tide of the Napoleonic Wars with his actions in
Portugal and Spain

◆

Nearly defeated by a surprise attack at Quatre Bras, Belgium, recovered
and fought to victory at Waterloo—the most famous military victory in
modern history

◆

Hand a strong hand in the structure of post-Napoleonic Europe

◆

Became an enduring example of the highest traditions of British arms

LIFE

Britain's "Iron Duke," Wellington is most famous as the commander who led the defeat of Napoleon at the Battle of Waterloo, thereby ending the Napoleonic Wars and the epoch of Napoleonic conquest.

Born Arthur Wellesley in Dublin, Ireland, the fifth son of the 1st Earl Mornington, the future Duke of Wellington was sent to Eton, where he gained an education he valued all of his life. As he once most famously declared when asked to account for the British triumph at Waterloo, the battle had been won "on the playing fields of Eton." Wellington also briefly attended a French military school at Angers. He was commissioned an ensign in the 73rd Regiment on March 7, 1787, and, on September 30, 1793, following the accepted practice of the day, purchased the rank of lieutenant colonel in command of the 33rd Regiment of Foot. At this time, he also served in the Irish Parliament for the family borough of Trim.

During 1793–1795, Wellesley led the 33rd in the Netherlands campaign of the Duke of York, proving himself an excellent commander and earning distinction for himself and his unit at the Battle of Hondschoote on September 8, 1793. Wellesley always showed the utmost concern for the welfare and morale of his men. He had less tolerance for his superiors, especially when they demonstrated—as many did—incompetence. In 1795, after being exposed to the blunders of high command in a campaign in Flanders, Wellesley abruptly resigned his commission in disgust. He was, however, appointed military undersecretary to the Lord Lieutenant of Ireland, Lord Camden, in May 1795, and then resumed command of his regiment in 1796. He took the 33rd to India, where his elder brother, Richard Wellesley, 2d Earl Mornington, had been appointed governor general.

It was in India that Wellesley earned his first national fame when, as commander of one of two columns sent against Tipu Sahib, Sultan of Mysore, he took part in the storming of Seringapatam. His spectacularly aggressive role in this operation resulted in the death of Tipu, in May 1799, and Wellesley's appointment as governor of Seringapatam. Next, during the Second Maratha War, Wellesley led British and allied forces in the Deccan campaign of 1803. He spearheaded the capture of Poona on March 20, 1803, and of Ahmadnagar on August 11. Engaging the Maratha army led by Daulat Bao Sindhia and the Raja of Besar at Assaye, Wellesley was victorious after an extremely hard-fought battle on September 23. He continued his record of triumph by defeating Sindhia again at Argaon on November 29, after which he stormed Gawilgarh on December 15. Together, these actions brought the war to a successful conclusion and made Wellesley its signal hero.

Wellesley returned to England in September 1805 and plunged into the Napoleonic Wars as brigade commander in the abortive Hanover expedition that December. After this disappointment, Wellesley withdrew from the military for a time and turned his attention to civilian politics, gaining election to Parliament as member for Rye in April 1806, sitting for St. Michael's, Cornwall, in 1807, and becoming Irish Secretary in March. But he found that he could not long resist field command. In summer 1807, he joined the expeditionary force sent to Denmark during July–September. Here he played a key role in the defeat of a French-allied Danish force at Kjoge on August 29 and was afterward dispatched to Portugal with a small force during July–August 1808. Using these troops, he defeated Marshal Jean Junot at Vimeiro on August 21, but was frustrated by the actions of

Sir Hew Dalrymple, an overly cautious commander who prevented Wellesley from capitalizing on his victory. Heartbroken and discouraged, Wellesley once again resigned his commission and returned to England to resume his post as Irish Secretary.

Yet again, with Napoleon always a menace, Wellesley found he could not stay away from military command for long. In April 1809, he was appointed to lead the remaining British forces in Portugal and, after obtaining reinforcements, defeated Marshal Nicolas Soult at Oporto on May 12. This was a major victory against the forces of the French, and, following it, in June, Wellesley led an invasion of Spain itself. There he defeated Marshal Claude Victor-Perrin and King Joseph at Talavera during July 27–28, pushing them back to Madrid. It was for this triumph that Wellesley was named Viscount Wellington in September 1809.

Wellington's victory proved short-lived, however. He was soon forced to fall back on Lisbon under the crushing weight of the enemy's superior numbers. He now demonstrated that he was as skilled and energetic in a defensive role as he had been on the attack. Wellington erected three fortified "lines of Torres Vedras" during the winter of 1809–10. After successfully defending against Marshal André Masséna's advance during July–October 1810, he halted the French advance at Bussaco on September 27. Following these actions, Wellington withdrew to the safety of the lines of Torres Vedras. From December 1810 to December 1811, he used his defensive lines as a base from which he prosecuted a patient and effective campaign along the Portuguese frontier. He managed to gain a narrow victory over Masséna, who commanded a larger force, at the Battle of Fuentes de Onoro on May 5, 1811. Though his triumph was slim, it was sufficient for Wellington to take the offensive early in 1812. He laid siege against Ciudad Rodrigo during January 7–20 and Badajoz during March 17–April 9. Victories here opened the road to Madrid.

Elevated to earl of Wellington in February, the commander defeated the army of Auguste Marmont at Salamanca on July 22, and then pushed on to Madrid, which fell to him on August 12. Named a marquess in October, he failed in his siege of Burgos during September 19–October 21, and had to fall back on Ciudad Rodrigo in November. Nevertheless, Wellington was named commander in chief of allied forces in northern Spain in March 1813 and proved his setbacks temporary by rapidly retaking Madrid on May 17.

Wellington made short work of the smaller army of King Joseph at the Battle of Vitoria on June 21, and then hammered away at Soult in the Battle of the Pyrenees during July 25–August 2. Wellington helped to capture San Sebastián after a siege that spanned July 9 to September 7. This opened the door to an invasion of France. Wellington fought to small-scale victories at Bidassoa and La Rhune during October 7–9, and then won a series of larger actions around Bayonne during December 9–13. Promoted to field marshal (the highest rank in the British military) in 1813, Wellington defeated Soult at Orthez on February 27, 1814, and pushed him out of Toulouse on April 10.

In May 1814, Wellington, who possessed the enviable ability to make the most of the momentum of victory, was named duke and, after Napoleon's first exile, was appointed British ambassador to the court of France's restored Bourbon king, Louis XVIII. He served as ambassador from August 1814 to January 1815, when he assumed Lord Castlereagh's place at the Congress of Vienna—charged with restoring Europe after the fall of Napoleon—during January–February.

Napoleon, however, was not through. He stunned the world by returning from exile on Elba in March 1815, reclaiming an army, and attempting a return to power in the so-called Hundred Days. Wellington, indefatigable, took command of an Anglo-Dutch army in Flanders. Working closely with a Prussian army under the fine general Gebhard von Blücher, Wellington prepared an invasion of France. He was, however, taken by surprise when Napoleon suddenly invaded Belgium. Wellington rapidly recovered and scrambled to repulse Marshal Michel Ney's violent jabs at Quatre Bras on June 16. Wellington succeeded in repulsing Ney, but at great cost. Undaunted, he decided to strike a decisive blow. He fought a dangerous holding action at Waterloo, awaiting the arrival of Prussian reinforcements under Blücher. Wellington held out against superior forces long enough to unite with the Prussians in achieving the single most famous victory in modern military history: the final defeat of Napoleon at Waterloo, Belgium, on June 18, 1815.

After his victory over Napoleon, Wellington was put in charge of the allied armies of occupation in northern France, during 1815–18. On his return to England, he devoted the rest of his life to politics. He was appointed master-general of the ordnance in 1818, and he served as British ambassador to the Congress of Vienna from 1822 to 1826, when he was appointed ambassador to Russia. The following year, he returned to England to accept appointment as commander in chief of the army after the death of the Duke of York in January 1827.

A committed conservative, Wellington resigned all of his offices in April 1827 when the celebrated liberal George Canning became prime minister. In January 1828, however, Wellington himself was named prime minister, but he resisted parliamentary reform so uncompromisingly that he was ousted on November 15, 1830. He served next as foreign secretary to Robert Peel from November 1834 to April 1835 and was again appointed commander in chief of the army in 1842. Wellington retired from government after the defeat of Peel in June 1846. He performed his last military service in 1848 when he organized resistance against the London Chartists, members of a British working-class movement for parliamentary reform.

Wellington was a fine strategist, so adept that he proved a worthy match for Napoleon and his marshals. Even more important was his command presence, his preternatural calm in the face of battle, and his demonstration at all times of dauntless courage. Despite his extreme political conservatism, he had great respect and regard for all the officers and men of his army and was at all times solicitous of their welfare.

IN HIS OWN WORDS

"My rule is to do the business of the day in that day."
—Quoted in Stanhope (Philip Henry, 5th earl of Stanhope), *Conversations with the Duke of Wellington,* 1888

"The whole art of war consists in getting at what lies on the other side of the hill, or, in other words, what we do not know from what we do know."
—Quoted in David Chandler, *Campaigns of Napoleon,* 1966

"Remember that you are a commander in chief and must not be beaten; therefore, do not undertake anything with your troops unless you have some strong hope of success."
—Letter, May 11, 1809

"When one is intent on an object, common sense will usually direct one to the right means."
—Quoted in Stanhope (Philip Henry, 5th earl of Stanhope), *Conversations with the Duke of Wellington,* 1888

"I attribute [my success] entirely to the application of good sense to the circumstances of the moment."
—Quoted in William Fraser, *Words of Wellington,* 1889

"The Spaniards make excellent soldiers. What spoils them is that they have no confidence in their officers—and how should the Spaniards have confidence in such officers as theirs?"
—Quoted in John Croker, *The Croker Papers,* 1884

"It requires time for a general to inspire confidence or to feel it; for you will never have confidence in yourself until others have confidence in you."
—Quoted in Stanhope (Philip Henry, 5th earl of Stanhope), *Conversations with the Duke of Wellington,* 1888

LEADERSHIP LESSONS

✦

In a leader, nothing counts more than character.

✦

To obtain superlative performance from those you lead, perform superlatively.

✦

Focus on anticipating your opponent's strategy; formulate your strategy accordingly.

✦

Make your first and last care the welfare of those you lead. This earns loyalty and the willingness to achieve excellence.

✦

Expect surprise. Maintain sufficient flexibility to recover from the unexpected.

✦

Act with aggressive energy. Never allow an opportunity to escape action.

William I the Conqueror

Born: ca. 1028   Died: 1087

Conqueror   Strategist   Tactician

LEADERSHIP ACHIEVEMENTS

✦

Thoroughly understood the nature of power in feudal Europe

✦

Seized every opportunity to advance and consolidate his position

✦

Used aggression against him as a means of achieving victory against the aggressors

✦

Having created a strong power base, successfully launched the conquest of England

✦

Began the transformation of England from Anglo–Saxon fragmentation and disorder to genuine nationhood

✦

Became the most powerful figure in northern Europe

LIFE

William, duke of Normandy, became William I, called William the Conqueror, after his epochal victory over Anglo–Saxon forces at the Battle of Hastings in 1066. As England's first Norman king, William I brought an unprecedented degree of central government and order to the feudal island realm.

William was born in Falaise, the illegitimate son of Robert I, duke of Normandy. As a bastard, William would have had no claim to his father's title, except that Robert I died without legitimate offspring in 1035 and explicitly named William his heir. This appointment displeased many Norman nobles, and William found himself the target of repeated attempts at assassination. While young William himself evaded harm, four of his guardians were murdered in the course of nine years. At last, in 1046, William's cousin, Guy of Burgundy, determined to remove the young man from the ducal throne once and for all, mounted a military campaign to overthrow William. Guy might well have succeeded, but for the support William received from his feudal overlord, Henry I, king of France. With the aid of the king's troops, William defeated Guy at the Battle of Val-es-Dunes in 1047. This victory effectively certified, in Norman eyes, William's right to rule. If anything, the actions of would-be usurpers only strengthened William's position. He dealt with them so decisively and effectively that even the most jealous and fractious lords were won over to his cause. Ultimately, William came to enjoy a harmonious relationship with the nobility that was almost unprecedented in tumultuously feudal Normandy. This allowed William to unite his realm and to make effective use of extensive military resources.

The downside of William's increasing power and popularity was the growing wariness of King Henry I of France. Fearing the rise of a powerful rival, Henry broke his previously amicable ties with the Norman duke and seized upon William's consanguineous marriage to Mathilda, daughter of the Count of Flanders, as an excuse to declare war against him. Henry allied himself with the powerful Count of Anjou, Geoffrey Martel, and attacked. William met the combined forces of the king and Martel twice—at the Battle of Mortemer in 1054 and again at the Battle of Varaville in 1058—and both times William emerged victorious. These triumphs gave William the independence from his royal overlord that allowed him to turn his attention to foreign conquest.

William focused on England, a weak, chaotic state ruled with difficulty by King Edward the Confessor. William approached the beleaguered Edward and pledged his support in return for being named Edward's successor to the English throne. William bolstered his claim on the English throne by striking a bargain with Harold Godwin, brother of Edward's wife. When Harold was shipwrecked in Normandy, William took him prisoner and then granted his release in exchange for a pledge to support his succession to Edward. With this matter secured, William awaited his moment for action. In 1060, both Henry I and Geoffrey Martel died, leaving William the dominant power in northern Europe. The moment had arrived.

William led an army into Anjou and conquered Maine before the Anjouan succession could be determined. With this conquest behind him and Anjou secured, he decided to advance against England. However, on his deathbed early in 1066, Edward broke his word to William by designating Harold as heir to the throne. Harold also abrogated his oath to

William and, in fact, assumed the throne. Undaunted, William raised an army and crossed the Channel, landing at Pevensey on the southern tip of England in September 1066. He advanced against Hastings, where he met and defeated Harold's forces on October 15, 1066, in what would be the most consequential battle in English history until Henry V's upset victory at Agincourt 350 years later.

Having defeated Harold, William quickly marched north, where he terrorized the English countryside into grudging submission. In December, he took London with little resistance. He was crowned William I, king of England, in Westminster Abbey on Christmas Day, 1066.

Many uprisings followed the coronation. William acted against them swiftly, certainly, and almost always brutally. By 1071, he had crushed all important rebellion and commenced rule over England and Normandy concurrently. In an age when travel between England and the continent was hardly a simple matter, William managed his two realms brilliantly. He introduced an unheard-of degree of order into English government and, for better or worse, imposed the Norman culture over that of the Anglo–Saxons. Shortly before his death in 1087, William designated his first son, Robert, as the heir to the Duchy of Normandy, and his third and favorite son, Rufus, as heir to the English throne. Reigning as William II, Rufus established the law of primacy henceforth to govern the succession of English monarchs, thereby eliminating a chronically debilitating source of conflict in English life.

LEADERSHIP LESSONS

◆

Define your goals. Assert your rights and prerogatives.
Focus. Never give up.

◆

Transform defense into offense. Exploit the errors and weakness of
aggressors to achieve victory and conquest.

◆

Be awake to new opportunities, but secure and consolidate your present
position before launching into new enterprises.

◆

Follow through. Conquest is never a matter of hit and run. It requires
patience, endurance, and a commitment to the long run.

◆

Maintain flexibility and a capacity to multitask. Do not allow a new
acquisition to blind you to long-standing commitments and needs.

Wilson, Woodrow

Born: 1856 Died: 1924

**Character model   Innovator   Mentor   Motivator   Problem solver
Strategist   Systems creator   Visionary**

LEADERSHIP ACHIEVEMENTS

◆

As president of Princeton, revolutionized a sleepy college and fashioned it
into one of the world's great universities

◆

Became an author, scholar, and teacher of great renown

◆

As the vigorous reform-minded governor of New Jersey, cleaned out
corrupt machine politics and ushered groundbreaking economic and social
legislation through the legislature

◆

As U.S. president, introduced a host of Progressive reforms, including the
federal income tax and worker protection

◆

Kept the United States out of World War I for three years

◆

As a war president, led the mobilization and war effort

◆

Was the leading architect of the armistice of November 11, 1918

◆

Fought, always valiantly, often futilely, for an equitable peace

LIFE

As the 28th U.S. president, Woodrow Wilson led the nation through important reforms during the Progressive Era and also through World War I, which saw the United States elevated to a position as one of the great powers among nations.

Born in the Shenandoah Valley town of Staunton, Virginia, Wilson was the son of a Presbyterian pastor. His family moved to Columbia, South Carolina, in 1870, and then, Wilmington, North Carolina. Wilson enrolled in Davidson College in North Carolina and then continued his education, beginning in 1875, at the College of New Jersey, which would become Princeton University. Wilson was not a brilliant student, but he was conscientious, and he developed a passion for history and for debate. As an undergraduate, he made the decision to "become a statesman" and enrolled at the Law School of the University of Virginia in 1879. Health problems forced him to withdraw, but he studied at home, opened a practice in Atlanta in June 1882, and was admitted to the bar shortly afterward.

Wilson soon discovered that he had little affinity for the practice of law, and he entered the Johns Hopkins University in September 1883, intent on becoming a professor of history and political science. In 1885, he published his first book, *Congressional Government,* an analysis of the weaknesses of leadership in the American constitutional system, and earned his Ph.D. 1886. Married on June 24, 1885, to Ellen Louise Axson (with whom he would have three daughters), Wilson became an associate professor of history at Bryn Mawr College and then moved on to Wesleyan University in 1888. Wilson not only published an important study in comparative government, *The State* (1889), he also coached one of the university's most outstanding football teams.

In 1890, he accepted a professorship at Princeton and taught there for the next dozen years, writing *Division and Reunion* (1893), a major study of the Civil War, and his popular *History of the American People* (1902) in addition to other works. In 1902, Wilson was appointed president of the university, a post in which he served through 1910. Under Wilson, Princeton blossomed into one of the nation's great universities. Wilson brought in more than 50 young scholars to implement what he called the "preceptorial system." Traditional lectures and rote instruction were supplemented by genuinely interactive discussion conferences conducted by the preceptors. Students were expected to become actively engaged in their education. Moreover, Wilson revised the university curriculum, creating an organically integrated program of study. He went on to institute new rules to liberalize and democratize the social life at the university and to minimize the exclusivity of the school's "eating clubs."

In 1910, Wilson accepted the invitation of James "Boss" Smith to run for governor of New Jersey on the Democratic ticket. Smith wholly anticipated that Wilson would make a distinguished but compliant puppet of the

Democratic machine, and so was stunned when the candidate aligned himself with the Progressive "good government" forces opposed to machine politics. Wilson's reform message struck a chord, and he won a stunning victory. Even before his inauguration, the governor-elect acted successfully to block Smith's own election to the U.S. Senate by the state legislature (in the days before direct popular election of senators). Almost immediately after his inauguration, Wilson introduced his program of reforms, relentlessly pressuring the legislature to pass in a single session almost everything he wanted. Suddenly, New Jersey had direct primaries, state regulation of public utilities, a system of workers' compensation, a slate of municipal reforms, and a fully reorganized school system. Later, Wilson was able to achieve passage of antitrust laws that ended the stranglehold of a small number of powerful New Jersey monopolies.

Wilson's progressive vigor catapulted him to national prominence and, in an uphill fight, gained him the Democratic presidential nomination in 1912 on the 46th ballot. In a three-way race against Republican incumbent William Howard Taft and third-party "Bull Moose" candidate Theodore Roosevelt, Wilson won a plurality, campaigning on a platform of what he called the New Freedom—a program to liberate American economic energies by drastic tariff reduction, by strengthening antitrust laws, and by liberalizing the banking and credit system. Wilson carried a Democratic Congress into office, which was a great aid in achieving passage of his many reforms.

Wilson's first term was jammed with bold new legislation. The income tax was introduced, a move not merely to raise federal revenues, but to make taxation more equitable by gearing it to the taxpayer's economic station in life. Protectionist tariffs were indeed lowered, and the Federal Reserve Act of 1913 reformed and liberalized currency and banking law. In 1914, antitrust legislation was bolstered by the Federal Trade Commission Act and the Clayton Anti-Trust Act, both aimed at preventing big business from gouging and strangling the people. In 1915, Wilson supported landmark legislation that federally regulated working conditions of sailors—the first of what would eventually be many federal mandates intended to create safe and decent conditions for American workers. In 1916, Wilson signed into law the Federal Farm Loan Act, which provided low-interest credit to farmers, and he introduced additional labor reforms with the Adamson Act, granting an eight-hour day to interstate railroad workers, and the Child Labor Act, curtailing children's working hours.

Wilson thus emerged as an activist president, a leader in economic and social reform. Yet as he focused on domestic policy, many dangers loomed on the international front. Wilson unsuccessfully tried to negotiate a pan–American pact to guarantee the mutual integrity of the Western Hemisphere, and he also found himself locked in a struggle with revolution-torn Mexico. At first, Wilson attempted to promote Mexican self-government by refusing to recognize the military dictatorship of General Victoriano Huerta and instead supporting the constitutionalist presidential contender Venustiano Carranza. But, in 1916, Wilson was forced to intervene against the revolutionary guerrilla leader Pancho Villa after Villa raided the border town of Columbus, New Mexico, killing 17 Americans. During this period, he also sent troops to rebellion-racked Haiti and Santo Domingo, where he established U.S. protectorates to safeguard American business interests in these volatile nations.

Most Americans highly approved of one key aspect of the Wilson foreign policy: strict neutrality in World War I, which had engulfed Europe since August 1914. In large part on the strength of his domestic reforms combined with the promise summed up in the campaign slogan "He kept us out of war," Wilson easily won a second term as president.

But it was not easy to keep America out of the war. On May 7, 1915, a German U-boat torpedoed the British passenger liner *Lusitania,* killing 1,200 people, including 128 Americans. This brought outraged cries for immediate U.S. entry into the war. Wilson attempted to cope diplomatically instead. During the early part of Wilson's second term, more incidents occurred, including Germany's resumption of unrestricted submarine warfare, which it had earlier pledged to discontinue. When, on February 3, 1917, the U.S. warship *Housatonic* was torpedoed and sunk by a German U-boat, Wilson severed diplomatic relations with Germany. The final straw came with the "Zimmermann Telegram," a coded message sent on January 19, 1917, from German foreign secretary Alfred Zimmermann to his nation's ambassador to Mexico outlining the terms of a proposed German–Mexican alliance against the United States. Wilson felt that neutrality was no longer an option and, on April 2, 1917, asked Congress for a declaration of war.

Wilson motivated and shaped the American war effort by proclaiming that the battle was "to make the world safe for democracy." With this single statement, he elevated the United States to the status of a true *world* power. But a nation with a puny army of only about 200,000 men was not much of a world power. Under the president's leadership, by the end of the war in November 1918, the army swelled to 4 million. The Wilson government created an array of special war agencies, which effectively placed private industry under federal control, so that war production reached unprecedented heights.

Woodrow Wilson was certainly no militarist, but, in the prosecution of the war, he backed his commanders fully, especially the commander in chief, General John J. Pershing. Pershing was faced with difficult demands from the French and British, who wanted him to relinquish control of American forces so that they could be deployed immediately, piecemeal fashion. Pershing refused to allow American soldiers to serve directly under foreign commanders, and he was determined not to deploy his troops until they had arrived in Europe in sufficient numbers and with sufficient training to serve as something more than cannon fodder. At the risk of imperiling the alliance, Wilson backed Pershing all the way, and, doubtless, the American Expeditionary Force was therefore a more effective fighting force than it would otherwise have been.

Well before the war was won, Wilson was thinking about—and attempting to design—the conditions of peace and an international political structure for a postwar world that would, he hoped, make future wars all but impossible. Hoping not only to "make the world safe for democracy," but to ensure that the Great War would be a "war to end all wars," he laid down his Fourteen Points as the "program of the world's peace . . . the only possible program." The Fourteen Points included the establishment of a "League of Nations," an international body in which disputes could be arbitrated and settled peacefully. It was, in all, a visionary program.

As the war drew to a close, Wilson was chiefly responsible for negotiating the armistice of November 11, 1918. He persuaded Germany to accept abject surrender, but with the promise that the ultimate settlement would be based upon his Fourteen Points. Wilson then became one of the "Big Four" with the heads of state of Great Britain, France, and Italy—the architects of the Treaty of Versailles, which dictated the ultimate terms of peace. Wilson instantly emerged as the leading figure among the Big Four, and he fought for principles that would be most likely to create enduring peace. Tragically, the other three heads of state were bent on exacting short-term vengeance on Germany, and the result, despite Wilson's efforts, was an extravagantly punitive treaty, which actually created the climate that would give rise to Hitler and Nazi militarism. Wilson did win some victories, including the prevention of the dismemberment of Germany in the west, the establishment of a new Poland, the acceptance of the principle that colonies should be administered in trust, and even a pledge of future general disarmament. He deemed his greatest triumph the creation of the League of Nations, and he believed that, with the United States leading the League, it would become a credible force for preventing war.

Unfortunately, isolationist Republicans, led by Senator Henry Cabot Lodge, chairman of the Foreign Relations Committee, blocked U.S. participation in the League of Nations. Fearing that the League would either be killed or compromised out of existence, Wilson decided to appeal directly to the American people and embarked on a tour of the West to stir up public demand for ratification. The president, already exhausted by the war and by his exertions at Versailles, pushed himself across some 8,000 miles of America and delivered 40 speeches. The strain caused his collapse following a speech at Pueblo, Colorado, on September 25, 1919. On his return to Washington, he suffered a stroke, which left him partially paralyzed and gravely ill. While he was incapacitated, Senate Republicans continued to push for unacceptable compromises. Wilson declared that the American people would decide the issue in the elections of 1920. The result was a landslide victory for the Republican ticket, and, with the succession of isolationist president Warren G. Harding, the death knell of the League of Nations, at least as far as America was concerned.

Although Wilson was awarded the Nobel Peace Prize late in 1920, he left office a deeply disappointed man. He retired with his second wife, Edith Bolling Galt (whom he married in 1915, after the sudden death of his first wife), and lived the final four years of his life in almost complete seclusion.

IN HIS OWN WORDS

"One cool judgment is worth a thousand hasty counsels. The thing to be supplied is light, not heat."

—Address, Pittsburgh, Pennsylvania, January 29, 1916

LEADERSHIP LESSONS

✦

The most effective leaders learn all they can and then apply that knowledge in practical ways to advance the enterprise they lead.

✦

A knowledge of relevant history is invaluable to leadership in the present and with an eye toward the future.

✦

If an idea or principle matters at all, it is worth fighting for.

✦

The person who presents the most rational and compelling program may expect to emerge as a leader.

✦

Taking leadership decisions to the people is a bold gamble. Know your constituents before you roll the dice.

✦

Failure is sometimes only a function of time. Wilson died in profound disappointment. Subsequent history, however, shows that people and nations greatly benefited from his work. Do not despair of temporary setbacks.

Yang Chien

Died: 604

**Conqueror Innovator Problem solver Profit maker Rescuer
Strategist Systems creator Tactician**

LEADERSHIP ACHIEVEMENTS

◆

Expanded China

◆

Brought unprecedented unity to China

◆

Reformed Chinese government in a fair, just, and efficient manner

◆

Ameliorated the cycle of agricultural abundance and famine through
administrative and practical means

◆

Increased revenues through an equitable system of taxation

◆

Created great public works: the expansion of the Great Wall and the
commencement of the Grand Canal

LIFE

Yang Chien was one of the great leaders of China. He not only did much
to unify the nation by creating a powerful and well-administered central
government, but he left his mark by continuing construction of the Great
Wall and beginning the Grand Canal. Very little is known about Yang
Chien's early life except that he was of mixed Chinese and Hsien-pi heritage and was a military commander in service to the Hsien-pi Northern
Chou dynasty in northern China. In this capacity he distinguished himself,
earning the title of Duke Sui. He went on to lead Chou forces against
Northern Ch'i, effectively reuniting northern China under the Chou in
577. After thus consolidating Chou dominion over northern China, Yang
acted quickly following the death of the Chou emperor and placed a 17-
year-old youth on the throne in 580, securing for himself the regency—the
true power behind the throne. Less than a year later, Yang forced the boy

to abdicate and installed himself as emperor, the first of the Sui dynasty. To ensure the absence of rivals for the throne, Yang arranged for the murder of the teenager he had displaced.

As emperor, Yang Chien acted to counter various forces threatening China. He mobilized against the Turkic tribes west of his realm, campaigning fiercely against them from 582 to 603. He failed to win a decisive victory against the tribes, but he did extend Chinese influence deep into central Asia. In 589, he also moved against Korea. Initially, his campaign was largely unsuccessful, but by the end of the year Yang's forces came to dominate the northern region of Korea.

Yang Chien's most important military campaign was against the Ch'en dynasty of southern China. Massing an army of tremendous size—historical tradition puts it at half a million—he defeated the Ch'en in 589, thereby unifying northern and southern China for the first time since the end of the Han dynasty three centuries earlier.

Many conquerors are military geniuses, but lack the administrative skills to maintain and successfully govern their conquests. Yang Chien, however, combined martial prowess with political acumen. He proved an extraordinarily skilled administrator. His reforms were productively backward-looking. Yang reintroduced the Han philosophy and methods of government, based on Confucianism. Always looming over China, Yang recognized, was the deadly cycle of harvest and famine, which caused great suffering and destabilized any government. Yang Chien ordered construction of massive centralized granaries as a bulwark against famine, and he introduced a just and productive system of taxes based on harvest yield.

The death of Yang Chien is shrouded in mystery. He died in 604, perhaps at the hand of his son, Yang Ti.

LEADERSHIP LESSONS

✦

Follow conquest with good administration. The proper price of assuming power is providing benefit.

✦

A leader is, first and foremost, a problem solver.

Index by Leadership Characteristic

PROBLEM SOLVER